readings in
abnormal psychology

readings in abnormal psychology

the problem of maladaptive behavior

edited by

Irwin G. Sarason
university of washington

Barbara R. Sarason

APPLETON-CENTURY-CROFTS
educational division / new york
MEREDITH CORPORATION

This book was printed on recycled paper.

72 73 74 75 76 / 10 9 8 7 6 5 4 3 2 1

Library of Congress Card Number: 73–184720

PRINTED IN THE UNITED STATES OF AMERICA

390–E–77708–0

contents

preface

The field of abnormal psychology is undergoing a major restructuring. The need for change arises from two circumstances. First, promising new concepts and methods are being brought to bear on clinical and research problems related to behavioral disorders. Second, it is becoming increasingly clear that limiting abnormal psychology to the traditional area of psychopathology or mental illness often means drawing arbitrary boundaries between personal and social problems. Defining abnormal psychology as the study of maladaptive behavior in no way restricts the analysis of such individual aberrations as neuroses and psychoses; it does broaden the purview of the psychologist to include the pervasive effects of societal variables (e.g., poverty, racial discrimination, the mass media) on individuals. These powerful variables are capable of producing a wide range of maladaptive behavior: "traditional" mental illness; intellectual stultification; vocational ineffectiveness; crime and violence.

Abnormal Psychology: The Problem of Maladaptive Behavior deals with the diversity of problems of living, the factors that bring them about, their treatment and prevention. This anthology contains clinical, research, and theoretical papers that deal with these topics. They provide the reader, and especially the beginning student, with insights into and in-depth examples of professional literature drawn from the field he seeks to comprehend. Through original articles, he gains exposure to the concepts, methods, and controversies that preoccupy contributors to the field.

This book is organized into five groups of articles. The first group deals with basic definitional problems concerning the nature of maladaptive behavior, society's response to it, and the professional roles of those who seek to modify it. Part II comprises articles reflecting four influential theoretical orientations that are often in conflict—psychodynamics, learning, sociology, and biology. The focus of Part III is clinical techniques, assessment of the client's problem behaviors, and evaluation of the therapeutic tactics employed by clinical workers. The diversity of personal and interpersonal problems confronted by clinical specialists is reflected in Part IV, which contains case studies, laboratory reports, clinical research investigations, and theoretical papers. Part V provides examples of research on several types of socially devalued behavior (crime, homosexuality, drug usage) and their determinants. In addition, this concluding section contains articles dealing with community psychology and the important problem of prevention.

We are indebted to the authors and publishers of the articles for permission to reprint their work. A specific acknowledgment accompanies each selection.

I. G. S.
B. R. S.

PART I
introduction

Concepts of maladaptive behavior vary according to both place and time. Each culture evaluates the behavior of its members within the context of distinctive values, aspirations, fears, and taboos. And within that culture ideas about devalued behavior change from one era to another. Over a period of not very many centuries, Western societies have moved from the belief that many forms of socially undesirable behavior are due to possession by the devil to the conviction that man's irrationality can be explained rationally through the application of scientific principles and methods.

With the ascendancy of scientific attitudes toward maladaptation has come an increase in humanitarian feelings toward those who are psychologically troubled or disabled. Tangible indications of these feelings can be seen in modern mentals hospitals and clinics that stress the use of nonpunitive methods. The rationale for these facilities has often been that devalued, deviant behavior is caused by mental illness. In the first article of Part I, Thomas Szasz attacks the idea of mental illness on several bases, one of which is that the idea is too often used as a *deus ex machina*. When this happens, deranged behavior is attributed to hidden mental aberrations for which the individual need not feel responsibility. In place of what he calls the myth of mental illness, Szasz proposes that maladaptive behavior be viewed as problems that people have in living and coping with the life situations that confront them.

David Ausubel agrees with Szasz that problems in living constitute a large and important group of the challenges confronting the clinical worker. He agrees also that hardheaded scientific analysis is superior to belief in myths. Yet, in his article, he is unable to go along with Szasz' stern rejection of the view that behavioral dysfunction is caused by mental illness. Ausubel argues that belief in the existence of mental illnesses need not necessarily be equated with belief in possession by the devil.

Szasz' second article, written a decade after the first one, is especially interesting for two reasons. First, it reflects his continued preoccupation with the definition of man's personal responsibility in a changing world. Second, it deals not just with psychiatric disorders such as phobias and schizophrenia, but also with criminal behavior. While crime generally elicits a much less benign response than do mental illnesses, there have been noticeable changes in social attitudes toward it. The direction of these changes has been toward humanitarian, therapeutic treatment of those who violate laws and widely agreed-upon standards of conduct. Szasz' second article is a contribution to the evolution of concepts of maladaptive behavior generally and of criminality in particular.

Social values and beliefs do not influence simply the types of problems that confront the clinical worker. They also exert significant influence over his professional identity and the therapeutic tactics that he employs. Murray and Adeline Levine show how social pressures, evidence provided by objective evaluations of clinical techniques, and the need to improve services offered to clients have combined in shaping new approaches to old problems, such as juvenile delinquency and the effects of socioeconomic deprivation. Charles Hersch's article, taking the same tack, focuses on one professional group, the clinical psychologists. Clinical psychology has perhaps been more susceptible to identity crises than most other professional groups because it is a relatively young field and because it has been committed both to the development of scientific knowledge and to its clinical application. Hersch's article exemplifies the sort of self-examination that characterizes professional groups which are viable, challenging, and changing. The question of the roles of the clinical psychologist in diagnosis, treatment, prevention, and social action continues to be debated actively.

the myth of mental illness

Thomas S. Szasz

My aim in this essay is to raise the question "Is there such a thing as mental illness?" and to argue that there is not. Since the notion of mental illness is extremely widely used nowadays, inquiry into the ways in which this term is employed would seem to be especially indicated. Mental illness, of course, is not literally a "thing"—or physical object —and hence it can "exist" only in the same sort of way in which other theoretical concepts exist. Yet familiar theories are in the habit of posing, sooner or later—at least to those who come to believe in them—as "objective truths" (or "facts"). During certain historical periods, explanatory conceptions such as deities, witches, and microorganisms appeared not only as theories but as self-evident *causes* of a vast number of events. I submit that today mental illness is widely regarded in a somewhat similar fashion—that is, as the cause of innumerable diverse happenings. As an antidote to the complacent use of the notion of mental illness (whether as a self-evident phenomenon, theory, or cause) let us ask this question: What is meant when it is asserted that someone is mentally ill?

In what follows I shall describe briefly the main uses to which the concept of mental illness has been put. I shall argue that this notion has outlived whatever usefulness it might have had and that it now functions merely as a convenient myth.

MENTAL ILLNESS AS A SIGN OF BRAIN DAMAGE

The notion of mental illness derives its main support from such phenomena as syphilis of the brain or delirious conditions—intoxication, for instance —in which persons are known to manifest various peculiarities or disorders of thinking and be-havior. Correctly speaking, however, these are diseases of the brain, not of the mind. According to one school of thought, *all* so-called mental illness is of this type. The assumption is made that some neurological defect, perhaps a very subtle one, will ultimately be found for all the disorders of thinking and behavior. Many contemporary psychiatrists, physicians, and other scientists hold this view. This position implies that people *cannot* have troubles—expressed in what are *now called* "mental illnesses"—because of differences in personal needs, opinions, social aspirations, values, and so on. *All problems in living* are attributed to physicochemical processes which in due time will be discovered by medical research.

"Mental illnesses" are thus regarded as basically no different than all other diseases (that is, of the body). The only difference, in this view, between mental and bodily diseases is that the former, affecting the brain, manifest themselves by means of mental symptoms; whereas the latter, affecting other organ systems (for example, the skin, liver, etc.), manifest themselves by means of symptoms referable to those parts of the body. This view rests on and expresses what are, in my opinion, two fundamental errors.

In the first place, what central nervous system symptoms would correspond to a skin eruption or a fracture? It would *not* be some emotion or complex bit of behavior. Rather, it would be blindness or a paralysis of some part of the body. The crux of the matter is that a disease of the brain, analogous to a disease of the skin or bone, is a neurological defect, and not a problem in living. For example, a *defect* in a person's visual field may be satisfactorily explained by correlating it with certain definite lesions in the nervous system. On the other hand, a person's *belief*— whether this be a belief in Christianity, in Com-

Reprinted from the *American Psychologist*, 1960, *15*, pp. 5–12. Copyright 1960 by the American Psychological Society and reproduced by permission.

munism, or in the idea that his internal organs are "rotting" and that his body is, in fact, already "dead"—cannot be explained by a defect or disease of the nervous system. Explanations of this sort of occurrence—assuming that one is interested in the belief itself and does not regard it simply as a "symptom" or expression of something else that is *more interesting*—must be sought along different lines.

The second error in regarding complex psychosocial behavior, consisting of communications about ourselves and the world about us, as mere symptoms of neurological functioning is *epistemological*. In other words, it is an error pertaining not to any mistakes in observation or reasoning, as such, but rather to the way in which we organize and express our knowledge. In the present case, the error lies in making a symmetrical dualism between mental and physical (or bodily) symptoms, a dualism which is merely a habit of speech and to which no known observations can be found to correspond. Let us see if this is so. In medical practice, when we speak of physical disturbances, we mean either signs (for example, a fever) or symptoms (for example, pain). We speak of mental symptoms, on the other hand, when we refer to a patient's *communications about himself, others, and the world about him.* He might state that he is Napoleon or that he is being persecuted by the Communists. These would be considered mental symptoms *only* if the observer believed that the patient was *not* Napoleon or that he was *not* being persecuted by the Communists. This makes it apparent that the statement that "X is a mental symptom" involves rendering a judgment. The judgment entails, moreover, a covert comparison or matching of the patient's ideas, concepts, or beliefs with those of the observer and the society in which they live. The notion of mental symptom is therefore inextricably tied to the *social* (including *ethical*) *context* in which it is made in much the same way as the notion of bodily symptom is tied to an *anatomical* and *genetic context* (Szasz, 1957a, 1957b).

To sum up what has been said thus far: I have tried to show that for those who regard mental symptoms as signs of brain disease, the concept of mental illness is unnecessary and misleading, for what they mean is that people so labeled suffer from diseases of the brain; and, if that is what they mean, it would seem better for the sake of clarity to say that and not something else.

MENTAL ILLNESS AS A NAME FOR PROBLEMS IN LIVING

The term "mental illness" is widely used to describe something which is very different from a disease of the brain. Many people today take it for granted that living is an arduous process. Its hardship for modern man, moreover, derives not so much from a struggle for biological survival as from the stresses and strains inherent in the social intercourse of complex human personalities. In this context, the notion of mental illness is used to identify or describe some feature of an individual's so-called personality. Mental illness —as a deformity of the personality, so to speak— is then regarded as the *cause* of the human disharmony. It is implicit in this view that social intercourse between people is regarded as something *inherently harmonious*, its disturbance being due solely to the presence of "mental illness" in many people. This is obviously fallacious reasoning, for it makes the abstraction "mental illness" into a *cause*, even though this abstraction was created in the first place to serve only as a shorthand expression for certain types of human behavior. It now becomes necessary to ask: "What kinds of behavior are regarded as indicative of mental illness, and by whom?"

The concept of illness, whether bodily or mental, implies *deviation from some clearly defined norm*. In the case of physical illness, the norm is the structural and functional integrity of the human body. Thus, although the desirability of physical health, as such, is an ethical value, what health *is* can be stated in anatomical and physiological terms. What is the norm deviation from which is regarded as mental illness? This question cannot be easily answered. But whatever this norm might be, we can be certain of only one thing: namely, that it is a norm that must be stated in terms of *psychosocial, ethical,* and *legal* concepts. For example, notions such as "excessive repression" or "acting out an unconscious impulse" illustrate the use of psychological concepts for judging (so-called) mental health and illness. The idea that chronic hostility, vengefulness, or divorce are indicative of mental illness would be illustrations of the use of ethical norms (that is, the desirability of love, kindness, and a stable marriage relationship). Finally, the widespread psychiatric opinion that only a mentally ill person would commit homicide illustrates the use of a legal concept as a norm of mental health. The norm from which deviation is measured whenever one speaks of a mental illness is a *psychosocial and ethical one*. Yet the remedy is sought in terms of *medical* measures which—it is hoped and assumed—are free from wide differences of ethical value. The definition of the disorder and the terms in which its remedy are sought are therefore at serious odds with one another. The practical significance of this covert conflict between the alleged nature of the defect and the remedy can hardly be exaggerated.

Having identified the norms used to measure deviations in cases of mental illness, we will now turn to the question: "Who defines the norms and hence the deviation?" Two basic answers may be offered:

(A) It may be the person himself (that is, the patient) who decides that he deviates from a norm. For example, an artist may believe that he suffers from a work inhibition; and he may implement this conclusion by seeking help *for* himself from a psychotherapist.

(B) It may be someone other than the patient who decides that the latter is deviant (for example, relatives, physicians, legal authorities, society generally, etc.). In such a case a psychiatrist may be hired by others to do something *to* the patient in order to correct the deviation.

In actual contemporary social usage, the finding of a mental illness is made by establishing a deviance in behavior from certain psychosocial, ethical, or legal norms. The judgment may be made, as in medicine, by the patient, the physician (psychiatrist), or others. Remedial action, finally, tends to be sought in a therapeutic—or covertly medical—framework, thus creating a situation in which, it is claimed, *psychosocial, ethical,* and/or *legal deviations* can be corrected by (so-called) *medical action*. Since medical action is designed to correct only medical deviations, it seems logically absurd to expect that it will help solve problems whose very existence had been defined and established on nonmedical grounds. I think that these considerations may be fruitfully applied to the present use of tranquilizers and, more generally, to what might be expected of drugs of whatever type, in regard to the amelioration or solution of problems in human living.

THE ROLE OF ETHICS IN PSYCHIATRY

Anything that people *do*—in contrast to things that *happen* to them (Peters, 1958)—takes place in a context of value. In this broad sense, no human activity is devoid of ethical implications. When the values underlying certain activities are widely shared, those who participate in their pursuit may lose sight of them altogether. The discipline of medicine, both as a pure science (for example, research) and as a technology (for example, therapy), contains many ethical considerations and judgments. Unfortunately, these are often denied, minimized, or merely kept out of focus; for the ideal of the medical profession as well as of the people whom it serves seems to be having a system of medicine (allegedly) free of ethical value. This sentimental notion is expressed by such things as the doctor's willingness to treat and help patients irrespective of their religious or political beliefs, whether they are rich or poor, etc. While there may be some grounds for this belief—albeit it is a view that is not impressively true even in these regards—the fact remains that ethical considerations encompass a vast range of human affairs. Making the practice of medicine neutral in regard to some specific issues of value need not, and cannot, mean that it can be kept free from all such values. The practice of medicine is intimately tied to ethics; and the first thing that we must do, it seems to me, is to try to make this clear and explicit. I shall let this matter rest here, for it does not concern us specifically in this essay. Lest there be any vagueness, however, about how or where ethics and medicine meet, let me remind the reader of such issues as birth control, abortion, suicide, and euthanasia as only a few of the major areas of current ethicomedical controversy.

Psychiatry, I submit, is very much more intimately tied to problems of ethics than is medicine. I use the word "psychiatry" here to refer to that contemporary discipline which is concerned with *problems in living* (and not with diseases of the brain, which are problems for neurology). Problems in human relations can be analyzed, interpreted, and given meaning only within given social and ethical contexts. Accordingly, it *does* make a difference—arguments to the contrary notwithstanding—what the psychiatrist's socioethical orientations happen to be; for these will influence his ideas on what is wrong with the patient, what deserves comment or interpretation, in what possible directions change might be desirable, and so forth. Even in medicine proper, these factors play a role, as, for instance, in the divergent orientations which physicians, depending on their religious affiliations, have toward such things as birth control and therapeutic abortion. Can anyone really believe that a psychotherapist's ideas concerning religious belief, slavery, or other similar issues play no role in his practical work? If they do make a difference, what are we to infer from it? Does it not seem reasonable that we ought to have different psychiatric therapies—each expressly recognized for the ethical positions which they embody—for, say, Catholics and Jews, religious persons and agnostics, democrats and communists, white supremacists and Negroes, and so on? Indeed, if we look at how psychiatry is actually practiced today (especially in the United States), we find that people do seek psychiatric help in accordance with their social status and ethical beliefs (Hollingshead and Redlich, 1958). This should really not surprise us more than being told that practicing Catholics rarely frequent birth control clinics.

The foregoing position, which holds that contemporary psychotherapists deal with problems in living rather than with mental illnesses and their cures, stands in opposition to a currently prevalent claim, according to which mental illness is just as "real" and "objective" as bodily illness. This is a confusing claim since it is never known exactly what is meant by such words as "real" and "objective." I suspect, however, that what is intended by the proponents of this view is to create the idea in the popular mind that mental illness is some sort of disease entity, like an infection or a malignancy. If this were true, one could *catch* or *get* a "mental illness," one might *have* or *harbor* it, one might *transmit* it to others, and finally one could get *rid* of it. In my opinion, there is not a shred of evidence to support this idea. To the contrary, all the evidence is the other way and supports the view that what people now call mental illnesses are for the most part *communications* expressing unacceptable ideas, often framed, moreover, in an unusual idiom. The scope of this essay allows me to do no more than mention this alternative theoretical approach to this problem (Szasz, 1957c).

This is not the place to consider in detail the similarities and differences between bodily and mental illnesses. It shall suffice for us here to emphasize only one important difference between them: namely, that whereas bodily disease refers to public, physicochemical occurrences, the notion of mental illness is used to codify relatively more private, sociopsychological happenings of which the observer (diagnostician) forms a part. In other words, the psychiatrist does not stand *apart* from what he observes, but is, in Harry Stack Sullivan's apt words, a "participant observer." This means that he is *committed* to some picture of what he considers reality—and he observes and judges the patient's behavior in the light of these considerations. This touches on our earlier observation that the notion of mental symptom itself implies a comparison between observer and observed, psychiatrist and patient. This is so obvious that I may be charged with belaboring trivialities. Let me therefore say once more that my aim in presenting this argument was expressly to criticize and counter a prevailing contemporary tendency to deny the moral aspects of psychiatry (and psychotherapy) and to substitute for them allegedly value-free medical considerations.

The diversity of human values and the methods by means of which they may be realized is so vast, and many of them remain so unacknowledged, that they cannot fail to lead to conflicts in human relations. Indeed, to say that human relations at all levels—from mother to child, through husband and wife, to nation and nation—are fraught with stress, strain, and disharmony is, once again, making the obvious explicit. Yet what may be obvious may be also poorly understood. This I think is the case here. For it seems to me that—at least in our scientific theories of behavior—we have failed to *accept* the simple fact that human relations are inherently fraught with difficulties and that to make them even relatively harmonious requires much patience and hard work. I submit that the idea of mental illness is now being put to work to obscure certain difficulties which at present may be inherent—not that they need be unmodifiable—in the social intercourse of persons. If this is true, the concept functions as a disguise; for instead of calling attention to conflicting human needs, aspirations, and values, the notion of mental illness provides an amoral and impersonal "thing" (an "illness") as an explanation for *problems in living* (Szasz, 1959). We may recall in this connection that not so long ago it was devils and witches who were held responsible for men's problems in social living. The belief in mental illness, as something other than man's trouble in getting along with his fellow man, is the proper heir to the belief in demonology and witchcraft. Mental illness exists or is "real" in exactly the same sense in which witches existed or were "real."

CHOICE, RESPONSIBILITY, AND PSYCHIATRY

While I have argued that mental illnesses do not exist, I obviously did not imply that the social and psychological occurrences to which this label is currently being attached also do not exist. Like the personal and social troubles which people had in the Middle Ages, they are real enough. It is the labels we give them that concerns us and, having labeled them, what we do about them. While I cannot go into the ramified implications of this problem here, it is worth noting that a demonologic conception of problems in living gave rise to therapy along theological lines. Today, a belief in mental illness implies—nay, requires— therapy along medical or psychotherapeutic lines.

What is implied in the line of thought set forth here is something quite different. I do not intend to offer a new conception of "psychiatric illness" or a new form of "therapy." My aim is more modest and yet also more ambitious. It is to suggest that the phenomena now called mental illnesses be looked at afresh and more simply, that they be removed from the category of illnesses, and that they be regarded as the expressions of man's struggle with the problem of *how* he should live. The last-mentioned problem is obviously a vast one, its enormity reflecting not only man's inability to cope with his environment, but even more his increasing self-reflectiveness.

By problems in living, then, I refer to that truly explosive chain reaction which began with man's fall from divine grace by partaking of the fruit of the tree of knowledge. Man's awareness of himself and of the world about him seems to be a steadily expanding one, bringing in its wake an ever larger *burden of understanding* (an expression borrowed from Susanne Langer, 1953). *This burden, then, is to be expected and must not be misinterpreted.* Our only *rational* means for lightening it is *more understanding*, and appropriate *action* based on such understanding. The main alternative lies in acting as though the burden were not what in fact we perceive it to be and taking refuge in an outmoded theological view of man. In the latter view, man does not

fashion his life and much of his world about him, but merely lives out his fate in a world created by superior beings. This may logically lead to pleading nonresponsibility in the face of seemingly unfathomable problems and difficulties. Yet if man fails to take increasing responsibility for his actions, individually as well as collectively, it seems unlikely that some higher power or being would assume this task and carry this burden for him. Moreover, this seems hardly the proper time in human history for obscuring the issue of man's responsibility for his actions by hiding it behind the skirt of an all-explaining conception of mental illness.

CONCLUSIONS

I have tried to show that the notion of mental illness has outlived whatever usefulness it might have had and that it now functions merely as a convenient myth. As such, it is a true heir to religious myths in general, and to the belief in witchcraft in particular; the role of all these belief-systems was to act as *social tranquilizers*, thus encouraging the hope that mastery of certain specific problems may be achieved by means of substitutive (symbolic–magical) operations. The notion of mental illness thus serves mainly to obscure the everyday fact that life for most people is a continuous struggle, not for biological survival, but for a "place in the sun," "peace of mind," or some other human value. For man aware of himself and of the world about him, once the needs for preserving the body (and perhaps the race) are more or less satisfied, the problem arises as to what he should do with himself. Sustained adherence to the myth of mental illness allows people to avoid facing this problem, believing that mental health, conceived as the absence of mental illness, automatically insures the making of right and safe choices in one's conduct of life. But the facts are all the other way. It is the making of good choices in life that others regard, retrospectively, as good mental health!

The myth of mental illness encourages us, moreover, to believe in its logical corollary: that social intercourse would be harmonious, satisfying, and the secure basis of a "good life" were it not for the disrupting influences of mental illness or "psychopathology." The potentiality for universal human happiness, in this form at least, seems to me but another example of the I-wish-it-were-true type of fantasy. I do believe that human happiness or well-being on a hitherto unimaginably large scale, and not just for a select few, is possible.

Our adversaries are not demons, witches, fate, or mental illness. We have no enemy whom we can fight, exorcise, or dispel by "cure." What we do have are *problems in living*—whether these be biologic, economic, political, or sociopsychological. My argument has been limited to the proposition that mental illness is a myth, whose function it is to disguise and thus render more palatable the bitter pill of moral conflicts in human relations.

REFERENCES

Hollingshead, A. B., and F. C. Redlich. *Social class and mental illness.* New York: Wiley, 1958.

Jones, E. *The life and work of Sigmund Freud.* Vol. III. New York: Basic Books, 1957.

Langer, S. K. *Philosophy in a new key.* New York: Mentor Books, 1953.

Peters, R. S. *The concept of motivation.* London: Routledge and Kegan Paul, 1958.

Szasz, T. S. Malingering: "Diagnosis" or social condemnation? *AMA Arch. Neurol. Psychiat.,* 1956, *76,* 432–443.

Szasz, T. S. *Pain and pleasure: A study of bodily feelings.* New York: Basic Books, 1957. (a)

Szasz, T. S. The problem of psychiatric nosology: A contribution to a situational analysis of psychiatric operations. *Amer. J. Psychiat.,* 1957, *114,* 405–413. (b)

Szasz, T. S. On the theory of psychoanalytic treatment. *Int. J. Psycho-Anal.,* 1957, *38,* 166–182. (c)

Szasz, T. S. Psychiatry, ethics and the criminal law. *Columbia Law Rev.,* 1958, *58,* 183–198.

Szasz, T. S. Moral conflict and psychiatry. *Yale Rev.,* 1959, *49,* 555–566.

personality disorder is disease

David P. Ausubel

In two recent articles in the *American Psychologist,* Szasz (1960) and Mowrer (1960) have argued the case for discarding the concept of mental illness. The essence of Mowrer's position is that since medical science lacks "demonstrated competence . . . in psychiatry," psychology would be wise to "get out" from "under the penumbra of medicine," and to regard the behavior disorders as manifestations of sin rather than of disease. Szasz's position, as we shall see shortly, is somewhat more complex than Mowrer's, but agrees with the latter in emphasizing the moral as opposed to the psychopathological basis of abnormal behavior.

For a long time now, clinical psychology has both repudiated the relevance of moral judgment and accountability for assessing behavioral acts and choices, and chafed under medical (psychiatric) control and authority in diagnosing and treating the personality disorders. One can readily appreciate, therefore, Mowrer's eagerness to sever the historical and professional ties that bind clinical psychology to medicine, even if this means denying that psychological disturbances constitute a form of illness, and even if psychology's close working relationship with psychiatry must be replaced by a new rapprochement with sin and theology, as "the lesser of two evils." One can also sympathize with Mowrer's and Szasz's dissatisfaction with prevailing amoral and nonjudgmental trends in clinical psychology and with their entirely commendable efforts to restore moral judgment and accountability to a respectable place among the criteria used in evaluating human behavior, both normal and abnormal.

Opposition to these two trends in the handling of the behavior disorders (i.e., to medical control and to nonjudgmental therapeutic attitudes), however, does not necessarily imply abandonment of the concept of mental illness. There is no inconsistency whatsoever in maintaining, on the one hand, that most purposeful human activity has a moral aspect the reality of which psychologists cannot afford to ignore (Ausubel, 1952), that man is morally accountable for the majority of his misdeeds (Ausubel, 1952), and that psychological rather than medical training and sophistication are basic to competence in the personality disorders (Ausubel, 1956), and affirming, on the other hand, that the latter disorders are genuine manifestations of illness. In recent years psychology has been steadily moving away from the formerly fashionable stance of ethical neutrality in the behavioral sciences; and in spite of strident medical claims regarding superior professional qualifications and preclusive legal responsibility for treating psychiatric patients, and notwithstanding the nominally restrictive provisions of medical practice acts, clinical psychologists have been assuming an increasingly more important, independent, and responsible role in treating the mentally ill population of the United States.

THE SZASZ–MOWRER POSITION

Szasz's (1960) contention that the concept of mental illness "now functions merely as a convenient myth" is grounded on four unsubstantiated and logically untenable propositions, which can be fairly summarized as follows:

1. Only symptoms resulting from demonstrable physical lesions qualify as legitimate manifestations of disease. Brain pathology is a type of physical lesion, but its symptoms, properly speaking, are neurological rather than psychological in nature. Under no circumstances, therefore, can mental symptoms be considered a form of illness. 2. A basic dichotomy exists between *mental*

symptoms, on the one hand, which are subjective in nature, dependent on subjective judgment and personal involvement of the observer, and referable to cultural–ethical norms, and *physical* symptoms, on the other hand, which are allegedly objective in nature, ascertainable without personal involvement of the observer, and independent of cultural norms and ethical standards. Only symptoms possessing the latter set of characteristics are genuinely reflective of illness and amenable to medical treatment.

3. Mental symptoms are merely expressions of problems of living and, hence, cannot be regarded as manifestations of a pathological condition. The concept of mental illness is misleading and demonological because it seeks to explain psychological disturbance in particular and human disharmony in general terms of a metaphorical but nonexistent disease entity, instead of attributing them to inherent difficulties in coming to grips with elusive problems of choice and responsibility.

4. Personality disorders, therefore, can be most fruitfully conceptualized as products of moral conflict, confusion, and aberration. Mowrer (1960) extends this latter proposition to include the dictum that psychiatric symptoms are primarily reflective of unacknowledged sin, and that individuals manifesting these symptoms are responsible for and deserve their suffering, both because of their original transgressions and because they refuse to avow and expiate their guilt.

Widespread adoption of the Szasz–Mowrer view of the personality disorders would, in my opinion, turn back the psychiatric clock twenty-five hundred years. The most significant and perhaps the only real advance registered by mankind in evolving a rational and humane method of handling behavioral aberrations has been in substituting a concept of disease for the demonological and retributional doctrines regarding their nature and etiology that flourished until comparatively recent times. Conceptualized as illness, the symptoms of personality disorders can be interpreted in the light of underlying stresses and resistances, both genic and environmental, and can be evaluated in relation to *specifiable* quantitative and qualitative norms of appropriately adaptive behavior, both cross-culturally and within a particular cultural context. It would behoove us, therefore, before we abandon the concept of mental illness and return to the medieval doctrine of unexpiated sin or adopt Szasz's ambiguous criterion of difficulty in ethical choice and responsibility, to subject the foregoing propositions to careful and detailed study.

Mental Symptoms and Brain Pathology

Although I agree with Szasz in rejecting the doctrine that ultimately some neuroanatomic or neurophysiologic defect will be discovered in *all* cases of personality disorder, I disagree with his reasons for not accepting this proposition. Notwithstanding Szasz's straw-man presentation of their position, the proponents of the extreme somatic view do not really assert that the *particular nature* of a patient's disordered beliefs can be correlated with "certain definite lesions in the nervous system" (Szasz, 1960). They hold rather that normal cognitive and behavioral functioning depends on the anatomic and physiologic integrity of certain key areas of the brain, and that impairment of this substrate integrity, therefore, provides a physical basis for disturbed ideation and behavior, but does not explain, except in a very gross way, the particular kinds of symptoms involved. In fact, they are generally inclined to attribute the *specific* character of the patient's symptoms to the nature of his pre-illness personality structure, the substrate integrity of which is impaired by the lesion or metabolic defect in question.

Nevertheless, even though this type of reasoning plausibly accounts for the psychological symptoms found in general paresis, various toxic deliria, and other comparable conditions, it is an extremely improbable explanation of *all* instances of personality disorder. Unlike the tissues of any other organ, brain tissue possesses the unique property of making possible awareness of and adjustment to the world of sensory, social, and symbolic stimulation. Hence, by virtue of this unique relationship of the nervous system to the environment, diseases of behavior and personality may reflect abnormalities in personal and social adjustment, quite apart from any structural or metabolic disturbance in the underlying neural substrate. I would conclude, therefore, that although brain pathology is probably not the most important cause of behavior disorder, it is undoubtedly responsible for the incidence of *some* psychological abnormalities *as well as* for various neurological signs and symptoms.

But even if we completely accepted Szasz's view that brain pathology does not account for any symptoms of personality disorder, it would still be unnecessary to accept his assertion that to qualify as a genuine manifestation of disease a given symptom must be caused by a physical lesion. Adoption of such a criterion would be arbitrary and inconsistent with both medical and lay connotations of the term "disease," which in current usage is generally regarded as including any marked deviation, physical, mental, or behavioral, from normally desirable standards of structural and functional integrity.

Mental versus Physical Symptoms

Szasz contends that since the analogy between physical and mental symptoms is patently fallacious, the postulated parallelism between physical and mental disease is logically untenable. This line of reasoning is based on the assumption that the two categories of symptoms can be sharply dichotomized with respect to such basic dimensions as objectivity–subjectivity, the relevance of cultural norms, and the need for personal involvement of the observer. In my opinion, the existence of such a dichotomy cannot be empirically demonstrated in convincing fashion.

Practically all symptoms of bodily disease involve some elements of subjective judgment—on the part of both the patient and the physician. Pain is perhaps the most important and commonly used criterion of physical illness. Yet any evaluation of its reported locus, intensity, character, and duration is dependent upon the patient's subjective appraisal of his own sensations and on the physician's assessment of the latter's pain threshold, intelligence, and personality structure. It is also a medical commonplace that the severity of pain in most instances of bodily illness may be mitigated by the administration of a placebo. Furthermore, in taking a meaningful history the physician must not only serve as a participant observer but also as a skilled interpreter of human behavior. It is the rare patient who does not react psychologically to the signs of physical illness; and hence physicians are constantly called upon to decide, for example, to what extent pre-cordial pain and reported tightness in the chest are manifestations of coronary insufficiency, of fear of cardiac disease and impending death, or of combinations of both conditions. Even such allegedly objective signs as pulse rate, BMR, blood pressure, and blood cholesterol have their subjective and relativistic aspects. Pulse rate and blood pressure are notoriously susceptible to emotional influences, and BMR and blood cholesterol fluctuate widely from one cultural environment to another (Dreyfuss and Czaczkes, 1959). Furthermore, anyone

who believes that ethical norms have no relevance for physical illness has obviously failed to consider the problems confronting Catholic patients and/ or physicians when issues of contraception, abortion, and preferential saving of the mother's as against the fetus' life must be faced in the context of various obstetrical emergencies and medical contraindications to pregnancy.

It should now be clear, therefore, not only that symptoms do not need a physical basis to qualify as manifestations of illness, but also that the evaluation of *all* symptoms, physical as well as mental, is dependent in large measure on subjective judgment, emotional factors, cultural–ethical norms, and personal involvement on the part of the observer. These considerations alone render no longer tenable Szasz's contention (1960) that there is an inherent contradiction between using cultural and ethical norms as criteria of mental disease, on the one hand, and of employing medical measures of treatment, on the other. But even if the postulated dichotomy between mental and physical symptoms were valid, the use of physical measures in treating subjective and relativistic psychological symptoms would still be warranted. Once we accept the proposition that impairment of the neural substrate of personality can result in behavior disorder, it is logically consistent to accept the corollary proposition that other kinds of manipulation of the same neural substrate can conceivably have therapeutic effects, irrespective of whether the underlying cause of the mental symptoms is physical or psychological.

Mental Illness and Problems of Living

"The phenomena now called mental illness," argues Szasz (1960), can be regarded more forthrightly and simply as "expressions of man's struggle with the problem of how he should live." This statement undoubtedly oversimplifies the nature of personality disorders; but even if it were adequately inclusive it would not be inconsistent with the position that these disorders are a manifestation of illness. There is no valid reason why a particular symptom cannot both reflect a problem in living *and* constitute a manifestation of disease. The notion of mental illness, conceived in this way, would not "obscure the everyday fact that life for most people is a continuous struggle . . . for a 'place in the sun,' 'peace of mind,' or some other human value." It is quite true, as Szasz points out, that "human relations are inherently fraught with difficulties," and that most people manage to cope with such difficulties without becoming mentally ill. But conceding this fact hardly precludes the possibility that some individuals, either because of the magnitude of the stress involved, or because of genetically or environmentally induced susceptibility to ordinary degrees of stress, respond to the problems of living with behavior that is either seriously distorted or sufficiently unadaptive to prevent normal interpersonal relations and vocational functioning. The latter outcome—gross deviation from a designated range of desirable behavioral variability—conforms to the generally understood meaning of mental illness.

The plausibility of subsuming abnormal behavioral reactions to stress under the general rubric of disease is further enhanced by the fact that these reactions include the same three principal categories of symptoms found in physical illness. Depression and catastrophic impairment of self-esteem, for example, are manifestations of personality disorder which are symptomologically comparable to edema in cardiac failure or to heart murmurs in valvular disease. They are indicative of underlying pathology but are neither adaptive nor adjustive. Symptoms such as hypomanic overactivity and compulsive striving toward unrealistically high achievement goals, on the other hand, are both adaptive and adjustive, and constitute a type of compensatory response to basic feelings of inadequacy, not unlike cardiac hypertrophy in hypertensive heart disease or elevated white-blood-cell count in acute infections. And finally, distortive psychological defenses that have some adjustive value but are generally maladaptive (e.g., phobias, delusions, autistic fantasies) are analogous to the pathological situation found in conditions like pneumonia, in which the excessive outpouring of serum and phagocytes in defensive response to pathogenic bacteria literally causes the patient to drown in his own fluids.

Within the context of this same general proposition, Szasz repudiates the concept of mental illness as demonological in nature, i.e., as the "true heir to religious myths in general and to the belief in witchcraft in particular," because it allegedly employs a reified abstraction ("a deformity of personality") to account in causal terms both for "human disharmony" and for symptoms of behavior disorder. But again he appears to be demolishing a straw man. Modern students of personality disorder do not regard mental illness as a cause of human disharmony, but as a co-manifestation with it of inherent difficulties in personal adjustment and interpersonal relations; and, insofar as I can accurately interpret the literature, psychopathologists do not conceive of mental illness as a cause of particular behavioral symptoms but as a generic term under which these symptoms can be subsumed.

Mental Illness and Moral Responsibility

Szasz's final reason for regarding mental illness as a myth is really a corollary of his previously considered more general proposition that mental symptoms are essentially reflective of problems of living and hence do not legitimately qualify as manifestations of disease. It focuses on difficulties of ethical choice and responsibility as the particular life problems most likely to be productive of personality disorder. Mowrer (1960) further extends this corollary by asserting that neurotic and psychotic individuals are responsible for their suffering, and that unacknowledged and unexpiated sin, in turn, is the basic cause of this suffering. As previously suggested, however, one can plausibly accept the proposition that psychiatrists and clinical psychologists have erred in trying to divorce behavioral evaluation from ethical considerations, in conducting psychotherapy in an amoral setting, and in confusing the psychological explanation of unethical behavior with absolution from accountability for same, *without* necessarily endorsing the view that personality disorders are basically a reflection of sin, and that victims of these disorders are less ill than responsible for their symptoms (Ausubel, 1952).

In the first place, it is possible in most instances (although admittedly difficult in some) to distinguish quite unambiguously between mental illness and ordinary cases of immorality. The vast majority of persons who are guilty of moral lapses knowingly violate their own ethical precepts for expediential reasons—despite being volitionally capable at the time both of choosing the more moral alternative and of exercising the necessary inhibitory control (Ausubel, 1952). Such persons, also, usually do not exhibit any signs of behavior disorder. At crucial choice points in facing the problems of living they simply choose the opportunistic instead of the moral alternative. They are not mentally ill, but they are clearly accountable for their misconduct. Hence, since personality disorder and immorality are neither coextensive nor mutually exclusive conditions, the concept of mental illness need not necessarily obscure the issue of moral accountability.

Second, guilt may be a contributory factor in behavior disorder, but is by no means the only or principal cause thereof. Feelings of guilt may give rise to anxiety and depression; but in the absence of catastrophic impairment of self-esteem induced by *other* factors, these symptoms tend to be transitory and peripheral in nature (Ausubel, 1952). Repression of guilt is more a consequence than a cause of anxiety.

Third, it is just as unreasonable to hold an individual responsible for symptoms of behavior disorder as to deem him accountable for symptoms of physical illness. He is no more culpable for his inability to cope with sociopsychological stress than he would be for his inability to resist the spread of infectious organisms. In those instances where warranted guilt feelings *do* contribute to personality disorder, the patient is accountable for the misdeeds underlying his guilt, but is hardly responsible for the symptoms brought on by the guilt feelings or for unlawful acts committed during his illness. Acknowledgment of guilt may be therapeutically beneficial under these circumstances, but punishment for the original misconduct should obviously be deferred until after recovery.

Last, even if it were true that all personality disorder is a reflection of sin and that people are accountable for their behavioral symptoms, it would still be unnecessary to deny that these symptoms are manifestations of disease. Illness is no less real because the victim happens to be culpable for his illness. A glutton with hypertensive heart disease undoubtedly aggravates his condition by overeating, and is culpable in part for the often fatal symptoms of his disease, but what reasonable person would claim that for this reason he is not really ill?

CONCLUSIONS

Four propositions in support of the argument for discarding the concept of mental illness were carefully examined, and the following conclusions were reached:

First, although brain pathology is probably not the major cause of personality disorder, it does account for *some* psychological symptoms by impairing the neural substrate of personality. In any case, however, a symptom need not reflect a physical lesion in order to qualify as a genuine manifestation of disease.

Second, Szasz's postulated dichotomy between mental and physical symptoms is untenable because the assessment of *all* symptoms is dependent to some extent on subjective judgment, emotional factors, cultural–ethical norms, and personal involvement of the observer. Furthermore, the use of medical measures in treating behavior disorders —irrespective of whether the underlying causes are neural or psychological—is defensible on the grounds that if inadvertent impairment of the neural substrate of personality can have distortive effects on behavior, directed manipulation of the same substrate may have therapeutic effects.

Third, there is no inherent contradiction in regarding mental symptoms both as expressions of problems in living *and* as manifestations of illness. The latter situation results when individuals are for various reasons unable to cope with such problems, and react with seriously distorted or maladaptive behavior. The three principal categories of behavioral symptoms—manifestations of impaired functioning, adaptive compensation, and defensive overreaction—are also found in bodily disease. The concept of mental illness has never been advanced as a demonological cause of human disharmony, but only as a co-manifestation with it of certain inescapable difficulties and hazards in personal and social adjustment. The same concept is also generally accepted as a generic term for all behavioral symptoms rather than as a reified cause of these symptoms.

Fourth, the view that personality disorder is less a manifestation of illness than of sin, i.e., of culpable inadequacy in meeting problems of ethical choice and responsibility, and that victims of behavior disorder are therefore morally accountable for their symptoms, is neither logically nor empirically tenable. In most instances immoral behavior and mental illness are clearly distinguishable conditions. Guilt is only a secondary etiological factor in anxiety and depression, and in other personality disorders either is not prominent or is conspicuously absent.

REFERENCES

Ausubel, D. P. *Ego development and the personality disorders.* New York: Grune and Stratton, 1952.

Ausubel, D. P. Relationships between psychology and psychiatry: The hidden issues. *Amer. Psychol.,* 1956, *11*, 99–105.

Dreyfuss, F., and J. W. Czaczkes. Blood cholesterol and uric acid of healthy medical students under the stress of an examination. *AMA Arch. intern. Med.,* 1959, *103*, 708.

Mowrer, O. H. "Sin," the lesser of two evils. *Amer. Psychol.,* 1960, *15*, 301–304.

Szasz, T. S. The myth of mental illness. *Amer. Psychol.,* 1960, *15*, 113–118.

justice in the therapeutic state

Thomas S. Szasz

The concept of justice and the concept of treatment belong to two different frames of reference or realms of discourse: the former to law and morals, the latter to medicine and health. Both justice and treatment articulate ideas basic to human life; both have dual uses, one popular, the other technical. Although justice is closely linked with, and receives its most precise meaning from, the workings of the legal system, the concept is not the "private property" of lawyers, but belongs to everyone. Similarly, although treatment is closely linked with, and receives its most precise meaning from, the workings of the medical profession, the concept is not the "private property" of physicians, but belongs to everyone. In this essay, I shall be concerned with examining the relations between these two concepts, in an effort to clarify current popular and prevalent attempts to assimilate jurisprudence to science, law to medicine, the judge to the physician, and justice to treatment.

Law and medicine are among the oldest and most revered professions. This is because each articulates and promotes a basic human need and value: social cooperation, in the case of law; health, in that of medicine. Simply put, the law opposes some types of social processes: it calls them "crimes" and inflicts punishment on those who commit them. Likewise, medicine combats some types of bodily processes: it calls them "diseases" and offers (or prescribes) treatment for those who suffer from them.

To exist as a man, as a person, is synonymous with existing as a social being. The regulation of social relations is an indispensable feature of every society and, indeed, of every coming together of two or more persons. The concept of justice is thus necessary both for the regulation of human relations and for judging the moral quality of the resulting situation. This is what is meant by the statement that without law there can be no justice, but that the law itself may be unjust.

What constitutes justice varies from place to place and from time to time. This does not prove that the concept is devoid of meaning or is "unscientific," as some contemporary social scientists claim. Instead, it shows that to the question "What is a good or proper social order?" mankind has given and continues to give not one but many answers. For example, in principle at least, capitalists believe that those who work harder, or produce more, or whose services are more valuable to the community should receive more for their work than those whose efforts are less productive. Communists believe that the products of all individuals should be pooled and distributed on the basis of absolute equality, and Marxists believe that labor and its products should be regulated by the formula "from each according to his abilities, to each according to his needs."

Framed as general rules of the game of life, contrasting concepts of justice, such as those listed above, would seem to have nothing in common. This is a fallacy, for what underlies all concepts of justice is a notion so basic to social intercourse that without it life would promptly degenerate into a Hobbesian war of all against all. The notion common to all diverse concepts of justice is *contract*, the expectation that we shall keep our promises to others and they shall keep theirs to us. "It is confessedly unjust," wrote John Stuart Mill, "to *break faith* with any one: to violate an engagement, either express or implied, or disappoint expectations raised by our own conduct. . . ." [1] More recently, Paul Freund has similarly sought to locate the core of justice in the concept of contract. He writes: ". . . the concept of

[1] Mill, J. S.: *Utilitarianism* (1863). *In* Lerner, M. (Ed.): *Essential Works of John Stuart Mill.* New York, Bantam, 1961, pp. 93–177; p. 95.

From *Comprehensive Psychiatry* (Fritz A. Freyhan, Ed.), 1970, *11*, pp. 433–444. Reprinted by permission of Grune & Stratton, Inc.

contract is a paradigm case of justice viewed as the satisfaction of reasonable expectations." [2]

Why is contract so all-important to human life? Because it is the foremost rational, nonviolent instrument for the equalization of social power. Contract is the social device par excellence that liberates the relatively powerless individual or group from domination by his more powerful superiors, thus freeing him to plan for the future. Conversely, lack of contract or systematic contract violation is an essential characteristic of oppression: deprived of the power to plan for the future, the inferior individual or group becomes subjected to the status derogation of dependency by his superiors. Thus, when the future arrives, the oppressed individual will be unable to care for himself and will be dependent on his "protectors" (for example, parents, politicians, psychiatrists).

To be sure, like all social arrangements, contract favors some members of the group and frustrates others. It favors the "weak" (that is, those who lack the power to coerce or, if they possess such power, the will to use it), and it frustrates the "strong" (that is, those who have such power or, if they lack it, strive to possess it). Generally contract favors the child as against the parent, the employee as against the employer, and the individual as against the State. In each of these relationships and in other similar situations, the superior member of the pair does not require contract to plan for *his* future; he can control his partner, by brute force if necessary. Contract expands the self-determination of the weak by constricting the powers of the strong to coerce him; at the same time, by placing the value of abiding by the terms of a contract above that of naked power, and by universalizing this value, contract tames not only the power of the strong to coerce but also that of the weak to counter-coerce.

In political life, the paradigm of contract is the Rule of Law, the principle that limits interference by the State in the conduct of the individual to circumstances that are clearly defined and known in advance to the individual. By avoiding law-breaking, the citizen can thus feel secure from unexpected interference by State power. This arrangement may be contrasted with despotic or tyrannical government, whose principal characteristic in its dealings with the individual is not harshness but rather arbitrariness. The brutality and terror of this kind of political arrangement

[2] Freund, P. A.: Social justice and the law. *In* Brandt, R. B. (Ed.): *Social Justice.* Englewood, N.J., Prentice-Hall, 1962, pp. 93–177.

lies precisely in the utter unpredictability with which the police power of the State may be deployed against the individual.

One more example of the fundamental role of contract in the concept of justice should suffice. It is an ancient legal maxim that there should be no punishment without law (*Nulla poena sine lege*). The principle that a man should not be punished for an act which was not prohibited by law, at the time when he engaged in it, shows dramatically that the concept of justice is rooted in ideas and sentiments that have more to do with the need to make behavior predictable than with the need to protect society from harm, for clearly a person may harm his neighbor without his behavior qualifying as an act prohibited by law. (A large part of what we nowadays call "mental illness" falls into this category of personal conduct.) Arguing from the "functional" or "scientific" point of view, the modern psychiatrist or behavioral scientist would hold that what is or ought to be important here is the proper restraint and remotivation of the malefactor, not the abstract idea of justice. From his point of view, the preexistence of law would not be a requirement for invoking the social sanction he calls "psychiatric treatment." It is precisely at this point that the behavioral scientist applies the analogy between misbehavior and illness by arguing that, just as a man may fall ill without his condition being officially recognized by medical science as a "diagnosis;" so, too, a man may engage in criminal conduct without his behavior being officially recognized by the law as a "criminal" act. In this view, what determines the existence of the undesired condition, whether it be illness or crime, and what justifies social intervention against it, whether it be treatment or punishment, is *the judgment of the expert, not a rule written down by lawmakers and legitimized by the judicial and political processes of government.*

These two fundamental principles of regulating human relations (the contractual and the discretionary) serve different aims. Each acquires its value from its "function": to foster the individual's capacity for independence by enabling him to plan for the future, in the case of contract; to enable the expert to act with optimal effectiveness by freeing him from the limitations of restricting rules, in the case of discretion. Since these are two radically different ends, it is hardly surprising that each requires different means for its attainment.

Man is not only a person, a social being; he is

also an animal, a biological organism. Hence, his biological equipment, that is, his body, which is a necessary but not a sufficient condition for his role as a person, will also be of paramount importance to him; for if a man's body is injured or becomes diseased, his ability to perform his social and personal functions will be altered, impaired, or even destroyed, and if his body ceases to function altogether, man ceases to exist as a member of the group or as a person. Just as the law has come into being to regulate and safeguard man's relations to his fellow man, so medicine has come into being to regulate and safeguard his relations to his own body.

Inasmuch as these two basic human needs are closely related (man's relations to his body *always* occurring in a context of preexisting social regulations), it is not surprising that law and medicine, their concepts, interventions, and sometimes their personnel are often intertwined and that, during various historical periods, each of these disciplines has made deep inroads into the territory of the other. In the Middle Ages, for example, when the religious ideology ruled undisputed over the minds of men, the scope and function of the medical healer was strictly circumscribed by the authority of the Church. Not only the dissection of bodies but also the use of drugs was thus forbidden, as contrary to the will of God. Hence it was that medicine, independent of the teachings and powers of the Church, was in the hands of Arab and Jewish physicians or was practiced illegally by white witches. Similarly, in our day, when a medical-psychiatric ideology rules undisputed over the minds of men, legal concepts and methods of social control are confused with and corrupted by medical concepts and methods of social control. The upshot is the transformation of the State from a legal and political entity into a medical and therapeutic one.[3]

The impetus that drives men to depoliticize and therapeutize human relations and social conflicts appears to be the same as that which drives them to comprehend and control the physical world. The history of this process, that is, the birth of modern science in the seventeenth century and its rise to ideological hegemony in the twentieth, has been adequately set forth by others.[4] I shall confine myself here to illustrating the incipient and developed forms of this ideology through quotations from the works of two of its most illustrious American protagonists: Benjamin Rush and Karl Menninger.

Benjamin Rush (1746–1813) signed the Declaration of Independence, was Physician General of the Continental Army, and served as Professor of Physic and Dean of the medical school at the University of Pennsylvania. He is the undisputed father of American psychiatry; his portrait adorns the official seal of the American Psychiatric Association. Without comment, I shall list below passages from Rush's writings showing how he transformed moral questions into medical problems and political judgments into therapeutic decisions.

Perhaps hereafter it may be as much the business of a physician as it is now of a divine to reclaim mankind from vice.[5]

Mankind considered as creatures made for immortality are worthy of all our cares. Let us view them as patients in a hospital. The more they resist our efforts to serve them, the more they have need of our services.[6]

The excess of the passion for liberty, inflamed by the successful issue of the war [of Independence], produced, in many people, opinions and conduct, which could not be removed by reason nor restrained by government. ... The intensive influence which these opinions had upon the understandings, passions, and morals of many of the citizens of the United States, constituted a form of insanity....[7]

In the year 1915, a drunkard, I hope, will be as infamous in society as a liar or thief, and the use of spirits as uncommon in families as a drink made of a solution of arsenic or a decoction of hemlock.[8]

... Miss H. L. .... was confined in our hospital in the year 1800. For several weeks she discovered every mark of a sound mind, except one. She hated her father. On a certain day, she acknowledged, with pleasure, a return of her

[3] Szasz, T. S.: *The Manufacture of Madness.* New York, Harper & Row, 1970. *Ideology and Insanity*, Garden City, N. Y., Doubleday-Anchor, 1970.

[4] Hayek, F. A.: *The Counter-Revolution of Science: Studies on the Abuse of Reason.* New York, Free Press, 1955; Matson, F.: *The Broken Image: Man, Science, and Society.* New York, Braziller, 1964.

[5] Rush, B.: Letter to Granville Sharp, July 9, 1774. *Amer. Studies* 1:20, 1967.

[6] Rush, B.: Letter to Granville Sharp, November 28, 1873. *Ibid.*

[7] Boorstin, D. J.: *The Lost World of Thomas Jefferson.* Boston, Beacon, 1948, p. 182.

[8] Binger, C.: *Revolutionary Doctor: Benjamin Rush, 1746–1813.* New York, Norton, 1966, p. 201.

filial attachment and affection for him; soon after she was discharged cured.[9]

Chagrin, shame, fear, terror, anger, unfit for legal acts, are transient madness. . . . Suicide is madness.[9]

Physicians best judges of sanity.[9]

Lying is a corporeal disease. . . . Persons thus diseased cannot speak the truth upon any subject.[10]

Terror acts powerfully upon the body, through the medium of the mind, and should be employed in the cure of madness.[10]

There was a time when these things [i.e., criticism of Rush's opinions and actions] irritated and distressed me, but I now hear and see them with the same indifference and pity that I hear the ravings and witness the antic gestures of my deranged patients in our hospital. We often hear of 'prisoners at large.' The majority of mankind are *madmen at large*. . . . Were we to live our lives over again and engage in the same benevolent enterprise [i.e., political reform], our means should be not reasoning but bleeding, purging, low diet, and the tranquilizing chair.[11]

Rush's foregoing views provide an early nineteenth century example of the medical–therapeutic perspective on political and social conduct. His statements cited above amply support my contention that although ostensibly he was a founder of American constitutional government, actually he was an architect of the Therapeutic State.[12] The leaders of the American Enlightenment never tired of emphasizing the necessity for restraining the powers of the rulers, that is, for checks and balances in the structure of government. Rush, on the other hand, consistently advocated rule by

benevolent despotism, that is, political absolutism, justified as medical necessity.

As the Constitution articulates the principles of the Legal State in which both ruler and ruled are governed by the Rule of Law, so Rush's writings articulate the principles of the Therapeutic State in which the citizen-patient's conduct is governed by the "clinical judgment" of the medical despot. The former constitutes a basis for expanding the personal liberty of the citizen; the latter, for expanding the political power of the government.

To bring into focus the ideology and rhetoric on which our present-day Therapeutic Society rests, I shall next present, in capsule form, the pertinent opinions of one of its foremost contemporary spokesmen, Karl Menninger, (1893–), a founder of the famed Menninger Clinic and Foundation, a former president of The American Psychoanalytic Association, the recipient of numerous psychiatric honors, and the author of several influential books in the mental health field. Like Rush before him, Menninger is one of the most prominent psychiatrists in America. His views illustrate the contemporary psychiatric mode of viewing all manner of human problems as mental illnesses, indeed, all of life as a disease requiring psychiatric care.

. . . The declaration continues about travesties upon *justice* that result from the introduction of psychiatric methods into courts. But what science or scientist is interested in *justice?* Is pneumonia just? Or cancer? . . . the scientist is seeking the amelioration of an unhappy situation. This can be secured only if the scientific laws controlling the situation can be discovered and complied with and not by talking of justice. . . .[13]

Prostitution and homosexuality rank high in the kingdom of evils. . . . From the standpoint of the psychiatrist, both homosexuality and prostitution—and add to this the use of prostitutes—constitute evidence of immature sexuality and either arrested psychological development or regression. Whatever it may be called by the public, there is no question in the minds of psychiatrists regarding the abnormality of such behavior.[14]

---

[9] Rush, B.: Lecture on the medical jurisprudence of the mind (1810). In Corner, G. W. (Ed.): *The Autobiography of Benjamin Rush: His "Travels Through Life" Together With His "Commonplace Book" for 1789–1812*. Princeton, N.J., Princeton University Press, 1948, pp. 348–351.

[10] Rush, B.: *Medical Inquiries and Observations upon the Diseases of the Mind* (1812). New York, Hafner, 1962, pp. 175, 255–256, 265.

[11] Rush, B.: *Letters of Benjamin Rush*, Vol. II. Princeton, N.J., Princeton University Press, 1951, p. 1090.

[12] Szasz, T. S.: *Law, Liberty, and Psychiatry: An Inquiry into the Social Uses of Mental Health Practices*. New York, Macmillan, 1963, pp. 212–222.

[13] Menninger, K.: *The Human Mind*. New York, Literary Guild of America, 1930, p. 428.

[14] Menninger, K.: *The Vital Balance: The Life Process in Mental Health and Illness*. New York, Viking, 1963, p. 197.

In the unconscious mind, it [masturbation] always represents an aggression against someone.[15]

The very word *justice* irritates scientists. No surgeon expects to be asked if an operation for cancer is just or not . . . behavioral scientists regard it as equally absurd to invoke the question of justice in deciding what to do with a woman who cannot resist her propensity to shoplift, or with a man who cannot repress an impulse to assault somebody. This sort of behavior has to be controlled; it has to be discouraged; it has to be *stopped*. This (to the scientist) is a matter of public safety and amicable coexistence, not of justice.[16]

Eliminating one offender who happens to get caught *weakens* public security by creating a false sense of diminished danger through a definite remedial measure. Actually, it does not remedy anything, and it bypasses completely the real and unsolved problem of *how to identify, detect, and detain potentially dangerous citizens.*[17]

[In a society properly informed by "behavioral science"], indeterminate sentences will be taken for granted, and preoccupation with punishment as the penalty of the law would have yielded to a concern for the best measures to insure public safety, with rehabilitation of the offender if possible, and as economically as possible.[18]

Being against punishment is not a sentimental conviction. It is a logical conclusion drawn from scientific experience. It is also a professional principle; we doctors try to relieve pain, not cause it.[19]

The principle of *no* punishment cannot allow of any exception; it must apply in every case, even the worst case, the most horrible case, the most dreadful case—not merely in the accidental, sympathy-arousing case.[20]

When the community begins to look upon the expression of aggressive violence as the symptom of an illness or as indicative of illness, it will be because it believes doctors can do something to correct such a condition. At present, some better-informed individuals do believe and expect this.[21]

All of the participants in this effort to bring about a favorable change in the patient . . . are imbued with what we may call *therapeutic attitude*. This is one in direct antithesis to attitudes of avoidance, ridicule, scorn, or punitiveness. Hostile feelings toward the subject, however justified by his unpleasant and even destructive behavior, are not in the curriculum of therapy or in the therapist. . . . Doctors and nurses have no time or thought for inflicting unnecessary pain even upon patients who may be difficult, disagreeable, provocative or even dangerous. It is their duty to care for them, to try to make them well, and to prevent them from doing themselves or others harm. This requires love, not hate.[22]

Do I believe there is effective treatment for offenders . . . ? *Most certainly and definitely I do*. Not all cases, to be sure. . . . Some provision has to be made for incurables—pending new knowledge—and these will include some offenders. But I believe the majority of them would prove to be curable. The willfulness and the viciousness of offenders are part of the thing for which they have to be treated. They must not thwart our therapeutic attitude. It is simply not true that most of them are 'fully aware' of what they are doing, nor is it true that they want no help from anyone, although some of them say so.[23]

Some mental patients must be detained for a time even against their wishes, and the same is true for offenders.[24]

As the foregoing quotations show, Menninger focuses systematically on the offender, or alleged offender, who, in his view, is either "punished" with hostile intention or "treated" with therapeutic intention. Accordingly, he urges that we abandon the legal and penological system with its limited and prescribed penalties and substitute

[15] Menninger, K.: *The Wolfenden Report: Report of the Committee on Homosexual Offenses and Prostitution.* New York, Stein & Day, 1964, pp. 5–7.

[16] Menninger, K.: *Man Against Himself.* New York, Harcourt, Brace, 1938, p. 69.

[17] Menninger, K.: *The Crime of Punishment.* New York, Viking, 1968, pp. 17, 262.

[18] *Ibid.,* p. 108.

[19] *Ibid.,* p. 139.

[20] *Ibid.,* p. 204.

[21] *Ibid.,* p. 207.

[22] *Ibid.,* p. 257.

[23] *Ibid.,* pp. 260–261.

[24] *Ibid.,* p. 265.

for it a medical and therapeutic system with unlimited and discretionary sanctions defined as
"treatments."

For centuries the "enlightened" and "scientific"
behavioral technologist has thus sought, and continues to seek, the destruction of law and justice
and their replacement by science and therapy.

Those who see the main domestic business of
the State as the maintenance of internal peace
through a system of just laws justly administered
and those who see it as the provision of behavioral
reform scientifically administered by a scientific
elite have two radically different visions of society
and of man. Since each of these groups strives
after a different goal; it is not surprising that each
condemns the other's methods. Constitutional
government, the rule of law, and due process are
indeed inefficient means for inspiring the personality change of criminals, especially if their
"crime" is not shoplifting (which is Menninger's
favorite example) but violating laws regulating
contraception, abortion, drug "abuse," or homosexuality. Similarly, unlimited psychiatric discretion over the identification and "diagnosis" of
alleged offenders, coercive "therapeutic" interventions, and life-long incarceration in an insane
asylum are neither effective nor ethical means for
protecting individual liberties or insuring restraints on the powers of the government, especially when the individual's "illness" is despair
over his inconsequential life and a wish to put an
end to it.

The legal and the medical approaches to social
control represent two radically different ideolo-
gies, each with its own justificatory rhetoric and
restraining actions. It behooves us to understand
clearly the differences between them.

In the legal concept of the State, justice is both
an end and a means. When such a State is just, it
may be said to have fulfilled its domestic function.
It then has no further claims on its citizens save
for defense against external aggression. What
people do (whether they are virtuous or sinful,
healthy or sick, rich or poor, educated or stupid)
is none of the State's business. This, then, is a
concept of the State as an institution of limited
scope and powers. (In such a State, the people
are of course not restrained from fulfilling their
needs, not met by the State, through voluntary
association.)

In the scientific–technological concept of the
State, therapy is only a means, not an end. The
goal of the Therapeutic State is universal health,
or at least unfailing relief from suffering. This
untroubled state of man and society is a quintes-
sential feature of the medical–therapeutic perspective on politics. Conflict among individuals,
and especially between the individual and the
State, is invariably seen as a symptom of "illness"
or psychopathology, and the primary function of
the State is accordingly the removal of such conflict through appropriate "therapy"—"therapy" imposed by force, if necessary. It is not difficult to
reognize in this imagery of the Therapeutic State
the old Inquisitorial, or the more recent Totali-
tarian, concept of the State, now clothed in the
garb of psychiatric treatment.[25]

Whether we want a society in which man has a
chance, however small, to develop his powers and
to become an individual, or whether we want one
in which such individualism is considered evil
and man, if we may call him that, is fashioned
into a plastic, compliant robot by his scientific
masters, is in the last analysis, a basic ethical
question to which we cannot, and need not, address ourselves here. Of course, all who feel
deeply about either of these alternatives believe
that they are championing man's dearest and most
authentic aspirations. According to the libertari-
ans, more than anything else man needs protection
from the dangers of unlimited government; according to the therapeutists, he needs protection
from the dangers of unlimited illness. As so often
happens when people become separated by an
ideological gulf, the advocates of these two points
of view are no longer on speaking terms. The
behavioral engineers and psychiatric therapists,
who have suceeded in defining their position as
the "progressive" and "scientific" one, have ceased
even to acknowledge the existence of a large body
of fact and thought critical of what I call "the
theory and practice of psychiatric violence." Nearly
200 years ago this was true of Rush who, in his
writings, never engaged those who opposed tyranny, whether priestly or medical, and it is true
now of Menninger who never confronts those who
fear and distrust the violence of psychiatrists no
less than of politicians.

Among the contemporary scholars who have
opposed the behavioristic–scientistic forces tending toward "the abolition of man," C. S. Lewis
stands high. Until his death in 1963, Lewis was
Professor of Medieval and Renaissance English at
Cambridge University. He is probably best known

[25] See footnote 3.

for his book, *The Screwtape Letters,*[26] which first established him as an influential spokesman for Christianity in the English-speaking world and a brilliant critic of modern science and technology as dehumanizing social institutions. I list below passages illustrative of Lewis's views pertinent to the relations between psychiatry and law.

I am not supposing them [the Conditioners] to be bad men. They are, rather, not men (in the old sense) at all. They are, if you like, men who have sacrificed their own share in traditional humanity in order to devote themselves to the task of deciding what "humanity" shall hence forth mean. . . . Nor are their subjects necessarily unhappy men. They are not men at all: they are artefacts. Man's final conquest has proved to be the abolition of man.[27]

There is no sense in talking about a 'just deterrent' or a 'just cure.' We demand of a deterrent not whether it is just but whether it will deter. We demand of a cure not whether it is just but whether it succeeds. Thus when we cease to consider what the criminal deserves and consider only what will cure him or deter others, we have tacitly removed him from the sphere of justice altogether; instead of a person, a subject of rights, we now have a mere object, a patient, a "case." [28]

The Humanitarian theory, then, removes sentences from the hands of jurists whom the public conscience is entitled to criticize and places them in the hands of technical experts whose special sciences do not even employ such categories as rights or justice. . . . The first result of the Humanitarian theory is, therefore, to substitute for a definite sentence (reflecting to some extent the community's moral judgment on the degree of ill-desert involved) an indefinite sentence terminable only by the word of those experts . . . who inflict it. Which of us, if he stood in the dock, would not prefer to be tried by the old system? [29]

It may be said that by the continued use of the word punishment and the use of the verb "inflict" I am misrepresenting Humanitarians. They are not punishing, not inflicting, only healing. But do not let us be deceived by a name. To be taken without consent from my home and friends; to lose my liberty; to undergo all those assaults on my personality which modern psychotherapy knows how to deliver: . . . to know that this process will never end until either my captors have succeeded or I grown wise enough to cheat them with apparent success—who cares whether this is called Punishment or not? That it includes most of the elements for which any punishment is feared—shame, exile, bondage, and years eaten by the locust—is obvious. Only enormous ill-desert could justify it; but ill-desert is the very conception which the Humanitarian theory has thrown overboard.[30]

Of all tyrannies a tyranny sincerely exercised for the good of its victims may be the most oppressive. . . . To be "cured" against one's will and cured of states which we may not regard as disease is to be put on a level with those who have not yet reached the age of reason or those who never will; to be classed with infants, imbeciles, and domestic animals. But to be punished, however severely, because we have deserved it, because we "ought to have known better," is to be treated as a human person made in God's image.[31]

For if crime and disease are to be regarded as the same thing, it follows that any state of mind which our masters choose to call "disease" can be treated as a crime; and compulsorily cured . . . but under the Humanitarian theory it will not be called by the shocking name of Persecution. . . . The new Nero will approach us with the silky manners of a doctor. . . . Even if the treatment is painful; even if it is life-long, even if it is fatal, that will be a regrettable accident; the intention was purely therapeutic.[32]

But the Humanitarians remain undaunted. Fifteen years after Lewis wrote the above, Menninger declared: "The secret of success in all [penological] programs, however, is the replacement of the punitive attitude with the therapeutic

[26] Lewis, C. S.: *The Screwtape Letters and Screwtape Proposes a Toast* (1943). New York, Macmillan, 1967.
[27] Lewis, C. S.: *The Abolition of Man* (1947). New York, Macmillan, 1965, pp. 76–77.
[28] Lewis, C. S.: The humanitarian theory of punishment. *Res Judicatae* (Melbourne University), 6:224–230, 1953.
[29] *Ibid.*, p. 226.
[30] *Ibid.*, pp. 226–227.
[31] *Ibid.*, p. 228.
[32] *Ibid.*, p. 229.

attitude. A therapeutic attitude is essential regardless of the particular form of treatment or help." [33]

The decision whether to treat others *justly* (fairly) or *therapeutically* (benevolently) is not a choice facing only jurists and psychiatrists; on the contrary, it is a choice everyone must make. The way an individual responds to this challenge, the choice he makes, largely shapes and defines his moral character. Some choose justice; they are regarded as competent and reliable by their friends and as unyielding by their enemies. Others choose benevolence; they are regarded as kindly and loving by their friends, and as despotic by their enemies. This is not to say that individuals cannot, in principle, be both just and benevolent; as persons, they may be both; but, when faced with concrete situations, they must often choose between these two values and types of conduct.

The same considerations hold for societies. Frankena puts this well when he asserts that "Societies can be loving, efficient, prosperous, or good, as well as just, but they may well be just without being notably benevolent, efficient, prosperous, or good." [34] He also notes, correctly, that there is an internal contradiction between a state being both "loving" and "just": the more loving it is, the more unjust it must become, and vice versa (unless "justice" is itself considered a form of "love"). A "just society," Frankena continues, restating the traditional definition, "is, strictly speaking, not simply a loving one. It must in its actions and institutions fulfill certain formal requirements dictated by reason rather than love: it must be rule-governed. . . ." [34] This puts the case of the Just State versus the Therapeutic State squarely before us. And it helps us see what I consider the fatal flaw, both empirically and ethically, in the argument for "love" over "justice."

As we saw earlier, justice, in its most basic sense, may be readily defined as the fulfillment of contracts (or expectations). Contracts, moreover, consist of performances and counterperformances, that is, of *overt acts*. They thus differ from intentions, sentiments, or states of mind which are private experiences. Accordingly, justice is open to public inspection, scrutiny, and judgment, whereas love is closed to such examination and evaluation. Hence, the claim that one is acting justly is a plea for the support of the good opinion of others, whereas the claim that one is acting

lovingly leaves no room for the judgment of others and in its zeal brooks no opposition. Although love appeals to the ideal of consideration for the *needs of others*, while justice appeals to the ideal of consideration for agreed-upon *rules*, in actual practice just actions afford more protection for the self-defined interests of others than do loving actions.

I have tried to show that justice and freedom are closely related concepts and that the value of the former is contingent on that of the latter. Thus, if freedom is debased, so is justice.

I use the term "freedom" to signify man's ability to make uncoerced choices. In this sense of the term, freedom is endangered from two different directions, by two different kinds of threats. One threat emanates from within the individual, from the limitations of his body, his mind, and his personality; for example, illness and stupidity diminish or impair freedom, by diminishing or impairing man's capacity to formulate or execute uncoerced choices. Another threat emanates from outside the individual, from the limitations of his wordly, and especially his social, circumstances; for example, other men, either acting as individuals or through the coercive apparatus of the Church or the State, diminish or impair freedom by diminishing or impairing man's capacity to formulate or execute uncoerced choices.

To confuse these two sources of danger to individual liberties is fatal to their cause, yet this is precisely what the modern "liberal" and "scientific" social critic and reformer often does. By stressing the similarities rather than the differences between man's vulnerability at the hands of Nature and of the State, between the injury inflicted on a person by an illness and by an individual, the behavioral scientist technicizes human problems and thus transforms man into a thing. Having done that at the outset, what is there left for him to protect? Nothing but an image, a shadow, which he then casts into the role of the alleged beneficiary of his spiritual munificence. In this way, the behavioral technologist authenticates himself as a great healer and a great scientist, but his performance is a tragic farce, a play act not unlike that of the child or so-called madman. In each of these cases, the performer *impersonates* an important or noble actor, whether he be fireman, Savior, or physician, and plays his part without regard to the participation of other actors or audience. It is this lack of confirmation by their respective "beneficiaries"—of child as fireman, of madman as Jesus, and of "humanitarian" forensic

---

[33] See footnote 17.

[34] Frankena, W. F.: The concept of social justice. *In* Brandt, R. B. (Ed.): *Social Justice.* Englewood Cliffs, N.J., Prentice-Hall, 1962, pp. 1–29; p. 3.

psychiatrist as healer—that defines each of these roles as counterfeit, but with this difference for the psychiatrist: Whereas child and madman lack the power to impose their role-playing on unconsenting others (thus usually having to confine their performances to their families), psychiatrists, invested with the coercive powers of the State, often impose their definitions of "reality" on others.[35] Hence, in the Therapeutic State, care, help and treatment are not what the involuntary "patients" request but what the "humanitarian" psychiatrists impose.

What, then, of Justice in the Therapeutic State? Its fate may be varied, but of this we can be certain: It will cease to exist as we have come to know it. Justice may thus be consigned to the history books as the relic of a barbarous age that valued individual freedom more highly than collective security, or it may be redefined, in the new-speak of our times, as Treatment.

[35] Szasz, T. S.: *The Myth of Mental Illness.* New York, Hoeber-Harper, 1961, pp. 241–258.

the climate of change

Murray Levine &
Adeline Levine

The field of mental health is currently in a state of ferment so strong that some have already termed the present period the beginning of its third major revolution. The first revolution dates from the time that Pinel removed the chains from mental patients, insisting they were sick and not sinful. The second revolution dates from Freud's introduction of psychodynamic concepts. The third revolution, which refers to the community mental health movement, is probably best dated by President Kennedy's address to Congress in 1963 in which he called for a radically new approach to the care of the mentally ill.

The radically new approach not only involves the *reintegration* of recovered mental patients into the community; it also involves the *prevention* of the personal waste and misery we term mental, emotional, or behavioral disorder, and the promotion of positive mental health. Positive mental health means more than the absence of symptoms. It means that state of well-being which enables the individual to pursue his personal fulfillment. These are bold and broad objectives for community mental health programs, for as soon as the field deals with concepts of positive mental health, the mental health professional must concern himself with studying and influencing those major institutions of society which create, perpetuate, or exacerbate personal waste and misery. In a sense, the whole quality of American life becomes his concern. The mental health professional retains his interest in the individual who is in distress, but in his role as helper he wishes also to influence the family, the schools, social agencies, the courts, industrial organization, community life, the legal and governmental structure, and the economic order. His role model changes from that of the physician and healer to that of educator, social critic, reformer, and social planner.

The contemporary community mental health movement must also be considered from the perspective of its place in American society. Its broad goals must be viewed as a product of the growing acceptance by American society of responsibility for the total welfare of all individuals. The contemporary period reflects the trends which began with the industrial revolution, which were accelerated with the rapid social changes induced by processes of industrialization and urbanization, and which continue today, powered by scientific and technical developments. Throughout our history, but particularly from the 1870's onward, the responsibility of government for the welfare of the people has become increasingly clear and increasingly pervasive. President Johnson spoke as a matter of national policy of the attainment of the Great Society, in which each individual would be freed of concern for material survival and enabled to achieve personal fulfillment.

In the mental health field, the change in the concept of governmental responsibility may be seen in the fate of federal legislation relating to the care of mentally ill. In 1854, President Franklin Pierce (Pierce, 1854) vetoed Dorothea Dix's bill to obtain a federally supported mental hospital on the grounds that the life conditions of individuals were no proper concern of government. In 1955, 101 years later, Congress appointed the Joint Commission on Mental Illness and Mental Health to study the problem and to make recommendations for federal action. When the Joint Commission recommended a narrow program in mental health to be built around the development and revitalization of the state men-

Reprinted from M. Levine and A. Levine, A *Social History of Helping Services: Clinic, Court, School, and Community,* pages 11–21. Copyright 1970 by Appleton-Century-Crofts and reproduced by permission.

tal hospital system, President Kennedy called for a completely new approach in which the federal government was to take the lead in the prevention and treatment of mental disorder. Federal support, on an unprecedented scale, was to be made available for the development of comprehensive, interlocking community services and facilities in order to identify and to satisfy a whole range of needs. Help was not to be limited to the provision of institutions which isolate the "repulsive" (to use the Joint Commission's apt, if harsh term) for their protection and for the protection of society. The concept of providing comprehensive services was embodied in the Community Mental Health Centers Act of 1963.[1]

The Joint Commission report (1961) stated what had long been known: that it is completely impossible with current patterns of mental health services to meet the needs of any but a tiny fraction of those who need help for mental and emotional problems. Surveys of adult populations (Veroff et al., 1960; Srole et al., 1962) and surveys of populations of children (White & Harris, 1961) show clearly that a distressingly large percentage of Americans suffer psychological complaints which at a minimum create personal misery, and which at worst are severely disabling. We cannot say that more people are disturbed now than at some former time because we do not have evidence.[2] However, we are certainly aware that the available mental health facilities, and particularly outpatient facilities, are overloaded. Almost every mental health clinic or social agency has a long waiting list. Private help is costly, in limited supply, and tends to be concentrated in a few large, urban centers.

Shortage of people and of facilities, not likely to be overcome by expanded training efforts, is one overriding factor in the mental health field.

[1] This act, which provides general guides for the type of service to be conducted, is singularly devoid of elements which might stimulate creative innovation. There is the distinct danger that the new community mental health center will turn out to be nothing more than the old psychopathic hospital with a few frills. Albee's (1965) evaluation of existing models of community mental health centers—"There is nothing on the inside except the same old performers going through the same old routines"—provides little cause for optimism that these centers will exert any important influence on the way in which people actually live.
[2] Goldhamer and Marshall (1953) have shown that rates of hospitalization for psychosis in the state of Massachusetts have not changed in 100 years.

There is little hope that educational facilities can be expanded to meet more than a small fraction of present and future needs for trained personnel (Albee, 1959). The overloading of present facilities is in part a consequence of the rapid increase in population. However, the near inevitability of shortage of treating personnel was recognized by the Commonwealth Demonstration Clinics in the mid-1920's, so it is clear the problem is a chronic one, and not solely the result of the current population explosion. Shortage, though, is a potent factor in opening the mental health field to change.

We have also become aware that the need is most acute in low-income populations. Surveys (Hollingshead & Redlich, 1958; Srole et al., 1962; Leighton et al., 1963) have indicated that emotional problems are both more frequent and more severe in low-income populations, particularly in areas noted for their social disorganization. Surveys of children indicate much the same (White & Harris, 1961). While there are arguments about the amount of unrecorded delinquency, and about differential enforcement of the law, it seems indisputable that low-income populations produce high rates of crime and delinquency. At another level, Knobloch and Pasamanick (1961) have argued that low-income populations have higher rates of prematurity, problems in pregnancy and birth associated with probable brain damage, and a variety of childhood disturbances including speech, reading, and behavioral disorders. The Coleman report (1956) confirms, on a national level, that low-income groups have educational deficits which presage a disastrous social and economic adjustment for these groups. Recently, Moynihan (1965) and Rainwater (1966) have documented a state of disorganization in lower-class Negro families which will perpetuate a variety of social and psychological problems.

While the need is clearly most acute, helping services reach low-income populations at best sparingly, and at worst ineffectively, or even destructively. For adult patients, Hollingshead and Redlich (1958) have shown clearly that low-income patients are most likely to receive custodial or somatic care, while upper-income patients are most likely to receive more intensive and personalized psychotherapy. Myers and Schaffer (1958) showed a similar phenomenon for patients applying for psychotherapy at an outpatient mental hygiene clinic. Upper-income patients were more likely to be accepted for psychotherapy, and when accepted, were most likely to be assigned to more experienced therapists. Class V patients, the lowest group, were more likely to be refused psychotherapeutic help, and when accepted for treatment, were more likely to be assigned to an inexperienced medical student who was to be at the clinic for a four-week period. In view of the questionable effectiveness of psychotherapeutic procedures, the evidence may reveal only that available services do not reach low-income groups in the same way they do other segments of the population. People may not be treated on the basis of what they need, but on the basis of who they are.

The reports of Furman (1965) and of Harrison et al. (1965) suggest that much the same is true for children seen in child guidance clinics in New York City. Low-income patients are generally underrepresented in clinic populations, and when they appear, they are less likely to receive treatment. When we think of the degree of family disorganization in lower-income Negro groups, when we think of the lower-class person's reluctance to deal with authority, and when we think of the requirements most clinics have that at least one, if not both parents, participate in treatment, it is not surprising that lower-income families are systematically screened out of existing child guidance services.

The Juvenile Courts were created with a broad mandate for child welfare and were among the first institutions to use psychiatric services. Now they rarely have treatment facilities. Social agencies rarely provide significant counseling help to their lower-income clientele. AFDC (Aid to Families of Dependent Children) programs generally supervise the purse strings of their clients but rarely if ever provide more personal interest and help to their families, as May (1964) has shown so movingly. Case reports of problems in the relationship of welfare agencies and the Juvenile Court to low-income populations may be found in Sarason et al. (1966).

The public school, another institution which might provide significant help to lower-income children, also has a dearth of services. Those services available have generally been directed to schools in better neighborhoods, according to Sexton's report (1961). Anti-poverty programs and federal aid to education may begin to reach more schoolchildren. However, established programs have not appeared in either the quantity or the quality which would give rise to an optimistic view of the future.

There is another set of internal professional pressures which have helped to create the climate of change. The most prestigious of the helping methods, psychotherapy, has come under strong attack, not only on the grounds that it does not reach the low-income patient, but also on the grounds that the procedures may be ineffective. Eysenck (1952, 1961) led the attack when he marshalled evidence which challenged psychotherapists to show that their efforts over a period of time produced change any more effectively than no special help or a minimum of help over an equal length of time. Levitt (1957) and Levitt, Beiser, and Robertson (1959) summarized similar evidence for psychotherapeutic work with children. While there are many questions about the basic studies, and while there are many unresolved issues of controls, it is perfectly clear that the burden of proof is upon the psychotherapist to demonstrate that his methods are effective. Serious question of the effectiveness of the helping technique obligates the professional to seek alternatives.

In clinical settings, particularly outpatient settings, we have also become aware that a highly significant number of patients drop out of treatment after relatively few interviews. Tuckman and Lavell (1959) reported an overall dropout rate of 58 percent for patients seen at 11 child guidance clinics in Philadelphia. Similar findings are reported by Furman (1965) for clinics in New York City, and there is an extensive literature on dropouts in therapy with adults (Reiss & Brandt, 1965). Some of these patients may benefit from brief contacts, and some eventually enter treatment elsewhere, but it is clear that a great deal of therapeutic and diagnostic time is wasted time. The careful intake of many outpatient facilities, which results in extensive waiting lists, is paradoxical in light of the high rate of discontinuance of treatment in many centers. Every clinician working in such a setting is painfully aware of the problem at some level, although some tend to justify the situation by arguing that therapeutic methods are effective only with those who demonstrate sufficient motivation to stay with treatment. Nonetheless, the existence of the problem in most outpatient settings must contribute to the professional mental health worker's willingness to reevaluate the nature of the services he is currently offering.

In the field of psychodiagnosis, the projective tests and clinical intuition and judgment have also come in for considerable questioning. In the decade of the 1950's innumerable Ph.D. theses and other researches failed to demonstrate that projective tests were of any significant worth. Much of that work is summarized in Rickers-Ovsiankina (1960), in Murstein (1963), and in Zubin, Eron, and Schumer (1965). Meehl (1954) unleashed a thunderbolt when he demonstrated that the clinician's vaunted clinical intuition was no better, and in many instances much worse, as a predictive device than a simple regression equation based upon standard, mechanical psychometric research. In subsequent years, Meehl (1960) continued his assault upon the clinical, psychodiagnostic enterprise showing that a clinician's appraisal of a case could not effectively influence a therapist's judgment. Therapists arrived at formulations of their cases within a relatively few hours and did not seem to need diagnostic tests after those few hours. While there still may be instances in which diagnostic tests may contribute significantly to decisions about treatment, evidence seems to suggest that a good deal of diagnostic testing is wasted, particularly in view of high dropout rates. There is not one study which shows that therapy was either reduced in length of time or was more effective as a consequence of diagnostic testing. The attack on the psychologist's functions has led to the reconsideration of the role and its clinical significance.

The role of the mental health professional is under pressure to change not only because of the inadequacies of current forms of treatment, but also because recent thinking in the field has suggested that aspects of practice may actually produce more mental health problems than are cured. The Joint Commission's report *Action for Mental Health* (1961) described the overcrowding and understaffing of the large mental hospitals which made for a custodial rather than a therapeutic orientation. Chronicity may be produced and encouraged by efforts to manage patients in the cheapest and most convenient ways in total institutions (Goffman, 1961) which remove the "repulsive" from the community. That society has been more interested in removing deviants from the community than in restoring them to the community is demonstrated in the lag in the development of aftercare services. At the present time, Connecticut, the home state of Clifford Beers and a pioneer in providing aftercare for mental patients, has minimal aftercare services. In New Haven, for example, it has been our experience that patients released from state mental hospitals typically will be seen once a month, if that often, for supervision of medication; more intensive care is almost impossible to obtain. We are not criticizing the quality of care in Connecticut facilities. We are simply using this enlightened state as an example to reveal the very limited aftercare which is available.

Not only is there a problem in finding facilities for aftercare, but a patient who returns after a sojourn in a mental hospital finds himself stigmatized by his community. Partly because of the problems which are caused by the huge state hospitals, the brand-new community mental health centers are experimenting with services and techniques intended to maintain the patient in the community with minimal dislocation in his life and in the lives of his family. Day hospitals, night hospitals, intensive treatment services, emergency care in crises, family therapy, and the inclusion of vocational rehabilitative services with mental hospital care all have as goals the integration of the patient (and the mental hospital) with the immediately surrounding community. The problem of stigma, so well described by Cumming and Cumming (1957; 1965), by Goffman (1963), and by Phillips (1967), is not entirely solved by such measures. Nonetheless, if the patient can be kept at home, and on his job, his reentry problem may be reduced considerably. The experimentation with new services and techniques requires that the mental health professional reorient himself to his role in the hospital and in the community, for he will be less likely to be living and working in the small, closed society of a psychiatric hospital or clinic.

The problem of the adult mental patient has received most of the attention, but no less severe a problem exists in the care of dependent, delinquent, mentally deficient, and mentally ill children. Residential treatment facilities are generally in short supply. The level of care in many of the institutions borders on the scandalous, and in not a few cases the borders have been crossed (Blatt & Kaplan, 1966). There is an increasing demand for residential services for children, but we have yet to see comparable concern about returning children to the community or maintaining them there. In our work with a local antipoverty agency we have come across instances of adolescents who spent their formative years in institutions with limited academic and vocational facilities, and then were released at age 18 into the community to fend for themselves. After 18, the state no longer had any formal legal responsibility for these boys. The few cases who came to our attention were living an aimless and lonely existence in a shabby midtown hotel. Recognizing the problems in the field of mental deficiency, Connecticut has developed the regional center concept (Sarason et al., 1966). Smaller institutions with a limited number of inpatient beds are located in population centers, with the mission of assisting the local community to maintain most of the retarded children in their own homes.

A still more subtle problem for the mental health field is raised by recent sociological thinking about mental illness as deviancy, and mental health facilities as agencies of deviance control. In this view, most recently explicated by Scheff (1966), psychiatric patients are seen as those who have engaged in what Scheff calls "residual rule-breaking." Residual rule-breaking refers to a variety of violations for which a society provides no explicit label. In our society the violators tend to get lumped together as mentally ill. This viewpoint enables one to consider the behavior called mental illness as bound to "culturally particular normative networks," and not as culture-free symptoms of disease. The social context in which symptoms appear then becomes vital, and the social context and the social norms are open to investigation as contributory to what we call mental illness.

Scheff (1966) argues that almost everyone engages in rule-breaking of various kinds, but only a small percentage of residual rule-breakers go on to deviant careers. That is, in only a very small percentage of the cases does the rule-breaking behavior become stabilized. Scheff wants to account for stabilized residual rule-breaking in terms of the societal reaction to it. The rule-breaking individual is defined as a patient, he takes on that role, and he is then subjected to all of the constraints which act in concert to prevent him from reentering the realm of the normal.

The implications of this view are profound. For one, the mental health professions, and psychiatry in particular, are viewed as contributing to the development of mental illness by providing the doctor role, the necessary complement to the patient role. In effect, by treating a patient in a separate treating institution, the doctor certifies that the patient is indeed a patient and is indeed mentally ill. If the social setting in which the residual rule-breaking occurred had some means of dealing with the problem behavior other than certifying the deviant as ill, the individual would be less likely to enter the sick role, and the deviant

behavior would be less likely to stabilize. Community-oriented approaches, in which normal caretakers, policemen, teachers, lawyers, ministers, and the like are encouraged to handle residual rule-breaking by means other than psychiatric referral might obviate considerably the problems of the sick role. A very new function, that of human relations consultant and advisor to the caretaker, is implied for the mental health professional, not only because the numbers problem demands it but because, in the end, it may prove a more effective way of helping.

There is a second implication in this sociological theory of mental illness. The mental health professionals must be viewed as agents of deviance control. Not only is the mental health professional the one who identifies the deviant; in the very doing he confirms the validity of the social norm violated. The mental health professional is accorded a position with considerable status and considerable wealth attached to it, but in turn the mental health professional confirms the norms of the society which rewards him. In periods of relative social stability, there may be little problem in the mental health professional acting to confirm societal norms. However, in periods of acute social change, *the mental health professional may contribute to the exacerbation of the dislocations people endure by becoming part of the process which induces and maintains cultural lag.* The mental health professional may be confirming social norms which no longer have viability in terms of the way in which people actually live in a changing society. . . .

The variety of forces we have described—population growth, social disorganization associated with personal misery, and the variety of inadequacies of the current pattern of services to serve that segment of the population with the greatest needs—are all factors currently creating both a climate of openness to change and an intense interest in community mental health. The phrase "community mental health" seems to be new. It seems to stand for a set of concepts and techniques as yet only half-formed. However, in the history of mental health services for children, the ideas defining contemporary concepts of community mental health programs are not new; and in fact they hark back to the very inception of a variety of professional services for children. . . .

The early clinical services for children developed with an orientation toward the community, and then changed directions. An examination of these clinical services and their history will enrich us in several ways. First, there are a number of valuable concepts which can be reexamined profitably in terms of the organization and actual practices of these services. Second, the clinical services changed over the course of time. If contemporary services are to learn anything from those experiences, and if we are to try to predict the future, a close examination of the kinds of changes which took place, and the rea-

sons for the change is in order. Third, we have stated the general thesis that social and economic conditions and the intellectual and political spirit of the times exert profound influences upon the mental health problems which occupy our attention, and upon the forms of help which develop and change. History can be the proving ground for such a thesis.

REFERENCES

Albee, G. W. *Mental health manpower trends.* New York: Basic Books, 1959.

Blatt, B., & Kaplan, F. *Christmas in purgatory.* Boston: Allyn & Bacon, 1966.

Coleman, J. S., Campbell, E. Q., Hobson, C. J., McPartland, J., Mood, A. M., Weinfeld, F. D., & York, R. L. *Equality of educational opportunity.* Supt. Documents, Catalog No. FS 5.238:38001. Washington, D.C.: U.S. Government Printing Office, 1966.

Cumming, E., & Cumming, J. *Closed ranks.* Cambridge: Harvard University Press, 1957.

Cumming, J., & Cumming, E. On the stigma of mental illness. *Commun. Mentl Hlth J.,* 1965, *1,* 135–143.

Eysenck, H. J. The effects of psychotherapy: An evaluation. *J. Consult. Psychol.,* 1952, *16,* 319–324.

Eysenck, H. J. The effects of psychotherapy. In H. J. Eysenck (Ed.), *Handbook of abnormal psychology.* New York: Basic Books, 1961.

Furman, S. S. Suggestions for refocusing child guidance clinics. *Children,* 1965, *12,* 140–144.

Goffman, E. *Asylums.* New York: Doubleday, 1961.

Goffman, E. *Stigma: Notes on the management of a spoiled identity.* Englewood Cliffs, N.J.: Prentice-Hall, 1963.

Harrison, S. I., McDermott, J. F., Wilson, P. T., & Schrager, J. Social class and mental illness in children: Choice of treatment. *Arch. General Psychiat.,* 1965, *13,* 411–417.

Hollingshead, A. B., & Redlich, F. C. *Social class and mental illness.* New York: Wiley, 1958.

Joint Commission on Mental Illness and Health. *Action for mental health.* New York: Basic Books, 1961.

Knobloch, H., & Pasamanick, B. Some thoughts on the inheritance of intelligence. *Amer. J. Orthopsychiat.,* 1961, *31,* 454–473.

Leighton, D. C., Harding, J. S., Macklin, D. B., Macmillan, A. M., & Leighton, A. H. *The character of danger: Psychiatric symptoms in selected communities.* New York: Basic Books, 1963.

Levitt, E. E. The results of psychotherapy with children: An evaluation. *J. consult. Psychol.,* 1957, *21,* 189–196.

Levitt, E. E., Beiser, H. R., & Robertson, R. E. A follow-up evaluation of cases treated at a community guidance clinic. *Amer. J. Orthopsychiat.,* 1959, *29,* 337–349.

May, E. *The wasted Americans.* New York: Signet Books, 1964.

Meehl, P. E. *Clinical versus statistical prediction.* Minneapolis: University of Minnesota Press, 1954.

Meehl, P. E. The cognitive activity of the clinician. *Amer. Psychologist,* 1960, *15,* 19–27.

Moynihan, D. P. *The Negro family: The case for national action.* Washington, D.C.: Office of Policy Planning and Research, U.S. Department of Labor, 1965.

Murstein, B. I. *Theory and research in projective techniques.* New York: Wiley, 1963.

Myers, J. K., & Schaffer, L. Social stratification and psychiatric practice: A study of an out-patient clinic. In E. Gartly Jaco (Ed.), *Patients, physicians and illness.* Glencoe, Ill.: The Free Press, 1958, pp. 501–506.

Phillips, D. L. Identification of mental illness. Its consequences for rejection. *Commun. Mentl. Hlth. J.,* 1967, *3,* 262–266.

Pierce, F. The Federal government—the great almoner? (1854) In R. E. Pumphrey & M. W. Pumphrey (Eds.), *The heritage of American social work.* New York: Columbia University Press, 1961, pp. 132–134.

Rainwater, L. Crucible of identity: The Negro lower-class family. *Daedalus,* Winter, 1966.

Reiss, B. F., & Brandt, L. W. What happens to applicants for psychotherapy? *Commun. Mentl. Hlth. J.,* 1965, *1,* 175–180.

Rickers-Ovsiankina, M. A. (Ed.) *Rorschach psychology.* New York: Wiley, 1960.

Sarason, S. B., Levine, M., Goldenberg, I. I., Cherlin, D. L., & Bennett, E. M. *Psychology in community settings: Clinical, educational, vocational, social aspects.* New York: Wiley, 1966.

Scheff, T. S. *Being mentally ill: A sociological theory.* New York: Aldine, 1966,

Sexton, P. C. *Education and income.* New York: Viking Press, 1961.

Srole, L., Langner, T. S., Michael, S. T., Opler, M.

K., & Rennie, T. A. C. *Mental health in the metropolis: The midtown Manhattan study.* New York: McGraw-Hill, 1962.

Tuckman, J., & Lavell, M. Attrition in psychiatric clinics for children. *Public Health Reports.* Public Health Service, 1959, *74,* 309-315.

Veroff, J., Feld, S., & Gurin, G. *Americans view their mental health.* New York: Basic Books, 1960.

White, M. A., & Harris, M. W. *The school psychologist.* New York: Harper, 1961.

Zubin, J., Eron, L. D., & Schumer, F. *An experimental approach to projective techniques.* New York: Wiley, 1965.

from mental health to social action: clinical psychology in historical perspective

Charles Hersch

Shortly after World War II clinical psychologists in the United States established for themselves a fairly clear set of roles as diagnosticians, therapists, and researchers in mental hospitals and clinics. In the next 20 years, however, there were dramatic expansions in the professional roles they came to play. At the heart of these developments were the psychologist's broadening concept of the field of mental health and his increasing concern over the social problems of our times. Bit by bit the domain of his involvement widened, as he moved into mental health consultation, community mental health, community psychology, planned social change, and social action.

During the 1950s the movement in this direction was gradual and not sharply focused. During the 1960s, however, the pressures pushing for change became more demanding, and the expansions in the participation of the clinical psychologist became more evident and more formalized. To be sure, not all of clinical psychology has followed this course. But the segment considered here represents a significant and growing trend, and it provides insights not only into the profession but into the society of which it is a part. The purpose of this article is to delineate some of the directions this trend has taken over the past two decades and to explore some of the historical and social factors that have brought it about.

ORIGINS

Clinical psychology of post–World War II was a child born of three parents: the United States

Paper read in symposium, "Psychology's Role in Social Action and Community Development Programs," at the XIIth Interamerican Congress of Psychology, Montevideo, Uruguay, April 1969.

Government, the profession of medicine, and academic psychology. The clinician was taught in the house of the academy and trained in the house of medicine, while the government, good provider that it was, paid the bills at both addresses.

Each of these forebears placed its stamp on the emerging profession. The relation to government, whose interest at this point was on the returning veteran, established clinical psychology's responsiveness to social needs, but at the same time its financial dependence upon an external influence. Medicine provided the new profession with models of service and a setting in which to work, but at the same time a professional situation that was soon felt to be unacceptable. Academic psychology provided it with the traditions of scientific inquiry and academic freedom, but also with dubious citizenship in the community of scholars and a legacy of guilt when its scientific responsibilities were not being fulfilled.

The character of the new profession was given its original form through the Shakow reports (APA, 1947; APA & AAAP, 1945) and through the conference held in Boulder, Colorado, in 1949 (Raimy, 1950). The clinician was to be educated in existing academic departments and trained in the agencies of the Veterans Administration and the United States Public Health Service. He would be a psychologist first and a clinician second. His clinical specialization in diagnosis and treatment would be reserved for the postdoctoral period. The Boulder model of the clinical psychologist as a scientist–professional was born.

But in the following years many clinical psychologists felt the influence of social and historical change forces that led them to move away from this model and into more broadly defined professional roles. I will discuss these factors making for change as they fall into the following four areas. One is the historical background of psychology itself. The second is the professional situation in which the clinical psychologist found himself during this period. The third involves the changes that took place within the mental health field in general. The fourth area concerns the developments in the American society at large.

IN THE BACKGROUND OF PSYCHOLOGY

The historical background of psychology was that of an independent scientific discipline, functioning in its own home as a full-fledged citizen having its established privileges and responsibilities. Its traditions included the principle of academic freedom, which is the intellectual equivalent of self-determination. Therefore, it was distasteful to the clinical psychologist when he found himself in a newly designated role as a secondary citizen under the jurisdiction of medicine. In the medical setting, the ground rules of what the clinical psychologist could do in his clinical practice and in his research function were determined outside the regulating power of psychology. In a short time, and increasingly so over the years, clinical psychology found these constraints and curtailments to be intolerable.

Another source of disquiet to the psychologist functioning in a clinical setting lay in his own scientific background, in particular in the attitude toward theory that the universities attempted to engrain. Ideally, any theory was to be seen as one among many trying to deal with the same body of facts. Each theory was to be evaluated on its merits, based on such principles as parsimony, breadth, logical consistency, and heuristic power. It was not expected that any one theory was going to encompass all of human existence. The nature of theory was to be analyzed abstractly, with principles originating in the philosophy of science. The psychologist took both theory and the process of theorizing as objects of study, especially romancing for some time with logical positivism. Theory was to be carefully distinguished from fact, and considerable discussion was devoted to the kinds of constructs that helped to maintain this distinction (Marx, 1951). It short, theory was to be regarded as an intellectual and disinterested ordering of the universe, rather than as a tool urgently needed in order to get on with one's day-to-day work. But the needs of the clinical setting were in many ways antithetical to this ideal

point of view toward theory. Service demands were immediate and pressing, and the "scientific attitude" was a luxury hardly to be afforded. Usable concepts and formulations were seized upon whether or not they were subject to test and verification, nor was the time for such verification available. There was a conflict between the psychologist's rigorous training in critical thinking and the facts of life in clinical work (Hathaway, 1958). Many psychologists experienced internal dissonance and discomfort as they were caught between an academic attitude and an applied attitude toward theory.

On the more positive side, another influencing factor was the range of content that fell within the body of psychology. In both his undergraduate and graduate education, the clinical psychologist was exposed to the variety of fields that constituted general psychology. His course work ranged from physiological to social psychology, and included along the way abnormal and developmental psychology, as well as learning, personality, and perceptual theory. The psychologist who had learned his lessons well had the facts and concepts to deal with phenomena at a variety of levels. Many of these learnings enabled him, when the time came, to move into the more community and socially oriented programs effectively. For example, the psychologist's background in learning theory, educational psychology, developmental psychology, and psychometrics made him the natural candidate among the mental health professionals to develop the role of mental health consultant to the schools.

On a broader level, social psychology provided a built-in consideration of social issues, as it touched upon such matters as interpersonal influence, group processes, social structures, and value systems. Woven into the fabric of this particular background was the question of the relationship between individual and social dynamics. This was expressed in a number of ways. Some graduate schools had a specialized curriculum incorporating personality and social psychology. At Harvard University the clinical psychology program was placed in the Department of Social Relations, which included social psychology, anthropology, personality theory, and sociology. The existence of *The Journal of Abnormal and Social Psychology* revealed psychology's recognition of the relationship between psychopathology and forces operating at the social-psychological level. Here we clearly have the antecedents to the presently emerging field of community psychology as it was recently described: "Community psychology . . . is devoted to the study of general psychological processes that link social systems with individual behavior in complex interaction [Conference Committee, 1966, p. 7]."

IN THE PROFESSIONAL SITUATION

I have already touched upon some of the elements in the professional situation that discomfited the clinical psychologist and led him to seek change. Fundamental, of course, was that the psychologist worked in a setting that was not his own but that belonged to another profession, medicine. A battle began between psychology and psychiatry that has continued in various forms over the years and in which neither side is to be commended for its maturity or rationality. Unfortunately for psychology, it was a battle that took place on the other fellow's home grounds and in which the antagonist had most of the weapons. Add to this the youth of clinical psychology, and the circumstances almost demanded the unhappy adolescent emotions and reactions that clinical psychology experienced. The new discipline insisted that it was as good as psychiatry, if not better; clamored for its freedom and independence; struggled against the constant control and supervision; and demanded that its individuality be respected. Psychiatry played out the complementary parental role, and the result was the mutual unreasonable posturing and the repetitious unproductive quarrels.

In his internal affairs, the clinical psychologist suffered from a discontinuity between his professional model and his practice, which was established at the Boulder Conference. The scientist–professional model—that is to say, the concept of a Renaissance psychologist—was not one that was readily converted into practice. Some psychologists conformed to the model; most did not. There is little to indicate that the motives and talents that predispose toward good research are the same as those that predispose toward good clinical performance, or that the two may comfortably coexist within the same person. There was also a curious double standard in regard to the two-headed model. The clinical psychologist who directed all of his efforts toward research was an acceptable member of the larger psychological community. The psychologist who devoted all of his time to clinical practice was regarded as reneging on his commitment to the profession and

as a prodigal who had fled the house of his fathers. The psychologist who moved into private practice was a particular object of dismay, for his specialization was additionally tainted by the touch of money. The Boulder model, then, established a residue of guilt that plagued many clinical psychologists over the next two decades.

There was a corresponding discontinuity between training and subsequent professional function. This was most marked in the limited relationship between what the student learned at the university and what he later had to do in the field. Meaningful clinical content was sparse in the academic courses, but even beyond that adequate role models and an orientation toward professionalism were generally lacking at the university. The practicum and internship placements were better in this regard, but, to the extent that they were, this contributed to the schizophrenic split between different portions of the student's development. The lack of adequate training in psychotherapy, the function to which the clinician particularly aspired and toward which he moved with all deliberate speed, was especially striking. But the discontinuity between training and role held not only for the practitioner side of the Boulder psychologist, it held for his research functioning as well. A few years ago Phillips (1964) described this end of the discontinuity vividly. He pointed to the failure of psychologists in clinical settings to conduct research in any significant quantity and at any distinguished level of leadership in the mental health field. He placed the blame for this state of affairs on an academic education for research that stressed methodological rigor and that focused on intrapsychic psychological processes, thereby laying a foundation that could not be appropriately transposed into the nonacademic setting.

The scientist–professional model was never scientific enough to suit the scientists and never professional enough to suit the professionals. But on the other hand, as it relates to the theme we are developing here, the model did engender flexibility. The clinical psychologist did have a multiplicity of functions, and he did not have to fall tightly into a particular niche. In spite of the disagreeable picture I have painted above, the clinical psychologist was still the research specialist in the mental health setting, was uniquely the diagnostic tester, and was also engaged in interviewing and therapy. Except for the definitely medical matters, such as the administration of drugs, the psychologist did a little bit of everything. He aspired to a range of competencies, and could shift when discomfort in a particular area reached the untenable level. In short, the very conflicts that made for difficulty and instability in his career developments also provided outlets and areas to move in when the difficulty and instability heightened.

IN THE MENTAL HEALTH FIELD

The changes that took place in the mental health field during this period were of such magnitude and such quality that they have been termed a revolution (Hobbs, 1964). I have discussed these changes in another place (Hersch, 1968), and I will summarize some of the major points here.

When the new clinical psychologist joined the mental health team after World War II, the professional situation could be described in fairly straightforward terms. The *patient* was readily defined as the person who suffered from a mental illness, or somewhat more broadly as the individual who appeared at the clinic or hospital seeking professional help. The *therapist* was essentially the psychiatrist, but he was soon joined by the psychologist and social worker in this role. The *process* of treatment was basically psychotherapy, and even the somatic therapies were regarded as facilitators of the therapeutic interview. The *goals* of treatment were the reduction of inner distress, the cure of mental illness or, more ambitiously, structural personality change; while mere symptom removal was not regarded as a meaningful or adequate goal. The *theory* guiding professional work was undisputedly psychoanalysis; the somatic therapies were essentially atheoretical. The *role* of the mental health professional was defined by the clinical tasks of diagnosis and treatment.

But in the ensuing years an explosion of discontent rocked the mental health field and shattered these relatively simple definitions. Changes took place in all directions, and diversity in principle and practice became commonplace. The concern of the mental health worker extended beyond the *patient* as previously defined, and came to include any member of the community who suffered from some degree of impairment; from here professional interest moved to "the improvement of the social well-being of the community at large [Rosenblum, 1968, p. 404]." The ranks of the *therapist* expanded to include other health pro-

fessionals, various community workers, specially trained mental health counselors, volunteers, and finally indigenous nonprofessionals. The *process* of treatment followed this diffusion as each group of helpers offered its services according to its own talents and limitations; and new treatment paradigms, such as behavior modification, appeared. Disagreements developed over the earlier *goals* of therapy, and new concepts of goal emerged. The existentialists stated that inner distress was part of the human condition. The behavior therapists declared that symptom removal was tantamount to cure. For many of those with psychotic conditions the hope was to have them function in the community rather than to have their psychoses disappear. The improvement of social competence and the promotion of positive mental health were cited as the desirable objectives of mental health intervention. As to *theory*, concepts derived from the experimental psychology of learning and from the philosophy–theology of existentialism joined psychoanalysis in guiding clinical work, and social science theories infused the mental health field. The *role* of the mental health professional expanded, moving from the clinical function with individual patients, to the indirect work of mental health consultation, and on to large-scale programs of prevention.

These overall changes in the mental health field represented fundamentally a shift from a clinical to a public health frame of reference. The move was from an intensive preoccupation with individuals to a concern over large populations. Programs came to orient themselves not only to intrapsychic pathology, but to a focus on the community. Attention was placed on the prevention of disability, not only upon its cure. But these concerns—with populations, with the community at large, and with prevention—soon became related to the problems of social systems, the institutions of the community, and the political process. The shift, therefore, brought the mental health professionals, the clinical psychologists among them, to an encounter with many new issues in regard to social and political action.

IN THE SOCIETY

Meanwhile, the American society was being torn by a panorama of urgent and critical problems. Our cities were burning; some of the finest of our youth were being wasted among the drug pads of San Francisco and elsewhere; crime rates had risen and the fear of assault was prevalent in our urban centers; promises to the American Negro were not being fulfilled and his wrath was accumulating; the poor rose to stake their claim for democratic participation and for control over their own destinies; a war that appealed to few and that was understood by even fewer was draining our material and human resources; and three of the most charismatic leaders of this century were shot down in public view. In spite of unprecedented affluence, scientific progress that baffled the common man, technology that seemed to outstrip the problems it was intended to solve, and a set of constitutional principles of government stating the highest of ideals—in spite of all this, the country felt itself beset by human problems that seemed beyond its management.

For the society was involved in a conflict between two intertwined and interdependent forces. On the one side there were the dehumanizing influences that were a consequence of technology, mobility, and urbanization, and that led to a breakdown of intimacy and stability in personal and community relationships. On the other side there was the wave of humanitarianism that was determined to bring reform and that repeatedly took on revolutionary fervor. The civil rights movement, the war on poverty, the hippie phenomenon, the general rising level of aspiration and demand for self-determination by those who felt themselves alienated from the society were all at least in part cut from this cloth. The rash of problems that were disrupting the society internally were the surface phenomena resulting from the clash of these two fundamental forces.

Central to the clash was the conflict between the status quo and the need for change. There was a virtual choosing up of sides by various segments of the community, as each strove either to maintain things as they were or to bring about the changes that were desired. Catch phrases took on double meanings, which varied according to the voice of the speaker. The phrase "law and order," for example, came to mean either a return to civilized living by undoing the wrongs that had been visited upon oppressed groups, or it was a signal to marshal the forces that would keep these oppressed groups in their place socially and economically.

The conflict between the status quo and the need for change was also felt in the professional world, as the center of gravity shifted from the problems of the individual to the problems of the social framework. Here too, twists of language became commonplace. Phrases that originally applied to the patients, and that in some instances smacked of the language of abuse rather than the language of diagnosis, were turned, with equal animosity, onto the serving agents. Instead of the school dropout we heard of the school pushout; instead of the hard-to-reach client we heard of the hard-to-reach agency; instead of the multiproblem family we heard of the multiproblem society. Before, when the mental health professional and his difficult patient had trouble coming to terms with each other, the burden of the problem was placed on the shortcomings of the patient; now it was being placed on the shortcomings of the professional and his institutional systems. Many professionals, therefore, became caught up in a conflict between an allegiance to these systems and an allegiance to their individual consciences, which, for the sake of their patients, asked that fundamental changes be wrought. And the scope of the conflict widened, as the awareness grew that these institutional systems had been set up so as to carry out the prevailing value sentiments of the society.

In short, as both a citizen of the community and as a professional, the mental health worker had his attention drawn to large-scale social issues.

THE PRESENT AND THE FUTURE

Where, then, is clinical psychology in the United States now? There are some discernible trends in the current scene. As I see these trends, they represent the range from a clinical service to a social action frame of reference, and I will present them here as points along such a continuum. It will be clear, however, that in actuality they overlap and shade into each other.

The first of these trends is to establish clinical psychology as an independent profession, freed from the constraints of both medicine and academic psychology. George Albee, the President of the American Psychological Association, has repeatedly called for clinical psychology to disengage itself from medicine, and to abandon both the illness model of personality disorder and the psychiatric setting as well. His suggestion that we establish psychological service centers, run by and for psychologists, is now well known, and a number of such centers have come into operation. In regard to education, there is a substantial body of opinion asking for training programs that are more pertinent to professional practice and less devoted to the academic traditions of research and scholarship. One of these programs has recently been created at the University of Illinois (Peterson, 1968). Its explicit goal is to prepare students for the professional practice of clinical psychology, and it offers a Doctor of Psychology degree rather than the PhD. It eliminates the dissertation and language requirements, and substitutes instead clinical laboratory courses, primarily in diagnosis and treatment. The student completes his doctoral training by spending his fourth year interning in clinical settings.

This first trend essentially has to do with the integrity of the profession. The second trend differs, in that it shifts its focus onto the nature of the public need for clinical services. It begins with the recognition that the model of clinical practice that developed following World War II is inappropriate for large segments of the population, and inappropriate as well in relation to the shortage of manpower. The aim of this trend is to create psychologists who can be broadly responsive to the needs of the community, and who can offer a variety of services in a variety of settings. Respecting the limitations of available manpower, these psychologists should be able to extend their effectiveness by offering brief forms of therapy, by working indirectly as mental health consultants, and by training mental health aides. Their efforts should be directed toward the previously neglected populations, such as the poor, the meagerly educated, and the mentally retarded. They should be able to man the new service delivery systems, which include the walk-in clinic, the emergency service, and the day-care center. The hallmark of the second trend, then, lies in its commitment to make the clinical skills of the psychologist socially responsible. These issues were given serious consideration at Harvard University as it established its new clinical psychology training program. The new program has been placed under an interdepartmental structure drawn from the faculties of Social Relations, Medicine, Education, and the Divinity School. The intent of the program is reflected in its title, "Clinical Psychology and Public Practice."

The next trend emerges out of the developments in the field of community mental health. These developments gave rise to the comprehensive community mental health center. This type of facility is intended to provide a range of services, offering continuity of care to the individual patient, as well as consultation and education programs to the rest of the community. Its plan is to provide for the localization and coordination of services that previously had been scattered both geographically and administratively. In discussing the psychologist of this trend, I will follow a recent paper by Rosenblum (1968). He states that the community mental health center psychologist, because of the setting in which he works, remains bound to the medical context, but there are considerable extensions in the roles that he plays, particularly in the areas of mental health consultation and education. The mental health center psychologist is described in the following way:

> He is aware of the need to bring community participation into a variety of mental health programs. It would be appropriate to say that he has added onto the clinical–medical model of mental health a public health approach and has developed an orientation toward the prevention of mental illness and the promotion of social well-being [p. 405].

Rosenblum goes on to list a range of functions or roles that are available to the psychologist in this setting. Some of these are traditional for the clinician, such as diagnostician, therapist, researcher and supervisor. Others, such as mental health consultant, embody the newer practices in the field. But other functions that he lists show an even broader scope. One of these is change agent participating in planned community change, in such areas as antipoverty programs and citizen committees on delinquency. Another is political lobbyist, promoting new legislation in areas touching on the welfare of the community. The role of the clinical psychologist in this setting, then, may extend appreciably into the domain of social intervention.

The fourth trend is the emergence of the field of community psychology. In May 1965 a conference was held on the education of psychologists for community mental health (Conference Committee, 1966). However, it promptly left behind both clinical psychology and community mental health, and gave birth to a new area altogether, community psychology. The participants at the conference agreed that the clinical orientation and the medical setting were too constricting, and that there was the need to move into much broader social change functions. The energizing power of this new field was drawn from clinical psychology and community mental health psychology, and from the frustration of its members in trying to deal with significant social and community problems from a traditional base. The desire was for new levels of involvement in bringing about change and for stronger positions from which to operate. The conference "emphasized that only by participation and involvement could the psychologist enrich the theory and technology of social intervention [Reiff, 1968, p. 525]." Community psychology was shortly thereafter established as a division within the American Psychological Association. This past year a new doctoral program in social community psychology was initiated at Boston College. Its purpose is to train professionals who can work toward social change by fostering and supporting the efforts of local populations to determine their own destinies.

The fifth and final trend is the most difficult for me to delineate clearly. It blurs into community psychology at one end and out of psychology altogether at the other. It is not confined to clinical psychology, although many clinical psychologists are involved, nor is it confined to psychology in general, for the movement has engaged many other professions, and other members of the community as well. In broad terms, I see this trend as the thrust to bring about major and basic changes in the society through social and political action. The trend is reflected in the formation in 1968 of the American Psychologists for Social Action. Their purpose is stated as follows:

> We psychologists feel a deep sense of social responsibility. This responsibility calls for action beyond talk and study. We seek ways of applying our knowledge and experience toward the resolution of the urgent social problems of our time. These include the problems of militarism, racism, and poverty. As human beings, we are confronted with the effects of violence and dehumanization that thwart the realization of human potential. As professionals, we are dedicated to bringing our influence to bear on society, to help solve these problems [APSA, 1968, p. 1].

Sylvia Scribner (1968) also captures much of this trend in her description of what she calls social movement psychologists:

> By this phrase I mean to refer to psychologists who identify themselves with the aims of political and social movements working for major change. It is their conviction that fundamental changes in society will only come about through the organized political struggle of sections of the population, and they have committed themselves to support the aggressive political action groups of today. . . . As psychologists, they are involved in working for social change in a political way [p. 4].

Psychologists who have moved in these directions may or may not work directly out of their institutional settings, often finding it better not to, and many of them have little concern for the distinction between professional and citizen roles.

I have presented a somewhat specialized history of clinical psychology, one that bears on the movement of clinical psychologists toward the framework of social action. But in a larger sense, the trends that I have discussed provide for me some general description of where clinical psychology is now. As to where it is going, I am too timid to hazard a prediction. It is unlikely that, 25 years ago, anyone could have foreseen the current face of clinical psychology. Where it will be 25 years from now will again be shaped by forces in its own background and in its professional and societal context. But what these forces will be and how they will blend we will have to wait and see. So let me hedge on prophesy, and simply quote the words of the grandfather of clinical psychology, Lightner Witmer, who at the turn of this century wrote: "But in the final analysis the progress of clinical psychology, as of every other science, will be determined by the value and amount of its contributions to the advancement of the human race [quoted in Reisman, 1966, p. 357]."

REFERENCES

American Psychological Association, Committee on Training in Clinical Psychology. Recommended graduate training program in clinical psychology. *American Psychologist,* 1947, *2,* 539–558.

American Psychological Association and American Association of Applied Psychology, Committees on Graduate and Professional Training. Subcommittee report on graduate training in clinical psychology. *Journal of Consulting Psychology,* 1945, *9,* 243–266.

American Psychologists for Social Action. APSA: Purpose, structure, function. *Social Action,* 1968, *1,* 1.

Conference Committee. *Community psychology: A report of the Boston conference on the education of psychologists for community mental health.* Boston:

Boston University and South Shore Mental Health Center, 1966.

Hathaway, S. R. A study of human behavior: The clinical psychologist. *American Psychologist*, 1958, *13*, 257–265.

Hersch, C. The discontent explosion in mental health. *American Psychologist*, 1968, *23*, 497–506.

Hobbs, N. Mental health's third revolution. *American Journal of Orthopsychiatry*, 1964, *34*, 822–833.

Marx, M. H. (Ed.) *Psychological theory*. New York: Macmillan, 1951.

Peterson, D. R. The doctor of psychology program at the University of Illinois. *American Psychologist*, 1968, *23*, 511–516.

Phillips, L. Specialized training for research. In L. Blank & H. P. David (Eds.), *Sourcebook for training in clinical psychology*. New York: Springer, 1964.

Raimy, V. C. (Ed.) *Training in clinical psychology*. (Boulder Conference) New York: Prentice-Hall, 1950.

Reiff, R. Social intervention and the problem of psychological analysis. *American Psychologist*, 1968, *23*, 524–531.

Reisman, J. M. *The development of clinical psychology*. New York: Appleton-Century-Crofts, 1966.

Rosenblum, G. The new role of the clinical psychologist in the community mental health center. *Community Mental Health Journal*, 1968, *4*, 403–410.

Scribner, S. What is community psychology made of? *Division of Community Psychology Newsletter*, 1968, *2*, 4–6.

PART II
views of
maladaptive
behavior

Contemporary students of abnormal psychology are committed to the scientific method, but they do disagree about which concepts and theoretical approaches will ultimately prove to be most productive. The articles of Part II provide examples of the four major theoretical orientations to the study of maladaptive behavior.

Two of these orientations are strongly psychological in character. They deal with the behaving individual and the antecedents—especially the environmental antecedents—of his activities. They differ in how they interpret the life conditions under which an individual lives and the internal events (thoughts, dreams) stimulated by them. The psychodynamic orientation stresses intrapsychic processes and is exemplified by psychoanalysis. However, neither the psychodynamic nor any other theoretical approach to maladaptation is unbending and monolithic. Within a given theoretical camp there may be sharp differences of opinion concerning the theory's tenets and its relationship to other theories.

Frieda Fromm-Reichmann's article offers a perspective of major components of the psychoanalytic viewpoint. Psychoanalysis was conceived by Freud as a broad framework within which all behavior can be understood. Fromm-Reichmann, who devoted much of her career to work with psychotic individuals, gives special emphasis to the clinical applications of Freudian concepts. Harry Stack Sullivan, like Fromm-Reichmann a psychiatrist, also worked extensively with psychotics. He believed that Freud had not paid sufficient attention to the important role played by interpersonal relationships in the formation of personality. As his approach to personality evolved, Sullivan modified the definition of many psychoanalytic terms and introduced several totally new ones. Sullivan's theory emphasizes the negative effects on personal adjustment of insecurity aroused by undesirable social experiences and de-emphasizes the Freudian preoccupation with instinctual impulses.

Learning theory provides another psychological orientation to the study of behavior disorders. Whereas psychodynamic theories have largely grown out of observational data gathered in clinical settings, learning theorists have relied more on the experimental method and laboratory investigations. A large group of learning theorists believes that clinical observations provide valuable leads which can be pursued most effectively under conditions better controlled than those obtaining in hospitals, clinics, and consulting offices. Writers such as Mowrer, Sears, and Dollard and Miller have pointed to the need for clearer and more verifiable definitions of the concepts introduced by psychoanalysts and other psychodynamically oriented clinicians. Taking a step in fulfilling this need, in his article O. H. Mowrer seeks to redefine one Freudian concept, that of anxiety. Mowrer argues that anxiety can be viewed more meaningfully in terms of identifiable stimulus events and the organism's reactions to them, than as an instinctive response.

Another group of learning theorists—B. F. Skinner is the most influential among them—believes that attempts like Mowrer's to sharpen psychoanalytic concepts are doomed to failure. Strict behaviorists are pessimistic because they see theoretical ideas referring to covert events (e.g., the defense mechanisms) as inhibiting the analysis of behavior into its objective components of stimulus and response. Whereas all learning theorists and most psychodynamic theorists (especially the psychoanalysts) believe in determinism—the idea that the causes of behavior can be uncovered through rational exploration—Skinner vigorously rejects explanations based on hidden causes such as repressed anxieties. In his article, he calls for a massive attack on the overt behavior of psychosis. Important questions that he propounds are: Which types of stimulus events are conducive to the acquisition of psychotic behavior? Which types contribute to its extinction?

A third theoretical orientation to abnormal psychology thrives among sociologists interested in deviancy. For them deviancy can be approached most effectively from a social systems viewpoint. Sociologists often criticize clinical and experimental psychological studies because these investigations sometimes do not take proper account of possible influence by social and cultural forces outside the individual's immediate environment. Thomas Scheff's paper outlines several sociological guidelines for the study of maladaptive behavior. Explicit or implicit in his discussion of mental disorders are the ideas that each person lives in many environments (family, school, circle of friends, country); that we may play quite different social roles in different environments; and that these different environments react differently to behavior that is socially unacceptable.

The article by Harold and Charlotte Raush is especially interesting because the authors deal with weaknesses both in psychoanalysis as a theory and in the social systems which have been developed by professions that provide clinical servies. These authors, like Scheff, hold that the variables of social systems are directly relevant to analysis of persons' maladaptive behavior. Believing, however, that the potential of psychoanalysis as a social force has not yet been realized, they continue to be intrigued by the roles played by hidden (Skinner would say fictitious) forces within each individual.

The fourth orientation concerns biophysical factors and their relationship to behavior. Man is both a social and a biological organism. In the history of scientific work on behavior, a number of landmark studies demonstrate the occasionally crucial role that biophysical variables can play in the causation of behavioral inadequacies. Perhaps the most dramatic discovery was the finding that the *Spirochaeta pallida* causes syphilis of the brain. This infection leads to deterioration of the brain, resulting in a variety of behavioral deficits (slurred speech, ideas of grandeur, overactivity). In his article Peter Wolff provides a strong caution against neglect of the biological dimensions of maladaptation. He pays special attention to the roles played by hereditary variables and their interaction with environmental factors.

This topic is also dealt with by Eiduson, Eiduson, and Geller, who discuss both the relationship between biochemical events and genetic transmission and the relationship between the result of that transmission and experience. As they point out, these relationships are almost always complicated and the student of behavior must guard against succumbing to the temptations of neat but oversimplistic explanations.

Despite doctrinal differences, the four orientations reflected in Part II are not necessarily in fierce competition with each other. Some champions of certain viewpoints are uncompromising in their theoretical commitments, but most students of behavior recognize the need to interrelate concepts and data that grow out of different assumptions and biases. Because the scientific exploration of maladaptive behavior is at an early stage of its development, the viewpoints presented in Part II are seen better as bases for charting explorations than as the products of them.

recent advances in psychoanalysis

Frieda Fromm-Reichmann

Before attempting any discussion of recent advances in psychoanalysis a brief review should be given of some basic concepts of classical psychoanalysis versus its modifications in recent modern dynamic psychoanalytic conceptual thinking, so that a useful frame of reference may be established.

Advances achieved in psychoanalysis in recent years are in relation to these conceptions, to the method and technique of therapy, and to the types of patients who can be treated by psychoanalytic psychotherapy. (1)

BASIC PSYCHOANALYTIC CONCEPTS

Psychoanalysis understands the functioning of the human mind as the result of the dynamic interaction between mental operations on various levels and with different qualities of awareness. (Freud: Conscious, preconscious, unconscious.) Thoughts and feelings which are incompatible with the standards of a person himself, with those of significant people in his environment or of his culture at large may be barred from awareness and recall ("repressed," "dissociated") because of the effect of anxiety they would produce were they to remain in awareness. Unknown to the person, these repressed experiences remain alive in his mind and influence his thoughts, feelings, and actions. At times, this is the reason for people expressing things which are seemingly not meaningful. As psychoanalysts have learned to realize that their origin is on other levels of awareness, hence qualitatively different from those in which the person communicates, they have learned to understand that all mental and emotional manifestations are meaningful and, at least potentially, understandable.

This dynamic conception of the modes of operation of the human mind is in contrast to the preanalytic, descriptive, psychiatric approach to an understanding of the working of the mind as a static entity. Poets and philosophers, of course, have known for centuries about the functional dichotomy of the human mind. It is the scientific discovery of its application to psychiatry and to psychology, and more specifically in the context of this paper, of its medical application to psychiatry, to psychotherapy, and to medicine at large (psychosomatic medicine), that I am discussing here.

To gain an understanding of human personality as characterized by psychoanalytic dynamic psychiatry, its functioning must be explored and understood genetically, that is, from its total history. The early developmental history of infancy and childhood plays a predominant role in the formation of character and personality and especially in the formation of patterns of human interrelationships. This early history is understood in terms of three elements complementing one another. They are: constitution, or that which a person brings with him, the influences of external circumstances at large, and, most of all, the specific important interpersonal experiences of the infant and young child with the significant people of his early environment. The latter play a portentous role, due to the length of time and the extent of the biological and psychological dependence of the human.

Unknown to the person, this pattern formation and its reappearance hold true also for the early traumatic interpersonal experiences which have been subjected to the process of dissociation or repression. Because they have been dissociated there can be no participation of such experiences in the growth and maturation of the rest of the personality. It is their reflection in the interpersonal experiences of later life which is the salience

Reprinted from *Journal of the American Medical Women's Association*, 1949, *4*, pp. 320–326. Reprinted by permission.

47

of many distorted evaluations of and responses to these experiences throughout life, on the one hand, and of the mental patient's unwitting, compulsive search for their repetition, on the other. Whether the connection of these early, unclarified interpersonal experiences is with love, hatred, pain, anxiety, or other feelings and emotions, their transference to the people of one's later life plays a very important role in all relationships.

So much, in brief, about the generally accepted basic psychoanalytic concepts of the functioning of the human mind and personality. I shall endeavor now to outline briefly a few highlights of the various psychoanalytic conceptions of human developmental history because they form the frame of reference for all genetically oriented psychoanalytic psychotherapy.

DEVELOPMENTAL HISTORY

The early developmental history as conceived by Freud is psychosexual in nature. (2, 3, 4, 5) He understands the various phases of a person's development to be the outcome of a response to the lust obtainable and the interpersonal expression available by means of the bodily zones of food intake and elimination. Consequently, Freud speaks of an oral, anal, and phallic state of one's pregenital psychosexual development, all of which precede the ability of a person to feel genital lust. The sexual energy manifesting itself in these psychosexual pregenital and genital interests and activities, Freud calls libido. He conceives the course of character development and personality in its ultimate mentally healthy outcome to be the result of this libidinal energy having run a complete and uninterrupted course, from the early oral state to the time at which the human gains the ability to feel primarily genital lust in relation to another person of the opposite sex.

According to Freud, a person matures as he learns to take care of the desexualization of his pregenital libido by means of sublimation, reaction formation, over-compensation, etc. Subsequently he develops the ability for orgastic genital experiences with a mature person of the opposite sex.

Oedipus Complex

This is done first in terms of the Oedipus complex, the situation in which the genitalization of libido is felt in connection with a tender and sexual

affection for the parent of the opposite sex and concomitant feelings of rivalry and hatred for the parent of the same sex. The Oedipus constellation in the mentally healthy is resolved by the child's tendency to use the parent of the same sex as a model for its own further developmental patterns and ideal formations, and the parent of the opposite sex as a person through whom it learns to develop friendly interpersonal relationships.

The ability to amalgamate feelings of emotional tenderness and of sexual attraction toward one and the same person is considered another evidence of matureness. Freud views love as an outcome and a concomitant feeling of sexual attraction to another person.

In the course of neurotic character development, according to Freud's concepts, the progress of libidinal energy from oral to genital primacy is interrupted and incomplete. The libidinal charge is fixated or attached emotionally to one of the pregenital levels of the psychosexual development. Also, the neurotic person has not succeeded in overcoming the early conflicts of the original Oedipus constellation. According to Freud, these early conflicts constitute one universally valid reason for the later development of neurotic disorders.

The doctrine of the ubiquitousness and of the sexual nature of the Oedipus complex has been revised by many psychoanalytic authors and cultural anthropologists. (Boehm [6], Fromm [7], Malinowski [8], Mullahy [9], et al.). They would demonstrate, first, that in matriarchal societies it may not be the father but an uncle who is the target for the little boy's hatred; second, that the boy's hatred against the father, where encountered, is much more frequently based upon his resentment of the authoritative prerogatives of the father figure and/or his envy of the interpersonal intimacy between the father and mother, than upon a sexual origin.

Sullivan viewed the various phases of developmental history in terms of the interpersonal experiences characteristic of each of these phases of development. (10) He referred to the period of infancy, the childhood period, the juvenile era, preadolescence, and, as a last developmental phase, adolescence.

The period of infancy he refers to as the time during which the human is in contact with the mothering one by empathic linkage, the state of non-verbal contact through nonsensory channels which is characteristic of the early mother–infant relationship. In varying degrees, empathy may operate in people throughout their lives. It is the quality due to which non-verbalized, meaningful communication is frequently successful and its operation becomes therapeutically important in the psychiatrist's dealings with his mental patients, especially with mute or inarticulate ones.

The childhood period, Sullivan characterizes by the development of mutual, verbalized communication, contentment in a communal life with authoritarian adults, and the more or less personalized pets, toys, and other objects.

The juvenile era is characterized by maturation of the need for compeers and of one's talents for such interpersonal phenomena as co-operation, competition, and compromise.

Preadolescence is a time during which the need for a chum to love is a predominant interpersonal factor. Love, as defined by Sullivan and Fromm (11), is the state of relatedness in which a person is as interested in the loved one's well-being, satisfaction, and security, growth, and maturation, as he is in his own.

Adolescence is the period that is characterized by the process of puberty, gradually producing a maturing sense of self-realization. This is the time when there is a need to break away from the authoritative people of childhood in a rather dramatic way, via the detour of exchanging them for dependence upon and admiration for one's heroes and heroines. In this way the ability to form independent evaluational judgments is finally gained and ultimately the capacity is developed for establishing durable relationships of intimacy.

PSYCHIATRY—THE SCIENCE OF INTERPERSONAL RELATIONSHIPS

This interpersonal concept of the developmental history is an illustrative part of Sullivan's total doctrine of psychiatry as being the art and science of interpersonal relationships, which means that human personality functions and can be understood only in terms of a person's actual or phantasy relationships and through the medium of a person's contacts and exchange with others.

The emotional importance of the bodily zones of intake and elimination and of their functions during early life is not denied, of course, by any of the modern psychoanalytic psychiatrists. (Fromm [12], Horney [13]) However, many of them do not believe that character and personality trends can be understood as the outcome

of various forms of desexualization, as has been described in the review of the basic classical psychoanalytic concepts. Fromm, for instance, sees the fundamental basis of character formation in the specific kind of relatedness of a person to the world as it is molded in childhood by the family, the psychic agent of society. His concept of a receptive, exploitative, hoarding, and marketing character versus a productive character who is able "to use his powers and to realize the potentialities inherent in him," in a positive, life-furthering sense are illustrative of his approach.

We see from these concepts, then, that modern developmental psychoanalytic theory is characterized by the maintenance of the paramount significance of the total developmental history and by the negation of its classical psychosexual interpretation.

Freud's conception of the emotional significance of immediate environmental influences for the understanding of human personality and for the treatment of human psychopathology has been broadened in the direction of the inclusion of cultural influences on a general scale versus his otherwise predominantly biological approach to human psychopathology. The concepts of Fromm (12, 14), Horney (13, 15), Kardiner (16), Sullivan (10, 17), et al., on the Oedipus constellation, may serve as an example for this development.

PSYCHOANALYTIC CONCEPTS OF ANXIETY

Another expression of the changes and advances in psychoanalytic thinking and therapy is with regard to some mental symptoms, among them the most outstanding one: anxiety. The study of the concepts of anxiety as developed in the various schools of psychoanalytic thinking is of greatest importance for any student and practitioner in the field, since the understanding and adequate handling of the patient's anxiety plays a crucial role in all psychopathology, hence in all psychoanalytic psychotherapy.

Freud has defined anxiety in his early writings as the correlate of repressed libidinal strivings. Later he saw it as a person's fear at the realization of culturally inacceptable inner strivings. (18) This definition is similar to the one Sullivan gives in his interpersonal frame of reference. (10, 19) In Sullivan's definition, anxiety is the discomfort which the child learns to feel in the presence of the disapproval of the significant adult who first uses the arousal of this discomfort as a tool while training the child to abide by the basic requirements of acculturation. With great variations as to the threshold of endurance, anxiety remains effective throughout people's lives in response to disapproval from important people which interferes with a person's security and prestige. Sullivan has taught the understanding of all mental disorders as an expression of and an attempt at warding off anxiety. Horney speaks of four principal modes of defense against anxiety: affection, submissiveness, power, withdrawal. She teaches that the craving for affection for power, and for control plays a paramount role in the development of neuroses and neurotic personalities.

Where there is anxiety there is insecurity; where there is insecurity there is lack of self-respect; where there is lack of self-respect there is lack of respect for others. Anxiety causes impairment of relatedness to others, fear of friendliness in giving and taking, loneliness and hostility, all well-known symptoms in mental patients.

This brief outline of psychoanalytic concepts may suffice as a background for the following discussion of the recent advances in the method and technique of psychoanalytic psychotherapy and the types of patients who may be treated by modern, dynamic psychoanalytic psychotherapy.

ETIOLOGY OF MENTAL DISORDER

In the light of the dynamic and genetic conceptions of the working of the mind, human psychopathology is understood by all dynamic psychiatrists as the outcome of early warp, thwarting experiences, and severe frustrations in relation to a significant person in the infant's or child's environment. In the upbringing of our present day, circumscribed as it is by family life, as a rule, it is a parent who is responsible for warping experiences, the threat of which is too great to be offset by other benign influences. The type of emotional disturbance which a person develops will depend upon the timing of the first decisive blow of a set of such traumatic experiences and from the presence or absence of other benign or malignant interpersonal influences. Many emotional experiences of his later life will be undergone, actually or by his interpretation, as if they were really repetitions of the original traumata in the childhood setting.

In other words, whenever a person who has undergone too severe or too frequent early traumatic experiences is exposed to later life experiences engendering pain, hostility, anxiety, etc., he has to cope not only with the actual experience as such, but in addition with its repetitional validity. This repetitional aspect stems from his early dissociated, therefore never satisfactorily integrated, traumatic experiences with all their immature misevaluation and their concomitant anxiety.

In order to avoid misunderstanding, I wish to state at this point, that in discussing the psychopathological effects of keeping emotional experiences from awareness, I do not mean to say that all dissociative or repressed processes are psychopathological in nature. The contrary is true. Man depends upon successful dissociations and processes of selective inattention for the mastery of his psychobiological existence. It is the surplus of painful and anxiety-rousing emotional experience, whose barring from awareness creates psychopathological problems. If a patient's original traumatic material is brought to awareness in psychotherapy, it can be submitted to revaluation on the present level of the patient's matureness, anxiety can be relieved and recent traumatic experience can be freed from the additional weight stemming from non-integrated previous experience. Hence, the bringing to awareness and the subsequent evaluation of repressed material must be an integral part of the psychotherapeutic process just as will the investigation of those feelings, the reflection of which will be transferred to the people of one's later life.

PSYCHOANALYTIC PSYCHOTHERAPY

In the situation of psychoanalytic psychotherapy these feelings, unknown to the patient himself, will be transferred to the psychotherapist and so they can be studied *in statu nascendi* by psychiatrist and patient. Otherwise, treatment must be directed toward resolving psychopathological repression and dissociation and understanding the patient's difficulties in terms of his developmental history. This aim is attained in using the following psychotherapeutic tools: collecting data from the patient regarding biographical and historical facts which the patient is able to offer; his presenting problems, previous problems and crisis situations; biographical data especially regarding his developmental history; his private mental experiences, such as dreams and daydreams, hallucinatory and delusional experiences.

The means for collecting the data are listening intelligently, as a participant observer, to all that the patient has to say; asking simply meaningful and pertinent questions; encouraging associative thinking; and picking up marginal thoughts and physical sensations, where direct information is failing. Further therapeutically valid material presents itself in the repetition and reactivation, during treatment, of the powers which originally motivated the patient's dissociative procedures. As mentioned before, this also takes place, and is of the essence for therapeutic use in the vicissitudes of the doctor–patient relationship, in its real and in its distorted, "parataxic," aspects—in classical terminology, in the patient's "transference" experiences. Once the pertinent data is carefully collected, interpretative collaboration between the patient and the psychotherapist follows, with regard to the understanding of the hidden meaning of the previously dissociated material, as to its genetics, dynamics, and content.

Interpretation

Interpretation means translating into the language of awareness, and thereby bringing into the open, that which the patient communicates, without being conscious of its contents, dynamics, revealing connections with other experiences or of various implications pertaining to its factual or emotional background.

At the present state of development in psychoanalytic psychotherapy, special interpretative attention is given to the clarification of the dynamic significance of the defense mechanisms, the security operations which the anxious mental patient uses, wittingly or unwittingly, in his dealings with his fellow men, including the psychotherapist. These security operations are directed against anxiety producing, real or alleged, threats to the patient's safety and prestige which he expects from the people of his environment. This makes it advisable that great attention be paid to the actual interpersonal experiences of the patient in his everyday life, both previous to and during the treatment situation, and that special attention be paid to the crises which may have precipitated his entering treatment, and as they recur while he is undergoing psychotherapy. (15, 10, 29)

Part of the previously hidden meaning of the patient's material reveals itself and part of his dissociations resolve themselves by the mere process of relating the data to the doctor, that is, by bringing his hitherto private covert experiences into contact with outward reality. Another part gets clarified in the course of the interpretative investigation of the patient's security operations. Only what remains unclarified by these two devices should be uncovered and revalued by direct interpretation of content. By and large, content interpretation, *per se*, is not considered as important today as it was in the early years of psychoanalysis, and it is used with ever-increasing thriftiness, caution, and discrimination.

No cure is accomplished according to present classical and modified psychoanalytic knowledge by any single, one-time understanding of any single symptom or any single previously dissociated experience. All emotional experiences which are made accessible to the patient's awareness and mature emotional judgment have to be recognized and accepted ("worked through") repeatedly in various contexts. In doing so, psychiatrist and patient should be guided by what gradually transpires as the patient's central problem. Working through should be continued until the time is reached when the intellectual understanding of this problem, its previously dissociated causes and its various interlocking mental and emotional ramifications are gradually transformed into real creative emotional insight.

Free Associations

The encouragement of the patient's "free associations" is considered to be a backbone of classical psychoanalytic therapy. It is designed to eliminate the patient's conscious control over his mental productions, thus bringing out previously repressed and dissociated material.

Since the psychoanalytic doctrine and method were first conceived, an impressive body of knowledge and experience as to the modes of operation and expression used in interpersonal processes which are outside of awareness has been collected. Therefore, many modern dynamic psychotherapists do not feel the indiscriminate use of the so-called method of "free association" to be a basic requirement in psychoanalytic therapy. This marks another change in psychoanalytic therapy.

Many psychoanalysts feel that a sufficient amount of recognizable dissociated material comes to the surface and may arise into awareness in more directed psychotherapeutic interchange and directed focused associative thinking.

Dream Interpretation

Scientific dream interpretation continues to be considered an important means of understanding many thoughts and feelings that the patient cannot express while awake, because of the fact that, during sleep, control and censorship of his mental processes are eliminated or at least great reduced. The extent to which dream interpretation may be used in any single psychotherapeutic process depends upon the therapeutic usefulness of both the nature of a patient's dreams and the understanding and interpretative skill of the psychotherapist.

Didactic Psychoanalysis

In this connection, emphasis may be placed upon the fact that the extent and nuance of the use of the various psychotherapeutic tools in each course of treatment will, of necessity, be co-determined by the assets and liabilities of both persons concerned, the patient and the doctor as participant observer. This being so, a personal psychoanalysis is among the training requirements for any psychiatrist who wishes to do psychoanalytic psychotherapy.

SET-UP IN PSYCHOANALYTIC PSYCHOTHERAPY

The trend toward more therapeutic attention being paid to the actual realities in the patient's life is responsible for several practical changes in the set-up of the treatment situation. Among these recent trends is the relinquishment, by many psychoanalysts, of the binding rule that the patient must lie on the couch, the doctor seated invisibly behind him. As is now understood by many psychoanalytic psychotherapists, this arrangement interfered, for quite a number of patients, with an experience of reality and spontaneity in the exchange between patient and doctor. This feeling of reality and a spontaneous interchange should be encouraged, notwithstanding the maintenance of the strictly professional character of the doctor–patient relationship. Present arrangements of many psychoanalysts allow for patients to sit or to lie down, depending upon the way it appears to work best with each patient.

With some patients this may be decided upon at once for the entire course of treatment, with others changes of position once or repeatedly may be advisable during the course of the treatment.

Brief Psychotherapy—Group Psychotherapy

Other recent changes in psychoanalytic psychotherapy stem from research and practical endeavor directed toward shortening the psychoanalytic process with a carefully selected group of patients. Important work in that direction is under way at one of the leading psychoanalytic training centers in this country, the Chicago Psychoanalytic Institute. (20, 21) The successful introduction of psychoanalytic concepts into group psychotherapy as it has been developed in many psychotherapy centers during and after the last war should also be mentioned in this connection. (22, 23, 24)

PSYCHOSOMATIC MEDICINE

The technique of psychoanalytic psychotherapy was originally created for the special application to psychoneuroses. Treatment of physical symptoms was in terms of an interpretative approach to the "conversion symptoms" of the hysteric. (2, 3, 4, 5) Modern developments in psychosomatic medicine are mainly due to psychoanalytic research. (25, 26, 27) Two sets of results, which have become of great significance for practically all branches of modern medicine, stem from this advance in psychoanalytic development. One is the psychotherapeutic approach to the emotional roots of the etiological factors of somatic symptomatology, where previously symptoms and syndromes were approached in terms of their clinical appearance. The other is the finding of certain laws governing the correlation between certain types of psychoneurotic personalities and their choice of bodily disturbances. The psychosomatic significance of high blood pressure, gastric ulcers, and the various types of colitis, asthma, and hay fever is by now known to every physician as representative of these findings.

PSYCHOSES

There is one more important progressive step in psychoanalytic psychotherapy, which is signified by a modification in the technique of psycho-analysis for the application to the psychoses. (28, 30) An early attempt at doing classical psycho-analysis with a manic depressive was made by Abraham. (31) Recently research and therapeutic endeavor focused around the manic depressive group has been done in England. (32) In this country severely disturbed schizophrenics have been approached with modified psychoanalytic techniques. This became possible in line with the previously described recent changes in psycho-analytic technique and as a result of the two aforementioned great discoveries of psychoana-lytic psychiatry: that all mental manifestations, including those of the mentally disordered, are potentially meaningful; and that there is inter-personal interaction between any two people who meet, including the mentally disturbed patient and the psychotherapist.

Out of this grew the psychopathologically significant insight: that the difference between healthy, neurotic, and psychotic people is much more one of degree than one in kind; that the mentally handicapped may have assets which may not be found in the healthy, and that the healthy may have liabilities not duplicated in the mentally disturbed. (32) In brief, that we are all "much more simply human than other-wise." (10)

Some psychoanalytic psychiatrists hope that it is not too optimistic to harbor the dream that this psychiatric insight may in time develop into a small contribution toward improving the mutual understanding between the people of the dis-turbed world of today.

REFERENCES

1. Fromm-Reichmann, F. Recent advances in psy-choanalytic psychotherapy, *Psychiatry*, May, 1941, *4*, 161–164.

2. Freud, S. *A general introduction to psycho-analysis.* New York: Boni & Liveright, 1920.

3. Brill, A. A. *The basic writings of Sigmund Freud.* New York: Modern Library, 1938.

4. Hendricks, I. *Facts and theories of psychoanal-ysis.* New York: Alfred Knopf, 1939.

5. Fenichel, O. *Outline of clinical psychoanalysis.* New York: W. W. Norton, 1934.

6. Boehm, F. *Intern. Ztschr. Psychoanalyse*, 1926, *12*, 66–79. Not translated.

7. Fromm, E., in *The Family, its function and des-tiny, a synthesis*, Anshen, Ruth Nanda (Ed.), Chap-ters XVII, XIX. New York: Harper & Brothers, 1949.

8. Malinowski, B. *Sex and repression in savage society.* New York: Harcourt, London: K. Paul, Trench Truebner & Co., 1927.

9. Mullahy, P. *Oedipus myth and complex.* New York: Hermitage Press, Inc., 1948 (offers orientation on the attitude of all psychoanalytic schools to the problem).

10. Sullivan, H. S. Conceptions of modern psy-chiatry; William Alanson White Memorial Lectures, *Psychiatry*, 1940, *3*, 1–117. Reprinted as monograph. The William Alanson White Psychiatric Foundation, Washington, D.C., 1947.

11. Fromm, E. Selfishness and self-love, *Psychiatry*, 1939, *2*, 507–523.

12. Fromm, E. *Escape from freedom.* New York and Toronto: Farrar and Rinehart, Inc., 1941.

13. Horney, K. *The neurotic personality of our time.* New York: W. W. Norton, 1937.

14. Fromm, E. *Man for himself; an inquiry into the psychology and ethics.* New York: Rinehart, 1947.

15. Horney, K. *New ways in psychoanalysis*, New York: W. W. Norton, 1939.

16. Kardiner, A. *The individual and his society.* New York: Columbia University Press, 1939.

17. Sullivan, H. S. A note on the implications of psychiatry, the study of interpersonal relations, for investigations in the social sciences, *American Journal of Sociology*, *43*, 848–861.

18. Freud, S. *The problem of anxiety.* New York: W. W. Norton, 1936.

19. Sullivan, H. S. The meaning of anxiety in psychiatry and in life, *Psychiatry*, 1948, *1*, 1–13.

20. Alexander, F., French, T. M., & others. *Psy-choanalytic therapy.* New York: Ronald Press, 1946.

21. Proceedings of the Psychotherapy Council, Chi-cago Psychoanalytic Institute, 1946.

22. Abraham, J. Group psychotherapy; remarks on its basis and application. *Medical Annals of the Dis-trict of Columbia*, 1947, *16*, 612–616.

23. Ackerman, N. W. Dynamic patterns in group psychotherapy, *Psychiatry*, 1944, 7, 341–348.

24. Slavson, S. R. *An introduction to group therapy.* London, Oxford: Commonwealth Fund, 1943.

25. *The Journal of Psychosomatic Medicine.* The Williams and Wilkins Company, Baltimore, Md.

26. Dunbar, H. F. *Emotions and bodily changes.* New York: Columbia University Press, 1938.

27. Weiss, E., & English, O. S. *Psychosomatic*

medicine. Philadelphia and London: W. B. Saunders Co., 1943.

28. Sullivan, H. S. Environmental factors in etiology and course under treatment of schizophrenia, *Medical Journal and Record,* 1931, *133,* 19–22.

29. Sullivan, H. S. Therapeutic investigations in schizophrenia, *Psychiatry,* 1947, *10,* 121–125.

30. Fromm-Reichmann, F. Notes on the develop-ment of treatment of schizophrenics by psychoanalytic psychotherapy, *Psychiatry,* 1948, *11,* 263–273.

31. Abraham, K. *Selected papers.* International Psychoanalytical Library, No. 13, p. 473 ff.

32. Klein, M. A contribution to the psychogenesis of manic–depressive states, *International Journal of Psycho-analysis,* 1935, *16,* 145–174.

interpersonal theory of mental disorder

Harry Stack Sullivan

In approaching the subject of mental disorder, I must emphasize that, in my view, persons showing mental disorder do not manifest anything specifically different in kind from what is manifested by practically all human beings. The only exceptions to this statement are those people who are very badly crippled by hereditary or birth injury factors. There is probably no particular difficulty in grasping this notion except when the disorder picture includes the reappearance of processes that properly pertain to late infancy and early childhood. From my viewpoint, we shall have to accept as a necessary premise that what one encounters in various stages of schizophrenia —the odd, awe-inspiring, terror-provoking feelings of vastness and littleness and the strange strewing-about of relevance—are part of the ordinary experience of these very early stages of personality development in all of us. Most of us, however, experience these processes in later life only as strange fragments carried over from sleep or in our fleeting glimpses of what I call anxiety.

The way in which these primitive types of mental operations become separated from our awareness is in the development of the self-system. The tracing of that development through the various eras of personality growth is absolutely essential to an understanding of my approach to mental disorder and I have already dwelt on it at some length. The self-system is struck off in the personality because of the necessity for picking one's way through irrational and un-understandable prescriptions of behavior laid down by the parents; in other words, the child has to be educated to a very complex social order, long before the reason and the good sense of the whole thing can be digested, long before it becomes understandable—if it ever does. And the self-system comes to be the organization that con-trols awareness; all the operations that are not primarily of the self go on outside awareness. That can be observed very clearly, however difficult it may be to reason it out with pellucid simplicity.

Early in the process of education and socialization, the self-system begins to emerge in personality; and from then on the diffuse referential processes of an early period usually begin to recede from awareness. From the time that the self-system begins to emerge, three aspects of the personality process can be rather readily distinguished: first, the waking and thoroughly active self; second, the part of the personality which is not readily accessible to awareness—the rest of the personality, which in another context can be considered as the whole personality with the self as the eccentric part; and finally, the period spent in sleep, in which the self is relatively dormant and many things are done which cannot be done when the self is functioning actively.

Now, in avoiding or minimizing the anxiety that is inherent in the unceasing struggle to protect the self-system from the diffuse referential processes that cannot be admitted into awareness, various specific processes, the dynamisms, come into play. In the following series of lectures I shall consider these dynamisms from this tripartite viewpoint as unitary abstractions that are useful both in thinking about what a patient is showing and in observing what is going on within ourselves. I use the word dynamism, you will observe, where other psychiatrists often use the term mechanism. Mechanism has never suited me because it always suggests a Diesel engine. And the one thing we are sure of in interpersonal relations is that there are processes which are dynamic; they are not static, mechanical entities. These processes have something in them of the element of energy and they are very apt to go on until something in the way of a goal, a terminal state, is reached, whereupon they cease for the time being and show no trace until they are next called forth.

When I speak of dynamisms of difficulty I mean those processes which, although they are a part of every personality, are at the same time the particular parts of the personal equipment that are often misused. In other words, these dynamisms go into action in situations or in fashions that do not achieve a goal, or that, at best, achieve only an unsatisfactory goal. As a result they tend to go on and on. Their frequent recurrence or their tendency to occupy long stretches of time characterizes the mentally sick as distinguished from the comparatively well.

It is the extraordinary dependence of a personality on a particular dynamism that is, I suppose, the fundamental conception to have in mind in thinking of mental disorder. The schizophrenic patient, for instance, is often a person who has in the past persistently shown the dynamism which we call dissociation as a means of resolving the conflict between powerful needs and the restrictions which the self imposes upon the satisfaction of these needs. That is, people who have dissociated anything as powerful as lust, for example, are in great danger of schizophrenic collapse.

We shall consider these dynamisms in an order roughly following that in which they appear in the evolution of personality. First, we shall discuss sublimation, which appears quite early in life, and then we shall take up the obsessional dynamism, which comes into being with the learning of language. Both of these dynamisms have a relation to the protection of the self-system from the appearance in consciousness of types of referential process, thought, or revery closely related to the schizophrenic-like processes of late infancy and early childhood; and we shall pause from time to time to consider their relationship to these earlier referential processes. In the juvenile era, the vast body of processes for controlling awareness which I refer to as selective inattention first becomes an important dynamism. From there we shall consider a number of other dynamisms, all part of the human paraphernalia for protecting the self-system from the minor but effective manifestations of anxiety and the more threatening possibility of the collapse of the self-system. And finally, as the last step in this survey of the dynamisms of difficulty, we shall consider the dissociative processes themselves and their relation to major personality disorder. We shall then be in a position to move on to the therapeutic implications and possibilities in terms of the major patterns of difficulties—the so-called clinical entities.

In considering the various dynamisms or processes of living we shall have to keep in mind that they are what has to go on from the very character of human nature in interpersonal situations. The situation exists because the tendency, the potentiality, or the possibility of the processes not only exists but has force; and this force shows in the tendency integrating the situation. Thus under certain circumstances, people are pulled together, situations are created so that something can work itself out. These situations may be integrated (1) by single, that is unitary, tendencies; (2) by several tendencies which are congruent and which can work in a unitary situation without peculiar things happening; or finally (3) by conflicting integrating tendencies. It is only now and then that one is lucky enough to find a situation that is simple, that is the product of *an* integrating tendency, instead of two or more congruent integrating tendencies or conflicting ones. In the event that there are congruent integrating tendencies, the processes are apt to be rather successful in the sense of all concerned coming out rather better than they went into the situation. When there are conflicting integrating tendencies, on the other hand, many things happen which in essence make up pretty nearly the sum total of human misery. So it is that complex situations and complex processes can be both pleasant and unpleasant, successful and quite otherwise.

Now I should like to consider the problem of where we look for information about these integrating tendencies. What are the basic ideas in attempting to define them?

Integrating tendencies may be defined, first, in terms of their goals, so that one might say that an integrating tendency is that sort of nature in two or more people which causes them to engage in reaching such and such an end state, which incidentally sets up the situation in which such processes can occur. For instance, the goal of the tendency to seek human intimacy, which I shall deal with as if it were a simple tendency at the moment, might be said to be reflected in all those situations in which two or more people tend to understand each other better, to come to a clearer grasp of their particular little differences of views, impulses, and so on. Thus the term, goal, however dubious philosophically, is quite an adequate term for describing this process since the culture is organized to think in terms of what you are doing this *for,* and *for* implies a goal. Time is another consideration here. Time reaches from here into the future and in a somewhat imaginary way, into the past; and a vast number of plans and operations going on now are clearly foreseen to lead to something in the future which we may quite properly describe, I think, as the goal of the activity without becoming too much preoccupied with more recondite problems of chance.

An even more striking approach to defining integrating tendencies, motives, or drives is in terms of what so-called "individual" people *feel* about these goals. All of you know that at times you feel hungry, at times some of you may even feel a little bit lustful, quite often some of you feel angry, and at other times some of you feel very kindly, in fact, positively loving. This felt component of the integrating tendencies that create situations with other people and move toward goals is so intimately related to what we term hunger, lust, anger, love, affection, and so on, that it is quite proper, if you do not get confused as to your unique individuality, to relate these terms that everybody knows to the integrating tendencies to which they pertain. For instance, in a situation in which love is the active force, the participants feel what they call love. One can indeed label integrating tendencies by the feeling that accompanies them—their "emotional" representation within awareness. The only trouble with that particular attempt to define them is that many of the integrating tendencies are not represented in awareness by any feeling; and very often integrating tendencies that are sometimes represented in awareness by feeling are very effective without any such representation, in other words, they are working unconsciously or externally to awareness. Thus integrating tendencies can be active and situations can exist without the participants *feeling* emotion.

And finally, and somewhat more obscurely, integrating tendencies can be defined in terms of the factors that they make relevant or—and this may sound a little paradoxical—in terms of the factors that make *them* relevant. In other words, since integrating tendencies pertain to the very tissue of life—to what goes on between people—you can understand that we can define them in terms of what the people concerned take

seriously when the integrating tendency is in effect, or, to express it another way, what the closely related factors in people are which lead them to be integrated into a particular situation.

In this attempt to define integrating tendencies, you will observe that the field of effort is never perfect because it is so extremely complex; but it is also never utterly obscure. And it is by this variety of approaches to such a complex area of study that we can, I believe, get clearer and clearer on what we are talking about, what we are thinking about, and actually what we are living.

Whichever way you approach a classification of integrating tendencies, you are on much safer ground if you consider two great general goals of the situation. These two grand divisions of goals have come into being from the most fundamental aspect of humanity itself—namely, that humanity and the human beings that make up humanity are extraordinary evolutions of very capable animals. Human beings are not animals, but they start as animals. And these animals are converted into human beings instead of merely members of the species *homo sapiens* by assimilating and becoming part of a vast amount of *culture*—culture being all that is man-made in this world, everything from scientific views and informal cultural and social organizations of people to the most holy traditions and institutions such as the state and the nation. All of these things are "remains" of human life that has been lived; but all of them are also an active living part of a lot of people. It is in the process of getting from the status of being born a vastly gifted animal to the status of being a person living with other people, and losing any such neat biological individuality as the infant *homo sapiens* had, that a great quantity of the traditions, principles of life, and what not that have been worked out by others in the historic period and that have been wished on us by our parents, teachers, companions, and so on, get into us and become in many ways the most striking thing about us. And it is in that process by which the human animal is converted into a human being—a subject of psychiatric interest instead of merely a subject of biological interest—that there comes about a great differentiation of the goals of behavior and therefore of the integrating tendencies that characterize interpersonal relations. This differentiation I shall discuss in terms of *satisfaction* and *security.*

We never have a chance of discovering what

a human animal who did not become a human being would be like, because human animals cannot live without help, and the help proceeds to bring them culture. And so, as you might surmise, this brings us to the other group of integrating tendencies—those which pertain to something markedly influenced by culture. This division of integrating tendencies is *not* clearly indicated in the biological heritage of the human animal; instead they are called out by the processes and are particularly relevant to the situations which are concerned with being a person in contradistinction to being an animal. They are, then, more clearly derivative of culture, of the assimilation of the man-made which has gone into one's education and so on; and when we have studied these, we find that they can be quite adequately placed under one heading—*security*. In contradistinction to the pursuit of satisfaction, these integrating tendencies of prevailingly cultural or educational origin pertain to the pursuit of security, or the maintenance of security, or the avoidance of insecurity. Each of you, when you think about it, will see that you have had experience in the past—and the effects of that experience are still manifest in the present —in which you were esteemed by somebody as good, important, worthy, or you were considered in an unfavorable, derogatory, or depreciatory way. The most general term I have ever found for the states which are attendant upon being valued, respected, looked up to, and so on, is a feeling of personal security; and the term, insecurity, works out even more impressively when one looks for a general term to encompass all the states and all the processes that are called out by situations in which that is not the case.

This differentiation between pursuits of satisfaction and the maintenance of security—that is, the avoidance of anxiety—is, I think, one of the most important classifying principles in all that we will have to say about living.

a stimulus-response analysis of anxiety and its role as a reinforcing agent

O. Hobart Mowrer

Within recent decades an important change has taken place in the scientific view of anxiety (fear),[1] its genesis, and its psychological significance. Writing in 1890, William James (1890) stoutly supported the then current supposition that anxiety was an *instinctive* ("idiopathic") reaction to certain objects or situations, which might or might not represent real danger. To the extent that the instinctively given, predetermined objects of anxiety were indeed dangerous, anxiety reactions had biological utility and could be accounted for as an evolutionary product of the struggle for existence. On the other hand, there were, James assumed, also anxiety reactions that were altogether senseless and which, conjecturally, came about through Nature's imperfect wisdom. But in all cases, an anxiety reaction was regarded as phylogenetically fixed and unlearned. The fact that children may show no fear of a given type of object, *e.g.*, live frogs, during the first year of life but may later manifest such a reaction, James attributed to the "ripening" of the fear-of-live-frogs instinct; and the fact that such fears, once they have "ripened," may also disappear he explained on the assumption that all instincts, after putting in an appearance and, as it were, placing themselves at the individual's disposal, tend to undergo a kind of oblivescence or decay unless taken advantage of and made "habitual."

Some years later John B. Watson (1928) demonstrated experimentally that, contrary to the James-ian view, most human fears are specifically relatable to and dependent upon individual experience. Starting with the reaction of infants to loud sounds or loss of physical support, which he refused to call "instinctive" but did not hesitate to regard as "unlearned" or "reflexive," Watson was able to show, by means of Pavlov's conditioning technique, that an indefinitely wide range of other stimuli, if associated with this reaction, could be made to acquire the capacity to elicit unmistakably fearful behavior. This was an important discovery, but it appears to have involved a basic fallacy. Watson overlooked the fact that "loud sounds" are intrinsically *painful,* and he also overlooked the fact that "loss of physical support," although not painful in its own right, is almost certain to be followed by some form of stimulation (incident to the stopping of the body's fall) that is painful. The so-called fearful reaction to loss of support—if not confused with an actual pain reaction—is, therefore, in all probability itself a learned (conditioned) reaction, which means that, according to Watson's observations, human infants show no innate *fear* responses whatever, merely innate *pain* responses.

Freud seems to have seen the problem in this light from the outset and accordingly posited that *all* anxiety (fear) reactions are probably learned;[2] his hypothesis, when recast in stimulus–response terminology, runs as follows. A so-called "traumatic" ("painful") stimulus (arising either from

[1] Psychoanalytic writers sometimes differentiate between anxiety and fear on the grounds that fear has a consciously perceived object and anxiety does not. Although this distinction may be useful for some purposes, these two terms will be used in the present paper as strictly synonymous.

[2] Freud (1936) has explicitly acknowledged the possibility of anxiety occurring, especially in birds and other wild animals, as an instinctive reaction; but he takes the position that in human beings, instinctive anxiety (not to be confused with "instinctual" anxiety, *i.e.,* fear of the intensity of one's own organic impulses) is probably nonexistent or is at least inconsequential.

external injury, of whatever kind, or from severe organic need) impinges upon the organism and produces a more or less violent defence (striving) reaction. Furthermore, such a stimulus–response sequence is usually preceded or accompanied by originally "indifferent" stimuli which, however, after one or more temporally contiguous associations with the traumatic stimulus, begin to be perceived as "danger signals," i.e., acquire the capacity to elicit an "anxiety" reaction. This latter reaction, which may or may not be grossly observable, has two outstanding characteristics: (i) it creates or, perhaps more accurately, consists of a state of heightened tension (or "attention") and a more or less specific readiness for (expectation of) the impending traumatic stimulus; and (ii), by virtue of the fact that such a state of tension is itself a form of discomfort, it adaptively motivates the organism to escape from the danger situation, thereby lessening the intensity of the tension (anxiety) and also probably decreasing the chances of encountering the traumatic stimulus. In short, *anxiety (fear) is the conditioned form of the pain reaction,* which has the highly useful function of motivating and reinforcing behavior that tends to avoid or prevent the recurrence of the pain-producing (unconditioned) stimulus.

In the mentalistic terminology that he characteristically employs, Freud (1936) has formulated this view of anxiety formation and its adaptational significance as follows:

Now it is an important advance in self-protection when this traumatic situation of helplessness [discomfort] is not merely awaited but is foreseen, anticipated. Let us call the situation in which resides the cause of this anticipation the danger situation; it is in this latter that the signal of anxiety is given. What this means is: I anticipate that a situation of helplessness [discomfort] will come about, or the present situation reminds me of one of the traumatic experiences which I have previously undergone. Hence I will anticipate this trauma; I will act as if it were already present as long as there is still time to avert it. Anxiety, therefore, is the expectation of the trauma on the one hand, and on the other, an attenuated repetition of it (pp. 149–150).

Affective [anxiety] states are incorporated into the life of the psyche as precipitates of primal traumatic experiences, and are evoked

in similar situations like memory symbols (p. 23). Anxiety is undeniably related to expectation; one feels anxiety *lest* something occur (pp. 146–147).

According to views expressed elsewhere by Freud, expectation and anxiety lie along a continuum, with the former merging into the latter at the point at which it becomes uncomfortably intense, i.e., begins to take on motivational properties in its own right. The preparatory, expectant character of anxiety is likely, however, to be obscured by the fact that danger situations sometimes arise and pass so quickly that they are over before the anxiety reaction—involving, as it does, not only an augmentation of neuromuscular readiness and tension but also a general mobilization of the physical energies needed to sustain strenuous action—has had an opportunity to occur. The result is that in situations in which danger is so highly transitory, as, for example, in near-accidents in motor traffic, anxiety is commonly experienced, somewhat paradoxically, *after* the danger is past and therefore gives the appearance of being indeed a useless, wasted reaction (*cf.* James). It must not be overlooked, however, that situations of this kind are more or less anomalous. The fact that in a given situation the element of danger disappears before flight, for which the anxiety-preparedness is most appropriate, has had time to occur, does not, of course, mean that anxiety-preparedness in the face of danger is not in general a very adaptive reaction.[3]

As early as 1903, Pavlov (1938a) expressed a point of view that bears a striking resemblance to the position taken by Freud in this connection. He said: "The importance of the remote signs (signals) of objects can be easily recognized in the movement reaction of the animal. By means of distant and even accidental characteristics of objects the animal seeks his food, avoids enemies, etc." (p. 52). Again, a quarter of a century later, Pavlov (1938b) wrote as follows:

It is pretty evident that under natural conditions the normal animal must respond not only to stimuli which themselves bring immediate benefit or harm, but also to other physical or chemical agencies—waves of sound, light, and the like—which in themselves only *signal*

---

[3] *Cf.* the discussion of the "startle pattern" by Landis and Hunt (1939).

the approach of these stimuli; though it is not the sight and sound of the beast of prey which is in itself harmful to the smaller animal, but its teeth and claws (p. 14).

Although both Pavlov and Freud thus clearly recognize the biological utility of anticipatory reactions to danger signals, there is, however, an important difference in their viewpoints. Pavlov emphasizes the mechanism of simple stimulus substitution (conditioning). According to his hypothesis, a danger signal (the conditioned stimulus) comes to elicit essentially the *same* "movement reaction" that has previously been produced by actual trauma (the unconditioned stimulus). It is true that the blink of the eyelids to a threatening visual stimulus is not greatly unlike the reaction made to direct corneal irritation. A dog may learn to flex its leg in response to a formerly neutral stimulus so as to simulate the flexion produced by an electric shock administered to its paw. And a small child may for a time make very much the same type of withdrawal reactions to the sight of a flame that it makes to actual contact with it. However, any attempt to establish this pattern of stimulus substitution as the prototype of all learning places severe restrictions on the limits of adaptive behavior: it implies that the only reactions that can become attached to formerly unrelated stimuli (*i.e.*, can be learned) are those which already occur more or less reflexly to some other type of stimulation.

According to the conception of anxiety proposed by Freud, on the other hand, a danger signal may come to produce any of an infinite variety of reactions that are wholly unlike the reaction that occurs to the actual trauma of which the signal is premonitory. Freud assumes that the first and most immediate response to a danger signal is not a complete, overt reaction, as Pavlov implies, but an implicit state of tension and augmented preparedness for action,[4] which he calls "anxiety." This state of affairs, being itself a source of discomfort, may then motivate innumerable random acts, from which will be selected and fixated (by the law of effect) the behavior that most effectively reduces the anxiety. Anxiety is thus to be regarded as a motivating and reinforcing (fixating) agent, similar to hunger, thirst, sex, temperature deviations, and the many other forms of discomfort that harass living organisms,

which is, however, presumably distinctive in that it is derived from (based upon anticipation of) these other, more basic forms of discomfort.[5]

By and large, behavior that reduces anxiety also operates to lessen the danger that it presages. An antelope that scents a panther is likely not only to feel less uneasy (anxious) if it moves out of the range of the odor of the panther but is also likely to be in fact somewhat safer. A primitive village that is threatened by marauding men or beasts sleeps better after it has surrounded itself with a deep moat or a sturdy stockade. And a modern mother is made emotionally more comfortable after her child has been properly vaccinated against a dreaded disease. This capacity to be made uncomfortable by the mere prospect of traumatic experiences, in advance of their actual occurrence (or recurrence), and to be motivated thereby to take realistic precautions against them, is unquestionably a tremendously important and useful psychological mechanism, and the fact that the forward-looking, anxiety-arousing propensity of the human mind is more highly developed than it is in lower animals probably accounts for many of man's unique accomplishments. But it also accounts for some of his most conspicuous failures.

The ostrich has become a proverbial object of contempt and a symbol of stupidity because of its alleged tendency, when frightened, to put its head in the sand, thereby calming its emotional agitation but not in the slightest degree altering the danger situation in its objective aspects. Such relevant scientific inquiry as has been carried out indicates, however, that infra-human organisms are ordinarily more realistic in this respect than are human beings. For example, if a dog learns to avoid an electric shock by lifting its foreleg in response to a tone, it will give up this response entirely when it discovers that the tone is no longer followed by shock if the response is not made. Human beings, on the other hand, are notoriously prone to engage in all manner of magical, superstitious, and propitiatory acts, which undoubtedly relieve dread and uncertainty (at least temporarily) but which have a highly questionable value in controlling real events.[6] The remarkable

[4] *Cf.* the revised theory of conditioning proposed by Culler (1938).

[5] Freud has never explicitly formulated this view in precisely these words, but it is clearly implied in various of his writings.

[6] Under some circumstances, *e.g.*, when warriors are preparing for battle, malevolent incantations or similar anxiety-reducing magical procedures may, of

persistence of such practices may be due, at least in part, to the fact that they are followed relatively promptly by anxiety-reduction, whereas their experienced futility at the reality level may come many hours or days or even months later.[7] The persistence of certain forms of "unrealistic" anxiety-reinforced behavior may also be due to the fact that in most societies there seem always to be some individuals who are able and ready to derive an easy living by fostering beliefs on the part of others in "unrealistic" dangers. For the common man protection against such "dangers" consists of whatever type of behavior the bogeymakers choose to say is "safe" (and which furthers their own interests).

Yet other forms of "unrealistic" anxiety-reinforced behavior are to be observed in the symptomatic acts of the psychoneuroses. According to Freud, anxiety is in fact "the fundamental phenomenon and the central problem of neurosis" (Freud, 1936, p. 111). He further says:

> Since we have reduced the development of anxiety to a response to situations of danger, we shall prefer to say that the symptoms are created in order to remove or rescue the ego from the situation of danger. . . . We can also say, in supplement to this, that the development of anxiety induces symptom formation—nay more, it is a *sine qua non* thereof, for if the ego did not forcibly arouse the pleasure–pain mechanism through the development of anxiety, it would not acquire the power to put a stop to the danger-threatening process elaborated in the id (Freud, 1936, pp. 112–113).

Willoughby (1935), in a scholarly, well-documented paper, has previously stressed the similarity of magical rites (including religion) and neurotic symptoms and has shown that both types of behavior spring from the common propensity of human beings to deal with their anxieties unrealistically, *i.e.*, by means which diminish emotional discomfort but do not adaptively alter external realities. This excellent study has, in the present writer's opinion, only one important weakness: it takes as its point of departure what Freud

has called his "first theory" of anxiety formation (1894), which he subsequently abandoned for the one outlined above. In brief, Freud's earlier supposition was that anxiety arose whenever a strong organic drive or impulse was prevented from discharging through its accustomed motor outlets. According to this view, inhibition was the primary state, anxiety the resultant. In all his more recent writings, on the other hand, Freud takes the position, here also adopted, that anxiety (as a reaction to a "danger signal") is primal and that inhibition, of anxiety-arousing, danger-producing impulses,[8] is a consequence (Freud, 1936). Reaction mechanisms (magic, symptoms, etc.) that contribute to this end tend, for reasons already given, to be reinforced and perpetuated. Willoughby's analysis is not of necessity predicated upon Freud's original view of anxiety formation and would seem to gain rather than lose cogency if based instead upon his more recent formulations.

Magical and neurotic practices constitute a very perplexing and challenging problem from the point of view of traditional psychological theory; but, as Allport (1937) has recently pointed out, so also do many other types of human activity that are commonly regarded as both rational and normal. Allport rightly stresses the inadequacies of the conditioned-reflex concept as a comprehensive explanation of learning and personality development in general. He also justly criticizes the view that all human conduct is to be accounted for in terms of trial-and-error striving to eliminate immediately felt organic needs. The plain fact is

---

[7] *Cf.* Hull's concept of the "goal gradient" (Hull, 1932).

course, be objectively efficacious, not, to be sure, in the supposed magical way, but in that they alter human conduct in crucial life situations (*i.e.*, make the warriors bolder and better fighters).

[8] One of Freud's most fundamental discoveries, basic to the understanding of reaction-formation, repression, projection, and other neurotic mechanisms, is that organic impulses, even though they are not consciously experienced and identified, may function as "danger signals" and thereby evoke anxiety. This relatively simple yet frequently misapprehended finding (Freud has himself contributed to the confusion by sometimes speaking as if anxiety *is* the "danger signal," instead of a *reaction* to it) can be readily translated into Pavlovian terminology by saying that an organic need, or drive, which has in the past led to overt behavior that was severely punished will tend upon its recurrence, even at low intensities, to elicit a conditioned pain (anxiety) reaction. Yet, as will be shown in a later paper on the so-called "experimental neurosis," Pavlov and his followers have largely ignored this possibility of internal, as well as external, stimuli acquiring "signal" value, *i.e.*, becoming "conditioned," and have consequently made apparent mysteries of some laboratory observations which, when viewed more broadly, seem completely intelligible.

that much of modern man's most energetic behavior occurs when his organic needs are ostensibly well satisfied. In an attempt to account for this state of affairs, without, on the other hand, falling back on a forthright mentalistic type of approach, Allport elaborates the view, previously advanced by Woodworth, that habits themselves have an on-going character, independent of the motivation that originally brought them into being, and that this type of habit-momentum constitutes a form of self-sustained motivation. Allport calls this the principle of "functional autonomy" and relies heavily upon it in developing his system of the "psychology of personality."

In the estimation of the present writer, "functional autonomy" is on a par with "perpetual motion." Its author clearly perceives an important psychological problem, but it seems unlikely that his is a scientifically tenable solution to it. The position here taken is that human beings (and also other living organs to varying degrees) can be motivated either by organic pressures (needs) that are currently present and felt *or* by the mere anticipation of such pressures and that those habits tend to be acquired and perpetuated (reinforced) which effect a reduction in *either* of these two types of motivation. This view rests upon and is but an extended application of the well-founded law of effect and involves no assumptions that are not empirically verifiable. It has the further advantage that it is consistent with common-sense impressions and practices and at the same time serves as a useful integrational device at the scientific level.

The present analysis of anxiety (anticipation, expectancy) and its role in shaping both "adaptive" and "mal-adaptive" behavior in human beings is also consistent with the growing tendency to eliminate the distinction between learning through "punishment" and learning through "reward." The earlier view was that so-called punishment "stamped out" habits and that reward "stamped" them in. This distinction now appears to have been spurious and to have depended upon a selectivity of emphasis or interest (Mowrer, 1938). If an individual is motivated by an internal discomfort or need (produced by his own metabolic processes), and if another individual provides the means of eliminating it, and if, in the process, the first individual acquires new behavior, this is called learning through "reward." But if a second individual supplies the need (by inflicting or threatening to inflict some form of discomfort),

and if the affected individual supplies the means of eliminating this discomfort (by flight, inactivity, propitiation, compliance, or the like), and if, in the process, this individual acquires new behavior, then this is called learning through "punishment." The truth of the matter seems to be that all learning presupposes (i) an increase of motivation (striving) and (ii) a decrease of motivation (success) and that the essential features of the process are much the same, regardless of the specific source of motivation or of the particular circumstances of its elimination.[9]

There is, however, one practical consideration to be taken into account. Although learning through "punishment" does not seem to differ basically from learning through "reward," inter-personal relationships are likely to be affected very differently in the two cases. If the method of "reward" is employed, inter-personal relationships are likely to be made more "positive" (*i.e.*, approach tendencies will be strengthened); whereas, if the method of "punishment" is employed, inter-personal relationships are likely to be made more "negative" (*i.e.*, avoidance tendencies will be strengthened). From a purely social point of view, it is therefore preferable to employ the method of "reward," whenever this is possible; but "punishment" may have to be resorted to if no *organic* needs are present to be "rewarded" or if means of rewarding them are not available. Punishment (or the threat of punishment, *i.e.*, anxiety) is particularly convenient in that it can be produced instantly; but this advantage is accompanied by disadvantages which cannot be safely disregarded (Mowrer, 1940).

Even the practical basis for distinguishing between learning through reward and through punishment just suggested becomes tenuous when one considers the type of situation in which one person withholds from another an expected reward. This, in one sense, is a form of "punishment," and yet its effectiveness is based upon the principle of

---

[9] According to this point of view, old habits are eliminated, not by being "stamped out" or extracted, as it were, "by the roots," but by the functional superimposition of new, more powerful, antagonistic habits (Mowrer, 1938). Anxiety may thus be said to exercise an "inhibitory" effect (see foregoing discussion of Freud's "first theory" of anxiety) upon established behavior trends mainly through its motivation and reinforcement of opposing behavior trends. In this way emphasis falls primarily upon the positive, habit-forming consequences of anxiety and only secondarily and indirectly upon its negative, inhibitory functions.

"reward." This complicated state of affairs seems especially likely to arise in the parent-child relationship and has implications that have been but slightly explored in stimulus-response terms.

SUMMARY

In contrast to the older view, which held that anxiety (fear) was an instinctive reaction to phylogenetically pre-determined objects or situations, the position here taken is that anxiety is a learned response, occurring to "signals" (conditioned stimuli) that are premonitory of (i.e., have in the past been followed by) situations of injury or pain (unconditioned stimuli). Anxiety is thus basically anticipatory in nature and has great biological utility in that it adaptively motivates living organisms to deal with (prepare for or flee from) traumatic events in advance of their actual occurrence, thereby diminishing their harmful effects. However, experienced anxiety does not always vary in direct proportion to the objective danger in a given situation, with the result that living organisms, and human beings in particular, show tendencies to behave "irrationally," i.e., to have anxiety in situations that are not dangerous or to have no anxiety in situations that are dangerous. Such a "disproportionality of affect" may come about for a variety of reasons, and the analysis of these reasons throws light upon such diverse phenomena as magic, superstition, social exploration, and the psychoneuroses.

Moreover, by positing anxiety as a kind of connecting link between complete wellbeing and active organic discomfort or injury, it is possible to reconcile the fact that much, perhaps most, of the day-to-day behavior of civilized human beings is not prompted by simultaneously active organic drives and the fact that the law of effect (principle of learning through motivation-reduction) is apparently one of the best-established of psychological principles. This is accomplished by assuming (i) that anxiety, i.e., mere anticipation of actual organic need or injury, may effectively motivate human beings and (ii) that reduction of anxiety may serve powerfully to reinforce behavior that brings about such a state of "relief" or "security." Anxiety, although derived from more basic forms of motivation, is thus regarded as functioning in an essentially parallel manner as far as its role as an activating and reinforcing agent is concerned. This analysis is consistent with the common sense view in such matters and does not conflict with any known empirical fact. Finally, it has the advantage of being open to objective investigation and of giving rise to a host of problems that have scarcely been touched experimentally (Mowrer, 1940).

REFERENCES

Allport, G. W. *Personality.* New York: Henry Holt and Company, 1937.

Culler, E. A. Recent advances in some concepts of conditioning. *Psychol. Rev.,* 1938, 45, 134–153.

Freud, S. *The problem of anxiety.* New York: W. W. Norton and Co., 1936.

Hull, C. L. The goal gradient hypothesis and maze learning. *Psychol. Rev.,* 1932, 39, 25–43.

James, W. *Principles of psychology,* Vol. II. New York: Henry Holt and Company, 1890.

Landis, C., & Hunt, W. A. *The startle pattern.* New York: Farrar & Rinehart, 1939.

Mowrer, O. H. Preparatory set (expectancy)—A determinant in motivation and learning. *Psychol. Rev.,* 1938, 45, 61–91.

Mowrer, O. H. Preparatory set (expectancy)—Some methods of measurement. *Psychol. Monogr.,* 1940, 52, No. 2.

Pavlov, I. P. *Conditioned reflexes.* (Translated by Anrep.) England: Oxford University Press: Humphrey Milford, 1938. (a)

Pavlov, I. P. *Lectures on conditioned reflexes.* (Translated by Gantt.) New York: International Publishers, 1938. (b)

Watson, J. B. Experimental studies on the growth of the emotions. Pp. 37–57, in *Psychologies of 1925.* Worcester, Mass.: Clark University Press, 1928.

Willoughby, R. R. Magic and cognate phenomena: An hypothesis. Pp. 461–519, in *A Handbook of Social Psychology.* Worcester, Mass.: Clark University Press, 1935, p. 1195.

what is psychotic behavior?

B. F. Skinner

A scientific program on "Newer Aspects of the Theory, Etiology, and Treatment of the Psychoses" marked the opening of the Renard Hospital, a psychiatric unit of the Washington University School of Medicine and the Barnes and Affiliated Hospitals, in St. Louis on October 10, 1955. As part of that program this paper was addressed primarily to psychiatrists and others concerned with mental health. The analysis, particularly as represented by the four figures and the accompanying text, has proved useful in a broader context.

Since my field of specialization lies some distance from psychiatry, it may be well to begin with credentials. The first will be negative. In the sense in which my title is most likely to be understood, I am wholly unqualified to discuss the question before us. The number of hours I have spent in the presence of psychotic people (assuming that I am myself sane) is negligible compared with what many of you might claim, and the time I have spent in relevant reading and discussion would suffer equally from the same comparison. I am currently interested in some research on psychotic subjects, to which I shall refer again later, but my association with that program in no way qualifies me as a specialist.

Fortunately, I am not here to answer the question in that sense at all. A more accurate title would have been "What is *behavior?*—with an occasional reference to psychiatry." Here I will list such positive credentials as seem appropriate. I have spent a good share of my professional life in the experimental analysis of the behavior of organisms. Almost all my subjects have been below the human level (most of them rats or pigeons) and all, so far as I know, have been sane. My research has not been designed to test any theory of behavior, and the results cannot be evaluated in terms of the statistical significance of such proofs. The object has been to discover the functional relations which prevail between measurable aspects of behavior and various conditions and events in the life of the

organism. The success of such a venture is gauged by the extent to which behavior can, as a result of the relationships discovered, actually be predicted and controlled. Here we have, I think, been fortunate. Within a limited experimental arrangement, my colleagues and I have been able to demonstrate a lawfulness in behavior which seems to us quite remarkable. In more recent research it has been possible to maintain—actually, to sharpen—this degree of lawfulness while slowly increasing the complexity of the behavior studied. The extent of the prediction and control which has been achieved is evident not only in "smoothness of curves" and uniformity of results from individual to individual or even species to species, but in the practical uses which are already being made of the techniques—for example, in providing baselines for the study of pharmacological and neurological variables, or in converting a lower organism into a sensitive psychophysical observer.

Although research designed in this way has an immediate practical usefulness, it is not independent of one sort of theory. A primary concern has been to isolate a useful and expedient measure. Of all the myriad aspects of behavior which present themselves to observation, which are worth watching? Which will prove most useful in establishing functional relations? From time to time many different characteristics of behavior have seemed important. Students of the subject have asked how well organized behavior is, how well adapted it is to the environment, how sensitively it maintains a homeostatic equilibrium, how purposeful it is, or how successfully it solves practical problems or adjusts to daily life. Many have been especially interested in how an individual compares with others of the same species or with members of other species in some arbitrary measure of the scope, complexity, speed, consistency, or other property of behavior. All these aspects may be quantified, at least in a rough way, and any one may serve as a dependent variable in a scientific analysis. But they are not all equally productive. In research which emphasizes prediction and control, the topography of behavior must be carefully specified. Precisely what is the organism doing? The most important aspect of behavior so described is its probability of emission. How likely is it that an organism will engage in behavior of a given sort, and what conditions or events change this likelihood? Although probability of action has only recently been explicitly recognized in behavior theory, it is a key concept to which many classical notions, from reaction tendencies to the Freudian wish, may be reduced. Experimentally we deal with it as the *frequency* with which an organism behaves in a given way under specified circumstances, and our methods are designed to satisfy this requirement. Frequency of response has proved to be a remarkably sensitive variable, and with its aid the exploration of causal factors has been gratifyingly profitable.

One does not engage in work of this sort for the sheer love of rats or pigeons. As the medical sciences illustrate, the study of animals below the level of man is dictated mainly by convenience and safety. But the primary object of interest is always man. Such qualifications as I have to offer in approaching the present question spring about equally from the experimental work just mentioned and from a parallel preoccupation with human behavior, in which the principles emerging from the experimental analysis have been tested and put to work in the interpretation of empirical facts. The formal disciplines of government, education, economics, religion, and psychotherapy, among others, together with our everyday experience with men, overwhelm us with a flood of facts. To interpret these facts with the formulation which emerges from an experimental analysis has proved to be strenuous but healthful exercise. In particular, the nature and function of *verbal*

behavior have taken on surprisingly fresh and promising aspects when reformulated under the strictures of such a framework.

In the long run, of course, mere interpretation is not enough. If we have achieved a true scientific understanding of man, we should be able to prove this in the actual prediction and control of his behavior. The experimental practices and the concepts emerging from our research on lower organisms have already been extended in this direction, not only in the experiments on psychotic subjects already mentioned, but in other promising areas. The details would take us too far afield, but perhaps I can indicate my faith in the possibilities in a single instance by hazarding the prediction that we are on the threshold of a revolutionary change in methods of education, based not only upon a better understanding of learning processes, but upon a workable conception of knowledge itself.

Whether or not this brief personal history seems to you to qualify me to discuss the question before us, there is no doubt that it has created a high probability that I will do so, as shown by the fact that I am here. What I have to say is admittedly methodological. I can understand a certain impatience with such discussion particularly when, as in the field of psychiatry, many pressing problems call for action. The scientist who takes time out to consider human nature when so many practical things need to be done for human welfare is likely to be cast in the role of a Nero, fiddling while Rome burns. (It is quite possible that the fiddling referred to in this archetypal myth was a later invention of the historians, and that in actual fact Nero had called in his philosophers and scientists and was discussing "the fundamental nature of combustion" or "the epidemiology of conflagration.") But I should not be here if I believed that what I have to say is remote from practical consequences. If we are now entering an era of research in psychiatry which is to be as extensive and as productive as other types of medical research, then a certain detachment from immediate problems, a fresh look at human behavior in general, a survey of applicable formulations, and a consideration of relevant methods may prove to be effective practical steps with surprisingly immediate consequences.

The study of human behavior is, of course, still in its infancy, and it would be rash to suppose that anyone can foresee the structure of a well-developed and successful science. Certainly no current formulation will seem right fifty years hence. But although we cannot foresee the future clearly, it is not impossible to discover in what direction we are likely to change. There are obviously great deficiencies in our present ways of thinking about men; otherwise we should be more successful. What are they, and how are they to be remedied? What I have to say rests upon the assumption that the behavior of the psychotic is simply part and parcel of human behavior, and that certain considerations which have been emphasized by the experimental and theoretical analysis of behavior in general are worth discussing in this special application.

It is important to remember that I am speaking as an experimental scientist. A conception of human behavior based primarily on clinical information and practice will undoubtedly differ from a conception emanating from the laboratory. This does not mean that either is superior to the other, or that eventually a common formulation will not prove useful to both. It is possible that questions which have been suggested by the exigencies of an experimental analysis may not seem of first importance to those of you who are primarily concerned with human behavior under

therapy. But as psychiatry moves more rapidly into experimental research and as laboratory results take on a greater clinical significance, certain problems in the analysis of behavior should become common to researcher and therapist alike, and should eventually be given common and co-operative solutions.

The study of behavior, psychotic or otherwise, remains securely in the company of the natural sciences so long as we take as our subject matter the observable activity of the organism, as it moves about, stands still, seizes objects, pushes and pulls, makes sounds, gestures, and so on. Suitable instruments will permit us to amplify small-scale activities as part of the same subject matter. Watching a person behave in this way is like watching any physical or biological system. We also remain within the framework of the natural sciences in explaining these observations in terms of external forces and events which act upon the organism. Some of these are to be found in the hereditary history of the individual, including his membership in a given species as well as his personal endowment. Others arise from the physical environment, past or present. We may represent the situation as in Figure 1.

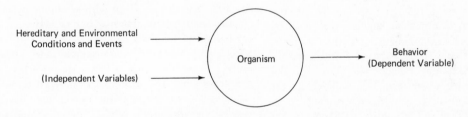

Figure 1

Our organism emits the behavior we are to account for, as our dependent variable, at the right. To explain this, we appeal to certain external, generally observable, and possibly controllable hereditary and environmental conditions, as indicated at the left. These are the independent variables of which behavior is to be expressed as a function. Both input and output of such a system may be treated with the accepted dimensional systems of physics and biology. A complete set of such relations would permit us to predict and, insofar as the independent variables are under our control, to modify or generate behavior at will. It would also permit us to *interpret* given instances of behavior by inferring plausible variables of which we lack direct information. Ad-

mittedly the data are subtle and complex, and many relevant conditions are hard to get at, but the program as such is an acceptable one from the point of view of scientific method. We have no reason to suppose in advance that a complete account cannot be so given. We have only to try and see.

It is not, however, the subtlety or complexity of this subject matter which is responsible for the relatively undeveloped state of such a science. Behavior has seldom been analyzed in this manner. Instead, attention has been diverted to activities which are said to take place within the organism. All sciences tend to fill in causal relationships, especially when the related events are separated by time and space. If a magnet affects a compass needle some distance away, the scientist attributes this to a "field" set up by the magnet and reaching to the compass needle. If a brick falls from a chimney, releasing energy which was stored there, say, a hundred years ago when the chimney was built, the result is explained by saying that the brick has all this time possessed a certain amount of "potential energy." In order to fill such spatial and temporal gaps between cause and effect, nature has from time to time been endowed with many weird properties, spirits, and essences. Some have proved helpful and have become part of the subject matter of science, especially when identified with events observed in other ways. Others have proved dangerous and damaging to scientific progress. Sophisticated scientists have usually been aware of the practice and alert to its dangers. Such inner forces were, indeed, the hypotheses which Newton refused to make.

Among the conditions which affect behavior, hereditary factors occupy a primary position, at least chronologically. Differences between members of different species are seldom, if ever, disputed, but differences between members of the same species, possibly due to similar hereditary factors, are so closely tied up with social and ethical problems that they have been the subject of seemingly endless debate. In any event, the newly conceived organism begins at once to be influenced by its environment; and when it comes into full contact with the external world, environmental forces assume a major role. They are the only conditions which can be changed so far as the individual is concerned. Among these are the events we call "stimuli," the various interchanges between organism and environment such as occur in breathing or eating, the events which generate the changes in behavior we call emotional, and the coincidences between stimuli or between stimuli and behavior responsible for the changes we call learning. The effects may be felt immediately or only after the passage of time—perhaps of many years. Such are the "causes"—the independent variables—in terms of which we may hope to explain behavior within the framework of a natural science.

In many discussions of human behavior, however, these variables are seldom explicitly mentioned. Their place is taken by events or conditions within the organism for which they are said to be responsible (see Figure 2). Thus, the species status of the individual is dealt with as a set of instincts, not simply as patterns of be-

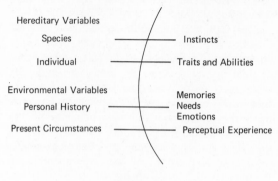

Figure 2

havior characteristic of the species, but as biological drives. As one text puts it, "instincts are innate biological forces, urges, or impulses driving the organism to a certain end." The individual genetic endowment, if not carried by body-type or other observable physical characteristic, is represented in the form of inherited traits or abilities, such as temperament or intelligence. As to the environmental variables, episodes in the past history of the individual are dealt with as memories and habits, while certain conditions of interchange between organism and environment are represented as needs or wants. Certain inciting episodes are dealt with as emotions, again in the sense not of patterns but of active causes of behavior. Even the present environment as it affects the organism is transmuted into "experience," as we turn from what is the case to what "seems to be" the case to the individual.

The same centripetal movement may be observed on the other side of the diagram (see Figure 3). It is rare to find behavior dealt with as a subject matter in its own right. Instead it is regarded as evidence for a mental

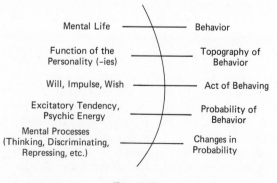

Figure 3

life, which is then taken as the primary object of inquiry. What the individual does—the topography of his behavior—is treated as the functioning of one or more personalities. It is clear, especially when personalities are multiple, that they cannot be identified with the biological organism as such, but are conceived of, rather, as inner behavers of doubtful status and dimensions. The act of behaving in a given instance is neglected in favor of an impulse or wish, while the probability of such an act is represented as an excitatory tendency or in terms of psychic energy. Most important of all, the

changes in behavior which represent the fundamental behavioral processes are characterized as mental activities—such as thinking, learning, discriminating, reasoning, symbolizing, projecting, identifying, and repressing.

The relatively simple scheme shown in the first figure does not, therefore, represent the conception of human behavior characteristic of most current theory. The great majority of students of human behavior assume that they are concerned with a series of events indicated in the expanded diagram of Figure 4. Here the hereditary and environmental conditions are as-

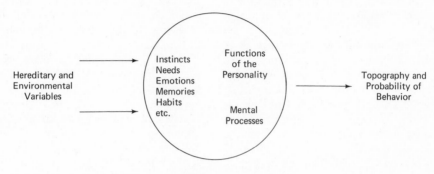

Figure 4

sumed to generate instincts, needs, emotions, memories, habits, and so on, which in turn lead the personality to engage in various activities characteristic of the mental apparatus, and these in turn generate the observable behavior of the organism. All four stages in the diagram are accepted as proper objects of inquiry. Indeed, far from leaving the inner events to other specialists while confining themselves to the end terms, many psychologists and psychiatrists take the mental apparatus as their primary subject matter.

Perhaps the point of my title is now becoming clearer. Is the scientific study of behavior —whether normal or psychotic—concerned with the behavior of the observable organism under the control of hereditary and environmental factors, or with the functioning of one or more personalities engaged in a variety of mental processes under the promptings of instincts, needs, emotions, memories, and habits? I do not want to raise the question of the supposed *nature* of these inner entities. A certain kinship between such an explanatory system and primitive animism can scarcely be missed, but whatever the historical sources of these concepts, we may as-

sume that they have been purged of dualistic connotations. If this is not the case, if there are those who feel that psychiatry is concerned with a world beyond that of the psychobiological or biophysical organism, that conscious or unconscious mind lacks physical extent, and that mental processes do not affect the world according to the laws of physics, then the following arguments should be all the more cogent. But the issue is not one of the nature of these events, but of their usefulness and expedience in a scientific description.

It can scarcely be denied that the expansion of subject matter represented by Figure 4 has the unfortunate effect of a loss of physical status. This is more than a question of prestige or "face." A subject matter which is unquestionably part of the field of physics and biology has been relinquished for one of doubtful characteristics. This cannot be corrected merely by asserting our faith in the ultimately physical nature of inner processes. To protest that the activities of the conscious and unconscious mind are only in some sense an aspect of the biological functioning of the organism will not answer the practical question. In abandoning the dimensional systems of physics and biology, we abandon the techniques of measurement which would otherwise be a natural heritage from earlier achievements in other sciences. This is possibly an irreparable loss. If we come out flatly for the existence of instincts, needs, memories, and so on, on the one hand, and the mental processes and functions of the personality on the other, then we must accept the responsibility of devising methods of observing these inner events and of discovering dimensional systems according to which they can be measured. The loss of the opportunity to measure and manipulate in the manner characteristic of the physical sciences would be offset only by some extraordinary advantage gained by turning to inner states or conditions.

It is possible, however, to argue that these inner events are merely ways of representing the outer. Many theorists will contend that a habit is only a sort of notation useful in reporting a bit of the history of the individual, just as so-called "mental processes" are ways of talking about changes in behavior. This is a tempting position, for we may then insist that the only dimensional systems required are those appropriate to the terminal events. But if we are to take that line, a great deal still needs to be done to put our house in scientific order. The concepts which one encounters in current behavior theory represent the observable events in an extremely confusing way. Most of them have arisen from theoretical or practical considerations which have little reference to their validity or usefulness as scientific constructs, and they bear the scars of such a history. For example, Freud pointed to important relationships between the behavior of an adult and certain episodes in early childhood, but he chose to bridge the very considerable gap between cause and effect with activities or states of the mental apparatus. Conscious or unconscious wishes or emotions in the adult represent the earlier episodes and are said to be directly responsible for their effect upon behavior. The adult is said, for example, to be suffering from conscious or unconscious anxiety generated when as a child he was punished for aggressive behavior toward a sibling. But many details of the early episode are glossed over (and may, as a result, be neglected) in attributing the disturbances in his behavior to a current anxiety rather than to the earlier punishment. The number of references to anxiety in treatises on behavior must greatly exceed the number of references to punishing episodes, yet we must turn to the latter for full details. If the details are not available, nothing can take their place.

Other kinds of independent variables provide similar examples. Everyone is familiar with the fact that, in general, organisms eat or do not eat depending upon a recent history of deprivation or ingestion. If we can establish that a child does not eat his dinner because he has recently eaten other food, there may seem to be no harm in expressing this by saying that "he is not hungry," provided we explain this in turn by pointing to the history of ingestion. But the concept of hunger represents quite inadequately the many features of schedules of deprivation and other conditions and events which alter the behavior of eating. In the same way the inner surrogates of hereditary variables function beyond the line of duty. We often have no other explanation of a given bit of behavior than that, like other features of anatomy and physiology, it is characteristic of a species; but when we choose instead to attribute this behavior to a set of instincts, we obscure the negative nature of our knowledge and suggest more active causes than mere species status warrants. Similarly, we accept the fact that individuals differ in their behavior, and we may, in some instances, show a relation between aspects of the behavior of successive generations, but these differences and relationships are optimistically misrepresented when we speak of hereditary traits and abilities. Again, the term *experience* incorrectly represents our information about a stimulating field. It has often been observed, for example, that some trivial incident generates a reaction altogether out of proportion to its magnitude. A person seems to be reacting, not to the physical world as such, but to what the world "means to him." Eventually, of course, the effect must be explained—for example, by pointing to some earlier connection with more important events. But whatever the explanation, it is almost certainly not adequately expressed by the notion of a momentary experience. There are obvious difficulties involved in representing a physical environment *plus a personal history* as a current psychological environment alone.

So far as our independent variables are concerned, then, the practice we are examining tends to gloss over many important details and complexities. The conceptual structure conceals from us the inadequacy of our present knowledge. Much the same difficulty is encountered with respect to the dependent variable, when observable behavior takes second place to mental functionings of a personality. Just as the physical environment is transmuted into experience, so physical behavior comes to be described in terms of its purpose or meaning. A man may walk down the street in precisely the same way upon two occasions, although in one instance he is out for exercise and in another he is going to mail a letter. And so it is thought necessary to consider, not the behavior itself, but "what it means" to the behaving individual. But the additional information we are trying to convey is not a property of behavior but of an independent variable. The behavior we observe in the two cases *is* the same. In reading meaning or intention into it, we are speculating about some of its causes. To take another example, it is commonly said that we can "see" aggression. But we "see" it in two steps: (1) we observe the behavior of an organism, and (2) we relate it to observed or inferred variables having to do with injurious consequences and with the kinds of circumstances which make such behavior probable. No behavior is itself aggressive by nature, although some forms of behavior are so often a function of variables which make them aggressive that we are inclined to overlook the inferences involved. Similarly, when we observe two or more behavioral systems in the same individual and attribute them to different personalities, we gain a considerable advantage for certain descriptive purposes. For example, we can then describe oppositions between such systems as we would between different persons. But we have almost certainly suggested a unity which is not justified by the observed systems of behavior, and we have probably made it more difficult to represent the actual extent of any conflict as well as to explain its origins. And when we observe that the behavior of a person is characterized by a certain responsiveness or probability of responding and speak instead of a given amount of psychic energy, we neglect many details of the actual facts and dodge the responsibility of finding a dimensional system. Lastly, mental processes are almost always conceived of as simpler and more orderly than the rather chaotic material from which they are inferred and which they are used to explain. The "learning process" in experimental psychology, for example, does not give us an accurate account of measured changes in behavior.

We look inside the organism for a *simpler* system, in which the causes of behavior are less complex than the actual hereditary and environmental events and in which the behavior of a personality is more meaningful and orderly than the day-to-day activity of the organism. All the variety and complexity of the input in our diagram seems to be reduced to a few relatively amorphous states, which in turn generate relatively amorphous functions of the personality, which then suddenly explode into the extraordinary variety and complexity of behavior. But the simplification achieved by such a practice is, of course, illusory, for it follows only from the fact that a one-to-one correspondence between inner and outer events has not been demanded. It is just this lack of correspondence which makes such an inner system unsuitable in the experimental analysis of behavior. If "hunger" is something which is produced by certain schedules of deprivation, certain drugs, certain states of health, and so on, and if in turn it produces changes in the probability of a great variety of responses, then it must have very complex properties. It cannot be any simpler than its causes or its effects. If the behavior we observe simply expresses the functioning of a personality, the personality cannot be any simpler than the behavior. If some common learning process is responsible for the changes observed in a number of different situations, then it cannot be any simpler than these changes. The apparent simplicity of the inner system explains the eagerness with which we turn to it, but from the point of view of scientific method it must be regarded as a spurious simplicity, which foreshadows ultimate failure of such an explanatory scheme.

There is another objection. Although speculation about what goes on with the organism seems to show a concern for completing a causal chain, in practice it tends to have the opposite effect. Chains are left incomplete. The layman commonly feels that he has explained behavior when he has attributed it to something in the organism— as in saying "He went *because* he wanted to go," or "He could not work *because* he was worried about his health." Such statements may have value in suggesting the relevance of one set of causes as against another, but they do not give a full explanation until it is explained *why* the person wanted to go, or *why* he was worried. Frequently this additional step is taken, but perhaps just as often these incomplete explanations bring inquiry to a dead stop.

No matter how we may wish to represent such a sequence of causal events, we cannot satisfy the requirements of interpretation, prediction, or control unless we go back to events acting upon the organism from without—events, moreover, which are observed as any event is observed in the physical and biological sciences. It is only common sense, therefore, as well as good scientific practice, to make sure that the concepts which enter into a theory of behavior are explicitly and carefully related to such events. What is needed is an operational definition of terms. This means more than simple translation. The operational method is commonly misused to patch up and preserve concepts which are cherished for extraneous and irrelevant reasons. Thus it might be possible to set up acceptable definitions of instincts, needs, emotions, memories, psychic energy, and so on, in which each term would be carefully related to certain behavioral and environmental facts. But we have no guarantee that these concepts will be the most useful when the actual functional relationships are better understood. A more reasonable program at this stage is to attempt to account for behavior without appeal to inner explanatory entities. We can do this within the accepted framework of biology, gaining thereby not only a certain personal reassurance from the prestige of a well-developed science, but an extensive set of experimental practices and dimensional systems. We shall be prevented from oversimplifying and misrepresenting the available facts because we shall not transmute our descriptions into other terms. The practical criteria of prediction and control will force us to take into account the complete causal chain in every instance. Such a program is not concerned with establishing the existence of inferred events, but with assessing the state of our knowledge.

This does not mean, of course, that the organism is conceived of as actually empty, or that continuity between input and output will not eventually be established. The genetic development of the organism and the complex interchanges between organism and environment are the subject matters of appropriate disciplines. Some day we shall know, for example, what happens when a stimulus impinges upon the surface of an organism, and what happens inside the organism after that, in a series of stages the last of which is the point at which the organism acts upon the environment and possibly changes it. At that point we lose interest in this causal chain. Some day, too, we shall know how the ingestion of food sets up a series of events, the last of which to engage our attention is a reduction in the probability of all behavior previously reinforced with similar food. Some day we may even know how to bridge the gap between the behavioral characteristics common to parents and offspring. But all these inner events will be accounted for with techniques of observation and measurement appropriate to the physiology of the various parts of the organism, and the account will be expressed in terms appropriate to that subject matter. It would be a remarkable coincidence if the concepts now used to refer inferentially to inner events were to find a place in that account. The task of physiology is not to find hungers, fears, habits, instincts, personalities, psychic energy, or acts of willing, attending, repressing, and so on. Nor is that task to find entities or processes of which all these could be said to be other aspects. Its task is to account for the causal relations between input and output which are the special concern of a science of behavior. Physiology should be left free to do this in its own way. Just to the extent that current conceptual systems fail to represent the relationships between terminal events correctly, they misrepresent the task of these other disciplines. A comprehensive set of causal relations stated with the greatest possible precision is the best contribution which we, as students of behavior, can make in the co-operative venture of giving a full account of the organism as a biological system.

But are we not overlooking one important source of knowledge? What about the direct observation of mental activity? The belief that the mental apparatus is available to direct inspection anticipated the scientific analysis of human behavior by many hundreds of years. It was refined by the introspective psychologists at the end of the nineteenth century into a special theory of knowledge which seemed to place the newly created science of consciousness on a par with natural science by arguing that all scientists necessarily begin and end with their own sensations and that the psychologist merely deals with these in a different way for different purposes. The notion has been revived in recent theories of perception, in which it has been suggested that the study of what used to be called "optical illusions," for example, will supply principles which help in understanding the limits of scientific knowledge. It has also been argued that the especially intimate empathic understanding which frequently occurs in psychotherapy supplies a kind of direct knowledge of the mental processes of other people. Franz Alexander and Lawrence

Kubie have argued in this manner in defense of psychoanalytic practices. Among clinical psychologists Carl Rogers has actively defended a similar view. Something of the same notion may underlie the belief that the psychiatrist may better understand the psychotic if, through the use of lysergic acid, for example, he may temporarily experience similar mental conditions.

Whether the approach to human behavior which I have just outlined ignores some basic fact, whether it is unable to take into account the "stubborn fact of consciousness," is part of a venerable dispute which will not be settled here. Two points may be made, however, in evaluating the evidence from direct "introspection" of the mental apparatus. Knowledge is not to be identified with how things look to us, but rather with what we do about them. Knowledge is power because it is action. How the surrounding world soaks into the surface of our body is merely the first chapter of the story and would be meaningless were it not for the parts which follow. These are concerned with behavior. Astronomy is not how the heavens look to an astronomer. Atomic physics is not the physicist's perception of events within the atom, or even of the macroscopic events from which the atomic world is inferred. Scientific knowledge is what people *do* in predicting and controlling nature.

The second point is that knowledge depends upon a personal history. Philosophers have often insisted that we are not aware of a difference until it makes a difference, and experimental evidence is beginning to accumulate in support of the view that we should probably not know anything at all if we were not forced to do so. The discriminative behavior called knowledge arises only in the presence of certain reinforcing contingencies among the things known. Thus, we should probably remain blind if visual stimuli were never of any importance to us, just as we do not hear all the separate instruments in a symphony or see all the colors in a painting until it is worth while for us to do so.

Some interesting consequences follow when these two points are made with respect to our knowledge of events within ourselves. That a small part of the universe is enclosed within the skin of each of us, and that this constitutes a private world to which each of us has a special kind of access can scarcely be denied. But the world with which we are in contact does not for that reason have any special physical or metaphysical status. Now, it is presumably necessary to learn to observe or "know" events within this private world just as we learn to observe or "know" external events, and our knowledge will consist of doing something about them. But the society from which we acquire such behavior is at a special disadvantage. It is easy to teach a child to distinguish between colors by presenting different colors and reinforcing his responses as right or wrong accordingly, but it is much more difficult to teach him to distinguish between different aches or pains, since the information as to whether his responses are right or wrong is much less reliable. It is this limited accessibility of the world within the skin, rather than its nature, which has been responsible for so much metaphysical speculation.

Terms which refer to private events tend to be used inexactly. Most of them are borrowed in the first place from descriptions of external events. (Almost all the vocabulary of emotion, for example, has been shown to be metaphorical in origin.) The consequences are well known. The testimony of the individual regarding his mental processes, feelings, needs, and so on, is, as the psychiatrist above all others has insisted, unreliable. Technical systems of terms referring to private events seldom resemble each other. Different schools of introspective psychology have emphasized different features of experience, and the vocabulary of one may occasionally be unintelligible to another. This is also true of different dynamic theories of mental life. The exponent of a "system" may show extraordinary conviction in his use of terms and in his defense of a given set of explanatory entities, but it is usually easy to find someone else showing the same conviction and defending a different and possibly incompatible system. Just as introspective psychology once found it expedient to train observers in the use of terms referring to mental events, so the education of experimental psychologists, educators, applied psychologists, psychotherapists, and many others concerned with human behavior is not always free from a certain element of indoctrination. Only in this way has it been possible to make sure that mental processes will be described by two or more people with any consistency.

Psychiatry itself is responsible for the notion that one need not be aware of the feelings, thoughts, and so on, which are said to affect behavior. The individual often behaves *as if* he were thinking or feeling in a given way although he cannot himself say that he is doing so. Mental processes which do not have the support of the testimony supplied by introspection are necessarily defined in terms of, and measured as, the behavioral facts from which they are inferred. Unfortunately, the notion of mental activity was preserved in the face of such evidence with the help of the notion of an unconscious mind. It might have been better to dismiss the concept of mind altogether as an explanatory fiction which had not survived a crucial test. The modes of inference with which we arrive at knowledge of the unconscious need to be examined with respect to the conscious mind as well. Both are conceptual entities, the relations of which to observed data need to be carefully reexamined.

In the long run the point will not be established by argument, but by the effectiveness of a given formulation in the design of productive research. An example of research on psychotic subjects which emphasizes the end terms in our diagram is the project already mentioned. This is not the place for technical details, but the rationale of this research may be relevant.[1] In these experiments a patient spends one or more hours daily, alone, in a small pleasant room. He is never coerced into going there, and is free to leave at any time. The room is furnished with a chair, and contains a device similar to a vending machine, which can be operated by pushing a button or pulling a plunger. The machine delivers candies, cigarettes, or substantial food, or projects colored pictures on a translucent screen. Most patients eventually operate the machine, are "reinforced" by what it delivers, and then continue to operate it daily for long periods of time—possibly a year or more. During this time the behavior is reinforced on various "schedules"—for example, once every minute or once for every thirty responses—in relation to various stimuli. The behavior is recorded in another room in a continuous curve which is read somewhat in the manner of an electrocardiogram and which permits a ready inspection and measurement of the rate of responding.

The isolation of this small living space is, of course, not complete. The patient does not leave his personal history behind as he enters the room, and to some extent what he does there resembles what he does or has done elsewhere. Nevertheless, as time goes on, the conditions arranged by the experiment begin to compose, so to speak, a special personal history, the important details of which are known. Within this small and admittedly artificial life space, we can watch the patient's behavior change as we change conditions of reinforcement, motivation, and to some extent emotion. With respect to these variables the behavior becomes more and more predictable and controllable or—as characteristic of the psychotic subject—fails to do so in specific ways.

The behavior of the patient may resemble that of a normal human or infrahuman subject in response to similar experimental conditions, or it may differ in a simple quantitative way—for example, the record may be normal except for a lower over-all rate. On the other hand, a performance may be broken by brief psychotic episodes. The experimental control is interrupted momentarily by the intrusion of extraneous behavior. In some cases it has been possible to reduce or increase the time taken by these interruptions, and to determine where during the session they will occur. As in similar work with other organisms, this quantitative and continuous account of the behavior of the individual under experimental control provides a highly sensitive baseline for the observation of the effects of drugs and of various forms of therapy. For our present purposes, however, the important thing is that it permits us to apply to the psychotic a fairly rigorous formulation of behavior based upon much more extensive work under the much more propitious control of conditions obtained with other species. This formulation is expressed in terms of input and output without reference to inner states.

The objection is sometimes raised that research of this sort reduces the human subject to the status of a research animal. Increasing evidence of the lawfulness of human behavior only seems to make the objection all the more cogent. Medical research has met this problem before, and has found an answer which is available here. Thanks to parallel work on animals, it has been possible, in some cases at least, to generate healthier behavior in men, even though at this stage we may not be directly concerned with such a result.

[1] Dr. Harry Solomon of the Boston Psychopathic Hospital has served as co-director of the project, although the preceding arguments do not necessarily represent his views. Dr. Ogden R. Lindsley is in immediate charge and responsible for much of the over-all experimental design as well as for the actual day-to-day conduct of the experiments. Support has been provided by the Office of Naval Research and by the National Institute of Mental Health. The work is being carried out at the Metropolitan State Hospital in Waltham, Massachusetts, with the co-operation of Dr. William McLaughlin, Superintendent, and Dr. Meyer Asakoff, Director of Research.

Another common objection is that we obtain our results only through an oversimplification of conditions, and that they are therefore not applicable to daily life. But one always simplifies at the start of an experiment. We have already begun to make our conditions more complex and will proceed to do so as rapidly as the uniformity of results permits. It is possible to complicate the task of the patient without limit, and to construct not only complex intellectual tasks but such interactions between systems of behavior as are seen in the Freudian dynamisms.

One simplification sometimes complained of is the absence of other human beings in this small life space. This was, of course, a deliberate preliminary measure, for it is much more difficult to control social than mechanical stimulation and reinforcement. But we are now moving on to situations in which one patient observes the behavior of another working on a similar device, or observes that the other patient receives a reinforcement whenever he achieves one himself, and so on. In another case the patient is reinforced only when his behavior corresponds in some way to the behavior of another. Techniques for achieving extraordinarily precise competition and cooperation between two or more individuals have already been worked out with lower organisms, and are applicable to the present circumstances.

This project has, of course, barely scratched the surface of the subject of psychotic behavior. But so far as it has gone, it seems to us to have demonstrated the value of holding to the observable data. Whether or not you will all find them significant, the data we report have a special kind of simple objectivity. At least we can say that this is what a psychotic subject did under these circumstances, and that this is what he failed to do under circumstances which would have had a different effect had he not been psychotic.

Although we have been able to describe and interpret the behavior observed in these experiments without reference to inner events, such references are, of course, not interdicted. Others may prefer to say that what we are actually doing is manipulating habits, needs, and so on, and observing changes in the structure of the personality, in the strength of the ego, in the amount of psychic energy available, and so on. But the advantage of this over a more parsimonious description becomes more difficult to demonstrate as evidence of the effectiveness of an objective formulation accumulates. In that bright future to which research in psychiatry is now pointing, we must be prepared for the possibility that increasing emphasis will be placed on immediately observable data and that theories of human behavior will have to adjust themselves accordingly. It is not inconceivable that the mental apparatus and all that it implies will be forgotten. It will then be more than a mere working hypothesis to say—to return at long last to my title—that psychotic behavior, like all behavior, is part of the world of observable events to which the powerful methods of natural science apply and to the understanding of which they will prove adequate.

the role of the mentally ill and the dynamics of mental disorder: a research framework

Thomas J. Scheff

Although the last two decades have seen a vast increase in the number of studies of functional mental disorder, there is as yet no substantial, verified body of knowledge in this area. A quotation from a recent symposium on schizophrenia summarizes the present situation:

> During the past decade, the problems of chronic schizophrenia have claimed the energy of workers in many fields. Despite significant contributions which reflect continuing progress, *we have yet to learn to ask ourselves the right questions.*[1]

Many investigators apparently agree; systematic studies have not only failed to provide answers to the problem of causation, but there is considerable feeling that the problem itself has not been formulated correctly.

One frequently noted deficiency in psychiatric formulations of the problem is the failure to incorporate social processes into the dynamics of mental disorder. Although the importance of these processes is increasingly recognized by psychiatrists, the conceptual models used in formulating research questions are basically concerned with individual rather than social systems. Genetic, biochemical, and psychological investigations seek

different causal agents, but utilize similar models: dynamic systems which are located within the individual. In these investigations, social processes tend to be relegated to a subsidiary role, because the model focuses attention on individual differences, rather than on the social system in which the individuals are involved.

Recently a number of writers have sought to develop an approach which would give more emphasis to social processes. Lemert, Erikson, Goffman, and Szasz have notably contributed to this approach.[2] Lemert, particularly, by rejecting the more conventional concern with the origins of mental deviance, and stressing instead the potential importance of the societal reaction in stabilizing deviance, focuses primarily on mechanisms of social control. The work of all of these authors suggests research avenues which are analytically separable from questions of individual systems and point, therefore, to a theory which would incorporate social processes.

The purpose of the present paper is to contribute to the formulation of such a theory by stating a set of nine propositions which make up basic assumptions for a social system model of mental disorder. This set is largely derived from the work of the authors listed above, all but two of the propositions (#4 and #5) being suggested, with varying degrees of explicitness, in the cited references. By stating these propositions explicitly, this paper attempts to facilitate testing of basic

This project was supported in part by the Graduate Research Committee of the University of Wisconsin. The help of many persons, too numerous to list here, who criticized earlier drafts is gratefully acknowledged.

[1] Nathanial S. Apter, "Our Growing Restlessness with Problems of Chronic Schizophrenia," in Lawrence Appleby, *et al., Chronic Schizophrenia*, Glencoe, Ill.: Free Press, 1958.

[2] Edwin M. Lemert, *Social Pathology*, New York: McGraw-Hill, 1951; Kai T. Erikson, "Patient Role and Social Uncertainty—A Dilemma of the Mentally Ill," *Psychiatry*, 20 (August, 1957), pp. 263–274; Erving Goffman, *Asylums*, New York: Doubleday-Anchor, 1961; Thomas S. Szasz, *The Myth of Mental Illness*, New York: Hoeber-Harper, 1961.

assumptions, all of which are empirically unverified, or only partly verified. By stating these assumptions in terms of standard sociological concepts, this paper attempts to show the relevance to studies of mental disorder of findings from diverse areas of social science, such as race relations and prestige suggestion. This paper also delineates three problems which are crucial for a sociological theory of mental disorder: what are the conditions in a culture under which diverse kinds of deviance become stable and uniform; to what extent, in different phases of careers of mental patients, are symptoms of mental illness the result of conforming behavior; is there a general set of contingencies which lead to the definition of deviant behavior as a manifestation of mental illness? Finally, this paper attempts to formulate special conceptual tools to deal with these problems, which are directly linked to sociological theory. The social institution of insanity, residual deviance, the social role of the mentally ill, and the bifurcation of the societal reaction into the alternative reactions of denial and labeling, are examples of such conceptual tools.

These conceptual tools are utilized to construct a theory of mental disorder in which psychiatric symptoms are considered to be violations of social norms, and stable "mental illness" to be a social role. The validity of this theory depends upon verification of the nine propositions listed below in future studies, and should, therefore, be applied with caution, and with appreciation for its limitations. One such limitation is that the theory attempts to account for a much narrower class of phenomena than is usually found under the rubric of mental disorder; the discussion that follows will be focused exclusively on stable or recurring mental disorder, and does not explain the causes of single deviant episodes. A second major limitation is that the theory probably distorts the phenomena under discussion. Just as the individual system models under-stress social processes, the model presented here probably exaggerates their importance. The social system model "holds constant" individual differences, in order to articulate the relationship between society and mental disorder. Ultimately, a framework which encompassed both individual and social systems would be desirable. Given the present state of knowledge, however, this framework may prove useful by providing an explicit contrast to the more conventional medical and psychological approaches, and thus assisting in the formulation of sociological studies of mental disorder.

THE SYMPTOMS OF "MENTAL ILLNESS" AS RESIDUALLY DEVIANT BEHAVIOR

One source of immediate embarrassment to any social theory of "mental illness" is that the terms used in referring to these phenomena in our society prejudge the issue. The medical metaphor "mental illness" suggests a determinate process which occurs within the individual: the unfolding and development of disease. It is convenient, therefore, to drop terms derived from the disease metaphor in favor of a standard sociological concept, deviant behavior, which signifies behavior that violates a social norm in a given society.

If the symptoms of mental illness are to be construed as violations of social norms, it is necessary to specify the type of norms involved. Most norm violations do not cause the violator to be labeled as mentally ill, but as ill-mannered, ignorant, sinful, criminal, or perhaps just harried, depending on the type of norm involved. There are innumerable norms, however, over which consensus is so complete that the members of a group appear to take them for granted. A host of such norms surround even the simplest conversation: a person engaged in conversation is expected to face toward his partner, rather than directly away from him; if his gaze is toward the partner, he is expected to look toward his eyes, rather than, say, toward his forehead; to stand at a proper conversational distance, neither one inch away nor across the room, and so on. A person who regularly violated these expectations probably would not be thought to be merely ill-bred, but as strange, bizarre, and frightening, because his behavior violates the assumptive world of the group, the world that is construed to be the only one that is natural, decent, and possible.

The culture of the group provides a vocabulary of terms for categorizing many norm violations: crime, perversion, drunkenness, and bad manners are familiar examples. Each of these terms is derived from the type of norm broken, and ultimately, from the type of behavior involved. After exhausting these categories, however, there is always a residue of the most diverse kinds of violations, for which the culture provides no explicit label. For example, although there is great cultural variation in what is defined as decent or real, each culture tends to reify its definition of decency and reality, and so provide no way of handling violations of its expectations in these areas. The typical norm governing decency or reality, therefore, literally "goes without saying" and its violation is unthinkable for most of its members. For the convenience of the society in construing those instances of unnamable deviance which are called to its attention, these violations may be lumped together into a residual category: witchcraft, spirit possession, or, in our own society, mental illness. In this paper, the diverse kinds of deviation for which our society provides no explicit label, and which, therefore, sometimes lead to the labeling of the violator as mentally ill, will be considered to be technically *residual deviance.*

THE ORIGINS, PREVALENCE AND COURSE OF RESIDUAL DEVIANCE

The first proposition concerns the origins of residual deviance. *1. Residual deviance arises from fundamentally diverse sources.* It has been demonstrated that some types of mental disorder are the result of organic causes. It appears likely, therefore, that there are genetic, biochemical or physiological origins for residual deviance. It also appears that residual deviance can arise from individual psychological peculiarities and from differences in upbringing and training. Residual deviance can also probably be produced by various kinds of external stress: the sustained fear and hardship of combat, and deprivation of food, sleep, and even sensory experience.[3] Residual deviance, finally, can be a volitional act of innovation or defiance. The kinds of behavior deemed typical of mental illness, such as hallucinations, delusions, depression, and mania, can all arise from these diverse sources.

The second proposition concerns the prevalence of residual deviance which is analogous to the "total" or "true" prevalence of mental disorder (in contrast to the "treated" prevalence). *2. Relative to the rate of treated mental illness, the rate of unrecorded residual deviance is extremely high.* There is evidence that grossly deviant behavior is often not noticed or, if it is noticed, it is rationalized as eccentricity. Apparently, many persons who are extremely withdrawn, or who "fly off the handle" for extended periods of time, who imagine fantastic events, or who hear voices or see visions, are not labeled as insane either by themselves or

others.[4] Their deviance, rather, is unrecognized, ignored, or rationalized. This pattern of inattention and rationalization will be called "denial."[5]

In addition to the kind of evidence cited above there are a number of epidemiological studies of total prevalence. There are numerous problems in interpreting the results of these studies; the major difficulty is that the definition of mental disorder is different in each study, as are the methods used to screen cases. These studies represent, however, the best available information and can be used to estimate total prevalence.

A convenient summary of findings is presented in Plunkett and Gordon.[6] This source compares the methods and populations used in eleven field studies, and lists rates of total prevalence (in percentages) as 1.7, 3.6, 4.5, 4.7, 5.3, 6.1, 10.9, 13.8, 23.2, 23.3, and 33.3.

How do these total rates compare with the rates of treated mental disorder? One of the studies cited by Plunkett and Gordon, the Baltimore study reported by Pasamanick, is useful in this regard since it includes both treated and untreated rates.[7] As compared with the untreated rate of 10.9 per cent, the rate of treatment in state, VA, and private hospitals of Baltimore residents was .5 per cent.[8] That is, for every mental patient there were approximately 20 untreated cases located by the survey. It is possible that the treated rate is too low, however, since patients treated by private physicians were not included. Judging from another study, the New Haven study of treated prevalence, the number of patients treated in private practice is small compared to those hospitalized: over 70 per cent of the patients located in that study were hospitalized even though extensive case-finding techniques were employed. The over-all treated prevalence in the New Haven

---

[3] Philip Solomon, *et al.* (eds.), *Sensory Deprivation,* Cambridge: Harvard, 1961; E. L. Bliss, *et al.*, "Studies of Sleep Deprivation—Relationship to Schizophrenia," *A.M.A. Archives of Neurology and Psychiatry,* 81 (March, 1959), pp. 348–359.

[4] See, for example, John A. Clausen and Marian R. Yarrow, "Paths to the Mental Hospital," *Journal of Social Issues,* 11 (December, 1955), pp. 25–32; August B. Hollingshead and Frederick C. Redlich, *Social Class and Mental Illness,* New York: Wiley, 1958, pp. 172–176; and Elaine Cumming and John Cumming, *Closed Ranks,* Cambridge: Harvard, 1957, pp. 92–103.

[5] The term "denial" is used in the same sense as in Cumming and Cumming, *ibid.*, Chap. VII.

[6] Richard J. Plunkett and John E. Gordon, *Epidemiology and Mental Illness,* New York: Basic Books, 1960.

[7] Benjamin Pasamanick, "A Survey of Mental Disease in an Urban Population, IV, An Approach to Total Prevalence Rates," *Archives of General Psychiatry,* 5 (August, 1961), pp. 151–155.

[8] *Ibid.,* p. 153.

study was reported as .8 per cent, which is in good agreement with my estimate of .7 per cent for the Baltimore study.[9] If we accept .8 per cent as an estimate of the upper limit of treated prevalence for the Pasamanick study, the ratio of treated to untreated cases is 1/14. That is, for every treated patient we should expect to find 14 untreated cases in the community.

One interpretation of this finding is that the untreated patients in the community represent those cases with less severe disorders, while those patients with severe impairments all fall into the treated group. Some of the findings in the Pasamanick study point in this direction. Of the untreated patients, about half are classified as psychoneurotic. Of the psychoneurotics, in turn, about half again are classified as suffering from minimal impairment. At least a fourth of the untreated group, then, involved very mild disorders.[10]

The evidence from the group diagnosed as psychotic does not support this interpretation, however. Almost all of the cases diagnosed as psychotic were judged to involve severe impairment, yet half of the diagnoses of psychosis occurred in the untreated group. In other words, according to this study there were as many untreated as treated cases of psychoses.[11]

On the basis of the high total prevalence rates cited above and other evidence, it seems plausible that residual deviant behavior is usually transitory, which is the substance of the third proposition. *3. Most residual deviance is "denied" and is transitory.* The high rates of total prevalence suggest that most residual deviancy is unrecognized or rationalized away. For this type of deviance, which is amorphous and uncrystallized, Lemert uses the term "primary deviation."[12] Balint describes similar behavior as "the unorganized phase of illness."[13] Although Balint assumes that patients in this phase ultimately "settle down" to an "organized illness," other outcomes are possible. A person in this stage may "organize" his deviance in other than illness terms, e.g., as eccentricity or genius, or the deviant acts may terminate when situational stress is removed.

The experience of battlefield psychiatrists can be interpreted to support the hypothesis that residual deviance is usually transitory. Glass reports that combat neurosis is often self-terminating if the soldier is kept with his unit and given only the most superficial medical attention.[14] Descriptions of child behavior can be interpreted in the same way. According to these reports, most children go through periods in which at least several of the following kinds of deviance may occur: temper tantrums, head banging, scratching, pinching, biting, fantasy playmates or pets, illusory physical complaints, and fears of sounds, shapes, colors, persons, animals, darkness, weather, ghosts, and so on.[15] In the vast majority of instances, however, these behavior patterns do not become stable.

If residual deviance is highly prevalent among ostensibly "normal" persons and is usually transitory, as suggested by the last two propositions, what accounts for the small percentage of residual deviants who go on to deviant careers? To put the question another way, under what conditions is residual deviance stabilized? The conventional hypothesis is that the answer lies in the deviant himself. The hypothesis suggested here is that the most important single factor (but not the only factor) in the stabilization of residual deviance is the societal reaction. Residual deviance may be stabilized if it is defined to be evidence of mental illness, and/or the deviant is placed in a deviant status, and begins to play the role of the mentally ill. In order to avoid the implication that mental disorder is merely role-playing and pretence, it is first necessary to discuss the social institution of insanity.

SOCIAL CONTROL: INDIVIDUAL AND SOCIAL SYSTEMS OF BEHAVIOR

In *The Myth of Mental Illness*, Szasz proposes that mental disorder be viewed within the framework of "the game-playing model of human behavior." He then describes hysteria, schizophrenia, and other mental disorders as the "impersonation" of sick persons by those whose "real" problem concerns "problems of living." Although Szasz states that role-playing by mental patients may

[9] Hollingshead and Redlich, *op. cit.*, p. 199.

[10] Pasamanick, *op. cit.*, pp. 153–154.

[11] *Ibid.*

[12] Lemert, *op. cit.*, Chap. 4.

[13] Michael Balint, *The Doctor, His Patient, and the Illness*, New York: International Universities Press, 1957, p. 18.

[14] Albert J. Glass, "Psychotherapy in the Combat Zone," in *Symposium on Stress*, Washington, D.C.: Army Medical Service Graduate School, 1953. Cf. Abraham Kardiner and H. Spiegel, *War Stress and Neurotic Illness*, New York: Hoeber, 1947, Chaps. III–IV.

[15] Frances L. Ilg and Louise B. Ames, *Child Behavior*, New York: Dell, 1960, pp. 138–188.

not be completely or even mostly voluntary, the implication is that mental disorder be viewed as a strategy chosen by the individual as a way of obtaining help from others. Thus, the term "impersonation" suggests calculated and deliberate shamming by the patient. In his comparisons of hysteria, malingering, and cheating, although he notes differences between these behavior patterns, he suggests that these differences may be mostly a matter of whose point of view is taken in describing the behavior.

The present paper also uses the role-playing model to analyze mental disorder, but places more emphasis on the involuntary aspects of role-playing than Szasz, who tends to treat role-playing as an individual system of behavior. In many social psychological discussions, however, role-playing is considered as a part of a social system. The individual plays his role by articulating his behavior with the cues and actions of other persons involved in the transaction. The proper performance of a role is dependent on having a cooperative audience. This proposition may also be reversed: having an audience which acts toward the individual in a uniform way may lead the actor to play the expected role even if he is not particularly interested in doing so. The "baby of the family" may come to find this role obnoxious, but the uniform pattern of cues and actions which confronts him in the family may lock in with his own vocabulary of responses so that it is inconvenient and difficult for him not to play the part expected of him. To the degree that alternative roles are closed off, the proffered role may come to be the only way the individual can cope with the situation.

One of Szasz's very apt formulations touches upon the social systemic aspects of role-playing. He draws an analogy between the role of the mentally ill and the "type-casting" of actors.[16] Some actors get a reputation for playing one type of role, and find it difficult to obtain other roles. Although they may be displeased, they may also come to incorporate aspects of the type-cast role into their self-conceptions, and ultimately into their behavior. Findings in several social psychological studies suggest that an individual's role behavior may be shaped by the kinds of "deference" that he regularly receives from others.[17]

One aspect of the voluntariness of role-playing is the extent to which the actor believes in the part he is playing. Although a role may be played cynically, with no belief, or completely sincerely, with whole-hearted belief, many roles are played on the basis of an intricate mixture of belief and disbelief. During the course of a study of a large public mental hospital, several patients told the author in confidence about their cynical use of their symptoms—to frighten new personnel, to escape from unpleasant work details, and so on. Yet these *same* patients, at other times, appear to have been sincere in their symptomatic behavior. Apparently it was sometimes difficult for them to tell whether they were playing the role or the role was playing them. Certain types of symptomatology are quite interesting in this connection. In simulation of previous psychotic states, and in the behavior pattern known to psychiatrists as the Ganser syndrome, it is apparently almost impossible for the observer to separate feigning of symptoms from involuntary acts with any degree of certainty.[18] In accordance with what has been said so far, the difficulty is probably that the patient is just as confused by his own behavior as is the observer.

This discussion suggests that a stable role performance may arise when the actor's role imagery locks in with the type of "deference" which he regularly receives. An extreme example of this process may be taken from anthropological and medical reports concerning the "dead role," as in deaths attributed to "bone-pointing." Death from bone-pointing appears to arise from the conjunction of two fundamental processes which characterize all social behavior. First, all individuals

---

[16] Szasz, *op. cit.*, p. 252. For discussion of type-casting see Orrin E. Klapp, *Heroes, Villains and Fools*, Englewood Cliffs, New Jersey: Prentice-Hall, 1962, pp. 5–8 and *passim*.
[17] Cf. Zena S. Blau, "Changes in Status and Age Identification," *American Sociological Review, 21* (April, 1956), pp. 198–203; James Benjamins, "Changes in Performance in Relation to Influences upon Self-Conceptualization," *Journal of Abnormal and Social Psychology, 45* (July, 1950), pp. 473–480; Albert Ellis, "The Sexual Psychology of Human Hermaphrodites," *Psychosomatic Medicine, 7* (March, 1945), pp. 108–125; S. Liberman, "The Effect of Changes in Roles on the Attitudes of Role Occupants," *Human Relations, 9* (1956), pp. 385–402. For a review of experimental evidence, see John H. Mann, "Experimental Evaluations of Role Playing," *Psychological Bulletin, 53* (May, 1956), pp. 227–234. For an interesting demonstration of the inter-relations between the symptoms of patients on the same ward, see Sheppard G. Kellam and J. B. Chassan, "Social Context and Symptom Fluctuation," *Psychiatry, 25* (November, 1962), pp. 370–381.
[18] Leo Sadow and Alvin Suslick, "Simulation of a Previous Psychotic State," *A.M.A. Archives of General Psychiatry, 4* (May, 1961), pp. 452–458.

continually orient themselves by means of responses which are perceived in social interaction: the individual's identity and continuity of experience are dependent on these cues.[19] Secondly, the individual has his own vocabulary of expectations, which may in a particular situation either agree with or be in conflict with the sanctions to which he is exposed. Entry into a role may be complete when this role is part of the individual's expectations, and when these expectations are reaffirmed in social interaction. In the following pages this principle will be applied to the problem of the causation of mental disorder.

What are the beliefs and practices that constitute the social institution of insanity? [20] And how do they figure in the development of mental disorder? Two propositions concerning beliefs about mental disorder in the general public will now be considered.

4. Stereotyped imagery of mental disorder is learned in early childhood. Although there are no substantiating studies in this area, scattered observations lead the author to conclude that children learn a considerable amount of imagery concerning deviance very early, and that much of the imagery comes from their peers rather than from adults. The literal meaning of "crazy," a term now used in a wide variety of contexts, is probably grasped by children during the first years of elementary school. Since adults are often vague and evasive in their responses to questions in this area, an aura of mystery surrounds it. In this socialization the grossest stereotypes which are heir to childhood fears, e.g., of the "boogie man," survive. These conclusions are quite speculative, of course, and need to be investigated systematically, possibly with techniques similar to those used in studies of the early learning of racial stereotypes.

Assuming, however, that this hypothesis is sound, what effect does early learning have on the shared conceptions of insanity held in the community? There is much fallacious material learned in early childhood which is later discarded when more adequate information replaces it. This question leads to hypothesis No. 5. *5. The stereotypes of insanity are continually reaffirmed, inadvertently, in ordinary social interaction.*

Although many adults become acquainted with medical concepts of mental illness, the traditional stereotypes are not discarded, but continue to exist alongside the medical conceptions, because the stereotypes receive almost continual support from the mass media and in ordinary social discourse. In newspapers, it is a common practice to mention that a rapist or a murderer was once a mental patient. This negative information, however, is seldom offset by positive reports. An item like the following is almost inconceivable:

> Mrs. Ralph Jones, an ex-mental patient, was elected president of the Fairview Home and Garden Society in their meeting last Thursday.

Because of highly biased reporting, the reader is free to make the unwarranted inference that murder and rape occur more frequently among ex-mental patients than among the population at large. Actually, it has been demonstrated that the incidence of crimes of violence, or of any crime, is much lower among ex-mental patients than among the general population.[21] Yet, this is not the picture presented to the public.

Reaffirmation of the stereotype of insanity occurs not only in the mass media, but also in

---

[19] Generalizing from experimental findings, Blake and Mouton make this statement about the process of conformity, resistance to influence, and conversion to a new role:

... an individual requires a stable framework, including salient and firm reference points, in order to orient himself and to regulate his interactions with others. This framework consists of external and internal anchorages available to the individual whether he is aware of them or not. With an acceptable framework he can resist giving or accepting information that is inconsistent with that framework or that requires him to relinquish it. In the absence of a stable framework he actively seeks to establish one through his own strivings by making use of significant and relevant information provided within the context of interaction. *By controlling the amount and kind of information available for orientation, he can be led to embrace conforming attitudes which are entirely foreign to his earlier ways of thinking.*

Robert R. Blake and Jane S. Mouton, "Conformity, Resistance and Conversion," in *Conformity and Deviation,* Irwin A. Berg and Bernard M. Bass (eds.), New York: Harper, 1961, pp. 1–2. For a recent and striking demonstration of the effect on social communication in defining internal stimuli, see Stanley Schachter and Jerome E. Singer, "Cognitive, Social, and Physiological Determinants of Emotional State," *Psychological Review,* 69 (September, 1962), pp. 379–399.

[20] The Cummings describe the social institution of insanity (the "patterned response" to deviance) in terms of denial, isolation, and insulation. Cumming and Cumming, *loc. cit.*

[21] Henry Brill and Benjamin Malzberg, "Statistical Report Based on the Arrest Record of 5354 Male Ex-patients Released from New York State Mental Hospitals During the Period 1946–48," mimeographed

ordinary conversation, in jokes, anecdotes, and even in conventional phrases. Such phrases as "Are you crazy?", or "It would be a madhouse," "It's driving me out of my mind," or "It's driving me distracted," and hundreds of others occur frequently in informal conversations. In this usage insanity itself is seldom the topic of conversation; the phrases are so much a part of ordinary language that only the person who considers each word carefully can eliminate them from his speech. Through verbal usages the stereotypes of insanity are a relatively permanent part of the social structure.

In a recent study Nunnally demonstrated that reaffirmation of stereotypes occurs in the mass media. In a systematic and extensive content analysis of television, radio, newspapers and magazines, including "confession" magazines, they found an image of mental disorder presented which was overwhelmingly stereotyped.

. . . media presentations emphasized the bizarre symptoms of the mentally ill. For example, information relating to Factor I (the conception that mentally ill persons look and act different from "normal" people) was recorded 89 times. Of these, 88 affirmed the factor, that is, indicated or suggested that people with mental-health problems "look and act different": only one item denied Factor I. In television dramas, for example, the afflicted person often enters the scene staring glassy-eyed, with his mouth widely ajar, mumbling incoherent phrases or laughing uncontrollably. Even in what would be considered the milder disorders, neurotic phobias and obsessions, the afflicted person is presented as having bizarre facial expressions and actions.[22]

DENIAL AND LABELING

According to the analysis presented here, the traditional stereotypes of mental disorder are solidly entrenched in the population because they are learned early in childhood and are continuously reaffirmed in the mass media and in every-

day conversation. How do these beliefs function in the processes leading to mental disorder? This question will be considered by first referring to the earlier discussion of the societal reaction to residual deviance.

It was stated that the usual reaction to residual deviance is denial, and that in these cases most residual deviance is transitory. The societal reaction to deviance is not always denial, however. In a small proportion of cases the reaction goes the other way, exaggerating and at times distorting the extent and degree of deviation. This pattern of exaggeration, which we will call "labeling," has been noted by Garfinkel in his discussion of the "degradation" of officially recognized criminals.[23] Goffman makes a similar point in his description of the "discrediting" of mental patients.[24] Apparently under some conditions the societal reaction to deviance is to seek out signs of abnormality in the deviant's history to show that he was always essentially a deviant.

The contrasting social reactions of denial and labeling provide a means of answering two fundamental questions. If deviance arises from diverse sources—physical, psychological, and situational—how does the uniformity of behavior that is associated with insanity develop? Secondly, if deviance is usually transitory, how does it become stabilized in those patients who became chronically deviant? To summarize, what are the sources of uniformity and stability of deviant behavior?

In the approach taken here the answer to this question is based on hypotheses Nos. 4 and 5, that the role imagery of insanity is learned early in childhood, and is reaffirmed in social interaction. In a crisis, when the deviance of an individual becomes a public issue, the traditional stereotype of insanity becomes the guiding imagery for action, both for those reacting to the deviant and, at times, for the deviant himself. When societal agents and persons around the deviant react to him uniformly in terms of the traditional stereotypes of insanity, his amorphous and unstructured deviant behavior tends to crystallize in conformity to these expectations, thus becoming similar to the behavior of other deviants classified as mentally ill, and stable over time. The process of becoming uniform and stable is completed when the traditional imagery becomes

document available from the authors; L. H. Cohen and H. Freeman, "How Dangerous to the Community are State Hospital Patients?", *Connecticut State Medical Journal*, 9 (September, 1945), pp. 697–701.

[22] Jum C. Nunnally, Jr., *Popular Conceptions of Mental Health*, New York: Holt, Rinehart and Winston, 1961, p. 74.

[23] Harold Garfinkel, "Conditions of Successful Degradation Ceremonies," *American Journal of Sociology*, 61 (March, 1956), pp. 420–424.

[24] Goffman, "The Moral Career of the Mental Patient," in *Asylums, op. cit.*, pp. 125–171.

a part of the deviant's orientation for guiding his own behavior.

The idea that cultural stereotypes may stabilize primary deviance, and tend to produce uniformity in symptoms, is supported by cross-cultural studies of mental disorder. Although some observers insist there are underlying similarities, most agree that there are enormous differences in the manifest symptoms of stable mental disorder *between* societies, and great similarity *within* societies.[25]

These considerations suggest that the labeling process is a crucial contingency in most careers of residual deviance. Thus Glass, who observed that neuropsychiatric casualties may not become mentally ill if they are kept with their unit, goes on to say that military experience with psychotherapy has been disappointing. Soldiers who are removed from their unit to a hospital, he states, often go on to become chronically impaired.[26] That is, their deviance is stabilized by the labeling process, which is implicit in their removal and hospitalization. A similar interpretation can be made by comparing the observations of childhood disorders among Mexican-Americans with those of "Anglo" children. Childhood disorders such as *susto* (an illness believed to result from fright) sometimes have damaging outcomes in Mexican-American children.[27] Yet the deviant behavior involved is very similar to that which seems to have high incidence among Anglo children, with permanent impairment virtually never occurring. Apparently through cues from his elders the Mexican-American child, behaving initially much like his Anglo counterpart, learns to enter the sick role, at times with serious consequences.[28]

ACCEPTANCE OF THE DEVIANT ROLE

From this point of view, then, most mental disorder can be considered to be a social role.

[25] P. M. Yap, "Mental Diseases Peculiar to Certain Cultures: A Survey of Comparative Psychiatry," *Journal of Mental Science,* 97 (April, 1951), pp. 313–327; Paul E. Benedict and Irving Jacks, "Mental Illness in Primitive Societies," *Psychiatry,* 17 (November, 1954), pp. 377–389.

[26] Glass, *op. cit.*

[27] Lyle Saunders, *Cultural Differences and Medical Care,* New York: Russell Sage, 1954, p. 142.

[28] For discussion, with many illustrative cases, of the process in which persons play the "dead role" and subsequently die, see Charles C. Herbert, "Life-influencing Interactions," in *The Physiology of Emotions,* Alexander Simon, *et al.,* eds., New York: Charles C. Thomas, 1961.

This social role complements and reflects the status of the insane in the social structure. It is through the social processes which maintain the status of the insane that the varied deviances from which mental disorder arises are made uniform and stable. The stabilization and uniformization of residual deviance are completed when the deviant accepts the role of the insane as the framework within which he organizes his own behavior. Three hypotheses are stated below which suggest some of the processes which cause the deviant to accept such a stigmatized role.

6. Labeled deviants may be rewarded for playing the stereotyped deviant role. Ordinarily patients who display "insight" are rewarded by psychiatrists and other personnel. That is, patients who manage to find evidence of "their illness" in their past and present behavior, confirming the medical and societal diagnosis, receive benefits. This pattern of behavior is a special case of a more general pattern that has been called the "apostolic function" by Balint, in which the physician and others inadvertently cause the patient to display symptoms of the illness the physician thinks the patient has.[29] Not only physicians but other hospital personnel and even other patients, reward the deviant for conforming to the stereotypes.[30]

7. Labeled deviants are punished when they attempt the return to conventional roles. The second process operative is the systematic blockage of entry to nondeviant roles once the label has been publicly applied. Thus the ex-mental patient, although he is urged to rehabilitate himself in the community, usually finds himself discriminated against in seeking to return to his old status, and on trying to find a new one in the occupational, marital, social, and other spheres.[31] Thus, to a degree, the labeled deviant is rewarded for deviating, and punished for attempting to conform.

8. In the crisis occurring when a primary deviant is publicly labeled, the deviant is highly suggestible, and may accept the proffered role of the insane as the only alternative. When gross de-

[29] Balint, *op. cit.,* pp. 215–239. Cf. Thomas J. Scheff, "Decision Rules, Types of Error and Their Consequences in Medical Diagnosis," *Behavioral Science,* 8 (April, 1963), pp. 97–107.

[30] William Caudill, F. C. Redlich, H. R. Gilmore, and E. B. Brody, "Social Structure and the Interaction Processes on a Psychiatric Ward," *American Journal of Orthopsychiatry,* 22 (April, 1952), pp. 314–334.

[31] Lemert, *op. cit.,* provides an extensive discussion of this process under the heading of "Limitation of Participation," pp. 434–440.

viancy is publicly recognized and made an issue, the primary deviant may be profoundly confused, anxious, and ashamed. In this crisis it seems reasonable to assume that the deviant will be suggestible to the cues that he gets from the reactions of others toward him.[32] But those around him are also in a crisis; the incomprehensible nature of the deviance, and the seeming need for immediate action lead them to take collective action against the deviant on the basis of the attitude which all share—the traditional stereotypes of insanity. The deviant is sensitive to the cues provided by these others and begins to think of himself in terms of the stereotyped role of insanity, which is part of his own role vocabulary also, since he, like those reacting to him, learned it early in childhood. In this situation his behavior may begin to follow the pattern suggested by his own stereotypes and the reactions of others. That is, when a primary deviant organizes his behavior within the framework of mental disorder, and when his organization is validated by others, particularly prestigeful others such as physicians, he is "hooked" and will proceed on a career of chronic deviance.

The role of suggestion is noted by Warner in his description of bone-pointing magic:

The effect of (the suggestion of the entire community on the victim) is obviously drastic. An analogous situation in our society is hard to imagine. If all a man's near kin, his father, mother, brothers and sisters, wife, children, business associates, friends and all the other members of the society, should suddenly withdraw themselves because of some dramatic circumstance, refusing to take any attitude but one of taboo . . . and then perform over him a sacred ceremony . . . the enormous suggestive power of this movement . . . of the community after it has had its attitudes (toward the victim) crystallized can be somewhat understood by ourselves.[33]

If we substitute for black magic the taboo that usually accompanies mental disorder, and consider a commitment proceeding or even mental hospital admission as a sacred ceremony, the similarity between Warner's description and the typical events

in the development of mental disorder is considerable.

The last three propositions suggest that once a person has been placed in a deviant status there are rewards for conforming to the deviant role, and punishments for not conforming to the deviant role. This is not to imply, however, that the symptomatic behavior of persons occupying a deviant status is always a manifestation of conforming behavior. To explain this point, some discussion of the process of self-control in "normals" is necessary.

In a recent discussion of the process of self-control, Shibutani notes that self-control is not automatic, but is an intricate and delicately balanced process, sustainable only under propitious circumstances.[34] He points out that fatigue, the reaction to narcotics, excessive excitement or tension (such as is generated in mobs), or a number of other conditions interfere with self-control; conversely, conditions which produce normal bodily states, and deliberative processes such as symbolization and imaginative rehearsal before action, facilitate it.

One might argue that a crucially important aspect of imaginative rehearsal is the image of himself that the actor projects into his future action. Certainly in American society, the cultural image of the "normal" adult is that of a person endowed with self-control ("will-power," "backbone," "strength of character," etc.). For the person who sees himself as endowed with the trait of self-control, self-control is facilitated, since he can imagine himself enduring stress during his imaginative rehearsal, and also while under actual stress.

For a person who has acquired an image of himself as lacking the ability to control his own actions, the process of self-control is likely to break down under stress. Such a person may feel that he has reached his "breaking-point" under circumstances which would be endured by a person with a "normal" self-conception. This is to say, a greater lack of self-control than can be explained by stress tends to appear in those roles for which the culture transmits imagery which emphasizes lack of self-control. In American society such imagery is transmitted for the roles of the very young and very old, drunkards and drug addicts, gamblers, and the mentally ill.

---

[32] This proposition receives support from Erikson's observations: Kai T. Erikson, *loc. cit.*

[33] W. Lloyd Warner, *A Black Civilization*, rev. ed., New York: Harper, 1958, p. 242.

[34] T. Shibutani, *Society and Personality*, Englewood Cliffs, N.J.: Prentice-Hall, 1961, Chapter 6, "Consciousness and Voluntary Conduct."

Thus, the social role of the mentally ill has a different significance at different phases of residual deviance. When labeling first occurs, it merely gives a name to primary deviation which has other roots. When (and if) the primary deviance becomes an issue, and is not ignored or rationalized away, labeling may create a social type, a pattern of "symptomatic" behavior in conformity with the stereotyped expectations of others. Finally, to the extent that the deviant role becomes a part of the deviant's self-conception, his ability to control his own behavior may be impaired under stress, resulting in episodes of compulsive behavior.

The preceding eight hypotheses form the basis for the final causal hypothesis. 9. *Among residual deviants, labeling is the single most important cause of careers of residual deviance.* This hypothesis assumes that most residual deviance, if it does not become the basis for entry into the sick role, will not lead to a deviant career. Most deviant careers, according to this point of view, arise out of career contingencies, and are therefore not directly connected with the origins of the initial deviance.[35] Although there are a wide variety of contingencies which lead to labeling rather than denial, these contingencies can be usefully classified in terms of the nature of the deviant behavior, the person who commits the deviant acts, and the community in which the deviance occurs. Other things being equal, the severity of the societal reaction to deviance is a function of, first, the degree, amount, and visibility of the deviant behavior; second, the power of the deviant, and the social distance between the deviant and the agents of social control; and finally, the tolerance level of the community, and the availability in the culture of the community of alternative nondeviant roles.[36] Particu-

larly crucial for future research is the importance of the first two contingencies (the amount and degree of deviance), which are characteristics of the deviant, relative to the remaining five contingencies, which are characteristics of the social system.[37] To the extent that these five factors are found empirically to be independent determinants of labeling and denial, the status of the mental patient can be considered a partly ascribed rather than a completely achieved status. The dynamics of treated mental illness could then be profitably studied quite apart from the individual dynamics of mental disorder.

CONCLUSION

This paper has presented a sociological theory of the causation of stable mental disorder. Since the evidence advanced in support of the theory was scattered and fragmentary, it can only be suggested as a stimulus to further discussion and research. Among the areas pointed out for further investigation are field studies of the prevalence and duration of residual deviance; investigations of stereotypes of mental disorder in children, the mass media, and adult conversations; studies of the rewarding of stereotyped deviation, blockage of return to conventional roles, and of the suggestibility of primary deviants in crises. The final causal hypothesis suggests studies of the conditions under which denial and labeling of residual deviation occur. The variables which might effect the societal reaction concern the nature of the deviance, the deviant himself, and the community in which the deviation occurs. Although many of the hypotheses suggested are largely unverified, they suggest avenues for investigating mental disorder different than those that are usually followed, and the rudiments of a general theory of deviant behavior.

---

[35] It should be noted, however, that these contingencies are causal only because they become part of a dynamic system: the reciprocal and cumulative inter-relation between the deviant's behavior and the societal reaction. For example, the more the deviant enters the role of the mentally ill, the more he is defined by others as mentally ill; but the more he is defined as mentally ill, the more fully he enters the role, and so on. By representing this theory in the form of a flow chart, Walter Buckley pointed out that there are numerous such feedback loops implied here. For an explicit treatment of feedback, see Edwin M. Lemert, "Paranoia and the Dynamics of Exclusion," *Sociometry*, 25 (March, 1962), pp. 2–20.

[36] *Cf.* Lemert, *op. cit.*, pp. 51–53, 55–68; Goffman, "The Moral Career of the Mental Patient," in *Asylums*,

op. cit., pp. 134–135; David Mechanic, "Some Factors in Identifying and Defining Mental Illness," *Mental Hygiene*, 46 (January, 1962), pp. 66–74; for a list of similar factors in the reaction to physical illness, see Earl L. Koos, *The Health of Regionville*, New York: Columbia University Press, 1954, pp. 30–38.

[37] *Cf.* Thomas J. Scheff, "Psychiatric and Social Contingencies in the Release of Mental Patients in a Midwestern State," forthcoming; Simon Dinitz, Mark Lefton, Shirley Angrist, and Benjamin Pasamanick, "Psychiatric and Social Attributes as Predictors of Case Outcome in Mental Hospitalization," *Social Problems*, 8 (Spring, 1961), pp. 322–328.

a look at the past: the impact of psychoanalysis

Harold L. Raush & Charlotte L. Raush

The history of madness and of the "sane" man's attempt to deal with it is intimately bound with man's conception of himself and his world. Reflected in his view of madness is man's cultural history, his cosmogony, theology and philosophy, his myths and his sciences. Whether the madman is seen as inspired or possessed, whether he is respected as a seer, burned as a witch or sorcerer, enchained as a lunatic, or hospitalized as a patient depends on the time he is born into. And the choice reflects not so much the body of knowledge of these times as it does their spirit.

The story is not yet ended.

Today the mad are called "sick." They suffer a "mental illness" which is "just like any other illness and certainly nothing to be ashamed of." If they are sufficiently disturbing to us, they are put into hospitals, some of which are devoted exclusively to the "treatment" of this "disease." Such hospitals are much like other hospitals—with the wards and beds, with the doctors, nurses, and attendants, and with the complex administrative apparatus of hospitals. In some ways mental hospitals differ from other hospitals, but these differences have not changed our views very much. We still, for example, use the language familiar to hospitals: even when calling for reforms, we are apt to note that "half of all hospital *beds* are occupied by the *mentally ill.*"

We have changed our terms for those who seek to guide the mad to pathways of return. No longer are they soothsayers as was David for Saul; no longer are they inquisitors exorcising the devils which infested the souls of the unwary from the Middle Ages to the end of the seventeenth century; no longer are they the puritan churchmen who struggled with the Devil for the souls of witches; no longer are they the tolerant physicians of the early nineteenth century, concerned with the dignity and the moral problems of those whom life had treated too harshly.

The age of science and its medical counterpart ushered in an era of medical treatment for madness. From the industrial revolution came urbanization and growing separation of work from family roles, creating increased difficulties in maintaining the psychologically alienated within the bounds of ordinary society. The mental hospital for the insane—an institution still less than two hundred years old—multiplied and grew in size and in distance from the working community. Furthermore, within the medical cosmogony it seemed reasonable that a syndrome of what are now called symptoms would have a specific etiology and would be subject to a specific course of treatment.

But somehow our system of medical treatment has, like the others, broken down. Notions of brain pathology, toxemias, nutritional deficiencies offered too few solutions to the mystery of madness, and the treatments based on these notions have now gone by the board. Heroic efforts are still being expended toward establishing specific etiologies and discovering specific treatments. But the etiology has given way to *mental* etiology, and the treatment to *mental* treatment.

We are just beginning to explore how daring this leap is. It is an unwilling exploration. We have tried to think of our psychological lives as similar to a collection of bodily organs—as relatively discrete and "treatable." Though faced with contradictions we have been, for the most part, unwilling to open a Pandora's box of new demons. We hold tight to our outmoded but familiar models. We speak of "patients" and "treatment" and "cure." Seeking comfort in familiar medical analogies, in our "treatment" of the mind we "employ" chemotherapy and psychotherapy (individual, group, conjoint and family).

We also have in our pharmacopoeia such ancillary "therapies" as rehabilitation therapy, milieu therapy, occupational therapy, recreational therapy, music therapy, dance therapy. And if you recommend a book to someone, that must be bibliotherapy. This proliferation is of course appropriate to our own age of fragmentation, specialization and expertise. Nonetheless the absurdities are being felt.

The notion of a multiplicity of therapies, each competing for title of "real cure," or all cooperating in the "total treatment" of an ill-understood disease, is becoming untenable. We are coming to recognize that, whatever their ultimate cause and etiology, the problems faced by the deranged concern the trials and vicissitudes of living in this world with oneself and with others. Those of us who are not quite mad have the same kinds of problems, and we too solve them in accord with our strengths and weaknesses and our virtues and vices. We are learning that for psychological functions terms like "illness" and "health" are analogical, and no more to be taken literally than are metaphors like "treating" a "sick" society. We are learning that the concept of "cure," in its purely medical sense, has outlived its usefulness. And that the prophet, the priest, the social reformer, the educator and the psychoanalyst—all those who ask us to change ourselves and the world around us—have models which are better suited to understanding and doing something about the vicissitudes of living. Perhaps our most appropriate models will come from the—unfelicitously named—social scientists, who, like Freud, destroy our most cherished and intimate illusions so that we may build more honest and useful lives. But that remains to be seen. . . .

The historical roots of medicine are in its response to the universal call for the alleviation of suffering. But as the boundaries of suffering move out from the interior milieu of the body to the regions of man's relation with man and to his relation with social institutions, the traditional approaches of medicine become progressively strained. So it was that Freud found himself forced away from the physicalistic biases of the psychiatry of his time. This course was indeed no easy choice for him. One has only to look at his early efforts to establish and maintain a physical rationale for psychological symptoms: his preoccupation with the pseudochemical theories of his friend Fliess (Jones, 1953; Freud, 1954), or his later attempt to attribute the primary

cause of anxiety to the blocking of the physical orgasm. Even when, after relinquishing a physical orientation, he embraced the notion of specific psychological trauma as causing the disturbances which he set himself to cure, he again suffered disappointment. The childhood events related by his patients had often, he found, never actually happened. Increasingly, despite his training and disposition, his observations led him to psychology. And although he never quite gave up hope for the eventual discovery of chemical foundations underlying the profounder mental disturbances, the revolution he created was in his unequivocal view of man as a psychological being.

Freud certainly made no pretense to a full understanding of the severe disturbances, the psychoses, or as he called them, the narcissistic neuroses. Nor did he reject ideas that genetic or chemical factors might contribute to the etiology of psychological disorders or that chemical means might eventually be found for mitigating psychological disturbances. These considerations, however, in no way lessened his convictions as to the psychological relevance of disturbed behavior. Mental suffering was to be understood in psychological, not physical terms. Phenomena senseless in physical terms made sense psychologically.

It is fashionable these days to criticize Freud for a bias toward physicalism, for ignoring man's culture and social environment, for neglect of the interpersonal, and for emphasis on the pathological. Such critiques carry enough truth to germinate the founding of new theories and movements. But none of these criticisms is wholly legitimate and most contemporary movements which emphasize a psychological approach to the amelioration of mental suffering are constructed on one or another cornerstone of the architectural foundation created by Freud.

At the base of psychoanalysis was Freud's insistence that there was always a kind of sense in what people felt and did. However seemingly nonsensical, however bizarre, behavior was not a random epiphenomenon of disordered neural circuits. Actions were meaningful in terms of the premises of the actor. The premises came from memories and distortions of memories, the residues of the culture in which the child was raised. The capacity for suffering from memories was part of the human condition. The premises, going back to origins in childhood, formed templates through which current realities were screened, sieved, and compared. Once and for all, the

seeming arbitrariness of behavior was given coherence.

How then does one "cure" memories? The
point is that one does not "cure" memories, in
any ordinary sense of the word *cure*. One can
come to recognize, reorganize, de-emphasize ("de-
cathect") memories, and perhaps even to forget
that which once was but no longer is relevant.
So in his "treatment" Freud was led ever farther
away from the paraphernalia of medicine, discarding the clinic atmosphere of Charcot, resign-
ing the costume and authority of the physician,
step by step abjuring the magic of physical
methods, of hypnosis, of suggestion. With the
method of free association, patient and therapist
became co-participant explorers. A major aspect
of the "cure" concerned the relation between the
two, a relation peculiarly structured to allow
fullest explorations of past interpersonal relations
through study of their current effects. "Cure"
was through understanding—psychological understanding.

If even the strangest behavior had meaning,
it could be understood, and hopefully that understanding could be used in effecting changes. But
there was yet another aspect of the psychoanalytic
viewpoint which had profound influence on the
position of the mentally disturbed. This was the
general dynamic theory of the unconscious, a
theory of forces and counter-forces. The specifics
of the theory need not concern us here. What is
relevant is that the general theory of psychic
function was applicable to both so-called "normal"
and "abnormal" phenomena. There was but one
psychopathology. The "normal" person did not
escape from it. It appeared in his dreams, his
humor, his slips of the tongue, and in his sometimes serious lapses from rationality. In an attenuated and usually somewhat controlled form,
he showed the "abnormalities" which were exaggerated in the more severely disturbed. The history he bore was a somewhat happier version of
equivalent events. We were all, patient and nonpatient, as Harry Stack Sullivan later put it, "more
simply human than otherwise."

The patient in the mental hospital was thus
rescued—if only theoretically—from his position
as member of a strange and alien species. His
mental processes and his actions, although difficult to fathom, were essentially no less comprehensible than our own. Psychoanalysis offered a
theory and a method for this understanding.
More than these, it offered a hope.

The influence of psychoanalysis on those confined in mental hospitals was slow to be felt.
On the one hand, the hope started a surge of
activity and humane concern such as had not
been seen since the early days of "moral" treatment. The impetus was most sharply felt following
the Second World War with the massive increase
in demands for psychiatric service and increase
in training for mental health workers. The new
young psychiatrists, psychologists and social workers were strongly influenced by the scope, breadth
and power of understanding offered by psychoanalysis. They were inspired by the pioneering
efforts of the few devoting themselves to the
herculean rescue of those humans who seemed
beyond human reach. The work of Paul Federn,
Frieda Fromm-Reichmann, Robert Knight, John
Rosen, and Harry Stack Sullivan was eagerly
absorbed. Although the theories of these pioneers
differed, all were psychoanalytic at the core. All
offered a path for work and for the adventure of
human understanding.

Failure of the new hope to become a social
force in modifying the lot of the hospitalized
lay less in the inadequacies of psychoanalytic
theory (though it is partly there) than in the
demands of the psychoanalytic method. Psychoanalysis evolved for those who were capable—
by virtue of their articulateness, their awareness,
their capacity for control, their economic and social stability—of meeting the psychological, social
and economic demands imposed by psychoanalytic treatment. For the severely disturbed, as for
children, the treatment model required modification. This Freud clearly recognized, as did every
psychoanalytic worker after him. But which parameters of treatment (Eissler, 1953) to modify
and how to modify them have never received any
fully satisfying answer.

The second basis for failure of psychoanalysis
as a social force in dealing with the severely disturbed lay in the demands psychoanalysis makes
on the practitioner. The requirements for training
of psychoanalysts—and indeed, for training of
any form of capable therapist—make it unlikely
that there will ever be a sufficient number of
practitioners to meet social demands. "In sum,
then," to quote *Action for Mental Health*, "psychoanalysis is adapted neither to the treatment
of the psychoses nor to mass application of any
kind (1961, p. 80)." Of course, acknowledge-
ment that the specific method cannot be applied
directly or en masse negates neither the contributions of the theory nor its social implications.

The major influence of psychoanalysis on social

approaches—such as the halfway house—to working with the psychologically alienated is in its emphasis on the unity of psychological suffering and in its focus on psychological determination. Psychoanalysis brought into scrutiny the reality of the psyche. Perhaps because the implications of such scrutiny were so massive, it gave little attention to the analysis of social reality. Yet the social situation, if not adequately emphasized by psychoanalysis, was not wholly neglected. Even in rather early writings (Freud, 1900), Freud described how actual experiences from the previous day (day-residues) influenced and helped form the dreams one had that night. The social situation received a similar, if secondary, focus in relation to psychopathology. Through its connection with previous memory traces, the current situation was seen as providing precipitating circumstances for the formation of symptoms. And in one of his last papers, *Analysis Terminable and Interminable* (1937), Freud gave explicit consideration to the limitations of psychoanalysis as related to environmental and other life circumstances. Moreover, present day psychoanalytic thought, particularly as exemplified by Erikson (1950, 1959), devotes considerable effort to exploring the relations of the social demands and opportunities in particular societies to individual patterns of personal development.

REFERENCES

Action for Mental Health. Final report of the Joint Commission on Mental Illness and Health, 1961. New York: Basic Books, 1961.

Eissler, K. R. The effect of the structure of the ego on psychoanalytic technique. *Journal of the American Psychoanalytic Association*, 1953, *1*, 104–143.

Erikson, E. H. *Childhood and society*. New York: Norton, 1950.

Erikson, E. H. Identity and the life cycle. *Psychological Issues*, 1959, *1*, 1–171.

Freud, S. Analysis terminable and interminable (1937). In Freud, S. *Collected Papers*. Vol. V. London: Hogarth, 1950. Pp. 316–358.

Freud, S. *The origins of psychoanalysis. Letters to Wilhelm Fliess, drafts and notes: 1887–1902*. London: Imago, 1954.

Jones, E. *The life and work of Sigmund Freud*. New York: Basic Books, 1953.

biology and behavior

Peter H. Wolff

Investigations into the biological basis of human behavior are, in a sense, equivalent to investigations of human behavior itself; therefore they touch on a range of topics that is far too extensive to be given even a cursory treatment in this brief communication. Within the limits suggested by the seminar's title it may, nevertheless, be useful to consider the extended boundaries of human behavior genetics, and to place the concrete contributions offered above within a general psychobiological framework. The empirical methods of behavior genetics, as well as the range of their applications to humans, have been discussed in several of the preceding presentations. Except for twin comparisons, correlations between major gene substitutions or chromosome defects and gross behavioral disturbances are as close as we can perhaps come today to the concrete analysis of genetic controls over human behavior. At best such correlations yield crude results. Yet they are nature's "experiments" on human subjects which at present must serve as substitutes for refined breeding experiments on animals (see Fuller and Collins elsewhere in this issue).

Other dimensions in behavior cannot be demonstrated as readily by the empirical methods of genetics, and may in fact be totally refractory to any precise genetic analysis. Nevertheless, they must be considered as part of any extended definition of the relation between genetics and behavior. These include the species characteristics of behavior that have been the major focus of ethology, and the group-variations within a species that result from inbreeding of natural mating groups (races or classes). (2)

Work for this report was completed while the author was supported by Career Development Award MH-K-3461 and Research Grant MH-06034, U.S. Public Health Service, National Institute of Mental Health.

An undue emphasis by contemporary psychology and cultural anthropology on the acquired (learned) characteristics of behavior has resulted in a parallel neglect of those intrinsic biological determinants of psychological development which were first suggested in broad sweep by Darwin (3, 4) and then pursued in greater detail by physical anthropologists, zoologists, and specifically ethologists, although mostly limited to nonhuman species. The extension of this inquiry to include human behavior is not only logical but essential.

Ethology is the study of species-specific behavior patterns. Its original aim was to refine zoological taxonomy by behavioral criteria whenever classification based on morphological criteria proved either insufficient or contradictory. Its primary realm has been the comparison of nonhuman species, and references to human behavior by ethologists have for the most part been speculations by analogy, unprejudiced by persuasive evidence. Although ethology has expanded the sphere of its investigations to include those behavior patterns which are determined as much by experience as by prefunctional organization (for example, the causal analysis of various "kinds" of learning), its close ties to evolutionary theory, and therefore indirectly to behavior genetics, have always been prominent.

The ethological approach to human behavior is made difficult by the fact that some of its essential tools, such as total isolation for extended periods of early development and selective breeding, are inapplicable to humans. Man's unique potential for elaborating stable cultures, moreover, determines the course of his development to such an extent that it is usually difficult and often impossible to separate biological and cultural determinants in those patterns of behavior which most distinguish man from other species.

From *Seminars in Psychiatry* (Milton Greenblatt and Ernest Artmann, Eds.), 1970, *2*, pp. 106–111. Reprinted by permission of Grune & Stratton, Inc.

The study of intraspecies racial variations, on the other hand, is limited by the fact that individual variations in behavior may be as great as group differences, that group differences can only be demonstrated on a statistical basis, and that demonstrated differences often pertain to features of behavior which on the surface appear trivial. From what we know about selective breeding for behavioral characteristics in animals, the possibility at least exists, however, that many shades of behavioral variation can appear in isolated human populations by a process of natural selection. Some apparently trivial features may have far reaching pleiotropic effects when considered in relation to local geographic and cultural variations. To entertain the possibility of biological contributions to such group differences does not commit us either to a precise definition of the concept of "race," or to the more extreme assumption that different human mating groups represent sub-species which have gone through independent evolutionary histories. (1) The concept of races is based on an arbitrary classification of inter-group differences that are sufficiently apparent to be easily recognized (physical stature, skin color, etc.), whereas less obvious differences are either ignored or classified as inter-individual differences. The distinction between "racial" and individual genetic variations is therefore arbitrary except in extreme cases. Yet morphological differences which distinguish mating groups along certain dimensions do exist, and they cannot be ignored, even for the sake of ethical principles. While these morphological variations are in no obvious way related to the fundamental categories of human behavior, they represent group differences that cannot be dismissed from our considerations until their possible indirect effects on behavior have been tested. Sexual dimorphism, for example, is far more clearly expressed in Caucasoid than Mongoloid peoples. That this variation would fundamentally alter the sexual life of the groups is highly unlikely. Directly or indirectly. however, it may influence the finer details of social life, aesthetic standards, mating preferences, etc., in the respective groups.

In a similar way, peoples of the Arctic and Antarctic regions have selectively bred so that when a limb is immersed in cold water, the peripheral circulation responds by vaso*dilatation* rather than by vasoconstriction as it does among individuals from temperate zones. This difference reflects a physiological adaptation in response to specific local circumstances; it may (or may not)

also be associated with other behavioral variations that could, for example, be relevant to developmental psychology. Skin pigmentation, the distribution of ABO blood-groups, steatopygy, large stature, and the like, are other physical features not randomly distributed across breeding groups. Whether or not, and to what extent, these physical features and their corresponding biochemical mechanisms are genetically or pleiotropically associated with behavioral variations, is again a matter of concrete investigation, but of investigations that fall within the sphere of behavior genetics.

As far as I know, there are no behavioral group differences whose direct genetic control has been demonstrated with the same assurance as that of some morphological variations listed above. Major dimensions of human behavior, such as intelligence and social cooperation, are probably so essential to man's survival that they leave no room for extensive genetic variations. Where genetics has discovered a single gene control of individual variations in behavior, the demonstrations have been limited to isolated traits that make little or no difference to the general conduct of human affairs, e.g., preferred motor rhythms, left-handedness, susceptibility to the autokinetic effect, etc. Where the incidence of genetically determined behavioral variations has been compared in different mating groups, as in the case of phenyl-thio-carbamide tasting, it was found to be distributed ubiquitously across different groups, with only quantitative local variations. (6)

Some hereditary metabolic diseases with a profound influence on the development of the nervous system, and associated with a major (single) gene substitution, are concentrated in specific mating groups (e.g., Tay-Sachs disease). Most group or individual variations in behavior for which any genetic control can be demonstrated, however, are polygenic in origin. The more complex the behavior in question, moreover, the less direct the causal chain from gene substitution to behavioral expression, and the more prominent the role of cultural and social factors shaping its phenotypic expression. Because the interaction of genetic and experiential determinants in human development is extraordinarily complex, few if any "racial" differences in behavior have been demonstrated that withstand the test of critical examination. Lack of concrete evidence, however, does not justify the conclusion that such differences do not exist.

Methodological difficulties alone cannot explain why we know so little about intrinsic group differences in behavior. A significant factor in this deficiency must be the reluctance of behavioral scientists to investigate biological contributions to behavioral group differences, for fear that their efforts will be construed as immoral, and that their results might imply that some people are better than others. As long as genetic studies are only concerned with innocent physical features such as stature or blood-groups they are not likely to draw adverse criticism, but whenever the biological basis of group differences pertains to behavioral variables, the lingering suspicion remains that one may be engaged in covert "Rassenkunde."

Yet if "equal" means "identical," neither all men nor all groups of men are created "equal." A demonstration of genetically determined differences in behavior cannot imply invidious value judgments any more when it applies to groups than when it applies to individuals. By the same token, a demonstration of group differences cannot imply value judgments any more when it applies to behavior than when it applies to physical features. Darlington stated the issue clearly when he wrote:

> All races, all classes, all mating groups, and all social units composed of mating groups, have their own genetic characteristics, they are all different. As soon as we answer the question and admit this difference, we appear to admit the propriety of a second question: Is one group better than another? In this general form the question, although it seems so obvious, is inadmissible. . . . We can compare men only for particular theoretical purposes defined for the sake of discussion. With this expressed restriction the comparison of men and races is of great value, indeed it is indispensable if we are to examine how humanity can manage its own future. (2)

The extended realm of human behavior genetics must therefore include the study of group, as well as individual, differences if it is to provide a comprehensive picture of the interaction between biological inheritance and ontogenetic adaptation. In the long run behavioral group differences may be reduced to biochemical variations. Our current knowledge about the dependence of behavior on biochemistry, however, is so primitive that it may be more fruitful to investigate group differences in behavioral characteristics directly instead of searching for underlying biochemical mechanisms. If such studies are to be undertaken at all, they must begin soon, because racially isolated groups that have remained untouched by international technological society are becoming fewer and fewer.

Of greater significance than the analysis of racial differences, when we are considering the extended boundaries of behavior genetics, is the study of those features in behavior that distinguish humans from other animals. Like genetics in general, behavior genetics must seek to account for inter-individual variations. In contrast, ethology (the study of species-specific behavior patterns) deals with units of behavior that are more or less uniformly distributed within the species. Despite this surface difference, ethology must base its analysis on species comparisons in order to determine what is unique within the species, just as genetics bases its analysis on inter-individual comparisons in order to demonstrate the genetic control over particular differences. Ethology cannot carry out direct evolutionary experiments. It is limited to contemporary comparisons: either "macro-comparisons" of behavioral competencies at all phylogenetic levels to demonstrate general trends in evolution; or "micro-comparisons" of behavioral differences of closely related species to demonstrate the radiation of particular behavior patterns from a common ancestor. (12)

The premature importation of ethological concepts from the observation of fish and birds to human psychology, caused a justified concern among zoologists who had demonstrated that major differences in behavior may occur even in closely related species. Since man unfortunately has no "close relations" in the animal kingdom, the evolutionary analysis of human behavior depends on comparisons with non-human primates, and these readily lend themselves to unwarranted generalizations. Field observations of primates in their natural habitat have, however, provided a broad base of information about species variations in social organization which indicates that a phylogenetic investigation of behavior need not be limited to instinctive action patterns observed at birth, in order to preserve its basically biological orientation. (5) From such field studies, augmented by laboratory experiments, we have learned, for instance, that group cooperation in the care of the young is not instinctive in the sense that it will appear totally independent of environmental circumstances. (8) Yet such social behavior varies systematically from species to species, and therefore must be partly determined by biological (genetic) factors. (10) Hallowell has gone farther to suggest that even the creation of stable cultures, sometimes considered the single most distinctive feature of human behavior, has its evolutionary counterparts in the social organization of primates:

A cultural level of adaptation could not arise *de novo*. There were prerequisites of various kinds. Simple forms of learning, some socialization of the individual, a social structure based on role differentiation in organized social groups, the transmission of some group habits and perhaps tool using, and a "non-syntactic" form of communication may be identified as necessary but not sufficient conditions for a human level of existence. The development of these conditions in combination provided a pre-adaptive or protocultural stage. But all of them were raised to a new level of functional organization and inclusiveness by the psychological restructuralization that must have occurred during the evolution of the Hominidae. . . .(7)

Our concern here, however, is not with the transition from nonhuman to human behavior, but with the fact, for example, that almost all human beings will acquire the natural language of their environment, that they share in and contribute to the development of technological societies, and that they acquire an operational form of thought which transcends the events of the concrete present. Most infants acquire these capacities regardless of race or individual differences and more or less independent of environmental variation.

Bipedal gait, refined tool making (as opposed to tool using), symbolization and operational thought are generally held to be uniquely human attributes which represent qualitative discontinuities within the evolution of human behavior. They may be regarded as specifically human attributes, although they require post-natal experience as much as biological potential to become actualities. From what we know about behavior genetic mechanisms in other animals, it is improbable that the phenotypic expression of these uniquely human competencies would be under demonstrable genetic control. The fact remains that all human infants except those suffering from gross organic defects or exposure to extreme pathologi-

cal environments, will acquire the natural language of their environment as well as the intermediate stages of operational thought, in Piaget's sense. (9) Once they reach sexual maturity, humans will, moreover, produce offspring who are endowed with the same potential for intellectual development. It is in this sense that Piaget regards symbolic (representational) intelligence as a specialized form of biological adaptation in general; (11) and that Lennenberg focuses the psychological problem of language acquisition on the biological question. "Why can only man learn to speak a natural language?"

While environmental variations may alter the rates of acquisition and the degrees of differentiation in mental activity, only human intelligence develops in a direction and to a degree that makes symbolic activity and rational thought possible. This human attribute is not preformed in the zygote; no blueprint of the stages in mental development, of logical operations, and of all natural languages is isomorphically given in the genetic code. Whatever the developmental potential of the human infant is, it can only be realized by an active interchange with the environment, and by a constant internal restructuring of what has been acquired. Nevertheless, some unlearned and probably unlearnable devices for structuring experiences, abstracting universals, and discovering logical relations among universals must be present in the prefunctional organization of the human nervous system if the infant is to develop into an adult member of his species. The form and function of this prefunctional organization must be sufficiently different from that of other animal infants to account for the fact that only the human infant becomes a logical, linguistic and cultural animal. This difference, in turn, cannot be attributed exclusively to the greater plasticity and storage capacity of man's essentially "empty" brain at birth; it cannot, in other words, be reduced to the circular reasoning that man is more susceptible to learning and cultural shaping than other animals because his behavior is less rigidly organized at birth. At the same time, the difference cannot be attributed to a fixed mosaic of genetic determinants which are isomorphic with the mental capacities of the mature organism. Yet the difference is a *biological* dimension of behavior that has its roots at once in the phylogeny of the species and the ontogeny of the individual. As such it belongs within the sphere of issues being considered by this seminar.

REFERENCES

1. Coon, C. S.: *The Origin of Races.* New York, Knopf, 1962.

2. Darlington, C. D.: *Genetics and Man.* New York, Schocken, 1969.

3. Darwin, C.: *The Origins of Species by Means of Natural Selection, or the Preservation of Favored Races in the Struggle for Life* (1859). New York, Collier, 1901.

4.—: *The Expression of the Emotions in Man and Animals.* London, Murray, 1872.

5. DeVore, I. (Ed.): *Primate Behavior.* New York, Holt, Rinehart and Winston, 1965.

6. Dunn, L. C., and Dobzhansky, Th.: *Heredity, Race and Society.* New York, New American Library, 1957.

7. Hallowell, A. I.: Self, society and culture in phylogenetic perspective. *In* Tax, S. (Ed.), *The Evolution of Man: Culture in phylogenetic perspective.* Chicago, Ill., University of Chicago Press, 1960, pp. 309–371.

8. Harlowe, H. F., and Harlowe, M. K.: Effects of various mother–infant relationships on Rhesus monkey behavior. *In* Foss, B. (Ed.), *Determinants of Infant Behavior,* Vol. IV. London, Methuen, 1969, pp. 15–36.

9. Inhelder, B., and Piaget, J.: *The Growth of Logical Thinking from Childhood to Adolescence.* New York, Basic Books, 1958.

10. Kaufman, I. C., and Rosenblum, L. A.: The waning of the mother–infant bond in two species of macaque. *In* Foss, B. (Ed.), *Determinants of Infant Behavior,* Vol. IV. London, Methuen, 1969, pp. 41–59.

11. Piaget, J.: *Biologie et Connaissance.* Paris, Gallimard, 1967.

12. Tinbergen, N.: Panel Discussion.: The evolution in mind. *In* Tax, S. (Ed.), *Issues in Evolution.* Chicago, University of Chicago Press, 1960.

biochemistry, genetics, and the nature-nurture problem

Bernice T. Eiduson, Samuel Eiduson, & Edward Geller

In a recent symposium on concepts in biology Spuhler said, "You hear very little now, outside of textbooks, about the heredity—environment controversy; the working people do not worry about this much anymore" (1). Psychologists arrived at a similar attitude 20 years ago. During the 1930's a large number of psychologists had been experimentally trying to parcel out the influence of heredity and environment in intelligence and other behavioral traits. Their results turned out to be equivocal; and this made most workers feel that research in this area was inevitably dogged by uncontrollable errors, statistical difficulties, and questionable controls (2). Anderson, in summarizing the data, suggested that nature—nurture was an unproductive area of research and advised psychologists to turn away from it, advice which most took.

In the intervening years, only a few papers have suggested its reconsideration. In these the trend has been to point out our need to conceptualize the heredity—environment problem differently, in ways that are more in line with some of the present theoretical formulations of biology, for example. If we followed these formulations, the question would no longer be simply how much heredity and how much environment, but rather the question would turn to their relevant contribution on each of the various levels or strata in terms of which the organism is conceived (3). Some psychologists (4) have suggested that perhaps behavioral data can contribute something to the mode or the mechanisms by which heredity and environment interact, for the fact of interaction is generally accepted, albeit more out of a feeling of helplessness at the complexity of the heredity—environment relationship than out of any real knowledge of the nature of the interplay.

Today some of the new experimental work in the biological sciences—embryology, genetics, biochemistry—is providing data about the nature—nurture factors and their interaction on the molecular level which elucidates the problem as it has been posed in regard to behavior. In the light of the new information, the assumptions generally held by psychologists about heredity turn out to be outdated, and even incorrect, and when the biological data about environment are considered along with the new findings in the behavioral sciences themselves, even the conceptions about the nurture side demand revision.

As we reviewed the nature of the interaction between the nature—nurture factors, we became aware that many convergences and possible identities existed between phenomena and process on the biological level, and those on the psychological. In fact, these turned up so regularly in the aspects we studied that we began to consider whether one model which had proved so useful on the molecular stratum could not be profitably transposed to the molar. We have taken the liberty of presenting our speculations about this at the end of this paper.

First, a look at the new and enhanced concept of the heredity mechanisms to which biological scientists are directing our attention: until recently psychologists have been prone to consider biological or constitutional factors as constants, establishing the limits or boundaries of behavior, but reflecting none of its variance or uniqueness. They have looked to environmental contacts for providing the bulk of the organism's information content. Elsasser suggests that this viewpoint stems from the strong influence of Darwinian notions on our scientific thinking (7). He, by contrast, feels that the bulk of the individual's information content is endogenous; and support for his position comes from the new genetic data which show that the hereditary mechanism itself can account for (at least has the potentiality for accounting for) all the vast differences that we see expressed in behavior (8). Biologists have now been able to show decisively that man has 23 pairs of chromosomes and they have been able, mathematically, to work out the possible combinations of chromosomes that can be transmitted by the parents to the child (9). It appears that the possibility for hereditary likenesses among children —even in the same family—is very small. The likelihood for two non-identical siblings in one family to have exactly the same genetic characteristics is only one chance in 64 trillion; the probability that two unrelated individuals will share the same genotype turns out to be effectively zero (10). While identical twins have the same genotype by definition, in fraternals or siblings there is still no question that the possible genic combinations make, as some geneticists have said, this inheritance game the "greatest lottery of all."

Moreover, we have thought until recently that some variability in heredity resided in discrepancies in the number of genic components transmitted from parent to child. Recent experimental work has shown that there are certain pathological disturbances which are produced by too many or too few chromosomes. Mongolism is one such disorder, the result of one extra autosomal chromosome. Kleinfelder's and Turner's diseases, which result in sexual aberration in boys and girls, are the results of one extra sex chromosome and one too few sex chromosomes respectively. Tarjan and his group at Pacific State Hospital in California are finding that mongolism and Kleinfelder's and Turner's diseases may actually be related to each other (11).

However, a more pertinent factor in normal and abnormal development is the composition of genic patterning, the sequential arrangement of the genetic components, and this turns out to be a highly intricate process, which is mosaic-like in its potential for variability. This has been most clearly elucidated in biochemical genetics, which is concerned with genetically-determined enzymes and thereby with the control of certain aspects of metabolic reactions. The "one gene: one enzyme" hypothesis, that each gene is a coded template by means of which one specific enzyme (more generally, protein) is synthesized, was elaborated some time ago. This formulation proved to be a first wedge into the understanding of the mechanisms of certain intraorganismic functions, but this has been shown to be only part of the story. Subsequent investigation with specific metabolic systems has shown that many reactions are not exclusively determined by the presence or the absence of the appropriate enzymes (12).

Few geneticists today uphold the hypothesis of the autonomous gene. Mendel originally postulated the notion of dominance as a principle determining whether or not a trait would be manifest in the phenotype of an organism, but techniques were not available to demonstrate the actual mechanism. Technological advance has resulted not only in a general investigation of this phenomenon, but in evidence indicating a host of other intragenetic relationships: suppressor genes and modifiers, which act as intensifiers, diluters, inhibitors; genes which exert their influences at early stages of development while the presence or identification of others can be recognized only when the organism reaches maturity, gene changes which may result in more than one observable change in the phenotype. For psychologists, it is particularly interesting to note that what changes are observed in this latter phenomenon (which is called pleitrophy) turn out to depend on the knowledge of the observer and the intensity with which the search was pursued (13).

The now well-known "inborn errors of metabolism" were the first inroads into the large area of pathological disturbance which we now accept as genetically determined (14). But with their exploration has come a host of syndromes which seem to be playing into a myriad of disorders in which classification of neither syndrome nor source is simple (15). Medical genetics has been able to elaborate many disturbances which are now recognized as genetically bound. As metabolic pathways are systematically mapped, their intricacies and circuitries become apparent, and the possibilities for distortion of function and resultant pathology seem to multiply with the complexities of the intermediary processes. In studying mutant individuals with hemophilia, for example, it has been shown that at least nine gene-controlled substances are required in the blood-clotting mechanism, and that each of the trace proteins involved may become dysfunctional through mutation (16).

Furthermore, medical genetics has shown that one cannot tell from the manifest behavior what has been the cause of the disturbance. In one individual an environmentally produced agent can lead to pathology; while, in another, an equivalent syndrome can be caused by genetically induced substances. Hemolytic anemia, for example, can be induced by certain drugs which makes it look environmentally determined but yet it is a genetically bound disorder. To further complicate the picture, the overt disease picture may give no clues as to its genesis.

The wide range of individual differences found in this work has alerted biochemists to the biochemical differences among individuals. We have long been familiar with interindividual physiological and anatomical differences, but until now attention has not been turned to how these differences in turn affect function, what intrasystemic differences exist, and how these make their appearance. Williams, in a systematic compilation of incidences of biochemical individuality, has shown, as one example, that the urinary amino acid profiles of individuals are considerably different (17).

The recognition that one form of mental deficiency could be a concomitant of the inability to convert one substance to another to form the proper metabolic product in the now well-known phenylpyruvic oligophrenia disorder, was an early encouragement to look for mental disturbances in genetic metabolic function. The subsequent search showed that this was only one of many ways in which interference with the necessary enzyme products can occur. Biochemists have found also partial lacks in enzymes; or overproduction of enzymes; or that metabolites are shunted off in such ways that they do not quite do their proper duties at the right time or at the right place. As the number of physical and mental disorders that can be reduced to inborn metabolic errors is steadily increasing, investigations are developing increasingly sophisticated models of intra-organismic function, and while our conceptual framework permits us to speculate that phenomena which exist side by side are probably highly correlated with each other, there are many more phenomena which are still extremely diffuse and vague, and as yet indefinable.

As the genetic factors do not operate in a vacuum but in an environment, attention has simultaneously been drawn to nature of the host, its participation in the intraorganism processes, and in the resultant behavior. Here, researchers have been confronted with an active factor or set of factors, which condition not only what is genetically determined, but often whether a genetic characteristic will make its appearance, and when. The biological studies make it quite evident that environment can no longer be defined as some-

thing outside the organism which affects or becomes part of the organism by internalization; environment must include intraorganismic factors as well, for the nature–nurture interaction is so meshed and interdependent even on the prenatal level that it becomes impossible to determine what is heredity and what is environment. Study of prenatal development has shown that development is a long process of continuous changes, starting with a given genetic array acting in a given environment. The first interaction product then constitutes the background (or the environment) for the next step of interaction with the environment. In the case of a given cell, this includes the interaction product of other cells, and in this manner all future reactions then are co-determined by all preceding steps and hence also by genetic endowment. Thus, at whatever point one arrests the sequential reactions for study, one can no longer, except arbitrarily, point to certain factors as genetic and others as environmental.

With the increasing knowledge of what goes on inside the organism, biologists have come to recognize the importance of the dimensions of time and space for even cellular phenomena. In the study of different metabolic needs of different cells, they have recognized that there are certain periods of sensitivity in cellular reactions—times at which things happen or interactions take place (19). Thus, even if all the structural components necessary for certain reactions to take place are in order, it is conceivable that these reactions just may not progress at the rate necessary to allow for a subsequent step to be instituted or systematically meshed with the first; or it is possible that certain reactions are physically separated by even so little as a fraction of a micron and that this may be enough to modify seriously a necessary and sequential relationship. Such dimensions are extremely significant in the elaborate system of regulatory relationships that exist in many metabolic processes. Feedback mechanisms, as in the case of hormonal regulation of pituitary response to stress, are well known. It has been found, additionally, that in nervous tissue a chemical substance apparently may induce that enzyme which it subsequently needs for its proper action in transmitting electrical impulses across the synapse (20). Acetylcholine, for example, functions as a chemical mediator. Once it has so operated, however, it has to be destroyed (hydrolyzed) so that the proper termination of the membrane depolarization can take place. Acetylcholine has now been suggested as the embryonic determinant for the elaboration of acetylcholinesterase, the enzyme which hydrolyzes it. Therefore, one sees here not only a built-in feedback system which permits proper functioning, but also a mechanism which appears to demand a more complex interpretation than simple feedback.

From the biologists we are also getting a picture of the kind of differential growth processes that are found prenatally. These are similar, we think, to the different capacities of the organism that have different maturational rates on the behavioral level. While in tissue growth there are presumably some metabolic requirements that are held in common for all tissues, the prenatal group processes do proceed differently in certain tissues and cells, so that different tissues develop with different metabolic needs (19). Some growth agents seem to effect only specific partial processes; others have a generalized effect. Some agents effect certain growth processes only at times when certain metabolic needs can be interfered with and these same agents will be ineffective at other times. Thus, the "sensitivity periods" may be also described as times when the likelihood of throwing processes out of gear seems to be much more probable. We learn, too, that different tissues progressively develop different metabolic needs, which permits us to elaborate the notion of differential growth processes on the cellular level.

These "sensitivity periods" of the biologists are particularly interesting, for they may be counterparts for the "critical periods" in development with which psychologists and ethologists are now becoming increasingly absorbed. Psychologists have found that there are specific times in ontogeny, or specific states, during which certain types of behavior normally first appear. If these times pass without the experiences having taken place, changes, and sometimes lags, in development occur which are never recoverable even though the "right" experiences are presented later. Lorenz's work on imprinting (21) and Thorpe's work (22) on bird songs have independently pointed to the importance of specific times for the occurrence of some kinds of species-specific behavior which subsequently becomes indelibly stamped as part of the psychological armamentarium of the animal. Once the time for experiencing this behavior has passed, its learning subsequently never takes place.

Considerable behavioral work on very early learning has emerged as scientists have given up their long indulgence in "instinctive behavior,"

which seems to have cloaked certain early learned behaviors which were considered innate since they seemed to be species-specific (24). When this "instinctive behavior" has been exposed to study, results have shown that even in those areas of behavior where the effective external influence may be practically nil, and where the behavior seems essentially unmodified by experience or unresponsive to environmental manifestation, the way that seemingly innate behavior is expressed or the conditions under which it is expressed depend upon experience (25). On whom the animal imprints, for example, is determined in some species by the environment, even if the fact of imprinting is not. The crucial importance of just this "environmental condition," or the person or thing imprinted, becomes evident as we see that this, and not the fact of imprinting by itself, determines in some species the character of adult sexual behavior in later life (21). Portielje, the curator at the Amsterdam Zoo, a trained zoologist, raised and had a male South American bittern imprinted to him. The bittern was subsequently placed in a cage which was covered very carefully. A female bittern put in the cage was his constant and only companion. Although at first the male would have nothing to do with the female, he finally accepted her and for two years subsequently the pair lived together. They were not further exposed to any other animals or human beings, even being fed through the cage. The animals mated and hatched a number of broods together. Two years later the curator to whom the male bittern had been imprinted in infancy entered the cage and the male bittern saw him for the first time in these two years. When the keeper entered the cage the female bittern happened to be sitting on a nest of eggs, but as soon as the male bittern saw the curator he chased the female off the nest and proceeded to try to woo the curator and to inveigle him onto sitting on the nest of eggs. He showed all of the usual nest relief and social behavior toward the curator. Needless to say, that brood of eggs was never hatched (26)! This example illustrates that a behavior like imprinting, that is thought to be genetically determined, is very much dependent on the sequential development of the organism for the character of its expression. However, it illustrates as well that whether a genetically-bound behavior is expressed at all is similarly dependent on the experience to which the organism is exposed after birth. The absence of a necessary stimulus which serves as a releasing mechanism may make it appear as if the behavioral trait were never transmitted genetically at all; or the absence of a later releasing stimulus may make what appeared to be an inevitably formative experience have no significance in adult life.

The cloak of ambiguity which "instinct" had thrown around early learning has had the further effect of drawing attention away from such factors as intra-uterine environmental conditions which influenced development. However, we today are becoming increasingly cognizant of the dependence of the phenotype on certain environmental conditions in the fetus, such as nutrition and temperature. Ephrussi and Herold have shown that the phenotype expression of drosophila is temperature-sensitive: W^{b1} flies have brown eyes at 30° and red-purple at 17° (27). Goldschmidt produced many phenocopies in wild type with temperature shocks (18). Thus, it is impossible to regard all intraorganismic phenomena as genetically determined, and therefore not susceptible to environmental influence. This position has received support, too, from the recent attempts to show the effect of environmental influence during the gestational period. Ginsberg and Hovda transferred fertilized ova from the female of a strain of mice, inbred for susceptibility to audiogenic seizure, to the uterus of a female of a seizure-resistant strain, and found that the resulting young showed an intermediate susceptibility (29). Thompson and Hochman changed the intrauterine environment and found differences in the emotionality of rats which they speculated might be due to possible changes in fetal material in the blood stream (30). In a water-maze learning situation, Thompson and Sontag showed that offspring of parent rats who were subjected to seizure were slowed in their response to this same task (31).

As the experimental data on the nurture side of the paradigm continue to support the biological work showing the early and inevitable interaction of nature and nurture, the definition of what is learned becomes more blurred than it once seemed. Previously, psychologists were very ready to label as learned those facets of behavior which were separate from central nervous system growth, responsive to experience and manipulation to change or extinction, characteristics which were distinguished by their variability and mutability, in contrast to hereditary mechanism which was more fixed and constant. This whole notion has been shown to be inappropriate in recent years. Sperry, the psychobiologist, tells us that in indi-

vidual development the central nervous system must be sufficiently complex for coordinating any level of behavior when behavior begins, and this inevitably involves learning (32). Thus, learning is indistinguishable from CNS growth.

The definition of what is learned has also become less clearcut as we have become aware of how much learning takes place without our being conscious of it. Experimental work, in discrimination and perception in both animal and human subjects, has suggested that the absence of normal amount of stimulation during developmental periods may result in an inability to respond effectively to sensory and perceptual cues when these cues become available. While much of the perceptual data is derived from studies of the visual modality, evidence demonstrates similar results with other sensory modes. The work on infant chimpanzees done by Nissen, Chow, and Semmes is in point (33): for when the chimp's normal tactual experiences on his own body and his environment were interrupted by placing mailing tubes over his hands and feet, no failure in development of primary sensory equipment of the skin was noted, but subsequently somatesthetic learning and localization of the tactual stimuli were defective. This implied that more or less random tactual experience is necessary for the normal development of somatesthetic perception. The experiments on pecking behavior response in chicks raised in darkness with consequent deficiencies in motor and sensory development is similarly vivid, in that such chicks never learned to peck and so were unable to feed themselves in times of starvation although they stood in the midst of plenty (34). The deprived and enriched environment studies on dogs and monkeys not only show how much facilitation is affected by conditions of early learning, but also point to the crucial period in development (the age) at which the deprivation or enrichment takes place (35). With human subjects one gets additional evidence that seemingly irrelevant and peripheral stimuli are taken in as part of the perceptual process and become part of learning even though no direct learning experience seems to have promoted this. In the Poetzl experiments, for example, some parts of exposed stimuli were so unconsciously perceived that they were not subject to direct recall, even though it was apparent from dreams and subsequent conscious behavior that they had been part of the input (36). In summarizing the experimental work on effects of early experience upon the behavior of animals, Beach and Jaynes point out that with all its equivocality and unde-termined reliability, the evidence suggests that habits formed in early life are persistent in adult behavior, that later perceptual capacities seem to be structured by early experiences, and that there seem to be certain stages in ontogeny during which certain types of behavior normally are molded and shaped for life (24).

Many years ago psychologists became aware that certain reactions like fear and rage, though admittedly unlearned, could not occur until the maturational development of the animal or infant had proceeded to a point where something in the environment could produce the innate response. Hebb has given the example of the infant chimp, who, though fearful of first strangers, only de-veloped such fears after he had reached an age where he was able to recognize his usual care-takers (usually around four months) (37). Even the chimp reared in darkness to an age where fear is normally at its peak will not be disturbed by the first sight of a stranger until he has had the opportunity to learn to differentiate those who care for him daily.

Piaget's and Buhler's studies on the develop-ment of human thinking similarly have shown the importance of understanding the maturation of universal modes of thought for interpreting why a child handles experiences differently at different times in his early life (38). The child a few months old will not be distressed when an object is removed from view; he behaves as if the toy ceased to exist. But a few months later he actively searches for the toy and tries to remove the ob-stacle which has taken it out of view. The child's response and his possible range of behaviors de-pends on his developmental level, and on the corresponding "mental structures" available to him. The child changes his behavior when the environment demands change; and yet the ma-turational level of the inherent "operatory struc-tures" determines the nature of the response which will be made. The parallel to tissue differ-entiation seems cogent; for, as Weiss has de-scribed, during maturation, tissue increasingly differentiates and metabolic needs are correspond-ingly altered; but during this innately determined process, the nature of its differentiation is respon-sive to the local experience it meets, and to the environmental demands made on it (18).

It becomes increasingly easy to draw such paral-lels with our extended knowledge—and increas-ingly provocative; and this has made us wonder if it would not be very profitable were such paral-

lels systematically extended. We have been im-pressed that with new data, more and more convergencies appear. Pre- and postnatal growth processes seem to be analogous in many aspects; and also the nature of the interaction of genetic and environmental factors seems similar on both molecular and molar levels. Therefore, taking our clue from general systems theory, we wonder if formal identities do not actually exist between the biological molecular processes, and the behav-ioral (39). Rapaport's finding that there was com-parability among diffusion of information (rumor) at the level of the social system, diffusion of matter or energy (infectious agents) in a biological sys-tem, and diffusion of neural impulses in an organ (the central nervous system) shows the value of transposing a hypothetical model from one sys-temic level to another (39).

We think that perhaps now we have the possi-bility of exploiting another model, that of bio-chemical genetics, for an exposition of the nature of the heredity–environment interaction on the behavioral strata. This would obviously be no simple job for psychology—for we would have to refine and recategorize some of our variables to make them suitable for the kind of differentiation that such a restudy would involve. Yet one gets the feeling that the time—and perhaps the means —are now ripe, for we have evidence that the inter-locked relationships of the nature–nurture factors is in itself important, and can be differentially broken down into distinguishable reaction pat-terns.

The biochemical genetic model has enabled the biologist to trace a number of pathways by which certain metabolic reactions proceed. Investigators can indicate what substances are given genetically and then show to some degree how certain se-quences are dependent on environmental agents normally, where these agents impinge, how they facilitate reactions or interfere with them. Once pathologies are set in motion, subsequent meta-bolic reactions can be studied, and eventually whole enzyme systems are, or in the future will be, mapped.

We are suggesting that such a model offers the potential for doing a similar job in psychology. Psychology has always assumed that development is sequential and reflects both heredity and en-vironment, but it has seldom considered that from the first postnatal moments, it is already looking at an interaction product with all behavior subse-quent to birth representing simultaneously modifi-cation of this product and the emergence of a new interaction phenomenon. To all intents and purposes the psychologists have assumed that heredity and environment factors were like dependent and independent variables with one albeit affecting the other, but with the results of these interacting effects not being taken into account as the changed stage on which a second subsequent behavioral segment is acted out.

To apply the biochemical genetic model in psychology, we would have to start with systematic observations on early development, draw our variables from these observations, and begin to trace their evolution. Clinical data have information which could be abstracted about interferences, distortions, and pathologies in postnatal growth processes—how they set in, the kinds of sequences that follow once an original abnormality or disturbance has resulted, and their subsequent development. Thus could whole psychological reaction systems be tentatively mapped out. This seems to us to offer a possibility for plotting the ontogenetic sequences of psychological diseases—an important job that has long been overdue. The advantage of such a model for psychology is obvious; but, additionally, if the convergencies between pre- and postnatal development continue to hold up, the psychological data based on postnatal observation and experimentation could conceivably offer to the biologist some clues about process in prenatal development, and suggest to him some new avenues for research.

REFERENCES

1. Spuhler, J. N. Behav. Sci., 1958, 3, 95.

2. National Society for the Study of Education. 39th Yearbook, 2. Chicago: 1940.

3. Fuller, J. L. Nature and nurture. A modern synthesis. New York: Garden City Books, 1954.

4. Anastasi, A. Psychol. Rev., 1958, 65, 197; A. Anastasi and J. P. Foley, Jr. Ibid., 1948, 55, 239.

5. Fenichel, O. Psychoanalytic theory of the neuroses. New York: W. W. Norton, 1945.

6. Hebb, D. O. Psychol. Rev., 1955, 62, 243.

7. Elsasser, W. M. Physical foundation of biology. New York: Pergamon Press, 1958.

8. Muller, H. J. Amer. J. Psychiat., 1956, 113, 483.

9. Hsia, D. Y. N. E. J. Med., 1960, 262, 1172.

10. Hirsch, J. Paper presented at AAAS meetings. Chicago: Sept. 1959.

11. Tarjan, G. In G. Kaplan (Ed.), Prevention of mental disorders in children. New York: Basic Books, 1959.

12. Snyder, L. H. Science, 1959, 129, 7.

13. Wagner, R. P., and H. K. Mitchell. Genetics and metabolism. New York: John Wiley and Sons, 1955.

14. Garrod, A. E. Lancet, 1908, 2, 142, 214.

15. Landing, B. H. Metabolism, 1960, 9, 198.

16. Graham, J. B. Amer. J. Hum. Genet., 1956, 8, 63.

17. Williams, R. J. Biochemical individuality. New York: John Wiley and Sons, 1957.

18. Weiss, P. In B. Mintz (Ed.), Environmental influences on prenatal development. Chicago: Univ. Chicago Press, 1958.

19. Mintz, B. (Ed.) Environmental influences on prenatal development. Chicago: Univ. Chicago Press, 1958.

20. Koelle, G. B. In A. D. Bass (Ed.) Evolution of nervous control from primitive organisms to man. AAAS, 1959, 52, 87.

21. Lorenz, K. Z. In C. H. Schiller, Instinctive behavior. New York: International Universities Press, 1957.

22. Thorpe, W. R. Learning and instinct in animals. Cambridge, Mass.: Harvard Univ. Press, 1956.

23. Eiduson, S. Amer. J. Orthopsychiat., 1960, 30, 1; N. T. Karki, R. Kuntzman, and B. B. Brodie, Fed. Proc., 1960, 19, 282.

24. Beach, F. A., and J. Jaynes, Psychol. Bull., 1954, 51, 239.

25. Simpson, A. In A. Roe and C. Simpson (Eds.), Behavior and Evolution. New Haven, Conn.: Yale Univ. Press, 1958.

26. Beckwith, W. C. Personal communication, 1961.

27. Ephrussi, B., and J. L. Herold. Genetics, 1945, 30, 62.

28. Goldschmidt, R. Physiological genetics. New York: McGraw-Hill, 1938.

29. Ginsberg, B. S., and R. B. Hovda. Anat. Rec., 1947, 99, 621.

30. Thompson, W. R., and C. H. Hochman. Influence of prenatal maternal anxiety on emotional behavior in rats. Paper read at Proc. East Psychol. Assoc., Atlantic City, Mar. 1956.

31. Thompson, W. R., and L. W. Sontag. J. Comp. Physiol. Psychol., 1956, 49, 454.

32. Sperry, R. J. In A. Roe and G. Simpson (Eds.), Behavior and evolution. New Haven, Conn.: Yale Univ. Press, 1958.

33. Nissen, H. W., K. L. Chow, and J. Semmes. Amer. J. Psychol., 1951, 64, 485.

34. Padilla, S. G. J. Comp. Physiol. Psychol., 1935, 20, 413.

35. Harlow, H. F. *Psychol. Rev.*, 1949, *56*, 51; J. R. Scott, E. Fredericson, and J. L. Fuller. *Personality*, 1951, *1*, 162; J. P. Scott and M. V. Marston. *J. Genet. Psychol.*, 1950, 77, 25.

36. Fisher, C. *J. Amer. Psychonal. Assoc.*, 1956, *4*, 5.

37. Hebb, D. O. *Brit. J. Anim. Behav.*, 1953, *1*, 43.

38. Piaget, J. *The construction of reality in the child.* New York: Basic Books, 1954; C. Buhler. *Kindheit und jugend.* Leipzig: Hirzel, 1931.

39. Miller, J. A. *Amer. J. Psychiat.*, 1956, *113*, 776.

PART III
the clinician
and the researcher

Clinical workers address themselves to two questions: "What is this person's problem?" "What can be done about solving it?" Of major importance is evaluation of the clinician's answers to these questions. This raises the issue of validity—the success with which problems are accurately defined and solved.

The articles by Donald Peterson and Harrison Gough deal with assessment or diagnosis. In assessment, behavior samples are obtained and conclusions drawn from them. Assessment can be no better than the tools the assessor has at his disposal. The fact that a test bears a title which sounds as though it can "do the job" is no guarantee that it can. For example, a poorly constructed, unreliable intelligence test does not provide a sound basis for making decisions about what school grade to place children in, or whether to assign someone to a program for the mentally retarded. Both Peterson and Gough make it clear that psychological assessment cannot be simply a mechanical process. Careful research must be carried out in order to arrive at an objective description of the types of behavior to be assessed, the most effective ways of assessing them, and an evaluation of the validity of the assessment process. Gough pays particular attention to the importance of the clinician's identifying for himself what his goals are as a diagnostician.

Peterson calls for an experimental approach to assessment and asks that the clinical worker be receptive to diagnostic approaches. Diagnostic tools may range from complex biophysical recording apparatus to readily available information such as a person's name and place of residence. The article by Charles Barthell and David Holmes shows the relationship between one piece of public information—descriptions of students' social activities in high school yearbooks—and the diagnosis of schizophrenia. In the course of their diagnostic work, clinical workers will almost never find it convenient to check high school yearbooks. Yet, it is important to realize that a great many more facts may be correlated with maladaptive behavior than we might at first think.

The article by David Shakow deals with classification. The clinician, having completed the assessment process, compares his present client with those with whom he has had past experience. Often this is done in an informal and unsystematic fashion; yet, as Shakow points out, it is important that an observer of behavior make such comparisons, not only with his own past observations but with those of others as well. Classification systems have been developed because they facilitate communication among clinicians who may be located far from one another. Another practical use of classification is in the maintenance and analysis of hospital records. For example, the incidences of hysteria and manic-depressive psychosis have declined significantly during this century. A reasonably stable diagnostic system enables an institution to chart long-term changes in its clientele. Along with these advantages, it is necessary to be aware of the limitations of present-day diagnosis, such as the danger of pigeon-holing people (sometimes for life) by attaching diagnostic labels to them, and the frequent unreliability of the labels which clinicians do attach to clients.

Treatment, like diagnosis, requires evaluation and objective study. A client comes to a clinician seeking help. Does he get it? Who decides whether or not he got it? If he was helped, which ingredients of the therapy were most responsible for bringing this about? Allen Bergin and Hans Strupp review important facets of the psychotherapy situation and review the types of research needed to identify its components. They are especially eloquent in their call for experimental studies capable of improving existing therapeutic methods and creating new, more powerful ones. For example, in traditional psychotherapy the therapist and the client engage in one-to-one verbal interchanges and play relatively circumscribed roles; Bergin and Strupp urge extensive inquiry into novel ways of structuring these roles and closer ties between the practice of psychotherapy and other areas of behavioral science.

The article on desensitization by Lang, Lazovik, and Reynolds illustrates how diversified the field of psychological therapies has become. Desensitization as described and evaluated by these experimenters seems to have several important advantages: it is less time-consuming than traditional "talking" therapy, the rate of success seems high, and the rate of relapse seems low. Yet, as Lang, Lazovik, and Reynolds recognize, many questions remain to be answered. Their experiment included a relatively homogeneous group of subjects, those with phobias about snakes. Might the procedures employed with snake phobics help persons with other types of problems?

Research and conjecture continue on this and other questions growing out of new approaches to behavior modification. The commentary by Cooper, Furst, and Bridger and the one by Levis illustrate the controversies as to the most reasonable interpretation of experiments such as that of Lang, Lazovik, and Reynolds. Cooper, Furst, and Bridger contend that success in treating snake fears may be quite irrelevant to the treatment of more severe clinical disorders. Levis, recognizing the danger of overgeneralizing from experimental demonstrations, rejects many of Cooper, Furst, and Bridger's arguments and discusses advantages of experimental research in developing new psychological therapies.

In the concluding article, Gordon Paul describes an experiment in which desensitization was used to help college students who were afraid of public speaking. This study showed that desensitization was effective in reducing or removing speech anxiety. This finding would seem to extend to a different kind of fear the results obtained by Lang, Lazovik, and Reynolds. Another significant aspect of Paul's research was its two-year follow-up, which revealed that subjects who had responded favorably to the original experimental conditions maintained their improvement.

the need for new approaches to clinical assessment

Donald R. Peterson

The clinical assessment of psychological problems has traditionally gone somewhat as follows. The social worker conducts an intake interview in which an attempt is made toward problem definition, a quick study of the individual, and a description of the social environment in which the individual is situated. A full social history may or may not be taken at this point, but in anything like a complete clinical evaluation, the facts of the applicant's life experience are covered in some detail.

The psychiatrist then conducts a psychiatric examination. This is also an interview of one kind or another. Depending on the past training and current proclivities of the psychiatrist, interview procedures may range from a completely unstructured free-associative narration by the patient to a rather tightly defined mental status outline. If medical problems are apparent or in question, appropriate physical examinations are also made though many psychiatrists prefer to send their patients to "real doctors" for study of this kind.

The psychologist performs a psychological evaluation. This may involve a brief interview but consists mainly of a battery of tests. Intelligence is usually assessed and any other functions thought to be important are evaluated by whatever methods the psychologist has learned to use. "Personality" is studied, ordinarily by means of the Rorschach, TAT, and other projective devices, and/or by means of structured tests like the MMPI.

Everybody writes a report. The reports are shared and typically the case is discussed in a staff conference where segmental information from the various specialists is synthesized. The product of this conference and the return from all the effort which has been invested in previous study is a diagnosis.

Let us be generous about what this can mean.

It may consist only of a Kraepelinian APA-style disease name such as "Schizophrenic reaction, paranoid type, with obsessive features, in a passive–aggressive personality," or "Personality pattern disturbance, cyclothymic type." This is a *typological* outcome. Or it may be composed of individual scores on a number of continua—a profile of traits. This is a *dimensional* outcome. Frequently the diagnosis is designed not merely to describe but to explain the disorder. The alleged explanation is ordinarily accomplished by reference to the underlying motives, conflicts, defenses and other dispositions of the patient, and is usually stated in psychoanalytic language. This is a *dynamic* outcome. Treatment recommendations, if any, are presumably based on the diagnostic summary.

But it is growing more and more apparent that there are serious flaws in the traditional approach to psychodiagnosis and that the means by which clinicians have studied personality need to be complemented and possibly replaced by improved procedures. For several decades evidence has been accumulating on the validity and utility of clinical personality measures. Over all, the results are discouraging. Kelly and Fiske (1951) found little predictive use in the usual kinds of clinical procedures. Little and Schneidman (1959) found recognized experts in use of the best known personality tests to disagree radically in the inferences they made from the tests. Meehl has reported that 83 percent of a sample of psychotherapists did not think the usual kinds of clinical diagnostic information were of much help in psychotherapy (Meehl, 1960). The pertinent chapters in the *Annual Reviews of Psychology* all look the same. So do those in Buros' *Mental Measurements Yearbook*. Each critic's list of studies is a little different from everyone else's but the general evaluations come out much alike. Personality tests are not doing as well as most people hoped they would.

There were some technical limitations in literally all the studies done so far on clinical assessment by means of tests. But the cumulative negative evidence is quite compelling and strong positive evidence for validity and utility is nowhere to be seen. A clinical psychologist who seeks to develop his professional identity as a diagnostician using psychological tests as the basic data source is taking a perilous risk. Use of tests for restricted purposes seems justified but there is no doubt at all any more about the need for major innovation in assessment procedures. It does not appear that further refinement of present devices will offer the precision or even the kinds of data needed. More and more, it looks as if entirely new approaches to the clinical study of behavior will have to be developed.

Psychiatry and social work have done no better than clinical psychology in the area of behavior study, and possibly not as well. Psychiatric diagnosis seems to be conducted in one of two extreme and equally questionable ways; either by following a mental status outline somewhat rigidly and arriving at a Kraepelinian diagnosis, or by encouraging free narration on the part of the patient and arriving at some kind of dynamic formulation of his inner mental condition. The promising and sometimes exciting innovations which have taken place under the name of social psychiatry have not been accompanied by any systematic attempt to develop revised improved diagnostic procedures, however piously each new grant request emphasizes the importance of program evaluation. Social work, which ought to have been doing the kinds of things proposed here, has been so concerned with professional status that needs for more effective procedures have gone unattended. Having subordinated themselves to psychiatrists, social workers fell into the trap of adopting the basic theories and viewpoints, mainly psychoanalytic, of their psychiatric leaders and began to engage in the professional activities, mainly psychotherapeutic, which were most prestigious in the eyes of their superiors. Social work is presently campaigning to upgrade standards and that is commendable, but at the very time when social workers should have been moving out into the community, honoring their traditions by developing better ways of dealing with man in society, many have been retreating comfortably into private offices, talking to individuals, calling it casework so nobody will punish them for treating the sick.

Clinical psychologists have reacted to the failure of their procedures and hence to the repudiation of a basic function and a loss of professional identity in three general ways. Some have turned to research. Others have devoted more and more of their time to treatment, particularly psychotherapy. Still others have continued to try to do diagnostic work, employing the same procedures their studies said had failed, and evidently reducing the consequent dissonance either by devaluating the research they had examined in graduate school or by developing a fairly bitter cynicism about the dilemma they and their profession have gotten themselves into. The negative findings about diagnostic techniques have had no material influence on the actual everyday practices of clinical psychologists. Sundberg's (1961) report on the diagnostic habits of clinicians suggests that the Rorschach and TAT are still going as strong as ever. Reports of the activities of VA psychologists have shown no particular shift over the past several years. The psychologists still say they spend most of their time in conventional diagnostics. A survey by McCulley (1965) of internship supervisors in approved agencies across the United States shows that they still employ projective techniques as much as ever, still demand that trainees learn to use the tests, and still insist that universities are obliged to teach them. One of the few changes in recent years is that trainees are doing *less research* than they formerly did on projective methods.

It is not plausible that the clinicians who have continued to do diagnostic work despite the limitations of available procedures have persisted in their ways wholly out of ignorance, self-deception, or temperamental perversity. It seems much more likely that they have continued to do diagnostic work because clinical decisions still have to be made, somehow, whether the methods in stock are effective or not. Clinicians have continued to use the familiar but fallible procedures because no better methods have appeared to supplement or supplant the old ones.

This failure, however, is more than a technological matter. It is increasingly clear that the flaws in clinical assessment are not only procedural but conceptual. Not only have we been using faulty methods, we have been trying to get the wrong kinds of data, in the framework of misleading conceptions of disordered behavior.

The main difficulty with the typological, disease-oriented approach to the study of human problems is simply that we are not dealing with disease types in the assessment and modification of disordered behavior. A child who strangles kittens or spits at his mother does not have a disease. He *does* something somebody defines as a problem, and this is so even when the behavior is covert and the judgment of the problem is subjective. The therapeutic need is to get the client to change his behavior, not to cure his illness, and the vital diagnostic need is for information contributory to the behavior changing enterprise.

The usefulness of a typology depends on three conditions. The first is *homogeneity within classes*. Members of each class must resemble one another closely in regard to the characteristics on which the typology is based. In traditional nosologies of psychiatric illness this requirement has only been imposed, much less met, for peripheral symptoms, but most psychiatric classification systems are also based on the assumption that homogeneity can ultimately be found at the level of central psychopathology, in lawful relationship with distal symptom clusters. The second requirement for a useful typology is *independence among classes*. If the types are not only cohesive within themselves, but distinct one from another, efficiency is gained in the structure of the descriptive system and clarity is gained in its application. The third requirement of a typology, or of any other clinically useful descriptive scheme for that matter, is *pertinence to treatment*. If membership in a disease class is to mean anything to the patients, differential treatment procedures must be available for the various forms of illness, and choice among these must be implied by the particular disorders patients are found to have. For syphilis, penicillin; for each mental disease, a proper mental treatment.

Unfortunately, clear-cut types of behavior disorders do not seem to occur in nature. None of the conditions stated above is met in fact by any present typology. This is fairly clear now both from clinical experience and from research. Efforts to employ Q-factor analysis as a means of identifying unitary, independent classes of behavior disorders have been conspicuously unprofitable. In one series of studies, for example, type-R factor analyses yielding three dimensions of delinquent behavior, namely psychopathy, neuroticism, and subcultural deviation (Peterson, Quay, & Tiffany, 1961) were accompanied by two attempts to reproduce the behavioral dimensions as classificatory types. In both studies, nearly random distributions

of subjects were found (Bowen, 1960; Tiffany, Peterson, & Quay, 1961). The dimensional traits could be identified with great dependability, but people did not fall into discrete classes as an effective typology requires. The more general literature on psychiatric typology is less conclusive, but a generalization about it can be ventured. The statement is in an extreme form to allow clear refutation if that is what the data eventually show: no Q-factor analysis to date, using even reasonably adequate procedures and tolerably unbiased samples of any general psychiatric population, has generated a nonrandom distribution of subjects in any psychiatrically meaningful descriptive hyperspace.

The failures which are slowly becoming apparent through the accumulation of negative research findings on psychiatric classification have been reflected for a long time in the day-to-day behavior of clinicians. Practitioners who have tried to use traditional nosologies as a basis for clinical description have had to add so many qualifiers to the basic disease labels they attach that they might as well forget entirely about the original classification system. Diagnosticians who try to describe the people they see in a conscientiously accurate and complete way have not been content to call people schizophrenic, manic–depressive or any other single thing and let it go at that. They have spoken instead of "schizo–affective reactions with paranoid features," or of "sociopathic personality disturbance, antisocial reaction, with schizoid features and occasional hysteroid manifestations." Violations of artificial class boundaries have been forced by the facts of clinical reality.

Dimensional formulations would appear to offer certain advantages over typology. In good psychometric tradition, we have assumed that anything which exists exists in some amount and can be measured. Objective tests can be developed for quantifying personality characteristics, and then the position of any subject can be established for whatever dimensions the investigator has chosen to define. Given continuous scales and an indefinite number of scales in the construct system, the individuality of any person can be taken into account and numerically expressed in his personality profile.

The most serious problem with presently available dimensional schemes appears to be that the traits involved are insufficiently general over method and situation to have much predictive utility. . . . Teacher ratings, for example, have little to do with self-ratings on dimensions which seem to represent the same dispositional tendency. The unitary traits we have so far defined seem to be determined more by the perceptual tendencies of observers than by the behavioral tendencies of the people under observation. And even if situation and method generality could be attained it is not immediately clear what the descriptions have to do with treatment. That is what we are up to, after all. No dimensional system available today is very useful in providing the kinds of information needed to help the people we labor so hard to describe.

Dynamic formulations of personality are designed to "penetrate the symptom facade" and reveal the (largely unconscious) psychic bases for the disorders people display. For the most part, these are based operationally on depth interviews, ordinarily of a free associative nature and on various projective tests, where unstructured stimuli are presented to elicit the latent personality tendencies of the individual. The data from tests and talks are usually interpreted in the framework of one version or another of psychoanalytic theory, and verbally fluent diagnosticians are capable of writing very compelling accounts of the inner mental life of the patients they see.

One needs to be skeptical, however, about the basic validity of such accounts, to say nothing of the reliability and generality of the methods used to generate the accounts. On all these scores, projective techniques have done very badly. Depth interviews have not been validated at all, nor can they be in their present amorphous state.

At best dynamic accounts are useful for planning certain kinds of individual psychotherapy. If we are going to invest most of our treatment capital in some other enterprise, elaborate dynamic accounts would probably be a waste. And even for individual psychotherapy, the utility can be questioned. Consider again the survey of therapists' opinions in which over 80 percent said the usual kinds of clinical diagnostic information were of little use in psychotherapy (Meehl, 1960). If Rorschach output is useless in planning psychotherapy, it may be worse than useless in planning a shift in the social reinforcement system or in other nonevocative forms of treatment.

Dissatisfaction with present methods does not immediately suggest a direction for new and better procedures. This demands a more fundamental logical analysis and a definition of the criteria an effective assessment system should meet.

IMPLICATIONS OF SOME RECENT DEVELOPMENTS IN TREATMENT PROCEDURE FOR THE CLINICAL STUDY OF BEHAVIOR

A clinically useful assessment system must above all yield information relevant to treatment. One way or another, the inquiry must generate decisions which will be helpful to the client. But the kinds of treatment which appear most promising today are different from those in widest use a few years ago, and assessment methods must take these innovations into account. Three very important changes have occurred in clinical treatment in the past several years. These were not unheralded by earlier efforts, but the major advances are quite recent. One is the development of social psychiatry, including principally the various milieu programs in mental health facilities as well as more general sociological shifts in community psychology. Another is the development of group procedures for treatment, particularly those approaches which employ natural primary groups, such as families and work crews, as the units in which treatment is done. The third is the development of behavioral approaches to the modification of disordered behavior; the effort to base treatment operations and procedural innovations on general behavior theory, notably on learning principles, rather than a separate theory of psychopathology.

The developments within social psychiatry which seem clinically most useful and most clearly accessible to systematic research are the social milieu programs which have been introduced at various mental hospitals. In institutions, the positions and roles and hence the socially influential behavior of personnel and residents apparently can be changed to the benefit of patients and staff alike. Custodial institutions have been transformed into active treatment agencies. When this is well done the effects are appreciable and appear to last.

In the field of group therapy, outcome research has been slow to appear, but some of the innovations in family treatment—family group and conjoint family therapy—and the quasi-therapeutic functioning of work groups appear quite promising.

The major implications for clinical assessment are clear. If one of the most effective things we can do for a disturbed or disturbing person is to alter his social environment, then we need to study the social environment systematically as an integral part of the assessment enterprise. In work with groups, there is an obvious need to study interpersonal transactions and relationships as well as individual behavior. In the study of milieu programs, we need to be concerned not only with the discrete interpersonal relationships between significant others and a person whose behavior is disordered, but with the organizational characteristics of the social systems in which the individual participates.

The many developments which have taken place under the name of behavior therapy have equally strong implications for changing assessment procedure. We are no longer just talking to people, trying to get them to understand themselves. Now we are trying to modify behavior explicitly and predictably by application of the principles of behavior which make up psychology itself. If learning is defined broadly enough (as any change whatever in covert or overt behavior) behavior therapy amounts exactly to the modification of behavior by the application of learning principles. This makes therapy a psychoeducational task. And it demands of assessment far more than a study of the individual, however profound or correct that study might be. The competent practice of behavior therapy requires knowledge of the conditions (external as well as internal) which arouse maladaptive responses, of the reinforcing consequences which sustain the maladaptive behavior, and of stimulus changes which might elicit and sustain a more acceptable pattern of activity. Designations of disease are useless. No profile of traits will do. No knowledge of dynamics is sufficient. One needs to accomplish a functional analysis of the problem behavior itself, i.e., a detailed study of problem behavior in relation to antecedents and consequences, by means of experimental, observational, and interrogative procedures.

SOME THEORETICAL CONSIDERATIONS AND THEIR MEANING FOR THE ASSESSMENT OF BEHAVIOR

The second basic condition for an effective assessment rationale is its pertinence to a general conception of behavior. Theoretical pertinence does not mean that each and every operation in the assessment system must relate to a definite proposition derived hypothetico-deductively from a comprehensive, fully articulated theory of human behavior. It means only that assessment efforts guided by some specified framework of behavioral concepts are likely to be more coherent and better defined, and hence may contribute more to knowledge about human behavior, than a battery of operations assembled without regard to theory. We are concerned not only with the clinical utility of diagnostic information but with promoting some general gain in knowledge about the human condition.

The conception we employ need not be very definite as to substance. We do not need to decide here and now what the hypothetical relationships might be among the variables we examine, although some manner of relationship is assumed if the characteristics are to be studied at all. We do not need to know, for instance, precisely how patterns of parental reinforcement are related to antisocial behavior on the part of children. That is what we are trying to find out. At this juncture all we need to know is that parental reinforcement patterns probably have some relationship to child behavior and hence are important to examine if we are interested in changing the antisocial activity. The level of theoretical specificity appropriate to our task is one which is sufficiently definite to tell us what variables to observe, but neutral regarding the exact relationships among variables.

The problem of defining a useful conception is not one of invention but of choice and synthesis—the supply of available theories is rich and plentiful. If we wish to integrate assessment with treatment, and treatment with theory, however, we can dispense with perhaps 90 percent of the formulations out of hand. For the reasons outlined above, I propose that we reject all typological–disease models, all dimensional–trait models, and all dynamic–intrapsychic models as the central bases for assessment, treatment, and research.

But what is left? What theory can offer the scope, the coherence, and the power needed for an effective clinical technology? There is only one answer. The conception we need must be as large as behavioral science itself. Parallel with developments in social psychiatry, treatment in natural primary groups, and the behavioral treatment of individuals, theoretical formulations concerning the organization of social systems, interpersonal transactions in groups, and individual action must be included. Concepts which have traditionally fallen within the scope of sociology, social psychology, and individual psychology are all required and some attempt at synthesis must be made.

The phenomena in all three classes require behavioral specification. A sociological concept of *communication system,* for example, must ultimately be defined by stipulating who-says-what-to-whom-under-what-conditions-to-what-effect. A social psychological concept like *relationship* must be stated in terms of recurrent transactions. Sooner or later, if one is to be clear about the nature of the relationship, he has to tell who does what to whom. Behavior theory thus lies at the core of the general conceptual system, and insofar as clinicians are concerned with treatment, the central concepts are those of learning. If concepts relating to individual action, group transaction, and social organization can all be given behavioral definition, then a basis for defining useful clinical assessment procedures may be provided, a system for continual self-correction may be established, and by the union between science and practice which this may accomplish, the enrichment and clarification of both may be achieved.

In developing improved conceptions of human behavior and in extending these to a technology for clinical assessment, it is important to take environmental factors as well as intrapersonal factors into systematic account. If one fact has become more painfully clear than others from recent research on personality, it is that we have been committing a very serious *organism error* in the study of personality. All along we have known that behavior was a function of the person *and* the environment in which he was situated, but in clinical diagnostic procedures and in research instrumentation alike we have continued to study the person alone. It is obviously necessary to begin taking the environment into orderly purview in procedures of clinical inquiry. The object of clinical study is not the individual alone nor his environment alone, but the individual-in-his-environment, as both aspects may be viewed in the context of general behavioral science and as both may be changed for the benefit of man and society alike.

PROCEDURAL CONSIDERATIONS

All assessment procedures need to be addressed to the same central issues, namely description of the problem and the conditions which affect it.

The study of individual behavior is procedurally fundamental to the study of sociological and social problems, as well as purely psychological problems. Diverse approaches, however, may be taken to the study of human behavior. If we abandon hope of developing global personality tests which will tell us all we need to know about a person, we are forced back to a rather primitive epistemology. If we are going to find out about a person's reactions to effective stimuli, we have to study his reactions to effective stimuli as directly as we can. Three general methods can be employed, namely observation, interview, and experimental manipulation.

Observations

We need to watch individuals behaving in situations that matter. We need to observe people interacting in groups and to obtain the most direct knowledge we can of organizational functions as expressed in the behavior of the people involved. The ideal observational method, of course, is a complete totally objective around-the-clock recording of every action subjects make in all the situations they enter. Clinicians are naturally unable to manage this, partly in principle (because some of the crucial observations would have to be made in the past, and because Heisenberg's ideas about indeterminacy apply with much greater force to psychological than to physical phenomena) and partly because of obvious limitations on practical feasibility.

The most that seems practicable in the usual clinical situation is a limited observation of the disturbed person in interaction with some significant others in his social world. Employment of parents, teachers, nurses, aides, or other informants as systematic observers offers considerable promise, but may present serious practical problems in many cases. Placement of a staff observer in crucial real-life situations frequently alters the event under observation, and is a difficult and expensive procedure even if no such effect occurs. We need to extend direct observational methods, but in practice this is hard to do.

Interviews

The methodological difficulties in direct observation require use of other procedures. Guided interviews offer some promise. As a general strategy, interviews may be conducted not only with the person under study but with others in the social systems of major importance to him. All these interviews should focus on the problem behavior under study, and on the social stimulus properties, as models, instigators, and reinforcers, of the significant others who are interviewed or about whom information is gained. The interview protocol must not be regarded as the "truth" about the individual and his environment, but as another form of data whose reliability, validity, and decisional utility must be subjected to the same kinds of scrutiny required for other modes of data collection.

Experimental Procedures

Given information from observations and interviews, some planned manipulative changes may be exercised in the person's stimulus situation, and changes in his behavior may be recorded. The stimulus changes can be general or specific, multiple or single, brief or extended—this will depend on the case—but only in an experimental way can some of the most important hypotheses concerning behavior disorders be examined. Thus if a mother's solicitous behavior appears to be sustaining tantrums on the part of a child, let us try to get the mother to change her way of treating the child and observe any shift in child behavior which may result. The resulting data are in the nature of *functional relationships* between disordered behavior and the conditions which influence it. Knowledge of such relationships is of obvious and direct relevance to treatment, and is therefore a more useful kind of information than any sort of typological, dimensional, or dynamic account whatever. In an analogous way, changes in group transactions and interpersonal relations may be deliberately and planfully altered, and a social system may be reorganized to improve functional effectiveness.

In a very basic sense, all forms of treatment, psychological, social, or sociological, are experimental procedures. This does not imply a loss of compassion or a lack of interest in human well-being. It does imply that the treatment be planned as carefully as available knowledge permits, that the treatment activity be specified as clearly as possible, that any changes which come about be faithfully recorded, that the information about functional relationships thus gained be employed in a reformulated appraisal of the problem, and that revised treatment measures then proceed in an indefinite cycle of diagnostic information and therapeutic action.

REFERENCES

Bowen, T. W., Typological analysis of conduct disorders. Unpublished master's thesis, Vanderbilt University, 1960.

Kelly, E. L., & Fiske, D. W. *The prediction of performance in clinical psychology.* Ann Arbor, Mich.: University of Michigan Press, 1951.

Little, K. B., & Schneidman, E. S. Congruencies among interpretations of psychological test and anamnestic data. *Psychological Monographs,* 1959, 73 (6, Whole No. 476).

McCulley, R. S. Current attitudes about projective techniques in APA approved internship training centers. *J. proj. Tech. pers. Assessment,* 1965, 29, 271–280.

Meehl, P. E. The cognitive activity of the clinician. *Amer. Psychologist,* 1960, 15, 19–27.

Peterson, D. R., Quay, H. C., & Tiffany, T. L. Personality factors related to juvenile delinquency. *Child Develpm.,* 1961, 32, 355–372.

Sundberg, N. D. Psychological testing in clinical services. *Amer. Psychologist,* 1961, 16, 79–83.

Tiffany, T. L., Peterson, D. R., & Quay, H. C. Types and traits in the study of juvenile delinquency. *J. clin. Psychol.,* 1961, 17, 19–24.

some reflections on the meaning of psychodiagnosis

Harrison Gough

Many psychologists tend to look on psychodiagnosis as mere ritual or wheelspinning. In Meehl's (1960) survey of therapists, the statement "It greatly speeds therapy if the therapist has prior knowledge of the client's dynamics and content from such devices as the Rorschach and TAT [p. 19]" was included; only 17% of 168 practitioners queried expressed agreement. Rotter (1964) asserts that the diagnostic approach is sterile and has yielded little in over 100 years of application. Rogerians have long since announced their release from the chains and constraints of diagnostic bondage (cf. Ford & Urban, 1963, p. 427; Rogers, 1957, pp. 101–102). These sentiments of disbelief, dubiety, and impatience are to be encountered in any center where psychologists work and study today.

Why then should anyone take diagnosis seriously? Why should psychologists be trained in the methods of appraisal and the ways of thinking that are involved in personality diagnosis? Why should we worry about this matter at all, except as a historical oddity such as phrenology or palm reading?

It is doubtful whether an answer can be formulated that will satisfy everyone, and it may well be true that disillusionment with diagnosis is fully justified. However, it is not the purpose of this article to dwell on the demise of diagnosis, nor in fact does the writer see the body as ready for interment. He is one of those peculiar souls who believes in diagnosis, as one might say, and therefore the obligation of this report is to delineate some of the reasons thought to justify this perhaps anachronistic point of view. To do this properly requires ranging over a number of ideas and topics —some well known and some not so well known.

Speech presented at a conference on personality assessment, Veterans Administration Hospital, Palo Alto, California, March 19, 1970.

For the former, the reader's indulgence is requested, and for the latter, his attention.

PURPOSE OF DIAGNOSIS

A first notion concerns what might be called the axiomatics of diagnosis. Courtesy in the evaluation of an idea suggests that we hold it for the claims it in fact makes, not for the claims we would like or misbelieve it to make. The goal of diagnosis, for example, is not to label or stigmatize; these outcomes may be unfortunate products or by-products of diagnosis, or they may be unfortunate effects of diagnosis abused. But diagnosis is not a form of lifemanship, whose goals are to put someone down or to score a debater's point.

The function of diagnosis is to identify the problem the patient has presented in such a way that an appropriate and restorative treatment may be carried out. It is easiest to think of this formulation in medical terms, and indeed the logic of diagnosis is probably most clearly illustrated in the medical treatment of physical illness. Complaints and symptoms may arise from many different sources, and depending on these sources the same treatment may be helpful, inconsequential, or dangerous. To treat abdominal distress with an aperient would be extremely unwise if the underlying condition was an inflammation of the vermiform appendix. Treatment, to be effective, must be addressed to the underlying condition as this is determined by accurate diagnosis.

Mere mention of the medical model, of course, is enough to set psychological teeth on edge, and the all too common reaction is one of phobic avoidance. Phobic response in the intellectual domain is as irrational and unproductive as in the behavioral, and doctrinaire beliefs about the independence and autonomy of psychology should not be permitted to interfere with rational analysis of the merits of diagnosis. In fact, there is a certain contradiction when those who oppose "labels" use the label "medical model" as a ploy for invalidating diagnostic concepts.

LOGIC OF CAUSATION

A second comment is that diagnostic thinking necessarily involves attention to the logical question of causation. This is a thorny issue, and could by itself discourage one from going very far into the intricacies of diagnosis. We might try to detoxify the problem by examining logical notions of causation to see if any could serve as a reasonable philosophical basis for the diagnostic approach.

A first sense of causation is that of the human agency or meditation. An individual causes a consequence, or is responsible for it, when in his voluntary action he brings it about. Cause in this sense usually signifies a sufficient antecedent condition, not a necessary one. Thus, to bring light into a room an individual can press a switch, light a match, or pull back the curtains from a window. The effect must be broadly conceived, as the quality of light produced by each of the causes will be different. The Latin word *causa*, as used in law, has to do with voluntary actions of this kind for which an individual can be held responsible.

A second sense of causality refers to causation in nature, and is an easy extension of the first. A cause is again a sufficient condition, and to discover the cause of an event is to discover something among its temporal antecedents such that, if it had not been present, the event would not have occurred. This is the sense of causation that is employed in the practical sciences; the procedure utilized by the practical scientist differs from that of the ordinary intelligent man only in that he needs to be more careful in his diagnosis of causes and in that he is assisted in this diagnosis by the availability of a large fund of formal and theoretical knowledge.

The ideas of J. S. Mill fall into this second category: the cause of a phenomenon is the antecedent or concurrence of antecedents on which it is invariably and unconditionally consequent. Mill's canons of induction require the analysis of complex events into factors and the discovery, by way of experiment and observation, of those factors that are invariably and un-

conditionally present when a certain phenomenon appears and absent when it does not occur. An assertion of cause, following this, is an expression of confident anticipation, based on the consistency of prior experience. The postulates of Robert Koch, the great bacteriologist, are addressed to this same purpose.

A third sense is to view cause as explanation. Now the distinction between antecedent and consequent becomes trivial, and reflects only the biases of experience. The essential notion is that of logical coherence and deducibility: given this set of conditions, this field of forces, this constellation of traits, etc., then these implications will obtain. The effect, that is, may be deduced from the cause.

Both the second and third senses of causality are relevant to the notion of therapy: in the second, the emphasis is on those antecedent conditions that will give rise to undesirable and unwanted consequences, and in the third, on the structure of the total field in which unfortunate components are to be found. Put in language more often used by diagnosticians, the search is for etiological factors in either prior circumstance or present situation.

The emphasis on prediction in the writing of some diagnostically minded psychologists can be related to this second notion of causality; that is, the purpose of diagnostic appraisal is to forecast what the subject will say or do at a later time. Leon Levy (1963) in his book *Psychological Interpretation* puts it this way:

> Psychodiagnosis is a descriptive venture, having as its ultimate goal the provision of a basis for the anticipation of the behavior of the patient under various contingencies. Unless it can be shown that this goal is accomplished by the use of a particular psychodiagnostic approach, continued use of that approach represents sheer ritual. Therefore, if the clinician is not to be found guilty of engaging in ritualistic behavior in the pursuit of his professional goals, he must be able to demonstrate that the product of his psychodiagnostic procedures permits predictions to be made about a patient's behavior at a higher level of accuracy than could otherwise be obtained [p. 157].

In practice, the steps taken in arriving at a diagnosis can be specified with little difficulty. First comes a recognition of the presenting problem or the presenting complaint. Second, facts relevant to the complaint are gathered—how long has the trouble been apparent, does the pain come and go, are there other symptoms, etc. Third, the clinician ponders this information and by induction hypothesizes possible explanations. Fourth, the implications of his hypotheses are checked back against the observations and if necessary new observations are gathered. And fifth, on the basis of confirmation and disconfirmation, a decision is made as to diagnosis.

Technical skill and apparatus are important in gathering information, but the capacity to think inductively is of paramount importance in the total sequence. Not everyone has what it takes to become a good diagnostician, just as not everyone has what it takes to become a good therapist or a virtuoso in any endeavor that requires a high order of talent and self-development.

OBSERVATION AND DIAGNOSIS

In gathering the relevant facts, there are more or less time-honored areas of attention. First comes the personal history of the patient. The diagnostician needs to know something of the family background, as certain conditions such as Huntington's chorea and Wilson's disease have known genetic linkage, and others such as diabetes and manic–depressive reactions tend to recur. The work situation is important, and the personal habits of the patient with respect to alcohol, drug usage, and other factors need to be explored.

The illness or presenting complaint must also be traced out. Pain is frequently a concomitant of physical illness, and an accurate description of the pain, if present, is needed: its location, duration, periodicity, quality, and the conditions under which it appears; sometimes just this information alone is sufficient to establish diagnosis, as in intermittent claudication.

The physical examination comes next, and it too follows a typical format. Visual inspection—of face, eyes, posture, gait, physique, etc.—is carried out. Palpation is a second method, and percussion a third. It is interesting to note that Leopold Auenberger, who first reported the method of percussion in his *Inventum Novum* in 1761, credits the method to his boyhood experiences in Graz, Austria, when he learned how to tell whether wine casks were filled or empty by tapping on them and listening to the reverberations.

Auscultation, a fourth method, proposed by Rene Laennec in 1819, also came to mind by way of a happy observation. According to his biographers, Laennec was watching a group of youngsters playing on a beam in the courtyard of the Louvre. One child scratched the beam with a pin, and the others, with ears pressed against the beam, called out every time he scratched. Laennec decided to try this on a patient, and took a sheet of paper, rolled it into a cylinder, applying one end to his patient's chest and his ear to the other. To his delight, he heard the heart sounds clearly, and at that moment the stethoscope was discovered.

The gradual development of more penetrating and precise aids to diagnosis can be illustrated in the succession of dates for these innovations: accurate timing of pulse rate, 1707; systematic data on body temperature in fevers, 1852; electrocardiograph, 1887; blood pressure cuff (sphygmomanometer), 1896; electroencephalography, 1929. New devices are being invented constantly, and advances in biochemical analyses, computer reduction of data, and other indirect aids are occurring with equal frequency.

Although the steps and illustrations just offered refer more to medicine than psychology, similar stages are applicable to the work of the psychodiagnostician. Mensh (1966) in his book *Clinical Psychology: Science and Profession* makes this statement:

> By means of data from interviews and from standard objective and projective test techniques, the clinical psychologist develops his inferences about the probable etiology of the behavior he is investigating, the complicating variables in the patient's life and his assets for handling life situations, and the probable optimal mode of treatment. He may also include data from school, work, family, or other sources, just as he also utilizes these avenues in his treatment approach [p. 12].

CRITICISMS OF DIAGNOSIS

One hopes that the text up to this point has given at least partially satisfactory answers to three of the criticisms often made of diagnostics. One of these criticisms is that diagnosis has as its aim the mere labeling of the problem, a kind of pigeonholing that helps to meet the therapist's need for order but that is of little value to the patient; the answer to this criticism is that the goal of diagnosis is to permit selection of that form of treatment which is most beneficial to the patient. A second criticism is that diagnosis is a philosophically naive enterprise and cannot hold up under logical scrutiny. The answer to this criticism is that diagnosis is but a special case of one of the most interesting and complex philosophical problems known to man—the problem of causality.

A third allegation is that diagnosis is a perfunctory endeavor, an easy and pedestrian task to be performed by individuals of modest endowment, who leave the more complicated challenges of therapy to their betters. The answer to this assertion is that diagnosis, properly conducted, is a complex and demanding task drawing on hard-to-acquire skills and a high degree of aptitude in its practitioners.

A fourth objection is that there is no need in treatment to attend to this or that specific factor, causative or otherwise. Why not, as some therapists announce, simply give the patient what we know will help him, no matter what his trouble may be. Thus, love is all you need say the Beatles —or unconditional regard say the Rogerians—and that is what you will receive. And after all, as the advertisements promise, Guinness is good for what ails you. Now it may be true that certain universal remedies may moderately enhance the well-being of all people, as for example an admonition to any American male to lose five pounds or the injunction *immer ohne schlag* to anyone from Vienna; but even if these instructions would enhance general well-being, they would not be of much help to someone suffering from Hodgkin's disease, tumor, or other illness in which the dietary factor is trivial or irrelevant.

Furthermore, therapy, if rational, should be cumulative in its wisdom, and a therapist should not in glorious ignorance or indifference recapitulate the errors, false starts, mistakes, and miscalculations of past relationships with each new patient. To build rationally on past experience, a method for relating the new to the old is needed, and this bridge is precisely what diagnosis is intended to supply.

LEVELS OF DIAGNOSIS

Up to this point, little has been said about the substantive side of diagnosis, and it is therefore time to turn to this issue. That is, if a diagnosis is not merely a classificatory word or phrase, what is it? To treat the matter properly, we must distinguish levels of diagnosis. Level 1 is that given by the clustering of symptomatic or phenotypical data. A clinician observes that certain behaviors or signs covary, such that when one is detected the others can usually be found. If the pattern recurs and is confirmed by others, it may be designated as a syndrome, as in the Libman-Sach's syndrome marked by persistent moderate fever, progressive anemia, and purpuric lesions of the skin.

The push in diagnosis, however, is on to a second level, that of pathology. Thus, whereas both malaria and polio may first be brought to visibility by way of the symptom of fever, the danger of pathological tissue damage in the first is to the spleen and liver and in the second to gray matter in the anterior horns of the spinal column. Insofar as treatment is concerned, relief of symptoms is about all that can be done for syndromes conceptualized at Level 1, barring a happy accident in the discovery of a frankly empirical specific, as for example chlorpromazine and the phenothiazines for some forms of schizophrenia. For illnesses conceptualized at the second level, the possibility of arresting the reaction by means of surgery or other forms of treatment is possible, and curative efforts may be directed at the underlying factor.

The third and most basic level of diagnosis is that in which the etiological factor is identified. Thus, malaria is known to be caused by the malarial parasite, transported by the anopheles mosquito, and polio by one of three kinds of virus. Once an illness is conceptualized on this third level, there is the possibility of prevention by way of vaccines or eradication of the conditions under which infection can occur.

To put this progression into a shorthand formula, we can therefore say that for reactions classified at the first level, therapy can provide relief; for those at the second, cure; and for those at the third, prevention. Thus, no clinical syndrome can ever be considered fully understood and fully controlled until the diagnostic formulation has been pushed on to the third level and confirmed.

One of the exceedingly interesting things that begins to happen, as a syndrome is conceptualized at a more basic level, is that what are called "false positives" and "false negatives" begin to appear. At Levels 1 and 2, a false-positive subject would be one showing the symptoms but not the pathology, and a false negative would be one free of the symptoms but suffering the pathology. Proper therapy for true positives and false positives might very well be different, and until the diagnostic differentiation is possible, the correct choice of differential treatment could not be made.

It is also interesting to observe the deepening of conceptualizations over time. In the early 1800's, a syndrome was observed involving symptoms such as dysarthria, shaky handwriting, alteration of sleep rhythms, pupillary abnormalities, etc. Some 50 years later, it was discovered that patients with this syndrome revealed a typical frontal lobe atrophy, with adhesions between arachnoid and cortex. At the turn of the century, it was established that the causative agent was the treponema pallidum, verifiable in the cortex. Treatment could then be directed against the invading organism (and was, with Ehrlich's "606"), and, since the discovery of penicillin, complete control of the illness—dementia paralytica—has been at least theoretically possible.

Not every illness in medicine has been conceptualized at this third level. Cancer, the second leading cause of death among Americans with a rate of 364.5 per 100,000, is an example. The symptomatology of cancer can take many forms: a slight cough, pain, swelling, alterations of skin tone and texture, bleeding, apparent indigestion, headache, etc. The pathology, on which diagnosis is based, is a form of malignant neoplasm manifesting invasiveness and a tendency to metastasize. The etiology, however, is not yet known; it may be caused by a virus, it could be nutritional, or even a kind of allergic reaction to foreign matter. As an illness conceptualized at Level 2, treatment by means of surgery or radiation therapy is possible, but prevention is not. Empirical knowledge relevant to incidence is available, as for example the statistics on lung cancer among smokers, but a valid etiological conception of the illness has not yet been developed.

Polio, on the other hand, is an example of an illness whose conceptualization at the third level was achieved fairly recently. Following the success of Enders, Weller, and Robbins in culturing polio virus, it was only a few years until the development of the Salk vaccine in 1954 and the Sabin oral vaccine in 1957.

PSYCHOLOGICAL DIAGNOSIS

These levels of diagnosis have a counterpart in the psychological realm, and the same push toward more fundamental understanding is as important in this realm as in the physical. The symptomatic–phenotypic level is much the same: clients have problems, difficulties, or other features of thought and behavior that are noted to covary. Symptomatic relief may be provided by way of palliatives such as reassurance, sympathy, etc., but with no assurance that these are directed at etiological factors.

At the second level, we encounter psychopathology. Thus, excessive dependence on the defense mechanism of repression may be the psychopathological factor underlying a clinical hysteria. Psychotherapy can then be addressed to the defense system, with a greater likelihood of stable improvement in the patient than if attention had been addressed to purely symptomatic phenomena.

Just as histological and biochemical analyses may be of great help in identifying these underlying pathological factors in physical illness, so may psychological tests be of help in identifying the psychopathological underpinnings of a presenting syndrome. One of the distinctions that is frequently made on the Minnesota Multiphasic Personality Inventory (MMPI)—between so-called symptomatic scales such as 7 and character scales such as 6—reflects this difference between Level 1 and Level 2 diagnoses. To the extent that an MMPI scale contains truly subtle items, the more certain we may be that it has penetrated through into the second level of psychopathology. A truly subtle item, incidentally, is one whose scale membership and scoring cannot be guessed by reading, and whose content is not necessarily associated with the domain of manifest concern ordinarily found among persons revealing the clinical picture.

One could go even further and say that empirical item analysis such as employed in MMPI scale construction is a reasonably powerful method for discovering whether a diagnostic syndrome at Level 1 does in fact have a psychopathological infrastructure. It may seem on reading Dahlstrom and Welsh (1960) that anything and everything can be scaled on the magic item pool of the MMPI. In fact, this is not the case, and there have been attempts to scale where the yield of subtle items was zero; a negative finding like this, following the aforementioned line of reasoning, suggests that the symptomatic syndrome is just that—a syndrome lacking a demonstrable psychopathological basis and hence one that should be abandoned or redefined.

An example can be taken from studies of alcoholics; item analyses of the MMPI against this symptomatic cluster nearly always turn out to be inefficient and indirect ways of finding the items in the inventory that say "I have used alcohol excessively." Thus, the empirical analysis confirms what most clinicians already suspect from other kinds of study: there is no single psychodynamic basis for the clinical syndrome.

Another example can be drawn from the study of headaches. A survey was made of patients complaining of headaches and for whom headache was a major symptom, contrasting them with other patients matched on age, sex, etc., but free of the complaint. The item analysis carefully brought to light all of the items in the inventory mentioning headaches, but not much else. Thus, from this probe it would appear that "headache" is not a very promising diagnostic concept, and should be left as a word in the symptomatic lexicon.

In interpreting tests like the MMPI, skilled workers draw heavily on these underlying or Level 2 notions. In a profile in which Scale 3 is elevated, an interpreter may say nothing whatsoever about manifest symptomatology, but a great deal about dependency and narcissism. On Scale 4, he may think more about inadequacies of attention span than of behavioral deviation. Complex interactions among test components, in fact, can often appear quite irreconcilable at the symptomatic level, but fully reasonable and revealing at Level 2. Diagnostic thinking at Level 2 is therefore superior to diagnostic thinking at Level 1, and instruments conceptualized at Level 2 are more valuable than those conceptualized at Level 1.

One should interject that these remarks do not apply only to tools intended for use in the clinic. The Strong Vocational Interest Bank (Strong, 1943) in the hands of skilled interpreters is read at Level 2 and not at Level 1, and the same assertion can be made for the California Psychological Inventory (CPI: Gough, 1957, 1968) whose scales are named for behavioral clusters observable in the ongoing currents of everyday social life.

PSYCHODIAGNOSIS AT LEVEL 3

The third level in psychodiagnosis is concerned with etiology, as found in the life history and family background. If, in the psychodiagnosis of

schizophrenia, we could discover just which factors of pseudo-mutuality and contradictory message-sending in the family were at the root of the schizoid reaction we could begin work on prevention. It is unlikely, of course, that single causative agents will be found at Level 3 in psychodiagnostic analysis but even though the conceptual problem will involve clusters and interactions of factors, the possibility of identifying the etiological progression remains. MacKinnon (1949), among others, has emphasized the need to go back to these root factors in the life history.

Our tools of appraisal should likewise be pushed back to this third level of understanding, where possible. Other things being equal, the more powerful the scale, the broader the range of life-history antecedents that can be deduced from variations of score on the measure.

Most of the psychodiagnostic concepts employed in psychology and psychiatry have been worked through to the second level, but not the third. Some have not even attained the second level, and as in the case of alcoholism may be essentially symptomatic descriptions rather than diagnostic notions. Anxiety may be another, and the relative inutility for personality assessment of scales for anxiety may reflect this fundamentally phenotypic status of the concept. The redefinition incorporated in the state-versus-trait distinction (Spielberger, 1966) could be the way out of this box. Depression, on the other hand, although it seems very symptomatic, has many features of a Level 2 concept. Asymptomatic depression, in other words, is not just a semantic contradiction, and most clinicians would probably grant that the idea has both validity and some interesting implications.

With respect to Level 3, life-history and family-background determinants of scores on personality measures, information is only slowly accumulating. The studies of more and less authoritarian children by Else Frenkel-Brunswik (1948) brought to light elements of family structure conducive to social and intellectual tolerance, and the work of Dale Harris (Harris, Clark, Rose, & Valasek, 1954) has shown that different childhood milieus are related to higher and lower scores on scales for responsibility in adolescence.

Retrospective accounts, although heuristic only, have also been assayed. In analyses at the Institute of Personality Assessment and Research in Berkeley, it was found that adult males scoring high on the MMPI D scale tended to describe their mothers as "generous," whereas those scoring low described her as "possessive." On the Rorschach W%, high-scoring males viewed their fathers as prudent and mild, but their mothers as nervous and worrying. On the CPI Socialization scale, high scorers saw their mothers as loving, whereas low scorers saw their mothers as criticizing.

ENHANCING DIAGNOSTIC SOPHISTICATION

If psychodiagnosis is to be practiced, it seems fair to say, it should therefore be addressed to the broader and more implicative concepts of Levels 2 and 3, and it should be aided by tools capable of generating information of this type (cf. Gough, 1965). Present-day psychometric sophistication and computer methodology are of great help in developing such tools, and current literature reveals a flourishing productivity. Thus, for specific syndromes such as depression, we have the Beck (Beck, Ward, Mendelson, Mock, & Ebaugh, 1961) and Zung (1965) scales for self-description and the Hamilton (1960) scale for use by an observer. For more general characterization, we have the Inpatient Multidimensional Psychiatric Scale of Lorr, Klett, McNair, and Lasky (1963), the Katz Adjustment Scales of Katz and Lyerly (1963), the Brief Psychiatric Rating Scale of Overall and Gorham (1962), the Hospital Adjustment Scale developed by Ferguson, McReynolds, and Ballachey (1953), and others.

Diagnostic interpretation of MMPI profiles is currently available from three sources—Roche Laboratories (Fowler, 1967), the Mayo Program (Rome et al., 1961) as handled by the Psychological Corporation, and the service provided by Alex Caldwell in Los Angeles—and a fourth, the Finney (1966) interpretational program of Lexington, Kentucky, is just becoming operational.

Decision-tree models of diagnostic interpretation are also being developed, using the coded interview materials and (potentially) test information. Best known among these at the present time is DIAGNO-II as developed in New York by Spitzer and Endicott (1969) and their colleagues. The Boston City Hospital Behavioral Check List developed by Peter Nathan (Nathan, Samaraweera, Ausberg, & Patch, 1968) is a close competitor. DIAGNO-II draws on a 96-variable input including age, sex, and 94 scaled judgments from an interview device called the Current and Past Psychopathology Scales (CAPPS). Fifty-seven decision points are programmed, leading to 46 different diagnostic classifications.

The flow chart or decision tree is modeled on the sequences of decisions actually made by the clinician when he reviews the evidence on a patient and attempts to arrive at a diagnosis. The correspondence between DIAGNO-II's conclusions and those of skilled clinical diagnosticians is remarkable. DIAGNO-II's output consists of 44 official diagnoses from the American Psychiatric Association handbook, augmented by *nonspecific illness with mild symptomatology* and *not ill*. The decision-tree model, however, could be applied to other kinds of diagnoses and to psychological classifications at Levels 2 and 3.

Psychologists can obviously play a part in these developments and are playing a part. Our training includes a greater emphasis on statistical technique than that of our fellow mental health professionals, and we are therefore in demand when this kind of analysis is indicated. Principles of learning and behavioral modification can also be invoked just as much for the training of a diagnostician as for the therapy of a patient with a problem. How should an apprenticeship in MMPI profile interpretation be conducted? With contingencies of reinforcement and lots of behavior being emitted, a learning theorist might say. Thus, not only in the analysis of how to approach diagnostic understanding, but in the building of tools and in the training of practitioners to use these tools, psychology has important contributions to make. Our help is needed, and let us hope there will always be enough of us with a knack for diagnostic work and an interest in it so that this vital tradition of psychological endeavor can be maintained and transmitted—intact and full of vigor—to each new generation of psychologists.

REFERENCES

Beck, A. T., Ward, C. H., Mendelson, M., Mock, J., & Ebaugh, J. An inventory for measuring depression. *Archives of General Psychiatry*, 1961, *4*, 53–63.

Dahlstrom, W. G., & Welsh, G. S. *An MMPI handbook: A guide for use in clinical practice and research.* Minneapolis: University of Minnesota Press, 1960.

Ferguson, J. T., McReynolds, P., & Ballachey, E. L. *Hospital adjustment scale.* Palo Alto, Calif: Consulting Psychologists Press, 1953.

Finney, J. C. Programmed interpretation of MMPI and CPI. *Archives of General Psychiatry,* 1966, *15,* 75–81.

Ford, D. H., & Urban, H. B. *Systems of psychotherapy: A comparative study.* New York: Wiley, 1963.

Fowler, R. D., Jr. Computer interpretation of personality tests: The automated psychologist. *Comprehensive Psychiatry,* 1967, *8,* 455–467.

Frenkel-Brunswik, E. A study of prejudice in children. *Human Relations,* 1948, *1,* 295–306.

Gough, H. G. *Manual for the California Psychological Inventory.* Palo Alto, Calif.: Consulting Psychologists Press, 1957.

Gough, H. G. Conceptual analysis of psychological test scores and other diagnostic variables. *Journal of Abnormal Psychology,* 1965, *70,* 294–302.

Gough, H. G. An interpreter's syllabus for the California Psychological Inventory. In P. McReynolds (Ed.), *Advances in psychological assessment.* Vol. 1. Palo Alto, Calif.: Science and Behavior Books, 1968.

Hamilton, M. A rating scale for depression. *Journal of Neurology, Neurosurgery, and Psychiatry,* 1960, *23,* 56–62.

Harris, D. B., Clark, K. E., Rose, A. M., & Valasek, F. The relationship of children's home duties to an attitude of responsibility. *Child Development,* 1954, *25,* 29–33.

Katz, M. M., & Lyerly, S. B. Methods for measuring adjustment and social behavior in the community: I. Rationale, description, discriminative validity, and scale development. *Psychological Reports,* 1963, *13,* 503–535.

Levy, L. H. *Psychological interpretation.* New York: Holt, Rinehart & Winston, 1963.

Lorr, M., Klett, C. J., McNair, D. M., & Lasky, J. J. *Inpatient multidimensional psychiatric scale.* Palo Alto, Calif.: Consulting Psychologists Press, 1963.

MacKinnon, D. W. Psychodiagnosis in clinical practice and personality theory. *Journal of Abnormal and Social Psychology,* 1949, *44,* 7–13.

Meehl, P. E. The cognitive activity of the clinician. *American Psychologist,* 1960, *15,* 19–27.

Mensh, I. *Clinical psychology: Science and profession.* New York: Macmillan, 1966.

Nathan, P. E., Samaraweera, A., Ausberg, M. M., & Patch, V. D. Syndromes of psychosis and psychoneurosis. *Archives of General Psychiatry,* 1968, *19,* 704–716.

Overall, J. E., & Gorham, D. R. The brief psychiatric rating scale. *Psychological Reports,* 1962, *10,* 799–812.

Rogers, C. R. The necessary and sufficient conditions of therapeutic personality change. *Journal of Consulting Psychology,* 1957, *21,* 95–103.

Rome, H. P., Swenson, W. M., Mataya, P., McCarthy, C. E., Pearson, J. S., Keating, F. R., Jr., & Hathaway, S. R. Symposium on automation techniques in personality assessment. *Proceedings of the Staff Meetings of the Mayo Clinic,* 1962, 37(3), 61–82.

Rotter, J. B. *Clinical psychology.* Englewood Cliffs, N.J.: Prentice-Hall, 1964.

Spielberger, C. D. Theory and research on anxiety. In C. D. Spielberger (Ed.), *Anxiety and behavior.* New York: Academic Press, 1966.

Spitzer, R. L., & Endicott, J. Diagno II: Further development in a computer program for psychiatric diagnosis. *American Journal of Psychiatry,* 1969, *125,* 12–21.

Strong, E. K., Jr. *Vocational interests of men and women.* Stanford: Stanford University Press. 1943.

Zung, W. W. K. A self-rating depression scale. *Archives of General Psychiatry,* 1965, *12,* 63–70.

high school yearbooks: a nonreactive measure of social isolation in graduates who later became schizophrenic

Charles N. Barthell &
David S. Holmes

Of the numerous hypotheses relating early social experience to the development of schizophrenia, none has been more frequently stated than that of "social isolation" (Faris, 1934; Kohn & Clausen, 1955). This hypothesis suggests that the preschizophrenic personality attempts to avoid painful exposure of his low level of self-esteem by reducing interpersonal contact or by rigidly controlling the nature of the interaction (Auerback, 1959; Sechehaye, 1956; White, 1956; Wolman, 1965). The individual consequently shuts himself off from communicative feedback and thus avails himself of fewer opportunities for reality testing. The avoidance of participation with others makes social participation progressively more difficult, and the individual falls further and further behind his peers in the development of social skills. It has been specifically suggested that "at adolescence, when various new social skills are required, such individuals are likely to drop fatally out of step and still further restrict their future development [White, 1956, p. 530]."

A number of studies have been conducted to determine the extent of social isolation among preschizophrenics while in high school (i.e., during adolescence). Schofield and Balian (1959) found that preschizophrenics, when compared with a "normal" control group, could be characterized by "higher rates of social withdrawal, lack of social adeptness and poise, and narrow interests [p. 225]." Further support for the social isolation hypothesis was provided by Bower, Shellhamer, and Daily (1960) who found that with few exceptions preschizophrenics could be characterized as

"tending toward the shut-in, withdrawing kind of personality [p. 728]." Finally, Kohn and Clausen (1955) found that roughly one-third of their schizophrenic sample reported a sufficient lack of activities and friendship patterns to lead the authors to classify them as isolates or partial isolates, whereas only 4% of the normals reported such patterns.

Although these studies support the social isolation hypothesis, an equal number of studies throw some doubt on its tenability. Bellak and Parcell (1946) found that in their study of the prepsychotic personalities of 100 cases diagnosed as dementia praecox,

> 35 had distinctly extrovert prepsychotic personalities, 28 had distinctly introvert prepsychotic personalities, and 37 had to be considered ambivert, or a mixture between extroversion and introversion [p. 630].

Morris, Soroker, and Burrus (1954) evaluated the current adjustment of 54 individuals who, when seen in a clinic from 16 to 27 yr. previously, had been described as "internal reactors." They found that these individuals were "relatively free of overt mental or emotional illness and getting along quite well [p. 749]." Last, in the follow-up study of Michael, Morris, and Soroker (1957), only 1 of the 10 Ss who carried the diagnosis of schizophrenia as an adult had been classed as an introvert from the social history collected at childhood.

It is clear then that there are inconsistencies and points of disagreement in the literature on the

Reprinted from *Journal of Abnormal Psychology*, 1968, 73, pp. 313–316. Copyright 1968 by the American Psychological Association and reproduced by permission.

relationship between schizophrenia and social withdrawal in the prepsychotic personality. One criticism of the previous studies, and a possible source of the inconsistencies, lies in the fact that in most studies the patient's social history was compiled by interviewing relatives and acquaintances after the patient had become psychotic, that is, retrospectively. This leaves the studies subject to a number of errors. First of all, inaccuracies may result from the fact that reliable informants may be difficult if not impossible to find, and their reports may have been distorted or changed with the passage of time. Second, if S had been identified as a patient (either as an adult or as a child who was later followed-up), informants may have been influenced in their reporting by what they had heard about mental disorders. Last, those studies in which information was gathered from patients may suffer from the disadvantage of unreliable information due to the patient's disorder and feelings about hospitalization.

Webb, Campbell, Schwartz, and Sechrest (1966) have recently outlined the value of using "nonreactive measures" such as archival material which would not be distorted by the passage of time or by the measurement process. With these measures there is no masking or sensitivity as there may be when the producer of the data knows he is being studied by some social scientist. According to Webb et al. (1966), "this gain by itself makes the use of archives attractive if one wants to compensate for the reactivity which riddles the interview and the questionnaire [p. 53]." In the present study, the activity summaries found in high school yearbooks were used as a means of determining the relative social isolation of the preschizophrenic and prepsychoneurotic individual.

METHOD

Subjects

A group of 20 hospitalized schizophrenics (14 males and 6 females) and a group of 20 hospitalized psychoneurotics (14 males and 6 females) were selected from the medical records of the Illinois State Psychiatric Institute. The criteria applied in S selection were the following: (a) All Ss were born between the years 1934 and 1944; (b) all Ss graduated from Chicago-area high schools between the years 1952 and 1962; (c) no S was selected who had been hospitalized within 2 yr. following the date of his high school graduation; (d) no schizophrenic patient was selected whose hospital stay was less than 3 mo. The 2-yr. period following graduation and prior to hospitalization was thought necessary in order to insure the fact that Ss were not overtly or incapacitatingly schizophrenic or neurotic while attending high school at which time the data were recorded. Schizophrenic Ss hospitalized for less than 3 mo. were excluded on the grounds that their schizophrenic break was more likely to be of a reactive nature, and less likely to be the culmination of a long-term developmental process.

A "normal" control group was selected using the method introduced by Bower, Shellhamer, and Daily (1960). At the time that data were being recorded from the yearbooks of each schizophrenic and psychoneurotic S, data were also collected for the student pictured next to him. This rule was followed unless the student pictured next to the patient S was of a different sex, of a different race, or of the same name indicating the possibility of a family relationship. In such cases, the next student pictured was selected as control S. Thus, for every schizophrenic or psychoneurotic S from a given high school, there was a control S from the same high school who had graduated in the same year and had been free to choose from the same number and types of activities offered by the high school at that time.

Procedure

A list of all of the activities in which each S had participated was taken from the index and/or the senior summary of each S's senior yearbook. Only high school graduates were used in this study since it is only in the senior year of high school that any extensive record is set down of the students' activities in school. At the time of the data collection, the experimenter knew to which group any one S belonged. Therefore, for each S, the entire list of activities was copied verbatim and was later analyzed blindly. Following the collection of the data, each S's activities were classified into one of the following categories: (a) social activities, (b) service activities, (c) performance activities, and (d) athletic activities. Those activities classified as social included all clubs, organizations, and activities whose primary purpose was a social one. Examples of activities classified as such included student-council or student-government organizations; language, academic, or special-interest clubs; and student publications. Those activities classified as service activities included activities in which some service was performed for the high school. Such activities were of the type that necessitated very little social interaction. Examples of activities classified under this heading included hall guard, office helper, library assistant, teacher's aide, and the like. Performance activities included musical or dramatic organizations, while athletic activities included all individual and team sports as well as intramurals and athletic associations. There was a 95% agreement between two independent judges on the classification of all of the activities into the above categories.

RESULTS AND DISCUSSION

Number of Activities

An analysis of variance was performed to test the significance of sex, diagnostic category, type of activity, and the interaction of these variables as related to number of activities participated in by Ss. The results of this analysis are presented in

TABLE 1.   Analysis-of-Variance Summary Table

Source of Variation	df	SS	MS	F
Sex (A)	1	10.29	10.29	2.32
Diagnostic category (B)	2	44.41	22.21	5.01*
A X B	2	1.32	.66	.15
Ss/SD groups[a]	74	327.60	4.43	
Type of activity (C)	3	102.08	34.03	17.54*
C X A	3	14.66	4.89	2.52
C X B	6	4.99	.83	.43
C X A X B	6	7.70	1.28	.66
C X Ss/SD groups	222	430.82	1.94	
Total	319	943.87		

[a]Ss within Sex Diagnostic group (nested design).
*$p < .01$.

Table 1. Both the variables of diagnostic category and type of activity were significant ($p < .01$). In light of the significant F for diagnostic categories, Kramer's (1956) multiple-range test for means based on unequal Ns was used to test the mean differences over all activities for the three diagnostic groups. The results of this analysis are presented in Table 2. This analysis indicated that the mean number of activities participated in by schizophrenics, as well as psychoneurotics, differed significantly from the mean number of activities for the control group ($p < .01$). There was, however, no significant difference found between the mean number of activities for the schizophrenic and psychoneurotic groups, although the difference was in the expected direction.

While schizophrenic Ss were found to differ significantly from normals in the mean number of activities in which they had participated, it is of interest to note that the mean number of activi-

ties for the schizophrenic group did not differ significantly from that of the psychoneurotic group. On the basis of these findings, one is forced to conclude, then, that *both* hospitalized groups showed a tendency toward withdrawal and iso-

TABLE 2. Significant Ranges for Kramer's Extension of Duncan's New Multiple-Range Test

	Schizophrenic	Neurotic	Normal
	Mean no. high school activities		
M	3.75	4.00	6.85
	Mean no. social activities		
M	1.60	1.95	2.83
	Mean no. service activities		
M	.75	.85	1.55
	Mean no. performance activities		
M	.65	.40	1.20
	Mean no. athletic activities		
M	.75	.80	1.28

Note: Any two means not underlined by the same line are significantly different at the .01 level. Any two means underlined by the same line are not significantly different.

lation when compared to the control group. It is important to remember, however, that the psychoneurotics used in this study were all hospitalized. Since psychoneurotics do not as a general rule require hospitalization, it might be that the psychoneurotics in this sample could be considered more severely disturbed than psychoneurotics in general. This fact might explain the similarity found between the two patient groups.

Type of Activity

A number of analyses on the mean differences between social, service, performance, and athletic activities for the three S groups were performed, again using Kramer's multiple-range test. The results of these analyses are presented in the lower part of Table 2. Significant differences were found between the mean number of social activities for the schizophrenic and normal groups ($p < .01$), while the mean of the psychoneurotic group fell between those of the schizophrenics and normals but did not differ significantly from either. There were no significant differences found between the means of the three groups on any of the other activity classifications: service, performance, or athletic activities.

From this data, it would appear, then, that social activity level forms a continuum, with schizophrenics and normals falling at the extreme ends and psychoneurotics in the middle. It is important to note that there were no significant differences between the groups on any of the other types of activities considered. That is, it was only when *social* activities per se were considered that schizophrenics were found to fall behind their peers in level of participation. This fact seems an important finding and lends support to those investigators who hypothesize that the individual who becomes schizophrenic is socially withdrawn and introverted during adolescence.

In general the results of this research which employed a nonreactive measure offered support for those studies which have found that individuals who became schizophrenic were less active in the social realm prior to being diagnosed as schizophrenic. Social isolation may not, however, be unique to schizophrenics, for in the present study psychoneurotics evidenced a similar trend.

REFERENCES

Auerback, A. (Ed.) *Schizophrenia, an integrated approach.* New York: Ronald Press, 1959.

Bellak, L., & Parcell, B. The pre-psychotic personality in dementia praecox. *Psychiatric Quarterly,* 1946, *20,* 627–637.

Bower, E. M., Shellhamer, T. A., & Daily, J. M. School characteristics of male adolescents who later became schizophrenic. *American Journal of Orthopsychiatry,* 1960, *30,* 712–729.

Faris, R. Cultural isolation and the schizophrenic personality. *American Journal of Sociology,* 1934, *40,* 155–169.

Kohn, M. L., & Clausen, J. A. Social isolation and schizophrenia. *American Sociological Review,* 1955, *20,* 265–273.

Kramer, C. Extension of multiple range test to group means with unequal numbers of replications. *Biometrics,* 1956, *12,* 307–310.

Michael, C. M., Morris, D. P., & Soroker, E. Follow-up studies of shy, withdrawn children: II. Relative incidence of schizophrenia. *American Journal of Orthopsychiatry,* 1957, *24,* 331–337.

Morris, D. P., Soroker, E., & Burrus, G. Follow-up studies of shy, withdrawn children: I. Evaluation of later adjustment. *American Journal of Orthopsychiatry,* 1954, *24,* 743–753.

Schofield, W., & Balian, L. A. comparative study of the personal histories of schizophrenic and non-psychiatric patients. *Journal of Abnormal and Social Psychology,* 1959, *59,* 216–225.

Sechehaye, M. *A new psychotherapy for schizophrenia.* New York: Grune & Stratton, 1956.

Webb, E. J., Campbell, D. T., Schwartz, R. D., & Sechrest, L. *Unobtrusive measures: Nonreactive research in the social sciences.* Chicago: Rand McNally, 1966.

White, R. W. *The abnormal personality.* New York: Ronald Press, 1956.

Wolman, B. B. (Ed.) *Handbook of clinical psychology.* New York: McGraw-Hill, 1965.

the role of classification in the development
of the science of psychopathology
with particular reference to research

David Shakow

D. Hack Tuke (1) in *A Dictionary of Psychological Medicine* published in 1892 introduced his section on Classification with the following remark: "The wit of man has rarely been more exercised than in the attempt to classify the morbid mental phenomena covered by the term insanity. The result has been disappointing." The present situation in psychiatric classification is, unfortunately, not very different.

In the present paper I wish to say something about the general attitude I believe the investigator should take in confronting the problem of classification. This will be followed by my own personal associations with the problem. By "personal" I mean the attempts to deal with classification that have occurred in the contexts of the programs with which I have been involved. This will present pertinent facts related to classification which have never been made public, and which I think belong in the history of this problem. I will then consider the various underlying issues of the classification problem as I see them.

GENERAL ATTITUDE

I do not understand how a psychologist can adopt a professional orientation which does not acknowledge classification as fundamental in dealing with the multiplicity of phenomena involved in the

From a paper prepared for the Conference on The Role and Methodology of Classification in Psychiatry and Psychopathology, Washington, D. C., 1965. Presented, in part, as the Helen Sargent Memorial Award Lecture at The Menninger Foundation, September 27, 1965.

diagnosis of mental disorder. Classification is essential whether it is being made for therapeutic or for research purposes, but it is especially important for the latter. The objections that are directed against a particular classification system usually arise because the criticized form of classification differs from the one used by the critic himself. No matter how vehemently a psychiatrist or psychologist may oppose an existing system of classification, he almost always has a personal method of categorizing patients.

Science is not possible without classification. It is essential to the objective investigation which is the core of the scientific method. The major objections to the classification of mental disorders that have been raised are the problems that almost inevitably result from any attempt at categorization. Such problems are reification—dealing with the abstract conception of the disorder rather than the actual behavior or symptoms presented by the individual patient; partialization—taking only a part for the total picture; privacy—the use of personal rather than public categories; and simplification—the substitution of a simple, easily comprehensible explanation for the complex of phenomena which are difficult to grasp in their intricacy. With the growing sophistication and critical self-evaluation of workers in the field, however, such obstacles are gradually being overcome.

Since the diagnostic aspect of the classification problem is so frequently emphasized and discussed, it is important to point out that there are really three different stages of the classification process in psychopathology which demand consideration: (1) The description of the phenomena exhibited by the patient, (2) the syn-dromization of these collected descriptions and (3) the actual process of assigning patients to different categories.

THE WORCESTER RESEARCH

My period of most intense involvement with the classification problem began in 1928 when I was at the Worcester State Hospital. One of my responsibilities as Chief Psychologist was the direction of the psychological investigations conducted by the Schizophrenia Research Service, a service which had been in existence for somewhat less than two years at the time of my arrival. Those first few years had been a kind of a "pseudopodic" period during which time the approaches had been highly probative. The program had relied on the part-time work of the psychiatrists of the regular hospital staff aided by Anton Boisen—then the Chaplain—and several of his associates.

At the time I joined the hospital staff, the research service was being expanded. Professional personnel from various relevant specialties were being recruited, and in a short time an extensive multidisciplinary activity was in operation. This work lasted for about 20 years and was probably the most continuous and extensive research program on chronic schizophrenia ever undertaken. Although the different groups of investigators examined the same patients, some of the work was unidisciplinary, some of it multidisciplinary (either concurrent or interrelated), and some of it truly interdisciplinary. In the last category I include those studies in which independent variables, whether physiological, psychological or psychiatric, were set up and in which patients were studied with regard to dependent variables in one of the other realms.

What did this effort in classification amount to —what results were achieved? It is my opinion that, in spite of its incompleteness and its many failings and inadequacies, the study was one of the most carefully carried-out, large scale projects ever attempted in the classification of chronic schizophrenia. Since our study was directed at the chronic group, our problem was made much easier than if we had been dealing with the whole range of mental disorders or even with only the full group of schizophrenic or schizophreniform conditions.

In general the atmosphere of the study fostered intimate knowledge of the individual patients,

accuracy in clinical investigation, more objective evidence in establishing the criteria for diagnosis as well as emphasizing the importance of unambiguous psychiatric categories. The research group developed a sensitivity both for the complexity of the problem and for the need for accurate characterization of the syndromes. The project resulted in the evolution of a common area of agreement about psychiatric classification among the psychiatrists, as well as in the rest of the staff, despite their different philosophic backgrounds, which varied from a psychoanalytic approach through a structural to an organic orientation. In short, we were thus able to reduce markedly the effectiveness of what is inevitably the Gresham's law of psychiatric discourse—the tendency for loose talk to drive out rigorous talk.

The specific effects of the project were many. First, criteria were developed which offered considerable reliability in evaluation. We were also able, on the basis of the evaluations and classifications, to establish reasonably homogeneous groups of psychiatric subtypes so that these subtypes correlated with quite independent psychological studies made of these same patients. We were able to differentiate the schizophrenic group both from other psychoses and from normal subjects, and even differentiate the various subtypes *within* the psychosis.

During an experiment using the play technique, Rosenzweig and I (2) observed how clearly normal, paranoid and hebephrenic subjects differentiated themselves from each other on the basis of their behavior in the assigned task. Having selected the subjects for our experiment according to their mental status and the other criteria used in the psychiatric classification, we were impressed with how distinctly the independent psychological data differentiated these categorized groups. Another specific result we achieved was a fairly high correlation between items on the mental status examination and the results of a wide variety of psychological experiments and tests.

Needless to say, the study was terminated before completion, which is almost inevitable with any project in this most complicated area. I am certain that even if we had obtained the necessary financial support for the much more elaborate study of the current mental status system which we then proposed, we would not have been able to achieve conclusive results. I am convinced that only from a long succession of such systematically organized careful studies will any meaningful solution of this problem be achieved.

Despite efforts such as those attempted at Worcester, studies which demand high standards and care for successful execution, I confess that I have frequently been left with an underlying sense of uneasiness and ambivalence about the process we followed. I have never been quite sure whether we were actually approaching the veridical through a process of mutual education in which the staff worked through the data and methodology to a generally acceptable system, or whether what we were engaged in was rather a form of indoctrination in which the observers were both consciously and preconsciously constrained into a form of nominalism—agreeing to call something by a certain name whether accurate or not.

The stages of the particular educational process involved in the development of a classification system seem to be essentially these: (1) the initial great differences in the criteria for diagnostic judgment which exist among the participants; (2) the minimization of these differences as a result of the participants' discussions of their differences in professional opinion, and the resulting achievement of an optimal degree of agreement and reconciliation; (3) the disclosure of a dilemma: Are the judgments veracious, or are they merely group-accepted stereotypes? In the end, I suppose, we must accept a minimal level of stereotypy which will not, I believe, be a critical disadvantage if the participants have already employed both self-criticism and mutual criticism in the attempt to clarify concepts.

BASIC DIFFICULTIES

Two basic difficulties have particularly plagued the field of classification—the tendency to adopt extreme attitudes, and uncertainty about the model to follow. In earlier years there was, perhaps, too strong a trend to accept passively the classification of mental disorders proposed by authoritative figures in psychopathology without either sufficient questioning or the utilization of empirical methods to evaluate their validity. In more recent years, however, a tendency to adopt uncompromising extreme positions in relation to classification has developed. Such extreme trends in the effort to classify mental disorders are reminiscent of what Franz Alexander (3) has labeled "dialecticism," and have resulted in either the acceptance of rigid categorization, or a nihilistic attitude expressed in the desire to discard all classificatory systems. The latter appears, at least

in part, to be a consequence of the contemporary emphasis on psychoanalysis, and the related stress on the idiographic approach to personality study which has characterized this same period. The combination of the two has resulted in a scepticism about classificatory systems. The consequence has been a heated controversy over the value of the standard categories which is reflected in the conflicting attitudes of a Mayer-Gross (4) and of a Karl Menninger. (5)

The other basic problem—considerably the more significant of the two—revolves around the question of which theoretical model should be employed in attacking the problem of classification. We touch here on a basic issue for psychiatry. For many reasons, the major ones being historical–vocational, psychiatry has naturally identified itself with the medical disease model in which psychiatrists are still trained. This is true although the actual practice of psychiatry has, from quite early days (compare the period of moral treatment of the early 19th century), followed a psychological–behavioral model. The resulting dissociation has plagued psychiatry almost from its beginnings and has resulted in a split like Santayana's characterization (6) of the 19th century which, according to him, "yearned with Rousseau or speculated with Kant, while it moved with Darwin, Bismarck, and Nietzsche. . . ." The problem, which has recently been intensified by both the important position that psychoanalysis has achieved in psychiatry and the more recent development of social psychiatry, has now reached an incandescent state. Eissler's recent book, *Medical Orthodoxy and the Future of Psychoanalysis,* (7) provides an elaborate statement of the effects of the split on psychoanalysis.

SIX DICHOTOMIES

There appear to me to be six major methodological dichotomies which have to be faced in the attack on the problem of classification. These are: (1) the multiple simple as opposed to the single recondite approach; (2) the direct as opposed to the inferential approach, as reflected in both the clinical and the test approaches; (3) the holistic–segmental dichotomy; (4) the nomothetic as opposed to the idiographic approach; (5) the literal as opposed to the metaphoric approach, whether in the aspects analogous to the shift in biological classification from the Linnaean type of empirical description to the system of more generalized evolutionary description, or the one reflected in the structural/dynamic descriptions introduced in large part by psychoanalysis, as opposed to the older tradition of empirical surface descriptions of symptoms; and finally (6) the emphasis on method as opposed to the emphasis on content.

In approaching any problem, the investigator has the choice of developing, on the one hand, a complicated multifaceted program which represents a complex fusion of methods and philosophies—what I might call the single recondite approach; or he can simultaneously attack the problem through a set of separate hypotheses or methods, each of which contributes to the total picture, but is relatively independent in original execution—what I call the multiple simple approach. I believe the second approach is the more fruitful.

The complexity of the problem cannot be denied. Almost from the time I started my work at Worcester, I have been convinced that problems of mental disorder, for instance schizophrenia, have to be dealt with on the basis of a group of multiple, relatively simple hypotheses. I was, therefore, recently gratified to come across an important early paper on this general topic, "The Method of Multiple Working Hypotheses," by Chamberlin, the famous geologist, originally written in 1890, but recently reprinted in *Science*. (8) I believe Chamberlin would have accepted my extrapolation of his argument for the use of multiple simple *hypotheses*, to the use of multiple simple *approaches* which the problems of classification call for. These are: the clinical psychiatric approach toward personality and behavior, the ward observer's behavior rating approach, the clinical psychologist's approach through tests and experiments, and the biochemist–physiologist's organic approach. It is only through their simultaneous use, and efforts to combine these various approaches, that we will eventually learn to deal satisfactorily with the problem of classification. When the data provided by these approaches have achieved an acceptable level of dependability, there is the further possibility for the use of computer techniques to deal with their separate and combinatory complexities.

The next methodological problem is that of the direct as opposed to the inferential approach. Anyone who has worked in this field recognizes the importance of inference in the mental status evaluation of patients, no matter which approach is employed. It is true, however, that some approaches to clinical evaluation depend to a far greater extent on inference than do others. Since mental status evaluation is very rarely as objective a task as reading points on an instrument dial (and psychology warns the investigator about numerous sources of error even here!), checks are called for in the area of direct observation of human behavior. Where inference plays a substantial role in the diagnostic process, the importance of controls becomes increasingly important. In addition to such controls as the use of original, agreed-upon criteria, and the use of independent judges and rating scales for direct observation, what is additionally necessary for the more inferential methods are both explicit and implicit norms, and repeated testing and cross-checking by several competent judges of hypotheses about the latent meanings of the manifest behavior. This is true both of the dynamic hypotheses originating from clinical practice and those derived from more controlled test performances, such as projective devices.

Still another methodological problem is that created by the holistic–segmental dichotomy. One aspect of this problem has often been characterized in medical literature as the differences in approach between the advocates of the Hippocratic approach to disease as opposed to those holding to the Platonic ideal. Interpreted in this way, it is difficult not to agree with the segmentalists in their recognition of the importance of the individual patient, as opposed to viewing disturbances as holistic entities in the Platonic sense. Classification, however, calls for subtle balancing of the holistic and the segmental so that the diagnosis of mental disorders recognizes the important individual and type variances which supersede fixed categories. A more modern approach to the holistic–segmental controversy should recognize both the total patient as a functioning unit and the patterns of individual traits which make up his totality; and that classification does not call for absolutes but rather for preponderances.

Associated with the next dichotomy, of the nomothetic as opposed to the idiographic approach, is the troublesome problem of the "single case" as opposed to a group of cases. Allport (9) has succinctly expressed this conflict in his question: Should scientific law be taken to refer to "any uniformity that is observed in the natural order" or should it be considered to involve only statements of "invariable association common to an entire class of subjects?" If prediction in science must, by definition, involve prediction across many individuals, then it is clear that the single case cannot be considered proper or adequate subject matter for scientific investigation. However, there have been stout representatives of the point of view that the *individual* may have his own laws. If we accept Kluckhohn's and Murray's neat characterization (10) of an individual's personality as being comprised of some characteristics like *all* other persons, some like *some* other persons, and some like *no* other person, then laws in psychological science have to take account of phenomena at these three levels: (1) universal, (2) type, and (3) individual. It is in relation only to the last level that controversy arises in our present context.

The dichotomy of the nomothetic and the idiographic (9) is only a more elaborate way of stating this fundamental problem. The nomothetic view calls for a discipline with uniform general laws, whereas the idiographic calls for a discipline concerned with particular events or particular individuals. Under limited circumstances, empirical prediction which does not involve intuition is possible for the individual. Psychology would, I believe, gain from the use of both of these approaches.

We have already considered some aspects of the literal–metaphoric dichotomy, particularly in the analogy I have mentioned of the shift from the Linnaean empirical description to evolutionary generalization as a basis for classification in biological taxonomy. I wish here, however, to emphasize a more direct aspect, that of the conflict between the literal–superficial descriptive as opposed to the structural–dynamic descriptive approach to the classification of mental disorders. One group indulges in a careful concern with minute discriminations and old-fashioned taxonomy in such detailed descriptions of psychiatric phenomena as seen in the studies of Langfeldt. (11) The opponents of detailed description of minutiae and rigid categorization often place excessive emphasis on dynamics. What the situation calls for is a combination of both of these approaches. The generalized interpretation of the dynamics of the patient's situation is important only when it is based on accurate description of the observed phenomena. Observation and description of the phenomena must precede generalizations, the core from which dynamic interpretations can be inferred.

Each of these relatively simple approaches calls for the same set of fundamental formal principles. The most basic of these is the accurate description of the patient's syndrome. This description should be made by experts who are trained in the particular approach and who have had considerable contact with the individual patient. Of the several methods of investigation, I consider, at least for the present, the psychiatric–clinical approach the most valuable.

I would, of course, expect the psychologists involved in classification to know their tests and experimental procedures thoroughly. But I would also expect them to be able, through general observation, to evaluate the nature of the reaction, the cooperation, and the motivation of the patient by both clearly defined diagnostic standards and through the "intuition" that comes from long acquaintance with mental patients.

A major contribution to the accurate description necessary for the development of a category of mental disorders is through the use of ward observers. Ward observation has, in general, been neglected. We have tended to depend either on formal tests or, more particularly, on the clinical impressions of psychiatrists who see the patients for relatively short periods of time.

The same kind of problems arise with the organic aspects. We must have personnel capable of giving the organic tests with great exactness while understanding the special need for careful experimental conditions with patients who, besides other difficulties, are often not cooperative or only passively so.

The last of the dichotomies I have included is that contrasting method with content, especially in the difference between the statistical and the pyschological techniques.

The best illustration I can give of the conflict is the difference between investigators who enter the field of classification with little or no background in psychopathology, but who merely possess a special statistical technique, usually a form of factor analysis, or a narrow experimental technique such as operant conditioning. These would-be "saviors," despite their lack of content knowledge about mental disorders, are not too infrequently "off-with-their-headers," prepared not only to decapitate the poor muddled psychopathologists who have wrestled futilely with the problems of their field without being able to understand or to categorize successfully the phenomena they observe, but also to rescue the field single-handedly with the magic of their statistical or empirical methodology.

I am, of course, far from objecting to the application of new methods. In fact, the field can advance only if such new methods are continuously being tested. Method is of value, however, only when content is already available to the user of that method. It appears most unrealistic as well as rather arrogant for "Johnny-come-latelys," without knowledge of psychopathology or awareness of the tremendous complexities involved, naively to enter this field, and expect to revolutionize it with sudden, significant solutions.

It is in connection with this topic that I wish to pay tribute to Helen Sargent, a major figure in the Menninger Psychotherapy Research Project, who was the possessor of a wealth of clinical experience which she contributed to the general field of clinical research of which the classification problem is only a part. Her major achievement was the emphasis she persistently placed on the importance of intrapsychic events as they are reflected in the judgments of clinicians, and how these subjective data might be objectively evaluated. Her further developments of quantitative methods, such as that based on the method of paired comparisons which she reconciled with the clinical approach, were major methodological contributions. She suggested (12) that criteria other than reliability and validity be used to evaluate the empirical status of clinical observation (p. 107); criteria such as *reality*, to be tested by agreement among observers; *relevance*, to be established by the relationship of observations to other known facts; *import*, thought of in terms of the hypotheses suggested by a given observation; and *utility*, as gauged by hypotheses supported or confirmed. These concepts are all of great relevance to clinical research and should be considered for their ultimate significance to the classification problem.

Above all I want to stress the guiding principle I learned from the Worcester studies in this area. It can be stated in just three words: Standards, Standards, Standards.

REFERENCES

1. Tuke, D. H.: *A Dictionary of Psychological Medicine*. Philadelphia, Blakiston, 1892, p. 229.

2. Rosenzweig, Saul, and Shakow, David: Play Technique in Schizophrenia and other Psychoses: II. An Experimental Study of Schizophrenic Constructions with Play Materials. *Amer. J. Orthopsychiat.* 7: 36–47, 1937.

3. Alexander, Franz: Psychology and the Interpretation of Historical Events. In *The Cultural Approach to History*, Caroline F. Ware, ed. New York, Columbia University, 1940.

4. Mayer-Gross, W., Slater, Eliot, and Roth, Martin: *Clinical Psychiatry*, Ed. 2. Baltimore, Williams & Wilkins, 1960.

5. Menninger, Karl, with Mayman, Martin, and Pruyser, Paul: *The Vital Balance*. New York, Viking, 1963.

6. Santayana, George: *Winds of Doctrine*. New York, Scribner, 1913, p. 7.

7. Eissler, K. R.: *Medical Orthodoxy and the Future of Psychoanalysis*. New York, International Universities, 1965.

8. Chamberlin, T. C.: The Method of Multiple Working Hypotheses. *Science 148*:754–759, 1965. Originally published in *Science* (old series), Vol. 15, 1890.

9. Allport, G. W.: *Personality: A Psychological Interpretation*. New York, Holt, 1937.

10. Kluckhohn, Clyde, and Murray, H. A.: Personality Formation: The Determinants. In *Personality in Nature, Society and Culture*, Ed. 2, Clyde Kluckhohn and H. A. Murray, eds. New York, Knopf, 1953, pp. 53–56.

11. Langfeldt, Gabriel: The Prognosis in Schizophrenia and the Factors Influencing the Course of the Disease. *Acta Psychiat., Kbh.*, Supplement 12–13, 1937.

12. Sargent, Helen: Intrapsychic Change: Methodological Problems in Psychotherapy Research. *Psychiatry 24*:93–108, 1961.

new directions in psychotherapy research

Allen E. Bergin &
Hans H. Strupp

Three national conferences on research in psychotherapy, held in Washington, D. C., 1957; Chapel Hill, 1961; and in Chicago, 1966, pointed up the need for investigators to pool their resources and to consider the design of research projects which might be executed on a collaborative basis. Precedents for such ventures were of course available in biomedical research, but had been conspicuously absent in psychotherapy. Informal suggestions at the first two conferences evidently were not followed by any action; the situation, however, was different at the Chicago conference. For one thing, a small group of investigators was more articulate about the problem; for another, the Clinical Research Branch of the National Institute of Mental Health—all three conferences had been supported by grants from the National Institute of Mental Health—was taking an active interest in the possibilities of collaborative research in this area.[1]

As a first step, John M. Shlien, the conference chairman, appointed an informal committee of conference participants to explore the feasibility of a collaborative study of psychotherapy. The following individuals were asked to explore the feasibility issue: Kenneth M. Colby, Jerome D. Frank, Howard F. Hunt, Joseph D. Matarazzo (Chairman), John M. Shlien, and A. Hussain Tuma.

Although the committee was informal and had no standing with any official group or organization, it consisted of researchers who believed that examination of the feasibility of coordinated or collaborative research was long overdue and that concerted action should be taken toward this end.

The committee met several times during the 18 mo. that followed the conference. At the initial meeting, it was concluded that an answer to the feasibility question required, as a first step, a critical review of the psychotherapy research literature. It seemed essential that a hard look at what the field had produced to date was necessary in order to determine whether studying other aspects of the feasibility issue would be fruitful.

The authors of the present report were asked by the committee to undertake this critical review of the literature and agreed to do so. We devoted the period from June through December 1967 to this undertaking, carried out under contracts from the National Institute of Mental Health. The results of our analysis were published as the February and March 1969 issues of the *International Journal of Psychiatry* (Bergin & Strupp, 1969; Strupp & Bergin, 1969a). A bibliography of research in psychotherapy was completed as a by-product (Strupp & Bergin, 1969b).

In our review, we reached the conclusion that the field might possibly be ready for one or more major collaborative studies, pending further feasibility testing and pilot work. Concomitantly, we outlined several studies which might prove fruitful.

We subsequently met with the originating committee in January 1968, by invitation of the Clinical Research Branch of the National Institute of Mental Health, and discussed future plans. Donald Kiesler, Nathaniel Raskin, and Charles Truax were also present. As a group, we discerned two possible next steps: (*a*) independent investigators might on their own pursue one or another of the Strupp–Bergin recommendations for promising lines of inquiry; or (*b*) further investigation of the feasibility issue in greater depth might be

---

[1] Reflecting this programmatic interest, A. Hussain Tuma attended the conferences as an official observer, and subsequently both he and Donald Oken, then Chief, Clinical Research Branch of the National Institute of Mental Health, worked with us closely throughout this effort.

undertaken. The latter would involve consideration of such problems as (*i*) kinds of variables to be studied, by whom, under what conditions, and in which settings; (*ii*) research designs which might most profitably be explored; (*iii*) consultants who might be approached for help on such matters as research design, statistical analysis, and professional and practical issues in collaboration; (*iv*) whether independent investigators could be persuaded and motivated to participate in a coordinated or collaborative study; and (*v*) whether such an undertaking would be economically feasible. Clearly, such an inquiry might also lead to the equally important conclusion that collaborative research, while perhaps desirable, is either not feasible or premature.

At this point, stimulated by our own previous work and the undeniable importance of the problem as reflected by the interest of the originating committee and the National Institute of Mental Health, the present authors decided to embark on an examination of the set of the aforementioned questions outlined under *b*. Accordingly, we submitted an application for a research grant to the National Institute of Mental Health, which received favorable consideration, and we began work on the project in the fall of 1968.

THE FEASIBILITY STUDY

In order to answer the questions posed by the present authors and the originating committee, we proposed to:

1. Explore in depth the relative merit and priority of several major psychotherapy research questions and relevant experimental designs in consultation with experts on substantive and methodological issues; and to scrutinize those designs which we had already identified as promising (in our review),[2] and determine the relative merits, power, feasibility, and potential contribution of the specific studies to the furtherance of knowledge in psychotherapy. This step involves the possible combination, amalgamation, modification, and specification of projects in an effort to arrive at optimal designs.

This phase of the planning began from the vantage point of a considerable body of past research and the thinking of many insightful investigators who seriously concerned themselves with (*a*) general problems of strategy and of individual efforts versus collective or coordinated efforts; (*b*) problems of experimental design, choice of variables, and their measurement; and (*c*) strategies of collaborative research on psychotherapy or other areas of investigation of comparable complexity, and who have acquired considerable sophistication and a general realization of the limitations of research in a complex area where, administratively, treatment studies are extremely difficult to implement and variables are hard to define, measure, control, or manipulate.

2. Inventory resources available at various centers in the nation for undertaking major responsibility for collaborative work. It was not our intention, at first, to begin organizing a large national network of collaborating centers nor to elicit specific commitments from them; rather, we planned to test, through visits and interviews with key personnel at differing levels in each center, the depth of interest and motivation for undertaking coordinated research and at the same time survey the clinical and research resources available. Through intensive work in conjunction with consultants and research centers, we hoped to arrive at progressive approximations representing a reasonable balance between such factors as precision of measurement, adequacy of controls, potential contribution to the advancement of basic knowledge, investment of manpower, facilities, and financial resources.

3. Keep a record of information and evaluations thus obtained which would eventually form the basis of a detailed report on the feasibility of specified collaborative research projects. With this goal in mind, we gave special attention to the following considerations: (*a*) that several models or designs for collaboration might prove feasible and they might or might not be like those implemented in other fields; (*b*) that the planning should aim for ends which could not be accomplished by individual investigators or agencies; (*c*) that master plans might include core variables and standardized measurements, but would not preclude measures preferred by or unique to any cooperating therapist or treatment center; (*d*) that it is important to be cognizant of the potential value of a variety of therapeutic techniques, influences, and innovations which have not yet been studied extensively but which might be profitably included in future research, such as any of a variety of group techniques, nonprofessional and natural therapeutic influences, personality

---

[2] These designs followed classical experimental models involving therapy, control, and other technique comparison groups along with rigorous selection procedures and preoutcome and postoutcome measures. They were heavily influenced by the tradition of outcome experimentation associated with H. J. Eysenck, C. R. Rogers, R. I. Watson, M. Scriven, D. J. Kiesler, etc.

change under induced emotional arousal, etc.; and (e) that a central coordinating mechanism for collaboration would have to evolve from our efforts and our report if one or more projects were actually implemented.

4. Devote the first year primarily to the testing of feasibility, development of a research plan (or several alternate plans), including identification of potential participants, investigators, clinical settings, and patient populations. Should a collaborative study of major consequence appear unfeasible, then the planning phase would terminate and a final substantive report would be submitted. However, should the indications be positive, the planning would move into the second year. We would then devote more of our energies to·actually working out specific details needed for mounting a study. This would involve obtaining specific commitments from potential collaborators and then deciding on a specific plan of study with appropriate design and specific measuring instruments, control variables, screening and selection procedures, procedures of selecting and training of raters, and the actual implementation of pilot work.

Consultants were selected in terms of their known expertise and their potential contribution to the objectives outlined in the foregoing. Prior to our visits, we sent each person a copy of our review, the grant proposal, and a set of 18 questions which we had formulated as stimuli for discussion.[3] Between October 1968 and July 1969, we spent from half a day to a full day with the following consultants: Arnold A. Lazarus, Lester Luborsky, Arthur H. Auerbach, Lyle D. Schmidt, Stanley R. Strong, Paul E. Meehl, Bernard F. Riess, Howard F. Hunt, Arnold P. Goldstein, Thomas S. Szasz, Gerald C. Davison, Bernard Weitzman, J. B. Chassan, Kenneth Mark Colby, Albert Bandura, Robert S. Wallerstein, Harold Sampson, Louis Breger, Howard Levine, Ralph Greenson, Milton Wexler, Carl R. Rogers, Joseph D. Matarazzo, Charles B. Truax, Neal E. Miller, Henry Linford, Peter Knapp (with Martin A. Jacobs, Louis Vachon, and Douglas M. McNair), John M. Shlien, David Bakan, Jerome D. Frank, Peter J. Lang, and Marvin Smith.

Following each visit, we independently prepared critical résumés based on notes taken during the meeting. In addition to exchanging these documents, we prepared various working papers, met

---

[3].Copies of the stimulus questions used during these interviews may be obtained from either of the authors. Résumés of the interviews will comprise a substantial portion of our third and final report.

at regular intervals for the purpose of assessing the progress of our endeavor, read extensively (often following up on suggestions made by the consultants), and shared our impressions with selected colleagues. The extent of this material is evidenced by approximately 500 pages of manuscript, which remain to be organized and digested for publication at a later date.

Publication of the present paper is based on a sense of urgency to communicate to colleagues our major conclusions at the earliest possible time. Pending later elaboration and documentation of our findings in the form of a more extensive publication, we are presenting our conclusions with a minimum of context and only limited justification. It should be emphasized that these conclusions represent a synthesis of our own views and those held by prominent persons in the field. Needless to say, we are expressing our personal interpretations and judgments concerning the status of the field, which are not necessarily shared by our consultants.

CONCLUSIONS REGARDING COLLABORATIVE STUDIES

(1) Based on a large number of convergent considerations, we have reluctantly reached the conclusion that large-scale, multifactorial studies of the kind sketched by other investigators and ourselves are not feasible at the present time or in the immediate future. On balance, we believe that the expectable returns, in terms of research findings that might contribute to the accretion of knowledge as well as practical applications of such findings, do not justify the very considerable investment of manpower and financial support which such studies would inevitably entail. In stating this decision, we are not saying that such studies are in principle futile or that all efforts at collaboration on large-scale ventures should be abandoned; however, we are asserting that the *likelihood* of success at the present time impresses us as low or at least incommensurate with the required expenditures in terms of effort, manpower, and funds. Major reasons supporting this judgment include the following:

(a) Because of the complex interactions among patient, therapist, technique, and socio-environmental variables, it will prove extraordinarily difficult to isolate the effects of one or a limited number of variables, with the result that large-scale multifactorial studies are almost certain to lead to "weak" results. As a corollary, the necessary experimental controls which would be required to counteract these tendencies are virtually impossible to achieve at the present time, a problem which is aggravated if studies are carried out in different locations by therapists of diverse theoretical orientations whose techniques (even within a given "school") are bound to be heterogeneous and on patient samples whose homogeneity may be questionable.

(b) Because the preceding weaknesses of large-scale studies will not be remediable in the near future, it is predictable that such studies will have minimal effect on prevailing practices and are not likely to sway clinicians from their personal beliefs.

(c) There are virtually no research centers which would be willing or able to observe meticulously the requirements called for by large-scale efforts.

(d) With few exceptions, we found insufficient motivation and commitment on the part of leading researchers and clinicians to design and execute such studies.

(e) The implementation of large-scale studies necessitates the creation of complex administrative machinery which would be costly to inaugurate and maintain. In view of the foregoing factors, it seems unlikely that a central coordinating agency, even if it had broad executive powers, would be able to effectively implement the necessarily stringent design and bring to a successful conclusion the elaborative data collection and analysis.

(f) Large-scale studies would at best serve as demonstrations that one set of techniques seems to be preferable to another set of techniques under broadly defined conditions, but they are not likely to shed much light on specific mechanisms of psychological change, specific techniques that might be necessary to produce such changes in patients of a certain "type," and the nature of therapeutic change. Stated otherwise, we believe that such studies will add only insignificant amounts to existing scientific knowledge.

(g) In view of the current state of knowledge and technology in the area, it is considered more desirable to encourage research developments along lines other than large-scale collaborative studies, such as systematic research on basic mechanisms, naturalistic observations of psychological change, and intensive study of single cases.

The foregoing conclusion will be more fully documented at a later time. At this point, it is important to note, however, that we approached the issue of collaborative research with a positive bias (Strupp & Bergin, 1969a) and came away with a much less optimistic conclusion.

(2) While collaboration on a large scale does not appear propitious at this time, more efforts at coordination should be encouraged. For one thing, it is considered essential to improve communication, exchange of research ideas, plans, and research findings among productive investigators, and to stimulate collaboration on smaller scale projects. We have begun to explore several possibilities and shall devote further effort toward this objective. Under such arrangements, investigators might begin to apply common measures in their respective studies, pool research data, and design coordinated studies which would directly further their research programs. A few attempts in this direction have already occurred, but more are needed. For our own part, we expect to devote a portion of our own future effort to the furtherance of this kind of small-scale collaboration.

CONCLUSIONS REGARDING OTHER DIRECTIONS OF THERAPY RESEARCH

While our primary goal was to determine the feasibility of large collaborative efforts, a corollary objective was to explore theoretical issues, research strategies, therapeutic techniques, and relevant variables in order to determine whether selective research emphases might possibly accelerate advances in the field. Some of our salient conclusions follow. Again, because of space limitations, they are presented without documentation; however, we believe that each assertion can be adequately defended, which will be a task for our final report.

(3) We have become convinced that further study of the therapeutic process and evaluations of outcomes resulting from traditional therapeutic practice offer little hope for significant scientific advance. While such studies may further expand our understanding of the therapeutic process and lead to refinements of traditional procedures, the potential yield resulting from pursuing other pathways appears incomparably greater. One exception would be to study the performance of unusual therapists. In this case, one might, through naturalistic study, succeed in extracting from their performance principles or strategies that make their therapeutic operations unusually effective.

Even here, however, the inquiry may be expected to lead rapidly to the formulation of new techniques on the basis of the principles so extracted.

The foregoing conclusion is of course a relative judgment. No doubt, further inquiry into psychotherapy as it is ordinarily practiced will continue to bear fruit, particularly if such studies are systematic and increasingly responsive to the special problems in the area. However, at present there is no "normal science" in Kuhn's (1962) sense in psychotherapy; therefore, research in the area is not likely to lead to a questioning of a "paradigm," and even less to a "revolution." In general, no field of scientific inquiry can probably be advanced by synthetic efforts, and lines of advance are impossible to predict. Nevertheless, we venture the prognostication that in psychotherapy, advances will not come from dissection of the therapeutic process as it generally occurs, no matter how precise or sophisticated such studies become. Instead, new departures appear called for. As we see it, this means a movement away from the gross, complex, and relatively nonspecific traditional therapeutic operations. Stated positively, we must achieve greater specificity and, concomitantly, greater power in the sense of making therapeutic operations and strategies count therapeutically. Efforts in this direction would also make technique more adequately teachable and learnable.

(4) While there is limited promise in the naturalistic study of the therapeutic process, there does seem to be a significant source of hypotheses and methods in the observation of spontaneous change processes which occur in the natural course of life events. It seems likely that a careful study of "the psychotherapy of everyday life" will yield valuable results. Accordingly, at the present stage of knowledge it may be valuable to study in greater depth "experiments of nature." Many examples in other sciences (e.g., the discovery of Vitamin C) underscore the merit of this approach. It has frequently been pointed out that the study of complex psychological processes requires approaches that are radically different from those employed in the physical and biological sciences, but the implications of this proposition still remain to be taken seriously. We have in mind studies that might deal with documentation of conditions under which personality changes occur "naturally," a "natural history of the neuroses," and similar investigations. Such work may also lead to new ideas regarding methods which will more effec-

tively and more straightforwardly produce desired personality change.[4]

(5) The influence of behavioristic therapies has become an important phenomenon of the 1960s and cannot be overlooked in stating conclusions about the status of the field. The new techniques, case study methodologies, research evaluations, and general style of inquiry and innovation which have been implemented by this group have stimulated considerable optimism and controversy. The number of new journals, research studies, and young people opting for this approach is impressive; however, all innovations are subject to a kind of fadism, and behavior therapy is clearly no exception. There are exaggerated claims and a certain zealousness or tendency to rigidify ideas and techniques; but in spite of these signs, which are held in common with most innovations, there appears to be more substance to this movement than is typical of fads.

While the behavioristic theories which presumably underlie this approach are difficult to justify and defend, there have been other conceptual contributions coming forth which are worth noting. The first of these is the notion of *specificity*. Not that human behavior or the human psyche is a collection of specific mechanical connections of the kind found in an automobile engine, but it is assumed that there are identifiable mechanisms which have reasonably homogeneous effects and which can be manipulated with a greater degree of specificity than has been historically associated with the practice of psychotherapy.

This manner of thinking, though it is spawned by a weak and probably irrelevant theory, is a most significant contribution in that it has dramatically brought the therapeutic domain within a much more objective frame of reference. Thus, while we may object to some of the exaggerated claims and theoretical weaknesses associated with this point of view, we must acknowledge the

[4] Up to this point, and again in Conclusions 15–21, the authors generally concur; however, on several specific points our emphases and interpretations differ. For this reason, Conclusions 5–14 were written independently and are presented with initials identifying the respective author. While we agreed on the major recommendation concerning the potential value of the intensive study of individual cases embodying experimental interventions (Bergin's Conclusion 9 and Strupp's Conclusion 14), the reasoning underlying this recommendation is partly based on divergent theoretical biases and interpretations of the current status of the field; therefore, we considered it advisable to present our respective formulations of that issue separately also.

power of its methodological contribution and its conceptual tools. These conceptual tools have to do with notions of simplifying nature and making it manageable.

Thus, the field may well owe the behaviorists a very real debt, but it is probably not the one which they would most like to be remembered for. Their demonstration that it is possible to focus on specific mechanisms within a highly complex context is a signal contribution. Surely the mechanisms and theories of the future will look far different from the picture thus far painted by arch-behaviorists, but the process by which we arrive at these new conceptions will have been facilitated and shaped to a great extent by the focused, penetrating work of these particular innovators. (AB)

(6) It is most interesting that the behavioral approach, in bringing about a focus on the mechanics of change, has elicited a new interest in cognitive processes. This new interest is evident in Bandura's (1969) emphasis on cognitive mediation processes, even though he still argues for a basically neobehavioral viewpoint; in the work of those doing cognitive desensitization (Davison & Valins, 1969; Marcia, Rubin, & Efran, 1969; Valins & Ray, 1967); in the use of conceptual and symbolic processes by the groups who are conducting instrumental conditioning of autonomic responses (Lang, Sroufe, & Hastings, 1967; Miller, 1969); and in the increasing evidence of cognitive mediation or control of classical conditioning processes in human Ss (Murray & Jacobson, 1970).

While this domain has only begun to be exploited and has hardly been conceptualized with rigor, it is further evidence of the notion that the behavioral style of inquiry can bear fruit with regard to discovering the mechanisms of change, even though these mechanisms may bear little relation to behavioral theory.

Thus, we may be on the threshold of discoveries within the realm of cognitive processes which will permit understanding and control over powerful change mechanisms. The intimations drawn thus far from preliminary experimentations are impressive. The fact that a man's heart rate can be modified by focusing his own symbolic processes on his bodily activity is an accidental by-product of conditioning studies which is intriguing. If this work is expanded and adequately replicated, we may be able to grasp the mechanics of personality and behavior change as it flows from conceptual reorganization. Thus, the behaviorists would have unintentionally provided new knowledge of a dominant process in traditional therapies, a process which had long been considered of fundamental importance in personality reconstruction. If that happens, it will be further proof that progress in complex domains is achieved by a zealous devotion to objectivity and by a willingness to simplify and experiment rather than simply sit back and watch the complex process flow naturally. (AB)

(7) Further evidence of the virtue of simplification and specificity is gained by observing the contributions which the client-centered group have made in extracting, measuring, and testing the effects of supposedly single variables like empathy or warmth. Even though it is now clear that these variables are more complex than originally appeared, the study of them has made a rich contribution to the therapeutic research literature, and the results have stimulated a renewed focus on relationship factors in the therapeutic enterprise. It seems unlikely that this knowledge would have developed if the researchers involved had not specified some particular influences and then studied them assiduously while at the same time ignoring much of the surrounding context and complexity. Indeed, some of the authors have made this point quite clear in referring to the fact that variables such as warmth and empathy account for only a minority of the variance in outcome. At the same time, these procedures seem to be powerful, and their potency has been brought out by isolating them from their context to an extent (Truax & Carkhuff, 1967).

While research in psychoanalysis and related interventions seems not to have produced a great deal in the way of empirical validity or technique innovation, this does not mean that the practice of these procedures is to be ignored. Clearly, many of the same processes which operate here must also operate in other therapies, and it is conceivable that powerful processes will yet be extracted and manipulated in a more experimental way from within this framework. (AB)

(8) The fruitfulness of attempts to simplify, isolate, extract, and manipulate new variables from the context of practice does not mean this is the only way to approach the study of the mechanisms of change. The potentialities for applying evidence from diverse areas of psychological research seem considerable. The recent efforts by the Goldstein group at Syracuse University (Goldstein & Simonson, 1970) provide one example from a social psychological frame of reference.

It seems equally likely that the study of cognitive processes, of human development, of motivation and emotion, etc., will prove equally fruitful in their yield of ideas, methods of inquiry, and new technologies.

A general conclusion may be drawn from the foregoing points, namely, that we are in a phase of our history in which we are moving rapidly away from the gross, placebo-laden, general doctor–patient relationship influence in therapy. We are moving more rapidly toward an understanding of the mechanisms of change and toward a more explicit technology of behavior and personality modification based on the substantive evidential base of the behavioral sciences. It seems that these efforts should be encouraged. They underline the importance of a departure from traditional procedures while at the same time not indulging in a premature commitment to fads. A commitment to the study of the mechanisms of change, their experimental refinement, and their practical elaboration will probably bear greater fruit than other potential approaches.

It is important to note here that the strategy of simplification need not and should not ignore the complexity of personality functioning and change. However, it is unlikely that the complex gestalt of behavior change in the clinic will ever be fully understood and placed under our control unless we first break it down into its part processes. Once this is achieved, we may then put the parts back together again, as building blocks, in order to match the degree of complexity required for practical purposes. This concept is discussed and illustrated in the next section. (AB)

(9) As for a general paradigm of inquiry, the individual experimental case study and the experimental analogue approaches appear to be the primary strategies which will move us forward in our understanding of the mechanisms of change at this point. Other strategies, such as the possible derivations from general psychology, the potential leads from the naturalistic study of "spontaneous" and traditional therapeutic change, and from field trials on large groups of cases will all be fruitful,

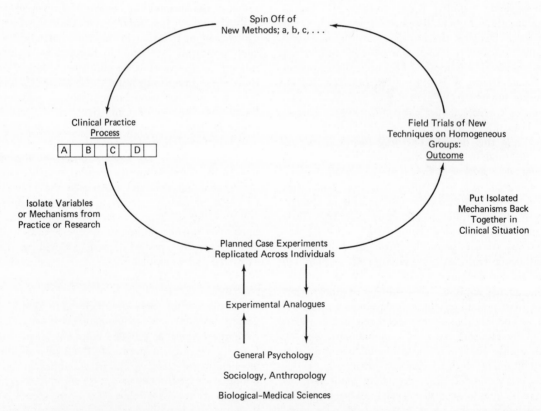

Figure 1. The process of therapy technique development and refinement. (The lower half of the diagram illustrates the process of isolating, testing, and manipulating change mechanisms, the upper half extrapolation from research programs to clinical practice.)

and they are all necessarily interrelated. However, the cycle of interrelationship which exists among these styles of inquiry will probably be put in motion more effectively at this time in history by a greater focus on the two processes just mentioned. Obviously, such a focus will have to be more a matter of emphasis than a matter of exclusion since it would be impossible to concentrate on them totally exclusively, for scientific fertility is bred by the natural interaction of this diverse range of approaches.

The details of the foregoing system of inquiry using the analogue and case study approaches as foci need substantial elaboration and discussion. While this will be one of the prime objectives of a later document, a further description of this schema is referred to in Figure 1.

It may be observed there that ideas about change mechanisms are likely to derive either from clinical phenomena or from behavioral science research. They may then be subjected to testing, experimentation, and refinement by means of analogue studies and single case experiments. For example, if empathic responding were the variable in question, its nature might be clarified by traditional laboratory-type empathy studies, and then variations in "live" empathy might be programmed into a case study in order to observe its specific clinical effects, as Truax and Carkhuff (1965) have done. Once the morphology of this therapeutic agent and its effects on given symptoms are defined by means of quantitative case studies, then field trials on larger samples of homogeneous cases could be conducted to demonstrate its clinical usefulness. After clinical validity was established, the procedure could be incorporated into the repertoire of clinical practices.

On the other hand, single case experiments could reveal that the procedure is ineffective or needs modification or amalgamation with other procedures. This might stimulate further analogue research or immediate modifications in the case study situation until a procedure is derived that does have the desired effects on given types of cases or symptoms. It should be clear, in any event, that the process is especially one of *technique building* and not simply *technique testing*, that this process of technique development is centrally located in the quantitative experimental case study where interventions are planned, their effects monitored, and their format modified until results are obtained. (AB)

(10) The preceding conclusions provide a clear basis for avoiding further classical therapy outcome studies of the type that compares changes due to a heterogeneous set of interventions called "psychotherapy" applied to a heterogeneous patient sample with changes in an equally diverse control group which exists under unknown psychological conditions (Bergin, 1970). This means a departure from old-technique testing to new-technique building and requires application of specific techniques to specific problems under controlled conditions of the type stipulated for experimental case studies and subsequent field trials.

It is hoped that action along the lines of Conclusions 9 and 10 would tend to mold research and practice together and thus bridge the traditional gap between the two which has retarded progress in this field. At the same time it should more readily yield new methods of therapy which will have more specific, differential applicability to given symptoms and syndromes than traditional broad spectrum, undifferentiated techniques. (AB)

(11) During the last decade, the field of psychotherapy has undergone considerable proliferation. Concomitantly, the classical model of psychotherapy, exemplified by the psychoanalytic situation, has receded to the background and largely lost its appeal to therapists and patients. Originally conceptualized as a form of medical treatment, the meaning of the term psychotherapy has become increasingly fuzzy and more than ever defies precise definition. Diverse human interactions, from individual psychotherapy to encounter groups, from aversive conditioning in the laboratory to token economies in mental hospitals, are subsumed under the heading of psychotherapy or under the new rubric, behavior modification. To characterize the field as chaotic is hardly an exaggeration.

Particularly noteworthy in this respect is the emergency of a wide diversity of new techniques and therapeutic modalities, most of which may be viewed as a response to modern man's insistent clamor for self-awareness, interpersonal intimacy, surcease from alienation, and the constraints of a "sick" society. New treatment methods in this area, it may be observed, do not arise from the efforts of researchers or as a result of experimentation in the laboratory; instead, they emerge in response to social needs which are met by the ingenuity or inventiveness of charismatic therapists whose individual temperament and philosophy of life are thoroughly intertwined with the therapeutic approach they espouse. The "system" or "theory of psychotherapy" propounded by them is inevitably a belated attempt to conceptualize what they have found to be of pragmatic value. Obviously, this is not to deny that theories of psychotherapy contain important psychological principles, although often, because of divergent conceptualizations, they are impossible to compare. It follows that (a) new techniques in psychotherapy, unlike new drugs, are not developed in the laboratory, tested, and then applied, but typically are "invented" and applied long before they are tested; (b) psychotherapeutic techniques are very loosely articulated to theories of psychotherapy, which largely preclude the testing of any theoretical formulation per se; (c) the researcher in psychotherapy, in comparison to the innovative clinician, has been relatively uninfluential as far as developments in the field are concerned; (d) the field of psychotherapy is at an extremely rudimentary stage of development, and it seems safe to predict that neither research nor clinical ingenuity are about to produce a dazzling technology for psychotherapeutic change (measured against what therapists have been able to accomplish in the past). This is not to assert that the field can afford to rest content with its achievements or that progress is impossible; however, it seems only realistic to recognize the formidable difficulties confronting both clinicians and researchers in this murky field.

I conclude that the field as a whole is currently beset with innumerable fads, considerable conceptual unclarity, muddy theories, and grossly unwarranted claims for the effectiveness of simplistic techniques. All of these factors have conspired to impede progress and to retard dispassionate examination of basic scientific issues. There exists at present a dire need for separating the wheat from the chaff, for taking full advantage of earlier insights which, in terms of their sophistication, often surpass contemporary formulations, and for discarding obsolete theoretical notions which have questionable relevance to empirical data. Withal, a serious return to empirical data is imperative. (HS)

(12) While the preceding conclusion has emphasized the arena of clinical practice, it is equally important to acknowledge the substantial growth of research in psychotherapy since the late 1950s, supported by a new wave of enthusiasm. The preponderance of this work has been inspired by behavior oriented researchers and, to a lesser extent, by client-centered investigators, whereas psychoanalytically oriented workers have all but abdicated serious research interest. It seems premature to assess the lasting value or promise of these endeavors, a fair segment of which must certainly be characterized as crude; however, there can be no doubt that the work has had the inestimable merit of providing a renewed focus on empirical data which had become all but lost in sterile discussions about the relative merits of theoretical propositions. Furthermore, there is an increasing recognition that psychotherapy (in the sense in which I propose to use the term) consists of a set of specifiable technical operations to reach specifiable objectives. If this assumption is granted, it follows that we must work toward the specification of problems we seek to solve as psychotherapists, the goals we aim to achieve, and the procedures we employ to reach these objectives. Thus, if psychotherapy in an important sense is a technology, we must concede that a set of technical operations can be more or less effective in reaching a particular goal. While psychotherapy is likely to remain a practical art for a long time, the task of the researcher is to document, with increasing precision, the conditions under which a therapeutic strategy or a set of techniques forming part of that strategy is relatively effective or ineffective. Accordingly, he must succeed in defining "the problem" (that is, the patient state to be modified), the kinds of personality and behavior changes to be achieved, and the procedures to be employed in reaching them. In short, the therapist and the researcher must become increasingly explicit about the operations of psychotherapy and the nature of the therapist's influence. Existing knowledge, while undoubtedly embodying important psychological principles, is altogether too general, broad-gauged, and imprecise. It can be concluded then that future research in this area must firmly rest on empirical data; it must tend toward increasing explicitness and specificity; and it must seek to isolate psychological principles embedded in, and often obscured by, divergent theoretical formulations. (HS)

(13) There has been insufficient clarity about the role of the researcher in psychotherapy and the kinds of contributions he may reasonably be expected to make. The fact is that to date

research has exerted little influence on clinical practice, and the clinical work of therapists has generally not been informed, much less altered, by empirical research results. It is possible that the researcher's insistence on empirical evidence and intersubjective verification has subtly modified the attitudes, at least of the younger therapists, toward the subject matter, but that influence appears to be rather intangible. An incisive examination of this issue would far exceed the scope of this paper, but, perhaps somewhat cavalierly, it may be concluded that the researcher has not provided the clinician with insights or useful information which he can employ in his daily work. However, there may be an important lesson from scores of studies that almost any set of procedures in the context of a benign human relationship, presented to, or viewed by, the patient as having therapeutic value, will result in psychological or behavior change describable as therapeutic. At times, such changes produced by nonspecific techniques may be quite impressive and rival in significance those attributed to planned technical interventions. As a corollary, it may be noted that the theoretical formulations invoked by the therapist to explain the effects of his work may grossly lack parsimony and be deficient on other grounds.

Despite certain appearances to the contrary, research in psychotherapy, as it has evolved since approximately 1940, has failed to provide incisive answers to important issues, such as the problem of outcome, the relative effectiveness of different techniques, etc. While a form of cultural lag may in part be responsible, the prevailing investigative model may not be the proper one to use. For example, the clinician has no way of using statistical trends based on mean differences between samples of broadly defined patient groups; he cannot be guided by findings that certain diffuse techniques *in general* tend to lead to certain patient responses under poorly defined conditions, etc. (This view is expanded in Conclusion 18.)

As one of our consultants, Colby, has pointed out, not everything can be a problem for the scientist at the same time, and for fruitful results to occur it is of crucial importance to ask questions which permit relatively unequivocal answers. In psychotherapy research, it appears, we have not yet reached great sophistication in asking the "right" questions. (HS)

(14) The field urgently needs greater collaboration of a different sort. We need improved communication between clinicians and researchers, and between researchers of divergent theoretical orientations. I believe Scriven (1964) is correct in asserting that progress in psychology is hampered not by a lack of knowledge but rather by a surfeit of commonsense knowledge shared by all individuals (e.g., the effects of reward or punishment on behavior). Since the time of Freud, largely as a function of his contributions which remain close to empirical observations, therapists have acquired a vast fund of knowledge, exemplified by man's ingenious tendencies to hide painful truths from himself, to disguise to himself and others primitive and self-defeating beliefs which profoundly influence the manner in which he construes himself and others, the profound but hitherto unrecognized effects of early traumatic experiences which have been "stored" in memory, etc. The therapist, above all, is an expert in decoding scrambled human communications which the patient continually sends to himself and others. This fund of knowledge is impressive, but it is largely ignored by researchers and others who restrict their focus to observable behavior. Thus, it is a strange phenomenon that the importance of "cognitive factors" is currently being rediscovered. The point is that clinicians and therapists build as yet insufficiently on each other's work, and because of theoretical or temperamental blinders they reject data which colleagues in other camps have to offer.

It is likewise important to record that the fund of clinical knowledge to which I have referred, poorly formulated as much of it is, has been acquired not through the study of mean differences between samples but through painstaking study of individual cases, by a process of "listening," which is closely akin to Polanyi's (1966) concept of indwelling. Man's capacity for discerning patterns, organization, and structure of beliefs, etc. in another person is infinitely greater than that of any man-made machine or rating instrument, and while the researcher can undoubtedly provide great help in systematizing and objectifying clinical observations, he hamstrings himself if he *substitutes* crude measuring devices for clinical insights instead of *articulating* his observations to the subtle functioning of the sensitive clinician. A wedding of clinical observation and research operations has yet to occur. From everything that has been said, it follows that significant increments in knowledge, at least within the therapeutic framework, are likely to come from the intensive study of individual cases in which disciplined observation is complemented by, and takes account of, the complex interaction of variables, a task which cannot be accomplished by statistical manipulations, although certain statistical techniques may be helpful in other respects.

It is conceivable that significant advances in the area will not come from within the traditional clinical framework, since it will prove extraordinarily difficult to disentangle the clinical complexities. It is also questionable whether "part processes" can be productively simulated in the laboratory or in quasi-therapeutic situations. Thus, it appears that new insights may come either from basic research in disparate areas, or, stated less esoterically, through a combination of clinical and experimental methods within the clinical context. In the latter kind of investigation, it may be possible to introduce, at selected points in time, specific experimental interventions whose effects, albeit in a relatively gross way, may then be assessed. This approach is reminiscent of the work of all clinical innovators, from Freud to Alexander to the behavior therapists, in which experimentation with relatively specific techniques occurs within the clinical situation. The current research on therapeutic learning through conditioning of autonomic responses (as pioneered by Miller, 1969) may be an important area for significant advances.

There is no question that greater specificity and a return to empirical data are absolutely essential, but it seems unlikely that the therapeutic process can effectively be broken down into "parts" which can be studied in isolation (e.g., the research on "empathy"), and then be "reassembled." The scientist, as Colby observed, must first isolate a problem he can do something about and he must then test its limits. The identification of important problems is solely a function of his ingenuity and intuition, and no prescriptions can be given.

As part of this effort, we need to achieve greater clarity concerning the principles of psychological change at work in all forms of psychotherapy and to articulate them to relatively specific therapeutic operations. Comparable to the researcher, the therapist must learn to recognize problems he can do something about and to employ better strategies to reach a particular goal. With varying degrees of emphasis, all forms of psychotherapy employ a limited number of psychological prin-

ciples, but the theoretical formulations in which they are couched typically obfuscate these commonalities. The task of reformulating these principles in terms which do greater justice to the phenomena in need of explanation remains an important assignment for the future. (HS)

(15) The foregoing set of conclusions embodies of course certain guidelines for the kinds of research directions we consider promising, investigations we ourselves might undertake or which we, as individual researchers, would find congenial. It would seem presumptuous, however, to make categorical assertions about the potential promise of research proposed or currently being carried forward by other investigators. No one can forecast future developments in as poorly developed a scientific discipline as psychotherapy, and as indicated previously, significant increments in knowledge may come from quite unsuspected sources. For this reason, too, it appears unwise at the present state of knowledge to propose complex research programs or to recommend the creation of research centers or institutes which might undertake concerted research efforts to "solve" specific problems in the area. Since we cannot identify the nature of the problems currently capable of solution and for other reasons, it appears best to leave the initiative for creative work with individual investigators who may succeed in bringing new ingenuity to bear on the field. However, we feel that the time for discerning a new gestalt in the multifarious concepts and bits of evidence may not be too far off. Intuitively, we feel that future research will build on and produce a closer integration between experimental and clinical approaches.

(16) The foregoing conclusions clearly imply certain negative recommendations, that is, classes of investigations which we consider to be of limited promise at the present time or in the foreseeable future. This list prominently includes large-scale collaborative studies, naturalistic studies of psychotherapy as it is usually practiced (see Conclusion 3), traditional outcome studies, comparative outcome studies pitting broad-gauged therapeutic techniques against each other, and studies attempting to evaluate the respective merits of divergent theoretical orientations. Our emphasis on studies dealing with the mechanisms of psychological change regardless of which particular "school" has laid proprietary claims to them suggest the desirability of "retiring brand names" (see Bandura's [1969] description) which

at present continue to befog major issues in the field.

(17) We also wish to note the great importance of wedding the study of change more closely to biological disciplines. The recent successes in instrumentally conditioning visceral responses and the advances in behavioral genetics are only two of several strands of evidence which have convinced us that research in therapy will be more fruitful when coordinated more closely with that of specialists in biological areas. We witness today a renewed emphasis on a holistic view of man which is beginning to take seriously the interaction between psychological variables and biological variables. Thus, increasing collaboration between psychologists and biologists should certainly be welcomed. We would like to see a center, for example, where the mechanisms of change were focused upon by various experts in the psychological, medical, and biological aspects of psychosomatic problems.

(18) Among researchers as well as statisticians, there is a growing disaffection from traditional experimental designs and statistical procedures which are held inappropriate to the subject matter under study. The judgment applies with particular force to research in the area of therapeutic change, and our emphasis on the value of experimental case studies underscores this point. We strongly agree that most of the standard experimental designs and statistical procedures have exerted, and are continuing to exert, a constricting effect on fruitful inquiry, and they serve to perpetuate an unwarranted overemphasis on methodology. More accurately, the exaggerated importance accorded experimental and statistical dicta cannot be blamed on the techniques proper—after all, they are merely tools—but their veneration mirrors a prevailing philosophy among behavioral scientists which subordinates problems to methodology. The insidious effects of this trend are tellingly illustrated by the typical graduate student who is often more interested in the details of a factorial design than in the problem he sets out to study; worse, the selection of a problem is dictated by the experimental design. Needless to say, the student's approach faithfully reflects the convictions and teachings of his mentors. With respect to inquiry in the area of psychotherapy, the kinds of effects we need to demonstrate at this point in time should be significant enough so that they are readily observable by inspection or descriptive statistics. If this cannot be done, no fixation upon statistical and mathematical niceties will generate fruitful insights, which obviously can come only from the researcher's understanding of the subject matter and the descriptive data under scrutiny.

This conclusion may be perceived as a rather broad and unwarranted repudiation of hard-won methods of rigor; but we are gratified to note the increasing concurrence in this viewpoint by knowledgeable statisticians (Bakan, 1969; Tukey, 1969).[5]

(19) There is a renewed appreciation that internal, intrapsychic, or experiential processes, whether they be of a feeling or of a cognitive nature, have considerable power to influence bodily processes, behavior, and the general state of the organism. Since these processes are obviously private and unobservable directly, their study will require development of a sophisticated technology for studying private experience. Massive denials of the problem since the time of J. B. Watson have not obviated its importance, and more than ever, it is with us demanding recognition. The revival of interest in cognitive processes is exemplified by recent studies of conditioning which have shown that verbal reports of various kinds are absolutely critical for an understanding of the processes under study. While the behaviorists have traditionally eschewed efforts to conceptualize or *objectify* inner experiences, there is no question that this task can no longer be avoided. To be sure, this is a major technical problem to which scores of psychologists and therapists have made notable contributions (e.g., in the heyday of the dynamic theories) but which has not been blessed by impressive breakthroughs. It will be absolutely necessary to take full account of intrapsychic processes as we seek to imbue the study of psychotherapeutic change with greater specificity, objectivity, and precision. This could be an exciting and productive area of future inquiry beckoning the imaginative researcher.

(20) We are impressed with the impoverished character of the major theories in the area. Running the gamut from psychoanalysis to behaviorism, we fail to see fertile theories emerging.

[5] We do not by this argument deny the significance of the distinctive contributions by psychologists to research on behavior, especially in basic fields, but the unique sophistication of psychologists in experimental design has led to compromises with crucial clinical issues, which implies that a new style of *clinical* research must emerge.

While the global theorizing which has dominated the field of personality has become largely defunct, more appropriate mini-theories centered around specific clusters of data have not emerged. We view the need for new theories as a vital one. Crucial concepts, such as "repression," "defense," "cognitive mediation," "conditioned response," and "experiencing" all need major overhauling or replacement. We view this as a prime task for advancing the field.

(21) We have been deeply impressed with the personal, human aspect of the scientific enterprise which became particularly vivid as a result of visiting a number of people in rapid succession. Largely because of this human element, we came to realize the virtual impossibility of artificially stimulating particular lines of investigation short of massive (and probably futile) external inducements. It is clear that proposals for programmatic inquiry, besides being contingent on a certain maturity of the field of inquiry, must match to a significant extent the basic motivations and personal styles of researchers. Collaboration of any kind must emerge from these personal bases and cannot be superimposed upon them. This is a vital lesson, learned at great expense by the designers of some previous collaborative efforts in other areas. It appears that crucial ingredients for successful collaboration include a confluence of intellectual interests, mutual need, and social rapport among collaborators which can neither be dictated nor deliberately "arranged." Any attempt to mount collaborative efforts must consider these variables to be as central as the scientific ones, regardless of the difficulties they pose.

Numerous addtional points could be made but perhaps these highlights will suffice to indicate the direction of our current thinking and provide interested colleagues with a general picture of our basic conclusions. This project has been a most illuminating experience for us, and we hope our digest adequately conveys to the reader the important shifts in direction we believe are now needed in this field.

REFERENCES

Bakan, D. *On method*. San Francisco: Jossey-Bass, 1969.

Bandura, A. *Principles of behavior modification*. New York: Holt, Rinehart & Winston, 1969.

Bergin, A. E. The evaluation of therapeutic outcomes. In A. E. Bergin & S. L. Garfield (Eds.), *Handbook of psychotherapy and behavior change*. New York: Wiley, 1970, in press.

Bergin, A. E., & Strupp, H. H. The last word (?) on psychotherapy research; a reply. *International Journal of Psychiatry*, 1969, 7, 160–168.

Davison, G. C. & Valins, S. Maintenance of self-attributed and drug-attributed behavior change. *Journal of Personality and Social Psychology*, 1969, *11*, 25–33.

Goldstein, A. P., & Simonson, N. R. Social psychological approaches to psychotherapy research. In A. E. Bergin & S. L. Garfield (Eds.), *Handbook of psychotherapy and behavior change*. New York: Wiley, 1970, in press.

Kuhn, T. S. *The structure of scientific revolutions*. Chicago: University of Chicago Press, 1962.

Lang, P. J., Stroufe, L. A., & Hastings, J. E. Effects of feedback and instructional set on the control of cardiac variability. *Journal of Experimental Psychology*, 1967, 75, 425–431.

Marcia, J. E., Rubin, B. M., & Efran, J. S. Systematic desensitization: Expectancy change or counterconditioning? *Journal of Abnormal Psychology*, 1969, 74, 382–387.

Miller, N. E. Learning of visceral and glandular responses. *Science*, 1969, *163*, 434–445.

Murray, E. J., & Jacobson, L. I. The nature of learning in traditional and behavioral psychotherapy. In A. E. Bergin & S. L. Garfield (Eds.), *Handbook of psychotherapy and behavioral change*. New York: Wiley, 1970, in press.

Polanyi, M. *The tacit dimension*. New York: Doubleday, 1966.

Scriven, M. Views of human nature. In T. W. Wann (Ed.), *Behaviorism and phenomenology*. Chicago: University of Chicago Press, 1964.

Strupp, H. H., & Bergin, A. E. Some empirical and conceptual bases for coordinated research in psychotherapy. *International Journal of Psychiatry*, 1969, 7, 18–90. (a)

Strupp, H. H., & Bergin, A. E. *A bibliography of research in psychotherapy: A critical review of issues, trends, and evidence*. Washington, D.C.: National Institute of Mental Health, 1969. (b)

Truax, C. B., & Carkhuff, R. R. The experimental manipulation of therapeutic conditions. *Journal of Consulting Psychology*, 1965, *29*, 119–124.

Truax, C. B., & Carkhuff, R. R. *Toward effective counseling and psychotherapy*. Chicago: Aldine, 1967.

Tukey, J. W. Analyzing data: Santification or detective work? *American Psychologist*, 1969, *24*, 83–91.

Valins, S., & Ray, A. Effects of cognitive desensitization on avoidance behavior. *Journal of Personality and Social Psychology*, 1967, 7, 345–350.

desensitization, suggestibility, and pseudotherapy

Peter J. Lang, A. David Lazovik, & David J. Reynolds

Positive change in psychotherapy has often been attributed to the relationship established between therapist and client, in the context of treatment. This phenomenon has been variously described as transference, suggestibility, the "hello-good-bye," or placebo effect. Lang and Lazovik (1963) demonstrated that phobic subjects who were briefly exposed to desensitization psychotherapy showed a significantly greater reduction in fear behavior than did untreated controls. The present experiment is an extension of this work, specifically to determine if the obtained change can be assigned to placebo effects.

A psychotherapeutic placebo is not as readily developed as the control medication of drug research. Psychological treatment is usually more prolonged; it involves a more complex interpersonal relationship, and the distinction between a placebo and the clinically effective agent can be less clearly delineated. Furthermore, the institution of a long pseudotreatment is generally impractical in the clinical situation. Not only is it wasteful of the patient's and therapist's time, but the necessary deception and delay of legitimate treatment can seldom be justified, and may be detrimental to the patient's future chances for cure.

These objections had considerably less validity in the experimental context considered here, which offered an opportunity to employ a stringent placebo control group. The subjects used in this research displayed phobic reactions to nonpoisonous snakes of considerable intensity. They systematically avoided snakes or places such as zoos or camping trips where they might be found. These individuals behaved so "unrealistically" as to react with anxiety not only to snakes themselves, but to pictures of snakes, artifacts (a snakeskin belt), similar shapes, or the mere mention of the word. Nightmares concerning snakes were not uncommon in this group. Such statements, descriptive of their fear, as the following have been recorded: "There's nothing in the world that I'm more afraid of than snakes." "I'm just weak when I see one." "I don't even want to look at them in books." In nearly all respects, except the degree to which the phobia is an omnipresent source of concern, this fear resembled those that patients themselves bring to the attention of psychiatrists and psychologists.

However, these subjects were not drawn from a clinical population, but were selected from among normal college students by a classroom questionnaire and subsequent interview (their frequency is approximately one or two per hundred students surveyed). They volunteered to participate in an experiment on psychotherapy. They were instructed that the procedures used might reduce or eliminate their fear, but that the main purpose of the project was a scientific evaluation of different therapy methods.

The advantages of working with this population are obvious. Treatment can be specific. The number of sessions may be arbitrarily controlled. The moral responsibility to choose the best treatment is not involved. As this phobia is not a central life problem and these subjects were generally more stable than patients, extratherapeutic incidents less frequently interfere with the therapy process. Most important, the necessary rigor of experimental procedure can be closely respected.

This research was supported by Public Health Service Grant M-3880, from the National Institute of Mental Health. The authors would like to thank J. Geer, R. Miller, R. Romano, and Jean Wilkinson, who participated as therapists in this project. Appreciation is also expressed to Lynne Norris and R. Wiater, who assisted in organizing the data collection and analysing the results.

Reprinted from *Journal of Abnormal Psychology*, 1965, *70*, pp. 395–402. Copyright 1965 by the American Psychological Association and reproduced by permission.

As in all translations of natural events into a laboratory context, something is lost in vivacity. In this case, some of the subject characteristics mentioned above, the rigidity of procedure, are obviously different from what is characteristically found in the consulting room. However, much can be gained in the exactness and clarity with which natural events are elucidated. Thus, the present study does not constitute a clinical test of desensitization therapy (clinical statistics have already been reported by Wolpe, 1958), but it is rather an attempt to illuminate through experiment the mechanism by which fear reduction is achieved in this method. Specifically, this research is designed to determine if placebo effects account for the positive results achieved by systematic desensitization therapy, and also to evaluate the overall contribution of suggestibility, as a personality trait, to progress in desensitization and posttherapy fear reduction.

METHOD

Desensitization Therapy

The procedure has been described in detail elsewhere (Lang & Lazovik, 1963; Lazovik & Lang, 1960). Each subject first experienced 5 training sessions. At this time an *anxiety hierarchy* was constructed—a series of 20 phobic situations graded from least to most frightening. The subject was also trained in hypnosis and deep-muscle relaxation (Jacobson, 1938). Subsequently he participated in 11 desensitization sessions. During these meetings he was hypnotized and instructed to vividly imagine the scenes described in the hierarchy.[1] The scenes were presented one at a time, starting with the least frightening, and repeated until the subject no longer reported coincident anxiety. This desensitization occurred in the context of deep-muscle relaxation, which is held to counter condition or "reciprocally inhibit" (Wolpe, 1958) the fear response. Sessions lasted approximately 45 minutes at the rate of 1 or 2 per week.

Pseudotherapy

An effort was made to involve the subject in a treatment procedure which was therapeutically neutral except for the therapist–client relationship. Because desensitization was to be eval-

[1] Six recently treated subjects experienced densitization without hypnosis.

uated, all procedures employed in that method were included in pseudotherapy. The subjects first experienced the same 5 training sessions as in desensitization, followed by 11 pseudotherapy sessions. The procedure for each of these latter sessions was the same. The subject was first hypnotized and then told to relax deeply. During the first 15 minutes of the therapy hour the subject was asked to imagine a series of scenes, which he had previously described as pleasant and relaxing. The last half hour was keyed to the hierarchy items. The items were taken in order during the course of therapy, and provided starting points for a discussion of nonanxiety evoking aspects of the subject's life. The therapist generally behaved in a nondirective manner. However, he did attempt to prevent phobic responses from being made in the context of the therapy hour. It was held that the occurrence of phobic verbal behavior could lead to positive change, for the same reason that theory predicts it in desensitization, that is, inhibition of anxiety by relaxation or comfort responses instigated by the therapist. Thus, the pseudotherapist gently steered the conversation away from phobic or other sensitive material— in the main, by reinforcing nonsensitive topics with nods and verbal signs of his attention, and failing to similarly reinforce comments directly pertinent to the subject's fear. For example, if the hierarchy item concerned a black snake at the farm of an uncle, the developing conversation might concern farms or farm animals, or experiences with the uncle, whatever the subject spontaneously brought up that did not directly refer to his anxieties.

The theoretical orientation given these subjects facilitated the pseudotherapist's task. In the first session the following explanation of procedure was offered:

"Perhaps if I impart a little bit of psychological theory to you, it will help you understand our next procedure. You have learned how to relax your muscles and this is going to be important in dealing with your fear. Previous research suggests that people with fears like yours have higher levels of autonomic tonus than others. What this means is that all the vegetative systems, digestive, circulatory, as well as the neural and muscular systems tend to overreact. They overreact mainly because they actually start from a higher level of tonus. Some psychologists hold that if this generally high tonus level could be reduced, the way would be paved for a general reduction in specific fears.

"What we hope to do in the rest of our sessions together is help you achieve a general lowering of the tonus levels. We will do this by first having you relax as you have learned to do. Then you will be hypnotized and even deeper relaxation will be achieved. To facilitate this process we will suggest pleasant scenes, from time to time, for you to concentrate on.

"As you probably know, fears such as yours are often related to situations which seem unimportant. After you are comfortable, that is deeply relaxed, we will want to begin a discussion with some of the items you used in the fear hierarchy. We will use these as starting points in our talks but plan to deviate from them. Our goal is to explore a number of areas of living, and produce a lowering of your overall tension levels. The theory holds that a person may overcome his fear if he obtains a better understanding of himself and learns to deeply relax."

The subjects participated eagerly. They came regularly and none discontinued treatment before the end of the experiment. Furthermore, no subject reported that he suspected he was involved in a nonviable treatment. The therapists reported consistently close, emphatic relationships with these subjects, comparable or superior to those achieved during desensitization.[2]

Subjects

This research has been underway continuously since September 1960, and the present report describes the total sample of 44 subjects. Included are 23 desensitization subjects, 11 untreated controls, and 10 subjects who participated in pseudotherapy.[3]

All subjects were introductory psychology students at the University of Pittsburgh. They

[2] Two factors probably helped considerably to insure that the pseudotherapist was not unmasked: (a) treatment was relatively brief, (b) metropolitan residents were being treated for a snake phobia. Therefore, subjects had little or no contact with the phobic object outside of the experimental situation. If subjects were treated for a more omnipresent fear over a longer time period, unfavorable feedback from the life situation might make the deception much more difficult to maintain.

[3] The untreated subjects and 13 desensitization subjects were described in a previous report (Lang & Lazovick, 1963). All desensitization subjects were combined as there was no significant difference between this 1963 group and subjects who have since participated, either in selection method or results on the major assessment variables. Change scores for the 1963 sample and all other subsequent desensitization subjects were, respectively: avoidance test, .23 and .32; fear thermometer, 2.47 and 2.38; FSS Number 38, 1.38 and 1.44.

rated their fear of nonpoisonous snakes as "intense," on a fear questionnaire, and were included in this research only if a psychological interview corroborated this statement. The subjects who appeared to have impairing physical disabilities or latent psychosis (based on the psychotic scales of the MMPI or the clinical judgment of the interviewer) were excluded. None of the subjects in this study were being seen elsewhere because of psychological problems.

Assignment to groups was essentially random, although some pretreatment effort to balance control variables was made. A more elaborate description of the selection battery has already been reported (Lang & Lazovik, 1963).

Procedure

After the selection tests and interviews, all subjects were administered the Stanford Hypnotic Susceptibility Scale Form A (SHSS; Weitzenhoffer & Hilgard, 1959). Subsequently all subjects except the untreated controls participated in the five therapy training sessions, after which SHSS Form B was administered. Fear intensity was measured both before and after the subsequent 11 desensitization or pseudotherapy trials. Untreated subjects were not seen, except for evaluation sessions.

The measures employed (Lang & Lazovik, 1963) were: The Fear Survey Schedule (FSS), FSS Number 38, an avoidance test, and the "fear thermometer." The FSS is a list of 50 phobias that subjects rate on a 7-point scale. Item Number 38 is the snake item. In the avoidance test the subject was confronted with an alive, tame blacksnake. He was invited to approach the animal, in a controlled setting. The closest point of approach to the animal provided the basis for his test score. If the subject held the animal, he achieved a score of 1, refusal to go to the test room and observe the snake yielded a score of 19. Immediately after this experience the subject rated his situational anxiety during the avoidance test on a 10-point "fear thermometer" (Walk, 1956). An open-ended fear interview provided additional qualitative information.

The experimenters in this research were all experienced psychotherapists. Most of the subjects were seen by two psychologists who have a full time psychotherapy practice. The same experimenters who saw the pseudotherapy subjects also treated desensitization subjects. Fear evaluation was conducted by an experimenter who participated in no other aspect of the procedure.

RESULTS

Mean fear behavior change scores from pretest to posttest are presented in Table 1. The similarity of the pseudotherapy and no-treatment means is readily apparent. The t tests yielded no significant differences between these groups for any measure of fear change (see Table 2). Furthermore, the change score frequency distributions for the two groups were normal and overlapping. Pseudotherapy and no-treatment subjects were therefore combined into a single control group for subsequent analyses.

Mean change scores for the combined control group and the desensitization group are presented in Table 1. Desensitization subjects showed significantly greater fear reduction than controls as measured by all three indices of snake phobic behavior. The t's are presented in Table 2 and de-

TABLE 1.   Mean Pre- to Posttreatment Change Scores for All Fear Measures

Group	Avoidance Test	Fear Thermometer	FSS Number 38	Fear Survey
Combined control (N = 21)	−.03	1.14	.48	12.14
Pseudotherapy (N = 10)	.14	1.30	.40	12.50
No treatment (N = 11)	−.19	1.00	.54	11.82
Desensitization (N = 23)[a]	.27	2.43	1.41	18.64
(hierarchy items completed)				
15 or more (N = 13)	.47	3.58	2.31	23.77
Less than 15 (N = 10)	.01	.89	.11	7.33

Note: The avoidance test score is the percentage change statistic previously described (Lang & Lazovik, 1963). All other change scores were simply the difference between pre- and posttests. The correlations between initial performance and fear change for all measures were insignificant and inconsistent in direction.

[a] Data were incomplete for three Ss. The Fear Thermometer and FSS Ns are 22 and 21, repectively.

sensitization and control frequency distributions are illustrated in Figure 1. Except for the avoidance test the control sample yielded essentially normal distributions of fear change. The desensitization subjects have a primary modal score in the same interval as the controls, but the distributions are skewed positively or are frankly bimodal.

Progress in systematic desensitization is directly

TABLE 2.   The t Tests of Mean Fear Change Scores from Pre- to Posttreatment

Group	Avoidance Test	Fear Thermometer	FSS Number 38	Fear Survey
Combined control versus desensitization	2.57*	2.12*	2.19*	1.25
Combined control versus 15 or more	3.26**	3.44**	3.99***	2.52*
Combined control versus less than 15	.14	.41	1.85	.41
Less than 15 versus 15 or more	2.33*	3.28**	5.00***	2.26*
Pseudotherapy versus no treatment	1.67	.48	.58	.12

Note: The desensitization group was subdivided into two groups on the basis of performance in therapy. "15 or more" and "less than 15" refers to the number of anxiety hierarchy items successfully completed by the group during desensitization.

*p < .05.
**p < .01.
***p < .001.

measured by the portion of the 20-item anxiety hierarchy completed in the 11 therapy sessions. Table 3 reveals that all measures of fear reduction are positively related to the number of hierarchy items successfully completed by each subject. No pretest measure of snake phobic behavior correlated-significantly with the number of items subsequently completed, although the first presentation of the FSS and items completed yielded an r of − .435, (p < .05). Number of items completed was wholly unrelated to any of the SHSS measures (see Table 3).

A previous review of part of these data (Lang & Lazovik, 1963) suggested that while subjects who completed 15 items or more showed considerable positive change, subjects completing less than 15 showed no more change than untreated subjects. The current enlarged sample confirmed this trend. It may be noted in Table 1, that subjects completing more than 15 items have the highest average change scores for all fear measures. Furthermore, Figure 1 shows that the 15 plus subjects clearly account for the positive skew of the distributions of experimental subjects. If the 15 plus group is eliminated, the remaining subjects are distributed normally around the con-

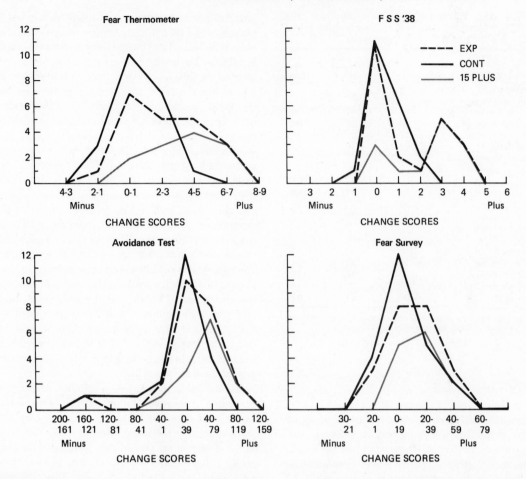

Figure 1. Fear change score frequency distributions for the combined control (CONT) and desensitization (EXP) samples. The shaded areas of the desensitization of groups' distributions define the subjects who successfully completed 15 or more anxiety hierarchy items.

trol mode. These impressions were assessed by the *t* test, and the results are reported in Table 2: 15 plus subjects show significantly more fear reduction than either controls or less than 15 sub-

TABLE 3: Pearson Correlations Between the Number of Anxiety Hierarchy Items Successfully Completed During Desensitization and Measures of Fear Change and the Stanford Hypnotic Susceptibility Scale

Fear Change	r	SHSS Form	r
Avoidance test	.40*	A	−.06
Fear thermometer	.50*	B	−.03
FSS Number 38	.60**		
Fear survey	.50*	Change	−.05

Note: SHSS change is the difference between Forms A and B.
*p < .05.
**p < .01.

jects. The latter group was not superior to the control group on any change measure.

The correlations between the pretest fear measures and SHSS Forms A and B, and the difference score, are at the top of Table 4. Inspection of these coefficients reveals that only the avoidance test is significantly related to suggestibility. Correlations between fear reduction and the SHSS measures are listed in the bottom half of Table 4. It may be noted that avoidance test change is unrelated to suggestibility for either the desensitization or control subject. For control subjects both the fear thermometer and FSS 38 change are positively related to measures of suggestibility, and the Fear Survey shows a tendency in this direction. There is no significant relationship between the desensitization group's SHSS scores and any fear change measure.

TABLE 4.   Pearson Correlations Between the Stanford Hypnotic Susceptibility Scale and the Initial Measures of Fear and Fear Change Scores

Fear measure	SHSS Form		
	A	B	Change
Total sample (N = 44)			
(Initial score)			
Avoidance test	−.34*	−.47**	−.06
Fear thermometer	−.14	−.22	.04
FSS Number 38	.10	.19	.11
Fear survey	.00	−.10	−.13
Control group (N = 21)			
(Change score)			
Avoidance test	.00	.12	.06
Fear thermometer	.33	.46*	.15
FSS Number 38	.47*	.48*	−.02
Fear survey	.29	.36	−.23
Desensitization group			
(N = 23)			
(Change score)			
Avoidance test	−.16	.11	.28
Fear thermometer	−.16	.18	.39
FSS Number 38	.07	.02	−.19
Fear survey	.08	.07	.02

Note: All correlational statistics were computed on the IBM 7090 at the University of Pittsburgh Data Processing Center.

*$p < .05$.

**$p < .01$.

DISCUSSION

Desensitization subjects clearly showed a significantly greater decrease in phobic behavior than did controls; subjects whose therapeutic experience was restricted to a placebo relationship yielded no more positive change than did the untreated group.

These results imply that the reduction in fear following desensitization does not stem from a suggestion to change implicit in being "in therapy." Both placebo and desensitization subjects were asked to participate in a procedure which had fear reduction as a goal, and both groups spent equal time at this task. The findings also indicate that hypnosis, training in muscle relaxation, hierarchy building, and their continued use in a therapeutic context, do not in themselves produce change in fear behavior. Finally, the results suggest that the relationship which developed between the experimenter and subject, with possible transference effects, was not in itself the vehicle of change.

The above inferences clearly depend on the extent to which the therapists kept their communications about goals the same for all subjects, and how well they succeeded in maintaining interpersonal relationships of comparable warmth and intensity with their client-subjects under both de-

sensitization and placebo conditions. A number of factors argue that a high degree of comparability was achieved. The formal, experimental setting in which this research was carried out certainly assisted in this task. Each step of the procedure was defined, and a considerable portion of the therapists' communications with the subject were read from a mimeographed program. Furthermore, it is unlikely that the therapists who saw most of the subjects in this study were personally committed to any outcome. They were paid for their participation, at the same rate per therapy hour regardless of the procedure administered, and they were involved in no other aspect of the experiment. It must also be mentioned that all subjects were seen by clinicians with considerable experience in interviewing and traditional psychotherapy, who would be well above average in their ability to meet the relationship requirements of the experiment. Finally, the posttherapy interviews with the subjects, and discussions with the therapists, did not suggest that placebo subjects were less closely involved, nor did they yield subjects who doubted the fact that a true therapeutic procedure was being undertaken.

On the other hand, the possibility of error in procedure can never be completely discounted, and is best detected by independent attempts at replication. Furthermore, despite the fact that many of the same procedures were used in both placebo therapy and desensitization, the way they were used undoubtedly influenced the character of the experimenter-subject relationship. Unlike the pseudotherapy group, desensitization subjects received regular feedback concerning progress through the hierarchy. Clearcut success experiences (as well as failures) were part of the therapeutic interaction. In this context, a good therapeutic relationship may be one in which the therapist has gained the properties of a reinforcer, and this capacity is in the service of a specific program of behavior change. Desensitization would then progress more rapidly if approval is given for the completion of items. The better the relationship, the more effective such reinforcement is likely to be. On the other hand, it should be pointed out that the completion of an item is in itself reinforcing and many subjects compliment themselves on their own progress. Thus, the quality of the relationship may be less relevant to a well-motivated subject's performance. These variables merit the continued attention of researchers.

While the desensitization subjects as a group showed considerable fear reduction, the change score distributions are skewed and some individual members changed no more than controls. The current experiment was limited to a brief 11 desensitization sessions, and it is, of course, possible that all subjects would have improved with a sufficient exposure. It is also possible that there are personality differences between those who profit and those who do not. As the sample size increases this contingency will be explored. In any event, suggestibility is clearly not one of the potential distinguishing traits. While a significant part of the control subject's fear change is attributable to the SHSS, no similar relationship between this scale and fear reduction was found for the experimental group. For desensitization subjects the positive effects of treatment were so overriding as to render undetectable any variance assignable to suggestibility.

All measures of fear change yielded high positive correlations with number of hierarchy items completed. Furthermore, subjects who completed at least 15 items showed significantly less fear than controls at the end of the experiment; subjects who failed to move this far along in the hierarchy were no different from pseudotherapy or untreated subjects. The correlations indicate that a general relationship exists between fear change and a measurable aspect of therapy process. It is unlikely that Item 15 represents a "critical point" in this process. However, given the measures used here, the data suggest that the therapeutic task must be well advanced before effects clearly greater than those achieved by control subjects are observed.

As would be predicted by an S–R theoretical model, fears other than the phobia treated showed less marked reduction. The desensitization group as a whole yielded significantly greater change than controls on FSS Number 38; an analogous result was not obtained for the entire FSS. Nevertheless, 15 plus subjects did show a significant reduction on the FSS when compared either to control subjects or to the less than 15 group. These findings suggest that the treatment was specific, as intended, and when it was successful that fear reduction generalized positively.

These findings are inconsistent with some predictions from psychoanalytic theory. Fear reduction occurred without exploration of the phobia's dynamic background. Posttreatment interviews revealed no examples of symptom substitution. Positive generalization of fear reduction was indicated, rather than an increase in other fears. Furthermore, a transference cure interpretation of the fear

change is weakened by the failure to find marked placebo effects.

Although the relationship by itself was shown to be less effective therapy than client-centered theorists have sometimes argued, this experiment does not constitute a test of that treatment method. A quasi-non-directive technique was employed as part of the pseudotherapy procedure, but its object was the opposite of client-centered therapy, to avert affect-laden statements rather than to encourage them. As was already suggested, theory would predict positive change in true client-centered treatment for the same reasons as for desensitization. Advocates of the latter treatment hold, of course, that behavior therapy is more specific and systematic, and therefore faster and more thorough. The present experimental design offers an excellent setting for a test of this assumption. Now that the level of placebo changes is known the way is open for meaningful, comparative evaluation of psychotherapies.

Both the limitations and the advantages of the subject population used in this experiment were mentioned at the outset, and they must be continually held in mind. However, the course of laboratory desensitization very closely followed the treatment process reported by clinical workers. Considerable success was achieved in 11 desensitization sessions, which compares favorably with the 11.6 average sessions per hierarchy reported by Wolpe (1958) for neurotic patients. Furthermore, many of the phenomena observed by the authors in clinical cases, and reported by others, were found with these experimental subjects. The systematic weakening of anxiety with repeated presentation of a hierarchy item was of course the typical result. However, subjects occasionally showed a perseveration of anxiety, and apparent summation with repetition, that presented all the difficulties that this situation creates when it occurs in a clinical case. Similarly, problems with visualization were frequently observed, as well as avoidance behavior when individual items were particularly upsetting. While these problems were undoubtedly fewer and less intense than would occur in clinical practice, they did not appear to differ in quality or kind.

Despite this apparent versimilitude, generalization to the clinic must be cautiously undertaken. Many issues are raised that need more intensive investigation. Nevertheless, the results obtained here encourage four important conclusions: (a) simply being in a therapeutic context and relating to a therapist (even when all the trappings of desensitization—hypnosis, hierarchy building, relaxation—are included) does not in itself effect the important changes in phobic behavior achieved by systematic desensitization; (b) successful desensitization is relatively independent of the subject's suggestibility; (c) change in verbal and motor indices of fear behavior may be directly predicted from measurable events that occur during desensitization therapy; (d) the systematic desensitization of a specific fear generalizes positively to other fears. These findings are further presumptive evidence that desensitization therapy process conforms to its theoretical model, that it is an adapting out or systematic counter-conditioning of fear responses to specific stimuli.

REFERENCES

Jacobson, E. *Progressive relaxation.* Chicago: Univer. Chicago Press, 1938.

Lang, P. J., & Lazovik, A. D. Experimental desensitization of a phobia. *Journal of Abnormal and Social Psychology,* 1963, *66,* 519–525.

Lazovik, A. D., & Lang, P. J. A laboratory demonstration of systematic desensitization psychotherapy. *Journal of Psychological Studies,* 1960, *11,* 238–247.

Walke, R. D. Self-ratings of fear in a fear-invoking situation. *Journal of Abnormal and Social Psychology,* 1956, *52,* 171–178.

Weitzenhoffer, A. M., & Hilgard, E. R. *Stanford Hypnotic Susceptibility Scale.* Palo Alto, Calif.: Consulting Psychologists Press, 1959.

Wolpe, J. *Psychotherapy by reciprocal inhibition.* Stanford: Stanford Univer. Press, 1958.

a brief commentary on the usefulness of studying fears of snakes

Allan Cooper, Joseph B. Furst, & Wagner H. Bridger

In this brief note, the authors suggest that evidence for the effectiveness of desensitization as a clinical technique should not be evaluated in studies of snake and rat phobias. The use of these animal studies initially appeared to be a brilliant stratagem. It provided a conveniently available phobic object that could be presented to a large pool of available Ss such as college students. The phobia was the same for all Ss. Change could be operationally defined in terms of distance from the snake that S could tolerate. However, despite all these apparent advantages, the usefulness of this type of study as an indicator of the effectiveness of desensitization in clinical practice was questioned. It is the authors' impression that both the type of S and the course of treatment are markedly different in college students who are fearful of snakes, and in people who are seen in actual clinical practice.

As part of a pilot study the authors successfully desensitized four students to their fear of harmless snakes or laboratory rats. These results replicated the findings of Lang, Lazovik, and Reynolds (1965) that desensitization can effectively cure a person's fear of snakes. Two other students served as control Ss. They were told that for the sake of science it was important to see if they could fool trained observers. They were instructed to act unafraid when a harmless snake was presented to them to hold. They were also told that by going through this procedure again and again, they would actually overcome their fears.

After an average of eight sessions the two control Ss were able to handle the snake and report that they were not afraid. Monitoring of their physiological reactions was in accord with their self-report.

Other investigators have reported results similar to those obtained with the control Ss in the present study. Strahley (1965) demonstrated that 16 Ss receiving "counterphobic" treatment were less afraid of a harmless snake than 16 Ss who received desensitization. Hogan and Kirchner (1967) report that significantly more of the 21 Ss treated with "implosion" were able to handle a laboratory rat after only one session than untreated control Ss.

One is impressed with all the various techniques that seem to be able to "cure" snake or rat phobias. However, the authors now suspect that the success of these techniques is due to "the natural fear extinction process" that one sees in human beings when they learn new skills. That is, when people learn to drive a car or dive into water, they soon overcome their fears with repeated exposure whether or not any "therapeutic" procedure is used to help them. It now appears that animal phobias in general are different from other clinical phobias. Marks and Gelder (1966) suggest that animal phobias have a much earlier onset, a more continuous course, come less frequently to psychotherapy, are associated with few or no other psychiatic symptoms, and respond better to behavior therapy. Moreover, the fear of snakes, in particular, is a fear that is not exposed to "the natural fear extinction process" since the person has little opportunity to encounter them in his daily life. In the case of fear of snakes, the therapeutic aspects of various procedures may be irrelevant to the cure. The therapy may simply operate by providing repeated contact with the feared object.

The therapeutic procedure may also operate by providing explicit or implicit suggestion that the person will overcome his fears. Agras, Leitenberg, and Barlow (1968) report that Ss treated with desensitization but not given therapeutically oriented instructions or social reinforcement did not differ significantly from an untreated control group, while a group which did receive these variables was able to make progress in overcoming their fear of snakes. Thus, suggestion seems to play a role in the curative process.

Ordinarily, when one invokes the concept of "suggestion" it often appears as if what is meant is that S has simply been fooled or tricked into getting better. A more complex statement as applied to the fear of snakes and rats is that the belief that a person will get better may be sufficient motivation for him to face the fear and thereby expose the fear to the natural fear extinction process.

Studying the effectiveness of "treatments" for curing fears of snakes and rats may be irrelevant to a knowledge of the treatment of clinical phobias. Any "technique" that helps a person confront the fear of snakes may "cure" him. However, clinical experience suggests that this procedure of confrontation by itself will not be effective in the treatment of clinical phobias. It is also the authors' experience that desensitization is not nearly as effective with patients in clinical practice as it is with college students who are afraid of snakes.

The authors therefore question studying techniques for the treatment of fear of snakes, if this is being done for the purpose of understanding the efficacy of these procedures in treating clinical phobias. It is suggested that despite the greater difficulty in procedures, only actual clinical phobias be studied to obtain data about techniques that are ultimately designed to treat clinical phobias.

SUMMARY

Therapy analogue studies, using Ss with fears of snakes or rats have been used by several investigators to evaluate types of behavior therapy. This technique has appeared to be an extremely convenient way of evaluating various therapies. However, as a result of curing two control Ss of their fear of snakes, the authors have come to the conclusion that studying the treatment of snake fears may be irrelevant to the understanding of treating clinical neuroses. Supporting evidence from other studies is cited.

REFERENCES

Agras, S., Leitenberg, H., & Barlow, D. H. Social reinforcement in the modification of agoraphobia. *Archives of General Psychiatry*, 1968, *19*, 423–427.

Hogan, R. A., & Kirchner, J. H. A preliminary report of the extinction of learned fears via short-term implosive therapy. *Journal of Abnormal Psychology*, 1967, *72*, 106–111.

Lang, P. J., Lazovik, A. D., & Reynolds, D. J. Desensitization, suggestibility, and pseudotherapy. *Journal of Abnormal Psychology*, 1965, *70*, 395–402.

Marks, I. M., & Gelder, M. G. Different ages of onset in varieties of phobias. *American Journal of Psychiatry*, 1966, *123*, 218–221.

Strahley, D. F. Systematic desensitization and counterphobic treatment of an irrational fear of snakes. Unpublished doctoral dissertation, University of Tennessee, 1965.

the case for performing research on nonpatient populations with fears of small animals: a reply to Cooper, Furst, and Bridger

Donald J. Levis

In the last decade, investigators interested in the theory and treatment techniques of the behavior therapist have engaged in research dealing with the "fears" of nonpatient populations. These studies, usually carried out in a laboratory setting with college students, have been labeled "analogue therapy" studies. The credibility of such research has recently been challenged by Cooper, Furst, and Bridger (1969), who concluded that "studying the treatment of snake fears may be irrelevant to the understanding of treating clinical neuroses [p. 414]."

When discussing the relevance of analogue studies, it is important to distinguish between two separate issues, both of which are raised by Cooper et al. The first issue involves making claims about a treatment technique which are not supported by data. It should be clearly understood that if the goal is to determine the efficacy of a treatment technique, then the utility of the technique being studied must in the *last analysis* be demonstrated on the population for which it was intended. Cooper et al. are quite correct in criticizing researchers who overgeneralize from data collected on nonpatient populations. The naïveté of some behavior therapists on this issue has also been pointed out by Breger and McGaugh (1965) and by Levis (1970). Nevertheless, it should be remembered that this dangerous jump from observation to generalization does not diminish markedly when the generalization is from one subgroup of a patient population to another.

Although not stated, the reader of the Cooper et al. article might gain the impression that most therapy analogue work is primarily carried out to demonstrate the efficacy of a treatment technique for patient populations. On the contrary, a review of the literature reveals that most investigators see laboratory studies as vehicles to obtain information about various treatment manipulations, to develop ideas or hypotheses, to clarify theoretical issues, or to check the validity of previous findings. These goals are reflected in the work of Lang, Lazovik, and Reynolds (1965) on suggestibility: in the work of Kirchner and Hogan (1966) and Lang (1970) on stimulus control and the therapist variable; in the work of Davison (1968) on the effects of relaxation; and in the work of Dee (1969) on instructional sets. The laboratory setting using nonpatient populations is employed because it permits the selection of homogeneous target behaviors, the equation of avoidance tendencies, the operational definition of independent and dependent measures, and the selection of appropriate control conditions. Such experimental precision is exceedingly difficult, if not impossible, when using patient populations. Anyone who has involved himself with therapy-outcome research is aware of the fantastic problems confronting the researcher in the execution of his study. Difficulty with the drug problem, administrators, ethical consideration, patient selection and participation, establishment of control groups, and the equating of therapists on such dimensions as experience, skill, and commitments are only a few of the frustrations facing the investigator. It is precisely because of this lack of experimental control that outcome research has not even begun to consider the questions raised at the analogue level of analysis. In fact, it is because of the control problem that outcome studies have not had much of an impact upon the scientific community.

The second issue involves profitability of using research populations different from the populations the treatment techniques are ultimately designed to aid. Cooper et al. tended to emphasize this issue throughout their article. In their words, "It is suggested that, despite the greater difficulty in procedures, only actual clinical phobias be studied to obtain data about techniques that are ultimately designed to treat clinical phobias [p. 414]." Such a statement implies the position that principles and techniques developed on nonpatient populations are not likely to be relevant for a patient population. This viewpoint, which is shared by many clinical psychologists, emphasizes the uniqueness of the patient population.

To substantiate their position, Cooper et al. presented two main arguments. The first was the belief that "the natural fear extinction process" can account for the success of those techniques that have been used to remove the fear of small animals. This conclusion was reached on the basis of the results of two pilot Ss and two literature reports. These authors considered the pilot data significant because two control Ss who were not desensitized by Wolpe's technique were able to handle a snake after they were (a) instructed to try to fool a trained observer; (b) instructed to act unafraid; (c) informed that the procedure of being exposed to the snake again and again would actually overcome the fears; and (d) given sessions in which they were exposed to the snake. Data were not provided on the strength of their control Ss' avoidance tendencies and on whether they equated all Ss on this variable prior to treatment manipulations. Furthermore, no attempt was made to separate the effects of in vivo exposure to the phobic test stimulus from the various instructional sets. Concerning the literature citations, the first study is unknown to this author because it is unfortunately unpublished (Strahley, 1965), and the second study (Hogan & Kirchner, 1967) did not manipulate in vivo exposure. However, for the sake of argument, let us assume that Cooper et al.'s suspicion is correct that "the natural fear extinction process" is the main principle operating in analogue studies. They then concluded that any "technique" that helps a person confront the fear of snakes may "cure" him. They went on to say, "However, clinical experience suggests that this procedure of confrontation by itself will not be effective in the treatment of clinical phobias [p. 414]." Although this may have been the experience of Cooper et al., the Hogan and Kirchner study which these authors cited was concerned with the technique of implosive therapy developed by Stampfl (see Stampfl & Levis, 1967). This technique is based, in part, on the principle of direct experimental extinction. The procedure employs a response prevention or confrontation technique of extinction and has been applied to patient populations with apparent success (Hogan, 1966; Levis & Carrera, 1967).

The second criticism offered by Cooper et al. concerning the target behavior of analogue studies is also best presented in their words, "both the type of S and the course of treatment are markedly different in college students who are fearful of snakes, and in people who are seen in actual clinical practice [p. 414]." Marks and Gelder (1966) were quoted to support this conclusion. Although Marks and Gelder did not make a comparison between college and patient populations and although they based the results of their study on interview material collected on adult patients, the possibility of differences between these two populations would most likely not be seriously disputed by anyone engaged in analogue research. The appropriate question, however, is, what are these differences and how do they affect the treatment technique? Viewing both populations, it is suggested that differences exist in motivation level for treatment; strength and intactness of avoidance behavior; interference with other behaviors; and accessibility, complexity, and intensity of conditioned stimuli. However, on the other hand, an equally long list of hypothesized *similarities* between the two populations can be constructed. Such lengthy lists of similarities and differences can also be constructed between any two subclasses of patient populations. Each of the preceding hypotheses is potentially testable, and once they are confirmed or rejected, new data may well be added to the understanding of psychopathology and to the improvement of treatment techniques.

Perhaps the feasibility of the analogue researcher's strategy can be best illustrated by calling to mind the history of genetic biology. It would be difficult, except for some recent work on human blood chemistry, to list even one fundamental genetic discovery in this field which was based on human research. Most of the work was carried out on the fruit-fly, *Drosophila*, an organism that is not considered close to man on the evolutionary scale. Yet the ideas and theories derived from these data have wide potential utility.

The choice of this population is based on essentially the same strategy that the psychologist has so intensively used to study the rat. This less complex organism may well be more advantageous for deciphering basic laws because it is expendable and subject to experimentation which for ethical reasons cannot be carried out on humans. The rat provides a population that is not only convenient but which is subject to better experimental control. Justified or not, such infrahuman data have already given impetus to the development of the behavior therapy techniques of operant conditioning, systematic desensitization, and implosive therapy.

Although in the last analysis, data must decide the fruitfulness of a particular strategy. Ford and Urban (1967) perhaps best stated the issue when they said:

One index of the viability and growth potential of a particular therapeutic approach may well be the extent to which it exposes itself to influences from, and attempts to utilize knowledge from, other domains. If the psychotherapy community does not adopt the responsibility for "bridge building," the therapy subject may be the victim [p. 338].

REFERENCES

Breger, L., & McGaugh, J. L. Critique and reformulation of "learning theory" approaches to psychotherapy and neurosis. *Psychological Bulletin*, 1965, *63*, 338–358.

Cooper, A., Furst, J. B., & Bridger, W. H. A brief commentary on the usefulness of studying fears of snakes. *Journal of Abnormal Psychology*, 1969, *74*, 413–414.

Davison, G. C. Systematic desensitization as a counter-conditioning process. *Journal of Abnormal Psychology*, 1968, *73*, 91–99.

Dee, C. K. The effect of instructions on the extinction of the fear of snakes in the context of implosive therapy. Unpublished doctoral dissertation, University of Iowa, 1969.

Ford, D. H., & Urban, H. B. Psychotherapy. *Annual Review of Psychology*, 1967, *17*, 333–372.

Hogan, R. A. Implosive therapy in the short term treatment of psychotics. *Psychotherapy: Theory, Research, and Practice*, 1966, *3*, 25–31.

Hogan, R. A., & Kirchner, J. H. Preliminary report of the extinction of learned fears via short-term implosive therapy. *Journal of Abnormal Psychology*, 1967, *72*, 106–109.

Kirchner, J. H., & Hogan, R. A. The therapist variable in the implosion of phobias. *Psychotherapy: Theory, Research, and Practice*, 1966, *3*, 102–104.

Lang, P. J. Stimulus control, response control, and the desensitization of fear. In D. J. Levis (Ed.), *Learning approaches to therapeutic behavior change*. Chicago: Aldine, 1970.

Lang, P. J., Lazovik, A. D., & Reynolds, D. J. Desensitization, suggestibility and pseudotherapy. *Journal of Abnormal Psychology*, 1965, *70*, 395–402.

Levis, D. J. Behavioral therapy: The fourth therapeutic revolution? In D. J. Levis (Ed.), *Learning approaches to therapeutic behavior change*. Chicago: Aldine, 1970.

Levis, D. J., & Carrera, R. N. Effects of 10 hours of implosive therapy in the treatment of outpatients: A preliminary report, *Journal of Abnormal Psychology*, 1967, *72*, 504–508.

Marks, I. M., & Gelder, M. G. Different ages of onset in varieties of phobias. *American Journal of Psychiatry*, 1966, *123*, 218–221.

Stampfl, T. G., & Levis, D. J. The essentials of implosive therapy: A learning-theory-based psychodynamic behavioral therapy. *Journal of Abnormal Psychology*, 1967, *72*, 496–503.

Strahley, D. F. Systematic desensitization and counterphobic treatment of an irrational fear of snakes. Unpublished doctoral dissertation, University of Tennessee, 1965.

insight versus desensitization in psychotherapy two years after termination

Gordon L. Paul

After a review of the difficulties of follow-up studies on psychotherapy, Sargent (1960) concluded that, "the importance of follow-up is equalled only by the magnitude of the methodological problems it presents." In the absence of a carefully designed outcome study on which to base follow-up investigations, the follow-up may be doomed from the start. Thus, in many studies, the methods of assessment at follow-up differ from those at pretreatment and posttreatment (e.g., Berle, Pinsky, Wolf, & Wolff, 1953; Cowen & Combs, 1950; Sinett, Stimput, & Straight, 1965). Other studies, especially of a retrospective nature, have used assessment procedures of questionable reliability and validity (e.g., Cooper, Gelder, & Marks, 1965; Sager, Riess, & Gundlach, 1964; Schmidt, Castell, & Brown, 1965). Still others have neglected to include appropriate no-treatment control groups for assessing change in the absence of treatment (e.g., Bookbinder, 1962; Fiske & Goodman, 1965; Rogers & Dymond, 1954). The follow-up also suffers, inherently, from the uncontrolled nature of client experiences during the posttreatment period. This is especially important when the time between treatment termination and follow-up is considerably longer

Appreciation is expressed to the Graduate College Research Board of the University of Illinois whose support made this study possible. The earlier data used in this paper were drawn from a study supported in part by Public Health Services Fellowship 1 F1 MH–19, 873, 01 from the National Institute of Mental Health, and in part by the Cooperative Research Program of the Office of Education, United States Department of Health, Education and Welfare, Contract No. 4–10–080, Project 006.

Thanks are extended to Tom Brudenell for his aid in collating and analyzing FU₂ data. Correlational analyses were performed by the IBM–7090 computer of the University of Illinois Computer Science Laboratory.

than the duration of treatment; environmental experiences during the posttreatment period may have more influence on Ss' status at follow-up than a brief program of treatment some months or years in the past. The greatest confounding comes from the fact that many Ss receive additional treatment of unknown nature during the posttreatment period, thus invalidating the design for determining cause–effect relationships for the specific treatment under investigation. This practical problem has limited the value of many follow-up studies (e.g., Braceland, 1966; McNair, Lorr, Young, Roth, & Boyd, 1964; Stone, Frank, Nash, & Imber, 1961).

Overshadowing all other problems of follow-up research is the practical difficulty of sample maintenance and attrition. Even adequately designed studies may not be able to obtain consistent follow-up data on treated Ss, let alone controls (e.g., Fairweather & Simon, 1963; Kogan, Hunt, & Bartelme, 1953; Lang & Lazovik, 1963). The problem of differential dropout and selective biasing of the sample cannot be ignored, since differences have been found between follow-up returnees and nonreturnees (Fiske & Goodman, 1965), and further, as May, Tuma, and Kraude (1965) point out, even if differences are not found, nonreturnees are clearly different in cooperation, mobility, or both. To highlight the magnitude of this problem, a thorough search of the literature failed to reveal a single study on individual treatment of noninstitutionalized adults which obtained data on all treated Ss 2 years or more after treatment termination, nor one which included an attempt to obtain such data on an appropriate group of control Ss.

The present study is a 2-year follow-up of an earlier investigation which was presented as a model design for the controlled evaluation of comparative therapeutic outcome (Paul, 1966). In the earlier study, a modified form of Wolpe's (1961) systematic desensitization was found to be significantly more effective in reducing maladaptive anxiety than insight-oriented psychotherapy or an attention-placebo treatment. Additionally, all three treated groups were found to show significant improvement over untreated controls. Although these effects were found at termination of treatment, under stress-condition assessment, and were maintained at a 6-week follow-up, the differing theoretical models from which the treatment techniques are derived make a long-term follow-up even more desirable than is usually the case.

Specifically, the disease-analogy model underlying the insight-oriented approach to psychotherapy would interpret the results obtained by systematic desensitization and attention-placebo treatments as suggestion or positive transference —in either case, results which would be regarded as merely symptomatic and temporary (e.g., Hendrick, 1958). According to this model, not only would Ss treated by either systematic desensitization or attention placebo be expected to show "relapse" after the "supporting contact with the therapist fades [Sargent, 1960]," but possibly harmful results would also be expected because of the necessary occurrence of symptom substitution (see Ullmann & Krasner, 1965). In fact, the minimal symptom-substitution effect expected would be an increase in anxiety, introversion, rigidity, or dependency (Fenichel, 1945). Additionally, some unsuccessful cases treated by insight-oriented psychotherapy might be expected to realize benefits at some time after treatment termination when their "insights" have had time to "consolidate" (Sargent, 1960). On the other hand, the learning model underlying systematic desensitization would predict no greater relapse for one group than another after treatment termination, since relapse would be expected to occur only on the occasion of unusual stress or if conditions favoring the relearning of anxiety were encountered. Further, this model would expect to find no change in behaviors that were not the specific focus of treatment, except through generalization or an increase in behavior previously inhibited by target behaviors. Thus, from the learning framework, if any change in anxiety, introversion, rigidity, or dependency were to occur at all after treatment termination, it would be in the opposite direction of that expected from the symptom-substitution hypothesis (Paul, 1966).

Although the findings at 6-week follow-up strongly favored the interpretation of the learning model, with none of the results expected on the basis of the disease model forthcoming, it is possible that the first follow-up period was too short to allow the expected processes to show their effects.

In the present study an attempt has been made to overcome the methodological and practical difficulties of follow-up research more adequately than previous attempts. By starting with a well-controlled outcome study, the same measures of assessment could be obtained from Ss at a consistent interval for long-term follow-up as were previously obtained at pretreatment and short-term follow-up. Persistent effort resulted in a greater return of data than has been reported before, not only for treated Ss, but for untreated controls as well. Additionally, specific frequency data were obtained to allow both the exclusion of Ss receiving additional treatment and the assessment of life stresses and possible symptom substitution during the posttreatment period. The major purpose of the present study was: (a) to determine the overall comparative effects of the different treatments from pretreatment to 2-year follow-up and (b) to examine the relative stability of improvement from the 6-week follow-up to the 2-year follow-up, particularly with regard to the questions of differential relapse and symptom substitution versus generalization, as predicted from the conflicting theories on which the treatments were based.

METHOD

Subjects

The Ss included in the present investigation consisted of three groups of 15 Ss each (10 males, 5 females) who received individual systematic desensitization, insight-oriented psychotherapy, or attention-placebo treatment and 44 Ss (32 males, 12 females) who composed an untreated control group. This included all Ss from the previous outcome study (Paul, 1966), except for a group of untreated controls who participated in a different therapy program in another context (Paul & Shannon, 1966). At pretreatment assessment all Ss were undergraduates (Mdn = sophomore) enrolled in a required public speaking course at the University of Illinois, ranging in age from 17 to 24 years (Mdn = 19). Each S was selected on the basis of indicated motivation for treatment, high scores on performance anxiety scales, and low falsification from a population of 380 students who requested treatment for interpersonal performance anxiety, as described in detail in the earlier report (Paul, 1966). Although the public speaking situation was reported to be the most stressful condition imaginable, anxiety was also reported in almost any social, interpersonal, or evaluative situation. As a group, the Ss also differed from the normal student population by obtaining higher general anxiety and emotionality scores and lower extroversion scores. The Ss' degree of anxiety in performance situations was strong to severe, and was reported to be of 2–20 years duration.

Procedure

Pretreatment assessment consisted of the administration of a battery of personality and anxiety scales to the students enrolled in the speech course the week following their first classroom speech. The battery was constructed specifically to assess focal treatment effects and to show symptom substitution or generalization if such processes were operating. The battery thus included forms of (a) IPAT Anxiety Scale (Cattell, 1957); (b) Pittsburgh Social Extroversion–Introversion and Emotionality Scales (Bendig, 1963); (c) Interpersonal Anxiety Scales (speech before a large group, competitive contest, job interview, final course examination) of the S–R Inventory of Anxiousness (S–R; Endler, Hunt, & Rosenstein, 1962); (d) a scale of specific anxiety in a referenced speech performance (PRCS; Paul, 1966).[1] Following initial selection and prior to treatment assignment, Ss underwent stress-condition assessment in which they were required to give a 4-minute speech before an unfamiliar audience which included four psychologists recording the presence or absence of 20 observable manifestations of anxiety during each 30-second period on a timed behavioral checklist. In addition, the palmar sweat index and pulse rate were obtained immediately before the stress speech, as was the Anxiety Differential (see Footnote 3). All Ss underwent stress evaluation except for an equated subgroup of controls initially used to evaluate the effects of the stress-condition assessment itself.

Following stress-condition evaluation the groups were formed, equating all groups on observable anxiety, with Ss randomly assigned to therapists. After a short screening interview,

[1] The original battery also included a form of the Anxiety Differential (Husek & Alexander, 1963). This form was excluded from follow-up analysis since an additional stress administration was not obtained.

during which standard expectations were established, the treatments began—4 weeks after pretreatment assessment. Five experienced psychotherapists (of Rogerian and Neofreudian persuasion) worked individually with three Ss (two males, one female) in each of the three treatment groups for five sessions over a 6-week period. All three treatments were conducted concurrently, with missed sessions rescheduled during the same week. Within the week following treatment termination, a posttreatment stress-condition assessment was obtained on treated Ss and no-treatment controls, including the same measures used in the pretreatment stress condition. The first follow-up (FU_1) data were then obtained by a second administration of the test battery to all Ss 6 weeks after treatment termination. Attitudinal and improvement ratings were also obtained from treated Ss and therapists. The details of all aspects of procedure and results through FU_1 are reported in the earlier study (Paul, 1966).

The 2-year follow-up (FU_2) procedure required tracking down the Ss for a third administration of the test battery which had been administered at pretreatment and FU_1. For FU_2 the test battery was augmented to obtain specific frequency data regarding the occurrence of stress during the posttreatment period; the frequency of external behaviors which might reflect predicted symptom-substitution effects of increased dependency, anxiety, or introversion, and information concerning additional psychological treatment or use of drugs which might affect S's behavior or response to the anxiety scales.

Information on external stress was obtained by requesting Ss to indicate the number of times each of a number of events occurred since the last contact (FU_1). These events covered five major areas of stress: (a) illness or death of loved ones; (b) conflict (with fiancé or spouse, with persons in authority); (c) change in family structure (engagement, marriage, separation, divorce, pregnancy, or birth); (d) personal illness or accident; (e) change in work or living arrangements (move to a different residence, move to a different city, take a new job, change vocational goals, leave college).

Behavioral frequencies regarding possible symptom substitution consisted of the following 13 items:

1. In the past *two weeks,* how many times did you seek advice, guidance or counsel from: friends?—; spouse/fiance?—; instructor/supervisor?—; parents?—; physician?—; others (please specify)? _____.

2. In the past *two weeks,* how many times

was advice, guidance, or counsel *offered* which you did *not* seek from: (same as #1).

3. In the past *two weeks,* how many times did you *accept* advice, guidance, or counsel when it was provided from: (same as #1).

4. Of your close friends and relatives, with how many different people would you currently feel that you could discuss personal problems should the need arise?—

5. To how many clubs or organizations do you currently belong?—

6. How many dances, parties, or similar social events have you attended in the *past month?*—

7. In the *past month,* how many events have you attended as a "spectator" (such as concerts, meetings, sporting events, etc.)?—

8. How many times in the *past month* have other persons been to your home (or room) to visit you?—

9. In the *past month,* how many times have you visited or "gone-out" with another person?—

10. Of the *different people* you have visited, gone-out with socially, or who have visited you in the *past month,* how many were: males?—; females?—

11. How many times have you participated in group discussion in the past month?—

12. In the last *three months,* how many times have you spoken or appeared before a group?—

13. How many *different* groups have you appeared before in the past 3 *months?*—

Additional information was requested regarding the date and audience size of public appearances in order to appropriately analyze the PRCS and S–R speech scales. The same self-ratings of specific and general improvement which were obtained from treated Ss at FU_1 were also included at FU_2.

The procedure for FU_2 contact ran as follows: 24 months from the date of treatment termination a packet containing the test battery, behavioral questionnaires, and rating scales was mailed to the last known address of each S. The packet was accompanied by a cover letter explaining the importance of participation for one last time and was otherwise designed to enlist cooperation, including an offer to furnish the results of the investigation. This letter set a date 3 weeks in the future by which the completed forms were to be returned in a stamped, self-addressed envelope which was provided. Those Ss not returning forms by the first due date were sent a personal letter which further stated the importance of their specific participation, and a new due date was set 2 weeks hence. The Ss not responding to the second let-

ter were then sent a complete new packet by registered mail, as were those Ss for whom new addresses were necessary. Those Ss not responding to the third letter were personally contacted by telephone and reminded of the importance of returning the data, and a promise was elicited to do so immediately. An arbitrary cut-off date was set exactly 27 months after treatment termination, for determining "nonreturnee" status of contacted Ss. Thus, although FU_2 was designated as a 2-year follow-up, the actual time from termination was 25–27 months, closer to 2 years from FU_2 than from treatment termination.

RESULTS

Return Rate

Of first concern was the adequacy of the follow-up procedure for locating Ss and eliciting their cooperation. Even though the sample was highly mobile (64% no longer in the local area, and 27% out of state or out of the country) all treated Ss and all but three control Ss were located. Complete data were returned by 100% of the treated Ss ($N = 45$), and 70% of the controls ($N = 31$). Of the 13 nonreturning controls (10 males, 3 females), 1 was deceased, 1 was in a mental hospital, 1 flatly refused, 7 failed to return after multiple contact, and 3 could not be located. Thus, the return rate was 79% for contacted controls who could return data, still significantly lower than the return rate for treated Ss ($p < .001$, Fisher exact probabilities test).

Since the purpose of the long-term follow-up was to determine the effects of the specific treatments included in the previous outcome study, Ss who received three or more sessions of psychological treatment during the posttreatment period were excluded from further analyses. On this basis, 3 Ss were excluded from the insight-oriented group, as were 1 each from systematic-desensitization and attention-placebo groups, and 12 returning controls; the difference between the proportion of treated Ss and controls receiving treatment during the follow-up period being highly significant ($\chi^2 = 9.87$, $df = 1$, $p < .01$). Additionally, one desensitization S was excluded because she was undergoing chemotherapy for a thyroid deficiency at FU_2, and one control was excluded on the basis of an extreme falsification score. While argument could be made either for including Ss who received additional treatment or for counting all such Ss as relapses, the data available on such additional treatment is unclear. It appears that most of the treated controls, two of the treated insight Ss, and the attention-placebo S did seek treatment for anxiety-related difficulties, while the desensitization S and one insight S sought primarily vocational counseling.

Although data obtained at pretreatment and FU$_1$ revealed no significant differences between the treated Ss who obtained additional treatment and those who did not, there is no question that the retained controls constituted a biased subsample of the original control group. The non-returning controls were found to differ from the retained controls in showing significantly greater increases from pretreatment to FU$_1$ (Pre–FU$_1$) on the general and examination anxiety scales, and a higher rate of academic failure over the follow-up period (78% versus 32%). Those controls excluded because they received treatment during the follow-up period also differed from retained controls by showing a greater Pre-FU$_1$ decrease in general anxiety, lower extroversion scores, and significantly greater increases on all specific anxiety scales. Even though there were no differences in demographic variables between retained controls and those lost or excluded, the retained controls appear to have improved more from pretreatment to FU$_1$, therefore raising the possibility that differences between treatment groups and controls at FU$_2$ may underestimate treatment effects. Likewise, if Ss excluded on the basis of additional treatment really were cases of relapse, the differential exclusion of these Ss would operate most in favor of the control group and, secondly, in favor of the insight-oriented group, while biasing results against systematic desensitization and attention-placebo treatments.

Comparative Treatment Effects from Pretreatment to FU$_2$ (Pre–FU$_2$)

The overall evaluation of treatment effectiveness is most reasonably made by a comparison of Pre–FU$_2$ changes between groups, since Pre–FU$_1$ changes had been subjected to detailed analysis earlier. Two scales of the battery (PRCS and S–R speech) focus specifically on performance anxiety in the speech situation, the specific treatment target. Unlike pretreatment and FU$_1$ assessments, however, there was no common reference speech for PRCS, and the size of audiences to which Ss had been exposed varied so widely that the separate consideration of S–R speech was no longer meaningful. Therefore, these two scales were converted to T scores and combined to form a Speech Composite score before analyses were undertaken. While the Speech Composite provides evaluation of specific treatment effects, the additional S–R scales report on performance anxiety in three different interpersonal-evaluative situations, none of which were the specific focus of treatment. These latter scales, along with the general scales on Social Extroversion, Emotionality, and General Anxiety, provide information on generalization or, conversely, symptom substitution. Before carrying out the main analyses on the data, the possibility of systematic differences attributable to the five participating therapists was investigated. As was previously found on pretreatment and posttreatment stress-condition data and Pre-FU$_1$ analyses, in no instance for any measure were significant or suggestive Pre-FU$_2$ differences found among the overall (main) effects achieved by the five therapists or among the effects achieved by different therapists with the three

TABLE 1. Mean Scores on Specific Anxiety Scales at Pretreatment, 6-Week Follow-up (FU$_1$), and 2-Year Follow-up (FU$_2$) for Subjects Retained at FU$_2$

		Scale							
		Speech Composite		S-R Interview		S-R Examination		S-R Contest	
Treatment	Testing	M	SD	M	SD	M	SD	M	SD
Desensitization	Pretreatment	115.5	9.74	43.2	11.01	46.8	10.32	35.6	7.92
(N = 13)	FU$_1$	85.0	16.10	37.4	8.82	43.2	10.81	35.5	7.28
	FU$_2$	82.5	16.07	31.5	8.79	36.5	9.28	30.5	6.68
Insight	Pretreatment	117.7	7.15	37.6	9.67	42.5	10.79	40.8	8.73
(N = 12)	FU$_1$	103.4	14.18	35.6	11.94	42.2	12.01	39.1	10.24
	FU$_2$	95.2	18.70	31.3	9.42	39.0	8.99	36.3	10.77
Attention-Placebo	Pretreatment	110.7	11.98	34.8	7.34	40.6	9.79	36.9	9.69
(N = 14)	FU$_1$	86.4	12.47	32.1	7.22	35.9	12.23	34.0	9.75
	FU$_2$	82.9	20.85	28.7	8.03	32.1	7.74	28.9	10.40
Control	Pretreatment	110.9	12.20	37.2	12.98	40.7	10.62	33.9	11.51
(N = 18)	FU$_1$	104.3	14.21	34.7	10.16	41.9	11.29	36.3	8.19
	FU$_2$	99.2	21.66	32.2	10.98	38.4	11.07	33.2	8.11

TABLE 2. Mean Scores on General Scales at Pretreatment, 6-Week Follow-up (FU$_1$), and 2-Year Follow-up (FU$_2$) for Subjects Retained at FU$_2$

		Scale					
		Extroversion-Introversion		Emotionality		IPAT Anxiety	
Treatment	Testing	M	SD	M	SD	M	SD
Desensitization	Pretreatment	14.1	7.58	19.8	6.03	40.7	10.69
(N = 13)	FU^1	17.9	8.45	18.9	6.16	38.2	11.18
	FU^2	19.9	6.18	17.5	7.08	32.0	10.01
Insight	Pretreatment	16.4	6.57	17.2	5.59	33.7	10.09
(N = 12)	FU^1	18.9	4.70	18.3	6.12	35.0	11.72
	FU^2	18.9	4.64	15.6	6.56	30.5	12.29
Attention-Placebo	Pretreatment	14.1	8.15	18.1	6.02	35.4	9.77
(N = 14)	FU^1	17.1	7.68	16.8	7.01	30.7	11.74
	FU^2	16.1	7.01	17.1	6.75	28.2	12.12
Control	Pretreatment	17.9	5.53	17.9	5.92	37.7	16.91
(N = 18)	FU^1	20.2	6.30	18.4	6.31	37.7	11.48
	FU^2	19.4	6.56	17.2	7.97	33.6	14.34

different treatment procedures (interactions). Consequently, the Ss within treatment groups have been pooled in the following analyses.

The Speech Composite and each of the additional scales from the test battery were subjected to three-way analyses of variance (Treatments, Pre–FU$_2$, Subjects) on the scores of Ss retained at FU$_2$. Means and standard deviations for all assessment periods are presented in Table 1 for specific anxiety scales and in Table 2 for general scales.

These analyses indicate highly significant Pre–FU$_2$ changes ($p < .01$; $df = 1/53$), not only for the Speech Composite ($F = 82.70$), but for all other specific anxiety scales ($F = 35.94$, 26.93, 10.39 for S–R Interview, Examination, and Contest, respectively) and general scales ($F = 12.69$ and 15.21, respectively, for Extroversion and IPAT Anxiety Scale) except Emotionality, which only approached significance ($F = 3.05$, $p < .10$). More important, significant Treatment × Pre–FU$_2$ interactions ($df = 3/53$) were obtained for the Speech Composite ($F = 3.68$, $p < .05$) and for S–R Interview ($F = 5.14$, $p < .01$), S–R Examination ($F = 6.96$, $p < .01$), and IPAT Anxiety Scale ($F = 3.46$, $p < .05$), indicating differential changes among groups from pretreatment to the 2-year follow-up. The nature of these changes may be seen in Figure 1, which presents the mean change for each group from pretreatment to FU$_1$ and FU$_2$ for all scales of the test battery. Unlike Pre–FU$_1$ changes, where significant overall effects were found only for speech anxiety and extroversion, the significant Pre–FU$_2$ main effects reported above reflect gen-

eral trends in the improved direction for all scales at FU$_2$.

Of the significant Pre–FU$_2$ interactions, of most interest is the Speech Composite, which reflects change in the focal area of treatment. Inspection of Figure 1 reveals that all four groups maintained their relative positions from FU$_1$ to FU$_2$, with slight addition shifts in the direction of lower mean anxiety scores for all groups. As was the case with Pre–FU$_1$ comparisons, all three treatment groups were found to show significant improvement over controls ($t = 3.70$, 2.04, and 2.38 for desensitization, insight, and attention-placebo groups, respectively; $p < .05$), with no significant difference between the mean anxiety reduction achieved by the attention-placebo group and the insight group ($t < 1$). Also, like Pre–FU$_1$ comparisons, Ss treated by systematic desensitization showed significantly greater mean Pre–FU$_2$ reductions in anxiety on the Speech Composite than Ss who were treated by insight-oriented psychotherapy ($t = 2.09$, $p < .05$). However, even though the magnitude of the difference between mean anxiety-reduction scores of the desensitization group and the attention-placebo group for Pre–FU$_2$ comparisons was the same as that of Pre–FU$_1$ comparisons, these differences were no longer found to be significant at FU$_2$ ($t < 1$). This was the result of greater variability in the Pre–FU$_2$ change scores of the attention-placebo group, primarily due to a drop of 71 points for one attention-placebo S. The overall effects between these two groups may be seen better in the individual data presented below.

Having found essentially the same results to

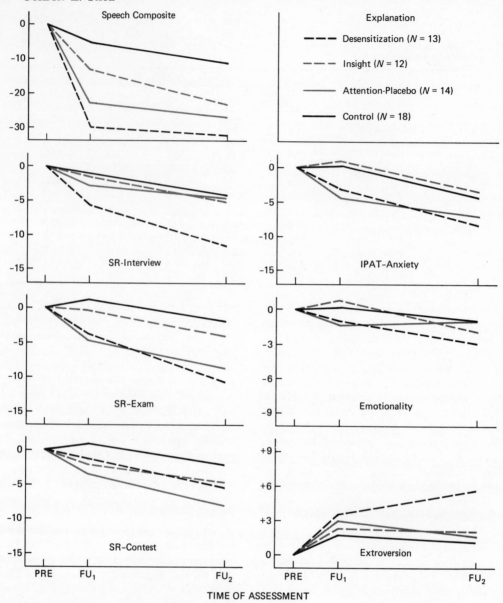

Figure 1. Mean change from pretreatment to 6-week follow-up (FU₁) and 2-year follow-up (FU₂) for Ss retained at FU₂.

obtain for focal treatment effects at the 2-year follow-up as at the 6-week follow-up, the significant interactions between groups and Pre–FU₂ change scores on the other scales of the test battery become of interest. Of the additional specific anxiety scales and general scales, a significant interaction effect was found only for IPAT Anxiety in the earlier analysis of the Pre–FU₁ data. The source of that interaction was found in significantly greater anxiety reduction for desensitization and attention-placebo groups than for controls. A significant overall increase in extroversion was also found on Pre–Fu₁ analysis, but no significant interaction was obtained over that time period. As indicated above, significant Pre–FU₂ interactions were again found for IPAT Anxiety and, in addition, for S–R Interview and Examination anxiety scales. Inspection of the nature of these changes (Figure 1) showed continued improvement over the follow-up period for the desensitization group on the S–R Interview scale, such that the Pre–FU₂ reduction for the desensitization group was significantly greater than that for controls ($t = 1.75$, $p < .05$) and approached significance when compared with insight and attention-placebo groups (respectively, $t = 1.39$, 1.61; $p < .10$). The source of the significant Pre–FU_2 interaction for S–R Examination was found in significantly greater reductions for both desensitization and attention-placebo Ss over controls ($t = 2.44$, 1.75; $p < .05$) and for desensitization over insight ($t = 1.72$, $p < .05$). Figure 1 shows that the significant interaction obtained on IPAT Anxiety at FU_2 is a result of the combined FU_2 reduction obtained by the desensitization and attention-placebo groups as compared to insight and control groups, although the latter two groups improved sufficiently from FU_1 to FU_2 that individual between-group comparisons alone were no longer significant. By the 2-year follow-up, the desensitization group had continued to show increased Social Extroversion scores to the point that the Pre–FU_2 increase in extroversion was significantly greater than that of the other three groups ($t = 2.06$, $df = 53$, $p < .05$). No other mean group comparisons approached significance from pretreatment to FU_2.

Although self-ratings of improvement by treated Ss had previously failed to discriminate between groups, direct ratings of perceived improvement were still included at FU_2 because of widespread usage in other follow-up studies. As before, in sharp contrast to the specific measures of anxiety reduction, no significant differences were found among groups on mean self-ratings of improvement. The Ss in all three treatment groups gave mean ratings ranging from "somewhat improved" to "much improved" for both specific reduction of performance anxiety and improvement in other areas.

Individual S Improvement from Pretreatment to FU_2

Since clinical workers are more often concerned with percentage improvement in individual cases than with mean group differences, and since negative treatment effects or symptom substitution would be more easily identified from data on individuals, all test data were further evaluated on the basis of individually significant Pre–FU_2 change scores. An individual case was classified as "significantly improved" on each scale if the Pre–FU_2 reduction in anxiety score or increase in extroversion score exceeded 1.96 times the standard error of measurement for the instrument

(two-tailed .05 level, as previously determined from a population of 523, Paul, 1966). Likewise, an individual case was classified as "significantly worse" on each scale if a Pre–FU_2 increase in anxiety score or decrease in extroversion score exceeded 1.96 times the standard error of measurement for the instrument.

TABLE 3. Percentage of Cases Showing Significant Change from Pretreatment to 2-Year Follow-up

Treatment	Significantly Improved	No Change	Significantly Worse
	Focal Treatment (Speech Composite)[a]		
Desensitization	85%	15%	—
Insight	50%	50%	—
Attention-Placebo	50%	50%	—
Control	22%	78%	—
	All Other Comparisons (Six Scales)[b]		
Desensitization	36%	64%	—
Insight	25%	71%	4%
Attention-Placebo	25%	70%	5%
Control	18%	74%	8%

Note: $N = 13$, 12, 14, and 18, respectively, for desensitization, insight, attention-placebo, and control. Classifications derived by two-tailed .05 cut-offs on each individual change score (see text).
[a] $\chi^2 = 11.64$, $p < .01$.
[b] $\chi^2 = 8.11$, $p < .05$.

Overall Pre–FU_2 improvement rates presented in Table 3 again disclosed significant differences between groups not only for focal treatment effects from the Speech Composite, but for all other comparisons as well. Particularly striking was the finding that not a single case retained at FU_2 in any group showed a significant increase in performance anxiety. Additionally, the percentage improvement of groups was remarkably consistent with a similar classification made earlier on the basis of pre- to posttreatment change from stress-condition data. By comparing the percentage of improved Ss in the attention-placebo group with untreated controls, it was possible to estimate the percentage of Ss responding favorably to merely undergoing treatment, over and above the base-rate improvement from extratreatment experiences throughout the 2.5-year period—28%. Similarly, by comparing the percentage of Ss improved under attention-placebo with those improved under insight-oriented psychotherapy and systematic desensitization, it was possible to estimate the percentage of additional Ss receiving lasting benefit from either the achievement of "insight" or "emotional re-education," over and above the nonspecific effects of undergoing treatment. For Ss receiving systematic desensitization, these comparisons revealed an additional lasting improvement of 35% for focal effects and 11% for generalized effects over that improvement expected from attention placebo. Again, no differences were found between the effects achieved by insight-oriented psychotherapy and attention-placebo treatment, although both produced better improvement rates than untreated controls. The "other comparisons" in Table 3 also favored a generalization interpretation of the effects of desensitization for changes found in areas which were not the specific focus of treatment, without the slightest suggestion of symptom substitution. Symptom substitution would be reflected in higher percentages in the "significantly worse" category for both attention-placebo and desensitization groups.

Comparative Relapse and Symptom Substitution over the Follow-up Period

While overall Pre–FU$_2$ evaluations gave no suggestive evidence to support the symptom-substitution hypothesis, nor any evidence that more Ss treated by desensitization and attention-placebo programs became significantly worse in any area, no information on relapse can be obtained from Pre–FU$_2$ comparisons. Rather, cases of relapse must be identified as those cases showing a significant increase in anxiety as reflected on the Speech Composite from FU$_1$ to FU$_2$. Similarly, if a symptom-substitution process were operating, a higher percentage of change in the "worse" direction should be obtained from FU$_1$ to FU$_2$ on nonfocal scales for desensitization and attention-placebo Ss who maintained improvement on the Speech Composite. As noted above, the data

presented in Figure 1 show no evidence of relapse or symptom substitution for the groups as a whole from FU$_1$ to FU$_2$.

Before concluding that the symptom-substitution effects and differential relapse predicted by the disease model had not occurred, a more sensitive analysis was made of the individual data from FU$_1$ to FU$_2$. A case was classified as significantly worse on each scale if from FU$_1$ to FU$_2$ an increase in anxiety on the Speech Composite (relapse) or other anxiety score (symptom substitution) or a decrease in extroversion score (symptom substitution) exceeded 1.65 times the standard error of measurement for the instrument (one-tailed .05 level cut-offs). The percentage of Ss maintaining status versus the percentage "getting worse" from FU$_1$ to FU$_2$ for each group is presented in Table 4. No significant differences between groups were found on any measure. In fact, as the figures for the Speech Composite demonstrate, there was not a single case which could be considered a relapse in any of the retained Ss from the three treatment groups. Additionally, the percentage of scores in the significantly worse direction, which would reveal symptom substitution, did not differ from the .05 level for any group. If Ss who received additional treatment during the follow-up period were to be included as cases of relapse, the figures would be even less in favor of the predictions based on the disease model, with 93% maintaining status for both desensitization and attention-placebo groups, as compared to 80% for insight and less than 40% for controls.

The frequency data obtained from the 13-item behavioral questionnaire specifically constructed to reveal hypothesized symptom-substitution effects also failed to provide any support for the symptom-substitution hypothesis. Kruskal-Wallis one-way analyses of variance by ranks over the four groups on each item produced an $H < 3.66$ ($p > .30$) on all items but one. On that item—No. 9, frequency of social exchange—the value of H approached the .10 level of significance and was in favor of the desensitization group. In fact, a significant coefficient of concordance ($W = .47$, $p < .01$) over all items was obtained, with the desensitization Ss receiving an equal mean rank with the insight Ss, both in the direction opposite to symptom-substitution effects. Similarly, Kruskal-Wallis analyses over the four groups for frequencies of each of the five areas of stress reported over the follow-up period failed to reveal significant differences between groups (all $H <$

TABLE 4. Percentage of Cases Showing Relapse or Symptom Substitution from 6-Week Follow-up to 2-Year Follow-up

Treatment	Maintained FU^1 status	Significantly Worse
Focal Treatment (Speech Composite)		
Desensitization	100%	—
Insight	100%	—
Attention-Placebo	100%	—
Control	89%	11%[a]
All Other Comparisons (Six Scales)		
Desensitization	97%	3%[b]
Insight	96%	4%[b]
Attention-Placebo	94%	6%[b]
Control	93%	7%[b]

Note: $N = 13$, 12, 14, and 18, respectively, for desensitization, insight, attention-placebo, and controls. Classifications derived by one-tailed .05 cut-offs on each individual change score (see text).
[a] "Relapse."
[b] "Symptom substitution."

3.66, $p > .30$; except C, "Change in family structure," where $H = 5.08$, $p < .20$). Thus while the occurrence of stress might be considered as evidence of symptom substitution or an external influence on relapse (Stone, et al., 1961), these questions need not be of concern in the present study, since no differences in the reported occurrence of stress approached significance between groups.

Interrelationships among Variables

Since the earlier study assessed specific improvement through several different instruments, persons, and situations in addition to the instruments on which FU_2 data were obtained, information relating to both predictive and construct validity of improvement may be gained through the correlation of previous improvement scores with those obtained at FU_2. For systematic agreement across different instruments, positive correlations would be expected between all change scores for each measure of performance anxiety. FU_1 improvement ratings of Ss and therapists should be positively correlated with Ss' ratings at FU_2. Further, FU_1 ratings of improvement should be negatively correlated with Pre–FU_2 performance-anxiety change scores. Opposite relationships would be expected for therapist posttreatment ratings of prognosis, since these scales were reversed.

Table 5 presents the correlations of pre- to

TABLE 5. Correlation of Prior Improvement Scores with all Change Scores from Pretreatment to 2-Year Follow-up

Prior improvement data	Subject FU_2 Rating of Improvement		Pre-FU_2 Change						
	Specific	Other	Speech Composite	S-R Interview	S-R Exam	S-R Contest	IPAT Anxiety	Emotionality	Extroversion
Pre- to posttreatment stress-condition change									
Physiological composite	-.33*	-.31*	.11	.13	.32*	.22	.46**	.38**	-.09
Behavioral checklist	-.34*	-.13	.61**	.07	.20	.17	.20	.15	-.25*
Anxiety differential	-.33*	-.27*	.44**	.28*	.22	.26*	.46**	.23	-.34*
Standardized therapist posttreatment rating									
Specific improvement	.30*	.15	-.51**	-.18	-.24	-.31*	-.38**	.04	.12
Other improvement	.02	.03	.01	.07	.00	.02	.08	-.10	-.24
Specific prognosis	-.35*	-.31*	.50**	.13	.30*	.11	.24	.02	-.17
Other prognosis	-.19	-.19	.25	.05	.01	-.11	.16	-.09	-.32
Subject FU_1 rating									
Specific improvement	.68**	.47**	-.56**	-.04	-.30*	-.19	-.18	.03	.34*
Other improvement	.56**	.65**	-.24	-.15	-.03	-.19	-.11	.08	.20

Note: $N = 44$ for stress condition; $N = 39$ for ratings.
*$p < .05$.
**$p < .01$.

posttreatment stress-condition change scores, therapist posttreatment ratings, and FU_1 ratings of treated Ss with FU_2 ratings of treated Ss and Pre–FU_2 change on the Speech Composite and all other scales of the test battery. Specific FU_2 improvement data (Ss' ratings, Pre–FU_2 Speech Composite) were significantly correlated in the expected direction, with all indicants of specific improvement at posttreatment and FU_1, except for the relationship between the Physiological Composite and the Speech Composite. Previous analyses had also failed to find significant relationships between physiological and self-report data, although physiological change was significantly correlated with observable manifestations of anxiety under stress conditions as assessed by the behavioral checklist.

Of the correlations presented in Table 5, the relationship of the behavioral checklist with Pre–FU_2 assessments is of a special importance. The behavioral checklist was the most objective measure of all instruments used and was highly reliable (interrater reliability = .96). Additionally, checklist data were obtained in a situation where target behaviors were most likely to occur, and pre- to posttreatment checklist change was consistently related to all other prior indicants of specific anxiety reduction. The correlation of .61 between pre- to posttreatment change on the behavior checklist with Pre–FU_2 change on the Speech Composite is strong evidence for both the construct validity of focal improvement at FU_2 and for the predictive validity of observable posttreatment improvement.

Table 5 also reveals discriminative relationships in the correlations of therapist and subject ratings with Pre–FU_2 improvement. Therapist ratings of specific improvement and prognosis were significantly correlated with Pre–FU_2 Speech Composite change and with FU_2 ratings of improvement by treated Ss. Conversely, therapists' ratings of general improvement and prognosis were not significantly related to specific improvement, although "other prognosis" was related to Pre–FU_2 change in extroversion. Likewise, Ss' ratings at FU_1 were significantly related to Pre–FU_2 change in a discriminative way, although "method factors" predominate in improvement ratings of Ss as they had earlier.

The correlation of specific improvement data from the earlier time periods with Pre–Fu_2 change on the scales of the test battery which were not directed towards focal treatment effects also showed several significant relationships. Inspection of the prime correlations among all variables presented in Table 5 found the source of covariation in every instance to result primarily from increased relationships at posttreatment and FU_2, with several of the prime correlations also reaching the .01 level of significance. The significant correlations presented in Table 5 may be interpreted as evidence for the stability of improvement and generalization effects, rather than as a result of relationships existing before treatment began. Further, when the specific posttreatment and FU_1 improvement variables from Table 5 were correlated with FU_1–FU_2 change for test battery scales, several low, but significant, coefficients were obtained ($Mdn\ r = .31$), all of which indicated that those Ss who showed greatest reduction in performance anxiety at posttreatment and FU_1 also showed greatest specific and generalized additional improvement over the period between FU_1 and FU_2. Since no significant correlations were obtained between pretreatment scores on the three general scales and change on the specific anxiety scales from Pre–FU_1, FU_1–FU_2, or Pre–FU_2, the slight additional improvement from FU_1 to FU_2 may be interpreted as the continuing effects of changes taking place during the treatment period, rather than as a function of pretreatment personality dimensions.

TABLE 6. Intercorrelations of Each Test Battery Scale Over the Three Testing Periods for Subjects Retained at FU_2

Scale	Stability Coefficient[a]		
	Pre-FU_1	Pre-FU_2	FU_1-FU_2
Speech Composite	.27	.29	.68
S-R Interview	.57	.53	.63
S-R Examination	.50	.52	.51
S-R Contest	.47	.43	.64
IPAT Anxiety	.76	.44	.63
Emotionality	.80	.64	.72
Extroversion	.82	.59	.71

Note: $N = 57$; $p = .05$, $r = 22$; $p = .01$, $r = .31$.
[a] Pearson r's.

Further information concerning the stability of scores for each scale of the test battery over treatment and follow-up periods may be seen in the test–retest correlations from Pre–FU_1, Pre–FU_2, and FU_1–FU_2 (Table 6). The greater stability of Speech Composite scores from FU_1 to FU_2, as compared to Pre–FU_1 and Pre–FU_2 relationships, again indicated the influence of treatment effects obtaining after pretreatment assessment, with Ss holding relative positions in a reliable manner over the 2 years following FU_1. However, it appears that relatively greater position changes in Extroversion and IPAT Anxiety occurred over the follow-up period than over the treatment period.

Intercorrelations of FU_2 scores for all scales of the test battery revealed essentially the same relationships as those reported earlier for FU_1 scores. Significant intercorrelations were obtained among all scales ($Mdn\ r = .51$), except Extroversion which was significantly related only to the Speech Composite ($r = .27$, $p < .05$). While the combined relationships reported above and in the earlier study support the assumption that FU_2 measures were internally consistent, the reliability of the Pre–FU_2 change for the primary measure can be directly estimated. The Pre–FU_2 changes for PRCS and S–R Speech (the scales which were converted to T scores and summed to obtain the Speech Composite) correlated .64, from which the reliability of the Speech Composite change can be estimated (by Spear-Brown formula) at .78.

Although no differences between groups were found for the 13 items of the behavioral questionnaire, indirect support for the validity of the items was obtained through correlational analyses. Moderate but significant correlations were found among the items, which clustered in the following way: Nos. 1, 2, and 3, ($Mdn\ r = .53$); Nos.

6, 9, and 10 (Mdn $r = .43$); Nos. 3, 5, 8, 11, 12, 13 (Mdn $r = .35$). Only No. 7 was unrelated to other items. Numerous significant correlations (Mdn $r = .32$) were found between the items of the second and third clusters and all scales of the FU_2 test battery, indicating that Ss obtaining lower anxiety scores and higher extroversion scores also tended to report having more close friends, belonging to more organizations, attending more social events, entertaining more, "going out" more, and more frequent group discussions and public appearances. Similarly, of the five areas of stress on which frequency data were obtained, all but one (change in family structure) were significantly intercorrelated (Mdn $r = .35$). With one exception, no significant correlations were found between reported stress frequencies and items of the behavioral questionnaire, nor between either FU_1–FU_2 or Pre–FU_2 change for any scale of the test battery and stress frequencies. The exception was a significant relationship between the reported frequency of occurrence of change in family structure and FU_1–FU_2 change in extroversion ($r = -.42$, $p < .01$); that is, those Ss increasing in extroversion from FU_1 to FU_2 tended to report less change in family structure over the same time period.

One last check on the symptom-substitution hypothesis was carried out by correlating Pre–FU_2 change on the Speech Composite with all other data. Several significant correlations were obtained between Pre–FU_2 Speech Composite change and items from the behavioral questionnaire, but all were in the opposite direction predicted by the disease model and favored a generalization interpretation. Intercorrelations of Pre–FU_2 change scores among all seven scales of the test battery revealed positive correlations between change on the Speech Composite and change on all other anxiety scales (Mdn $r = .34$) and a negative correlation with change in Extroversion ($r = -.30$). Similar relationships were found among the other scales, with positive correlations among all anxiety and emotionality change scores and negative correlations between the latter and change in Extroversion. Of the 15 correlations, 10 achieved statistical significance (Mdn $r = .29$).

DISCUSSION

In general, the combined findings from individual and group data as well as correlational analyses

showed the relative gains in focal treatment effects found earlier to be maintained over the 2-year follow-up period. Some additional relative improvement in related areas was found for Ss treated by systematic desensitization and, to a lesser extent, for those treated by attention placebo. Like the finding at 6-week follow-up, in no instance were the long-term effects achieved through insight-oriented psychotherapy significantly different from the effects achieved with attention-placebo treatment, although both groups showed significantly greater treatment effects than untreated controls. As a group, the systematic desensitization Ss continued to show greater positive treatment effects than any other group, with evidence of additional generalization, and no evidence even suggestive of symptom substitution. In fact, the comparative findings at 2-year follow-up are so similar to the findings at posttreatment and 6-week follow-up that the detailed discussion of results in relation to previous research, theoretical hypotheses concerning factors and effects within treatments, and methodological implications for research and clinical practice which were presented earlier (Paul, 1966, pp. 71–99) require no modification and need not be reiterated here.

The finding that effects of systematic desensitization are maintained over the follow-up period with evidence of additional improvement through generalization is consistent with the results of the only other controlled follow-up of systematic desensitization therapy (Lang & Lazovik, 1963) and with the suggestive findings from follow-up reports of accumulated case studies (Lazarus, 1963; Wolpe, 1961). Although all previous long-term follow-up studies have suffered considerably from the methodological problems described at the beginning of this report, the general trend of results for psychological treatment of noninstitutionalized adults has been for treatment effects to be maintained or slightly improved over the follow-up period (Stone et al., 1961). Consistent with this trend, the present investigation found no relapse for any of the retained treated Ss, no matter what treatment they had received.

While these findings were somewhat surprising for systematic desensitization and insight-oriented psychotherapy, the stability of improvement resulting only from the nonspecific effects of attention-placebo treatment was almost completely unexpected. This was especially true since previous studies of placebo responsiveness had not only found relapse on 3–6-month follow-up (Gliedman, Nash, Imber, Stone, & Frank, 1958), but further, that Ss who improved most at the time of their initial placebo experience were more likely to relapse than those who improved least (Frank, Nash, Stone, & Imber, 1963). The difference between the latter effects of pure placebo (inert medication) and lasting effects of the attention-placebo treatment of the present investigation may lie in changes in attitudes and expectancies resulting from the interpersonal relationship with the therapist functioning as a "generalized reinforcer" (Krasner, 1955). Stone et al. (1961) point out that the long-term success of any form of treatment depends in large part on the extent to which changes that are accomplished are supported by the client's subsequent life experiences. This fact might be extended to suggest that no matter how change is brought about, it is likely to be maintained in a supportive environment which reinforces resulting behavior, and it is not likely to be maintained if the resulting behavior is not reinforced or if new aversive consequences or extreme stress reinstitute negative emotional responses. While systematic desensitization produced a more direct modification of the emotional reactions associated with interpersonal performance situations, resulting in significantly higher improvement rates, the emergent behaviors of Ss experiencing anxiety reduction from all three treatments were likely to be regarded as socially appropriate and were likely to be rewarded, independently of the manner in which change initially came about.

The usual concern with "spontaneous remission" rates from other populations need not be considered in this investigation, since an untreated control group from the same population was assessed on the same instruments as were the treatment groups. Even though results were favorably biased towards the controls, due to differential loss of Ss, superior long-term effects for all treatment groups were still obtained. Additionally, the 22% "improved" without treatment at the 2-year follow-up for a favorably biased untreated subgroup seriously questions the "two-thirds spontaneous remission" rate so frequently quoted (e.g., Eysenck, 1966). Of course, Lesse (1964) notes:

The concept of anything that is labeled as "spontaneous" must be considered in the light of the fact that it is spontaneous only because we do not understand the causes for the change or are at the present time unable to measure various factors that influence it. In all probability, therefore, so-called spontaneous remis-

sions are probably not spontaneous at all [p. 111].

There is no reason to believe that factors other than the same environmental influences which maintained improvement for treated Ss were involved in the improvement and stability of untreated controls. In fact, processes similar to desensitization may take place through environmental interaction in the absence of formal treatment (Stevenson, 1961), and considerable nonspecific therapy may be expected without contacting a socially designated psychological helper (Goldstein, 1960).

While this investigation was able to overcome methodological difficulties more adequately than previous attempts, it still suffered from difficulties inherent in the nature of follow-up studies. The tight control procedures maintained during the earlier outcome study were not possible once Ss were "turned loose" after the 6-week follow-up. When control is not possible, attempts at assessment are a second-best choice. Although Ss were asked to indicate whether or not treatment had been received during the follow-up period, only 5 indicated that they had, when a total of 17 were actually identified as having received treatment through a survey of clinics and therapists. Considering the high return rate for this investigation, the problem of Ss not reporting additional treatment in other studies could be astronomical. Even though a higher return rate was obtained than in previous follow-up studies, total assessment of cause–effect relationships for treatment groups was not possible due to the necessity of S exclusion. Additionally, untreated controls were known to be a favorably biased subgroup which may have underestimated treatment effects and overestimated (un)spontaneous remission. Although the assessment instruments used possessed adequate reliability and validity for determining effects, the mobility of the sample precluded use of the instrument which was known to provide the most objective evaluation (i.e., the behavioral checklist).

These inherent difficulties have led some investigators to question the value of long-term follow-ups. May et al. (1965) point out:

formal, controlled studies are doomed to depreciate progressively with the passage of time from the end of the controlled treatment period with much of their discriminating power being eroded by contamination . . . it is inevitable that the longer the follow-up, the more all treatments approximate the same end result [p. 762].

On the basis of their own research, Stone et al. (1961) state further that, "evaluation of different forms of psychotherapy should be primarily in terms of their immediate results [p. 420]." In essential agreement, the stability of treatment effects over the 2-year follow-up period in the present study, combined with the failure to find a single case which could be considered evidence of relapse or symptom substitution for any treated S, suggests that the short-term follow-up provided adequate evaluation of comparative treatment effects. Thus, for the evaluation of psychological treatment with noninstitutionalized adults, more scientifically useful information is likely to be obtained if future efforts are directed towards short-term follow-ups, in which total sample assessment of treated Ss may be obtained, rather than longer follow-ups, which suffer from differ-

ential attrition and the effects of uncontrolled environmental influences. The number and timing of follow-ups should be determined by the nature of the population and problem, rather than preconceived theoretical notions (Paul, in press).

However, the methodological difficulties of follow-up studies should not overshadow the major findings of the present investigation. Namely, that modified systematic desensitization produced significant and lasting reductions in maladaptive anxiety, not only on an absolute level, but also in comparison with other treatment and control groups. None of the effects predicted on the basis of the traditional disease-analogy model were forthcoming, while considerable evidence was found for a learning model. Results as consistent as these are rare in the psychotherapy literature and require not only replication, but also an extension of evaluations across differing populations of clients, therapists, and problems, as well as parametric investigations of the mechanics involved.

REFERENCES

Bendig, A. W. Pittsburgh scale of social extroversion–introversion and emotionality. *Journal of Psychology,* 1962, *53,* 199–210.

Berle, B. B., Pinsky, R. H., Wolf, S., & Wolff, H. E. Appraisal of the results of treatment of stress disorders. Research Publications Association for Research in Nervous and Mental Disease, 1953, *31,* 167–177.

Bookbinder, L. J. Follow-up versus discharge status of psychiatric inpatients. *Journal of Clinical Psychology,* 1962, *18,* 501–503.

Braceland, F. J. (Ed.) Special section: Follow-up studies. *American Journal of Psychiatry,* 1966, *122,* 1088–1124.

Cattell, R. B. *The IPAT Anxiety Scale.* Champaign, Ill.: Institute for Personality and Ability Testing, 1957.

Cooper, J. E., Gelder, M. G., & Marks, I. M. Results of behavior therapy in 77 psychiatric patients. *British Medical Journal,* 1965, *1,* 1222–1225.

Cowen, E. L., & Combs, A. W. Follow-up study of 32 cases treated by nondirective psychotherapy. *Journal of Abnormal and Social Psychology,* 1950, *45,* 232–258.

Endler, N. S., Hunt, J. McV., & Rosenstein, A. J. An S–R inventory of anxiousness. *Psychological Monographs,* 1962, *76* (17, Whole No. 536).

Eysenck, H. J. *The effects of psychotherapy.* New York: International Science Press, 1966.

Fairweather, G .W., & Simon, R. A further follow-up of psychotherapeutic programs. *Journal of Consulting Psychology,* 1963, *27,* 186.

Fenichel, O. *The psychoanalytic theory of neuroses.* New York: Norton, 1945.

Fiske, D. W., & Goodman, G. The posttherapy period. *Journal of Abnormal Psychology,* 1965, *70,* 169–179.

Frank, J. D., Nash, E. H., Stone, A. R., & Imber, S. D. Immediate and long-term symptomatic course of psychiatric outpatients. *American Journal of Psychiatry,* 1963, *120,* 429–439.

Gliedman, L. H., Nash, E. H., Imber, S. D., Stone, A. R., & Frank, J. D. Reduction of symptoms by pharmacologically inert substances and short-term psychotherapy. *A.M.A. Archives of Neurology and Psychiatry,* 1958, *79,* 345–351.

Goldstein, A. P. Patient's expectancies and nonspecific therapy as a basis for (un)spontaneous remission. *Journal of Clinical Psychology,* 1960, *16,* 399–403.

Hendrick, I. *Facts and theories of psychoanalysis.* New York: Knopf, 1958.

Husek, T. R., & Alexander, S. The effectiveness of the Anxiety Differential in examination situations. *Educational and Psychological Measurement,* 1963, *23,* 309–318.

Kogan, L. S. Hunt, J. McV., & Bartelme, P. A *follow-up study of the results of social casework.* New

172 GORDON L. PAUL

York: Family Service Association of America, 1953.

Krasner, L. The use of generalized reinforcers in psychotherapy research. *Psychological Reports*, 1955, *1*, 19–25.

Lang, P. J., & Lazovik, A. D. Experimental desensitization of a phobia. *Journal of Abnormal and Social Psychology*, 1963, *66*, 519–525.

Lazarus, A. A. The results of behaviour therapy in 126 cases of severe neuroses. *Behaviour Research and Therapy*, 1963, *1*, 69–79.

Lesse, S. Placebo reactions and spontaneous rhythms: Their effects on the results of psychotherapy. *American Journal of Psychotherapy*, 1964, *18* (Monogr. Suppl. No. 1), 99–115.

May, P. R. A., Tuma, A. H., & Kraude, W. Community follow-up of treatment of schizophrenia—issues and problems. *American Journal of Orthopsychiatry*, 1965, *35*, 754–763.

McNair, D. M., Lorr, M., Young, H. H., Roth, I., & Boyd, R. W. A three-year follow-up of psychotherapy patients. *Journal of Clinical Psychology*, 1964, *20*, 258–263.

Paul, G. L. *Insight vs. desensitization in psychotherapy: An experiment in anxiety reduction*. Stanford: Stanford University Press, 1966.

Paul, G. L. Behavior modification research: Design and tactics. In C. M. Franks (Ed.), *Assessment and status of the behavioral therapies and related developments*. New York: McGraw-Hill, in press.

Paul, G. L., & Shannon, D. T. Treatment of anxiety through systematic desensitization in therapy groups.

Journal of Abnormal Psychology, 1966, *71*, 124–135.

Rogers, C. R., & Dymond, R. F. (Eds.) *Psychotherapy and personality change*. Chicago: University of Chicago Press, 1954.

Sager, C. J., Riess, B. F., & Gundlach, R. Follow-up study of the results of extramural analytic psychotherapy. *American Journal of Psychotherapy*, 1964, *18*, (Monogr. Suppl. No. 1), 161–173.

Sargent, H. D. Methodological problems of follow-up studies in psychotherapy research. *American Journal of Psychotherapy*, 1960, *30*, 495–506.

Schmidt, E., Castell, D., & Brown, P. A retrospective study of 42 cases of behavior therapy. *Behaviour Research and Therapy*, 1965, *3*, 9–19.

Sinett, E. R., Stimput, W. E., & Straight, E. A five-year follow-up study of psychiatric patients. *American Journal of Orthopsychiatry*, 1965, *35*, 573–580.

Stevenson, I. Processes of "spontaneous" recovery from the psychoneuroses. *American Journal of Psychiatry*, 1961, *117*, 1057–1064.

Stone, A. R., Frank, J. D., Nash, E. H., & Imber, S. D. An intensive five-year follow-up study of treated psychiatric outpatients. *Journal of Nervous and Mental Disease*, 1961, *133*, 410–422.

Ullmann, L. P., & Krasner, L. (Eds.) *Case studies in behavior modification*. New York: Holt, 1965.

Wolpe, J. The systematic desensitization treatment of neuroses. *Journal of Nervous and Mental Disease*, 1961, *132*, 189–203.

PART IV
personal and interpersonal problems

This group of articles deals with personal problems ranging in intensity from neurosis to psychosis, from conditions requiring relatively superficial counseling to those for which hospitalization is indicated. These disorders affect people of all ages and situations. Nearly everyone faces some of these problems during his life, either in himself or in a close friend or family member.

The first three articles illustrate the range of maladaptive behaviors that people bring to clinicians for assessment and treatment. Charles Shaw and Alexander Lucas describe the traditional psychiatric approach in the case of an eight-year-old boy whose behavior and family situation led to his hospitalization. Joseph Cautela's article presents a case illustrating recent applications of learning theory concepts to clinical cases. Their study involved a 33-year-old man who experienced strong fear on the job and in other situations. Both desensitization and reinforcement were used in an effort to overcome his neurotic fears; aspects of insight-oriented therapy were also employed. Thelma Alper's article provides a unique opportunity to read a firsthand account of what it is like to receive one of the more widely used clinical therapies, electric shock treatment. The patient, a young man, suffered from a manic-depressive disorder, a condition often treated effectively and dramatically by electric shock.

Donald Peterson's case study differs from the three just mentioned in that the "client" was an institution rather than one person. Elba State Hospital had many characteristics typical of the state hospital in the United States. Peterson's aim in describing his work at Elba is not to criticize but rather to illustrate the useful consultative role which a psychologist can play with agencies that treat disturbed individuals. The increased concern in recent years with community psychology has heightened awareness of the need to improve not only the effectiveness of individuals but also that of social institutions, including hospitals and clinics. Peterson presents a provocative social-psychological analysis of life at Elba State Hospital.

The follow-up study is a valuable tool at the disposal of clinical researchers. What happens to children after they are treated at child guidance clinics? Do patients discharged from state hospitals make successful adjustments when they return to the community? The follow-up is a longitudinal study; an individual is assessed at two points in time, which may be widely separated. Its focus may be evaluative (was the hospital doing its rehabilitative job successfully?) or descriptive (do youngsters with school phobias continue to have personality problems in adult life?). In her article, Lauretta Bender reports the results of a follow-up study of a group of schizophrenic children. Although this condition is now receiving increased attention from researchers, childhood schizophrenia continues to be a puzzling disorder. It is especially challenging because of its severity and the difficulty in interpreting the behavior of the uncommunicative psychotic child. Bender's study suggests that while the psychotic children who were followed up continued to show behavioral disturbances as adults, the disturbances took a wide variety of forms.

Lee Robins, in her article, reports the results of follow-up of another group of troubled children, those described as being antisocial. She examines such questions as: Do the clinics to which "antisocial" children are brought help these youngsters? She cautions against too simplistic answers to this question, for it is not immediately obvious what the meaning of "help" is. The meaning will vary depending upon who is asked the question and the real-world constraints under which the child in question must live. One of Robins' findings is that traditional clinical efforts at modifying the behavior of antisocial children do not seem to be very effective. This failure suggests the need for long-term follow-up of antisocial children treated with novel and well specified treatments.

Lovaas, Schreibman, Koegel, and Rehm took an experimental tack in approaching the behavior studied by Bender. They explored the effects of specified interventions in the lives of autistic children. These researchers were particularly interested in the ability of psychotic children to attend to environmental cues. Why is the child so unresponsive to his environment? If he is not paying attention to the stimuli most people attend to, with which stimuli is he preoccupied? Lovaas and his colleagues used conditioning procedures in teaching discrimination to autistic, retarded, and normal children. Their results support efforts aimed at analyzing psychosis and social withdrawal in terms of selective, maladaptive attention to stimuli. Learning experiments may open up paths to the acquisition of more conventional attentive behavior.

Sarnoff Mednick reports on one aspect of a pioneering investigation of schizophrenia. The subjects in the study, which is still going on, are children of schizophrenic mothers. The study is prospective and seeks to determine longitudinally the quality of the personal and social adjustments of these children. A major question for students of schizophrenia is that of the relative contributions to schizophrenia of genetic and environmental factors. To these factors Mednick's research has added a third, perinatal factor. His study shows that two circumstances—a genetic predisposition (which by itself might not lead to a serious behavior disorder) and anoxia (oxygen deficiency) at birth—combine to increase significantly the probability of a serious behavioral disturbance. While it will be many more years before Mednick can draw definitive conclusions from his study, results such as those reported in his article appear likely to shed some valuable light on the multiple causes of schizophrenia.

Leonard Heston's article presents the results of careful inquiry into the genetics of schizophrenia. Taking into account the preponderance of research carried out over a number of years, Heston finds inevitable the conclusion that schizophrenia has a genetic basis. However, as he makes clear, this conclusion leads only to other pressing questions such as the nature of genetic transmission. Studies of identical twins and fraternal twins have provided leads in this regard. Another question concerns the roles played by modifying factors, the most notable of which are environmental conditions. Along with Mednick, Heston believes that only through joint study of genetic predispositions and perinatal and environmental factors can scientists learn to predict the appearance of schizophrenic reactions.

Paul Meehl seeks to integrate knowledge about schizophrenia into a coherent theoretical formulation. A theoretical formulation is not an unchanging entity;

rather, it is a tentative statement based on the best data available and offered for use in directing future research efforts. Meehl's article, written before Mednick's or Heston's findings became available, is a durable contribution whose influence will continue to be felt by researchers and clinicians and whose ideas will generate empirical inquiry.

The concluding article by Stanley Schachter is provocative for at least two reasons: it demonstrates convincingly that animal studies are relevant to an understanding of human behavior, and it deals with a common human weakness, overeating. Many writers and clinicians have interpreted obesity as a psychosomatic disorder; they see overeating as caused by repressed anxiety and psychological complexes. Schachter carried out a reasoned analysis of the components of eating behavior; he concluded that certain variables, such as the stimulus conditions under which food intake occurs, are potent and can be manipulated experimentally. His laboratory studies of human beings and animals led to several results that had not previously been predicted. Through his experiments Schachter may have laid the groundwork for developing retraining methods to help obese people.

neurosis in an eight-year-old boy

Charles R. Shaw &
Alexander R. Lucas

Billy S. was first brought to the psychiatrist by his mother at the age of 8 because of progressive anxiety, extreme fearfulness, night terrors, and phobias. He had been unable to attend school for the previous eight months because of these symptoms. At home he spent most of his time with his mother or playing and reading alone in his room, although occasionally he would play with his one good friend in their clubhouse in the backyard. He had many interests and was seldom bored. He liked to make things with his hands, was inventive and imaginative, and most of the time appeared content. However, his panic attacks and apprehension would come on at least once every day. These seemed worse when they happened in the evening at about the time his father was due to come home, or later at bedtime. Sometimes he would lie awake in his room in utter terror, imagining that there were strange creatures in the closet, or that the shadows in the room were moving, and he would hold his breath for fear that he might be heard. Sometimes, after lying rigid for a long time, he would suddenly leap out of bed and rush into his parents' room.

Billy had other symptoms which annoyed the family and which interfered with their daily living. He was phobic about dirt, germs, and bugs. He would meticulously wash his hands before each meal or whenever he had touched anything which he considered dirty. He had many somatic complaints and would often develop a headache, or a stomachache, or say that he was tired, or sometimes just that "I feel bad all over."

FAMILY HISTORY

Billy's parents were both older people. Mrs. S., by a previous marriage, had a son 16 years older than Billy. She was thin, bright, cheerful, and an out-going person. She was also rather tense and emotional, given to occasional episodes of "nervous exhaustion," and she suffered from severe bronchial asthma which incapacitated her much of the time each winter. Mr. S., by contrast, was a stoical, apathetic but quick-tempered man who worked as a laborer, had few interests and limited ambition, and whose life consisted of going daily to work, eating his meals, reading the evening newspaper, and sleeping. To Billy, his father was a stranger who, for most of his hours at home, sat silently in his chair but who would suddenly and unaccountably burst into loud and terrifying anger. Billy lived in fear of his father, could only relax when he was out of the house, and would begin to get tense as the afternoon wore on and it became time for his father to return home.

Between Billy and his mother there was a close bond. She recognized that she was overprotective, and that the relationship was abnormally close, but, as she explained to the psychiatrist, "What else can a mother do when her child is so wretched and unhappy?" The overinvolvement between them was further enhanced by the mother's asthma. During her severest attacks both she and Billy were fearful that she might die. At these times he would remain by her for hours on end, or, if she were in the hospital, he would sit alone in her room at home in a kind of deathwatch. The onset of his severe symptoms and his refusal to attend school had occurred at the time of her worst asthma attack eight months prior to his psychiatric evaluation.

PERSONAL HISTORY

Billy's birth and early development were normal. However, in his first year of life he was far from healthy. He had severe colic which continued long past the usual three-month period. His mother said that he screamed almost constantly during his first year of life, seldom being able to sleep longer than two or three hours at a time.

It was apparent early that Billy was an unusually bright child. Language developed precociously; he soon became quite verbal and used words far beyond his years. He developed an excellent sense of humor, engendered by his mother's somewhat wry, understated humor. He was sensitive, empathic, an altogether charming and appealing little boy, well liked by adults, but never at home in the society of his peers. He would spend long hours in his room with a book; here he felt comfortable and safe and would allow nobody to interfere. By the age of seven he had expressed the concept that you couldn't "trust" anybody; he had been disappointed and hurt so often, and the solution seemed to be to stay away from people.

In school, Billy did well, but not as well as he was capable of doing. The teachers noted that he was often preoccupied and that he could not "apply himself," so that his work was often incomplete. He was frequently late to school and also late getting home; he dawdled and was painfully slow in nearly everything, to the exasperation of his teachers and parents.

PRESENT ILLNESS

Things became progressively worse. His schoolwork fell off badly, his panic attacks and social isolation increased. Matters came to a head with his mother's most severe asthma attack. This coincided with the time between semesters at school, and when school resumed Billy became upset, cried, and refused to leave home. His mother, by her own account, was "too sick to insist," so Billy stayed home, and thus the pattern was set. When his mother's health improved, in about a month, she tried to get him to return to school, but he only cried and begged to stay home. The family physician eventually referred him to the psychiatric clinic, and he was admitted to the inpatient unit at age eight years, three months.

COURSE IN THE HOSPITAL

At first, as was expected, Billy was terribly homesick. However, almost immediately his night ter-

rors disappeared. The first night, he went to bed readily in his new room and went immediately to sleep, sleeping the entire night. This improvement in the night terrors persisted throughout his hospitalization, with only an occasional mild relapse. He went to the inpatient school his first day and participated readily, and it was immediately apparent that he would be a superior student. He learned a great deal during the nine months of his hospitalization and easily caught up academically, so that he was able to resume his regular class when he returned home.

Socially, Billy also made impressive gains, although not as rapidly as in the academic sphere. He never became close friends with any of the other children, and while he participated in many of the games and other activities, he continued to be a peripheral member of the group. He avoided rough play, such as wrestling and football, and rarely got into a fight. However, he learned vicariously to enjoy the roughness and the fighting of the other children. This was also true of the profanity, the foul language, and the displays of anger in which many of the children indulged. At such times, Billy could be seen quietly observing, often with a small grin. He never came to use profanity himself, but he expressed to his therapist that, while the language of the other children had at first shocked and upset him, he later came to "not mind it so much."

However, if Billy could not allow his language to become dirty, the same could not be said of his person. His meticulousness and his compulsiveness soon disappeared. He began literally to wallow in dirt with complete abandon and obvious enjoyment; he became for a time one of the filthiest children at the Center (no minor achievement). Later, in his personal cleanliness he swung back to a middle-of-the-road policy.

For the first half of his hospitalization, Billy's relationship with his therapist was friendly but distant. The therapy hours were spent almost entirely in conversation. Unlike most younger children, Billy preferred not to, as he himself put it, "waste the time playing," so that such things as games and drawing had little part in his therapy. From the beginning, Billy wanted to talk about his symptoms. He wanted desperately to understand them, and to learn how to make them "disappear." He wanted to go straight to the heart of the matter and could not accept that it was helpful to talk to his therapist about such things as his friends back home, his daily activities, and his roommate in the cottage. He enjoyed these conversations, and his sense of humor was superb, but it was obvious that he was dissatisfied with the therapy, that he felt he was somehow being cheated, and that his therapist was putting him off.

The major step in Billy's treatment occurred dramatically one morning in the sixth month of his hospitalization. He had been in bed with a severe cold for three days, was to return to school that morning, but after breakfast had been found sitting alone on his bed, crying. His therapist went to see him, and, when he asked what was wrong, Billy burst into tears, and said, "Everything has gone wrong." They talked for a while. Billy began to cheer up a bit, but when the therapist suggested that perhaps he should go down to school rather than sit around in the cottage, he again burst into tears saying, "That's what the trouble was before I came here. When my nerves were like this, I didn't feel like going to school but they made me go and then I would feel worse."

At this point it was felt that Billy wanted desperately to relate with the therapist, and that his reserve was gone. It was suggested that he might like to come down to the office, and he eagerly accepted. There, he poured out all of his feelings and thoughts which he had kept to himself for so long, and told in great detail the fears that he had felt, especially toward his father, fears that his father might kidnap him, that he might do terrible things to him. He had fantasies that the father was a member of a bandit gang and that at times when they were out driving in the car, the father intended to deliver him to this gang. He felt that his mother wanted to protect him, but that she had to give in to the father's will. He resented her for this weakness and felt that she had failed him.

He talked of other fears and said that all his life he had seemed to be afraid of things. "As far back as I can remember, when I heard about witches and things, I would get scared. Sometimes walking along the street if I saw a woman walking toward me I would think she was a witch. Even when people were mad at somebody else and weren't mad at me, I'd get scared, and would feel like they would turn on me next." He said that his mother had told him about his having colic as an infant, and it seemed to him that he could even remember those very early times, that he could remember screaming and being afraid and that the earliest memories he had were of being afraid.

At length, he began to talk of his great need to tell somebody about all these fears and of the awful feeling he had that he could never be close enough to anyone to confide in them, that nobody could really understand or accept his feelings, and that, if he told somebody, they would laugh at him, or at least would not be able to understand him, so that he would feel even worse, and would be more lonely. The word that he used often was "trust," and he said that he had never felt that he could "really trust anyone." Finally I asked him (here a secret is revealed: the writer is the therapist) if he trusted me, and he looked directly at me and said with real feeling, "Not completely." I asked if he was afraid of me and he said "Sometimes. I don't entirely trust you, and I think I should tell you about things but I couldn't." I pointed out that he was telling me about many things at this time, and he said, "Yes, and you're the only person I could tell these things to. I couldn't tell them to my mother or dad or any other doctor or any other counselors, or anybody." I then told him that the fact that he could now tell me these things was a very good sign. He looked thoughtful, then smiled and said, "Maybe I can get to trust you, then it will spread to other people and then I will get better."

This interview continued for over two hours. It had obviously been a major emotional experience for Billy, and he recognized this openly and said that he wanted to go back to his room and think about all the things that had been said. As he left, he referred to his great misery at the beginning of the morning and said, "I was sitting there on my bed feeling terrible, then I saw the door open and I saw these trousers and jacket coming in and I thought 'Here is more trouble coming.' Then I looked up and saw that it was you, and it seemed like a miracle."

When Billy said that his feeling of trust would spread to other people and that he would get better he had previewed the eventual outcome of his illness. He did indeed get better. He returned home and to school. There were some bad times, some recurrences of the old fears, but he mastered them. He continued as an outpatient, returning for weekly visits for about a year. Then his family moved out West, partly for the climatic benefits for the mother's asthma, partly to start a new life in another community. This has worked out well, and the annual letters from the mother disclose that Billy has continued to be a good student, is maturing normally, is well liked by his peers, and plans to go to medical school. This wish of his to become a doctor is the only apparent remaining link with his therapist. He does not write, and, according to his mother, he seldom mentions Hawthorn Center [the institution at which Billy was treated]. All this is as it should be. This is one of the ironies of the practice of psychiatry—those patients whom we help the most are those that most completely abandon us. A major aspect of their health is a capacity to dissociate themselves from the troubled and unhappy past. And good therapy consists not only in being able to give the patient good treatment when he needs it, but also in being able to let him go when he no longer needs it.

the application of learning theory "as a last resort" in the treatment of a case of anxiety neurosis

Joseph R. Cautela

INTRODUCTION

In recent years investigators such as Eysenck (3, 4, 5), Wolpe (12), Rachman (11), and Yates (13), have given conclusive evidence that the application of learning theory principles has been very effective in the treatment of abnormal behavior. Though the evidence is there for all to see, many psychologists engaged in some kind of therapeutic endeavor have not attempted to apply learning theory principles in the treatment of their patients. This writer has been a prime example of a sort of intellectual schizophrenia. The author has taught learning theory for a number of years and has been quite familiar with the recent literature on behavior therapy, but has never attempted to apply learning theory principles in the treatment of behavior problems. In retrospect, the main reason for this lack of transfer was that the learning theory approach seemed too simple for maladaptive behavior that appeared to develop in a very complex manner. Experience indicated that this undesirable behavior was due to faulty multiple causal relationships that existed for a relatively long time. It seemed logical that if the causal nature of the illness was complex and existed for some time, then the elimination of the illness has to be long and arduous. Actual work with behavior problems showed that this indeed seemed to be the case. This attitude on the part of the writer persisted until the remaining portion of a patient's maladaptive behavior seemed quite resistive to treatment. Then, learning theory was applied as "a last resort" and was successful. The details of the case are presented below.

CASE HISTORY

A 33-year-old male was referred by an industrial nurse. The patient had recently changed jobs within his plant, and soon after developed such a high degree of anxiety that he felt that he could no longer function in his work. An examination of the patient's history revealed that he suffered from chronic anxiety for the last five years. He became "dizzy and faint" in crowds, and in a store even if it was almost empty. If he had to stop at a traffic light and had to wait, he became extremely fearful and wanted to run out of the car. It seemed that any situation in which he had to relate to unfamiliar people made him tremble and he would feel like fainting. The patient revealed that he felt like a failure and was never able to complete anything he started out to accomplish. He resented his wife because she did not understand him and told him his fears were "all in his head." She thought his fears were a sign of weakness. The patient resented his wife's ability to relate well with other people. He changed jobs from a janitor to an inspector on an assembly line (he had seniority which allowed him to make the choice) to please his wife by making more money and having a more prestige position. Soon after he made the change to the new job his anxiety behavior became exacerbated and he reported his complaints to the plant nurse.

It became immediately evident that his parents, especially his mother, were a major factor in his illness. His mother was a neurotic woman who incessantly screamed at the children, always criticized them severely for any failure, and never praised them. No matter what the patient did the mother never perceived it as good enough or successful. Regardless of the outcome of his problem-solving attempts they were almost always perceived as failures by the mother and now by the patient himself.

After the first interview with the patient, he arranged to have his old job back. He was treated for two years by arriving at the dynamics of his

Reprinted by permission from the *Journal of Clinical Psychology*, 1965, 21, pp. 448–452.

problems and working them through. At the end of this two-year period he was no longer fearful in crowds and no longer experienced panic while parked and waiting for the light to change. He enjoyed shopping and felt quite at ease in social relations. His relationship with his wife became very satisfactory. All his friends were amazed at the change in his behavior.

The one remaining problem area was his work. Though he was less nervous on his job than ever before and was able to appear well adjusted while working, he still complained about fear of going to work. He was still afraid that the foreman would criticize him or ask him to do something outside of his janitorial duties. The patient was still fearful that his fellow workers would discover that he was anxious and therefore take advantage of him. Leaving his job was no solution, for we both agreed he would be even more fearful in a new position. At least as janitor, when the anxiety became too great, he could go somewhere and be by himself. Even though all his non-work behavior was very satisfactory, it was reasoned that there must be some dynamic factor or factors that had been overlooked. These had to be discovered and worked through. Six months of trying to discover the proper dynamic factors that would eliminate this remaining maladaptive behavior proved fruitless. It as then decided "as a last resort" to try a learning theory approach.

The first problem to consider was apparent lack of adequate generalization of extinction of the S(people)–R(anxiety) relationship from all other areas of the patient's life to the work situation. That there was some generalization there was no doubt. The patient did have less anxiety in the work situation than ever before, but apparently the generalization was not enough to overcome the reaction threshold.

From the beginning of the treatment the one apparent adaptive aspect of his behavior was his ability to enter into situations even though they were anxiety provoking. He continued his driving through the whole course of treatment. He used to go to dances with his wife. He never quit work (though he changed jobs within the plant). The repeated exposures to the anxiety-producing situations led to many reinforced trials and therefore to a strong development of habit strength. Though repeated exposures to one situation would generalize to other situations, each situation had its own habit strength. It can only be concluded that the thousands of reinforced trials over a five-year period in work led to the highest development of

habit strength. The great habit strength resulted in very high reaction potential which was not sufficiently inhibited by extinction generalized from the other situations.

The problem then was to directly reduce the reaction potential (readiness to respond with anxiety) to work (S) situation. According to Guthrie (6), one way to weaken or eliminate a particular S–R relation is to present the S and prevent the R from occurring so that another R may be connected to the original S. In the Hullian model (7), the reaction potential to a stimulus may be forced below the reaction threshold by either building up total inhibitory potential or by reinforcing a competing response tendency to a greater degree than the original. A combination of the interference method of Guthrie and the reinforcement method of Hull has been adapted by Wolpe (12) in his reciprocal inhibition therapy. The first part of the treatment in this case encompassed both the interference and reinforcement model.

The patient was taught relaxation and autosuggestion. In the first session, while in a state of deep relaxation and autosuggestion in the therapist's office, the patient was asked to picture various scenes while at work in the plant. He was asked to suggest to himself that it was a pleasant feeling to be at the plant. He was instructed to smile when he felt pleasant while imagining his presence in the plant. When he smiled he was asked to visualize the foreman greeting him in a friendly way and joking with him. He was asked to smile when he felt at ease with this visualization. The same procedure was repeated for his relations with his fellow employees. In the second session, a week later, the above procedures were repeated for the first half hour. In the second half of the session it was suggested that even though his foreman and fellow employees were friendly toward him they sometimes would tease him and criticize him. He was asked to imagine that he would take the teasing good-naturedly and respond to the criticisms without fear. The procedure of the second session was followed in the next four sessions during the following four weeks. After the first session he was asked to repeat the procedures once a day at home.

The second part of the treatment consisted in asking the patient, after the first session, to eat a candy bar whenever he felt fearful at work. He had previously indicated he liked candy bars, and his janitorial work was flexible enough so that he could eat a candy bar almost any time. A vending machine was available on each floor for the purchase of the candy. It was reasoned that anxiety acted both in a response and drive producing capacity; thus starting a spiral of total drive (D) increasing reaction potentiality which caused a further increase in drive followed by an even further increase in reaction potential. Eating food would act to reduce the total drive state and to introduce a pleasant competing response to the fear stimulus. This is similar to the classic case described by Jones (8) and similar to the method of Lazarus (9). The hope was that this would stop the spiral effect and establish competing responses to allow autosuggestion techniques to exert their influence.

There was a problem involved in the candy bar procedure. Habit strength could generalize outside the work situation and cause obesity. To prevent the development of a strong anxiety–food habit, two procedures were adopted. The patient was told that the use of candy bars was specific to this situation while the autosuggestion procedure was being employed. He was also told that the candy bars would help him relax in this situation so that the autosuggestion could take over. The writer did not expect this technique to be very effective since the kind of conditioning involved in the anxiety–food situation was not on a verbal level. As a further check on the possible development of a habit that might lead to obesity, the patient was asked by some pretext not related to the treatment procedure to report his weight every week.

RESULTS AND DISCUSSION

At the end of the first week the patient reported little or no change in his apprehension at work. By the middle of the second week, he began to notice that he wasn't as tense going to work as he had been previously. He also stated that he felt a little better at work. At the end of the third week, he reported a noticeable change in feelings at work. He seemed much less fearful than ever before. He didn't tremble so much when he talked to his foreman or fellow workers. By the end of the sixth week he reported that although he was not enthusiastic about his work, he had experienced whole days without an anxiety response.

Once when he was criticized by his boss, his initial response was anxiety, but he recovered immediately and discussed the problem calmly with his foreman. At the end of the six-week period he was asked to continue the procedure on his own. At the end of the second week on his own, he reported that his job was no longer a problem as far as fear was concerned; but he would like to change jobs and felt confident that his fear responses would not generalize to another job. He left his job and began his new job with confidence. Six months after he started his new position he reported little or no anxiety in his working relationships. He reported that the work problem was all behind him now. He did not appear to have developed any other symptoms.

After the first session, the patient was asked to keep careful count of the number of candy bars he ate each day and to note it on a pad supplied to him. On the first day after the instructions concerning the candy bars the patient ate four bars. On the second day he consumed eight bars. The rise on the second day was probably due to the reinforcing effect of the candy during the first day. The rest of the week's intake varied from five to seven bars a day. There was a noticeable decrease the last week. One day he had two bars, the other days either one or no bars. It is difficult to ascertain whether the decrease in candy bar consumption was due to the decrease in anxiety-provoking stimuli or due to a satiation effect. No weight change was reported during the six-week period.

The lack of adequate control procedures in a case such as described in this paper calls for caution in interpreting the results. It is possible that the patient was in a state of latent learning before the learning theory principles were applied and the desired behavior might have emerged because of the previous therapeutic attempt using more conventional techniques. Also of course there is the possibility of spontaneous remission. The only reasons that allow for the interpretation of success due to the application of learning theory principles concern the reported successes by others (1, 2, 9, 10, 12) with the techniques used here with similar cases. Also, the coincidental gradual diminution of maladaptive behavior when the learning theory (behavior therapy) was used appears to be more than just a chance relationship.

REFERENCES

1. Ashem, B.: The treatment of a disaster phobia by systematic desensitization. *Behav. Res. Ther.*, 1963, *1*, 81–84.

2. Clark, D. F.: The treatment of monosymptomatic phobia by systematic desensitization. *Behav. Res. Ther.*, 1963, *1*, 63–68.

3. Eysenck, H. J.: Personality and behavior therapy. *Proc. Royal Soc. Med.*, 1960, *53*, 504–508.

4. Eysenck, H. J.: *Behavior Therapy and the Neuroses.* Oxford: Pergamon Press, 1960.

5. Eysenck, H. J.: *Handbook of Abnormal Psychology.* London: Pitmans, 1960.

6. Guthrie, E. R.: *The Psychology of Learning.* New York: Harper, pp. 70–73, 1935.

7. Hull, C. L.: *A Behavior Theory Concerning the Individual Organism.* New Haven: Yale University Press, 1952.

8. Jones, M. C.: A laboratory study of fear: The case of Peter. *Pedagog. Sem.*, 1924, *31*, 308–315.

9. Lazarus, A.: The elimination of children's phobias by deconditioning. In Eysenck, H. J., (Ed.) *Behavior Therapy and the Neuroses.* Oxford: Pergamon Press, 1960, pp. 181–187.

10. Meyer, V.: The treatment of two phobic patients on the basis of learning theory. *J. abn. soc. Psychol.*, 1957, *55*, 261–265.

11. Rachman, S.: Treatment of anxiety and phobic reaction by desensitization. *J. abn. soc. Psychol.*, 1959, *102*, 421–427.

12. Wolpe, J.: *Psychotherapy by Reciprocal Inhibition.* Stanford: Stanford University Press, 1958.

13. Yates, A. J.: The application of learning theory to the treatment of tics. *J. abn. soc. Psychol.*, *56*, 175–182.

an electric shock patient tells his story

Thelma G. Alper

Although electric shock therapy has been widely used in the treatment of many types of psychotic and of psychoneurotic illnesses since 1938, very little case material is available for understanding the patient's subjective reactions to it. Yet without such material it is difficult, if not impossible, to evaluate some of the current theories of cure.[1] Judging from the patient's behavior, the trembling, the profuse sweating, and the impassioned verbal pleas for help and release, it would appear that most patients find at least the preparatory phase of the treatment very unpleasant. So marked are these overt anxiety reactions that they have been accepted by many investigators as basic to psychogenic theories of cure. It has been suggested, for example, that the treatment threatens the patient with death and offers him an opportunity of rebirth cleansed of previous fears, anxieties, and confusions; or, that the treatment is a form of punishment which absolves the patient from overwhelming guilt feelings. Evidence in support of such theories, however, is not very great and, to date, neither psychogenic nor organic theories of cure have been generally acceptable (7).

Only a few investigators have tried to test any of the psychogenic theories by soliciting pre- and post-treatment accounts from their patients [cf. Fraser and Sargant (3), Millet and Mosse (10), Mosse (11), and Silbermann (12)]. Unfortunately, however, most of the accounts published by these authors are fragmentary, and of only limited usefulness for understanding the psychological elements in the curative process. Typically, the patient is too ill, or too anxious, both before and after treatment, to cooperate with the therapist.[2] This may be one reason why so few studies in this field include accounts by patients. But another, and perhaps even more basic, reason for the dearth of published case material written by patients themselves may be that therapists have not been sufficiently aware of the potential usefulness of such personal documents for understanding the dynamics of the individual illness or for predicting the likelihood of a successful cure by electric shock therapy.

An unusual opportunity to procure a personal document from a former patient presented itself to the writer when a student in an elementary psychology course offered to write an account of his own manic–depressive episodes and reactions to electric shock therapy. His story, written in the summer of 1946 during a lucid interval between recurrent manic–depressive attacks, appears below. Some suggestions as to how such material could be used for prognostic purposes in the individual case, and a brief discussion of the relation of this material to current psychogenic theories of shock, follow the patient's story.[3]

[2] Gillespie (5) and Wiedeking (14) have attempted to supplement studies of patients by investigating the reactions of normal Ss to shock treatment. Such studies have yielded material consistent with patient material though their usefulness for the interpretation of patient reactions is limited. The normal person, by definition, is typically neither anxiety ridden nor disoriented before "treatment" is instituted.

[3] Liberties have been taken only with the introductory portions of the document. These consist primarily of rearranging certain portions of the material in order to present a clearer chronology than the document originally afforded. The original document was written in the third person. For present purposes it was recast into the first person.

[1] See Stainbrook (13) and Kalinowsky and Hoch (8) for summaries both of the empirical findings and the theoretical discussions in this area.

Reprinted from *Journal of Abnormal and Social Psychology*, 1948, *43*, pp. 201–210. Copyright 1948 by the American Psychological Association and reproduced by permission.

MY ELECTRIC SHOCK TREATMENT

Introduction: the Course of the Illness

In 1940–41, I was a senior at college. I had already gone through mild episodes of both elation and depression but I had managed to get my work done and to stay in college. If I could stick to the end of the year I would graduate in June.

But the spring of 1941 was different. Before it was over things got out of hand. I took my divisionals but I was convinced that I had flunked them, that I would never graduate, that I would never be able to hold down a job, that I would be a continual burden upon my parents. I left college without taking a final course examination and without waiting to hear about my divisionals.

By the middle of that summer things had gotten much worse. I was severely depressed. Such tasks as getting out of bed in the morning had taken on the proportions of hard labor. Sitting in a deep chair looking at the pictures in old copies of *Life Magazine* was about all I was able to manage. My family accounted for my blues by the sudden death of my father a month after my failure to graduate from college. I had also lost the job I had procured for myself that summer because the plant was closed down by a strike. And it remained shut down for three and one-half months.

But as the fall drew nearer my family thought things were going better and they decided that I should return to college for one semester. I *had* passed my divisionals. In fact, I had done surprisingly well on them. But since I had so sold myself on the idea that I had flunked and had not taken the final exam, I did not complete my course in Freshman Physics.

When September finally came around, and I was to return to college, I was out of control. For example, I had decided that the building material of the twentieth century should be diatomite, a rock made up of the skeletons of million of microscopic organisms. Deposits of diatomite were known in every state of the union, with one source of supply in Lompac, California that extended over several counties and had a known thickness of almost three quarters of a mile. I worked on my plans diligently, frequently staying up without sleep for 48 hours at a time until I was able to work 64 hours straight without a break, except to drink several glasses of milk to keep myself going. I was making elaborate plans to prefabricate small houses from diatomite blocks. My family realized that hospitalization was required, and instead of returning to college that fall, I was committed to the State Hospital.

The Hospital Period

I was in the hospital for a large part of the next three years. During this time I had studied myself until I could catalogue every move. I was a textbook example of a manic–depressive. Perfect. I enjoyed reading about manic–depressives in elementary psychology books. It was as though the author was watching me, jotting down all of my thoughts and actions. I had learned all about my cycle, and how it affected me. I boasted that I could tell the day of the year, the time of the day, by asking myself how I felt. This was a joke, but it wasn't the exaggeration it sounds. My cycle was as regular as a chronometer: three months elation, six weeks normalcy, six months of depression, six weeks of normalcy, and another year had gone by, but the cycle continued, and it took exactly a year for it to make one revolution. I knew that for the three months of my elation I would be locked up in the hospital; when I was depressed I would be out on pass. In spite of this I always looked forward to the elation; it was the depression that scared me. On two different occasions I bet with my brother that by the fifteenth of the coming September I would be back at the hospital. In each case I won. The first time I missed the date by eleven days, but the second time I was off by only two days.

I knew the game, knew it cold, nothing could surprise me. But in March of 1944 at one of the Friday afternoon hospital dances I had a new experience. I began to "hear voices." There was a great deal of conversation, noise, and general confusion. But suddenly every noise, every word was aimed at *me*. Everything that was being said, was being said about me. Everything that was being done, was being done because of me. For a short time I did my best to cope with this unusual situation. I tried to answer every remark, I tried to meet action with its proper counteraction. But in a short time it overwhelmed me. I knew something was radically wrong, and I told the attendant, who had brought me to the dance that I must see the doctor immediately. We started back to the ward together. On the way it slowly dawned on me that it would be impossible to see the doctor in my present "disturbed condition." The only other rational thought I had was that this situation must be brought to an end. I must get myself knocked out. The simplest way of accomplishing this was to go after an attendant. As soon as I got to the ward I made a beeline for my old friend, Mac.[4]

I have no clear recollection of the following two weeks, my last memory of the incident was running down the long corridor to get Mac. He told me all about it afterwards, but this is the only period in the entire three years that still remains vague, confused, distorted.

The next thing I remember was lying in the tub with my head resting on a small straw-filled, canvas-covered pillow. I was not at all surprised to find myself in the tubs. I could vaguely remember going haywire, but I couldn't recall any of the subsequent details. I could remember the experience of hearing voices; I would never forget it. I could remember the beginning of it all, but nothing else. I wasn't surprised at being in the tubs but I was surprised that I wasn't strapped in a hammock. The tubs were rather pleasant when you aren't rolled up in canvas so that you can scarcely blink your eyes. You can loll around, read magazines, if you don't get them too wet, you can even smoke cigarettes if you can bum them from the attendants. The only thing is that you can't quite go to sleep. Eight hours is a long time, and sleep is the ideal way to pass time.

There were five tubs in the white-tiled room, and in the five tubs were the five worst patients of the one hundred and fifty in the Reception Building. At least one was always raising the roof. I wondered if I had been that bad, but obviously I hadn't, or else I wouldn't be splashing around so comfortably. I dreamed and dreamed, and the morning passed. I didn't dare think about myself, for the first time I was scared, really scared. I thought of the autobiography I was writing. I had started it back in 1941 sometime after I first came to the hospital. Two hundred pages were already written but I decided now that at last I had written the final period. This was the end. I'd be spending my life here in the hospital. So I started to dream again, the wilder the dream the better.

[4] Mac was a former alcoholic patient, a great big jovial fine-looking Irishman, and all in all one of the finest attendants the hospital ever had. When Mac and I had been patients together we became good friends. In the violent ward there are only a few patients that you can talk to. Mac had a parole, and before long we were allowed to go for long walks together through the extensive, beautifully landscaped hospital grounds. We were even allowed to go to town. We were together continually and when Mac became an attendant our friendship was only strengthened.

At lunch time Hap, the little Irishman in charge, passed out sandwiches and eggnog. Hap brought me my sandwiches first and asked:

"What the hell's been the matter with you?"

"I don't know, Hap."

"You went after Mac."

"I know I did."

"Mac's your best friend. What the hell did you do that for?"

"I don't know, Hap. What else did I do?"

"Oh, you've been making a damn fool of yourself. You've got more sense than that. Well, take it easy for a while. You'll be all right, fella."

Take it easy for a while. Three years of taking it easy for a while. I'd be all right. I'd be just dandy. But don't think; dream.

About one-thirty in the afternoon Mac came in carrying a county bathrobe, yellow county pajamas, and black felt carpet slippers. This meant that I had come down to the tubs wrapped in a sheet, that I had spent the night naked in a seclusion room and not in my regular bed in the dormitory. But, then, I couldn't expect to spend the night in the bridal suite at the Waldorf.

Mac said, "What do you say, Pal? You're looking better."

"Hi, Mac."

"We've got to take a cardiograph. Dr. S—— is going to give you shock treatment."

No other attendant would have bothered with this explanation. Electric shock, this was another surprise. Electric shock treatment had been suggested before for me but it never was seriously discussed. It was "too severe," "too drastic," a "last resort." When all else fails, try electric shock and hope for the best. Well, here it was. What would they try after electric shock failed? It would be worse if they gave up entirely. But don't think about it.

I got out of the tub, dried myself in a clean sheet, put on the pajamas and slippers, and holding the bathrobe close about me, I went down the corridor with Mac. Mac didn't seem mad at me, and even went so far as to make conversation, being careful to avoid referring to the entire business.

One of the doctors whom I didn't know, and a nurse whom I knew only by sight, made the necessary preparations for taking a cardiograph. There were a few feeble jokes about being electrocuted, and it was over. I expected to go back to the tubs, but Mac took me up to the Ward.

We stopped in at the office where the charge was admiring his new teeth in a small hand mirror. The charge had been a sergeant in the cavalry in the first World War. Mac said, "Sarge, our old college chum looks better today."

"How are you feeling, Ted?"

"Oh, pretty good, Sarge."

But this was a lie; I felt lousy. They could have taken me out in the field and buried me for fertilizer and I'd have made no kick.

"Do you want to sit around in the Ward for a while?" Sarge asked.

"Yeah, that'd be fine."

"O.K., fella. Take it easy."

I went down the long polished linoleum corridor to the day room. Another attendant was sitting in a rocker in the hallway.

"Hi, Ted. Sit down. Take it easy."

I sat down beside the attendant but there wasn't much talk. In a few minutes Mac came down the ward, and the three of us sat together.

"I hear he'll be getting shock treatment," the other attendant said.

"Yeah," Mac said.

The other attendant started off, "I'd be damned if I'd let any doctor give a relation of mine shock treatment."

"Why not?" Mac asked.

The attendant answered, "I've studied electricity long enough to know that it develops heat when it meets resistance." This man had been an electrician and had studied at Princeton for a short time, so you couldn't entirely laugh him off.

Mac said, "Dr. S—— wouldn't use it if it did any harm."

The attendant said, "What the hell does Dr. S—— know about electricity?"

It doesn't take much to get Mac mad when Dr. S——'s judgment is being bandied about and he said, in a fighting voice, "Well, he knows plenty more about it than you do, and I'll tell it to your face. If you know so much about electricity why don't you go out and get a job as an electrician? It'll pay a lot more than this lousy job."

"Well, all I know is that it generates heat, and heat will burn, and you can't tell me it doesn't destroy some of the brain cells."

"I wouldn't tell you anything," Mac said, and the conversation stopped.

Well, this was good. Electricity equals heat, equals burn. I'd never heard of a burned brain, but I was learning a lot lately, just when I thought nothing new could happen to me.

The next morning at six o'clock I was told to stay in bed. There would be no breakfast this morning because I was getting shock treatment.

I already knew quite a bit about shock treatment. I had helped them give it to other patients many times. I worked in the dormitory, helping to lift the unconscious patients into bed from the wagon, covering them up, checking that no one swallowed the bandage gag that prevented the patient from biting his tongue or chipping his teeth, tying a man in bed if necessary, and occasionally holding the patient down in bed when things got really tough. It wasn't easy work and in a way I was glad not to be doing it this morning.

At half past six Mac came on duty. He came right up to my bed.

"Good morning, Ted. How are you feeling?" Mac asked with a big grin. You couldn't help smiling when Mac was feeling good.

At nine o'clock the doctor came on the Ward. The doctor was a good friend of mine and it was a nice feeling to know that someone was doing his best to help me. But at this moment I was none too happy. I hoped that I'd be the first on the list to get treatment. Yet I was glad to see another patient wheeled out first. I was scared and there was no getting around it. I tried to tell myself that I was just hungry. But I wasn't hungry at all. I tried to tell myself that I had had a bad night. But I'd slept like a log, as I always did. I wondered if I was going to burn, and if I did burn, whether I'd smell. But by this time there was an awful cry down the hall and I knew that the first patient's shock treatment had begun.

Soon a man was pushed into the dormitory and lifted into bed while another man on another wagon was pushed into the visiting room where the shock was administered. They had a system. Fifteen patients could be given shock treatment in an hour, easily.

Now it was my turn. I climbed up on the high wagon and stretched out. Three sand bags in the form of a pyramid stuck into the small of my back to expand my chest. Many of the men squirmed and fidgeted and fooled with the sand bags trying to make themselves comfortable. But you were never on the wagon long. A counterpane was pulled up to my neck and a small straw pillow, though covered with a clean towel, was wet with the sweat of the men who had gone before. I was wheeled out into the hall to wait my turn. There was another scream and a gurgling coughing groan, and the patient ahead of me was moved out down the hall and into the dormitory, with arms and legs and head flopping around. Before I realized it I was zooming down the hall. Mac was pushing me, and Mac was in a hurry.

The wagon bumped over the thick rubber matting that formed a hollow rectangle for the wagon to fill. The doctor was looking down, smiling.

"Hello there, young fellow."

"Good morning, Sir."

Sarge was rubbing some sticky stuff on my head beside my ears. I had seen tubes of the stuff in the office, "electrode jelly." After all you had to make a good contact—to burn. I was mighty scared and there was no use kidding about it. Mac held my right arm and pressed hard with the elbow just inside my shoulder muscle. Sarge had the other arm. Another attendant climbed up on the wagon and lay across my knees gripping the side of the wagon with hands and toes. The three attendants would hold me down during my convulsion. The theory was: the more severe the convulsion, the better the results.

I heard the doctor give the pretty blonde nurse a set of numbers, and I knew that she was setting the dials.

"God, don't let her give me an overdose."

Mac's face was about eight inches above my own. I looked up into Mac's eyes. Mac wasn't smiling a bit. I stared up into Mac's eyes and slowly said over and over to myself, "Mac, you big Irish lug, take care of me now." Very deliberately, very slowly a black shade came up over my eyes.

I woke up sometime later feeling completely refreshed, not tired or logy, or drugged with sleep, just ready for a big day. I started thinking what I would do today but I could think of nothing. I began looking around. I was in a large cream colored room with fifteen or twenty beds neatly made, and covered with white counterpanes. It looked like a hospital, but why should I be in a hospital? There were large windows all along one wall. The room looked strangely familiar. I shut my eyes and tried to think. But nothing came.

"What is the date?" I asked myself.

"I haven't any idea."

"What day of the week is it?"

"Don't be silly."

"What month is it?"

"I don't know."

"What year is it?"

That shouldn't be hard. But I wasn't sure. It was later than 1941. I tried to outsmart myself by asking how old I was and then figuring one year. But I didn't know how old I was.

"What season of the year is it?"

I looked out the window. I couldn't see much, but I realized I didnt have on my glasses. I must have lost them. I rubbed my eyes. I wasn't alarmed at all. What difference did it make? I went back to sleep.

Then someone was shaking me.

"Come on, Pud." Mac sometimes called me Pudd'n'head.

"Good morning, Mac."

Mac laughed.

"Well, you remember my name anyhow."

"Why shouldn't I remember your name?"

"What else do you remember, smart boy?"

"I remember everything."

Mac laughed again.

"Where are you now?"

"I'm with you, I must be at O——."

"That doesn't say much for me, Pud, does it?"

I didn't feel quite up to snappy sayings.

"It's time to get up, Ted."

Going down the corridor I looked at the clock. Ten-thirty. It must have stopped. The ward was almost empty, and it was quiet. I didn't try to think much, I just watched. The first meal of the day was lunch. I began to pick up some of the details of the ward. Lunch was over by twelve. I started to help clean up the dishes, but there was too much confusion, so I went down back to the day room.

At one almost everyone went off to Occupational Therapy. The ward was again empty and quiet. I found a few old copies of *Life*. I looked at the pictures. There was a war going on. The date was 1944 or later.

By that evening I had gained enough confidence to sit with the attendants out in the hall. This was one of my privileges. But I didn't talk much, and I didn't ask any questions. I mostly listened.

I had two more shock treatments in the following five days. They didn't bother me as much as the first one, but I never looked forward to them. I always looked up at Mac's eyes above mine and thought, "Stick with me, old side kick. Don't let me down now."

At six-thirty the morning of my fourth treatment, Mac came over to my bed and said: "You're not getting treatment this morning, Ted. Dr. S—— has taken you off the list."

"Why? I've only had three." There were six treatments to a series.

"You don't need any more. You're coming along fine."

"Shall I help give treatment this morning?"

"No. Take it easy for a while."

This was the first time in years that I hadn't resented "take it easy for a while."

After breakfast I got another piece of paper from Sarge and started the routine which had become daily since my first day of shock treatment: my chronology—

1919—born
1920—1 year old
1921—2 years old

Very shortly I worked my way up to 1944. So I was twenty-four years old. But I had a hard time believing it. It must be so, but I couldn't remember my last birthday. I knew I had been in the hospital at that time. My mother would have visited me. My sister would have baked me a delicious chocolate birthday cake with an orange filling. She always did. My mother would have a big basket of fruit and presents from the rest of the family. I couldn't remember the cake, I couldn't remember the presents, I couldn't even remember the fruit and my mother always brought me a big basket of fruit, every week, often two or three times a week. Fruit was good for me, non-fattening, and I always gave it away.

Slowly I began to work out the chronology again. Slowly I began to remember things. Some things I couldn't remember at all. But this didn't worry me. All things came in time.

One day I realized that I was normal. I wasn't depressed, but I sure wasn't elated. I checked with the calendar. I should be normal. Damn the cycle. In a week or two I found I was getting depressed. This was mighty discouraging.

Mac came down the hall.

"Dr. S—— wants to see you, Ted," Mac said. Mac looked pretty pleased.

I followed Mack into Dr. S——'s office.

Dr. S—— said, "Sarge and I have been talking it over, and we've decided that you're ready to go to work. You can go to work as an attendant here and work right with Mac and Sarge. We all know you can swing it. You've been working in the Ward as an unofficial attendant for a good part of three years, only now you'll be paid for it. Think it over, talk it over with your mother and let me know what you decide."

I went back down the hall and thought. I didn't want the damned job, but they would have to discharge me before they hired me. I had never before been discharged, and this would certainly be a big step in the right direction. Always before, when I left the hospital, I had been on Pass.

Four days later I was working as an attendant, white coat and all. I was still depressed and it was getting worse, but I was beginning to hold my head up. I was legally sane. I was supporting myself. I was saving a little money.

Six weeks later I broke my leg in a scramble. A patient fell on me sidewise. I went up to 57, the infirmary ward. I realized my days of attending were over and I felt fine. I had known that sooner or later I would get hurt, then I'd never work as an attendant again, if for no other reason than that my mother wouldn't allow it. I laughed for the first time in some months. A broken leg. That's cheap. I had been afraid that my eyes would be injured. I had to wear glasses, and on a lively day those glasses would spin across the smooth linoleum floor at a great rate. I stretched out in bed and decided to be lazy for at least four weeks. I had made a habit of asking myself how I felt, checking up on myself. I felt great. This was strange, for according to the calendar I should still be depressed. But I was way off my cycle, there was no denying it. I had been depressed for only three months, not six months. I watched myself. No elation followed. My cycle was a thing of the past. Get Thee behind me.

What threw me off my cycle? Was it shock treatment? Probably. But I was depressed following the shock treatment, even if only for a short time. What had the shock treatment done for me? It had given me a new chance. I was able to start over fresh. With no memory, no delusions, no fears. Or at least I had no memory of them for that period of days before I could again remember the details of my life. In that time I had been reoriented. I was on the right track for the first time in some years. I had been offered a job on a silver platter. In fact it had been forced upon me. That was a very smart move on Dr. S——'s part. And I was discharged as sane.

When my leg healed I left the hospital and got a job as a laboratory assistant. After a year I got a better job as a chemist. In February 1946 I returned to college. On June 6, 1946, I graduated. Four days later I had my diploma framed.

Conclusion: My Understanding of Shock Treatment

Electric shock treatment was successful in my case because there existed a "love relationship," a relationship similar to that between father and son, between myself and Mac, a relationship such as is established between psychiatrist and patient in narcosynthesis. I believe that this lucky accident proved to be the focal point of the entire treatment. This relationship must be reaffirmed and strengthened during the short period of complete loss of memory, following the awakening from unconsciousness, if the treatment is to be used with best results.

The personal document ends at this insightful point. The subsequent history is based on brief interviews and letters.

After graduation, the patient returned home and resumed his old job as a chemist. During a lull at the plant when the men were laid off for a few days, the patient completed his personal document and sent it off to the writer. With it came a letter dated June 24, 1946. In the letter he spoke of "working leisurely on the book." His family was encouraging him in this and wanted him to finish it. He ended the letter with the remark, "So I guess I have no choice."

Nothing further was heard from him until September 18, 1946. Then a brief note came saying, "I am sorry to write that I am once again back at the hospital as a patient. I went haywire July 23. I have had six shock treatments, and, as before, they have done me a great deal of good."

In November, 1946 he left the hospital on Pass and went back to his old job as a chemist. "Normally" the excited phase of the cycle would have caught up with him by June, 1947. But in a letter dated late in July he reported that he had "safely passed the June date." He was certain that the shock treatments were responsible for this but he himself raised the question as to whether the cycle had merely been delayed by the treatments, as had occurred in the past, or whether a permanent cure had been effected.

In November, 1947 he visited briefly with the writer. He was still holding down his job as a chemist. He was "feeling fine." It had been a good summer—plenty of fun and relaxation on weekends spent lazily drifting down inland streams. Would he stay well? He wasn't sure, but he was hopeful.

It is not possible, of course, to predict with certainty what the outcome in this case will be. If one checks the facts with the prognostic signs listed by Gold and Chiarello (6) as portending a good prognosis, the outlook is not too happy. In the present case, though the youthfulness of the patient is in his favor, he already has had more than one series of attacks, and at least one series of unsuccessful shock treatments. Moreover, it is not clear that exogenic factors played a significant role in precipitating the illness. There is also evidence from interviews that the patient had been fairly restricted in his interpersonal relations even before the illness. According to the criteria set forth by Gold and Chiarello, this combination of factors would seem to mitigate against a permanent recovery.

These authors also mention that personality factors, in addition to the nature of the patient's interpersonal relations, mitigate against recovery. They suggest that the prognosis is poor if the patient has "personality defects." They do not make clear, however, what the nature of these defects might be. Nor have other investigators of shock therapy treated the role of personality factors in this form of therapy any more extensively. The evidence from the personal document alone, in the present case, is, of course, inadequate for estimating whether or not there are "personality defects" here. A much more intensive case record, including the results of projective techniques and interview material, would be required. On the basis of the personal document alone, however, certain tentative hypotheses can be formulated.

Perhaps the clearest needs of this personality are in the nature of strong passive, dependent needs. Others decide things for him and he considers it right that they should: the family decides that he is to go back to college, that he should finish the book, and he has "no choice"; the mother, not he, will decide whether he should go back to work - after the accident in the hospital. All of this he takes for granted. He even takes the horrors of the treatment for granted, pinning his hopes on his good friend Mac who will take care of him. He learns that he may end up with a "burned brain." He knows that electric shock treatment is a "last resort," that other patients dread it. Yet he does not resist it. The pain and fear of treatment would seem to serve not so much as a death threat, or as punishment, but rather as inevitable and to be endured because the good parent can be trusted here, as well as with respect to other details of his life. Whether the psychosis in this case is basically a giving-in to these passive dependent needs, or not, cannot categorically be stated. On the other hand, recognizing the existence of these needs one must also recognize that electric shock therapy alone does nothing to alter this patient's psychogenic need-structure. If anything, one might expect it to *increase* his dependency and to increase the likelihood of subsequent episodes.

On the other hand, the fact that the two sets of shocks did "throw the cycle off," that the period of depression was shortened and the period of normalcy was lengthened, is a hopeful sign. Even if subsequent attacks should occur, it may be that the duration of each attack can be considerably shortened if treatments are instituted at the first signs of manic breakdown [cf. Geoghegen (4)]. Moreover, if, along with the electric shock treatment, psychotherapy which is more than mere supportive therapy can be given, as is recommended in the recent report (7) of the Committee on Therapy of the Group for the Advancement of Psychiatry, the prognosis may be reasonably good. Somehow the personality needs to be strengthened. It is not enough merely to be given a "new chance, to start over fresh," as he himself puts it, "with no memory, no delusions, no fears." Unfortunately, the amnesia, as is typical in these cases, wears off and, without psychotherapy, the inner and outer life-situation of the patient remains essentially unchanged.

One further point needs to be stressed here. In spite of the confusion and seeming disorientation of the patient, it cannot be assumed that he is unaware of the discomfitures of other patients and of the attitudes and conversations of staff members. Clifford Beers (2) called this to our attention many years ago. Kindwell and Kinder (9) have written more recently. Shock treatment, whether it is insulin (1) or electric shock, is a terrifying experience for the patient. It has not yet been conclusively shown that the results of the wholesale use of electric shock therapy warrant inflicting such terror on the patient.

REFERENCES

1. Anonymous: Insulin and I. *Amer. J. Orthopsychiat.*, 1940, *10*, 810–814.

2. Beers, C.: *A mind that found itself: An autobiography.* New York: Longmans Green, 1908.

3. Fraser, R., and Sargant, W.: The subjective experiences of a schizophrenic illness. *Character & Pers.*, 1940–41, *9*, 139–151.

4. Geoghegen, J. J.: Manic depressive psychosis and electroshock. *Canadian Med. Ass. J.*, 1946, *55*, 54–55.

5. Gillespie, J. E. O. N.: Cardiazol convulsions, the subjective aspect. *London Lancet*, 1939, *1*, 391–392.

6. Gold, L., and Chiarello, C. J.: The prognostic value of clinical findings in cases treated with electric shock. *J. Nerv. Ment. Dis.*, 1944, *100*, 577–583.

7. Group for the Advancement of Psychiatry. Report #1. Formulated by Committee on Therapy. Sept. 15, 1947.

8. Kalinowsky, L. B., and Hoch, P. H.: *Shock treatments and other somatic procedures in psychiatry*, New York: Grune & Stratton, 1946.

9. Kindwell, J. A., and Kinder, E. F.: Postscript on a benign psychosis. *Psychiatry*, 1940, *3*, 527–534.

10. Millet, J. A. P., and Mosse, E. P.: On certain psychological aspects of electroshock therapy. *Psychosom. Med.*, 1944, *6*, 226–236.

11. Mosse, E. P.: Electroshock and personality structure. *J. Nerv. Ment. Dis.*, 1946, *104*, 296–302.

12. Silbermann, I.: The psychical experiences during the shocks in shock therapy. *Int. J. Psychoanal.*, 1940, *21*, 179–200.

13. Stainbrook, E.: Shock therapy: Psychologic theory and research. *Psychol. Bull.*, 1946, *43*, 21–60.

14. Wiedeking, I.: Selbstbeobactungen in hypoglykämischen Zustand. *Z. Ges. Neurol. Psychiat.*, 1937, *159*, 417.

the study of a social system: Elba State Hospital

Donald R. Peterson

This case study concerns a state hospital where I have worked as a consultant for several years, and in particular a program for children and adolescents which is under development there.

Elba State Hospital is fairly typical of the "asylums" which were built throughout the country around the turn of the century to house the "insane" of an earlier generation. The hospital is situated on the outskirts of a small city, by the bend of a gentle river. It must have seemed an ideal location to the people who selected the site, a haven where madmen could escape the filth and barbarity which would otherwise have been theirs in the jails and poorhouses of the day.

But as our society expanded and changed, and as conceptions of disordered behavior changed, Elba State Hospital, like the other institutions it resembles, became less and less effective as a treatment center for disturbed and disturbing human beings. The buildings, poorly maintained through several economic depressions and two world wars, gradually deteriorated, and to the medieval character established directly by the stone walls of the buildings, the pillared gate, the iron fence around the grounds, and the high tower of the administrative center, was added the authenticity of decay.

The staff deteriorated too. Once Adolf Meyer worked at Elba. The administrators still trade on his name. But now the wards are run by less distinguished physicians, nearly all of whom are foreign-born, and many of whom scarcely know the language, let alone the cultural traditions of the people they are supposed to be helping. The superintendent is of Eastern European extraction. His English is not bad, by the standards of most physicians there, but nearly every time we meet he asks "Why don't you send me more Ph's?" I have never quite been able to keep from recoiling when I hear that, nor have I ever had the courage or the kindness to tell him that the correct designation, if he cannot say "psychologist," is "Ph.D." For all that, he is very strongly interested in getting Elba State Hospital accredited by the American Medical Association, he is beset with the nearly impossible demands of providing adequate treatment for the patients and responsible protection of society on an operating budget of about $5.25 per patient per day, and I believe he is running the hospital as well as he knows how.

Besides the physicians, the staff at Elba is like that in most hospitals of the kind. For a population of about 3500 patients, there are 18 workers in Social Service, only three of whom have Master's degrees; 34 in the Activities Service, five of them college trained and the rest not; three graduate nurses; 52 registered nurses; and 594 aides, none of whom have more than the most rudimentary training in modern treatment procedures. There are six psychologists on the staff. The Chief Psychologist has a doctoral degree. So does another, a research psychologist whose functions are quite distinct from those of the clinical psychology department itself. The rest of the psychologists have Master's degrees and in some cases many years of clinical experience, but until very recently their numbers have been so few, their training so limited, and their positions so narrowly defined that they have spent most of their working time in routine diagnostics. Functionally, this has meant the administration and interpretation of psychological tests, designation of diseases and dynamics, discussion of test results at case conferences, and entry of the material in the files. The diagnostic work has had no obviously beneficial effect on patients.

Despite many recent efforts toward improvement, the hospital is still organized more for convenience as a custodial center than for effectiveness as a treatment agency. It is divided administratively into two main sections, a so-called Acute Intensive Treatment Service (AITS) and a Continuous Treatment Service (CTS). Titles notwithstanding, little real treatment goes on in either place. Group therapy meetings are held regularly on three of the five AITS wards. These are conducted by psychologists with varying degrees of training and experience, and of the most diverse ideological persuasions. Drugs are used abundantly and the medical and nursing staffs seems more preoccupied with matters of dosage and kind of drug than with any other aspect of planned treatment. Beyond chemotherapy they mainly cope as well as they can with the emergencies which arise from hour to hour in any mental hospital. The doors are locked on most of the wards and light physical restraints are used as needed.

The patients take part in various aspects of the general intramural program in effect at the hospital. Activities of several kinds are offered; volunteers associated with various programs periodically appear and do what they can. For the most part, however, the 200 to 250 patients who enter the Intensive Treatment Service each month spend their time waiting for the diagnostic workup to be accomplished. By state and hospital policy, this must be done by team enterprise and signed by the physician in charge. Whatever else may go into the record, the emphasis is on a typological diagnostic label stated in the terms of official American Psychiataric Association nosology. Most of the staff still refer to the AITS as diagnostics and I think this is more than a verbal habit.

If for some undiscernable reason a patient on the diagnostic service improves during his stay there, he may be discharged, and Social Service actively tries to articulate the release with action by the patient's family or by agencies with whom the patient has been associated in the past. This is very difficult, however, since about 90 percent of the patients come from the Chicago area, about 60 miles away, and basic changes in the situations which played a part in causing the disorders to begin with are only very rarely made.

If AITS patients do not improve within three months they are sent to one of the CTS wards for continued treatment. The assignments are made partly on the basis of sex—female patients go to the north wards and males to the south wards—partly by age—male and female geriatric services are in operation and a juvenile unit is being formed—and partly by the characteristics of the disorder a person displays. Except for alcoholism and definite physical illness, this last criterion reduces operationally to the ease with which nursing management can be accomplished and determines whether the patient goes to a maximum security ward or one of the very few open wards on the grounds. The final and in many ways the most decisive factor in assigning any patient to a chronic ward is the availability of bed space. If one ward has more room than another it is likely to get the main flow of new patients until it is full.

The same hospital services which are given to new admissions are also offered to patients on the Continued Treatment Service. Except for the most severely regressed patients and some of the maximum security cases, they have activity programs too; patient government meetings are now held on many of the wards; volunteer programs are in formal effect. But volunteers, like most of the staff, tend to prefer patients who are socially more interesting, who smell better and are esthetically more attractive than the average chronic mental patient at Elba, so most of those people live on year after year with little more to their benefit than drugs and minimal care for purely physical needs.

Except for drugs, the life of a patient on one of the regressed wards at Elba is not much better than it was fifteen years ago, and in many ways not as good as it was a hundred years ago. I visited one of these wards again last month, to talk to some aides and to remind myself again of the nature of my reality. It was the female regressed ward, "3-North" at Elba, and the view I had on entering must not have been very different from the sight which confronted Pinel at Le Bicêtre. The paint on the walls was chipped and peeling, tile had been picked off the floor wherever a piece came loose. Little light came through the screened windows and the air was fetid in the heavy oppression of a hot summer afternoon. Most of the patients were seated on the hard oak chairs and benches lined up in the middle of the dayroom, staring ahead, rocking now and then, obviously under heavy sedation. A few were shuffling around the ward, mumbling to themselves. A scrawny white-haired woman who appeared to be above seventy years old was lying in her own excrement near a water fountain. One of the two aides on duty tried to clean this up while I was there. The smell was overpowering. I have visited wards like this many times since I became a psychologist, but I have never gotten used to the smell of human urine in the back wards of mental hospitals, and I still must fight down a swell of nausea whenever I enter one. Maybe it would be different if I worked there every day. I am as enthusiastic as anyone I know about the ideals of social psychiatry and community psychology. That is where the main hope lies for improving conditions such as these. But the difference between the ideal and present reality is very harsh. Do not sing me any pretty songs about the accomplished wonders of community action. The back wards at Elba smell just as bad as they ever did.

Despite the dreariness of the situation I have just described, some very real progress has recently been made at Elba and in the Illinois mental health system more generally. In 1960, a referendum provided $150,000,000 for capital improvements in the mental health facilities of the state. A favorable political climate at that time encouraged the appointment of a competent and energetic psychiatrist as Director of the Illinois Department of Public Welfare, and shortly thereafter a distinct, professionally oriented Department of Mental Health was created. The Director and the staff he soon collected put into motion the acts required for establishment of a zone system of mental health services in the state. This involved as a major feature the construction of seven new facilities along lines recommended by the Joint Commission on Mental Illness and Health in their 1961 report (*Action for Mental Health*). The zone centers are distinguished from traditional mental hospitals mainly by their location near major population centers, their relatively small size, and the comprehensiveness and the community orientation of the services to be offered there. At this writing, only one of the centers is actively in operation in Illinois. The rest are still under construction, and in the zone where Elba State Hospital is located the effect of the zone system on the operation of the hospital was negligible at the time observations for the present account were being made.

Improvements are underway continuously in the hospital. Many of the older buildings are being extensively remodeled. The daily per capita expenditure for patients has risen from less than $3.25 per day in 1955 to approximately $5.25 in 1965. Some of the wards are open now where once none were. Patient government and group therapy meetings occur with some regularity where a few short years ago scarcely anything of the kind took place. Staff salaries are gradually being increased. A research psychologist has been appointed at Elba, a hospital improvement project for aide training has been approved, and if additional grant funds are awarded a major behavior modification project will soon be set in motion. My appointment as a consultant, and the appointment of others like me from Chicago and the University of Illinois, is evidence of the interest State Department of Mental Health staff have in the constructive criticism and improvement of clinical services.

But there is a paradox in this, for all these efforts at improvement of the state hospital take place in a situation where the smaller urban zone centers are supposed to make the state hospitals obsolete. At one and the same time the hospitals are supposed to be improving and liquidating themselves, and this anomalous identity, this uncertainty of direction, affects all programs which take place within and revolve about the hospital. It is in such a context that the children's program at Elba must be understood.

It is hard to say just when the program began. About two years ago, a psychologist who had been conducting group therapy meetings on one of the AITS wards began to hold special sessions for a number of adolescent patients in his charge. The youngsters seemed to have certain common problems, distinct from those of the older patients, and the meetings, as the saying goes, seemed to be quite profitable. As some patients moved onto the chronic wards, however, their wishes to continue with the group work were administratively difficult to fulfill. Some casual and accidental conversation between the psychologist, the school principal and an activities supervisor led to the discovery that all of them were having similar problems in dealing with the children at Elba. An informal survey conducted at that time revealed approximately 50 patients under 21 years of age scattered over 17 different wards of the hospital, under the care of 12 different ward physicians, two clinical directors, three different chiefs of service, and an indeterminate but very large number of aides and nurses. It did not take an especially penetrating inquiry to show that little was being done for the children by way of treatment at the time, aside from school for those who were able to attend, group meetings for those who happened to have passed through the wards where the meetings went on, and the minimal custodial care a typical state hospital provides. It was equally obvious that no coherent program could be mounted as long as the children were scattered as widely as they were among the wards and services of the institution.

I talked with the psychologist at the time and agreed to work with him and with his colleagues in planning a children's program. We recognized from the start that the residential location of adolescents within institutions is a somewhat controversial matter. Some people maintain that it is best to keep the younger patients with adults, to approximate the extra-hospital world somewhat and to prepare the children for the adult life they should soon be entering. At Elba, however, this issue was academic. The children there were not being prepared for adult life outside the hospital in any systematic way. They were simply being housed with the adults, and not even the rudiments of an adequate program for them had ever been set in motion. Issues concerning the desirability of institutionalization were also academic. It is of course debatable whether children should ever be sent to a state hospital, but the question became coldly senseless at Elba. The children were there already. Some had been there for several years and there was no sign that the flow of new patients would cease in the foreseeable future. We had to do the best we could for them there, within the walls of Elba, however appealing a more general solution might seem to others and to us in our moments of higher idealism.

A proposal to transfer all patients under 18 years of age to a separate unit, along with a tentative treatment plan for them, was therefore drawn up and presented to the superintendent. After about a week's delay, he approved the general proposal, and appointed a Committee on Juvenile Patients' Affairs to coordinate the program in the months ahead. The committee included the psychologist, the school principal, and the activities supervisor who had started the whole operation, along with three clinical directors—all physicians, three social workers, two other activities workers, a chief nurse, and the Director of Volunteer Services at the hospital. Aides on the various shifts were invited to attend as their work schedules might allow and some of them have in fact attended on an irregular basis ever since. One of the clinical directors who spends almost all his time at the hospital in administrative committee work was appointed Chairman of the group. I introduced myself to this man, offered to work as a consultant with him and with the Committee, and after the matter had been taken under consideration for a short time, was invited to do so.

At first, the main task simply was to get all the youngsters together and to find other placements for those who were unlikely to profit from the program. An early census showed that about 40 percent of the patients were mentally retarded by both legal and psychometric criteria, and the staff, especially the social workers, spent very large amounts of time and effort in the first weeks trying to make other arrangements for these children. Where possible, they were sent to non-institutional locations. Many were sent to state schools, but some were not relocated at all because other facilities were not available. The population of children at Elba therefore still contains about fifteen children who are mentally retarded in a legal sense, who got into the state hospital for several more or less gratuitous reasons, but who continue to make the establishment of an effective program more difficult than it might be if all the patients were of adequate intellectual competence. For the time being at least, this is one of the conditions we have to live with.

For the next two months, almost the only thing that happened by way of program development was that the committee continued to meet regularly. The problems they considered were many in number, various in kind, and ranged in gravity from questions of carpentry (most of one session was occupied with a discussion of the relative merits of Dutch doors versus single doors for the clothing room) to the basic philosophy of the treatment program. A study of the minutes of the committee meetings suggested that little was being proposed, much less done, by way of improved treatment for the children, so I undertook a more thorough study of the program at that time.

I talked with many people, from the Zone Director to the patients, and I stayed long enough on the wards to gain some reasonably stable and consistent beliefs about the daily lives of patients there. Clearly very little was going on by way of active treatment. One of the girls whom I had asked to describe a typical day on the ward said she got up about six in the morning, had breakfast, and cleaned her room. People with ground passes were let out then but most of the people did not have these, and the restricted patients spent the rest of the morning "just watching TV, when it works—it ain't working now—or just sitting around." At eleven, they "had medicine," and at twelve they had lunch. After noon, those who went to school were let out for that; the rest just sat around the ward again. At four the school pupils returned to the ward, had dinner an hour or so later, and then were confined through the evening until medicine and bedtime came around again. She said, "It gets pretty bad around here sometimes. We fight because there's nothing else to do. Sometimes we bug the aides. . . . At least there's something going on that way."

The aides were clearly preoccupied with matters of control. One of them showed me a table knife she had taken away from a patient and said "This can be a lethal weapon." She then told me, with a good deal of emotion, that she "loved kids" but didn't know how much longer she could "take it" in this ward.

The other personnel with whom I talked emphatically stressed the great difficulty they were having getting anything done for the children. More child care workers had been promised but none had appeared. A special training program for them had been approved but nothing had been done to get this underway. New space was needed for an activities program but none had been found. It was clear from all my inquiries that fundamental administrative support for the program was less than enthusiastic, so I went to see the Superintendent.

There was, I learned from him, a basic ambivalence about the children's program which he personally experienced and which had roots in higher level administrative indecision about psychiatric care for children. The history of all this was fantastically complex. The outcome was that no one in power had ever really decided whether there were to be children's services in the state hospitals or not, and that the Superintendent wanted to "do something for the kids" but was reluctant to move forward too rapidly until he "got the word from the Center Office." He said if he really got a program going at Elba and everybody knew about it, he would be overwhelmed by a flood of disturbed children from Chicago. The mental health facilities there were woefully inadequate to accommodate the need, but sending the unmanageable horde to Elba did not seem to offer a very helpful solution to the problem either.

Conversation with the Zone Director showed that he was personally opposed to developing a large children's program at Elba. He believed that it would be vastly preferable to "turn off the flow from Chicago," and was working toward that end with the staff in the central office.

This impasse clearly had to be overcome, one way or another, if progress toward an effective program were ever to be made. At about that time, a commission had been established by the State Director of Mental Health to study the problem of children's psychiatric services. The members had recommended that quantitatively limited but clearly defined children's units be set up in all state hospitals, and the Director had asked for comments from a great many of the people who would be involved in the programs.

I wrote a letter to the Director suggesting that the administrative miracles which would stop the flow of juvenile patients into state hospitals did not seem in prospect of occurring in the immediate future though we all were committed to that as an ultimate goal. It seemed a good idea in the meantime to develop the most effective programs available resources would permit. With all possible emphasis, I said that whatever decisions were reached should be stated with sufficient force to guarantee dependable support for any actions people might begin to undertake in the hospitals themselves. I am sure other people expressed opinions too, and that not all of them were in favor of developing explicit children's programs in the state hospital system, but the ultimate decision of the Director was to encourage programs of this kind.

In a phone conversation with the Zone Director a short time later, I was told that there would be a distinct children's unit at Elba, and indeed that funds for construction of cottage facilities for children had been given a high priority in the capital budget for the next biennium. The Superintendent at Elba then released one floor of a very large building for use as a gymnasium by the juvenile patients, and a number of other program developments very quickly began to transpire.

Within three months' time, regular patient–staff meetings were occurring on all the wards, a rather full activities schedule had been planned for the children, a group of volunteers from a nearby Catholic school had begun to come in one afternoon each week to assist with the activities program, arrangements had been made to take the children swimming at the local YMCA, and an explorer scout troop had been organized.

I was not especially concerned with any elegancies of program evaluation at this time. The first job was to get a program of some kind going, and to initiate action where there had been none before. I did everything I could do to encourage development of the program right then, no matter how chaotic it all seemed to the scientist in me. The changes were allowed to consolidate for approximately three more months, and then another informal inquiry was undertaken. The length of hospital stay was determined for the very first group of children who had been assembled in a single location when the program began. There were 14 patients in this sample and the mean length of hospitalization was 10.09 months. This value was compared with that for a sample of 66 patients who had entered the juvenile unit around 18 months later, after the various kinds of program enrichment mentioned above had been put into effect. The average length of hospitalization for this group was 6.27 months and the difference between that and the mean of 10.09 months for the earlier sample is not only statistically reliable but appears to be of some clinical and administrative importance.

The difference itself, of course, says nothing about origin. There is no way of telling whether the effect was created by the volunteers, the milieu therapy meetings, the increased involvement of the children in extra-hospital community life, the mere fact that hospital administrators noticed the children more now that so many of them were all together instead of allowing them to get lost in the hospital bureaucracy, or some indeterminant combination of these and other factors.

From additional observations on the wards and particularly from talking with the staff, it became obvious that while "things were much better now," the program left much to be desired by way of coherence and clarity. The aides were uncertain about their positions in the program. They were not supposed to be the passive-authoritarian custodians they had been before, but no one had really told them what else to be. They spoke of a "lack of communication" and of "working blind" with the children. The three shifts operated quite independently of one another "like three different hospitals," as one aide put it, and neither the staff nor the children knew quite what to expect from one another.

Manifestly the program required a better statement of objectives, a clearer delineation of staff positions, an improved means of communicating useful information among the various agencies and people who were working with the children, a better means of training personnel, and as usual a more orderly way of evaluating the program than had been achieved so far. Progress toward all these ends was considerably furthered by two new developments. One was the appointment of a permanent Unit Director to provide the functional leadership the program had previously lacked. Three different physicians had adminis-

tered the program over its history. None of them had much training in psychiatry, let alone child psychiatry; none had any experience working with children; and not one of them, despite their good intentions, really knew what to do in shaping the program. The Unit Director now in charge of the unit has had two years of residential training in psychiatry and two additional years of experience working on the children's unit of another state hospital. He shows a strong desire to develop the best program possible for the children at Elba; he is intelligent, willing to acknowledge deficiencies and remedy defects when these appear, and above all he tends to agree with me about the basic features of the program. We work together very well, and I cannot pretend my favorable regard him is uncolored by that fact.

The second major development, beyond appointment of the Unit Director, was the institution of a behavioral merit system for the children. I encouraged development of the general concept as strongly as I could, and incidentally found the phrase *merit system* much more acceptable to most hospital personnel than such terms as *token economy*, though the basic principles and operations are much the same. The concrete definition of behavior classes and the tactics of administration, however, were left to the Unit Director and his working staff. I think it is far more important to gain the personnel involvement of the people who are going to do the work in an enterprise of this kind than to define the substantive and tactical details of the action in a compulsively careful way. The classes of behavior which emerged from the discussion of the Unit Director and his staff thus seem less than ideal with regard to such desiderata as behavioral specificity and independence among classes, and they reflect the interests of aide management in a predictably unilateral way. The Director and the aides decided to rate the children on good grooming, room care, peer relationships, response to authority, punctuality, cooperation, and courtesy. When I saw the list, I said "Great! That's fine! Let's get it going!" in the knowledge that we could change it later on, and indeed that the need for changes would probably become self-evident as the work progressed.

In additional staff meetings, the details of a six-point scale from extremely good performance (5) to total failure (0) were worked out; it was agreed that grounds passes should be employed as the major incentive for good behavior, or from another viewpoint, the privilege to be earned by demonstrated responsibility on the part of the children.

The privilege contingency itself was deferred one week, however, while the aides familiarized themselves with the ratings and baseline data were obtained. Then the merit system was announced to the children at one of their regular patient government meetings. They were told how many points they would have to accumulate for a grounds pass and what they would have to do behaviorally to earn the ratings.

The procedure has now been in effect for six weeks on the adolescent boys' ward. It has only been in use for a week on the wards for younger boys and for girls, so only the results for the older male patients are reported. The main findings are shown in Figure 1. During the first baseline week, ratings averaged only slightly more than 2.00, a poor performance as the scale was de-

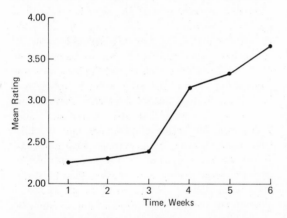

Figure 1. Increase in mean rating of ward behavior following institution of a merit system.

fined. During the second and third weeks, after the privilege system was in effect, very little happened to the ratings, and there was no reason to suppose that any changes were actually taking place in the behavior of the children. I talked with some of them at this time, and found that many did not really believe their own behavior would determine what happened to them. One said, "They're going to let me out when they feel like it, just like they always did." A few began "making points" in earnest, however, and the variance in ratings was significantly higher in the second and third weeks than in the first. The major changes took place in the fourth, fifth, and sixth weeks. By then the children had seen for themselves that the Unit Director meant what he

said; the children who had visibly shaped up were given freedom and a certain responsible status which others were denied, and more and more of them began to show average to good behavior. The mean rating for the sixth week of the program is significantly different from that for the first week $(P_t < .01)$ without even taking the substantial correlation between first- and sixth-week scores into account.

Through interviews with several aides, I learned that they were pleased with the changes which had taken place in the behavior of the children, and hence in the general situation on the ward. In the typical comments of one woman, "It really works great . . . now I know how the kids are doing on the night shift and maybe over at school too. They'll call me if somebody really fouls up. . . . There's better communication than there used to be." She cited a number of examples of children who had changed considerably in the short time the system had been in effect, but added, "Some of these kids are just little con men. They're out to make points, but they aren't really changing." I avoided philosophical argument with her on this point, but tried to find out what she would regard as a real change. We finally agreed that if a child was not just putting us on with his good behavior, but had adopted the goals as his own, and especially, if he would continue to show the improved behavior in other places and for a reasonably long time after he left the ward, the change would be about as real as human behavior changes ever get.

The merit system was not evaluated with complete favor by the children, but all of those I talked to agreed that changes had occurred and most of them approved of the way things were going on the ward at the time. One said, "It's a lot stricter around here than it used to be, but I like it better. . . . You know what to expect." Other signs of change were also evident. The aides and children reported far less fighting on the ward than took place before, and property damage had been visibly reduced. Before the merit system went into effect, an average of eight windows per week were broken on the boys' adolescent ward. Only two have been broken in the past three weeks.

Just a week ago, two other organizational changes were made at Elba. Both are aspects of the general shift to unit operation, and they seem likely to have considerable effect on the children's program in the future. After extensive discussion, the Committee on Juvenile Patients' Affairs voted itself out of existence, probably the most decisive action it has ever taken, and the authority for day-to-day operational affairs has been transferred formally and firmly to the unit staff, with the Director in administrative charge. This change was accompanied by general agreement that decisional power should be decentralized as much as possible, with the children themselves ultimately taking as much responsibility for their own lives as their capabilities and the constraints of circumstance would allow.

The second organizational change concerns the input of patients. In the past they have gone just to the diagnostic service, where they have spent an average of three weeks, waiting for the study to be completed. Now they are to be placed directly in the children's unit, and at least the administrative precondition for continuity and immediacy of treatment as well as for improved unity in the assessment and modification of behavior has finally been met.

It is too early to say what the effects of these measures will be, but I am quite certain that they will shorten the hospital stay still further and faster with more effective help for the children than has been available in the past.

That is where we stand now. For all the shortcomings of the program, it is fair to say that some changes have taken place, and in fact the contrast with conditions two years ago is rather marked. There have been some changes in the basic aims of treatment. At the time when the children were scattered throughout the hospital, the real goal of institutional management went very little beyond custodial care and coping with crises. To a very appreciable extent now, the aides, the physicians, the activities workers, and all the others who work with the children have a more definite and higher objective. It is to change the behavior of the children in ways which will help them get along better in their lives within and beyond the hospital. The number of people who regard this as an aim in which they have an important personal part to play has been increased. The aides are involved to a degree they were not before, and the children are coming to realize the part they themselves must take in the attainment of personal responsibility and social competence. The organizational structure of the children's unit has progressed from literally no organization at all, through a long period of formation by a central committee, to a reasonably accurate facsimile of local unit operation today. The procedures used to accomplish collective aims within this structure

have changed from the custodial nursing of the early continued treatment service, through a phase of vigorous but chaotic program development, to the somewhat greater coherence provided by the merit system now in effect. And the statements of staff and patients alike offer reason to say that some changes have taken place in the belief systems, in the cultural assumptions, on which the aims, the organizations, and the procedures all are based. I have not once in the past three months heard the aides talk about mental illness. To an increasing extent, they are talking instead about the ways the children are behaving, and are asking what they can do to improve the behavior.

These claims can be made with no denial of remaining faults in the program. Elba is not the dumpheap it once was, but it is not exactly a showplace of psychiatric excellence either. The merit system, for example, can be improved and extended in many ways. The need for individual behavior assessment is still unmet. As the code is now defined, some generally desirable forms of action have been stipulated from the viewpoint of the Unit Director, the aides, and the hospital management generally. But no one yet is trying very hard to identify desired behavior changes for each child, to assure that patients and staff alike know what the target behaviors are, and to establish effective ways to encourage their emission. It will be far easier to do this as a part of the general merit system now in effect than it would have been before. All we need to do is add a column or two for individual changes, and this could be accomplished at no clerical cost by eliminating some of the redundant characteristics which staff now have to evaluate. The intercorrelations among *peer relationships, cooperation,* and *response to authority,* for example, range from .93 to .97, and one rating will obviously do for them all. Inclusion of individually defined target behaviors should help fortify each child's conviction that the people in the hospital are trying to help *him* get better, and would qualify more truly as a therapeutic system in effect at the present time.

It would be a fairly simple matter to bring reinforcing consequences closer to behavior by manipulating grounds privileges on a daily rather than a weekly basis. A week's restriction is a hazy lifetime for some of these children, but they may be able to look a day ahead and pattern their behavior accordingly. A token system might be in-

avior of certain designated kinds on the part
atients and staff alike, and regular surveys of
patients and staff, to find out what the major
lems are in the operation and to identify pos-
useful ways of solving the problems.

believe these all will be helpful measures to
though getting them into effect will be no
affair. A consultant, for that matter any
ge agent, is only one influence among many
he degree of effect and order he may expect
to attain is inherently limited. I think there is no
way to order life completely, either by way of
comprehension or control. What I have learned
from the Elbas . . . of my experience is that I
come for a time into the lives of others, learn
what I can about them, change something if I
can and hope it is for the better, and then move
out again while the people and the groups and
the organizations I have known go on somehow
without me.

stituted. Other incentives and deterrents could be employed. Disturbed twelve-year-olds tend to have the utmost contempt for anyone who will work for lollypops, but they really do like candy bars, and properly offered and well delivered, a hundred dollars' worth of incentive material might go a long way in encouraging the children's need to develop in their own self interest. A camping trip has already been held as a privilege to be earned by mature behavior rather than as a necessarily salubrious activity which every child should enjoy as a matter of right. Movies, trips to the swimming pool, and other experiences could be regulated in a similar way. We can also do more than we have to generalize the present merit system, or some revised version to be developed in the future, across and beyond the hospital. The teachers and activities workers can take part in the rating operation. They too can know, encourage, and help define the kinds of behavior to be expected of every child, and a more coherent treatment program can be extended over all situations and through all the hours of the daily lives of the patients. A well defined merit system can also serve as the vehicle for extending treatment into the community. The children who come to Elba are not generally blessed with intact and effective families or they would probably never have gotten to Elba in the first place. But sooner or later every child is released to some kind of familoid group, and a change in social service procedure might readily be made to transfer the information and techniques developed in the hospital to the people in charge outside. A talk with those involved, telling them what had been set as the behavioral goals at Elba, how these were accomplished if indeed they were, and what the parents or others might do to keep the action going and maybe to increase benefits still further, should be feasible even within present limits of time and personnel, and might be the opening wedge of a more generally effective community program in which work in the hospital is related more closely to work outside than it has ever been before.

The need for better training of personnel is woefully evident. We must train a larger sector of the staff with emphasis on aides and nurses, but with proper attention to other personnel, including the physicians, if we can get to them. The aides, nurses, teachers, and others must not only be told that they are to take more active roles in treatment than before, but they must be shown how.

A training program of sorts
for aides and nurses. About h
to the children's unit have
lecture-discussions by Unive
chology consultants, and ha
about behavioral approach
ment. I believe the accept
merit system is related to
training of aides is contr
Service, however, and the
still stresses medication ar
too emphatic a way. Seve
the Director of Nurses' T
and I think that a more
ally oriented training pr
into effect if we can get t
power to do it. This mo
and interpersonal aspe
plexity, but in general I
will be accepted by h
portion to the progra
There may be delays,
time, patience, and
skill, but the people
have most of the sa
genuine contribution
tively, they tend to
own way, with a ca
ence. Other "new
problem" have be
previous consultan
astically by the h
into the system as
tible advantage.
found field pers
not impervious to
and I believe we
stantially the tra

The procedur
be extended, sy
more general o
So far, I have
operation who
tems analysis,
evaluation. T
gram evaluat
machinery o
Psychologist
along these
one source
for the co
mind. The
fined, but

a longitudinal study of schizophrenic children with autism

Lauretta Bender

Childhood schizophrenia is an early manifestation of schizophrenia as it appears in adolescents and adults. It is an endogenous disorder of the total organism. The inherited predisposition may remain latent or may develop into some form of schizophrenic illness. When such decompensation occurs in early childhood, it is the result of a combination of inherited tendencies and noxious or traumatic events, intrauterine or perinatal. The combination leads to a global disorganization in physiological and psychological functions that appear as maturational lags or embryonic immaturities and are characterized by plasticity in patterning, in boundaries, and in relationships.

Because schizophrenic decompensation in early childhood occurs partly as a result of intrauterine or perinatal events, such children usually also show evidence of developmental defects; sometimes there is brain damage, usually minimal. Their ever-present core anxiety requires some defense mechanism, often autistic withdrawal.

Many but not all young schizophrenic children present some of the features of infantile autism described by Leo Kanner. He spoke of an innate disturbance in the first and second year of life, characterized by extreme autistic aloneness; an obsessive desire for unchanging environment, daily routine, and personal experiences; and language disturbance, with muteness or noncommunicative language such as echolalia, bizarre speech, evidence of thought disturbances, and failure to use the first-person pronoun. The child also has a poor object relationship, except with nonhuman objects, and low intellectual functioning on tests, although such children often show isolated areas of high cognitive ability.[1]

Kanner saw early infantile autism as a specific syndrome, not necessarily part of a schizophrenic illness. In the United States, unfortunately, every young child who fails to develop normally may be labeled autistic, whether his failure is caused by developmental defects, organic brain pathology, mental retardation, or schizophrenia. That leads to the belief that the failure was caused by infantile deprivation of emotional, social, and sensory stimulation, and therefore could be corrected by appropriate psychotherapy, especially in a one-to-one relationship. Heart-breaking experiences resulting from this illusion have not been recorded as often as they should have been. Recently, however, John Kysar dramatized such an experience in a paper "The Two Camps in Child Psychiatry: A Report from a Psychiatrist–Father of an Autistic and Retarded Child."[2]

Similar errors have been made about children born very prematurely who have suffered blindness from retrolental fibroplasia and who function at a very low level. The blindness results from hyperoxia in extensive incubator care at a critical period in the development of the eye. The low functioning is ascribed to autism. It is even called schizophrenia and is said to be caused by sensory, social, and emotional deprivation due to the incubation, blindness, and assumed rejection by the parents. However, studies by Karl Andermann and myself of 22 such children showed that they had all suffered brain damage, probably early in the mother's pregnancy, and that their low functioning was due to brain defects and damage.[3]

In my view, autism is a defense by withdrawal in a young child who suffers from disorganization,

[1] Kanner, Leo, "Problems of Nosology and Psychodynamics of Early Infantile Autism," *American Journal of Orthopsychiatry*, Vol. 19, July 1949, pp. 416–426.

[2] Kysar, John E., "The Two Camps in Child Psychiatry: A Report from a Psychiatrist–Father of an Autistic and Retarded Child," *American Journal of Psychiatry*, Vol. 125, July 1968, pp. 103–109.

[3] Bender, Lauretta, & Andermann, Karl, "Brain Damage in Blind Children with Retrolental Fibroplasia," *Archives of Neurology*, Vol. 12, June 1965, pp. 644–649.

Reprinted by permission from *Hospital and Community Psychiatry*, August, 1969, pp. 28–35.

disturbed patterning, and maturational disorders, and the resulting anxiety that occurs in schizophrenia, brain defects and pathology, or other severe traumata.[4] Often all these conditions occur in one severely ill child. If one is to adequately diagnose, treat, and prognosticate the life course of a child who has started life with infantile autism or childhood schizophrenia with autism and is to guide his parents, one must recognize all the factors.

A group of children, diagnosed childhood schizophrenics before the age of 12, who were on the children's ward of Bellevue Psychiatric Hospital between 1935 and 1952, have been the subjects of repeated follow-up studies. From that pool of 200 cases, 50 who met the criteria of infantile autism described by Kanner [5] have been selected. Those children, after their initial period of study and treatment at Bellevue, and several subsequent follow-up studies,[6] are again having their life course reviewed to the present time. Many are in state institutions where they and their records are accessible to me. A report of these 50 autistic schizophrenic children is in press.[7]

[4] See Margaret S. Mahler, *On Human Symbiosis and the Vicissitudes of Individuation*, Vol. I, International Universities Press, New York City, 1968, p. 2.

[5] Kanner, *op. cit.*

[6] Bender, Lauretta, & Freedman, Alfred M., "A Study in the First Three Years in the Maturation of Schizophrenic Children," *Quarterly Journal of Child Behavior*, Vol. 4, July 1952, pp. 245–272. Alfred M. Freedman and Lauretta Bender, "When the Childhood Schizophrenic Grows Up," *American Journal of Orthopsychiatry*, Vol. 27, July 1957, pp. 553–565. Lauretta Bender, Alfred M. Freedman, Alvin E. Grugett, Jr., and William Helme, "Schizophrenia in Childhood: Confirmation of Diagnosis," in *Transactions of the American Neurological Association*, Vol. 77, 1952, pp. 67–73. Lauretta Bender and Saul Gurevitz, "Results With Psychotherapy With Young Schizophrenic Children," *American Journal of Orthopsychiatry*, Vol. 25, January 1955, pp. 162–170. Lauretta Bender, "Diagnostic and Therapeutic Aspects of Childhood Schizophrenia," in *Mental Retardation: Proceedings of the First International Medical Conference*, edited by Peter W. Bowman and Hans V. Mautner, Grune & Stratton, New York City, 1960, pp. 453–468. Lauretta Bender, "The Origin and Evolution of the Gestalt Function, the Body Image, and Delusional Thoughts in Schizophrenia," in *Recent Advances in Biological Psychiatry*, Vol. V, edited by Joseph Wortis, Plenum Press, New York City, 1963, pp. 38–62. Lauretta Bender, "Twenty-Five-Year View of Therapeutic Results," in *Evaluation of Psychiatric Treatment*, edited by Paul Hoch and Joseph Zubin, Grune & Stratton, New York City, 1964, pp. 129–142.

[7] "The Life Course of Children With Autism," in *Psychiatric Approaches to Mental Retardation in*

For this paper I will analyze the life course of 30 of the 50, who, if alive, now range in age from 22 to 42. To make a meaningful comparison, we must consider them in two groups: the 17 patients (3 women) with predominant organicity, who are in chronic institutional care except for 6, all males, who died between the ages of 18 and 40; and 13 individuals who have made a social adjustment in the community.

The data came from the Bellevue records, and from records available to me from New York State institutions, where I have been a consultant since 1956, and from the repeated follow-up studies. The records give us the cultural, socioeconomic, and hereditary background of the patients; the organic factors of the mothers' pregnancies, the perinatal period, and the early infancy of the patients; and their early developmental factors, especially their speech and the autistic features observed in early childhood. The records also describe their mid-childhood, when many of them were seen at Bellevue, diagnosed as schizophrenic, and given various forms of treatment; their adolescence, after they left Bellevue, with the variable patterns of home, school, and institutional experiences; and finally, their adulthood, when I came into repeated contact with many of them in various institutions for the mentally ill or retarded or in correctional institutions.

One might expect that the cultural and religious origins of the 30 individuals would reflect those of the New York population of the 1930s and 1940s, when as children the subjects were referred to the city hospital under an unrestricted admission policy. However, that is not so. Of the total group of 30 children, 13, or 43 per cent, came from homes where the parents were European Jews, first- or second-generation Americans; 8, or 27 per cent, had Italian or Irish Catholic parents; and the parents of 8, or 27 per cent, were of mixed Western-European and Protestant origin and not recent immigrants. There was one black child of Haitian parentage.

I have previously noted that a relatively high percentage of young schizophrenic children referred for professional care are Jewish, while few are American Negroes.[8] We do not believe that indicates a different incidence of schizophrenia

Childhood, edited by Frank J. Menolascino, Basic Books, New York City (in press).

[8] Bender, Lauretta, & Grugett, Alvin E. Jr., "A Study of Certain Epidemiological Factors in a Group of Children With Childhood Schizophrenia," *American Journal of Orthopsychiatry*, Vol. 26, January 1956, pp. 131–145.

in the two ethnic groups, but rather that Jewish middle-class and professional parents are more aware of deviations in child development and seek earlier medical help for their children. The low number of poverty-class Negro patients represents a failure in case-finding.

When we compared the two groups in this study, we found that 6, or 30 per cent, of the 17 patients with predominant organicity and 7, or 54 per cent, of the 13 who have made a social adjustment as adults had Jewish parents. Bernard Rimland relates the high incidence of autistic children with Jewish parents to a high degree of intellectual eminence among Jews. He speculates that children with infantile autism are born of a special type of highly intellectual parents.[9] Kanner, too, claimed that the parents of children with infantile autism were highly intelligent but emotionally cold and detached.[10] The Bellevue case material does not confirm either's assumption.

Although most children treated at Bellevue Hospital came from families of a marginal or dependent income level, only 20 per cent of the autistic group did. Eleven of the 30 children had parents in the professions; 13 had parents who had small businesses or worked for others; and 6 came from low-income families. The socioeconomic difference between the autistic and other child patients is largely a reflection of the parents' awareness. The more affluent and educated families were most likely to identify their child's deviant development and to learn of our program, which was one of the few available for schizophrenic children at that time.

Of the 17 children with predominant organicity, 7 had parents in the professions, compared with 4 of the 13 patients who made a social adjustment. Among the latter group, 2 families were on welfare and 4 fathers worked at jobs below their educational level because of schizoid traits. Two patients had been born out of wedlock and raised in foster homes.

Since the histories given of emotional disorders among the families must be considered minimal, the data are quite impressive. The 30 children had 7 psychotic siblings, 6 psychotic mothers, 5 psychotic fathers, and 12 collateral relatives with psychoses. They also had 10 relatives with seriously deviant personalities, although they had not been diagnosed in a medical facility as being psychotic.

[9] Rimland, Bernard, *Infantile Autism*, Appleton-Century-Crofts, New York City, 1964.
[10] Kanner, *op. cit.*

That total of 40 mentally disordered relatives represents 1.3 per child. Seven of the 30 patients had no history of familial mental illness: 5, or 29 per cent, of the 17 patients with organicity, compared with 2, or 15 per cent, of the 13 socially adjusted patients. That difference seems to suggest some relationship between organicity and less familial mental disorder. However, the other hereditary differences between the two groups of patients were not significant. The socially adjusted group had a total of 16 psychotic and 4 socially deviant relatives, and the other group had 14 psychotic and 6 deviant family members.

In general, the genetics of childhood schizophrenia as shown in the Bellevue studies [11] is similar to what was shown by Franz Kallmann and Bernard Roth, who studied prepuberty schizophrenia in 52 pairs of twins (17 monozygotic and 35 dizygotic) and 50 singletons, and compared the family backgrounds of these patients with those of a comparable sample of adult patients. They found that for the children, 12.5 per cent of the parents and 12.2 per cent of the siblings were schizophrenic; that compares with a rate of 9.2 per cent of the parents and 14.3 per cent of the siblings of the adult schizophrenics.[12] Kallmann and Roth also confirmed the Bellevue experience that the incidence of schizophrenia before puberty is always higher in boys than in girls, although that relationship is reversed after puberty. The fact has been attributed to the lesser capacity of the young male to maturate smoothly; a similar relationship has been shown for many other developmental deviations in children.[13]

For the 17 patients in our study who had predominant organicity, 12 normal gestation periods and 13 normal births were recorded. There was one stormy pregnancy during which abortives were used, and one pregnancy with bleeding; one mother had surgery for sinus infection during her pregnancy, another had suffered three miscarriages, and one mother had previously had a tubal pregnancy. Two premature births and one postmature birth occurred; one child was delivered in

[11] Bender, Lauretta, "Mental Illness in Childhood and Heredity," *Eugenics Quarterly*, Vol. 10. March 1963, pp. 1–11.
[12] Kallmann, Franz, & Roth, Bernard, "Genetic Aspects of Preadolescent Schizophrenia," *American Journal of Psychiatry*, Vol. 112, February 1956, pp. 599–606.
[13] Falek, Arthur, book review of *A Clinical and Genetic Population Study* by T. Larsson and T. Sjogren, *American Journal of Human Genetics*, Vol. 12, September 1960, pp. 379–380.

a cyanotic condition with the cord around his neck. Additional complications during pregnancy or birth may have gone unrecorded, because the information was obtained 20 or 30 years ago by a mixed staff of varied backgrounds.

Of the 17 children, 10 had congenital defects: 3 were microcephalic, 2 had internal hydrocephalus, 2 had birth weights below five pounds, one was a pituitary (Levi-Lorain) dwarf, another was acromegalic, and one had pes cavus, with other defects. Furthermore, only 3 of the 17 were reported to have been normal infants before the age of 2. The others were reported to have been sickly babies with severe respiratory and intestinal disorders, generalized allergic eczema, calcium tetany, and head injuries. Most important, 4 had infantile convulsions. All of the 17 subjects showed at least one form of pathology at some time during gestation, birth, or the first two years. One underwent a mastoidectomy at 30 months; another had acute encephalitis at 40 months. Besides the 4 incidences of infantile convulsion, 8 children had convulsions in adolescence. (One child had convulsions in both infancy and adolescence.)

There was an even higher rate of pathological gestation reported for the 13 patients who as adults made a social adjustment in the community. Only 6 of the mothers claimed to have had normal pregnancies. Two others had attempted abortion; one of them had bleeding in the second and eighth months, and the infant was jaundiced at birth. One mother, pregnant for the first time at age 39, carried the infant three weeks past term before labor was induced; the infant's birth-weight was nearly 12 pounds, and his head had instrument marks, but he seemed normal during his first year. One mother was a severe alcoholic, and the baby was placed in a foundling home at birth and later in a foster home; the mother had three more children, who developed normally, before she was placed in a mental hospital.

One mother had a tubal pregnancy and a tumor, but the birth was normal; however, the baby had severe intestinal and respiratory disorders and during his first month was constantly ill with diarrhea. Another mother had previously had a tubal pregnancy and a miscarriage, and the infant developed autistically from birth. Still another mother, an x-ray technician, was exposed to an erythematous dose of radiation in early pregnancy and two weeks before birth received an accidental electric shock that stopped fetal movements for a week; the baby was born at seven and

a half months and looked premature although he weighed seven pounds.

The 13 patients in this group also had a high rate of other physical disorders during infancy, including respiratory infections, gastrointestinal disturbances, measles, and whooping cough; 4 had to have mastoidectomies. However, only one patient in this group was ever reported to have suffered a convulsion, compared with 11 of the 17 patients with marked organicity. That patient had a single convulsion at the age of 9 years and 9 months and showed an atypical epileptogenic electroencephalogram.

Kanner, in his original series of cases of infantile autism, measured the severity of the illnesses by the child's capacity to use language by the age of 5. That proved to be a useful predictor of school adjustment in adolescence. His description of the "irrelevant and metaphorical language" in infantile autism is well known and has been widely reprinted.[14]

None of the 13 autistic schizophrenic children in this study had normal communicative use of language at the age of 5. Of the 17 with marked organicity, 13 showed a slow development of language and retarded language at age 5; 3 were reported to have developed language normally until they were 2½ or 3½ years and then regressed and used language in a retarded and schizophrenic fashion at age 5; one was precocious in language development but used it in a schizophrenic and non-communicative fashion.

Of the 13 children who ultimately made a social adjustment, 6 had a history of slow development of language, 5 of normal early development, and 2 of precocious development before 3½ years. But at 5 years, they had all regressed and used language in a schizophrenic and non-communicative fashion. Using Kanner's criterion of useful and communicative language, we found that all but one of the 13 who later made a social adjustment had developed speech before 5 years, 2 of them

[14] Leo Kanner's original article (1943), "Autistic Disturbance in Affective Contact," has recently been reprinted in *Acta Paedopsychiatrica*, Vol. 35, Fasc. 4-8, 1968, pp. 98–136. For the follow-up of these children into adolescence, see Leo Kanner and Leo Eisenberg, "Early Infantile Autism 1943–1955," in *Stress; Experimental Psychology; Child Psychiatry*, Psychiatric Research Report No. 7, American Psychiatric Association, Washington, D.C., 1957, pp. 55–65; and for the paper on language disturbances, see Leo Kanner, "Irrelevant and Metaphorical Language in Early Infantile Autism," *American Journal of Psychiatry*, Vol. 103, September 1946, pp. 242–246.

precociously. Four had lost it before age 5. The exception was a boy who had echolalia but could make average scores on performance tests. Two boys who had developed the ability to speak and then lost it had regained schizophrenic language by age 5; 2 others did not regain speech until a later age.

Many different forms of language disturbance occurred. Often a child's language varied from time to time, perhaps over a period of months. Some became mute, either with full understanding of heard language or with total inattention. Some failed to use the first-person pronoun. Some employed neologisms; others mumbled incoherent language used egocentrically; yet others used explosive obscenities, private language, or echolalia. They asked repetitive questions without waiting for an answer, most often about time, place, identity of self, and body-image distortions. Except for the greater proportion of children with retarded language development among those with organic impairment, there appeared to be no relationship between language development and use at the age of 5 years and the final outcome in this series of patients.

Repeated psychometric tests of intelligence were made on most of the individuals. Verbal scores on the Wechsler Intelligence Scale for Children, the Wechsler Adult Intelligence Scale, or the Stanford-Binet were used.

Among the children tested several times before they reached 15, both groups showed some variability in intellectual function.[15] But a general difference between the two groups is evident. The patients with predominant organicity either died or have spent their lives in institutions; they tended to deteriorate in intelligence after childhood and adolescence. Patients who have been able to adjust outside, even though they may have spent much of their childhood and adolescence in institutions, tended to maintain good intelligence and to increase their verbal intelligence score even when it was as low as 30 in early childhood.

Recently Milada Havelkova has claimed that "childhood psychosis is a serious illness resulting in ultimate intellectual deficits which can be only partially prevented by treatment."[16] However,

[15] Wechsler, David, & Jaros, Eugenia, "Schizophrenic Patterns on the WISC," *Journal of Clinical Psychology*, Vol. 31, July 1965, pp. 288–291.

[16] Havelkova, Milada, "Follow-up Study of 71 Children Diagnosed as Psychotic in Preschool Age," *American Journal of Orthopsychiatry*, Vol. 38, October 1968, pp. 846–857.

her study was only a 4- to 12-year follow-up and thus did not extend beyond adolescence, when some of her patients might be expected to show the same spontaneous rise in intelligence quotient our patients did. It is clear, however, that a combination of organic factors and schizophrenia from an early age, as in autistic schizophrenia, does interfere with intellectual development.

The life course of the 17 predominantly organic patients has been one of progressive deterioration, in most cases combined with schizophrenia. In 1968 the surviving 11 were chronically institutionalized: 6 men and 2 women were in institutions for the retarded, one woman was in a mental hospital, and 2 men were in hospitals for the criminally insane, where they were transferred because they became dangerously violent during convulsions. Two of the patients had shown early symptoms of autism and severe infantile illnesses, one with acute encephalitis, after which they seemed to regress and to settle in institutions. One boy whose mother was mentally ill developed precociously and was a dramatic case of infantile autism with bizarre behavior. Another child had a schizophrenic mother and sister. His birthweight at full term was 5 pounds 3 ounces. He never developed mentally beyond the 2-year level and has been epileptic from adolescence on. He and his schizophrenic sister were observed and diagnosed together at 6 and 8 years of age. His sister had not shown any early infantile autism and was less defective than he. She was able to return to and remain in her home, while the boy has spent his life in an institution for the retarded.

Seven of the 11 surviving patients have had convulsions, 2 in infancy and 5 in adolescence, including the 3 women. One woman is a microcephalic defective with a head circumference of 18½ inches. Although she was thought to present some autistic features in childhood, her course has been that of a low-grade defective; she acquired a few words of speech, but lost them after a mastoidectomy at 2½ years. Another woman is a twin whose sibling died. She had been born prematurely, was always sickly, and developed poorly. She was autistic in early childhood and bizarrely schizophrenic in adolescence, and has had one convulsion. There is no history of schizophrenia in either family. The third girl, the oldest of three schizophrenic siblings, had a head circumference of 19½ inches in childhood. Her language was bizarre, she was psychologically untestable, and her behavior was always stereotyped and ritualistic. She has spent her entire life in a mental hospital with a diagnosis of schizophrenia.

Fifteen of the predominantly organic patients, including those who died, received convulsive therapy, seven by Metrazol, and eight by electroshock. Two had no convulsive treatment, and both developed severe epilepsy in adolescence. Two of those who did receive convulsive treatment had isolated convulsions in adolescence, perhaps associated with phenothiazines.

Four of the 15 appeared unaffected by convulsive treatment; 5 improved in habit-training, speech, and general behavior, and one of them in early puberty showed a dramatic remission from a severe psychotic state. Five received anticonvulsant medication, and all have received various tranquilizers during the past ten years, resulting in varying degrees of control of their disturbed behavior.

Six of the eight patients in institutions for the retarded were diagnosed as mentally retarded; one was diagnosed as schizophrenic and the other as psychotic with organic brain disease. Together with the current medical staff of the institutions, I have re-examined all these patients and have agreed that three were organically defective and probably never schizophrenic, although they showed some autistic features in early childhood. In the other five, we agreed to reconfirm the earlier diagnoses of schizophrenia, together with organic disorders and mental deficiency. Of the three patients in state hospitals for the mentally ill or criminally insane, two were diagnosed as schizophrenic and one as psychotic with encephalitis.

Two of the six deceased subjects died in convulsive episodes at ages 18 and 30 years. One of them had strong schizophrenic features and a family history of mental illness as well as infantile organic illnesses; the other, who had a family history of probable schizophrenia, showed early autistic features with congenital internal hydrocephalus and a steady course of organic deterioration. Three others, with no family history of schizophrenia, were markedly dysplastic from birth and had a life history of organic disease; they died of cardiac failure, cardiac dysplasia, and general inanition at the ages of 18, 30, and 40 years.

The sixth patient died of drowning at the age of 22 in an effort to escape from an island hospital; this youth, the Levi-Lorain dwarf, had a strong family history of schizophrenia and had received a diagnosis of infantile autism in three medical centers besides Bellevue; in puberty he was also diagnosed as having a pleuriglandular syndrome. When he was 9 years old his schizophrenia exacerbated into acute psychosis following possible meningitis. He was then in Bellevue, where he received 26 Metrazol shock treatments; they resulted in a marked but short-lasting remission, during which his intelligence was scored in the average range. He spent seven years in a state hospital, with a diagnosis of hebephrenic schizophrenia; he received insulin shock with little benefit.

The life course of the 13 patients now living at home differed considerably from that of the 17 predominantly organic patients, although their history of pathology in pregnancies, births, and early infancy was comparable. It may be significant that the histories of 5 of the 13 contain statements that the child was very much wanted and loved by the parents, who made heroic efforts to keep him at home. They included a boy who had lived with the same foster parents since the age of one month.

These children first came to our attention at Bellevue between the ages of 31 months and 10½ years, after they had been evaluated and treated in private physicians' offices, public clinics, or pediatric services in hospitals. On the children's psychiatric ward at Bellevue, they took part in ward activities, schoolwork, art, music, and puppet shows. Some had extensive psychotherapy during and after their hospital stay. Nine received electroconvulsive treatment, and two had convulsive treatment by Metrazol; one had insulin coma therapy in addition to Metrazol. The remaining child did not receive electroconvulsive treatment until he entered a state hospital at age 15. All the patients spent some time in special residential schools, institutions for the retarded, or state or private mental hospitals, but by 1968 were living at home in some degree of adjustment ranging from psychotic dependency to social and financial independence.

All of them had begun to display autistic behavior during their first or second year of life. Some were quiet and undemanding, but generally immature; some were irritable and anxious, cried frequently, and demanded constant attention. Some became severely regressed or increasingly phobic and anxious for no evident reason or following an apparently precipitating event, such as pneumonia at 9 months, a severe fright and fall at 2 years, or a marked change in the family pattern.

After the age of 2, the children's behavior was characterized by disturbance in motility, withdrawal from sensory stimuli and social contact, various language disorders, outbursts of disturbed behavior, a demand for ritualistic sameness in daily routine, bizarre compulsive habits, and clinging symbiotic attachments to the mother. A few showed precocities in language, structured play, or drawings. Two boys with more normal behavior and speech had a short remission, but three others became more disturbed and regressed between the ages of 3½ and 4, following traumatic incidents. They included a change in foster home, separation from the mother when she had a new baby, and a case of measles and otitis media.

All of the 13 were able to be intellectually evaluated on psychometric tests at an early age; none were recorded as "untestable" at any time, and none deteriorated intellectually. On the contrary, wherever several psychometric tests were recorded and after a period of variability in functioning before 15 years, the trend is for an increase in the verbal intelligence quotient.

All initial IQ scores were above 60, except for one boy who scored 38 at age 5; he had normal speech between the ages of 2 and 3. During adolescence his IQ gradually reached 76, and he received schooling and vocational training in an institution for the retarded. After receiving maximum benefit from that program, he returned home at age 27 and is employed full time. One boy had an initial score of 106 at age 4, and later developed an IQ of 169, but he has spent his life in rehabilitation and psychotherapy programs. Another boy whose IQ was estimated at 62 at age 4 later developed an IQ of 118 and completed college, although he required psychiatric treatment during his last year there and has since been living with his overly protective mother.

A boy whose parents are in the professions was carefully placed in a series of residential schools suited to each phase of his life. He is independently employed and has an active social life through a special organization. Although his level of functioning is below his family's expectations, he has become a contented and well-adjusted individual.

Two boys were never placed in state institutions, although both had several months of care in private psychiatric hospitals and were treated with insulin and electroconvulsive therapy. For the most part they were kept at home by protective mothers, even during periods of catatonic excitement and withdrawal. One boy remains dependent on his mother, who says she does not want him to die in a mental hospital as his father did. The other boy, after staying at home for years in a deteriorated schizophrenic state, had a sudden remission. He passed a civil service examination and has been employed as a park attendant for several years.

Five others were in mental hospitals with diagnoses of schizophrenia until they were 18, 23, 24, 25, and 27. They have since been living at home on tranquilizers, unemployed and dependent on their families. One, a recognized homosexual, had a stormy career in hospitals, including Matteawan State Hospital. He was trained as a beautician at Matteawan and has adjusted outside the hospital since he was 27.

In reviewing the 30 case histories, we find that the subjects, all of whom presented a picture of autism before the age of 2, show a wide range of schizophrenic disorders in adulthood. Only 3, from among the organically defective group, appear not to be schizophrenic but mentally retarded with organic defects, with and without convulsions. Others from the same group were concurrently diagnosed as mentally retarded, but in February 1969 were reevaluated by the present clinical staff, who have agreed that the diagnoses are schizophrenia with mental retardation.

As noted earlier, these 30 cases were from a series of 200 schizophrenic children seen at Bellevue from 1935 to 1952 and followed to adulthood. By the age of 30, one-third of them, including the 13 socially adjusted individuals described here, were doing fairly well, and one-third, including the 17 with predominant organicity, were chronically defective or regressed institutionalized patients. The other third fluctuated from a poor to fair adjustment, most of them living in institutions.

Those proportions are comparable with the outcomes reported by others doing similar research in this country and abroad. In September 1966, at the Fourth World Congress of Psychiatry in Madrid, I discussed papers from five countries on the prognosis of infantile psychoses and neuroses.[17] Among them were Walter Spiel's follow-up studies in Austria, in which he found that one-half of the patients remain deeply regressed, one-third are socially stabilized as neurotics, and one-sixth appear to be practically cured. (The best one-

[17] Bender, Lauretta, "Discussion: Prognosis of Infantile Psychosis and Neurosis," *Excerpta Medica International Congress*, Series No. 150, 1968, pp. 124–126.

sixth of our 200 patients might compare with Spiel's.)

At the congress I also analyzed 12 reports that appeared in the literature during the past 20 years describing studies from the United States, England, Sweden, and Russia. Those studies covered a total of 759 cases followed from childhood to late adolescence or adulthood; 229 subjects, or 31.5 per cent, were said to be making an adequate or normal social adjustment.[18]

In his book *The Empty Fortress*, Bruno Bettelheim reported on the results of "the most intensive and sustained therapy we were able to provide." [19] He compared them with Eisenberg's follow-up of Kanner's original 63 patients with infantile autism, in which one-third were said to function in adolescence at a fair to good social level.[20]

Bettelheim's group worked with 46 autistic children. However, he excluded 6, including one of the 3 reported on in detail in *The Empty Fortress*, because she was removed from treatment after a year and failed to improve, and one who, unbeknown to him, previously had electroshock treatment. He excluded the other 4 because he thought they had not been in treatment long enough. Such exceptions have not been made in any of the other 20 to 25 follow-up studies. If one includes all 46 autistic children in Bettelheim's program and accepts his evaluation of good results in 17 and fair results in 15, and assumes that the remaining 14 (excluding the 6 he excluded) had poor results for whatever reason, his results are similar to those of other researchers. Incidentally, of the 13 autistic schizophrenic children I have here reported to have made an adult social adjustment, 9 had electroshock and 3 Metrazol-induced convulsive therapy in childhood.

C. Gary Merritt has written a careful critique of Bettelheim's follow-up report and questions his conclusions partly, as I have, for excluding poor results, and partly because his report of results did not permit the reader to understand what was meant by "fair" and "poor" results. Bettelheim replied without clarifying the issues.[21]

In her recent report from Toronto, Havelkova analyzes the results of 4- to 12-year follow-up studies of 71 autistic and pseudoneurotic schizophrenic children. The original assessment of 64 of them included a month of observation and therapeutic trial in a day care center; the other 7 children had previously been assessed by Havelkova at Toronto's Hospital for Sick Children. Children with autism secondary to gross brain damage or obvious mental defect were not included in the study. In the original assessments, made during the children's preschool years, 17 were considered severely affected, 29 moderately, and 25 mildly. Six of the mildly affected and 17 of the moderately affected had been treated in a special program at the day center, and another 8 moderately and 8 mildly affected subjects were treated elsewhere; the remaining patients had no formal therapy. At the time of follow-up, the children were between the ages of 8 and 17; of the severe group, 2 were at home and 15 in institutions; of the moderate group, 16 were at home, 9 in institutions, and 4 in residential treatment centers; of the mild group, 20 were at home, 2 in institutions, and 3 in treatment centers. Of the 38 children living at home, 9 of the moderately affected and 8 of the mildly affected attended normal classes in school.

Havelkova avoids categorical conclusions, but she comments, "Our general impression is that childhood psychosis is a serious illness resulting, in most cases, in ultimate intellectual deficit of different degrees that can be only partially prevented by treatment. . . . Changes in the clinical form of childhood psychosis . . . appear to occur on a maturational basis in the less severely ill children irrespective of therapeutic procedures." [22] Although this study does not follow most of the children beyond childhood, it is a careful, insightful, and important report.

As the several studies show, there is no single life pattern for schizophrenic children with infantile autism. As adults they are still schizophrenic, often with some form of organic defect, but they show a great variety of life adjustments and varying degrees of dependency.

[18] *Ibid.*

[19] Bettelheim, Bruno. *The Empty Fortress*, Free Press, New York City, 1967, pp. 413–416.

[20] Kanner & Eisenberg, *op. cit.*

[21] Merritt, Gary C., review of *The Empty Fortress* by Bruno Bettelheim, in *American Journal of Orthopsychiatry*, Vol. 38, October 1968, pp. 926–930. Reply by Bruno Bettelheim, pp. 930–933.

[22] Havelkova, *op. cit.*

the adult development of the antisocial child

Lee N. Robins

"Where have all the young men gone,
Long time passing,
Where have all the young men gone,
Long time ago?"

*—Pete Seeger**

The distribution by sex and complaint in the ordinary psychiatric clinic is vastly different from the distribution an adult clinic. The children's clinic contains a high proportion of boys, while the adult clinic has about equal proportions of men and women, with a slight excess of women aged 25 to 35. (8, 31) A large proportion of the referrals to children's clinics are for acting-out behavior (personality disorders), particularly among boys. Personality disorder in adult clinics is similarly seen mostly in men, but constitutes only a relatively small proportion of the total referrals.

What are we to make of these characteristic differences? One possible explanation is that most of the antisocial behavior of childhood is a transient phenomenon, perhaps a product of boys being forced into school situations where their natural proclivities run afoul of rules established by proper middleclass teachers. If this is the source of many referrals to children's clinics, we would expect the problem for most boys to disappear once they reached the legal age for leaving school.

Another possibility is that antisocial boys continue to be seen in clinics as adults, but form a much smaller proportion of the total clinic population as they are outnumbered by the neuroses,

predominantly female, which have their onset in late adolescence and adulthood.

A third possibility is that while the flood of female neuroses explains the change in the sex ratio, the decline in personality disorders among men results from a transformation with aging of their antisocial symptoms into the symptoms of psychosis and neurosis.

A final possibility is that the antisocial boys who were known to children's clinics continue to show antisocial behavior as adults, but are no longer considered psychiatric cases. Instead of appearing in adult psychiatric clinics, they become the clients of parole officers and social workers, once they reach the age at which they are presumed "responsible" for their own behavior.

Comparing the patients in children's and adult clinics in a cross-sectional study does not allow choosing among these possible explanations. Instead, we need studies which start with antisocial children and follow them into adulthood to learn how many continue to require psychiatric care and under what diagnostic categories they are classified, how many recover, and how many become the clients of nonpsychiatric professionals. A satisfactory answer requires comparing their adult outcomes with the outcomes of normal children and of children with other disorders.

Follow-up studies of antisocial children have been done both on children who received psychiatric care and on children identified as antisocial in school or through contact with the courts. Comparing the adult outcomes of antisocial children who did not receive early psychiatric care

Supported in part by NIMH Special Fellowship No. 36,598. The work of the author referred to herein was done with the support of the Foundations Fund for Research in Psychiatry, and NIMH research grants MH-1400, MH-07126, and MH-09247.

* "Where Have All the Flowers Gone?" Library of Congress No. 63–11133.

Reprinted by permission of Grune & Stratton, Inc. from *Seminars in Psychiatry* (Milton Greenblatt and Ernest Artmann, Eds.), 1970, *2*, pp. 420–433.

with the outcomes of those known to children's clinics allows us to evaluate the effect of treatment in childhood. It also allows us to learn to what extent the entry of antisocial children *into* psychiatric care for the first time as adults compensates for the flow of antisocial children out of treatment with recovery or with delivery into the hands of courts and social agencies.

Follow-up studies of antisocial children can do more than help to explain the striking epidemiological finding of differences between the sex and diagnostic patterns encountered in psychiatric facilities for children and adults. They can also help to identify the characteristics of the antisocial child's own behavior, his family setting, and his socioeconomic situation which predict which of these routes a particular antisocial child will follow: to recovery, to continuation in psychiatric care as a personality disorder, to continuation in psychiatric care with some other diagnosable syndrome, or to the adult role of welfare case or criminal.

In this paper, we will discuss findings from 23 studies that traced the outcomes of antisocial children at least 10 years after their initial identification. The publication dates of these studies range from 1926 to 1970. Some of the children were identified as antisocial in clinics, some by their contacts with police, some by their school behavior. Each of the studies has determined adult outcome from records (hospitals, clinics, police, vital statistics, social agencies) and/or interviews with the subjects or their relatives.

The questions that these studies provide answers to are: How many antisocial children recover? How long does it take? Do antisocial children contribute more than their share to the pool of adult psychiatric patients? Into what diagnostic groups do they fall as adults? Do they differ from normal children or children with other kinds of disorders in the frequency of adult adjustment problems that may not come to psychiatric attention? What kinds of efforts at therapy or control appear to influence their outcome? What characteristics of the child and of his family and social background predict *which* antisocial children will mature into healthy, competent adults and which will remain antisocial or develop other syndromes?

We will summarize what can be learned from these studies to answer these questions. The studies vary in the size and representativeness of their samples and in the rigorousness of their data collection and analysis. Their authors represent a broad range of disciplines (law, criminology, psychiatry, psychology, sociology, pediatrics). Despite the diversity of technique and discipline, where various studies have attacked the same question, their answers show remarkable agreement. This agreement is evidence, I believe, of the value of the long-term follow-up study. The requirement that data be collected at two widely separated points in time does wonders to dim any possible halo effect and to reduce the impact on the findings of the researcher's particular set of preconceptions. This is not to say that all the questions raised above can be satisfactorily answered at the present time. But the results from follow-up studies over the last 45 years do provide a fairly clear picture of the kinds of outcomes to be expected for antisocial children.

How Many Antisocial Children Recover and How Soon?

Of all the questions listed above, this is the least well answered. The difficulty lies in the absence of satisfactory criteria for recovery and in the lack of uniformity in choosing the time period during which the subject must be free of problems in order to qualify as recovered. That period can be as brief as the weeks or month preceding the follow-up interview or as long as the total interval between initial contact and the follow-up, or some period between these two extremes.

Two studies of hospitalized children (7, 10) and one study of male reformatory inmates (2) report rates of improvement at follow-up, but do not specify whether the criteria for adequate functioning have been met for only a very brief period or for longer. Among the reformatory inmates, (2) 25 per cent were classified as successes. Masterson (10) reports 55 per cent of 20 adolescents who had been diagnosed psychopaths to have a "good outcome" after 5 to 19 years. Kochman (7) had 62 children diagnosed psychopathic whom he followed more or less continuously for 20–30 years. At follow-up, 75 per cent were judged recovered, although some of them had been convicted of crimes earlier in the follow-up interval. It is not clear whether the higher recovery rate in the last study is a truly different result or whether it stems from requiring a briefer period free of symptoms or from different diagnostic criteria in designating the children as psychopaths originally. The Kochman study appears to define psychopathy in the Kurt Schneider tradition, including neurotics, infantile personality, and "show offs" along with classically antisocial children. Children who would probably have been excluded by American or British psychiatrists constituted 42 per cent of Kochman's "psychopaths." Although differences between the studies should warn us against making too much of the exact proportions found recovered, all show that *some* antisocial children did recover even when they were originally sufficiently disturbed to be hospitalized or placed in a reformatory.

Three follow-up studies of children seen in child guidance clinics (22, 33) or hospitalized (34, 35) reviewed either the whole follow-up interval or the whole interval since age 18. When the children had antisocial behavior as presenting symptoms, only 34 per cent of 62 English hospitalized children followed 6–10 years were considered well throughout. (34, 35) Swedish clinic patients classified as delinquents (33) were well throughout in only 40 per cent of cases. Lowest rates of all for being well throughout adulthood were reported for antisocial child guidance clinic patients in St. Louis (16%). (22) Since the patients in the last study had been followed about three times as long as the other two samples, and had had more sources of information explored, it is not surprising that more of them were found to have displayed positive symptomatology in the interval. When one bases success rates on the *non*occurrence of symptoms, treatment, or crime in an interval, the length of the interval and the number of sources of information will obviously greatly influence the findings.

Although the criteria for improvement, the intervals during which the criteria must be met, the populations from which the antisocial samples were drawn, and the sources of follow-up information vary among these six studies, all found that *some* antisocial children had recovered. And when these studies compared the outcomes of the antisocial with outcomes for children presenting with other problems, (7, 10, 22, 23, 35) all agreed that the antisocial children recovered more often than psychotics, and much less often than children presenting with "neurotic" problems such as fears, eating and sleeping problems, psychosomatic complaints or speech difficulties. We have then found some evidence favoring our first hypothesis about the reason for a decline in antisocial cases in adult clinics: some of the antisocial children seen will have recovered before reaching adulthood. But we have no reason to believe this explanation a very important one, since half or fewer appear to be well throughout follow-up, and

since neurotic children seen in the same clinics recover much more often than the antisocial children. It seems unlikely, then, that recovery alone explains the marked disappearance of antisocial males from older clinic populations.

Estimates of how long antisocial behavior endures before it dissipates, if it does, are seldom made. Sundby (33) estimated a median duration for all nonpsychotic, nonfeebleminded disorders of 6.5 years. The longest duration of antisocial symptoms followed by recovery was 14 years. Morris (17) and Robins (22) were concerned with the age at recovery rather than the duration of illness. Morris pointed out that among hospitalized antisocial children, if recovery had not occurred by 19 it was unlikely to occur. Robins agreed that if serious symptoms were present after 18, recovery occurred in only a minority, but found improvement and remissions occurring right up until follow-up at age 45.

Do Antisocial Children Become Adult Psychiatric Patients?

In the preceding section, we found disagreements about how many antisocial children recover, but we also found that within each study the likelihood of recovery was always greater for antisocial children than for psychotics and poorer for antisocial children than for neurotics.

The same pattern of erratic estimates but stable within-study comparisons holds for studies investigating the probability that an antisocial child will have an adult psychiatric hospitalization. The proportion hospitalized during follow-up was 17 per cent in one study for antisocial children who had been hospitalized initially (17) and approximately the same rate was found during the adult follow-up period of antisocial children in a child guidance clinic population (17% for males, 14% for females). (22) Other studies, however, report much lower rates. In a long-term follow-up study of a Dallas child guidance clinic population, (16) only 5 per cent of the antisocial children (here called ambiverts and extraverts) were found to have been hospitalized or to have had lunacy hearings. The Gluecks' study of delinquents (3) did not report total hospitalizations, but found only 0.7 per cent of delinquents in psychiatric hospitals at follow-up at age 31. Comparable figures from the St. Louis study (22) were 3 per cent of antisocial males and 1 per cent of antisocial females in a psychiatric hospital at follow-up (approximate age 43). The levels of hospitalization reported depend, of course, on how thoroughly hospital records have been traced. The Dallas and Glueck studies had access only to public hospital information in one state, while the St. Louis study asked in interview about hospitalizations, as well as searching for records wherever the subject had moved.

Within a single study, information about treatment has been obtained from the same sources and with the same degree of effort for all subjects. Consequently, much greater consistency of results is found in comparing relative rates for subsamples within studies than between studies. The Dallas and St. Louis studies both found more hospitalization for antisocial children than for children with referral for neurotic complaints (5% versus less than 1% in Dallas; 17% versus 9% for men in St. Louis; 14% versus 5% for women in St. Louis). Both the Glueck and the St. Louis studies found more hospitalizations at follow-up for antisocial boys than for normal controls (0.7% versus 0.2% for the Gluecks at follow-up; 3% versus none in the St. Louis samples).

The finding that antisocial behavior is associated with adult hospitalization is further substantiated in a "follow-back" study of patients in Massachusetts public hospitals who were located in the files of the Judge Baker Clinic. (21) The childhood clinic records of these hospitalized patients showed more antisocial behavior than did the records of matched clinic patients who were not hospitalized as adults. A similar study (1) of Illinois mental patients diagnosed schizophrenics who had been seen as children in the Institute for Juvenile Research found that the hospitalized patients exceeded a matched control patient group in antisocial symptoms (running away and lying, particularly), although they had no more referrals for antisocial behavior.

While we find an association between childhood antisocial behavior and adult psychiatric hospitalization, no such association is found with adult outpatient care. In St. Louis, (22) equal proportions of men from all three groups, the antisocial, the neurotic, and the normal, had received outpatient psychiatric care (7%, 5%, 6% respectively). Among women, the neurotics had the most outpatient psychiatric care (12% of the neurotics versus 7% of the women antisocial in childhood and 3% of the normal controls). Now, perhaps, we have found one reason that antisocial behavior is more common in child than in adult outpatient clinics: after antisocial children grow up, they are more likely to receive treatment as inpatients

than as outpatients. The reasons for this are probably related both to their class status and their behavior. Psychiatry is seen as the proper source of help for tension states and other internalized discomfort chiefly by the well-educated middle class. But antisocial children, as we shall see, are usually both ill-educated and poor as adults, and therefore unlikely voluntarily to seek psychiatric help in clinics. Second, the kind of behavior they exhibit frequently leads to hospitalization rather than outpatient care, because confinement and control of behavior is necessary. The St. Louis study (22) found that the common reasons for adult hospitalization of former antisocial children were a threat to do bodily harm to others or to himself, drug or alcohol intoxication, and creating a disturbance or being suspected of malingering while incarcerated. These reasons resulted in hospitalization rather than outpatient care, either because the behavior was life-threatening or because the patient had to be kept in custody for a corrections official. A possible additional factor, for which present studies offer no direct evidence, is that clinics, many of which rely on psychotherapy as their treatment of choice, may discourage the attendance of the adult antisocial patient, because they believe him a poor prospect for psychotherapy.

What Diagnostic Groups Do Antisocial Children Fall Into as Adults?

Information about the adult disorders that antisocial children develop comes from diagnoses found in adult hospital records or from evaluations by the researcher based on the history obtained by interview and by abstracting a variety of records.

Hospital diagnoses were reported in three "follow-back" studies, (20, 21, 36) which identified adults in treatment and then sought childhood records for them. In the Boston hospital study referred to previously, (21) men with the adult diagnoses of schizophrenia, alcoholism, and "impulsive character" (behavior disorders) were sought in the files of the Judge Baker Clinic. Antisocial behavior was found to a greater degree in the childhood records of men who had each of these diagnoses than in the records of matched clinic patients who were not hospitalized later. Since no search was made for patients with other hospital diagnoses as adults, this study does not tell us whether these were the most frequent adult diagnoses for antisocial children, but only that they all occurred.

Wittman and Steinberg (36) used all diagnostic groups in an Illinois state hospital, and looked for their names in the Chicago Child Study Bureau. Most referrals to the Child Study Bureau had been for educational problems, but there were also referrals for school behavior problems. The diagnoses of adult patients who had been behavior problem children were most often psychopath and organic brain syndrome. (Educational problems were more often associated with schizophrenia and mental defect; depressed adult patients did not appear in the Child Study Bureau records.)

Pritchard and Graham (20) chose 75 adults seen at the Maudsley Hospital who had also been seen there as children, and compared their adult and childhood complaints. Of the 25 who were antisocial as children, 40 per cent showed violence or criminality, compared with only 10 per cent of the adults who were not antisocial children. Antisocial children also fell into all the other adult diagnostic categories, but with no greater frequency than did nonantisocial children.

We mentioned earlier that Frazee (1) had found antisocial children when searching for childhood records of adult schizophrenics. The Dallas study (16) found that about 40 per cent of those antisocial children who had been hospitalized had received a diagnosis of schizophrenia.

Three studies (3, 22, 35) made a psychiatric evaluation based on follow-up interviews and a variety of adult records. Warren's study (35) found 45 per cent of the antisocial children, but only 8 per cent of the neurotic children, diagnosable as adult antisocial personality (psychopathy). The Gluecks (3) found a strikingly greater incidence of antisocial personality in their delinquents than in their normal controls (18% versus .5%) and a slightly elevated rate of psychosis (5% versus 2%). They found no difference in rates of neurosis. The St. Louis study (22) agreed in finding a greatly elevated rate of adult antisocial personality (or sociopathy) (28% of the antisocial referrals, as compared with only 4% of other referrals and 2% of the normal controls). The rate of alcoholism was also somewhat high among antisocial children (8% versus 6% of neurotics and 2% of controls). Among girls, antisocial behavior was also associated with the adult diagnosis of hysteria, while other adult neuroses were relatively infrequent among persons who had been antisocial as children. Schizophrenia was also somewhat more common among patients with a history of antisocial behavior than among children with exclusively neurotic symptoms.

Each of these studies has found clinically diagnosable antisocial personality unusually common among people with a history of antisocial behavior in childhood, and rare or nonexistent in children without such an early history. Other diagnoses are less clearly associated with antisocial behavior, but alcoholism, schizophrenia, chronic brain syndrome, and hysteria have been found to follow antisocial childhoods at a rate somewhat above chance. Manic depressive disorder and anxiety neurosis occur as rarely or more rarely in the adult lives of antisocial children than of normal controls.

Do Antisocial Children Have Adult Adjustment Problems That May Not Come to Psychiatric Attention?

Interviews and records other than psychiatric hospital records give information about adult adjustment. Among records studied for antisocial children are death records, school, police, military, and social agency records. The results of searches of such records show a poor adult outcome much more dramatically than do psychiatric records. We noted above that while antisocial children come to psychiatric attention somewhat more often than neurotic or normal children, still only a minority are seen by psychiatrists after they become adults. A very high proportion of them, on the other hand, come to police attention. Records of rearrest between ages 17 and 25 were found for 81 per cent of the reformatory inmates in the Glueck study, (3) while only 10 per cent of their nondelinquent control subjects were arrested in this age period. Similarly, in the St. Louis study, 72 per cent of males who were antisocial patients as children were arrested after 18 while only half as many male (36%) expatients with other childhood complaints had adult arrests, and only 26 per cent of male controls. Women were less frequently arrested, no matter what their childhood behavior, but female arrests, even more than male arrests, were almost exclusively confined to persons with an antisocial childhood (30% of the antisocial girls, 8% of the other patients, and only 3% of controls were arrested after 18). Among antisocial girls, many of the adult arrests were for prostitution and drunkenness; among antisocial boys, adult arrests were primarily for theft and drunkenness. (2, 22) Even among women, who are known to be relatively immune to arrest and more likely than men to seek medical care, childhood antisocial behavior was more likely to be followed by adult arrests than by psychiatric help.

The Warren study, (35) the Dallas study (14, 15) and the Cambridge-Somerville Youth Study (11) all confirm the high rate of later arrest among antisocial boys. The Dallas and Cambridge-Somerville studies are particularly important, because they report arrest rates for antisocial boys who had had no police contact prior to referral. Their findings show that childhood *behavior* is an important predictor of later arrest, in addition to the possible effects of having come to police attention as a child.

School records show that antisocial children have high rates of school dropout. Both the Glueck (3) and the St. Louis follow-up (22) found that only about 2 per cent of their delinquents graduated from high school; but one might assume that becoming involved with the Juvenile Court, particularly if the court sent the child to a correctional institution, would itself interfere with schooling. That dropping out is predicted by the child's behavior, and not merely by his court contact, is shown by the high rate of dropouts among St. Louis antisocial children who were *not* seen in court. (25) Only 20 per cent of these children graduated from high school, compared with 52 per cent of those patients without antisocial behavior.

The antisocial children studied by the Gluecks had been sent to a reformatory and those in the St. Louis study had been sent to a psychiatric clinic. Both samples were, therefore, presumably at the extreme end of the normal range of antisocial behavior. One wonders whether the same relationship between educational achievement and antisocial behavior would be found in an ordinary school population. The River City study (4) shows that it is. Children in the highest quartile with respect to aggressiveness at age 11 graduated from high school in 43 per cent of cases; those in the lowest quartile graduated in 82 per cent. The overall graduation level is higher for both antisocial and normal children than in the previous studies because the sample is both more middle class and younger. (High school graduation has increasingly become the expected level of education in the last 25 years.) But the relationship between antisocial behavior and failure to graduate remains strong.

Any childhood variable that simultaneously predicts little education and a criminal record must inevitably also be linked to chances for military service and for having a successful occupational career. Roff (30) the Gluecks, (3) and the St. Louis study (22) all found that men who had been antisocial children were more often rejected by the Armed Services on grounds of educational deficit, psychiatric diagnosis, and criminality.

Similarly, the jobs held by people with an antisocial history were low level, (3, 22) as compared with the jobs of both other patients and control subjects.

Both the Glueck and St. Louis samples were white, of predominantly lower-class origins, and sufficiently deviant to come to official attention. One wonders whether the influence of antisocial behavior on occupation would be equally striking in populations unselected for extremes in deviant behavior and either better off (i.e., white middle class) or more disadvantaged (black lower class). The Terman study of high IQ children selected from school records provides a gifted white middle-class sample without striking pathology. Predictors of occupational status were sought in parents' and teachers' comments in childhood for the most and least occupationally successful of these subjects. (18) The least successful were found to have been more often described as imprudent and headstrong children (38% versus 13%), suggesting an association even in this gifted middle-class sample between rather mild antisocial behavior in childhood and occupational failure.

A second study in St. Louis investigated childhood predictors of occupational status in young black men whose names had been chosen from public school records, and who were therefore not identified as an abnormal sample with respect to childhood deviance. Men who in elementary school both had markedly excessive absences (absent more than 20% of school days in 5 or more quarters) and had been held back at least one semester, reported holding poorer jobs in their thirties than men without such serious elementary school behavior problems (mean Duncan Socioeconomic Index score 25.7 versus 36.7). Illegal behavior in adolescence was also important. For instance, black men who used drugs in adolescence held poor jobs as adults (74% had a Duncan score of less than 30 versus 45% of nonusers), even though drug users had not had conspicuous behavior problems in elementary school. (27)

The low job level of antisocial children might be a direct effect of dropping out of school and being arrested. Better jobs require more education, and employers avoid hiring people with criminal records. While the direct effect of these events is undoubtedly important, an additional factor is the antisocial behavior still present in these men as adults. Evidence for this comes from the observation that delinquents and antisocial boys who had *not* been rejected by the Armed Services had much stormier military careers as measured by disciplinary action, demotions, and dishonorable discharges than did control subjects or neurotic children. (22, 28) When employed in civilian jobs they were more often fired and more often quit. (3, 22)

It should be no surprise, then, since being fired and quitting lead to extensive unemployment, that antisocial children are particularly likely to swell the rolls of welfare and other social agencies. The Gluecks (3) found four times as many ex-delinquents as normals on the rolls of Massachusetts social service agencies: and an association between antisocial behavior and adult financial dependency was also found in the St. Louis study, (22) particularly for women, more than half of whom had received financial assistance, compared with one-third of women who had been neurotic children, and only 10 per cent of the controls.

One of the striking findings about antisocial children is the frequency with which they drink heavily and smoke. In the four studies that made the comparison, alcohol abuse was more frequent in people who had been antisocial children than in those who had not. One-fourth of the Gluecks' delinquents (3) later had alcohol-associated arrests. In the St. Louis study (24) almost half (45%) of the juvenile delinquents seen in the clinic were judged probable alcoholics as adults, compared with only 15 per cent of patients without antisocial behavior. The McCords (12) found that the children in the Cambridge-Somerville study who were later identified as alcoholic were those who had been described as aggressive, indifferent to their siblings, and hostile toward their mothers.

The same association between drinking and childhood behavior was found for black schoolboys in St. Louis. (26) Later problems with alcohol occurred in two-thirds of the boys who had both truanted and been held back in elementary school, compared with less than half of the boys without serious elementary school problems. At age 33 one-third of the men with these serious elementary school problems were still having trouble with drinking, as compared with 15 per cent of the men who had had less serious school problems. The consistent finding of an association

between alcoholism and early antisocial behavior throws into question the psychodynamic interpretation of alcoholism as a defense against passivity and dependency. The passive alcoholic undoubtedly occurs, but seems to account for a smaller proportion of the alcoholic population than does the alcoholic with a history of overt acting-out behavior.

We noted that among black boys, antisocial behavior early in the school career predicted problem drinking. A study of normal white children studied early in elementary school (9) found that rebelliousness remarked upon as early as kindergarten and first grade predicted smoking in adulthood. The relationship was found for both sexes, but was stronger for men.

Except for smoking, the nonpsychiatric outcomes we have examined thus far are associated with major social problems: crime, poverty, alcoholism. But antisocial children are disadvantaged in interpersonal and intrapersonal areas as well. As compared with persons with normal or neurotic childhoods, they have less social interaction with family and friends, more often move about the country and from house to house within the same geographic area, and have unstable marriages, with consequent high rates of divorce and illegitimate children. (3, 22) A study of normal children from birth to adulthood (6) found that aggressiveness toward the mother, aggression toward peers, and overactivity in childhood were associated with greater adult sexual freedom and greater adult aggressiveness and anger. Indeed, of all the childhood traits explored in this study, aggressive behavior was the most persistent.

Subjective distress, as well as interpersonal difficulties, is common in the adult lives of antisocial children. The Gluecks (3) found half of the delinquents to be discontented adults compared with only one-fifth of the normal controls, and to report themselves in poorer health (17% said their health was not good versus 8% of normal controls). Asked whether they had experienced any of a long series of psychiatric symptoms, including somatic complaints, anxiety, depression, and fears, women in the St. Louis study (22) who had been antisocial children reported more symptoms than did women who had been either neurotic or normal children (a mean of 11.7 versus 9.6 and 6.0). Among men, patients of either type had more symptoms than normals but did not differ between themselves.

Not only ill health and discomfort, but mortality is greater among antisocial boys. In the St. Louis child guidance clinic study, (22) 17 per cent of the antisocial boys died before follow-up in their mid-forties, compared with 9 or 10 per cent of the other patients and the controls. Differences were even more striking for black school-boys, (23) 11 per cent of whom had died by age 33 when they were both truant and held back in elementary school, compared with only 1.3 per cent of those free of elementary school problems. For both whites and blacks, the excess deaths were chiefly by violent means.

What Kinds of Effort at Therapy or Control Appear to Influence the Later Outcome of Antisocial Boys?

Since we are considering only follow-up studies in which outcome is measured at least 10 years after identification of the child as antisocial, we cannot report on the effectiveness of the newer treatment techniques. The studies available report the effects of correctional institutionalization, (5, 13, 22) treatment in a traditional child guidance clinic, (22) and a program offering friendship and guidance. (22) None of the three seemed measurably to improve the outcome of the children, and correctional institutions in all three studies reporting on them seemed to do considerable harm. It is difficult in such studies to separate the effects of institutionalization from the effects of factors *leading to* institutionalization. Institutionalized delinquents, as compared with those placed on probation, have committed more crimes, more serious crimes, crimes against outsiders rather than against family and friends, and also they more often come from families judged inadequate to supervise them. Although controls may not be ideal, when efforts were made to control for number and seriousness of prior offenses and family background, the finding was not wiped out that delinquents sent to the reformatories then available had worse prognoses than those put on probation.

To say that the reformatories and clinics of the 1920s and 1930s and counseling in the 1940s had no impressive results does not mean that antisocial behavior is necessarily untreatable by other methods. There are optimistic reports of short-term successes with drugs and behavior therapy with which there will soon be sufficient experience to warrant long-term evaluation. At the present time, we simply do not have a treatment for which effectiveness has been demonstrated by long-term follow-up.

What Factors in the Child's Behavior, His Family, and His Social Background Predict Recovery or Later Psychiatric Disorder and Social Maladjustment?

With traditional treatments found unsuccessful, one looks at differences between antisocial children who recover and those who do not for crucial factors that might lend themselves to incorporation into a treatment scheme. Certainly the most persistent finding is that the milder the original disorder the better the prognosis. Fewer and milder symptoms were found to predict good outcome in Morris' (17) and Masterson's (10) hospitalized children, and in child guidance clinic patients in Chicago, (5) Boston, (21) Minneapolis, (28) and St. Louis. (22)

Later onset was found favorable by Morris (17) and Otterstrom. (19) In St. Louis, (22) onset between 8 and 10 years had the worst prognosis for boys, after 14 years of age for girls.

Differences by sex are not consistent. Morris (10) and Robins (22) found fewer girls completely well at follow-up, but Otterstrom (19) and Healy and Bronner (5) report better outcomes for women. This probably is simply a matter of criteria for recovery. If one uses adult crime, (5) women do better; if one uses number of subjective symptoms and marital stability, men do better. (22)

There is general agreement on the advantages of having adequate parents. An absence of antisocial behavior in the parents was found to predict good outcome by Otterstrom, (19) the McCords, (11) Havighurst, (4) and Robins, (22) and the parents exercising adequate discipline was found important by the McCords (11) and Robins. (22)

Good relationships with peers and avoidance of delinquent friends is noted as predicting recovery by the McCords, (11) Roff, (29) Ricks and Berry, (21) and Havighurst. (4)

Good school performance predicted good outcome in Masterson's study (10) and in Robins' for both white and black children. (22, 23, 25, 26)

These factors predicting poor outcome seem almost self-evident—the worse the child and the worse his family, the worse the future. But when one notes the factors that were *not* important, the feeling that these studies have produced nothing that is not banal disappears. Many of the easy "common sense" assumptions are toppled.

Roff (28) found that the guidance clinic psychiatrists' psychodynamic interpretation had no prognostic value for performance in the Armed Services. The widely accepted notion that low social status leads to poor outcome failed in every study in which it was investigated. (5, 11, 22, 35) The famous "broken home" theory proved equally untenable. (5, 11, 22) Tested intelligence was not prognostic, at least below the superior level. (11, 18, 19, 22, 35) Gang experiences did not increase the risk of adult criminality for antisocial children. (22) While the antisocial father was important, an antisocial mother without an antisocial father was found to make little difference, perhaps only because such family patterns are rare. (11, 22) Early illness, head injuries, birth difficulties were not helpful in prediction. (5, 11, 22) Neurotic symptoms were common in antisocial children (contrary to some popular beliefs) but predicted neither increased difficulty nor improvement. (11, 22, 33) Indeed, no symptoms appearing before the age of 5 seemed helpful. (6, 35) Parental deprivation, that time-honored scapegoat for children's problems, made no measurable difference, not even a *positive* difference when the separation was from a criminal father. (11, 19, 22)

This list of unimportant variables is formidable, and goes against many of our convictions. A word of caution is necessary here. It should be remembered that we are discussing factors that failed to influence the future outcome for *antisocial* children. Some of these factors may well have contributed to the initial appearance of antisocial behavior in childhood. If one had started with a random sample of children, unselected with respect to behavior problems, we would indeed have found that the children with impoverished backgrounds, broken homes, and neglectful mothers had worse outcomes than unselected children *without* such backgrounds. What the studies summarized here have shown is that once the child is defined as antisocial, whatever the causes of his antisocial behavior, these factors provide no *additional* insights into his probable later outcome. Some of these variables which did not predict adult outcomes for antisocial children *were* predictive for children without antisocial behavior, but these children's outcomes are not being discussed in the present paper.

CONCLUSIONS

One inescapable conclusion from the review of these 23 studies of the outcomes for antisocial children is that the antisocial behavior of child-

hood is often not at all transitory. Some antisocial children do disappear from psychiatric attention because they recover, particularly those who were not seriously antisocial in the first place and whose parents were not themselves antisocial nor negligent in disciplining them. Competent parents and mild symptoms often appear together in the same clinic patients, because such parents are likely to bring a child to psychiatric attention before symptoms are acute enough to lead to school expulsion or arrest. The parent who is himself antisocial is more negligent and less well informed about treatment possibilities. He seldom initiates treatment for the child; and the child, therefore, appears only when his behavior is so intolerable to the school and society that agents outside the family refer him. Such children have very poor prognoses compared with other children in the clinic.

The fact that antisocial adults make up only a small portion of clinic patient loads results not only from the recovery of milder cases, but also in part from early death, prolonged incarceration, and inpatient treatment. Another source of loss is the rediagnosis of antisocial children as hysterics, schizophrenics, and chronic brain syndromes.

While all these factors appear important, they are not the only factors. Another is the disappearance from care altogether, without recovery. The school is a powerful screening agent for disturbed children. Once out of school, no such agency functions for the more mildly disordered adult. When disorders are not perceived by their victim as requiring psychiatric attention, as most personality disorders are not, the person affected may spend the years between prison sentences and agency help in personal distress—unable to make friends or hold a job, drinking excessively, moving about the country—without any care at all. The family, which is likely to see that the depressed or anxious patient gets help, does not function for the antisocial adult, because he has long since lost their good will and broken off contact with them.

Noting that the antisocial child once grown up rarely gets psychiatric care even when he does not recover, should not inspire us to try to persuade him to attend clinics, because we now have little proven effective treatment for him either as a child or as an adult. His great need for help should, however, provide an incentive to seek new treatments and carefully to evaluate recent ones that seem to offer promise. One hopeful fact is that childhood antisocial behavior is recognizable at extremely young ages. Although the average

age at first becoming a delinquent is 14 or 15, the patterns predicting delinquency and antisocial behavior can be identified in the first school grades. The boys detectable in these early years have been shown to have particularly bad long-term prognoses. Among the earliest signs are rejection of the teacher's authority, school failure, and discipline problems in school. Some of the newer techniques of behavior modification are reported to attack such symptoms with rapid suc-

cess. It is important to know whether interrupting such symptoms in the early school years can interrupt or head off the disastrous later life patterns so clearly spelled out by these follow-up studies.

The studies of the effect of therapy have been discouraging in these studies. But the unanimity with which these follow-up studies have shown that older methods fail gives us hope that a successful method can just as unanimously and unequivocally be shown effective.

REFERENCES

1. Fraze, H. E.: Children who later became schizophrenic. *Smith Coll. Stud. Social Work* 23:125–149, 1953.

2. Fuchs-Kamp, A.: Lebensschicksal u. Persönlichkeit, ehemaliger Fursorgezöglinge. Berlin, 1929. *In* Otterström, E.: Delinquency and children from bad homes. *Acta. Paediat.* (Stockholm) 33: Suppl. 5, 1946.

3. Glueck, S., and Glueck, E.: *Delinquents and nondelinquents in perspective.* Cambridge, Harvard University Press, 1968.

4. Havighurst, R. J., Bowman, P. H., Liddle, G. P., Matthews, C. V., and Pierce, J. V.: *Growing Up in River City.* New York, Wiley, 1962.

5. Healy, W., and Bronner, A. F.: *Delinquents and criminals: Their making and unmaking.* New York, Macmillan, 1926.

6. Kagan, J., and Moss, H. A.: *Birth to Maturity.* New York, Wiley, 1962.

7. Kochmann, R.: Uber diagnose und prognose besonders der psychopathie in der kinderpsychiatrie. *Acta Paedopsychiat.* 30: 21–28, 1963.

8. Kramer, M.: Some implications of trends in the usage of psychiatric facilities for community mental health programs and related research. Presented at the Annual Meeting of American College of Neuropsychopharmacology, San Juan, Puerto Rico, December, 1965.

9. Livson, N., and Peskin, H.: Prediction of adult psychological health in a longitudinal study. *J. Abnorm. Psychol.* 72:509–518, 1967.

10. Masterson, J. F., Jr.: Prognosis in adolescent disorders. *Amer. J. Psychiat.* 114:1097–1103, 1958.

11. McCord, W., and McCord, J.: *Origins of Crime.* New York, Columbia University Press, 1959.

12. ———, and ———: *Origins of Alcoholism.* Stanford, Calif., Stanford University Press, 1960.

13. McKay, H. D.: Subsequent arrests, convictions, and commitments among former juvenile delinquents. Submitted to the President's Commission on Law Enforcement and Administration of Justice, Washington, D.C., 1967.

14. Michael, C. M.: Follow-up studies of introverted children: III. Relative incidence of criminal

behavior. *J. Crim. Law, Criminology and Police Sci.* 47:414–422, 1956.

15. ———: Relative incidence of criminal behavior in long term follow-up studies of shy children. *Dallas Med. J.* January, 1957. (unpaged).

16. ———, Morris, D. P., and Soroker, E.: Follow-up studies of shy, withdrawn children: II. Relative incidence of schizophrenia. *Amer. J. Orthopsychiat.* 27:331–337, 1957.

17. Morris, H. H., Jr., Escoll, P. J., and Wexler, R.: Aggressive behavior disorders of childhood: A follow-up study. *Amer. J. Psychiat.* 112:991–997, 1956.

18. Oden, M. H.: The fulfillment of promise: 40-year follow-up of the Terman gifted group. *Gen. Psychol. Monog.* 77:3–93, 1968.

19. Otterström, E.: Delinquency and children from bad homes. *Acta Paediat.* (Stockholm), 33: Suppl. 5, 1946.

20. Pritchard, M., and Graham, P.: An investigation of a group of patients who have attended both the child and adult departments of the same psychiatric hospital. *Brit. J. Psychiat.* 112:603–612, 1966.

21. Ricks, D. F., and Berry, J. C.: Family and symptom patterns that precede schizophrenia. *In* Roff, Merrill, and Ricks, David F. (Eds.): *Life History Research in Psychopathology.* Minneapolis, The University of Minnesota Press, 1970, pp. 31–50.

22. Robins, L. N.: *Deviant children grown up: A sociological and psychiatric study of sociopathic personality.* Baltimore, Williams & Wilkins, 1966.

23. ———: Negro homicide victims—who will they be? *Trans-action* 5:15–19, 1968.

24. ———, Bates, W. M., and O'Neal, P.: Adult drinking patterns of former problem children. *In* Pittman, D. J., and Snyder, C. R. (Eds.): *Society, Culture and Drinking Patterns.* New York, Wiley, 1962, pp. 395–412.

25. ———, Gyman, H., and O'Neal, P.: The interaction of social class and deviant behavior. *Amer. Sociol. Rev.* 27:480–492, 1962.

26. ———, Murphy, G. E., and Breckenridge, M. B.: Drinking behavior of young urban Negro men. *Quart. J. Stud. Alc.* 29:657–684, 1968.

27. ———, Darvish, H. S., and Murphy, G. E.: The long-term outcome for adolescent drug users: A follow-up study of 76 users and 146 non-users. *In* Zubin, J., and Freedman, A. (Eds.): *The Psychopathology of Adolescence.* New York, Grune & Stratton, 1970, 159–178.

28. Roff, M.: Relation between certain preservice factors and psychoneurosis during military duty. *U.S. Armed Forces Med. J. 11:*152–160, 1960.

29. ———: Childhood social interactions and young adult psychosis. *J. Clin. Psychol. 19:*152–157, 1963.

30. ———: Juvenile delinquency and military service. *In* Little, R. W. (Ed.): *Selective Service and American Society.* New York, Russell Sage Foundation, 1969, pp. 109–138.

31. Rosen, B. M., Bahn, A. K., and Kramer, M.: Demographic and diagnostic characteristics of psychiatric clinic outpatients in the U.S.A. 1961. *Amer. J. Orthopsychiat. 34:*455–468, 1964.

32. Stewart, L., and Livson, N.: Smoking and rebelliousness: A longitudinal study from childhood to maturity. *J. Consulting Psychol. 30:*225–229, 1966.

33. Sundby, H. S., and Kreyberg, P. C.: *Prognosis in child psychiatry.* Baltimore, Williams & Wilkins, 1968.

34. Warren, W.: A study of adolescent psychiatric in-patients and the outcome six or more years later: I. Clinical histories and hospital findings. *J. Child Psychol. Psychiat. 6:*1–17, 1965.

35. ———: A study of adolescent psychiatric in-patients and the outcome six or more years later: II. The follow-up study. *J. Child Psychol. Psychiat. 6:* 141–160, 1965.

36. Wittman, M. P., and Steinberg, D. L.: A study of prodromal factors in mental illness with special reference to schizophrenia. *Amer. J. Psychiat. 100:*811–816, May, 1944.

selective responding by autistic children to multiple sensory input

O. Ivar Lovaas, Laura Schreibman, Robert Koegel, & Richard Rehm

The unresponsivity of autistic children serves as one of the main criteria for their diagnosis. This unresponsiveness is typically apparent in a child during the first year of life when he behaves as if he were blind and deaf, causing his parents to seek professional opinion. Kanner (1944) describes such behavior in one of his patients as follows:

> When spoken to, he went on with what he was doing as if nothing had been said. Yet one never had the feeling that he was willingly disobedient or contrary. He was obviously so remote that the remarks did not reach him. [p. 212].

Rimland (1964, cf. pp. 94–96) has presented several other illustrations of such unresponsivity. Description of the phenomenon points to a large variability which can be observed within a particular modality. For example, it may be impossible to observe a response in these children to a

This investigation was supported by United States Public Health Service Research Grant 11440 from the National Institute of Mental Health. The authors express their appreciation for the help of: James Q. Simmons, Associate Program Director of Clinical Training for the Mental Retardation Center, Neuropsychiatric Institute, University of California, Los Angeles; Thomas Ball, of the Department of Psychology, Pacific State Hospital, Pomona, California; and Norbert Rieger, Superintendent of Children's Services, Camarillo State Hospital, Camarillo, California. They are grateful to B. Henker, W. E. Jeffrey, and I. Maltzman for their helpful comments on an earlier draft. They also wish to thank Bodil Sivertsen for her assistance in this research.

The essentials of this paper were presented at the Annual Meeting of the National Society for Autistic Children, San Francisco, California. June 24–27, 1970.

very loud (100-db.) sound, yet they may respond excessively to a barely audible siren. The child who behaves as if he does not see the person who greets him, or other objects in his environment, may spot a sugar-coated corn flake some 20 ft. away. There also exists some speculation (Rimland, 1964) that the unresponsiveness may vary across modalities, such that visual, auditory, and pain stimulation are less likely to elicit a response than tactual, gustatory, or olfactory stimuli.

An example from our own laboratory serves to illustrate how such unresponsivity interferes with these children's treatment. We attempted to teach mute autistic children language by beginning with a program on the teaching of verbal imitation (Lovaas, Berberich, Perloff, & Schaeffer, 1966). We have tried to facilitate such imitations by providing the child with visual cues as well as auditory ones. Thus, the child can clearly see the teacher's face when she presents the various sounds, such as "mm," which has auditory and visual cues quite distinct from "ah." The child will learn under these conditions; that is, he comes to reliably emit the vocal response in apparent imitation of the teacher. Following this, the teacher presents the sounds while the child is looking away, or while she is purposely covering her face. Strikingly, the child remains mute. He only attended to the visual cues. It is as if he had never heard the sounds despite thousands of trial exposures.

Figure 1 presents an example from a large number of such instances in our speech training program. The figure is based on data from a patient, Johan, an 8-yr.-old mute boy diagnosed as a "textbook example of autism." He was trained to imitate the sound "ah" with full visual exposure to the teacher's face. Percentages of correct repro-

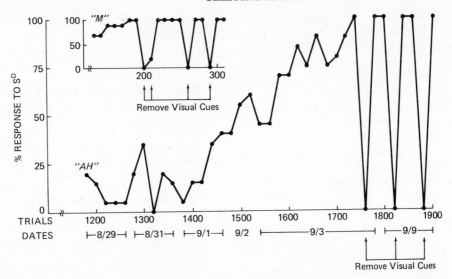

Figure 1. Acquisition of "Ah" and "Mm" trained with auditory and visual cues. (Percentages of correct reproductions of *E*'s presentations are plotted on the ordinate with trials plotted along the abscissa. Arrows indicate trials where visual cues were removed.)

ductions (*S*'s "ah" to *E*'s "ah") are given on the ordinate, and trials are given along the abscissa. The *S* had 1,180 trials preceding those which are plotted here, but his performance reflected no learning until after 1,400 trials. At this point he improved, and by Trial 1,740 he gave an onlooker the impression that he was listening to *E* and imitating what he had heard. However, when *E* removed the visual cues associated with the sound (Trials 1760–1780, 1800–1820, and 1840–1860), *S*'s performance fell to zero. It is as if he had never heard *E*'s voice.

The insert in the figure shows the same loss when visual cues are removed from the training of Johan's second sound, "mm." Eventually, as in the case of guttural sounds (e.g., "g," "k") without distinct visual components, the child learns to discriminate (imitate) the auditory cues. This acquisition is very slow. These observations raise several questions. Are the children particularly unresponsive to auditory cues? Are they unresponsive to auditory cues when these are presented together with visual cues? Do they have difficulty attending to any one cue in a multiple cue input, etc.?

The clinical observations that these children respond to cues in a particular modality on one occasion while not responding to these cues on another occasion have led to inferences regarding deficiencies in attentional, rather than sensory, mechanisms. These deficiencies in attentional mechanisms have been given a central, explana-

tory role in the child's failure of cognitive, social, or emotional development. For the reader who feels that there may be a similarity between attentional deficit in adult and childhood schizophrenia, excellent reviews of theories of attentional deficit in adult schizophrenia have been provided by Buss and Lang (1965), Lang and Buss (1965), and Feigenberg (1969).

There are two main etiologies which have been proposed to underlie the attentional deficiencies in autism. One of these is based on developmental models and draws heavily on Sherrington's work (1906). He postulated a transition from near-receptor dominance in lower organisms to far-receptor dominance in higher organisms. He considered, furthermore, that the far receptors are prerequisite for the development of complex psychological processes. This conceptualization has been employed by Goldfarb (1964) in his postulation of a distorted hierarchy of receptor dominance in autistic children, with motor–tactile orientation dominating auditory and visual inputs. Subsequent experimental studies (cf. Schopler, 1966) have failed to verify the propriety of this model in describing receptor orientation in autistic children.

The other proposed etiology of these attentional deficits is based on hypothesized deviations in their social history and draws heavily on psychodynamic formulations. The children's primary difficulty is seen to arise from inadequate early mother–child interactions, with a consequent failure in the development of perceptual activity, or it may be selective, largely restricted to social stimuli. As was the case with the developmental theories based on Sherrington's work, there has been a similar failure for research to confirm psychodynamic interpretations.

Much of the empirical work here has been carried out by Hermelin and O'Connor (summarized by Hermelin, 1966) and usually involved exposing the children to various stimulus displays, obtaining preferences for certain inputs as a function of the amount of their visual or tactual attending behavior. The conclusion which can be drawn from these studies is that, in contrast to normals, autistic children look less at the experimental stimuli, but do not selectively avoid social ones. Young (1969) found that they may attend proportionately less to complex, incongruous stimuli.

Although descriptions of visual attending behavior, which comprise the bulk of research in this area, may provide leads in understanding the psychopathology, such studies are quite inferential. That is, they require a model which relates visual attending to learning, or to some other behavior change. This is feasible since a person can visually attend to an environment without learning anything about it. Receptor orientation is necessary, but not sufficient, for learning. Viewed in that context, a discrimination learning situation may be a superior procedure for the study of attentional deficits, since it incorporates learning. We have employed such a procedure in the study we shall describe below.

The situation we constructed was as follows: the child was reinforced for responding in the presence of a stimulus display and was not reinforced for responding in the absence of that display. One can argue that the child attends to (is controlled by) certain stimuli when independent variation of these stimuli is associated with concurrent change in the child's behavior. We employed a multidimensional stimulus display, that is, a display which contained auditory, visual, tactual, and temporal cues. The study was designed such that, after the child's behavior was brought under the control of the display, separate components of that display could be presented singly so as to assess to which aspects the child was responding. One could then find out if certain components of the display were more functional than others, how many components had become functional, whether certain components had failed to acquire any function, etc.

METHOD

Subjects

We ran three groups of Ss. The autistic group consisted of five boys and one girl, with mean CA of 7.2 yr. (range of 4–10 yr.). These children had been diagnosed by agencies not associated with the experiment. Four of the Ss were mute and would utter only unintelligible sounds without communicative intent. They gave sporadic response to the most elementary commands (e.g., "sit down," "close the door"). They were untestable on standard psychological tests. Two of the Ss were not toilet-trained, and other social and self-help skills were minimal. For example, they did not dress themselves; they did not play with toys; and they did not play with peers. Three had early histories of suspected deafness. They were inpatients, and in all likelihood faced permanent hospitalization. In short, they were extremely regressed and fell within the lower third of the psychotic continuum. The fifth child, Danny, differed from the rest in that he was echolalic, expressed simple demands, and was behaviorally more advanced so that he remained at home and made a marginal adjustment to a class for severely retarded children. Like the others, he would frequently act as if he did not see or hear adults. All Ss demonstrated bizarre self-stimulatory behavior (stereotyped motor acts).

The second group contained five mentally retarded children, four boys and one girl, with a mean CA of 8 yr. (range of 7–10 yr.) and a mean MA of 3.7 yr. (range 3.5 to 4.0 yr.). Four of these Ss were institutionalized. Two had been diagnosed as Mongoloid, two as retarded due to birth trauma, and one as retarded from an unknown genetic origin. One of the retarded Ss had a history of suspected (but unconfirmed) deafness, while all other Ss had displayed normal responsiveness to external stimulation.

A normal control group consisted of five children with mean CA of 6.4 yr. (range of 6.0–7.5 yr.). These Ss, two boys and three girls, were obtained from parents working at the university.

Apparatus

The S was seated in a 7 × 8 ft. experimental room in front of a 2½-ft.-high table holding a box with a 3-in. bar protruding from its front. The box also housed a Davis Model 310 universal feeder which delivered candy, potato chips, etc., to S through a chute at the left side of the box. Sound equipment and one-way vision screens connected the experimental room to an observation room from which E would present the various experimental manipulations. The experimental room was lighted by a 40-w. light, giving a dim illumination level of .50 ftc. The room was sound attenuated.

We employed four kinds of stimuli. (*a*) A visual stimulus, which consisted of a 150-w. red floodlight, was mounted on the ceiling behind S's back and out of his view. This light raised the room illumination level from .50 to 2.50 ftc. as measured by a Weston illumination meter, Model 756 (these readings were made on the front panel of the box which faced S). (*b*) An auditory stimulus, consisting of white noise, was fed from a tape recorder into a speaker located above S. The noise level generated was 63 db. (measured by a General Radio Co. sound-level meter, Type No. 1551-B, set at 20-kc. weighting). Since white noise consists of all frequencies, the possibility of Ss being differentially sensitive to particular frequencies was eliminated. (*c*) A tactile stimulus was applied by forcing air into a blood pressure cuff fastened around S's left calf. The cuff was attached by a rubber tube to an automobile tire pump operated by E. The arrangement allowed E to deliver a rather discrete tactile pressure (20 mm. of mercury), retain that pressure for the desired interval, and instantly remove (deflate) it. (*d*) A temporal cue was arranged by presenting all the stimuli for a 5-sec. interval every 20 sec. That is, S could obtain reinforcement simply by hitting the bar as a function of time elapsed since last reinforcement (a temporal cue) rather than on the basis of the three other cues.

The S was run in two kinds of sessions, training and testing. During training sessions, he was taught a discrimination where his bar presses were brought under the control of the stimulus complex. During the subsequent test sessions, he was presented with the various components of the stimulus complex to assess which one(s) had acquired functional control.

Training

The S was seated before the bar and instructed that if he pressed it he would get candy. If S failed to respond to the instructions, E prompted the response manually. As soon as S had emitted two unassisted bar presses within 1 min., he was left alone in the experimental room and presented with the S^D (stimulus complex). The S^D was presented for 10 sec. or until it was terminated by a single bar press. When S had

responded to the S^D on three successive presentations, the duration of the S^D period was gradually decreased in 1-sec. units to the ultimate 5-sec. S^D interval. At the same time, the reinforcement schedule was gradually changed from FR-1 to FR-4. In the final stages of training, S would eventually respond with a burst of four bar presses within the 5-sec. S^D period. The fourth bar press terminated the S^D. S^Δ was set to last for 20 sec. When S failed to give any evidence of decreased rate of response during the S^Δ interval after the first training session, E would deliver a loud "no" over the intercom contingent on such response. All steps, including the onset and timing of the S^D and S^Δ intervals, operation of the feeder, recording of the bar presses, etc., were carried out automatically through Davis relay programming equipment and a Davis Model CRRC 133 cumulative recorder. Session lengths, which varied between 20 and 50 min., were determined by the length of time it required S to obtain 36 reinforcements (which emptied the dispenser). The Ss received not more than two sessions per day, not more than 3 days apart. The discrimination training was considered complete, and test trials were begun, when S had completed two consecutive sessions in which at least 90% of his bar presses fell within the S^D interval.

Testing

Upon completion of the training phase, each autistic and retarded S received 10 test sessions. Testing for the normal Ss was terminated after two successive tests showing 100% response to the auditory, visual, and tactile cues. The test sessions were of the same duration as the training sessions and were distributed such that S received no more than two tests a day nor less than one every third day. In the test trials, the single stimuli were randomly interspersed between training trials (trials with all the stimulus components present) except that: (*a*) each test trial was always preceded and followed by at least one training trial, and (*b*) E did not run more than three training trials in a row. The density of the training trials helped to maintain the discrimination. The S was reinforced if he responded correctly on a test trial. To test for temporal discriminations, the S^Δ interval was altered from 20 to 10, 15, 25, and 30 sec. The intervals with presentations occurring prior to 20 sec. potentially provided evidence for responses to individual stimuli in the absence of the normal temporal cue. The intervals greater than 20 sec., however, allowed S to respond on the basis of a temporal cue without the influence of the external stimuli. The S received, on the average, seven presentations of each individual stimulus in a test session. The temporal intervals were randomly selected among the 10, 15, 25, and 30 sec. Altogether, he received approximately 70 test trials on any one stimulus, distributed over 10 sessions.

RESULTS

There was a great deal of variability in the acquisition of the discrimination. The normal Ss learned to respond to the complex input within a matter of minutes. The retarded Ss required, on the average, less than five 30-min. training sessions, while the autistic group required approximately twice as many sessions as the retardates. One autistic child, Leslie, was run for a total of 3 mo., five sessions a week, and still could not maintain the discrimination (she responded less than 80% of the time to the S^D, and had large bursts of S^Δ responding). Her discrimination of the complex input was so poorly maintained that tests for component control were meaningless; hence her data are not included.

Once S had learned to discriminate the stimulus complex, the main question became centered on which stimuli within the complex were controlling his responding. The S's responding to the separate components will be presented as a percentage derived from the number of actual responses to a given stimulus over the total number of opportunities to respond to that stimulus. For example, if in a particular test session S gave eight bar presses to the tactile stimulus, and that stimulus was presented eight times during that session, which would allow for 32 possible responses (4 responses per presentation), his score would equal 25%. This value is used as an index of S's sensitivity to a particular stimulus element. There will be no discussion of the temporal cue since no evidence for a temporal discrimination was observed for any of the Ss.

The most general conclusion which can be made from the data is that autistic Ss respond primarily to one stimulus component, retardates to two, and normals to all three. We derived this conclusion from a statistical analysis which was carried out as follows: we divided the Ss' responses into three levels—high, medium, and low—on the basis of the amount of responding to the separate stimuli. High was the stimulus component to which S responded most (was most functional), medium was the next most functional, and

low the least functional. The magnitude of these differences was tested as follows. If there was no significant difference in the amount of responding between these levels, then it could be inferred that S had not responded differently to the three stimuli. On the other hand, a significant difference between these levels would indicate differential control by the stimulus components. For example, a significant difference between high and medium and a lack of difference between medium and low would indicate that only one cue had acquired control.

The statistical analysis was performed on the first test session only. We limited the analysis to this test session because with additional sessions S received increasing reinforcement for responding to single cues.

TABLE 1. Analysis of Variance on Level of Responding to the Single Cues

Source	df	MS	F
Diagnosis (D)	2	1217	.548
Ss within groups	12	2218	
Level of responding (L)	2	9487	43.1*
D X L	4	1677	7.62*
L X Ss within groups	24	220	

*$p < .005$.

Table 1 shows the analysis of variance. There was a significant ($p < .01$) interaction between diagnosis (autistic, retarded, and normal) and level of responding (high, medium, and low). There was no significant difference in regard to overall level of responding. A Newman-Keuls test on the means enabled a closer analysis of the individual populations. The result of that analysis has been presented in Table 2.

TABLE 2. Results of the Newman-Keuls Test on the Mean Levels of Responding for Autistic, Retarded, and Normal Ss

Ss	Level of Response	p <
Autistics	High vs. medium	.05
	Medium vs. low	ns
	High vs. low	.01
Retardates	High vs. medium	ns
	Medium vs. low	.01
	High vs. low	.01
Normals	High vs. medium	ns
	Medium vs. low	ns
	High vs. low	ns

As Table 2 shows, there was no significant difference in the amount of responding to the separate stimuli for the normal Ss. The normals gave no evidence for a preference among the cues, or that they were selectively attending to some cues and not others. For the autistics, the significant difference between the high and medium cues and lack of significant difference between the medium and low cues show the dominance of one cue. The retardates differ from the autistics in that they responded to two of the cues. They did not show a significant difference between the two most functional cues (high versus medium), while the difference between these cues and the third cue (medium versus low) was significant.

The data from all the test sessions for the autistic Ss are presented in Figure 2. Percentages of correct responding are presented on the ordinate, while the test sessions are plotted along the abscissa. It is perhaps best to split these data into two parts. The first part can be limited to Test Session 1 and provides data on which cues had acquired control over S during training, when he was reinforced for responding to the stimulus complex. The second part of the data provides information about change in S's responding to the

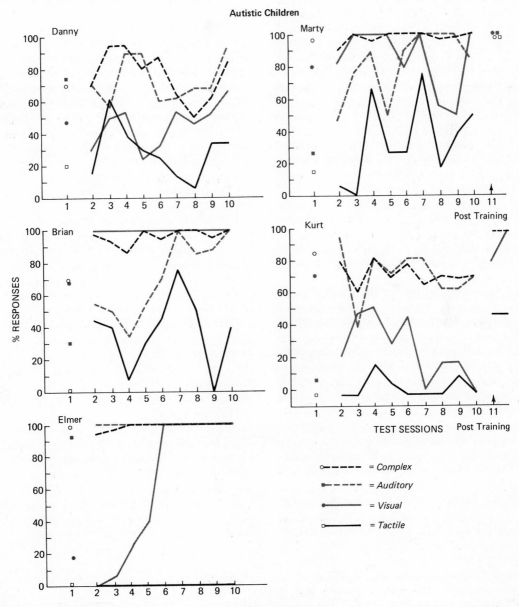

Figure 2. Test sessions for the autistic Ss. (Percentages of correct response to the stimuli are plotted on the ordinate and test sessions are plotted along the abscissa.)

separate stimuli with continuation of testing conditions, when S was reinforced for responding to the separate presentations of these stimuli.

If we inspect the data from Test Session 1 in Figure 2, we observe that the performance on only one of the single cues lies close to the complex cue, and the response to the remaining two cues is very weak or absent altogether. This is clearly shown in regard to the tactile cue for all Ss. It is also apparent in Elmer and Kurt's minimal response to the visual cue, while Marty and Brian responded minimally to the auditory cue.

If we now look at the data with continuation of testing (Session 2 on), one can observe much variability in Ss' response to the separate stimuli. Elmer's record is the least variable. He was initially under auditory control only, but as he received reinforcement for responding to the separate presentation of the visual cue, that cue acquired control. Similar effects can be observed in Brian's and Marty's records. They were initially under visual control and later began responding to the auditory stimulus. This effect, however, is unpredictable. Thus, despite Kurt's reinforcement for responding to the visual cue, that cue eventually ceases to control him. Similar failures of separate elements to acquire control, despite reinforcement for responding in their presence, can be observed in Danny's response to the visual cue, and in Brian's, Marty's, and Danny's response to the tactile cue.

Since we were testing for the possible acquisition of temporal cues, we could not maintain the conditions for the suppression of S^Δ responding. One may therefore question whether response to the least functional cue(s) reflects control by that cue, or random responding. We attempted to answer this question by examining the correlation between S^Δ responding preceding an S^D trial and response during that trial. This analysis was performed on the data of three of the autistic Ss. For each S, we correlated S^D and S^Δ to the two least functional stimuli and to the complex stimulus. This was done for five of the tests of each of the three Ss. Of the 45 correlations, only 6 were significant. However, these 6 were based on few observations, thus increasing the possibility of the analysis reaching significance by chance. We therefore concluded that S^Δ responding was not an important factor in determining S's level of responding to the least functional stimuli.

At the end of the test sessions, we took the cue which had not become functional in the earlier training (visual for Kurt, tactile for Marty) and attempted to establish it as functional by presenting it repeatedly with a variable S^Δ interval. Thus, in contrast to the test sessions, reinforcement could only be obtained by responding to the nonfunctional cue since none of the other cues were presented. Upon reaching criterion, S was reintroduced to the test sessions as before. The data from this training are presented as Posttraining Trial 11 for Marty on the tactile cue and Posttraining Trials 11 and 12 for Kurt on the visual cue. When the previously nonfunctional cues are trained separately, they do acquire control.

Data from the normal Ss are presented in Figure 3. The normal Ss differed from the autistics in three ways. First, they quickly acquired the discrimination and, second, their data show little variability. Third, while the autistic Ss responded differentially to certain components of the complex, the normals responded uniformly to all. Four of the normal Ss appeared to have formed a pattern discrimination, treating the separate components as different from the complex. With continuation of testing, this discrimination is broken, allowing for a demonstration of the equal control acquired by the separate cues.

Individual responding of the retarded Ss is presented in Figure 4. David's (Mongoloid), Tony's (genetic origin) and Colleen's (birth trauma) responding conform to the statistical analysis (Table 1) in that their response to two of the cues parallels their response to the complex. By the end of testing, Jeffrey's (only outpatient) record resembles a normal child, while Roberto's (Mongoloid) graph most closely resembles that of an autistic in that he responded to only one of the cues. These children, like most retardates, present heterogeneous behavioral repertoires, and we have no way of accounting for the variability in their performance.

At the end of testing, we trained a nonfunctional stimulus separately (the auditory stimulus for Colleen and Roberto) in the same manner as we had for the autistic children. The data are presented in Session 11 for both children. The separate training established the cues as functional and allows us to rule out more easily understood problems in sensory deficiency.

DISCUSSION

Three groups of children were reinforced for responding to a complex stimulus involving the

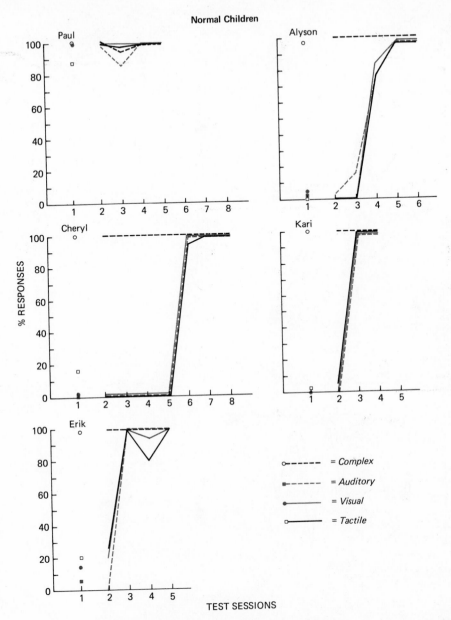

Normal Children

Figure 3. Test sessions for the normal Ss. (Percentages of correct response to the stimuli are plotted on the ordinate and test sessions are plotted along the abscissa.)

simultaneous presentation of auditory, visual, and tactile cues. Once this discrimination was established, elements of the complex were presented separately to assess which aspects of the complex stimulus had acquired control over the child's behavior. We found that (*a*) the autistics responded primarily to only one of the cues; the normals responded uniformly to all three cues; and the retardates functioned between these two extremes.

(*b*) Conditions could be arranged such that a cue which had remained nonfunctional when presented in association with other cues could be established as functional when trained separately.

Our data failed to support notions that any one sense modality is impaired in autistic children, or that a particular sense modality is the "preferred" modality. Our data can perhaps best be understood as the autistics' problem of dealing

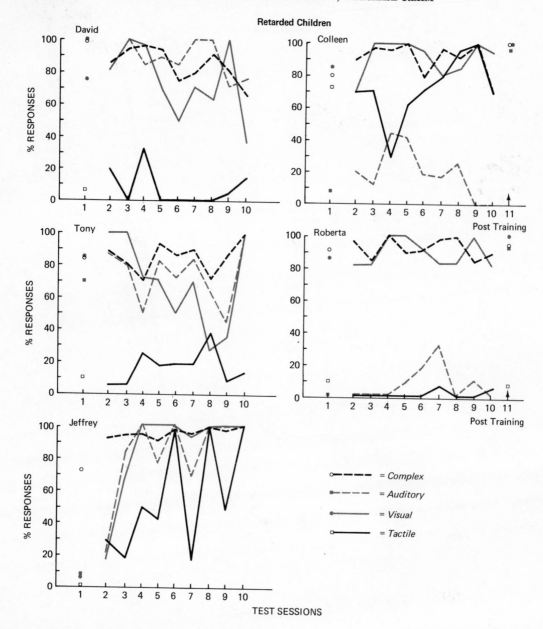

Figure 4. Test sessions for the retarded Ss. (Percentages of correct response to the stimuli are plotted on the ordinate and test sessions are plotted along the abcissa.)

with stimuli in context, a problem of quantity rather than quality of stimulus control. One can call this a problem of stimulus *overselectivity*.

There are some obvious qualifications which one has to impose upon these data. One pertains to the potentially unstable nature of Ss' responding with increased exposure to the training stimuli. This is left unclear in our experiment, since the stimuli were taken out of context

and presented singly (from Test Session 1 on). But one may observe different results with different amounts of training prior to testing.

Perhaps the most important qualification centers on the choice of Ss and the bases of their diagnoses. It is noteworthy that we have worked with the most regressed of autistic children, and that different results may have been obtained had we used children who were more advanced, having, for example, speech development. This problem may be even more pronounced with the retarded Ss who show much heterogeneity. Roberto, for example, though he was diagnosed as retarded, responded like an autistic.

Similarly, we may qualify our data in regard to the *intensity* of the stimuli. Prior to the experiment we attempted to correct for unequal subjective intensities by choosing intensities which college students had rated as having "equal impact." It would have been more ideal to have autistic Ss perform this task, but that would be extremely difficult to do. The results could also be a function of the particular *kind* of stimuli we employed. Perhaps it is the tactile cue which blocks response to other cues. One can also think of other qualifications, such as Ss' motivational level, except that the retarded Ss appeared motivated, yet show parts of the deficiency. Training under more stress, however, as when the child is anxious or inhibiting self-stimulation, may wipe out the effect.

Although these results could be interpreted in several ways, the data conform closely to a selective attention, or stimulus selection, hypothesis. Selective attention refers to the process in which an organism, when presented with multiple cues, attends to, or comes under the control of, only a portion of the available stimuli. This fact has led to the distinction between "nominal" or perceived stimulus variables which consist of the total set of available elements and "functional" or effective stimuli which are those elements actually controlling behavior.

There has been a great deal of research on this differentiation, and excellent reviews of such research are available in recent texts by Fellows (1968) and Trabasso and Bower (1968). A comprehensive presentation will not be attempted here, but a short comment is appropriate.

Long ago, Pavlov (1927) found that the conditioned response to one element (the dominant) of a complex stimulus was as large as the response to the complex, leaving the response to the other elements negligible. Warren (1953) taught monkeys to discriminate between two objects differing in size, color, form, two, or all three of these dimensions. He found that although learning was facilitated by the inclusion of more relevant cues, the color cue alone was the most dominant. Similar results have been reported in other studies with animals (Harlow, 1945: Warren, 1954) and with children (Suchman & Trabasso, 1966). Studying nursery and kindergarten children, Suchman and Trabasso found that when color, size, and form cues were simultaneously available for discrimination, younger children preferred the color cue while the older children preferred the form cue. Working within the operant training paradigm presented here, Reynolds (1961) trained two pigeons to discriminate two white forms on differently colored backgrounds (red or green). In extinction test periods, it was found that one pigeon responded only to the white form and the other pigeon responded only to the colored background. Orlando (1961) reported similar instances of stimulus selection in the learning of retarded children. In a task in which a cue for S^D and S^Δ periods was employed, he found that one of these cues was not only sufficient, but exclusively functional in maintaining the discrimination.

There have been various mechanisms thought to underlie selective responding in normals. Sometimes the underlying mechanism is considered genetic, in that a particular cue emerges as the dominant for the great majority of members within a species. One can also manipulate learning experiences in such a fashion as to render a cue dominant. Both Kamin (1968) in a classical conditioning paradigm and Trabasso and Bower (1968) in a redundant relevant cue (RRC) paradigm have demonstrated blocking effects, finding that a first-learned cue blocks the learning of another relevant cue which was added during overtraining.

"Stimulus blocking" is said to occur when attention to one stimulus in a complex stimulus situation blocks or inhibits the attention to another cue also present. Trabasso and Bower (1968) suggested that the observed dominance or selection in RRC tasks could be due to the blocking of a slower learned cue by a faster learned cue when both cues are present from the beginning of training. They see overshadowing as resulting when an S by chance responds to a particular cue and because he is reinforced does not broaden his learning to the other relevant cues.

One conclusion from all the work on normal children using RRC procedures is that normal children display stimulus selection and thus often come under the control of only a portion of the available stimuli. It is important, therefore, to use a control group of normal Ss to better assess selective responding in autistics. Our failure to observe selective responding in the normal children, which others so often report, was probably based on the nature of the task. In most RRC tasks all the elements fall within one modality, rather than being distributed across modalities as was the case in our study. We also kept the number of stimuli small. Levine (1967) and Eimas (1969) have presented data which suggest that by the time normal children have reached the age of the Ss in this experiment, they will generally attend to about three or four simultaneous cues during discrimination learning. In contrast to the normal children, the autistic children showed an extreme degree of stimulus selection, leaving large segments of their environment essentially neutral.

Perhaps the first questions to be raised by this study regard a more accurate description of the stimulus overselectivity. For example, one may wonder whether the selectivity is a function of the kinds and number of cues in the complex stimulus; whether it is present also when all cues are presented in one modality; or whether it also presents itself when the cues are nonoverlapping but closely spaced in time. Studies are now in progress in our laboratory to investigate some of these questions.

The second line of questions deals with assessing some of the mechanisms which may underlie stimulus overselectivity. Perhaps the autistics tend to respond only to one cue because of a failure in "switching" behavior. Lindsay, Taylor, and Forbes (1968) and Treisman (1969) have suggested that normals seem to attend to only one stimulus component at a time and analyze complex cues by very rapidly switching attention to different aspects of the complex, going quickly through sets of "alternative analyzers." Autistics may not adequately sample stimuli, but settle on one stimulus which "blocks" the others. The problem with this line of reasoning can be easily seen when one considers the possibilities that inadequate switching may result in stimulus blocking, or, conversely, that stimulus blocking may result in inadequate switching. Either direction seems equally plausible.

A third line of questions may be directed toward a better description of stimulus selectivity among groups with different pathology. We included a retarded group to help isolate those peculiarities associated with autistic functioning. The retarded Ss showed less stimulus selectivity than the autistics. They also showed less behavioral deficiency (higher IQ scores, social adjustment, etc.). Perhaps future research will suggest that this kind of discrimination task differentiates between children with different degrees of behavioral deficiencies.

It may be of interest to speculate on how our findings may relate to the pathology in autistic children. Before we present this speculation, two considerations must be made. First, the pathology in autism is so profound and extensive that it is unlikely any one finding will provide insight into it all. Second, the speculations we make presuppose that our inference of stimulus overselectivity best describes the data. Additional studies will be needed to strengthen this inference.

Implications for Understanding Autism

A necessary condition for much learning involves a contiguous or near-contiguous presentation of two stimuli. Such contiguous stimulus presentations are clearly present in classical conditioning when the CS is presented in close proximity to the UCS. In fact, this is a necessary condition for optimal learning. Contiguous presentations are also present in those aspects of operant conditioning where one seeks a shift in stimulus control. In these instances the training stimulus is presented simultaneously with a prompt. Since this contiguous presentation of two stimuli involves presenting the child with a stimulus complex, it may be assumed that the autistics' response to one of these stimuli is blocked, overshadowed, or otherwise has failed to occur. Let us consider some of the implications of this assumption for certain kinds of learning.

1. One can consider that the acquisition of most human behavior, like language, interpersonal, and intellectual behavior, is based on the prior acquisition of conditioned reinforcers. A failure in this acquisition would lead to a failure in behavioral development (Ferster & DeMyer, 1962). If it is the case that conditioned reinforcers acquire strength by contiguous association with primary ones, then our finding should help to further describe the failure for such conditioning to take place in autistic children (Lovaas, Freitag, Kinder, Rubenstein, Schaeffer, & Simmons, 1966).

2. The autistic child's failure to give appropriate affect is well-known. The mechanisms for establishing appropriate affect may well be very similar to those involved in establishing conditioned reinforcers: contiguous presentation of two stimulus events which enables the affect, elicited by one of these events (the UCS), to be elicited by the other (the CS).

3. Many autistic children have topographically elaborate speech (echolalia), but it appears without "meaning." One can argue that the speech exists without meaning to the extent it has an impoverished context. The acquisition of a context for speech probably involves a shift in stimulus control. To the extent that this involves simultaneous presentations of auditory with visual, tactile, or some other cue, one may expect that the autistic child would "overselect" and fail to learn.

4. From a consideration of the data in Figure 1, which illustrates the difficulties in the establishment of imitative behavior, it is also possible that such stimulus overselectivity as we have de-

scribed might contribute importantly to the autistic child's failure in the acquisition of new behavioral topographies. In fact, the usual way we train new skills is to "aid" the child by adding large numbers of extra cues to the training situation. This, of course, may be exactly what makes it so difficult for the autistic child to learn what we want him to.

5. Whenever one postulates blocking of incoming stimuli, learning as well as performance should be impaired. Stimulus overselectivity may also be a factor which underlies the sporadic, highly variable nature of these children's responses to already functional stimuli. A number of other possibilities suggest themselves, which probably are best discussed in light of more extensive data.

REFERENCES

Buss, A., & Lang, P. Psychological deficit in schizophrenia. I. Affect, reinforcement, and concept attainment. *Journal of Abnormal Psychology*, 1965, 70, 2–24.

Eimas, P. Multiple-cue discrimination learning in children. *Psychological Record*, 1969, 19, 417–424.

Feigenberg, I. Probalistic prognosis and its significance in normal and pathological subjects. In M. Cole & I. Maltzman (Eds.), *A handbook of contemporary Soviet psychology*. New York: Basic Books, 1969.

Fellows, B. J. *The discrimination process and development*. London: Pergamon Press, 1968.

Ferster, C. B., & DeMyer, M. A method for the experimental analysis of the behavior of autistic children. *American Journal of Orthopsychiatry*, 1962, 32, 89–98.

Goldfarb, W. An investigation of childhood schizophrenia. *Archives of General Psychiatry*, 1964, 11, 620–634.

Harlow, H. F. Studies in discrimination learning in monkeys. VI. Discriminations between stimuli differing in both color and form, only in color, and only in form. *Journal of General Psychology*, 1945, 33, 225–235.

Hermelin, B. Recent psychological research. In J. K. Wing (Ed.), *Early childhood autism*. London: Pergamon Press, 1966.

Kamin, L. J. Attention-like processes in classical conditioning. In M. R. Jones (Ed.), *Miami Symposium on the Prediction of Behavior, 1967: Aversive stimulation*. Miami: University of Miami Press, 1968.

Kanner, L. Early infantile autism. *Journal of Pediatrics*, 1944, 25, 211–217.

Lang, P. J., & Buss, A. H. Psychological deficit in schizophrenia. II. Interference and activation. *Journal of Abnormal Psychology*, 1965, 70, 77–106.

Levine, M. The size of the hypothesis set during

discrimination learning. *Psychological Review*, 1967, 74, 428–430.

Lindsay, P. H. Taylor, M. M., & Forbes, S. M. Attention and multidimensional discrimination. *Perception and Psychophysics*, 1968, 4, 113–117.

Lovaas, O. I., Berberich, J. P., Perloff, B. F., & Schaeffer, B. Acquisition of imitative speech in schizophrenic children. *Science*, 1966, 151, 705–707.

Lovaas, O. I., Freitag, G., Kinder, M. I., Rubenstein, B. D., Schaeffer, B., & Simmons, J. Q. Establishment of social reinforcers in schizophrenic children using food. *Journal of Experimental Child Psychology*, 1966, 4, 109–125.

Orlando, R. The functional role of discriminative stimuli in free operant performance of developmentally retarded children. *Psychological Record*, 1961, 11, 153–161.

Pavlov, I. P. Lectures. In, *Conditioned reflexes*. Oxford: University Press, 1927.

Reynolds, G. S. Attention in the pigeon. *Journal of the Experimental Analysis of Behavior*, 1961, 4, 203–208.

Rimland, B. *Infantile autism*. New York: Appleton-Century-Crofts, 1964.

Schopler, E. Visual versus tactual receptor preference in normal and schizophrenic children. *Journal of Abnormal Psychology*, 1966, 71, 108–114.

Sherrington, C. S. *The integrative action of the nervous system*. London: Cambridge University Press, 1906.

Suchman, R. G., & Trabasso, T. Color and form preference in young children. *Journal of Experimental Child Psychology*, 1966, 3, 177–187.

Trabasso, T., & Bower, G. H. *Attention in learning*. New York: Wiley, 1968.

Treisman, A. Strategies and models of selective attention. *Psychological Review*, 1969, 76, 282–299.

Warren, J. M. Additivity of cues in visual pattern discrimination by monkeys. *Journal of Comparative and Physiological Psychology*, 1953, *46*, 484–488.

Warren, J. M. Perceptual dominance in discrimination learning in monkeys. *Journal of Comparative and Physiological Psychology*, 1954, *47*, 290–292.

Young, S. Visual attention in autistic and normal children: Effects of stimulus novelty, human attributes, and complexity. Unpublished doctoral dissertation, University of California, Los Angeles, 1969.

breakdown in individuals at high risk for schizophrenia: possible predispositional perinatal factors

Sarnoff A. Mednick

In 1962–63 in Copenhagen, Denmark, Dr. Fini Schulsinger and I intensively examined 207 "normally functioning" children with a high risk

This article is adapted from an address delivered at the annual meeting of the Society for Research in Child Development in Santa Monica, Calif. on March 27, 1969.

The author wishes to express his appreciation to Drs. Donald Kenefick, Daniel Kimble, Neal Miller, Fini Schulsinger and Peter Venables for their advice and criticism. This research project has been supported in part by the National Association for Mental Health and the Scottish Rite Committee for Research in Schizophrenia.

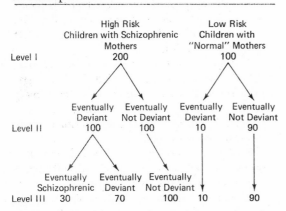

	High Risk Children with Schizophrenic Mothers		Low Risk Children with "Normal" Mothers	
Level I	200		100	
	Eventually Deviant	Eventually Not Deviant	Eventually Deviant	Eventually Not Deviant
Level II	100	100	10	90
	Eventually Schizophrenic	Eventually Deviant	Eventually Not Deviant	
Level III	30	70	100	10	90

of becoming schizophrenic. (They have chronic and severely schizophrenic mothers.) We also examined 104 controls. The study is prospective and longitudinal. We intend to follow these 311 subjects for 20–25 years. During the course of these years we estimate that approximately 100 of the high-risk children will succumb to some form of mental illness, twenty-five to thirty should become schizophrenic.

Figure 1 presents a schematic picture of the research design of this type of study. There are certain research advantages in the longitudinal study of such high-risk populations.

1. They have not yet experienced many aspects of the schizophrenic life such as hospitalizations and drugs. Thus, these factors do not yet color their reactions.

2. The researchers, relatives, teachers and the subject himself do not know that he will become schizophrenic. This relieves the data of a certain part of the burden of bias. The bias is certainly not greater for the future schizophrenic than for other high-risk subjects who do not succumb.

3. The information we gather is current, not retrospective. That part of our inquiry which is

Figure 1. The design can be conceptualized as developing at three levels. At the first level we can study the distinguishing characteristics of children with schizophrenic mothers in comparison with children with no familial psychiatric background. At the second level we can estimate that about 50% of the high-risk children will become seriously socially deviant. Rather good controls for these deviants are the children with schizophrenic mothers who do not become deviant. At the third level we can estimate that perhaps 30 of the 100 high-risk deviants will be diagnosed schizophrenic. The remaining 70 high-risk deviants may be considered appropriate controls for these 30 schizophrenics, as may the non-deviant, high-risk children and the low-risk children.

Such a study may not be readily or at least easily replicated. Others using even the same design may not be attracted to the same variables. In view of this fact a form of replication can be built into the design. At level II the 100 eventually deviant individuals may be conceived of as suffering breakdown in five waves of 20 subjects each. Thus, there are four potential replications of the first data analysis. (It should be mentioned that the precision of the replication might be attenuated if the waves differ in age of breakdown or diagnosis.) At level III the 30 schizophrenics may be conceived of as suffering breakdown in two waves of 15 subjects each.

Reprinted by permission from *Mental Hygiene*, 1970, *54*, pp. 50–63.

retrospective is less so than it would be if the subjects were adults.

4. The data are uniformly and systematically obtained. This is in contrast to retrospective studies which make use of childhood and school records concernings adult schizophrenics. (A detailed discussion of the high-risk design may be found in Mednick and McNeil). (38)

Since 1962, 20 of our high-risk children have suffered severe psychiatric breakdown. I will briefly summarize the 1962 premorbid characteristics that distinctly differentiated these 20 sick children from controls.

METHODS

The high- and low-risk samples were matched, individual for individual, for certain variables. (Table 1).

As may be seen, the average age of the sample was 15.1 years (range was 9–20 years). There would have been some advantage in testing a younger group; however, it will take 20–25 years for the present sample to pass through the major risk period for schizophrenia. The subjects' mean age was selected so as to maximize the probability that the investigators would still be alive at the conclusion of this risk period. Studies of three-year-old and ten-year-old high-risk samples are being undertaken. A study of prenatal high-risk children is being planned.

TABLE 1. Characteristics of the Experimental and Control Samples

	Control	Experimental
Number of cases	104	207
Number of boys	59	121
Number of girls	45	86
Mean age §	15.1	15.1
Mean social class†	2.3	2.2
Mean years education	7.3	7.0
Percent of group in children's homes (5 years or more)£	14%	16%
Mean number of years in children's homes (5 years or more)£	8.5	9.4
Per cent of group with rural residence∅	22%	26%

§Defined as age to the nearest whole year.
†The scale runs from 0 (low) to 6 (high) and was adapted from Svalastoga (1959).
£We only considered experience in children's homes of 5 years or greater duration. Many of the Experimental children had been to children's homes for brief periods while their mothers were hospitalized. These experiences were seen as quite different from the experience of children who actually had to make a children's home their home until they could go out and earn their own living.
∅A rural residence was defined as living in a town with a population of 2500 persons or fewer.

PROCEDURES

In addition to weight and height the following measures were taken in the intensive 1962 examination:

1. *Physiological–conditioning–extinction testing.* Continuous recording was made of heart rate, muscle tension, respiration, and galvanic skin response (GSR) during rest, conditioning, generalization and extinction procedures. The CS was a 54 db tone of 1000 cps. The UCS (also considered the stress stimulus) was a very irritating, loud (96 db) noise presented via earphones.

2. *Wechsler Intelligence Scale for Children.* (Danish adaptation). All subtests were administered.

3. *Personality Inventory.* This consisted of a group of items translated from the MMPI.

4. *Word Association Test.* This was a translation of the Kent-Rosanoff list.

5. *Continuous Association Test.* We observed the flow of the subject's associations to a single word over a one-minute period. Thirty stimulus words were used.

6. *Adjective Check List.* A list of 241 items was used by professional personnel to describe the subject. The subject also described himself using the same list.

7. *Psychiatric Interview.* A pre-coded psychiatric interview was included for diagnostic purposes and to elicit reports from the subject on his current social and interpersonal functioning. A rating of Level of Adjustment was made for each subject.

8. *Parent Interview.* A pre-coded interview was conducted with the individual with major responsibility for the child's rearing.

9. *School Report.* A questionnaire was obtained from the teacher that knew each subject best.

10. *Midwife's Report.* This is a detailed, legally required, standard form prepared by the midwife attending the subject's birth.

More detailed statements of methodology may be found in Mednick and Schulsinger. (29, 30, 31)

RESULTS

As of last year, the first wave of 20 breakdowns (which we call the Sick Group) had been identi-

TABLE 2. Descriptions of Conditions of Sick Group

1. Male, born 16 March 1953. Extremely withdrawn, no close contacts, 2 months' psychiatric admission following theft, currently in institution for boys with behavior difficulties, still performing petty thieveries.

2. Female, born 19 January 1943. Married, one child, extremely withdrawn, nervous. Evidence of delusional thinking, pulls her hair out, has large bald area.

3. Female, born 29 March 1946. Promiscuous, highly unstable in work, no close contacts, confused and unrealistic, psychiatric admission for diagnostic reasons, recent abortion, some evidence of thought disorder.

4. Male, born 1 July 1946. Under minor provocation had semipsychotic breakdown in Army, expresses strange distortions of his body image, thought processes vague, immature.

5. Male, born 2 May 1944. Severe difficulties in concentrating, cannot complete tasks, marked schizoid character, marginally adjusted.

6. Male, born 3 June 1947. Lonely in the extreme, spends all spare time at home. Manages at home only by virtue of extremely compulsive routines. No heterosexual activity, marked schizoid character.

7. Male, born 1 October 1953. No close contact with peers, attends class for retarded children, abuses younger children, recently took a little boy out in the forest, undressed him, urinated on him and his clothes, and sent him home.

8. Male, born 17 January 1954. Has history of convulsions, constantly takes antiseizure drug (Dilantin), nervous, confabulating, unhappy, sees frightening "nightmares" during the day, afraid of going to sleep because of nightmares and fear that people are watching through the window, feels teacher punishes him unjustly.

9. Female, born 18 March 1944. Nervous, quick mood changes, body image distortions, passive, resigned. Psychiatric admission, paranoid tendencies revealed, vague train of thought.

10. Male, born 14 March 1952. Arrested for involvement in theft of motorbike. Extremely withdrawn, difficulties in concentration, passive, disinterested, father objected to his being institutionalized, consequently he is now out under psychiatric supervision.

11. Male, born 19 October 1947. Level of intellectual performance in apprenticeship decreasing, private life extremely disorderly, abreacts through alcoholism.

12. Male, born 20 January 1944. Severe schizoid character, no heterosexual activity, lives an immature, shy, anhedonic life, thought disturbances revealed in TAT.

13. Female, born 25 May 1947. Psychiatric admission, abortion, hospital report suspect pseudoneurotic or early schizophrenia, association test betrays thought disturbance, tense, guarded, ambivalent. Current difficulties somewhat precipitated by sudden death of boy friend.

14. Male, born 13 August 1950. Sensitive, negativistic, unrealistic. Recently stopped working and was referred to a youth guidance clinic for evaluation. Is now under regular supervision of a psychologist.

15. Male, born 28 May 1947. History of car stealing, unstable, drifting, unemployed, sensitive, easily hurt, one year institutionalization in a reformatory for the worst delinquents in Denmark.

16. Female, born 1 June 1945. Psychotic episode, one year of hospitalization. Diagnoses from 2 hospitals: (1) schizophrenia, (2) manic psychosis.

17. Male, born 3 September 1946. Severe schizoid character, psychotic breakdown in Army, preceded by arrest for car thievery. Now hospitalized.

18. Male, born 28 January 1953. Perhaps border-line retarded. Psychiatric admission for diagnostic reasons, spells of uncontrolled behavior.

19. Male, born 23 June 1948. Repeatedly apprehended for stealing, severe mood swings, sensitive, restless, unrealistic, fired from job because of financial irregularities.

20. Female, born 5 July 1941. Highly intelligent girl with mystical interests. Very much afflicted by mother's schizophrenia. TAT reveals thought disorder. Receiving psychotherapy.

fied. Their clinical status is described very briefly in Table 2. Thirteen have been admitted to psychiatric hospitals with many diagnoses including schizophrenia. The seven not admitted include some who are clearly schizophrenic. The clinical status of these individuals was ascertained by our follow-up procedures. To each of these 20 we have matched another high-risk subject (Well Group) of the same age, sex, social class, and institutional rearing status. In addition we have matched these subjects for the psychiatrist's 1962 Level of Adjustment rating. We tried as much as possible to select individuals for the Well Group who, since 1962, had shown some improvement in Level of Adjustment. Also, 20 Controls were selected from the low-risk group for comparison purposes. This matching yielded two groups of high-risk subjects. In 1962, both were judged to be equal in Level of Adjustment. Yet since 1962 one group has improved in level of mental health, the other group has suffered severe psychiatric breakdown. Why? Part of the answer could lie with the predisposing characteristics measured in 1962 at the time of the intensive examination.

The most important characteristics distinguishing the Sick Group from the Well and Control Group were:

1. The Sick Group lost their schizophrenic mother to psychiatric hospitalization much earlier in their lives than did the other two groups. These early-hospitalized mothers were also more severely schizophrenic. The Well Group lost their mothers at approximately the same time as did the Control Group. In view of the greater severity

of illness of the mothers who left their home early, these data may be interpreted in relatively genetic or environmental terms.

2. The teachers' reports indicate that the Sick subjects tended to be disturbing to the class. They were disciplinary problems, domineering, aggressive, created conflicts and disrupted the class with their talking. This was true of 53% of the Sick Group, 18% of the Well Group, and 11% of the Control Group.

3. On the Continual Association Test, where the subject is asked to give, in one minute, as many single-word associations as he can to a stimulus word, the Sick Group showed two distinctive patterns. They had a strong tendency to rattle off a whole series of words which were interrelated but contextually relatively irrelevant, "Opremsning," in Danish. Their associations also tended to "drift" away from the stimulus word. Contrary to instructions and cautions they might begin responding to their own responses; for example to the stimulus word "Table" they might respond "Chair, top, leg, girl, pretty, sky. . . ." Those in the Sick Group who do not evidence drifting can apparently manage to avoid this only by restricting themselves to one or two responses per stimulus word for the entire one-minute period.

4. Some of the variables most sharply differentiating the Sick Group from the Well and Control Groups were the electrodermal measures taken during the psychophysiological testing. These measures largely reflect the functioning of the body's stress mobilization mechanisms.

a) The latency of the GSR was substantially faster for the Sick Group than for either of the other two groups.

b) The GSR latency for the Sick Group did not show any signs of habituation. This was especially marked in their responses to the nine UCS stress stimulus trials. The Control and Well Groups' rapid habituation of latency was seen in the progressive increase of their response latencies from the first to the last of the stress trials. The latencies of the Sick Group progressively decrease suggesting a negative habituation or even increasing irritability. Moving from UCS trials I–IX, 69% of the Well Group exhibit a slowing of response latency (habituation); 75% of the Sick Group actually increase the speed of their response.

c) A well-documented characteristic of conditioned GSR behavior is the rapidity with which it demonstrates experimental extinction and/or

adaptation. In both the Well and Control Groups electrodermal responsiveness was already dropping off by the end of the stress stimulus trials. Following those stress trials we presented a series of nine nonreinforced test trials for generalization and speed of extinction of the conditioned response. The Well and Control Groups evidenced very rapid extinction, i.e., they responded to only one or two of the extinction test trials. The Sick Group exhibited great resistance to extinction, in many cases responding with tenacity until the very end of the extinction series.

d) The Sick Group showed remarkably fast recovery from momentary states of autonomic imbalance. Once a GSR was made we measured the rate at which recovery to basal level proceeded. (This measure and its theoretical significance has been reported previously in this Journal. [33]) On some trials rate of recovery almost perfectly separated the Sick and Controls Groups. The pooled Sick and Well Groups' distributions for rate of recovery typically found 70% of the Sick and 30% of the Well Group above the median.

The above material may be found discussed in greater detail in Mednick and Schulsinger. (31)

5. In a previous report of the differences between the Sick, Well and Control Groups we pointed out that while in our analyses of data on birth complications "there was a slight general tendency for the Sick Group to have had a more difficult birth, none of the differences reached statistical significance." (31) Subsequent, more careful, examination of these data revealed that while it was true that no single complication significantly differentiated the groups, 70% of the members of the Sick Group had suffered one or more serious pregnancy or birth complication (PBC). This contrasted sharply with the 15% of the Well Group and 33% of the Control Group with PBCs. The PBCs included anoxia, prematurity, prolonged labor, placental difficulty, umbilical cord complication, mother's illness during pregnancy, multiple births, and breech presentations. Careful perusal of these data brought out an additional striking relationship within the Sick Group (and the entire high-risk group). There is a marked correspondence between PBC and the anomalous electrodermal behavior reported above. All the GSR differences between the Sick and Well Groups could be explained by the PBCs in the Sick Group. In the Control Group and low-risk group the PBCs were not strongly associated with these extreme GSR effects. This suggests

that the PBCs trigger some characteristic which may be genetically predisposed. The PBCs seem to damage the modulatory control of the body's stress-response mechanisms. PBCs are associated with rapid response onset, poor habituation of the response, poor extinction of the conditioned electrodermal response, and very rapid recovery from the response. In terms of the theoretical orientation guiding this project (Mednick [27, 28, 32]) this lack of modulation may be viewed as an important etiological factor in the development of mental illness, especially schizophrenia.

The finding that immediately raised fertile questions was the high frequency of PBCs in the Sick Group. What damage might these PBCs have done and where? We first sought for inklings of brain sites particularly sensitive to being damaged by PBCs. We then examined animal studies in which analogous damage had been inflicted by surgical lesion to particularly sensitive brain sites. The reports of the behavior of animals suffering surgically inflicted lesions to these same areas were then searched for instances of behavior similar to that which we observed in our PBC-Sick subjects. We hoped in this manner to generate hypotheses regarding specific sites of brain lesions in our PBC subjects.

Brain Sites of Selective Vulnerability

PBCs result in future difficulties for the fetus chiefly because of the great sensitivity of neural tissue to anoxia. (Mechanical damage probably plays a less significant role, although through vascular obstruction it can also lead to anoxia.) Researchers have singled out particular brain structures as being "selectively vulnerable" to the effects of anoxia. These areas include most prominently, the hippocampus, and Purkinje cells of the cerebellum. (2) Of these two areas, Spectator (46) singles out the hippocampus as being the most vulnerable. He evaluates the effects of anoxia by studying "biochemical lesions," i.e. "the initial chemical changes in tissues following the application of harmful agents and preceding anatomical evidence of damage." The chemical changes he has studied as a function of anoxia have been losses in certain enzymes which precede "histological evidence of cell injury by approximately 10 hours. It is noteworthy that chemical changes appear in the hippocampus immediately after anoxia, whilst the other areas show earliest loss of enzymes after 1–6 hours. The enzyme loss in the hippocampus involved the

neurones and was not apparent in the glia or neuropil. This observation suggests that, in this site at least, the neurones are more susceptible than are the surrounding cells to oxygen lack" (552–553).

Friede (12) also indicates that the hippocampus (Ammons Horn) represents one of "the most striking examples of selective vulnerability in the brain and in particular Sommer's Sector, H 1 is known to be a characteristic site for anoxic damage." (Friede links this vulnerability of H 1 to relatively low levels of lactate dehydrogenase in Sommer's Sector).

Animal Ablation Literature

Thus, with the hippocampus as our chief, and most likely suspect, and the amygdaloid and the cerebellum (Purkinje cells) as an additional suspect we next turned to the animal ablation literature. The strategy here was to see if we could find any similarity between the behavior of our Sick subjects with PBCs and the behavior of animals with circumscribed lesions to each of these suspect areas. Conditioning and extinction behaviors are frequent dependent variables in animal ablation studies. This facilitated comparisons with our data since our subjects have gone through a conditioning and extinction session.

Briefly stated, the literature on the Purkinje cells did not strongly relate to the conditioning data of our PBC subjects. On the other hand the behavior of hippocampus animals was in some surprising ways like that of our PBC-Sick subjects. At this point we must sound a strong note of caution; below we will be relating rat, instrumental, and human, classical conditioning data. It is doubtless a questionable procedure to draw analogies across two species and two types of conditioning. In this case it has proven of great value for hypothesis formation. These ideas are presented in this spirit.

There are several aspects of the behavior of hippocampal rats which are of interest to us in the present context.

1. Rats with hippocampal lesions manifest relatively fast response latency. (19, 41, 45)

2. Rats with hippocampal lesions evidence very poor habituation of the latency of their responses. While normal and cortically damaged control groups exhibit habituation by responding with increasing latencies across a series of test trials, the response latencies of the hippocampal rats do not slow down. They continue to respond as

though they were experiencing the stimulus for the first time. (17)

3. Rats with hippocampal lesions evidence great resistance to the experimental extinction of conditioned behavior. (15, 37)

4. Rats with hippocampal lesions are hyperactive. (16, 45)

5. Rats with hippocampal lesions acquire a conditioned avoidance response in a shuttle box more quickly than control or cortically damaged rats. (15, 18, 45)

In comparing these characteristics with the characteristics described above for the Sick Group we can detect some considerable similarity. Both the Sick subjects with PBCs and the hippocampal rats evidence fast response latency, very poor habituation and poor extinction of a conditioned response. We can also tentatively link the hyperactivity of the hippocampal rats to the unruly classroom behavior of our Sick Subjects. The two points that do not immediately relate to each other are the fast avoidance conditioning of the hippocampal rats and the fast GSR recovery of the Sick Group with PBCs. In terms of some of the components of a theory of schizophrenia advanced earlier (31, 32) these seemingly independent points may actually be closely related. Thus, if we assume that the fast GSR recovery of the Sick Group with PBCs is also characteristic of the hippocampal rats we can postulate some basis for the puzzling and consistent finding of unusually fast avoidance learning on the part of the hippocampal rats. Whether one takes a reinforcement or contiguity position, one crucial variable influencing speed of avoidance conditioning in a shuttle box is the rapidity and amount of fear reduction following a successful avoidance response. After the avoidance response has been made, the speed and the amount of reinforcement depends in large part, on the speed of fear reduction and hence on the rate of recovery from the stress response. (57) Any rat who recovers unusually rapidly from a stress response will receive a correspondingly rapid reward of fear reduction when he leaps from the shuttle box' electrified grid floor into the safe compartment. His reinforcement will be greater than that of a rat with normal recovery rate or slow recovery rate. Fast recovery from stress response could conceivably explain the otherwise rather mysterious rapid avoidance learning of hippocampal rats. If such fast recovery were directly demonstrated,

the similarity of hippocampal rats to our PBC-Sick subjects would be striking. In the light of the sensitivity of the human hippocampus to the anoxic effects of PBCs, this similarity would suggest the hypothesis that the PBCs in our high-risk children have resulted in damage to their hippocampus. What is further suggested is the possibility that the resultant behavioral anomalies are in some way predispositional to psychiatric breakdown and schizophrenia in individuals with schizophrenic mothers.

IMPLICATIONS

In summary:

1. The most likely site of brain damage resulting from PBCs seems to be the hippocampus, especially Sommer's Sector, H 1.

2. High-risk children who have suffered PBCs exhibit a specific and unique pattern of conditioning, habituation, extinction and GSR behavior. (This pattern is also exhibited by low-risk children with PBCs but at a diminished level).

3. This pattern is strikingly similar to the conditioning, habituation and extinction behavior of rats who have experienced surgical lesions to the hippocampus. These surgical lesions encompass what in the human would be Sommer's Sector H 1. (19)

Another important aspect of behavior which is characteristic of hippocampal rats has been observed in infants who may have suffered anoxia and hence hippocampal damage at birth. Kimble (17) indicates that "damage to the hippocampus should impair the process of habituation to novel stimuli, as has been reported (Leaton, 1965)." This same failure of habituation to novel stimuli has been reported for infants at the ages of two days, five days and 30 days in those cases where the mother had undergone heavy anaesthesia during delivery. Controls were infants of the same age where the mothers had undergone mild or no anaesthesia. (6) Maternal heavy anaesthesia during delivery can affect the fetus, producing retarded respiration and anoxia. (36) In the context of this general discussion it is tempting to postulate that in this study anaesthesia-induced anoxia produced some hippocampal damage in these children which, in turn, manifested itself in the form of a failure of habituation.

We are suggesting the existence of a relationship between a pattern of observed habituation–

conditioning–extinction findings in our PBC-Sick Group and hypothesized hippocampal damage. It is tempting to consider what biochemical and neurophysiological mechanisms could possibly be at the basis of this hypothesized relationship. One interesting lead is recent evidence of a link between hippocampal functioning and ACTH secretion. Damage to the hippocampus has been shown to result in a failure of inhibition of ACTH released by the pituitary gland. (20, 21) Weiss, McEwen and DeSilva (personal communication) have evidence that this inhibitory influence is only called into play during states of stress reaction. During such stress states a damaged hippocampus does not provide an adequate inhibitory influence on the pituitary gland and thus permits an oversecretion of ACTH. Interestingly enough, such ACTH oversecretion may be expected to prolong the extinction of a conditioned response. (7, 8, 9) Such prolonged extinction effects were, of course, observed in our PBC-Sick subjects and are observed in hippocampal rats. It may be suggested that one basis for this failure of extinction was an oversupply of circulating ACTH due to the failure of a damaged hippocampus to sufficiently inhibit ACTH-pituitary secretion during the stressful psychophysiological session.

This failure to inhibit ACTH secretion because of hippocampal inadequacy may also partially explain the state of hyperarousal that seems characteristic of the schizophrenic. (1, 5, 14, 25, 35, 42, 52, 53, 56) The explanation of the state of hyperarousal may also follow a relatively non-biochemical, neurophysiological route. On the basis of a series of studies observing cortically evoked potentials to visual and auditory stimuli, while concurrently stimulating the hippocampus, Redding (43) concluded that the hippocampus exerts an inhibitory influence on the brain stem reticular formation. An inadequate hippocampus exerting a less than normal inhibitory influence on the reticular formation could contribute to the existence of a chronic state of hyperarousal in an individual. Mechanisms by means of which this hyperarousal and fast GSR recovery and latency could translate themselves into the clinical symptoms and life condition of schizophrenia have been elaborated in detail in earlier publications including this Journal and need not be repeated here. (27, 28, 31, 32)

We are, perhaps, now at a point where we can hypothesize that PBC factors lead to defective hippocampal functioning which in combination with genetic and environmental factors could conceivably play a vital predispositional role in at least some forms of schizophrenia. This linking of hippocampal functioning and schizophrenia is not an entirely new idea. Necrosis of neural tissue in Sommer's Sector of the hippocampus has been very regularly found in neuropathological studies of the epileptic. (2) Chapman (3) and Slater, Beard and Glithero (47) among others have pointed to the great similarity of epileptic states of consciousness, especially psychomotor epilepsy, to the disturbances of consciousness in the schizophrenic. Roberts (44) conceptualized schizophrenia "as a disordering of an entire brain system . . . correlated with malfunction in the dorsal hippocampal limbic system." There has also been a considerable amount of research linking PBCs with serious behavioral disturbances and schizophrenia in children (22, 39, 40, 50) and adults. (23, 49) There are studies in the literature which have demonstrated "typical" hippocampal-lesion behavior in the schizophrenic. Milstein, Stevens and Sachdev (34) demonstrated very poor habituation and very fast latency of the alpha attenuation response for chronic adult schizophrenics. As early as 1937, Cohen and Patterson reported poor habituation of the cardiac response in schizophrenics. Zahn (56) has reported poor habituation of the GSR in chronic schizophrenics. Vinogradova (55) has demonstrated that chronic schizophrenics take an unusually large number of trials to extinguish a conditioned plethysmograph response.

The adjective "chronic" has been used above to modify the noun "schizophrenia." It may well be that hippocampal dysfunction is an important contributing predispositional factor in only some types of schizophrenia. These may be the more typical, process, chronic, or poor premorbid types. Our Sick subjects tend to be "early onset" cases suggesting that many of them may have a relatively poor prognosis. It is also possible that degree of hippocampal dysfunction will relate to degree of seriousness of illness.

The emphasis on neurophysiological, biochemical and traumatic variables and materials in this paper should not be read as a denigration of the capability of genetic forces to produce identical hippocampal insufficiency or a disregard for the necessity of an appropriate environment to cultivate the learning of schizophrenic modes of behavior and thought. The emphasis on PBCs should not be read as denying the possibility that postnatal injury or high fever could also produce similar brain damage. Finally we have dealt exclusively with the possible impact of hippocampal injury. We could have also brought the septum and other limbic areas into the discussion. The functioning of the entire temporal lobe is also not irrelevant in this area. However, for reasons that are made evident above, the hippocampus seems the best candidate for our attention.

IMPLICATIONS FOR FUTURE STUDY

In terms of the theoretical orientation of the author, the condition of schizophrenia (predisposed by a variety of conditions and circumstances) is a pattern of well-learned avoidance responses. In terms of treatment considerations, such well-learned avoidance responses are difficult to extinguish. Every time an avoidance response is successfully made it is automatically and immediately reinforced. In animal research a shuttle-box-avoidance response can be extinguished by physically preventing the rat or dog from performing the avoidance response in the presence of the avoidance stimulus and not delivering the punishment. However, the bulk of the schizophrenics' avoidance responses are thoughts. These are difficult if not truly impossible to prevent or control. Thus, for theoretical as well as practical and humane reasons our research thinking centers on primary prevention rather than treatment. In view of our findings, one potentially useful field of intervention that suggests itself is the pregnancy and birth process. If a sound hippocampus is a prerequisite for sound mental health and if we can avoid PBCs in high-risk populations, we may avert hippocampal damage and hence reduce the probability of mental illness. A research project on this very matter is currently being planned. Secondly, in view of the possible involvement of poorly modulated hormonal secretions, research on psychopharmacological intervention at an early premorbid age would seem indicated. Such a study is now in its early stages. We are also conducting further prospective studies on the long-term consequences of PBCs in children with schizophrenic parents.

REFERENCES

1. Ax, A. F., Beckett, P. G. S., Cohen, B. D., Frohman, C. E., Tourney, G., and Gottlieb, J. S., Physiologic patterns in chronic schizophrenia. In Wortis, B. (Ed.), *Recent advances in biological psychiatry*, Vol. IV, New York, Plenum Press, 1962.

2. Blackwood, W., McMenemey, W. H., Meyer, A., Norman, R. M., and Russell, D. S., *Greenfield's Neuropathology*, Baltimore, Williams & Wilkins, 1967.

3. Chapman, J., The early symptoms of schizophrenia, *British Journal of Psychiatry, 112*:225–251, 1966.

4. Cohen, L. H., and Patterson, M., Effect of pain on the heart rate of normal and schizophrenic individuals, *Journal of General Psychology, 17*:273–289, 1937.

5. Conn, J. W., Aldosteronism in man, *Journal of the American Medical Association, 183*:775–781, 1963.

6. Conway, R., and Brackbill, Y., Effects of obstetrical medication on infant sensorimotor behavior. Paper presented at meeting, Society for Research in Child Development, Santa Monica, 1969.

7. De Weid, D., Inhibitory effect of ACTH and related peptides on extinction of conditioned avoidance behavior in rats, *Proceedings of the Society of Experimental Biological Medicine, 122*:28–32, 1966.

8. De Weid, D., The influence of the posterior and intermediate lobe of the pituitary and pituitary peptides on the maintenance of a conditioned avoidance response in rats, *International Journal of Neuropharmacology, 4*:157–167, 1965.

9. De Weid, D., and Bohus, B., Long term and short term effects on retention of a conditioned avoidance response in rats by treatment with long acting pitressin and MSH, *Nature, 212*:1484–1486, 1966.

10. Fowles, D. C., and Venables, P. H., Endocrine factors in palmar skin potential, *Psychonomic Science, 10*:387–388, 1968.

11. Fowles, D. C., and Venables, P. H., The effects of epidermal hydration and sodium reabsorption on palmar skin potential, *Psychological Bulletin*, In press.

12. Friede, R., The histochemical architecture of Ammons Horn as related to its selective vulnerability, *Acta Neuropathologica, 6*:1–13, 1966.

13. Ganong, W. F., Biglieri, E. G., and Mulrow, P. J., Mechanisms regulating adrenocortical secretion of aldosterone and glucocorticoids, *Recent Progress in Hormone Research, 22*:381–430, 1966.

14. Goldstein, L., Sugerman, A. A., Stolberg, H., Electro-cerebral activity in schizophrenic and non-psychotic subjects: Quantitative EEG Amplitude analysis, *Electroencephalography and Clinical Neurophysiology, 19*:350–361, 1965.

15. Isaacson, R. L., Douglas, R. J., and Moore, R. Y., The effect of radical hippocampal ablation on

acquisition of an avoidance response, *Journal of Comparative and Physiological Psychology, 54:*625–628, 1961.

16. Kimble, D. P., The effects of bilateral hippocampal lesions in rats, *Journal of Comparative and Physiological Psychology, 56:*273–283, 1963.

17. Kimble, D. P., Hippocampus and internal inhibition, *Psychological Bulletin, 70:*285–295, 1968.

18. Kimble, D. P., and Gostnell, D., Role of the cingulate cortex in shock avoidance behavior of rats, *Journal of Comparative and Physiological Psychology, 65:*290–294, 1968.

19. Kimble, D. P., Personal communication, 1969.

20. Knigge, K. M., and Hays, M., *Proceedings of the Society for Experimental Biological Medicine, 114:*67–69, 1963.

21. Knigge, K. M., Abstracts, 2nd international Congress on Hormonal Steroids, Milan, 1966.

22. Knobloch, H., and Pasamanick, B., Etiological factors in early infantile autism and childhood schizophrenia, paper presented International Congress of Pediatrics, Lisbon, Portugal, 1962.

23. Lane, E., and Albee, G. W., Comparative birth weights of schizophrenics and their siblings, *Journal of Psychology, 64:*227–231, 1966.

24. Leaton, R. N., Exploratory behavior in rats with hippocampal lesions, *Journal of Comparative and Physiological psychology, 59:*325–330, 1965.

25. Malmo, R. B., Shagass, C., and Smith, A. A., Responsiveness in chronic schizophrenia, *J. Personality, 19:*359–375, 1951.

26. McEwen, B. S., Weiss, J. M., and Schwartz, L. S., Selective retention of corticosterone by limbic structures in rat brain, *Nature, 220:*911–912, 1968.

27. Mednick, S. A., A learning theory approach to research in schizophrenia, *Psychological Bulletin, 55:*316–327, 1958.

28. Mednick, S. A., Schizophrenia: a learned thought disorder, in G. Nielsen (Ed.) *Clinical Psychology,* Proceedings of the XIV International Congress of Applied Psychology, Copenhagen: Munksgaard, 1962.

29. Mednick, S. A., and Schulsinger, F., A longitudinal study of children with a high risk for schizophrenia: a preliminary report, in S. Vandenberg (Ed.) *Methods and goals in human behavior genetics,* New York, Academic Press, 1965.

30. Mednick, S. A., and Schulsinger, F., Children of schizophrenic mothers, *Bulletin of the International Association of Applied Psychology, 14:*11–27, 1965.

31. Mednick, S. A., and Schulsinger, F., Some premorbid characteristics related to breakdown in children with schizophrenic mothers, *Journal of Psychiatric Research, 6:*(supplement 1), 267–291, 1968.

32. Mednick, S. A., A longitudinal study of children with a high risk for schizophrenia, *Mental Hygiene, 50:*522–535, 1966.

33. Mednick, S. A., and McNeil, T. F., Current methodology in research on the etiology of schizophrenia, *Psychological Bulletin, 70:*681–693, 1968.

34. Milstein, V., Stevens, J., and Sachdev, K., Habit-uation of the alpha attenuation response in children and adults with psychiatric disorders, *Electroencephalography and Clinical Neurophysiology, 26:*12–18, 1969.

35. Mirsky, A. F., Neuropsychological bases of schizophrenia, *Annual Review of Psychology, 20:*321–348, 1969.

36. Moya, F., and Thorndike, V., The effects of drugs used in labor on the fetus and newborn, *Clinical Pharmacology and Therapeutics, 4:*628–638, 1963.

37. Mulrow, P. J., Metabolic effects of adrenalmineralocordicoid hormones, in A. B. Eisenstein (Ed.), *The adrenal cortex,* Boston, Little, Brown, 1967.

38. Niki, H., The effects of hippocampal ablation on the inhibitory control of operant behavior in the rat, *Japanese Psychological Research, 7:*126–137, 1965.

39. Pasamanick, B., Rogers, M., and Lilienfeld, A. M., Pregnancy experience and the development of childhood behavior disorder, *American Journal of Psychiatry, 112:*614–618, 1956.

40. Pollack, M., and Woerner, M. G., Pre- and perinatal complication and "childhood schizophrenia": A comparison of 5 controlled studies, *Journal of Child Psychology and Psychiatry, 7:*235–242, 1966.

41. Rabe, A., and Haddad, R. K., Acquisition of 2-way shuttle box avoidance after selective hippocampal lesions, *Physiology & Behavior, 4:*319–323, 1969.

42. Ray, T. S., Electrodermal indications of levels of psychological disturbance in chronic schizophrenics, *American Psychologist, 18:*393, 1963.

43. Redding, F. K., Modification of sensory cortical evoked potentials by hippocampal stimulation, *Electroencephalography and Clinical Neurophysiology, 22:*74–83, 1967.

44. Roberts, D. R., Functional organization of the limbic systems, *International Journal of Neuropsychiatry, 2:*279–292, 1966.

45. Roberts, W. W., Dember, W. N., and Brodwick, M., Alternation and exploration in rats with hippocampal lesions, *Journal of Comparative and Physiological Psychology, 55:*695–700, 1962.

46. Silveira, J. M., The deficit in the disinhibition of attention after bilateral hippocampal lesions: Brightness discrimination and reversal in the hippocampectomized rat, unpublished master's thesis, University of Oregon, 1967.

47. Slater, E., Beard, A. W., and Glithero, E. Schizophrenia-like psychoses of epilepsy, *International Journal of Psychiatry, 1:*6–30, 1965.

48. Spector, R. G., Enzyme chemistry of anoxic brain injury, in C. W. M. Adams (Ed.), *Neurohistochemistry,* New York, Elsevier, 1965.

49. Stabenau, J. R., and Pollin, W., Early characteristics of monozygotic twins discordant for schizophrenia, *Archives of General Psychiatry, 17:*723–734, 1967.

50. Taft, L., and Goldfarb, W., Prenatal and perinatal factors in childhood schizophrenia, *Developmental Medicine and Child Neurology, 6:*32–43, 1964.

51. Venables, P. H., Input dysfunction in schizophrenia. In B. A. Maher (Ed.), *Progress in Experimental Personality Research*, Vol. I, New York, Academic Press, 1964.

52. Venables, P. H., Psychophysiological aspects of schizophrenia, *British Journal of Medical Psychology*, *39*:289–297, 1966.

53. Venables, P. H., and Wing, J. K., Level of arousal and the subclassification of schizophrenia, *Archives of General Psychiatry*, *7*:114–119, 1962.

54. Venables, P. H., Personal communication, 1969.

55. Vinogradova, N. V., Protective and stagnant inhibition in schizophrenics, *Zhurnal Vysshei Nervnoi Deaietelnostni*, Imeni L. P. Pavlova, 1962.

56. Zahn, T. P., Autonomic reactivity and behaviour in schizophrenia, *Psychiatric Research Reports*, *19*:156–171, 1964.

57. Zeaman, D., and Wegner, N., The role of drive reduction in the classical conditioning of an autonomically mediated response, *Journal of Experimental Psychology*, *48*:349–354, 1954.

the genetics of schizophrenic and schizoid disease

Leonard L. Heston

The contribution of genetic factors to the etiology of schizophrenia has been confirmed decisively. Because the investigations that have led to this result have uncovered questions cutting across several fields of inquiry, a fresh look at some central aspects of the schizophrenia problem is warranted. These questions and the factual background underlying them are the main concerns of this article. Because emphasis is placed on formulating testable hypotheses, the evidence is organized in support of a particular genetic theory.

THE BASIC EVIDENCE

During the first half of this century, systematic family studies demonstrated that the distribution of schizophrenia is that of a genetic disease. Relatives of schizophrenics were found to be afflicted with the illness much more frequently than members of the general population. The child of a schizophrenic parent, for example, was found to have a risk of schizophrenia about 15 times that of a member of the population at large. It was found that, among all classes of relatives, the closer the genetic relationship to a schizophrenic proband (or index case) is, the greater is the likelihood of schizophrenia in the relative. Finally, and most telling of all, monozygotic twins were found to be concordant with respect to schizophrenia about four times as often as dizygotic twins. Several authorities have critically reviewed these basic data (1, 2). But, despite the supporting evidence, a genetic etiology for schizophrenia was not widely accepted, especially in this country. It was pointed out that the investigators did not pay enough attention to important procedural matters, such as providing sampling safeguards

I thank James Shields, John Price, Irving Gottesman, and Russell Noyes, who commented on various phases of this manuscript.

and insuring against bias on the part of the investigator. But the paramount objection to a genetic interpretation of the evidence was the objection that the whole research strategy was faulty. The results of these studies, it was held, were just as compatible with transmission of schizophrenia through the social environment as with transmission through genes. The closer the genetic relationship, the closer the social relationship. Were genes or was noxious social learning responsible for the familial clustering of schizophrenia?

Recently, several studies have been aimed at closing those methodological and conceptual gaps. In these newer studies diagnoses either were made by raters who did not know the genetic background of the subjects or were taken unchanged from medical records. Care was taken to remove sampling biases, and, most importantly, control groups were used. The strategy permitted separation of the effects of genes from the effects of social environment through the use, as subjects, of children reared in adoptive or foster homes.

The results of one such study are shown in Table 1 (3). The experimental subjects were individuals born to schizophrenic mothers, and the controls were individuals born to parents who had no record of psychiatric disturbance. The members of both groups had been permanently separated from their biological mothers in the first month of life and reared mainly in foster or adoptive homes. The subjects, as adults, were assessed through psychiatric interviews and review of every available record—for example, school, police, Veterans Administration, and medical—and then evaluated by a team of clinicians. The significant excess of schizophrenia found among those subjects whose biological mothers were schizophrenic seems impossible to explain except on a genetic basis. Moreover, among those same experimental subjects, and thus also linked to schizophrenia by the evidence, was an even greater excess of vari-

TABLE 1. Results of a Study of Individuals Born to Schizophrenic Mothers and Reared in Adoptive or Foster Homes, and of Controls Born to Normal Parents and Similarly Reared.

Item	Control	Experi-mental	Exact Probability (Fisher's test)
Number of subjects	50	47	
Number of males	33	30	
Age, mean (years)	36.3	35.8	
Number adopted	19	22	
MHSRS, means*	80.1	65.2	0.0006
Number with schizophrenia	0	5	.024
Number with mental deficiency (I.Q. < 70)†	0	4	.052
Number with antisocial personalities	2	9	.017
Number with neurotic personality disorder‡	7	13	.052
Persons spending more than 1 year in penal or psychiatric institution			
Number	2	11	.006
Total years incarcerated	15	112	
Number of felons	2	7	.054
Number serving in armed forces	17	21	
Number discharged from armed forces on psychiatric or behavioral grounds	1	8	.021
Social group, first home, mean§	4.2	4.5	
Social group, present, mean§	4.7	5.4	
I.Q., mean	103.7	94.0	
Years in school, mean	12.4	11.6	
Number of children, total	84	71	
Number of divorces, total	7	6	
Number never married, > 30 years of age	4	9	

*The MHSRS is a global rating of psychopathology moving from 0 to 100 with decreasing psychopathology. Total group mean, 72.8; S.D., 18.4.

†One mental defective was also schizophrenic; another had antisocial personality.

‡Considerable duplication occurs in the entries under "neurotic personality disorder"; this designation includes subjects diagnosed as having various types of personality disorder and neurosis whose psychiatric disability was judged to be a significant handicap.

§Group 1, highest social class; group 7, lowest.

ous apparently nonschizophrenic disorders. The latter finding, which is reflected in nearly every entry in Table 1, is a central concern throughout this article.

The preliminary results from a very similar study which stressed exemplary investigative safeguards were much the same. Rosenthal *et al.* (4) reported that biological children of schizophrenics reared in adoptive homes exhibited "schizophrenic spectrum" disorders in significant excess over similarly reared controls. The "schizophrenic spectrum"—an expression coined in a quite reasonable attempt to find a term that would encompass the various disorders seen among biological relatives of schizophrenics—included schizophrenia, possible schizophrenia, borderline states, certain paranoid disorders, schizoid disorders, and the condition known as inadequate personality.

Karlsson (5), as one result of his study of schizophrenia in Icelandic families, found that 6 of 29 persons, some of them siblings, born to a schizophrenic parent but reared in foster homes developed schizophrenia. None of their 28 foster sibs who were reared in the same homes developed schizophrenia. This difference, too, is significant. Karlsson did not ascertain any disorders

other than typical schizophrenia among his subjects.

In two ingeniously designed research projects, adopted individuals served as the starting point. Wender *et al.* (6) studied the biological and adoptive parents of ten adopted schizophrenics and the adoptive parents of ten normal persons. The biological parents of the schizophrenics were found to exhibit significantly more psychopathology than either group of adoptive parents. In a similar but wider-ranging study conducted by Kety *et al.* (7), psychopathology, again reported as "schizophrenic spectrum" disorders, was found to be concentrated in significant excess among the biological relatives of adopted schizophrenics. The adoptive families of schizophrenics were indistinguishable from the adoptive and biological families of adopted controls. Since the psychopathology found in these studies was significantly greater among the group of biological relatives of the schizophrenic probands than among the adoptive relatives who actually lived with them, this evidence too strongly favors genetic over social transmission of schizophrenia.

The results of the studies of adopted and foster children—results which are strikingly consistent from study to study, considering the vagaries of research in this area—present seemingly insurmountable difficulties for adherents of environmental theories of schizophrenia. The evidence must surely compel acknowledgment of a genetic contribution to schizophrenia, and probably to related disorders as well. To go further, however, requires information on other types of genetic relationships and larger numbers of subjects. Happily, the older family studies can now meet these needs. For perhaps the most important contribution of the recent studies of adopted and foster children is the fact that they have confirmed the results of the older studies in all material respects. The familial clustering of psychopathology that had been documented in such detail has been linked to one critical variable, a genetic relationship to schizophrenia.

The presence of so much psychopathology other than typical schizophrenia among relatives of schizophrenics was first noticed by physicians on visiting days in the earliest asylums. Isaac Ray, writing in 1863, gave a good description (8). Because the relatives' disabilities resembled schizophrenia, investigators associated with the Munich school called these disabilities "schizoid" (schizophrenic-like). Describing the schizoid individual, delimiting schizoid from psychiatric and general populations, and placing the schizoid in relation to the schizophrenic were central concerns of the psychiatry of that day. After perhaps the longest detour in the modern history of science, we have come full circle in returning to the same concerns. Meanwhile, problems of nomenclature have developed.

To me, "schizoid" and "schizophrenic spectrum" seem to denote precisely the same disabilities, except that the latter term also includes schizophrenia. One consideration that may have led Kety (7), Rosenthal (4), Wender (6), and their co-workers to coin the new term is the obvious danger of confusing "schizoid" with "schizoid personality." The latter term, a diagnosis in the American Psychiatric Association and World Health Organization nomenclature, although descended from descriptions of the abnormal relatives of schizophrenics, has evolved and changed in meaning so that it is no longer applicable to most of those relatives. For example, it was not often applied to relatives of schizophrenics by the rating clinicians in the studies of adopted and foster children. But other diagnoses currently considered applicable to such individuals also fit these relatives imperfectly, so no formal categori-

zation is now available. Because of a central trait of the schizoid—his clinical resemblance to the schizophrenic—and because of the desirability of maintaining continuity with older studies, I use the term "schizoid" as a name for the schizophrenic-like disabilities seen in relatives of schizophrenics, or for the individual manifesting such disabilities.

Nearly all observers of the schizoid have noted his clinical resemblance to the schizophrenic, but clinical criteria adequate to reliably distinguish the schizoid from members of a general or a psychiatric population or even from other kinds of abnormal persons with a coincidental genealogical connection to a schizophrenic are most imperfect (9). Though unsatisfactory, the only means of identifying many—perhaps most—schizoids remains genealogical, and a clinical understanding of the schizoid can best be gained by reading descriptions of abnormal relatives of schizophrenics (see references 10–13 for good examples). The circularity thus introduced is regrettable but inescapable. The schizoid exists, and he sometimes shows as much impairment psychiatrically as a typical schizophrenic.

Several problematical behaviors have been associated with the schizoid. Among males, antisocial behavior has been found commonly enough to warrant the older subdesignation "schizoid psychopath." Entries in the police records of the schizoid psychopaths in my study reflected impulsive, seemingly illogical crime such as arson, unreasoning assault, and poorly planned theft (3). Social isolation, heavy intake of alcohol, and sexual deviance have been noted frequently. Other schizoids, both male and female, have been described as eccentric, suspicion-ridden recluses. The main disability of still other schizoids, mostly females, has been found to be incapacitating attacks of panic or unreasoning fear in response to ordinary social challenges.

On a more technical level the resemblance to schizophrenia is more apparent. Rigidity of thinking, blunting of affect, anhedonia, exquisite sensitivity, suspiciousness, and a relative poverty of ideas—in variable combinations and intensities—characterize both the schizoid and the schizophrenic, though such characteristics are less prominent in the former. Though schizoids do not show a well-marked thought disorder, delusions, and hallucinations, descriptions of some of the behavioral lapses of schizoids, especially the schizoid psychopath, are bizarre enough to suggest micropsychotic episodes.

TABLE 2. Explicatives Used by Relatives of Schizophrenics in Describing Their Schizoid Relatives (After Slater [*13*])

Paranoid eccentricities: suspicious, sensitive, sullen, touchy, grouchy, morose, resentful, unforgiving, difficult, quarrelsome, self-conscious, jealous, litigious, critical, and others.
    Eccentricities: giggly, opinionated, pedantic, narrow-minded, meticulous, obstinate, humorless, rigid, little-minded, spiritualists, and many others.
    Lack of feeling: passive, cruel, calculating, placid, hard and stingy, unsympathetic, cold, withdrawn, little-feeling, and others.
    Reserve: shy, serious, haughty, snobbish, studious, unforthcoming, taciturn, unsociable, seeks solitude, and so on.
    Anergic: dependent, tired, slack, unreliable, subservient, and so on.

Slater took a different approach. He listed a series of explicatives, partially reproduced in Table 2, used by relatives of schizophrenics when describing their abnormal but nonschizophrenic relatives (13). Slater went on to say (13, p. 83) that "the same or similar words or phrases occur in descriptions of abnormal personalities from other kinds of families, but much less frequently, not in such concentrated form, and they are usually submerged by descriptions of a very different tone."

Because Kallmann's investigations of the families of schizophrenics were by far the most extensive that have been made, his concept of the schizoid is of critical importance (11). From his description (11, p. 102) it is clear that he relied heavily on the schizoid's clinical resemblance to the schizophrenic. Kallmann regarded the distinguishing features of the schizoid to be the "fundamental symptoms of schizophrenia in the milder form of characterological abnormalities . . . dominating the personality of the individual in question." Kallmann also looked analytically at traits other than those obviously associated with schizophrenia or schizoidia that seemed to occur in excess among relatives of schizophrenics, with the aim of including or excluding them from the group of schizoid traits. On various grounds he excluded all the traits that he considered.

One of the traits which Kallmann considered and rejected, mental deficiency, perhaps deserves another look. About 6 to 10 percent of schizophrenics (see 14) and their first-degree relatives (see 3, 11) are mentally subnormal, as compared with 3 percent of the general population. The expected reciprocal relationship, an excess of schizophrenics among mental defectives or their relatives, was found by Penrose (15) and Böök (16) among mental defectives but not by Reed and Reed (17) in their monumental survey of the relatives of mental defectives. Also, Kallmann found a much higher rate of mental deficiency (10.8 percent) among relatives of simple schizophrenics, where there is a clinical commonality of

sorts, than among relatives of other subtypes in the Kraepelinian classification. The evidence for or against an association between schizophrenia and mental deficiency is inconclusive, and more data are needed before the matter can be decided.

Obviously there is much yet to be learned before we can describe and delimit schizoidia. However, the same thing can be said of schizophrenia itself, and in this regard study of the schizoid may lighten some dark corners. Schizophrenia is defined operationally, not etiologically. It is the clinician who determines whether schizophrenia is present. But of course the limits of the clinical entity may not correspond to those of the etiological entity. In fact the linking of schizoidia to schizophrenia by genetic evidence raises serious questions about the etiological reality of the clinical definition of schizophrenia. There has always been a fuzzy border about schizophrenia along which several named entities, including abortive, ambulatory, borderline, latent, pseudoneurotic, pseudopsychopathic, and reactive schizophrenia and the "schizotype" of Meehl (18) have seemed to lie. These terms may best be viewed as attempts to cope with an operationally defined border between schizoidia and schizophrenia that is clinically imprecise because it is biologically unreal.

QUANTITATIVE ASPECTS

Given a schizophrenic who has a monozygotic twin, the empirical probability that his twin will also be schizophrenic has been found to be about 0.46 (Table 3). Most of the remaining 54 percent of monozygotic twins of schizophrenics have also been found to be abnormal. From clinical descriptions included in five studies (12, 13, 19–21) it appears that nearly all of the abnormal though nonschizophrenic co-twins were schizoid. Overall, only about 13 percent of the monozygotic twins of schizophrenics have been regarded as normal or nearly normal, and, because most of the errors

TABLE 3. Data on Monozygotic Twins of Schizophrenics

Investigator	Pairs (No.)	Schizophrenia (No.)	Other Significant Abnormality* (No.)	Normal, or Mild Abnormality (No.)
Essen-Möller (*19*)	9	0	8	1
Slater (*13*)	37	18	11	8
Tienari (*41*)	16	1	12	3
Kringlen (*12*)	45	14	17	14
Inouye (*42*)	53	20	29	4
Gottesman and Shields (*23*)	24	10	8	6
Kallmann† (*43*)	174	103	62	9
Totals	358	166 (46.4%)	147 (41.1%)	45 (12.6%)

*Investigators' diagnoses: ? schizophrenia, schizophreniform, transient schizophrenia, reactive psychosis, borderline state, schizoid, suicide, psychopathic, neurosis, and variations of these diagnoses.
†From Shields, Gottesman, and Slater (*44*).

inherent in this sort of research tend to increase the proportion of apparent normals, this is surely an overestimate. But, while a critic could easily quibble about any of the proportions in Table 3, a crude but critical conclusion is inescapable: monozygotic twins of schizophrenics are about as likely to be schizoid as schizophrenic. What then is inherited? These considerations led Essen-Möller (19) to regard schizoidia as the basic inherited trait, and Kringlen, in a careful and sensitive analysis of twin research, including his own major study, seems to have reached a similar conclusion, although he regarded the predisposition as less specific (12). At the very least a prima facie case has been made for considering the whole group of schizoid and schizophrenic disorders as alternative expressions of a single genotype. Moreover, because monozygotic twins are identical genetically, there is presumptive evidence that the range of variability within pairs can in principle be accounted for by environmental factors. The genes allow a range of outcomes.

A critical point to be established is the proportion of schizoids or schizophrenics among the first-degree relatives (parents, sibs, children) of schizophrenics. Table 4 gives Kallmann's results. No

one else has investigated so many relatives of schizophrenics, and few others have conducted field studies intensive enough to identify schizoids. The more intensive modern studies have tended to show somewhat larger proportions of afflicted relatives (3, 10, 22). So did Slater among dizygotic twins of schizophrenics (13). The proportions found by Gottesman and Shields (23) and by Ödegård (24) were somewhat smaller. Kallmann's values may be taken as fair average estimates of the proportion of schizoids or schizophrenics among first-degree relatives of schizophrenics.

Table 4 also shows the results of four studies of the children of two schizophrenics. An estimated 66 percent of the children of these matings were schizoid or schizophrenic; again, this is surely an underestimate because the subjects were still quite young. The results of one such study, that of Lewis (25), was not included. Lewis did not give ages, and he stated that his follow-up was incomplete. Rosenthal has recently reviewed these studies (26).

An important unknown must now be considered There is no adequate estimate of the proportion of schizoids in the general population. Then, is

TABLE 4. Percentages of First-Degree Relatives Found to be Schizophrenic or Schizoid

Relationship	Number of Individuals	Schizophrenia* (%)	Schizoid (%)	Total: Schizoid Plus Schizophrenic (%)
Children†	1000	16.4	32.6	49.0
Siblings‡	1191	14.3	31.5	45.8
Parents‡	2741	9.2	34.8	44.0
Children of two schizophrenics§	171	33.9	32.2	66.1

*Age-corrected rates.
†From (*11*).
‡From (*43*).
§From Kallmann (*11*), Kahn (*45*), Schulz (*46*), and Elsässer (*47*).

the clustering of schizoids, among relatives of schizophrenic greater than might occur by chance? Although the proportion of schizoids found in families of schizophrenics is surely greater than that expected by even the most pessimistic observer of the general population, a better answer is that neither the relatives of other kinds of psychiatric patients nor the controls used in psychiatric studies have been found to be afflicted in significant numbers with disorders of a schizoid character or with any kind of behavioral disorder to the extent seen in relatives of schizophrenics. Further evidence—the small proportion of schizoids found among descendants of normal relatives of schizophrenics—is discussed below.

While the lack of data for the general population and the related lack of data for the families of schizoid probands preclude estimates of gene frequency, it should be noted that schizoid disorders surely afflict a large proportion of the population. With only isolated exceptions, schizophrenia afflicts about 1 percent of any population. If each schizophrenic has five living first-degree relatives (about the number in Kallmann's study), a simple extrapolation yields an estimate of 4 percent for the proportion of schizoids plus schizophrenics in the general population. This crude estimate can only make the point that any population, and especially any psychiatric population (persons identified because they came to psychiatric clinics or hospitals), is likely to contain large numbers of schizoids. One of the most neutral implications of this conclusion has an obvious application to the choosing of control groups for research in schizophrenia.

GENETIC HYPOTHESIS

The most parsimonious explanation of the data is given by the hypothesis that a defect in a single autosomal gene accounts for the genetic contribution to both schizoid and schizophrenic disease (the "dominance hypothesis"). By including schizoid disease (schizoidia), this hypothesis extends that of Slater (27). The view that schizoidia and schizophrenia are a single disease genetically is supported by their clinical similarity and is virtually required by the finding that the disorders occur with equal probability in monozygotic twins of schizophrenics. Further support for the hypothesis is presented in Figure 1. The proportions of affected first-degree relatives fit reasonably well

with the theoretical proportions expected under the dominance hypothesis.

Kallmann presented some data on second-degree relatives (11). Among 822 grandchildren of his schizophrenic probands he found 4.3 percent to be schizophrenic and 22.8 percent to be schizoid. The corresponding rates for nephews and nieces were considerably lower (3.9 and 6.2 percent). However, Kallmann pointed out that the normal sibs of his schizophrenic probands contributed many more nephews and nieces than the schizoid or schizophrenic sibs did. While the total of 27.1 percent for affected grandchildren is certainly close to the 25 percent expected under the dominance hypothesis, the proportions of affected nephews and nieces may or may not be compatible with that hypothesis.

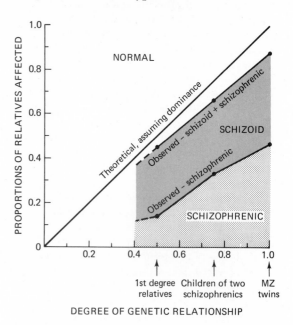

Figure 1. Observed and expected proportion of schizoids and schizophrenics.

The segregation of schizophrenia and schizoidia within families fits well with the dominance hypothesis. In Kallmann's study, which included three generations, the normal children of his schizophrenic probands produced few schizophrenic or schizoid children (1.8 and 2.6 percent, respectively), no more than might be expected in a general population. This is in contrast to the corresponding values of 13.7 and 33.4 percent for the children of the schizoid or schizophrenic children of Kallmann's schizophrenic probands (11).

The matter cannot be so simple, of course. The

mechanisms involved in a disease like schizoidia–schizophrenia will surely be found to be extremely complex. Even phenylketonuria, which only a few years ago provided a prototype of rigorous simplicity for behavioral genetics, has turned out to be enormously complicated by secondary biochemical effects and by other, mostly unknown, factors (28). Heterogenity is also likely. Probably the most completely known genetic disease in humans, glucose-6-phosphate dehydrogenase deficiency, occurs in at least 18 variants, each one presumably due to an amino acid substitution at a different place in the same enzyme (29). But research must proceed from hypotheses based on present understanding. From that viewpoint, and for practical purposes, it is not at all unreasonable to proceed on the working assumption that most schizoidia–schizophrenia is associated with defects in a single basic biochemical or physiological pathway, transmitted by a single mode of inheritance. It matters little that new research will no doubt turn up complexities that cannot even be imagined today.

Apart from insights gained from analogies to other genetic diseases, there are factual reasons for expecting that many elements in addition to a single main gene go into the mix that results in schizoidia–schizophrenia. First of all, there remain small deviations from the theoretical expectations under the dominance hypothesis, deviations which have been cited by Shields (2). These mainly take the form of a greater resemblance between relatives than can be explained by simple dominance. For example, the monozygotic twin of a severely afflicted individual is more likely to be schizophrenic than the twin of a mildly affected individual. If only a single gene were involved one would expect the risk of schizophrenia for a monozygotic twin of any schizophrenic to be equal to that of any other. Likewise, the larger the proportion of schizophrenic relatives is, the greater is the risk of schizophrenia for any given individual. Another sort of problem is that of accounting for the variability seen among schizophrenics; this becomes more difficult when schizoids are included. Although there are no grounds for expecting any particular degree of resemblance between affected persons, it has often been argued that, if only one gene were involved, the range of observable phenotypes should be smaller than is the case. And the persistence of schizophrenia presents a problem. Before the introduction of antipsychotic drugs, schizophrenics reproduced at a rate 30 percent lower (16), and schizoids at a

rate 22 percent lower (11), than the rate for the general population. Such reproductive deficits should have lowered the rates of occurrence of a disorder due to a main gene of large effect far below the presently observed rates for schizophrenia.

Attempts to account for such findings have led to widespread espousal of polygenic theories of schizophrenia (12, 24, 30). As Gottesman and Shields have pointed out (31), the facts are explained adequately by polygenic theory. Most polygenic theorists have regarded schizophrenia as a threshold trait. But clinically schizoidia and schizophrenia seem to form a continuum of psychopathology, much as first described by Kretschmer (32). If there is a threshold it probably falls between the schizoid and the normal condition, but it seems that any such "threshold" is as likely to be a function of lack of diagnostic precision as a function of the disease. It is not necessary to consider other aspects of the polygenic argument here. Known modifiers of the phenotypic expression of the disease point toward plausible solutions of the problems encountered by the dominance hypothesis and toward resolution of the apparent differences between main-gene and polygenic theories.

MODIFYING FACTORS

One class of modifiers must be environmental events in the broadest sense—events occurring from conception onward that produce some change in the organism. The nature–nurture dilemma is unreal. It is change in the environment of the cell that induces change in the genetically mediated metabolic systems of the cell. The functional state of the cell is a result of the interplay of these determinants. But realization that phenotypic traits depend on interaction between gene and environment imposes conditions on research aimed at assessing the environment contribution. Genes function within cells. They interact with chemical, thermal, or other physical events and not with the abstractions ("stress," for example) that too often have passed for environmental data. The ultimate questions implicit in the concept of gene–environment interaction are, for example: How does a noxious learning experience alter the environment of the cell? What response is elicited from the genetic program of the cell? How is the later operation of the cell modified? Of course, such questions cannot be approached directly today. But unless the environmental contribution is too variable from case to case to allow generalization, it should be possible to build up a series of associations between environment and behavior that would point toward the environmental events that enter into the gene–environment interaction. The critical requirement is that such associations be potentially translatable into events that occur at the level of the gene. Despite all the research that has been done on the effects of environment on the development of schizophrenia, and despite the scope for environmental factors demonstrated by the differences between members of monozygotic twin pairs, practically no associations that meet this requirement have been established. Clinicians have learned to predict the effects of environmental features on their patients, but it is difficult to see any etiological clues in this body of experience. On general clinical grounds it makes sense to continue to study the effects of environmentally stimulated autonomic and endocrine responses. An association between lower birth weight and the development of schizophrenia in one member of a monozygotic twin pair has been reported (21), but it must be quite imperfect in view of the failure of other investigators to confirm it (12, 23). Perhaps differences in autonomic responses among children of schizophrenics that were described in a preliminary report from a wide-ranging prospective study (33) are the most promising associations so far defined. Almost everything remains to be done.

A second class of modifiers consists of complex traits that have been linked to schizophrenia by decades of empirical research. Somatotype has been found by several investigators to be associated with major modification of schizophrenia. Mesomorphs are underrepresented among schizophrenics, and especially underrepresented among schizophrenics younger than 25. Ectomorphs are correspondingly overrepresented. Schizophrenic mesomorphs are predominantly paranoid and have a shorter mean period of hospitalization than other schizophrenics. Parnell (34), who has reviewed the subject and contributed his own data, found all these associations to be statistically significant. A relation between intelligence and the prognosis in schizophrenia is well known: the higher the intelligence the better the prognosis. But higher intelligence may also affect the expression of schizophrenia. Lane and Albee (35) found that the I.Q. of children who later became schizophrenic was seven points lower than that of their siblings who remained nonschizophrenic. There are a host of other established associations between complex traits and schizophrenia—for example, patterns of autonomic nervous system reactivity, immunological phenomena, resistance to certain chronic diseases, and tolerance of wound shock. Some such traits appear to be only oddities, given our present knowledge; others are known to be linked to favorable or unfavorable prognosis in schizophrenia, and still others are known only to be more frequent or infrequent among schizophrenics. Several reviews of these findings are available (36).

The large number of such complex traits and the magnitude of the modification of schizophrenia associated with some of them must mean that they have a significant role in the ecology of the disease. For one thing, they suggest a plausible solution to the puzzle posed by the persistence of high rates of schizophrenia. Sir Julian Huxley et al. (37) postulated that the gene responsible for schizophrenia conferred sufficient physiological or reproductive advantages to maintain a balanced polymorphism. They listed several physiological traits found in schizophrenics that could be due to pleiotropism. Although the number of traits listed seems large, widespread pleiotropism might result from a mutation at a regulatory locus (38). But many modifying traits are clearly not due to pleiotropism, and some of those—particularly differences in somatotype and intelligence—which demonstrably affect the outcome in schizophrenia must have conferred general biological advantages through much of man's history as well. In either event, schizophrenics possessing advantageous traits would be expected to reproduce at relatively higher rates than those not possessing such traits. Over time, the evolutionary process would theoretically, act to establish sets of favorable traits that, on the average, would tend to accompany schizophrenia. Theory aside, the popular association between genius and insanity, thought to be erroneous by Kallmann, was given some substance by Karlsson's finding that creative achievements and schizophrenia occurred in the same family lines (39). I reported a similar impression: however, the evidence was not gathered systematically (40). Although the problem posed by the persistence of schizophrenia remains theoretical and unsolved, further exploration of modifying traits provides as likely a path as any other now in view toward solution of the puzzle.

Modifying traits also suggest an approach to

the problem of deviations from strict expectations under the dominance hypothesis. As pointed out above, polygenic theory can account for such deviations. But traits like somatotype and intelligence are themselves almost certainly polygenic. Polygenic modifiers of a single main gene explain the same facts, and indeed would yield the same mathematical results as simple additive polygenic theory per se. A multitude of genes summating to produce schizophrenia directly or a single main gene plus groups of genes summating to produce modifying traits account equally well for findings such as the tendency of monozygotic twins to be concordant with respect to severity of illness.

CONCLUSION

A main gene of large effect modified by multiple factors, including polygenic traits, suggests a number of testable hypotheses. Biochemical or other effects of a main gene should be present in schizoids as well as in schizophrenics. In family studies, the critical test of the place of the schizoid would be his reproductive performance in matings with normal individuals; 50 percent of the offspring of such matings should be schizoid or schizophrenic. However, polygenic modifiers should, on the average, maintain lesser degrees of disability in particular families. Thus, schizoid parents should have fewer schizophrenic but more schizoid children than schizophrenic parents. There is incomplete support for this contention in Kallmann's study (11) of the grandchildren of his schizophrenic subjects: the schizoid children of his schizophrenic probands had more schizoid and fewer schizophrenic children than their schizophrenic siblings, but members of the third generation, the grandchildren of the probands, were too young to yield decisive evidence. Along the same lines, it would be expected that nearly all schizophrenics should have at least one schizoid or schizophrenic parent. Although the work of Kallmann and the intensive family studies of Alanen (10) and Lidz (22) support this expectation, more rigorous evidence is needed. The traits that favorably modify schizophrenia should be more apparent among schizoid than among schizophrenic relatives of schizophrenics. One would hypothesize, for example, that the more mesomorphic or more intelligent among the children of schizophrenics would tend to have less severe illnesses and to have more children than the less mesomorphic or less intelligent. These hypotheses, and many more that are implicit in the preceding discussion, constitute a significant refinement of the genetic hypotheses so far explored in schizophrenia.

SUMMARY

The importance of genetic factors in the development of schizophrenia has by now been established beyond reasonable dispute, although it is clear that environment too plays its etiologic role. The results of recent research have refocused attention on schizoid disorders, a term applied to psychiatric disorders resembling schizophrenia which afflict relatives of schizophrenics. The many conceptual and research problems presented by the schizoid are considered.

Schizoids and schizophrenics occur with about the same frequency among monozygotic twins of schizophrenics. About 45 percent of the sibs, parents, and children of a schizophrenic are schizoid or schizophrenics, as are about 66 percent of the children of two schizophrenics. From the known risk of schizophrenia for the population as a whole, it is estimated that at least 4 percent of the general population will be afflicted with schizoid–schizophrenic disease.

Since monozygotic twins are identical genetically, it appears that the same genotype is compatible with either schizophrenic or schizoid disease. The proportions of affected first-degree relatives and the segregation of affected individuals within families closely approximate theoretical expectations based on the hypothesis of a defect in a single autosomal dominant gene. However, modifying traits play a significant role; this is discussed and integrated into the main genetic hypothesis. Emphasis is placed on hypotheses testable by future research.

REFERENCES

1. E. Slater, in *The Transmission of Schizophrenia*, D. Rosenthal and S. Kety, Eds. (Pergamon, Oxford, 1968); D. Rosenthal, in *The Origins of Schizophrenia*, J. Romano, Ed. (Excerpta Medica Foundation, New York, 1967).

2. J. Shields, in *The Transmission of Schizophrenia*,

D. Rosenthal and S. Kety, Eds. (Pergamon, Oxford, 1968).

3. L. L. Heston, *Brit. J. Psychiat. 112*, 819 (1966).

4. D. Rosenthal, P. Wender, S. Kety, F. Schulsinger, L. Östergard, J. Welner, in *The Transmission of Schizophrenia*, D. Rosenthal and S. Kety, Eds. (Pergamon, Oxford, 1968).

5. J. Karlsson, *The Biological Basis of Schizophrenia* (Thomas, Springfield, Ill., 1966).

6. P. Wender, D. Rosenthal, S. Kety, in *The Transmission of Schizophrenia*, D. Rosenthal and S. Kety, Eds. (Pergamon, Oxford, 1968).

7. S. Kety, D. Rosenthal, F. Schulsinger, P. Wender, *ibid*.

8. I. Ray, *Mental Hygiene* (Hafner, New York, new ed., 1968).

9. K. Planansky, *J. Nerv. Ment. Dis. 142*, 318 (1966); E. Essen-Möller, *Mschr. Psychiat. Neurol. 112*, 258 (1946).

10. Y. O. Alanen, *Acta Psychiat. Scand., Suppl. No. 189* (1966).

11. F. J. Kallmann, *The Genetics of Schizophrenia* (Augustin, New York, 1938).

12. E. Kringlen, "Heredity and Environment in the Functional Psychoses," *Norwegian Monogr. Med. Sci. Univ. Oslo* (1967).

13. E. Slater, with the assistance of J. Shields, "Psychotic and Neurotic Illness in Twins," *Med. Res. Counc. (Great Brit.) Spec. Rep. Ser. No. 278* (1953).

14. B. Hallgren and T. Sjögren, *Acta Psychiat. Neurol. Scand., Suppl. No. 140* (1959).

15. L. S. Penrose, *A Clinical and Genetic Study of 1280 Cases of Mental Defect* (Her Majesty's Stationery Office, London, 1938).

16. J. A. Böök, *Acta Genet. 4*, 1 (1953).

17. E. W. Reed and S. C. Reed, *Mental Retardation: A Family Study* (Saunders, Philadelphia, 1965).

18. P. E. Meehl, *Amer. Psychol. 17*, 827 (1962).

19. E. Essen-Möller, *Acta Psychiat., Suppl. No. 23* (1941).

20. P. Tienari, *Acta Psychiat., Suppl. No. 171* (1963).

21. W. Pollin, J. R. Stabenau, J. Tupin, *Psychiatry 28*, 60 (1965).

22. T. Lidz, S. Fleck, A. Cornelison, *Schizophrenia and the Family* (International Universities Press, New York, 1966).

23. I. I. Gottesman and J. Shields, *Brit. J. Psychiat. 112*, 809 (1966).

24. Ö. Ödegard, *Acta Psychiat., Suppl. No. 169* (1963), p. 94.

25. A. Lewis, *Acta Genet, 7*, 349 (1957).

26. D. Rosenthal, *J. Psychiat. Res. 4*, 169 (1966).

27. E. Slater, *Acta Genet. 8*, 50 (1958).

28. C. Johnson, *J. Iowa Med. Soc. 59*, 27 (1968).

29. H. Harris, *Brit. Med. J. 2*, 135 (1968).

30. D. Rosenthal, *The Genain Quadruplets* (Basic Books, New York, 1963).

31. I. Gottesman and J. Shields, *Proc. Nat. Acad. Sci. U.S. 58*, 199 (1967).

32. E. Kretschmer, *Physique and Character* (W. Sprott, Trans.) (Paul, Trench and Trubner, London, 1925).

33. S. Mednick and F. Schulsinger, in *The Transmission of Schizophrenia*, D. Rosenthal and S. Kety, Eds. (Pergamon, Oxford, 1968).

34. R. Parnell, *Behavior and Physique* (Arnold, London, 1958).

35. E. A. Lane and G. W. Albee. *Amer. J. Orthopsychiat. 35*, 747 (1965).

36. E. Gellhorn and G. Loofbourrow, *Emotions and Emotional Disorders: A Neurophysiological Study* (Harper & Row, New York, 1963); W. Ross, J. Hay, M. McDowal, *Psychosom. Med. 12*, 170 (1950); P. Huston and M. Pepernik, in *Schizophrenia, A Review of the Syndrome*, L. Bellak, Ed. (Logos, New York, 1958); C. Rosenbaum, *J. Nerv. Ment. Dis. 146*, 103 (1968); H. Freeman, in *Schizophrenia, A Review of the Syndrome*, L. Bellak, Ed. (Logos, New York, 1958); L. Rees, in *Schizophrenia: Somatic Aspects*, D. Richter, Ed. (Macmillan, New York, 1957).

37. J. Huxley, E. Mayr, H. Osmond, A. Hoffner, *Nature 204*, 220 (1964).

38. R. J. Britten and E. H. Davidson, *Science 165*, 349 (1969).

39. J. Karlsson, in *The Transmission of Schizophrenia*, D. Rosenthal and S. Kety, Eds. (Pergamon, Oxford, 1968).

40. L. Heston and D. Denney, *ibid*.

41. P. Tienari, *ibid*.

42. E. Inouye, in *Proceedings, Third World Congress of Psychiatry* (Univ. of Toronto Press, Montreal, 1961), vol. 1, p. 524.

43. F. J. Kallmann, *Amer. J. Psychiat. 103*, 309 (1946).

44. J. Shields, I. Gottesman, E. Slater, *Acta Psychiat. Scand. 43*, 385 (1967).

45. E. Kahn, *Monogr. Gesamtgeb. Neurol. Psychiat. 36*, 1 (1923).

46. B. Schulz, *Z. Gesamte Neurol. Psychiat. 168*, 322 (1940).

47. G. Elsässer, *Die Nachkommen geiteskranker Elternpaare* (Thieme, Stuttgart, 1952).

schizotaxia, schizotypy, schizophrenia

Paul E. Meehl

In the course of the last decade, while spending several thousand hours in the practice of intensive psychotherapy, I have treated—sometimes unknowingly except in retrospect—a considerable number of schizoid and schizophrenic patients. Like all clinicians, I have formed some theoretical opinions as a result of these experiences. While I have not until recently begun any systematic research efforts on this baffling disorder, I felt that to share with you some of my thoughts, based though they are upon clinical impressions in the context of selected research by others, might be an acceptable use of this occasion.

Let me begin by putting a question which I find is almost never answered correctly by our clinical students on PhD orals, and the answer to which they seem to dislike when it is offered. Suppose that you were required to write down a procedure for selecting an individual from the population who would be diagnosed as schizophrenic by a psychiatric staff; you have to wager $1,000 on being right; you may not include in your selection procedure any behavioral fact, such as a symptom or trait, manifested by the individual. What would you write down? So far as I have been able to ascertain, there is only one thing you could write down that would give you a better than even chance of winning such a bet —namely, "Find an individual X who has a schizophrenic identical twin." Admittedly, there are many other facts which would raise your odds somewhat above the low base rate of schizophrenia. You might, for example, identify X by first finding mothers who have certain unhealthy child-rearing attitudes; you might enter a subpopulation defined jointly by such demographic variables as age, size of community, reli-

gion, ethnic background, or social class. But these would leave you with a pretty unfair wager, as would the rule, "Find an X who has a fraternal twin, of the same sex, diagnosed as schizophrenic" (Fuller and Thompson, 1960, pp. 272–283; Stern, 1960, pp. 581–584).

Now the twin studies leave a good deal to be desired methodologically (Rosenthal, 1962); but there seems to be a kind of "double standard of methodological morals" in our profession, in that we place a good deal of faith in our knowledge of schizophrenic dynamics, and we make theoretical inferences about social learning factors from the establishment of group trends which may be statistically significant and replicable although of small or moderate size; but when we come to the genetic studies, our standards of rigor suddenly increase. I would argue that the concordance rates in the twin studies need not be accepted uncritically as highly precise parameter estimates in order for us to say that their magnitudes represent the most important piece of etiological information we possess about schizophrenia.

It is worthwhile, I think, to pause here over a question in the sociology of knowledge, namely, why do psychologists exhibit an aversive response to the twin data? I have no wish to argue *ad hominem* here—I raise this question in a constructive and irenic spirit, because I think that a substantive confusion often lies at the bottom of this resistance, and one which can be easily dispelled. Everybody readily assents to such vague dicta as "heredity and environment interact," "there need be no conflict between organic and functional concepts," "we always deal with the total organism," etc. But it almost seems that clinicians do not fully believe these principles in any concrete sense, because they show signs of thinking that *if* a genetic basis were found for schizo-

Address of the President to the seventieth Annual Convention of the American Psychological Association, St. Louis, September 2, 1962.

From *American Psychologist*, 1962, 17, pp. 827–838. Copyright 1962 by the American Psychological Association and reproduced by permission.

phrenia, the psychodynamics of the disorder (especially in relation to intrafamilial social learnings) would be somehow negated or, at least, greatly demoted in importance. To what extent, if at all, is this true?

Here we run into some widespread misconceptions as to what is meant by *specific etiology* in nonpsychiatric medicine. By postulating a "specific etiology" one does *not* imply any of the following:

1. The etiological factor always, or even usually, produces clinical illness.

2. If illness occurs, the particular form and content of symptoms is derivable by reference to the specific etiology alone.

3. The course of the illness can be materially influenced only by procedures directed against the specific etiology.

4. All persons who share the specific etiology will have closely similar histories, symptoms, and course.

5. The largest single contributor to symptom variance is the specific etiology.

In medicine, not one of these is part of the concept of specific etiology, yet they are repeatedly invoked as arguments against a genetic interpretation of schizophrenia. I am not trying to impose the causal model of medicine by analogy; I merely wish to emphasize that *if* one postulates a genetic mutation as the specific etiology of schizophrenia, he is not thereby committed to any of the above as implications. Consequently such familiar objections as, "Schizophrenics differ widely from one another" or "Many schizophrenics can be helped by purely psychological methods" should not disturb one who opts for a genetic hypothesis. In medicine, the concept of specific etiology means the *sine qua non*—the causal condition which is necessary, but not sufficient, for the disorder to occur. A genetic theory of schizophrenia would, in this sense, be stronger than that of "one contributor to variance"; but weaker than that of "largest contributor to variance." In analysis of variance terms, it means an interaction effect such that no other variables can exert a main effect when the specific etiology is lacking.

Now it goes without saying that "clinical schizophrenia" as such cannot be inherited, because it has behavioral and phenomenal contents which are learned. As Bleuler says, in order to have a delusion involving Jesuits one must first

have learned about Jesuits. It seems inappropriate to apply the geneticist's concept of "penetrance" to the crude statistics of formal diagnosis—if a specific genetic etiology exists, its phenotypic expression in *psychological* categories would be a quantitative aberration in some parameter of a behavioral acquisition function. What could possibly be a genetically determined functional parameter capable of generating such diverse behavioral outcomes, including the preservation of normal function in certain domains?

The theoretical puzzle is exaggerated when we fail to conceptualize at different levels of molarity. For instance, there is a tendency among organically minded theorists to analogize betweel catatonic phenomena and various neurological or chemically induced states in animals. But Bleuler's masterly *Theory of Schizophrenic Negativism* (1912) shows how the whole range of catatonic behavior, including diametrically opposite modes of relating to the interpersonal environment, can be satisfactorily explained as instrumental acts; thus even a convinced organicist, postulating a biochemical defect as specific etiology, should recognize that the causal linkage between this etiology and catatonia is indirect, requiring for the latter's derivation a lengthy chain of statements which are not even formulable except in molar psychological language.

What kind of behavioral fact about the patient leads us to diagnose schizophrenia? There are a number of traits and symptoms which get a high weight, and the weights differ among clinicians. But thought disorder continues to hold its own in spite of today's greater clinical interest in motivational (especially interpersonal) variables. If you are inclined to doubt this for yourself, consider the following indicators: Patient experiences intense ambivalence, readily reports conscious hatred of family figures, is pananxious, subjects therapist to a long series of testing operations, is withdrawn, and says, "Naturally, I am growing my father's hair."

While all of these are schizophrenic indicators, the last one is the diagnostic bell ringer. In this respect we are still Bleulerians, although we know a lot more about the schizophrenic's psychodynamics than Bleuler did. The significance of thought disorder, associative dyscontrol (or, as I prefer to call it so as to include the very mildest forms it may take, "cognitive slippage"), in schizophrenia has been somewhat de-emphasized in recent years. Partly this is due to the greater interest in interpersonal dynamics, but partly also to the realization that much of our earlier psychometric assessment of the thought disorder was mainly reflecting the schizophrenic's tendency to underperform because uninterested, preoccupied, resentful, or frightened. I suggest that this realization has been overgeneralized and led us to swing too far the other way, as if we had shown that there really *is* no cognitive slippage factor present. One rather common assumption seems to be that if one can demonstrate the potentiating effect of a motivational state upon cognitive slippage, light has thereby been shed upon the etiology of schizophrenia. Why are we entitled to think this? Clinically, we see a degree of cognitive slippage not found to a comparable degree among nonschizophrenic persons. Some patients (e.g., pseudoneurotics) are highly anxious and exhibit minimal slippage; others (e.g., burnt-out cases) are minimally anxious with marked slippage. The demonstration that we can intensify a particular patient's cognitive dysfunction by manipulating his affects is not really very illuminating. After all, even ordinary neurological diseases can often be tremendously influenced symptomatically via emotional stimuli; but if a psychologist demonstrates that the spasticity or tremor of a multiple sclerotic is affected by rage or fear, we would not thereby have learned anything about the etiology of multiple sclerosis.

Consequent upon our general assimilation of the insights given us by psychoanalysis, there is today a widespread and largely unquestioned assumption that when we can trace out the motivational forces linked to the content of aberrant behavior, then we understand why the person has fallen ill. There is no compelling reason to assume this, when the evidence is mainly our dynamic understanding of the patient, however valid that may be. The phrase "why the person has fallen ill" may, of course, be legitimately taken to include these things; an account of how and when he falls ill will certainly include them. But they may be quite inadequate to answer the question, "Why does X fall ill and not Y, granted that we can understand both of them?" I like the analogy of a color psychosis, which might be developed by certain individuals in a society entirely oriented around the making of fine color discriminations. Social, sexual, economic signals are color mediated; to misuse a color word is strictly taboo; compulsive mothers are horribly ashamed of a child who is retarded in color development, and so forth. Some color-blind individuals (not all, perhaps not most) develop

a color psychosis in this culture; as adults, they are found on the couches of color therapists, where a great deal of *valid* understanding is achieved about color dynamics. Some of them make a social recovery. Nonetheless, if we ask, "What was basically the matter with these patients?" meaning, "What is the specific etiology of the color psychosis?" the answer is that mutated gene on the X chromosome. This is why my own therapeutic experience with schizophrenic patients has not yet convinced me of the schizophrenogenic mother as a specific etiology, even though the picture I get of my patients' mothers is pretty much in accord with the familiar one. There is no question here of accepting the patient's account; my point is that *given* the account, and taking it quite at face value, does not tell me why the patient is a patient and not just a fellow who had a bad mother.

Another theoretical lead is the one given greatest current emphasis, namely, *interpersonal aversiveness.* The schizophrene suffers a degree of social fear, distrust, expectation of rejection, and conviction of his own unlovability which cannot be matched in its depth, pervasity, and resistance to corrective experience by any other diagnostic group.

Then there is a quasi-pathognomonic sign, emphasized by Rado (1956; Rado and Daniels, 1956) but largely ignored in psychologists' diagnostic usage, namely, *anhedonia*—a marked, widespread, and refractory defect in pleasure capacity which, once you learn how to examine for it, is one of the most consistent and dramatic behavioral signs of the disease.

Finally, I include *ambivalence* from Bleuler's cardinal four (1950). His other two, "autism" and "dereism," I consider derivative from the combination of slippage, anhedonia, and aversiveness. Crudely put, if a person cannot think straight, gets little pleasure, and is afraid of everyone, he will of course learn to be autistic and dereistic.

If these clinical characterizations are correct, and we combine them with the hypothesis of a genetic specific etiology, do they give us any lead on theoretical possibilities?

Granting its initial vagueness as a construct, requiring to be filled in by neurophysiological research, I believe we should take seriously the old European notion of an "integrative neural defect" as the only direct phenotypic consequence produced by the genic mutation. This is an aberration in some parameter of single cell function, which may or may not be manifested in the functioning of more molar CNS systems, depending upon the organization of the mutual feedback controls and upon the stochastic parameters of the reinforcement regime. This neural integrative defect, which I shall christen *schizotaxia*, is all that can properly be spoken of as inherited. The imposition of a social learning history upon schizotaxic individuals results in a personality organization which I shall call, following Rado, the *schizotype*. The four core behavior traits are obviously not innate; but I postulate that they are universally learned by schizotaxic individuals, given any of the actually existing social reinforcement regimes, from the best to the worst. If the interpersonal regime is favorable, and the schizotaxic person also has the good fortune to inherit a low anxiety readiness, physical vigor, general resistance to stress and the like, he will remain a well-compensated "normal" schizotype, never manifesting symptoms of mental disease. He will be like the gout-prone male whose genes determine him to have an elevated blood uric acid titer, but who never develops clinical gout.

Only a subset of schizotypic personalities decompensate into clinical schizophrenia. It seems likely that the most important causal influence pushing the schizotype toward schizophrenic decompensation is the schizophrenogenic mother.

I hope it is clear that this view does not conflict with what has been established about the mother–child interaction. If this interaction were totally free of maternal ambivalence and aversive inputs to the schizotaxic child, even compensated schizotypy might be avoided; at most, we might expect to find only the faintest signs of cognitive slippage and other minimal neurological aberrations, possibly including body image and other proprioceptive deviations, but not the interpersonal aversiveness which is central to the clinical picture.

Nevertheless, while assuming the etiological importance of mother in determining the course of aversive social learnings, it is worthwhile to speculate about the modification our genetic equations might take on this hypothesis. Many schizophrenogenic mothers are themselves schizotypes in varying degrees of compensation. Their etiological contribution then consists jointly in their passing on the gene, *and* in the fact that being schizotypic, they provide the kind of ambivalent regime which potentiates the schizotypy of the child and raises the odds of his decompensating. Hence the incidence of the several parental genotypes among parent pairs of diag-

nosed proband cases is not calculable from the usual genetic formulas. For example, given a schizophrenic proband, the odds that mother is homozygous (or, if the gene were dominant, that it is mother who carries it) are different from those for father; since we have begun by selecting a decompensated case, and formal diagnosis as the phenotype involves a potentiating factor for mother which is psychodynamically greater than that for a schizotypic father. Another important influence would be the likelihood that the lower fertility of schizophrenics is also present, but to an unknown degree, among compensated schizotypes. Clinical experience suggests that in the semicompensated range, this lowering of fertility is greater among males, since many schizotypic women relate to men in an exploited or exploitive sexual way, whereas the male schizotype usually displays a marked deficit in heterosexual aggressiveness. Such a sex difference in fertility among decompensated cases has been reported by Meyers and Goldfarb (1962).

Since the extent of aversive learnings is a critical factor in decompensation, the inherited anxiety readiness is presumably greater among diagnosed cases. Since the more fertile mothers are likely to be compensated, hence themselves to be relatively low anxiety if schizotaxic, a frequent parent pattern should be a compensated schizotypic mother married to a neurotic father, the latter being the source of the proband's high-anxiety genes (plus providing a poor paternal model for identification in male patients, and a weak defender of the child against mother's schizotypic hostility).

These considerations make ordinary family concordance studies, based upon formal diagnoses, impossible to interpret. The most important research need here is development of high-validity indicators for compensated schizotypy. I see some evidence for these conceptions in the report of Lidz and co-workers, who in studying intensively the parents of 15 schizophrenic patients were surprised to find that "minimally, 9 of the 15 patients had at least one parent who could be called schizophrenic, or ambulatory schizophrenic, or clearly paranoid in behavior and attitudes" (Lidz, Cornelison, Terry, and Fleck, 1958, p. 308). As I read the brief personality sketches presented, I would judge that all but two of the probands had a clearly schizotypic parent. These authors, while favoring a "learned irrationality" interpretation of their data, also recognize the alternative genetic interpretation. Such facts do not permit a decision, obviously; my main point is the striking difference between the high incidence of parental schizotypes, mostly quite decompensated (some to the point of diagnosable psychosis), and the zero incidence which a conventional family concordance study would have yielded for this group.

Another line of evidence, based upon a very small sample but exciting because of its uniformity, is McConaghy's report (1959) that among nondiagnosed parent pairs of 10 schizophrenics, subclinical thought disorder was psychometrically detectable in at least one parent of every pair. Rosenthal (1962) reports that he can add five tallies to this parent-pair count, and suggests that such results might indicate that the specific heredity is dominant, and completely penetrant, rather than recessive. The attempt to replicate these findings, and other psychometric efforts to tap subclinical cognitive slippage in the "normal" relatives of schizophrenics, should receive top priority in our research efforts.

Summarizing, I hypothesize that the statistical relation between schizotaxia, schizotypy, and schizophrenia is class inclusion: All schizotaxics become, *on all actually existing social learning regimes,* schizotypic in personality organization; but most of these remain compensated. A minority, disadvantaged by other (largely polygenically determined) constitutional weaknesses, and put on a bad regime by schizophrenogenic mothers (most of whom are themselves schizotypes) are thereby potentiated into clinical schizophrenia. What makes schizotaxia etiologically specific is its role as a *necessary* condition. I postulate that a nonschizotaxic individual, whatever his other genetic makeup and whatever his learning history, would at most develop a character disorder or a psychoneurosis; but he would not become a schizotype and therefore could never manifest its decompensated form, schizophrenia.

What sort of quantitative aberration in the structural or functional parameters of the nervous system can we conceive to be directly determined by a mutated gene, and to so alter initial dispositions that affected individuals will, in the course of their childhood learning history, develop the four schizotypal source traits: cognitive slippage, anhedonia, ambivalence, and interpersonal aversiveness? To me, the most baffling thing about the disorder is the phenotypic heterogeneity of this tetrad. If one sets himself to the task of doing a theoretical Vigotsky job on this list of psychological dispositions, he may manage part of it

by invoking a sufficiently vague kind of descriptive unity between ambivalence and interpersonal aversiveness; and perhaps even anhedonia could be somehow subsumed. But the cognitive slippage presents a real roadblock. Since I consider cognitive slippage to be a core element in schizophrenia, any characterization of schizophrenic or schizotypic behavior which purports to abstract its essence but does not include the cognitive slippage must be deemed unsatisfactory. I believe that an adequate theoretical account will necessitate moving downward in the pyramid of the sciences to invoke explanatory constructs not found in social, psychodynamic, or even learning theory language, but instead at the neurophysiological level.

Perhaps we don't know enough about "how the brain works" to theorize profitably at that level; and I daresay that the more a psychologist knows about the latest research on brain function, the more reluctant he would be to engage in etiological speculation. Let me entreat my physiologically expert listeners to be charitable toward this clinician's premature speculations about how the schizotaxic brain might work. I feel partially justified in such speculating because there are some well-attested general truths about mammalian learned behavior which could almost have been set down from the armchair, in the way engineers draw block diagrams indicating what kinds of parts or subsystems a physical system *must* have, and what their interconnections *must* be, in order to function "appropriately." Brain research of the last decade provides a direct neurophysiological substrate for such cardinal behavior requirements as avoidance, escape, reward, drive differentiation, general and specific arousal or activation, and the like (see Delafresnaye, 1961; Ramey and O'Doherty, 1960). The discovery in the limbic system of specific positive reinforcement centers by Olds and Milner in 1954, and of aversive centers in the same year by Delgado, Roberts, and Miller (1954), seems to me to have an importance that can scarcely be exaggerated; and while the ensuing lines of research on the laws of intracranial stimulation as a mode of behavior control present some puzzles and paradoxes, what *has* been shown up to now may already suffice to provide a theoretical framework. As a general kind of brain model let us take a broadly Hebbian conception in combination with the findings on intracranial stimulation.

To avoid repetition I shall list some basic assumptions first but introduce others in context and only implicitly when the implication is obvious. I shall assume that:

When a presynaptic cell participates in firing a postsynaptic cell, the former gains an increment in firing control over the latter. Coactivation of anatomically connected cell assemblies or assembly systems therefore increases their stochastic control linkage, and the frequency of discharges by neurons of a system may be taken as an intensity variable influencing the growth rate of intersystem control linkage as well as the momentary activity level induced in the other systems. (I shall dichotomize acquired cortical systems into "perceptual–cognitive," including central representations of goal objects; and "instrumental," including overarching monitor systems which select and guide specific effector patterns.)

Most learning in mature organisms involves altering control linkages between systems which themselves have been consolidated by previous learnings, sometimes requiring thousands of activations and not necessarily related to the reinforcement operation to the extent that perceptual-to-instrumental linkage growth functions are.

Control linkage increments from coactivation depend heavily, if not entirely, upon a period of reverberatory activity facilitating consolidation.

Feedback from positive limbic centers is facilitative to concurrent perceptual–cognitive or instrumental sequences, whereas negative center feedback exerts an inhibitory influence. (These statements refer to initial features of the direct wiring diagram, not to all long-term results of learning.) Aversive input also has excitatory effects via the arousal system, which maintain activity permitting escape learning to occur because the organism is alerted and keeps doing things. But I postulate that this overall influence is working along with an opposite effect, quite clear from both molar and intracranial experiments, that a major biological function of aversive-center activation is to produce "stoppage" of whatever the organism is currently doing.

Perceptual–cognitive systems and limbic motivational control centers develop two-way mutual controls (e.g., discriminative stimuli acquire the reinforcing property; "thoughts" become pleasantly toned; drive-relevant perceptual components are "souped-up").

What kind of heritable parametric aberration could underlie the schizotaxic's readiness to acquire the schizotypic tetrad? It would seem, first

of all, that the defect is much more likely to reside in the neurone's synaptic control function than in its storage function. It is hard to conceive of a general defect in storage which would on the one hand permit so many perceptual–cognitive functions, such as tapped by intelligence tests, school learning, or the high order cognitive powers displayed by some schizotypes, and yet have the diffuse motivational and emotional effects found in these same individuals. I am not saying that a storage deficit is clearly excludable, but it hardly seems the best place to look. So we direct our attention to parameters of control.

One possibility is to take the anhedonia as fundamental. What is *phenomenologically* a radical pleasure deficiency may be roughly identified *behaviorally* with a quantitative deficit in the positive reinforcement growth constant, and each of these—the "inner" and "outer" aspects of the organism's appetitive control system—reflect a quantitative deficit in the limbic "positive" centers. The anhedonia would then be a direct consequence of the genetic defect in wiring. Ambivalence and interpersonal aversiveness would be quantitative deviations in the balance of appetitive–aversive controls. Most perceptual–cognitive and instrumental learnings occur under mixed positive and negative schedules, so the normal consequence is a collection of habits and expectancies varying widely in the intensity of their positive and negative components, but mostly "mixed" in character. Crudely put, everybody has *some* ambivalence about almost everything, and everybody has *some* capacity for "social fear." Now if the brain centers which mediate phenomenal pleasure and behavioral reward are numerically sparse or functionally feeble, the aversive centers meanwhile functioning normally, the long-term result would be a general shift toward the aversive end, appearing clinically as ambivalence and exaggerated interpersonal fear. If, as Brady believes, there is a wired-in reciprocal inhibiting relation between positive and negative centers, the long-term aversive drift would be further potentiated (i.e., what we see at the molar level as a sort of "softening" or "soothing" effect of feeding or petting upon anxiety elicitors would be reduced).

Cognitive slippage is not as easy to fit in, but if we assume that normal ego function is acquired by a combination of social reinforcements and the self-reinforcements which become available to the child via identification; then we might say roughly that "everybody has to learn *how* to think straight."

Rationality is socially acquired; the secondary process and the reality principle are slowly and imperfectly learned, by even the most clear headed. Insofar as slippage is manifested in the social sphere, such an explanation has some plausibility. An overall aversive drift would account for the paradoxical schizotypic combination of interpersonal distortions and acute perceptiveness of others' unconscious, since the latter is really a hypersensitivity to aversive signals rather than an overall superiority in realistically discriminating social cues. On the output side, we might view the cognitive slippage of mildly schizoid speech as originating from poorly consolidated second-order "monitor" assembly systems which function in an editing role, their momentary regnancy constituting the "set to communicate." At this level, selection among competing verbal operants involves slight differences in appropriateness for which a wash-out social reinforcement history provides an insufficiently refined monitor system. However, if one is impressed with the presence of a pervasive and primary slippage, showing up in a diversity of tests (cf. Payne, 1961) and also on occasions when the patient is desperately trying to communicate, an explanation on the basis of deficient positive center activity is not too convincing.

This hypothesis has some other troubles which I shall merely indicate. Schizoid anhedonia is mainly interpersonal, i.e., schizotypes seem to derive adequate pleasure from esthetic and cognitive rewards. Secondly, some successful psychotherapeutic results include what appears to be a genuine normality of hedonic capacity. Thirdly, regressive electro-shock sometimes has the same effect, and the animal evidence suggests that shock works by knocking out the aversive control system rather than by souping up appetitive centers. Finally, if the anhedonia is really general in extent, it is hard to conceive of any simple genetic basis for weakening the different positive centers, whose reactivity has been shown by Olds and others to be chemically drive specific.

A second neurological hypothesis takes the slippage factor as primary. Suppose that the immediate consequence of whatever biochemical aberration the gene directly controls were a specific alteration in the neurone's membrane stability, such that the distribution of optional transmission probabilities is more widely dispersed over the synaptic signal space than in normals. That is, presynaptic input signals whose spatiotemporal configuration locates them peripherally in the neurone's signal space yield transmission probabilities which are relatively closer to those at the maximum point, thereby producing a kind of dedifferentiation or flattening of the cell's selectivity. Under suitable parametric assumptions, this synaptic slippage would lead to a corresponding dedifferentiation of competing interassembly controls, because the elements in the less frequently or intensely coactivated control assembly would be accumulating control increments more rapidly than normal. Consider a perceptual–cognitive system whose regnancy is preponderantly associated with positive-center coactivation but sometimes with aversive. The cumulation of control increments will draw these apart; but if synaptic slippage exists, their difference, at least during intermediate stages of control development, will be attenuated. The intensity of aversive-center activation by a given level of perceptual–cognitive system activity will be exaggerated relative to that induced in the positive centers. For a preponderantly aversive control this will be reversed. But now the different algebraic sign of the feedbacks introduces an important asymmetry. Exaggerated negative feedback will tend to lower activity level in the predominantly appetitive case, retarding the growth of the control linkage; whereas exaggerated positive feedback in the predominantly aversive case will tend to heighten activity levels, accelerating the linkage growth. The long-term tendency will be that movement in the negative direction which I call *aversive drift*. In addition to the asymmetry generated by the difference in feedback signs, certain other features in the mixed-regime setup contribute to aversive drift. One factor is the characteristic difference between positive and negative reinforcers in their role as strengtheners. It seems a fairly safe generalization to say that positive centers function only weakly as strengtheners when "on" continuously, and mainly when they are turned on as terminators of a cognitive or instrumental sequence; by contrast, negative centers work mainly as "off" signals, tending to inhibit elements while steadily "on." We may suppose that the former strengthen mainly by facilitating postactivity reverberation (and hence consolidation) in successful systems, the latter mainly by holding down such reverberation in unsuccessful ones. Now a slippage-heightened aversive steady state during predominantly appetitive control sequences reduces their activity level, leaves fewer recently active elements available for a subsequent Olds-plus "on" signal to consolidate. Whereas a slippage-heightened Olds-plus steady state during predominantly aversive control sequences (a) increases their negative control *during* the "on" period and (b) leaves relatively more of their elements recently active and hence further consolidated by the negative "off" signal when it occurs. Another factor is exaggerated competition by aversively controlled sequences, whereby the appetitive chains do not continue to the stage of receiving socially mediated positive reinforcement, because avoidant chains (e.g., phobic behavior, withdrawal, intellectualization) are getting in the way. It is worth mentioning that the schizophrenogenic mother's regime is presumably "mixed" not only in the sense of the frequent and unpredictable aversive inputs she provides in response to the child's need signals, but also in her greater tendency to present such aversive inputs *concurrently* with drive reducers—thereby facilitating the "scrambling" of appetitive-and-aversive controls so typical of schizophrenia.

The schizotype's dependency guilt and aversive overreaction to offers of help are here seen as residues of the early knitting together of his cortical representations of appetitive goals with punishment-expectancy assembly systems. Roughly speaking, he has learned that to want anything interpersonally provided is to be endangered.

The cognitive slippage is here conceived as a direct molar consequence of synaptic slippage, potentiated by the disruptive effects of aversive control and inadequate development of interpersonal communication sets. Cognitive and instrumental linkages based upon sufficiently massive and consistent regimes, such as reaching for a seen pencil, will converge to asymptotes hardly distinguishable from the normal. But systems involving closely competing strengths and automatized selection among alternatives, especially when the main basis of acquisition and control is social reward, will exhibit evidences of malfunction.

My third speculative model revives a notion with a long history, namely, that the primary schizotaxic defect is a quantitative deficiency of inhibition. (In the light of Milner's revision of Hebb, in which the inhibitory action of Golgi Type II cells is crucial even for the formation of functionally differentiated cell assemblies, a defective inhibitory parameter could be an alternative basis for a kind of slippage similar in its consequences to the one we have just finished discussing.) There are two things about this somewhat moth-eaten "defective inhibition" idea which I find appealing. First, it is the most direct

and uncomplicated neurologizing of the schizoid cognitive slippage. Schizoid cognitive slippage is neither an incapacity to link, nor is it an unhealthy overcapacity to link; rather it seems to be a defective *control* over associations which are also accessible to the healthy (as in dreams, wit, psychoanalytic free association, and certain types of creative work) but are normally "edited out" or "automatically suppressed" by those superordinate monitoring assembly systems we lump together under the term "set." Secondly, in working with pseudoneurotic cases one sees a phenomenon to which insufficient theoretical attention has been paid: Namely, these patients cannot turn off painful thoughts. They suffer constantly and intensely from painful thoughts about themselves, about possible adverse outcomes, about the past, about the attitudes and intentions of others. The "weak ego" of schizophrenia means a number of things, one of which is failure of defense; the schizophrenic has too ready access to his own id, and is too perceptive of the unconscious of others. It is tempting to read "failure of defense" as "quantitatively deficient inhibitory feedback." As mentioned earlier, aversive signals (whether exteroceptive or internally originated) must exert both an exciting effect via the arousal system and a quick-stoppage effect upon cortical sequences which fail to terminate the ongoing aversive signal, leading the organism to shift to another. Suppose the gene resulted in an insufficient production (or too rapid inactivation) of the specific inhibitory transmitter substance, rendering all inhibitory neurones quantitatively weaker than normal. When aversively linked cognitive sequences activate negative limbic centers, these in turn soup up the arousal system normally but provide a subnormal inhibitory feedback, thereby permitting their elicitor to persist for a longer time and at higher intensity than normal. This further activates the negative control center, and so on, until an equilibrium level is reached which is above normal in intensity all around, and which meanwhile permits an excessive linkage growth in the aversive chain. (In this respect the semicompensated case would differ from the late-stage deteriorated schizophrenic, whose aversive drift has gradually proliferated so widely that almost any cognitive or instrumental chain elicits an overlearned defensive "stoppage," whereby even the inner life undergoes a profound and diffuse impoverishment.)

The mammalian brain is so wired that aversive

signals tend to produce stoppage of regnant cognitive or instrumental sequences without the aversive signal having been specifically connected to their controlling cues or motivational systems. E.g., lever pressing under thirst or hunger can be inhibited by shock-associated buzzer, even though the latter has not been previously connected with hunger, paired with the discriminative stimulus, nor presented as punishment for the operant. A deficient capacity to inhibit concurrent activity of fringe elements (aversively connected to ambiguous social inputs from ambivalent mother) would accelerate the growth of linkages between them and appetitive systems not hitherto punished. Sequential effects are here especially important, and combine with the schizophrenogenic mother's tendency not to provide differential cues of high consistency as predictors of whether aversive or appetitive consequences will follow upon the child's indications of demand.

Consider two cortical systems having shared "fringe" subsystems (e.g., part percepts of mother's face). When exteroceptive inputs are the elicitors, negative feedback from aversive centers cannot usually produce stoppage; in the absence of such overdetermining external controls, the relative activity levels are determined by the balance of facilitative and inhibitory feedbacks. "Fringe" assemblies which have already acquired more aversive control, if they begin to be activated by regnant perceptual–cognitive sequences, will increase inhibitory feedback; and being "fringe" they can thereby be held down. The schizotaxic, whose aversive-feedback stoppage of fringe-element activity is weakened, accumulates excessive intertrial Hebbian increments toward the aversive side, the predominantly aversive fringe elements being more active and becoming more knit into the system than normally. On subsequent exteroceptively controlled trials, whenever the overdetermining stimulus input activates predominantly aversive perceptual–cognitive assemblies, their driving of the negative centers will be heightened. The resulting negative feedback may now be strong enough that, when imposed upon "fringe" assemblies weakly activated and toward the appetitive side, it can produce stoppage. On such occasions the more appetitive fringe elements will be retarded in their linkage growth, receiving fewer Hebbian increments. And those which do get over threshold will become further linked during such trials to the concurrent negative center activity. The result is twofold: a retarded growth of appetitive perceptual–cognitive linkages; and a progressive drawing of fringe elements into the aversive ambit.

"Ambiguous regimes," where the pairing of S+ and S− inputs occurs very unpredictably, will have a larger number of fringe elements. Also, if the external schedule is dependent upon regnant appetitive drive states as manifested in the child's instrumental social acts, so that these are often met with mixed S+ (drive-relevant) and S− (anxiety-eliciting) inputs, the appetitive and aversive assemblies will tend to become linked, and to activate positive and negative centers concurrently. The anhedonia and ambivalence would be consequences of this plus–minus "scrambling," especially if the positive and negative limbic centers are mutually inhibitory but here deficiently so. We would then expect schizotypic anhedonia to be basically interpersonal, and only derivatively present, if at all, in other contexts. This would in part explain the schizotype's preservation of relatively normal function in a large body of instrumental domains. For example, the acquisition of basic motor and cognitive skills would be relatively less geared to a mixed input, since "successful" mastery is both mechanically rewarded (e.g., how to open a door) and also interpersonally rewarded as "school success," etc. The hypercathexis of intellect, often found even among nonbright schizotypes, might arise from the fact that these performances are rewarded rather "impersonally" and make minimal demands on the reinforcing others. Also, the same cognitive and mechanical instrumental acts can often be employed both to turn on positive center feedback and to turn off negative, an equivalence much less true of purely social signals linked to interpersonal needs.

Having briefly sketched three neurological possibilities for the postulated schizotaxic aberration, let me emphasize that while each has sufficient merit to be worth pursuing, they are mainly meant to be illustrative of the vague concept "integrative neural defect." I shall myself not be surprised if all three are refuted, whereas I shall be astounded if future research shows no fundamental aberration in nerve-cell function in the schizotype. Postulating schizotaxia as an open concept seems at first to pose a search problem of needle-in-haystack proportions, but I suggest that the plausible alternatives are really somewhat limited. After all what does a neuron do to another neuron? It excites, or it inhibits! The schizotypic preservation of relatively normal function in selected domains directs our search toward some minimal deviation in a synaptic control parameter, as opposed to, say, a gross defect in cell distribution or structure, or the kind of biochemical anomaly that yields mental deficiency. Anything which would give rise to defective storage, grossly impaired transmission, or sizable limitations on functional complexity can be pretty well excluded on present evidence. What we are looking for is a quantitative aberration in synaptic control—a deviation in amount or patterning of excitatory or inhibitory action—capable of yielding cumulative departures from normal control linkages under mixed appetitive–aversive regimes; but slight enough to permit convergence to quasi-normal asymptotes under more consistent schedules (or when massive repetition with motive-incentive factors unimportant is the chief basis for consolidation). The defect must generate aversive drift on mixed social reinforcement regimes, and must yield a primary cognitive slippage which, however, may be extremely small in magnitude except as potentiated by the cumulative effects of aversive drift. Taken together these molar constraints limit our degrees of freedom considerably when it comes to filling in the neurophysiology of schizotaxia.

Leaving aside the specific nature of schizotaxia, we must now raise the familiar question whether such a basic neurological defect, however subtle and nonstructural it might be, should not have been demonstrated hitherto? In reply to this objection I shall content myself with pointing out that there are several lines of evidence which, while not strongly arguing *for* a neurological theory, are rebuttals of an argument presupposing clear and consistent *negative* findings. For example: Ignoring several early European reports with inadequate controls, the literature contains a half-dozen quantitative studies showing marked vestibular system of dysfunction in schizophrenics (Angyal and Blackman, 1940, 1941; Angyal and Sherman, 1942; Colbert and Koegler, 1959; Freeman and Rodnick, 142; Leach, 1960; Payne and Hewlett, 1960; Pollock and Krieger, 1958). Hoskins (1946) concluded that a neurological defect in the vestibular system was one of the few clearcut biological findings in the Worcester studies. It is of prime importance to replicate these findings among compensated and pseudoneurotic cases, where the diffuse withdrawal and deactivation factor would not provide the explanation it does in the chronic, burnt-out case (cf. Collins, Crampton, and Posner, 1961). Another line of evidence is in the work of King (1954) on psychomotor deficit, noteworthy for its careful use of task simplicity, asymptote performance, concern

for patient cooperation, and inclusion of an outpatient pseudoneurotic sample. King himself regards his data as indicative of a rather basic behavior defect, although he does not hold it to be schizophrenia-specific. Then we have such research as that of Barbara Fish (1961) indicating the occurrence of varying signs of perceptual–motor maldevelopment among infants and children who subsequently manifest clinical schizophrenia. The earlier work of Schilder and Bender along these lines is of course well known, and there has always been a strong minority report in clinical psychiatry that many schizophrenics provide subtle and fluctuating neurological signs of the "soft" variety, if one keeps alert to notice or elicit them. I have myself been struck by the frequent occurrence, even among pseudoneurotic patients, of transitory neurologic-like complaints (e.g., diplopia, localized weakness, one-sided tremor, temperature dyscontrol, dizziness, disorientation which seem to lack dynamic meaning or secondary gain and whose main effect upon the patient is to produce bafflement and anxiety. I have seen preliminary findings by J. McVicker Hunt and his students in which a rather dramatic quantitative deficiency in spatial cognizing is detectable in schizophrenics of above-normal verbal intelligence. Research by Cleveland (1960; Cleveland, Fisher, Reitman, and Rothaus, 1962) and by Arnhoff and Damianopoulos (1964) on the clinically well-known body-image anomalies in schizophrenia suggests that this domain yields quantitative departures from the norm of such magnitude that with further instrumental and statistical refinement it might be used as a quasi-pathognomonic sign of the disease. It is interesting to note a certain thread of unity running through this evidence, which perhaps lends support to Rado's hypothesis that a kinesthetic integrative defect is even more characteristic of schizotypy than is the radical anhedonia.

All these kinds of data are capable of a psychodynamic interpretation. "Soft" neurological signs are admittedly ambiguous, especially when found in the severely decompensated case. The only point I wish to make here is that *since* they exist and are at present unclear in etiology, an otherwise plausible neurological view cannot be refuted on the ground that there is a *lack* of any sign of neurological dysfunction in schizophrenia; there is no such lack.

Time forces me to leave detailed research strategy for another place, but the main directions are obvious and may be stated briefly: The clinician's Mental Status ratings on anhedonia, ambivalence, and interpersonal aversiveness should be objectified and preferably replaced by psychometric measures. The research findings on cognitive slippage, psychomotor dyscontrol, vestibular malfunction, body image, and other spatial aberrations should be thoroughly replicated and extended into the pseudoneurotic and semicompensated ranges. If these efforts succeed, it will be possible to set up a multiple sign pattern, using optimal cuts on phenotypically diverse indicators, for identifying compensated schizotypes in the nonclinical population. Statistics used must be appropriate to the theoretical model of a dichotomous latent taxonomy reflecting itself in otherwise independent quantitative indicators. Family concordance studies should then be run relating proband schizophrenia to schizotypy as identified by

this multiple indicator pattern. Meanwhile we should carry on an active and varied search for more direct neurological signs of schizotaxia, concentrating our hunches on novel stimulus inputs (e.g., the stabilized retinal image situation) which may provide a better context for basic neural dysfunction to show up instead of being masked by learned compensations or imitated by psychopathology.

In closing, I should like to take this unusual propaganda opportunity to play the prophet. It is my strong personal conviction that such a research strategy will enable psychologists to make a unique contribution in the near future, using psychological techniques to establish that schizophrenia, while its content is learned, is fundamentally a neurological disease of genetic origin.

REFERENCES

Angyal, A., & Blackman, N. Vestibular reactivity in schizophrenia. *Arch. Neurol. Psychiat.*, 1940, *44*, 611–620.

Angyal, A., & Blackman, N. Paradoxical reactions in schizophrenia under the influence of alcohol, hyperpnea, and CO_2 inhalation. *Amer. J. Psychiat.*, 1941, *97*, 893–903.

Angyal, A., & Sherman, N. Postural reactions to vestibular stimulation in schizophrenic and normal subjects. *Amer. J. Psychiat.*, 1942, *98*, 857–862.

Arnhoff, F., & Damianopoulos, E. Self-body recognition and schizophrenia: An exploratory study. *J. Gen. Psy.* 1964, *70*(2), 353–361.

Bleuler, E. *Theory of schizophrenic negativism.* New York: Nervous and Mental Disease Publishing, 1912.

Bleuler, E. *Dementia praecox.* New York: International Universities Press, 1950.

Cleveland, S. E. Judgment of body size in a schizophrenic and a control group. *Psychol. Rep.*, 1960, *7*, 304.

Cleveland, S. E., Fisher, S., Reitman, E. E., & Rothaus, P. Perception of body size in schizophrenia. *Arch. gen. Psychiat.*, 1962, *7*, 277–285.

Colbert, G., & Koegler, R. Vestibular dysfunction in childhood schizophrenia. *AMA Arch. gen. Psychiat.*, 1959, *1*, 600–617.

Collins, W. E., Crampton, G. H., & Posner, J. B. The effect of mental set upon vestibular nystagmus and the EEG. *USA Med. Res. Lab. Rep.*, 1961, No. 349.

Delafresnaye, J. F. (Ed.) *Brain mechanisms and learning.* Springfield, Ill.: Charles C. Thomas, 1961.

Delgado, J. M. R., Roberts, W. W., & Miller, N. E. Learning motivated by electrical stimulation of the brain. *Amer. J. Physiol.*, 1954, *179*, 587–593.

Fish, Barbara. The study of motor development in infancy and its relationship to psychological functioning. *Amer. J. Psychiat.*, 1961, *117*, 1113–1118.

Freeman, H., & Rodnick, E. H. Effect of rotation on postural steadiness in normal and schizophrenic subjects. *Arch. Neurol. Psychiat.*, 1942, *48*, 47–53.

Fuller, J. L., & Thompson, W. R. *Behavior genetics.* New York: Wiley, 1960. Pp. 272–283.

Hoskins, R. G. *The biology of schizophrenia.* New York: Norton, 1946.

King, H. F. *Psychomotor aspects of mental disease.* Cambridge: Harvard Univer. Press, 1954.

Leach, W. W. Nystagmus: An integrative neural deficit in schizophrenia. *J. abnorm. soc. Psychol.*, 1960, *60*, 305–309.

Lidz, T., Cornelison, A., Terry, D., & Fleck, S. Intrafamilial environment of the schizophrenic patient: VI. The transmission of irrationality. *AMA Arch. Neurol. Psychiat.*, 1958, *79*, 305–316.

McConaghy, N. The use of an object sorting test in elucidating the hereditary factor in schizophrenia. *J. Neurol. Neurosurg. Psychiat.*, 1959, *22*, 243–246.

Meyers, D., & Goldfarb, W. Psychiatric appraisals of parents and siblings of schizophrenic children. *Amer. J. Psychiat.*, 1962, *118*, 902–908.

Olds. J., & Milner, P. Positive reinforcement produced by electrical stimulation of septal area and other regions of rat brain. *J. comp. physiol. Psychol.*, 1954, *47*, 419–427.

Payne, R. S., & Hewlett, J. H. G. Thought disorder in psychotic patients. In H. J. Eysenck (Ed.), *Experiments in personality.* Vol. 2. London: Routledge & Kegan & Paul, 1960. Pp. 3–106.

Payne, R. W. Cognitive abnormalities. In H. J. Eysenck (Ed.), *Handbook of abnormal psychology.*

New York: Basic Books, 1961. Pp. 248–250.

Pollack, M., & Krieger, H. P. Oculomotor and postural patterns in schizophrenic children. *AMA Arch. Neurol. Psychiat.*, 1958, 79, 720–726.

Rado, S. *Psychoanalysis of behavior.* New York: Grune & Stratton, 1956.

Rado, S., & Daniels, G. *Changing concepts of psychoanalytic medicine.* New York: Grune & Stratton, 1956.

Ramey, E. R., & O'Doherty, D. S. (Ed.) *Electrical studies on the unanesthetized brain.* New York: Hoeber, 1960.

Rosenthal, D. Problems of sampling and diagnosis in the major twin studies of schizophrenia. *J. psychiat. Res.*, 1962, 1(2), 116–134.

Stern, K. *Principles of human genetics.* San Francisco: Freeman, 1960. Pp. 581–584.

some extraordinary facts about obese humans and rats

Stanley Schachter

Several years ago, when I was working on the problem of the labeling of bodily states, I first became aware of Stunkard's (Stunkard & Koch, 1964) work on obesity and gastric motility. At that time, my students and I had been working on a series of studies concerned with the interaction of cognitive and physiological determinants of emotional state (Schachter, 1964). Our experiments had all involved manipulating bodily state by injections of adrenaline or placebo and simultaneously manipulating cognitive and situational variables that were presumed to affect a subject's interpretation of his bodily state. In essence, these experiments had demonstrated that cognitive factors play a major role in determining how a subject interprets his bodily feelings. Precisely the same set of physiological symptoms—an adrenaline-induced state of sympathetic arousal—could be interpreted as euphoria, or anger, or anxiety, or indeed as no emotional state at all, depending very largely on our cognitive and situational manipulations. In short, there is not an invariant, one-to-one relationship between a set of physiological symptoms and a psychological state.

This conclusion was based entirely on studies that manipulated bodily state by the exogenous administration of adrenaline or some other agent. My interest in Stunkard's research was generated by the fact that his work suggested that the same conclusion might be valid for endogenous physiological states. In his study, Stunkard had his subjects do without breakfast and come to his laboratory at 9:00 A.M. They swallowed a gastric balloon, and for the next four hours, Stunkard continuously recorded stomach contractions. Every 15 minutes, he asked his subjects, "Do you feel hungry?" They answered "Yes" or "No," and that is all there was to the study. He has then a record

of the extent to which stomach contractions coincide with self-reports of hunger. For normally sized subjects, the two coincide closely. When the stomach contracts, the normal subject is likely to report hunger; when the stomach is quiescent, the normal subject is likely to say that he does not feel hungry. For the obese, on the other hand, there is little correspondence between gastric motility and self-reports of hunger. Whether or not the obese subject describes himself as hungry seems to have almost nothing to do with the state of his gut. There are, then, major individual differences in the extent to which this particular bodily activity—gastric motility—is associated with the feeling state labeled "hunger."

To pursue this lead, we (Schachter, Goldman, & Gordon, 1968) designed an experiment in which we attempted to manipulate gastric motility and the other physiological correlates of food deprivation by the obvious technique of manipulating food deprivation so that some subjects had empty stomachs and others full stomachs before entering an experimental eating situation. The experiment was disguised as a study of taste, and subjects had been asked to do without the meal (lunch or dinner) that preceded the experiment.

When a subject arrived, he was, depending on condition, either fed roast beef sandwiches or fed nothing. He was then seated in front of five bowls of crackers, presented with a long set of rating scales and told, "We want you to judge each cracker on the dimensions (salty, cheesy, garlicky, etc.) listed on these sheets. Taste as many or as few of the crackers of each type as you want in making your judgments; the important thing is that your ratings be as accurate as possible."

The subject then tasted and rated crackers for 15 minutes, under the impression that this was a taste test, and we simply counted the number of crackers that he ate. There were, of course, two types of subjects: obese subjects (from 14% to

The research reported has been supported by National Science Foundation Grant GS 732.

75% overweight) and normal subjects (from 8% underweight to 9% overweight).

To review expectations: If it is correct that the obese do not label as hunger the bodily states associated with food deprivation, then this manipulation should have no effect on the amount eaten by obese subjects; on the other hand, the eating behavior of normal subjects should directly parallel the effects of the manipulation on bodily state.

It will be a surprise to no one to learn, from Figure 1, that normal subjects ate considerably

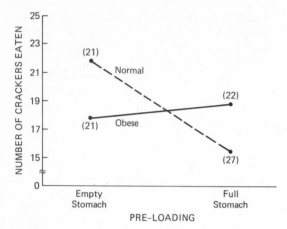

Figure 1. The effects of preloading on eating.

fewer crackers when their stomachs were full of roast beef sandwiches than when their stomachs were empty. The results for obese subjects stand in fascinating contrast. They ate as much—in fact slightly more—when their stomachs were full as when they were empty. Obviously, the actual state of the stomach has nothing to do with the eating behavior of the obese.[1]

In similar studies (Schachter, 1967; Schachter et al., 1968), we have attempted to manipulate bodily state by manipulating fear and by injecting subjects with epinephrine. Both manipulations are based on Cannon's (1915) and Carlson's (1916) demonstrations that both the state of fear and the injection of epinephrine will inhibit gastric motility and increase blood sugar—both peripheral physiological changes associated with low hunger. These manipulations have no effect at all on obese

[1] The obese subject's failure to regulate when preloaded with sandwiches or some other solid food has now been replicated three times. Pliner's (1970) recent work, however, indicates that the obese will regulate, though not as well as normals, when preloaded with liquid food.

subjects, but do affect the amounts eaten by normal subjects.

It seems clear that the set of bodily symptoms the subject labels "hunger" differs for obese and normal subjects. Whether one measures gastric motility as Stunkard did, or manipulates motility and the other physiological correlates of food deprivation, as I assume my students and I have done, one finds, for normal subjects, a high degree of correspondence between the state of the gut and eating behavior and, for obese subjects, virtually no correspondence.

Whether or not they are responsive to these particular visceral cues, the obese *do* eat, and the search for the cues that trigger obese eating occupied my students' and my attention for a number of years. Since the experimental details of this search have been published (Schachter, 1967, 1968, 1971), and I believe are fairly well known, I will take time now only to summarize our conclusions—eating by the obese seems unrelated to any internal, visceral state, but is determined by external, food-relevant cues such as the sight, smell, and taste of food. Now, obviously, such external cues to some extent affect anyone's eating behavior. However, for normals these external factors clearly interact with internal state. They may affect what, where, and how much the normal eats, but chiefly when he is in a state of physiological hunger. For the obese, I suggest, internal state is irrelevant, and eating is determined largely by external cues.

As you may know, there have been a number of experiments testing this hypothesis about the external sensitivity of the obese. To convey some feeling for the nature of the supporting data, I will describe two typical experiments. In one of these, Nisbett (1968a) examined the effects of the sight of food. He reasoned that if the sight of food is a potent cue, the externally sensitive, obese person should eat just as long as food is in sight, and when, in effect, he has consumed all of the available cues, he should stop and make no further attempt to eat. In contrast, the amounts eaten by a normal subject should depend on his physiological needs, not on the quantity of food in sight. Thus, if only a small amount of food is in sight but the subject is given the opportunity to forage for more, the normal subject should eat more than the obese subject. In contrast, if a large amount of food is in sight, the obese should eat more than the normal subject.

To test these expectations, Nisbett provided subjects, who had not eaten lunch, with either one or three roast beef sandwiches. He told them to help themselves and, as he was leaving, pointed to a refrigerator across the room and said, "There are dozens more sandwiches in the refrigerator. Have as many as you want." His results are presented in Table 1. As you can see, obese subjects

TABLE 1. Effect of Quantity of Visible Food on Amounts Eaten

Subjects	No. Sandwiches	
	One	Three
Normal	1.96	1.88
Obese	1.48	2.32

Note: From Nisbett (1968a).

ate significantly more than normals when presented with only one sandwich.

In another study, Decke (1971) examined the effects of taste on eating. She reasoned that taste, like the sight or smell of food, is essentially an external cue. Good taste, then, should stimulate the obese to eat more than normals, and bad taste, of course, should have the reverse effect.

In a taste test context, Decke provided her subjects with either a decent vanilla milk shake or with a vanilla milk shake plus quinine. The effects of this taste manipulation are conveyed in Table 2 where, as you can see, obese subjects drank

TABLE 2. Effect of Taste on Eating

Subjects	Ounces Consumed in	
	Good taste	Bad taste
Normal	10.6	6.4
Obese	13.9	2.6

Note: From Decke (1961).

more than normals when the milk shake was good and drank considerably less when the milk shake had been laced with quinine.

Now, anyone who sees Decke's milk shake data and who is familiar with physiological psychology will note that this is precisely what Miller, Bailey, and Stevenson (1950) found and what Teitelbaum (1955) found in the lesioned hyperphagic rat. For those of you who are unfamiliar with this preparation, let me review the facts about this animal. If you make bilateral lesions in the ventromedial nuclei of the hypothalamus, you are likely to get an animal that will eat prodigious amounts of food and will eventually achieve monu-

mental weight—a creature of nightmares. This has been demonstrated for rats, cats, mice, monkeys, rabbits, goats, dogs, and sparrows. Classic descriptions of these preparations portray an animal that immediately after the operation staggers over to its food hopper and shovels in food. For several weeks, this voracious eating continues, and there is, of course, very rapid weight gain. This is called the dynamic phase of hyperphagia. Finally, a plateau is reached, at which point the animal's weight levels off, and its food intake drops to a level only slightly above that of the normal animal. This is called the static phase. During both the static and the dynamic stages, the lesioned animal is also characterized as markedly inactive, and as irascible, emotional, and generally bitchy.

Now it turns out that though the lesioned animal is normally a heavy eater, if you add quinine to its food it drastically decreases its intake to levels far below that of a normal animal's whose food has been similarly tainted. On the other hand, if to its normal food you add dextrose, or lard, or something that is apparently tasty to a rat, the lesioned animal increases its intake to levels considerably above its regular intake and above the intake of a control rat whose food has also been enriched.

The similarity of these facts about the finickiness of the lesioned rat to Decke's findings in her milk shake experiment is, of course, striking, and many people (notably Nisbett, 1968a, 1971) have pointed to this and other similarities between our data on obese humans and the physiologist's data on the obese rat. In order to determine if there was anything more to this than an engaging, occasional resemblance between two otherwise remotely connected sets of data, Judith Rodin and I decided to treat the matter dead seriously and, where possible, to make a point-for-point comparison of every fact we could learn about the hypothalamic, obese rat with every fact we could learn about the obese human. Before describing the results of our work, I would like, however, to be sure that you are aware of the areas of my expertise. I am not a physiological psychologist. Though I am pretty sure that I've eaten a hypothalamus, I doubt that I've ever seen one. When I say something like "bilateral lesions of the ventromedial nuclei of the hypothalamus," you can be sure that I've memorized it. I make this personal confession because of the dilemma that Rodin, also a physiological innocent, and I faced in our work. Though we couldn't have succeeded, we attempted to read *everything* about the ventromedial lesioned rat. If you've ever made this sort of attempt, you may have been seized by the same despair as were we when it sometimes seemed as if there were no such thing as a fact that *someone* had not failed to confirm. (I include in this sweeping generalization, by the way, the apparent fact that a ventromedial lesion produces a hyperphagic, obese animal—see Reynolds, 1963, and Rabin and Smith, 1968.) And it sometimes seemed as if there were no such thing as an experiment which *someone* had not failed to replicate. Since I happen to have spent my college physics lab course personally disproving most of the laws of physics, I cannot say that I find this particularly surprising, but if one is trying to decide what is the fact, it is a depressing state of affairs. In our own areas of expertise, this probably isn't too serious a problem. Each of us in our specialties knows how to evaluate a piece of work. In a field in which you are not expert, you simply cannot, except in the crudest of cases, evaluate. If several experimenters have different results, you just don't know which to believe. In order to cope with this dilemma, Rodin and I decided to treat each of our facts in batting average terms. For each fact, I will inform you of the number of studies that have been concerned with the fact and the proportion of these studies that work out in a given direction. To be included in the batting average, we required only that a study present all or a substantial portion of its data, rather than report the author's impressions or present only the data of one or two presumably representative cases. I should also note that in all cases we have relied on the data and not on what the experimenter said about the data. It may seem silly to make this point explicit, but it is the case that in a few studies, for some perverse reason, the experimenter's conclusions simply have nothing to do with his data. Finally, I should note that in all comparisons of animal and human data, I will consider the data only for animals in the static phase of obesity, animals who, like our human subjects, are already fat. In general, however, the results for dynamic and static animals are quite similar.

As a shorthand method of making comparisons between studies and species, I shall throughout the rest of this article employ what we can call a Fat to Normal (F/N) ratio in which we simply get an index by dividing the magnitude of the effect for fat subjects by the magnitude of the effect for normal control subjects. Thus, if in a particular study the fat rats ate an average of 15 grams of food and normal rats ate 10 grams, the F/N ratio would be 1.50, indicating that the fat rats ate 50% more food than normal rats.

To begin our comparisons, let us return to the effects of taste on eating behavior. We know that fat human beings eat more of a good-tasting food than do normal human beings and that they eat less of bad-tasting food than do normals. The physiologists have done almost identical experiments to ours, and in Line 1 of Table 3 we can

TABLE 3. Effects of Taste on Eating

	Animals		Humans	
Condition	Batting Average	Mean F/N	Mean F/N	Batting Average
Good food	5/6	1.45	1.42	2/2
Bad food	3/4	.76	.84	1/2

Note: F/N = Fat to normal ratio.

compare the effects of good-tasting food on lesioned animals and on men. You will notice on the left that Rodin and I found six studies on lesioned animals, in this case largely rats. Batting average: five of the six studies indicate that lesioned, static, obese animals eat more of a good-tasting food than do their normal controls. The average F/N ratio for these six studies is 1.45, indicating that fat rats on the average eat 45% more of good-tasting food than do normal rats. On the right side of the table, you can see that there have been two human studies, and that both of these studies indicate that fat humans eat more of good-tasting food than do normal humans. The average F/N ratio for humans is 1.42, indicating that fat humans eat 42% more of good-tasting food than do normally sized humans.[2]

Incidentally, please keep in mind throughout this exercise that the left side of each table will always contain the data for lesioned animals, very largely rats, that have been abused by a variety of people named Epstein, and Teitelbaum, and Stellar, and Miller, and so on. The right side of each table will always contain the data for humans, mostly Columbia College students, nice boys who go home every Friday night, where, I suppose, they too are abused by a variety of

[2] The technically informed reader undoubtedly will wish to know precisely which studies and what data are included in Tables 3 and 4. There are so many studies involved that, within the context of this paper, it is impossible to supply this information. Dr. Rodin and I are preparing a monograph on this work which will, of course, provide full details on such matters.

people named Epstein, and Teitelbaum, and Stellar, and Miller.

In Line 2 of Table 3, we have the effects of bad taste on consumption. For both animals and men, in all of these studies bad taste was manipulated by the addition of quinine to the food. There are four animal studies; three of the four indicate that fat animals eat less than normal animals, and the average F/N ratio is .76. There are two human studies: one of the two indicates that fats eat considerably less bad food than normals; the other indicates no significant difference between the two groups, and the mean F/N ratio for these two studies is .84. For this particular fact, the data are more fragile than one would like, but the trends for the two species are certainly parallel.

To continue this examination of parallel facts: the eating habits of the lesioned rats have been thoroughly studied, particularly by Teitelbaum and Campbell (1958). It turns out that static obese rats eat on the average slightly, not considerably, more than normal rats. They also eat fewer meals per day, eat more per meal, and eat more rapidly than do normal animals. For each of these facts, we have parallel data for humans. Before presenting these data, I should note that for humans, I have, wherever possible, restricted myself to behavioral studies, studies in which the investigators have actually measured how much their subjects eat. I hope no one will be offended, I assume no one will be surprised, if I say that I am skeptical of the self-reports of fat people about how much they eat or exercise.[3] For those of you who feel that this is high-handed selection of studies, may I remind you of Stunkard's famous chronic fat patients who were fed everything that, in interviews, they admitted to eating daily, and who all steadily lost weight on this diet.

Considering first the average amount eaten per

day when on ad-lib feeding of ordinary lab chow or pellets, you will note in Line 1 of Table 4 that consistently static obese rats eat somewhat (19%) more than do their normal counterparts. The data for humans are derived from all of the studies I know of in which eating is placed in a noshing, or ad-lib, context; that is, a bowl of ordinary food, usually nuts or crackers is placed in the room, the experiment presumably has nothing to do with eating, and the subject is free to eat or not, as he chooses, just as is a rat in its cage. In two of the three experiments conducted in this context, obese subjects eat slightly more than do normals; in the third experiment, the two groups eat precisely the same number of crackers. For both humans and rats, then, the fat subject eats only slightly more than the normal subject.

Turning next to the number of meals per day, we note on Line 2 of Table 4 that for both rats and humans, fatter subjects consistently eat fewer meals per day. (A rat meal is defined by Teitelbaum and Campbell, 1958, as "any burst of food intake of at least five pellets separated by at least 5 min. from any other burst [p. 138]." For humans, these particular data are based on self-report or interview studies, for I know of no relevant behavioral data. In any case, again the data for the lesioned rat and the obese human correspond very closely indeed.

From the previous two facts, it should, of course, follow that obese subjects will eat more per meal than normal subjects, and, as can be seen in Line 3 of Table 4, this is the case for both lesioned rats and obese humans. The data for rats are based on two experiments that simply recorded the amount of food eaten per eating burst. The data for humans are based on all experiments in which a plate of food, usually sandwiches, is placed before a subject, and he is told to help himself to lunch or dinner.

Our final datum on eating habits is the speed of eating. Teitelbaum and Campbell (1958) simply recorded the number of pellets their animals ate per minute. Since there is nothing else to do when you are sitting behind a one-way screen watching a subject, Nisbett (1968b—data not reported in paper) recorded the number of spoonfuls of ice cream his subjects ate per minute. The comparison of the two studies is drawn in Line 4 of Table 4, where you will note an unsettling similarity in the rate at which lesioned rats and obese humans outspeed their normal counterparts.[4]

TABLE 4. Eating Habits

	Animals		Humans	
Variable	Batting Average	Mean F/N	Mean F/N	Batting Average
Amount of food eaten ad lib	9/9	1.19	1.16	2/3
No. meals per day	4/4	.85	.92	3/3
Amount eaten per meal	2/2	1.34	1.29	5/5
Speed of eating	1/1	1.28	1.26	1/1

Note: F/N = Fat to normal ratio.

[3] In three or four such self-report studies, fat people report eating considerably less food than do normals.

[4] Fat rats do not drink more rapidly than do normals. There are no comparable data for humans.

All told, then, in the existing literature, Rodin and I found a total of six items of behavior on which it is possible to make rather precise comparisons between lesioned rats and obese humans. These are mostly nonobvious facts, and the comparisons drawn between the two sets of experiments do not attempt to push the analogies beyond the point of common sense. I do not think there can be much debate about pellets versus spoonfuls of ice cream consumed per minute as equivalent measures of eating rate. For all six facts in the existing literature, the parallels between the species are striking. What the lesioned, fat rat does, the obese human does.

In addition to these facts, we identified two other areas of behavior in which it is possible to draw somewhat more fanciful, though still not ridiculous, comparisons between the species. These are the areas of emotionality and of activity. Though there has been little systematic study of emotionality, virtually everyone who has worked with these animals agrees that the lesioned animals are hyperexcitable, easily startled, overemotional, and generally bitchy to handle. In addition, work by Singh (1969) and research on active avoidance learning do generally support this characterization of the lesioned animal as an emotional beast.

For humans, we have two experiments from which it is possible to draw conclusions about emotionality. In one of these (Schachter et al., 1968), we manipulated fear by threat of painful electric shock. On a variety of rating scales, fat subjects acknowledged that they were somewhat more frightened and anxious than did normal subjects. In a second experiment, Rodin (1970) had her subjects listen to an audio tape while they were working at either a monitoring or a proofreading task. The tapes were either neutral (requiring the subject to think about either rain or seashells) or emotionally charged (requiring the subject to think about his own death or about the bombing of Hiroshima). The emotionally charged tapes produced dramatic differences between subjects. On a variety of rating scales, the obese described themselves as considerably more upset and disturbed than did normal subjects; they reported more palpitations and changes in breathing rate than did normals; and performance, at either the proofreading or monitoring tasks, deteriorated dramatically more for obese than for normal subjects. Again, then, the data are consistent, for both the lesioned animal and the obese human seem to react more emotionally than their normal counterparts.

Finally, on activity, numerous studies using stabilimeter cages or activity wheels have demonstrated that the lesioned animal is markedly less active than the normal animal. This is not, I should add, a totally trivial fact indicating only that the lesioned animal has trouble shlepping his immense bulk around the cage, for the dynamic hyperphagic rat—who though not yet fat, will be—is quite as lethargic as his obese counterpart. On the human side, Bullen, Reed, and Mayer (1964) have taken movies of girls at camp during their scheduled periods of swimming, tennis, and volleyball. They categorize each camper for her degree of activity or exertion during these periods, and do find that the normal campers are more active than are the obese girls.

All told, then, Rodin and I found a total of eight facts, indicating a perfect parallel between the behavior of the lesioned rat and the obese human. We have, so far, found no fact on which the two species differ. Now all of this has proved such an engaging exercise that my students and I decided to play "real" scientist, and we constructed a matrix. We simply listed every fact we could find about the lesioned animals and every fact we could find about obese humans. I have told you about those facts for which parallel data exist. There are, however, numerous holes in the matrix—facts for rats for which no parallel human data have yet been collected, and vice versa. For the past year, we have been engaged in filling in these holes—designing for humans, experiments that have no particular rhyme or reason except that someone once did such an experiment on lesioned rats. For example, it is a fact that though lesioned rats will outeat normal rats when food is easily available, they will not lift a paw if they have to work to get food. In a Skinner box setup, Teitelbaum (1957) finds that at FR1, when one press yields one pellet, fat lesioned rats outpress normal. As the payoff decreases, however, fat rats press less and less until at FR256, they do not manage to get a single pellet during a 12-hour experimental session, whereas normal rats are still industriously pressing away. Similarly, Miller et al. (1950) found that though lesioned rats ate more than normal controls when an unweighted lid covered the food dish, they ate less than did the controls when a 75-gram weight was fastened to the lid. They also found that the lesioned rats ran more slowly down an alley to food than controls did and pulled less hard when temporarily restrained by a harness. In short, fat rats will not work to get food.

Since there was no human parallel to these studies, Lucy Friedman and I designed a study in which, when a subject arrived, he was asked simply to sit at the experimenter's desk and fill out a variety of personality tests and questionnaires. Besides the usual student litter, there was a bag of almonds on the desk. The experimenter helped herself to a nut, invited the subject to do the same, and then left him alone with his questionnaires and nuts for 15 minutes. There were two sets of conditions. In one, the nuts had shells on them; in the other, the nuts had no shells. I assume we agree that eating nuts with shells is considerably more work than eating nuts with no shells.

The top half of Table 5 presents for normal

TABLE 5. Effects of Work on the Eating Behavior of Normal and Fat Subjects

Nuts Have	Number Who	
	Eat	Don't Eat
	Normal Subjects	
Shells	10	10
No shells	11	9
	Fat Subjects	
Shells	1	19
No shells	19	1

subjects the numbers who do and do not eat nuts in the two conditions. As you can see, shells or no shells has virtually no impact on normal subjects. Fifty-five percent of normals eat nuts without shells, and 50% eat nuts with shells. I am a little self-conscious about the data for obese subjects, for it looks as if I were too stupid to know how to fake data. I know how to fake data, and were I to do so, the bottom half of Table 5 certainly would not look the way it does. When the nuts have no shells, 19 of 20 fat subjects eat nuts. When the nuts have shells on them, 1 out of 20 fat subjects eats. Obviously, the parallel to Miller's and to Teitelbaum's rats is perfect. When the food is easy to get at, fat subjects, rat or human, eat more than normals; when the food is hard to get at, fat subjects eat less than normals.

Incidentally, as a casual corollary of these and other findings, one could expect that, given acceptable food, fat eaters would be more likely

than normals to choose the easiest way of eating. In order to check on this, Lucy Friedman, Joel Handler, and I went to a large number of Chinese and Japanese restaurants, categorized each patron as he entered the restaurant as obese or normal, and then simply noted whether he ate with chopsticks or with silverware. Among Occidentals, for whom chopsticks can be an ordeal, we found that almost five times the proportion of normal eaters ate with chopsticks as did obese eaters—22.4% of normals and 4.7% of the obese ate with chopsticks.

In another matrix-hole-filling experiment, Patricia Pliner (1970) has demonstrated that obese humans, like lesioned rats, do not regulate food consumption when they are preloaded with solids but, again like the rats, do regulate when they are preloaded with liquids.

In addition to these experiments, we are currently conducting studies on pain sensitivity and on passive versus active avoidance learning—all designed to fill in more holes in our human–lesioned rat matrix. To date, we have a total of 12 nonobvious facts in which the behaviors of lesioned rats parallel perfectly the behaviors of obese humans. Though I cannot believe that as our matrix-hole-filling experiments continue, this perfect parallelism will continue, I submit that even now these are mind-boggling data. I would also submit, however, that we have played this enchanting game just about long enough. This is, after all, science through analogy—a sport I recommend with the same qualifications and enthusiasms with which I recommend skiing—and it is time that we asked what on earth does it all mean? To which at this point I can only answer ruefully that I wish to God I really knew.

On its most primitive level, I suppose that I would love to play doctor and issue pronouncements such as, "Madam, you have a very sick hypothalamus." And, indeed, I do know of one case of human obesity (Reeves & Plum, 1969) accompanied by a precisely localized neoplasm that destroyed the ventromedial hypothalamus. This is an astonishing case study, for the lady reads like a lesioned rat—she ate immense amounts of food, as much as 10,000 calories a day, grew impressively fat and was apparently a wildly emotional creature given to frequent outbursts of laughing, crying, and rage. Now I am not, of course, going to suggest that this lady is anything but a pathological extreme. The only vaguely relevant study I know of is a morphological study

(Maren, 1955) of the hypothalami of genetically obese mice, an animal whose behavior also resembles the lesioned rat's, which found no structural differences between obese and normal mice.

Mrosovsky (1971) has been developing a more sober hypothesis. Comparing the hibernator and the ventromedial lesioned rat, Mrosovsky has been playing much the same analogical game as have I, and he, too, has noted the marked behavioral similarities of his two species to the obese human. He hypothesizes that the unlesioned, obese animal, rodent or human, has a ventromedial hypothalamus that is functionally quiescent. Though I would be willing to bet that when the appropriate biochemical and electrophysiological studies are done, Mrosovsky will be proven correct, I do not believe that this is a fact which is of fundamental interest to psychologists. Most of us, I suspect, have long been convinced, psychodynamics notwithstanding, that there is *something* biologically responsible for human obesity, and to be able suddenly to point a finger at an offending structure would not really put us much ahead. After all, we've known about the adrenal medulla and emotion for more than 50 years, and I doubt that this particular bit of knowledge has been of much help in our understanding of aggression, or fear, or virtually any other emotional state.

If it is true that the ventromedial hypothalamus is functionally quiescent, for us the question must be, for what function, psychologically speaking, is it quiescent? What processes, or inputs, or outputs are mediated by this particular structure? Speculation and theorizing about the functions of this area have tended to be cautious and modest. Essentially, two suggestions have been made—one that the area is a satiety center, and the other that the area is an emotionality center. Both Miller (1964) and Stellar (1954) have tentatively suggested that the ventromedial area is a satiety center—that in some fashion it monitors the signals indicating a sufficiency of food and inhibits the excitatory (Eat! Eat!) impulses initiated in the lateral hypothalamus. This inhibitory-satiety mechanism can account for the hyperphagia of the lesioned animals and, consequently, for their obesity. It can also account for most of the facts that I outlined earlier about the daily eating habits of these animals. It cannot by itself, however, account for the finickiness of these animals, nor can it, as I believe I can show, account for the apparent unwillingness of these animals to work for food. Finally, this hypothesis is simply irrelevant to the demonstrated inactivity and hyperemo-

tionality of these animals. This irrelevance, however, is not critical if one assumes, as does Stellar, that discrete neural centers, also located in the ventromedial area, control activity and emotionality. The satiety theory, then, can account for some, but by no means all, of the critical facts about eating, and it has nothing to say about activity or emotionality.

As a theoretically more ambitious alternative, Grossman (1966, 1967) has proposed that the ventromedial area be considered the emotionality center and that the facts about eating be derived from this assumption. By definition, Grossman's hypothesis accounts for the emotionality of these animals, and his own work on active avoidance learning certainly supports the emotionality hypothesis. I must confess, however, that I have difficulty in understanding just why these emotional animals become fat. In essence, Grossman (1966) assumes that "lesions in or near the VMH sharply increase an animal's affective responsiveness to apparently all sensory stimuli [p. 1]." On the basis of this general statement, he suggests that "the 'finickiness' of the ventromedial animal might then reflect a change in its affective response to taste." This could, of course, account for the fact that lesioned animals eat more very good- and less very bad-tasting food than do normals. However, I simply find it hard to believe that this affective hypothesis can account for the basic fact about these animals—that for weeks on end, the lesioned animals eat grossly more of ordinary, freely available lab chow.

Grossman (1967) attributes the fact that lesioned animals will not work for food to their "exaggerated response to handling, the test situation, the deprivation regimen, and the requirement of having to work for their daily bread [p. 358]." I suppose all of this is possible; I simply find it farfetched. At the very least, the response to handling and to the deprivation regime should be just as exaggerated whether the reinforcement schedule is FR1 or FR256 and the lesioned animals do press more than the normals at FR1.

My skepticism, however, is irrelevant, and Grossman may be correct. There are, however, at least two facts with which, it seems to me, Grossman's hypothesis cannot cope. First, it would seem to me that an animal with an affective response to food would be likely to eat more rather than less often per day, as is the fact. Second, it is simply common sense to expect that an animal with strong "affective responsiveness to all sensory stimuli" will be a very active animal indeed, but the lesioned animal is presumably hypoactive.

None of the existing theories, then, can cope with all of the currently available facts. For the remainder of this article, I am going to try my hand at developing a hypothesis that I believe can cope with more of the facts than can the available alternatives. It is a hypothesis that derives entirely from our work on human obesity. I believe, however, that it can explain as many of the facts about ventromedial-lesioned rats as it can about the human obese. If future experimental work on animals proves this correct, it would certainly suggest that science by analogy has merits other than its entertainment value.

The gist of our findings on humans is this—the eating behavior of the obese is under external, rather than internal, control. In effect, the obese seem stimulus-bound. When a food-relevant cue is present, the obese are more likely to eat and to eat a great deal than are normals. When such a cue is absent, the obese are less likely to try to eat or to complain about hunger. Though I have not, in this article, developed this latter point, there is evidence that, in the absence of food-relevant cues, the obese have a far easier time fasting than do normals, while in the presence of such cues, they have a harder time fasting (Goldman, Jaffa, & Schachter, 1968).

Since it is a little hard to believe that such stimulus-binding is limited to food-relevant cues, for some time now my students and I have been concerned with the generalizability of these facts. Given our starting point, this concern has led to some rather odd little experiments. For example, Judith Rodin, Peter Herman, and I have asked subjects to look at slides on which are portrayed 13 objects or words. Each slide is exposed for five seconds, and the subject is then asked to recall what he saw. Fat subjects recall more objects than do normal subjects. The experiment has been replicated, and this appears to be a reliable phenomenon.

In another study, Rodin, Herman, and I compared fat and normal subjects on simple and on complex or disjunctive reaction time. For simple reaction time, they are instructed to lift their finger from a telegraph key as soon as the stimulus light comes on. On this task, there are no differences between obese and normal subjects. For complex reaction time, there are two stimulus lights and two telegraph keys, and subjects are instructed to lift their left finger when the right light comes on and lift their right finger when the left light comes on. Obese subjects respond more rapidly and make fewer errors. Since this was a little hard to believe, this study was repeated three times—each time with the same results—the obese are simply better at complex reaction time than are normals. I do not pretend to understand these results, but they do seem to indicate that, for some reason, the obese are more efficient stimulus or information processors.

At this stage, obviously, this is shotgun research which, in coordination with the results of our eating experiments, seems to indicate that it may be useful to more generally characterize the obese as stimulus-bound and to hypothesize that any stimulus, above a given intensity level, is more likely to evoke an appropriate response from an obese than from a normal subject.

Our first test of implications of this hypothesis in a noneating setting is Rodin's (1970) experiment on the effects of distraction on performance. She reasoned that if the stimulus-binding hypothesis is correct, distracting, irrelevant stimuli should be more disruptive for obese than for normal subjects when they are performing a task requiring concentration. Presumably, the impinging stimulus is more likely to grip the attention of the stimulus-bound obese subject. To test this guess, she had her subjects work at a simple proofreading task. In one condition, the subjects corrected proof with no distractions at all. In the three other conditions, they corrected proof while listening to recorded tapes that varied in the degree to which they were likely to grip a subject's attention, and therefore distract him. The results are presented in Figure 2, where, as you can see, the obese are better at proofreading when

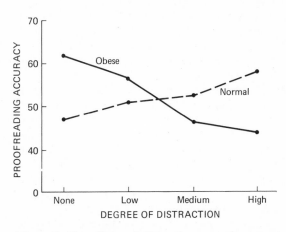

Figure 2. The effects of distraction on performance (from Rodin, 1970).

undistracted but their performance seriously deteriorates as they are distracted until, at extreme distraction, they are considerably worse than normals. Rodin finds precisely the same pattern of results, by the way, in a similar study in which she uses the complex reaction time task I have already described rather than the proofreading task. For humans, then, there is evidence, outside of the eating context, to support the hypothesis.

Let us return to consideration of the ventromedial-lesioned animal and examine the implications of the hypothesis that any stimulus, above a given intensity level, is more likely to evoke an appropriate response from a lesioned than from an intact animal. This is a hypothesis which is, in many ways, similar to Grossman's hypothesis and, on the face of it, would appear to be vulnerable to exactly the same criticisms as I have leveled at his theory. There are, however, crucial differences that will become evident as I elaborate this notion. I assume it is self-evident that my hypothesis can explain the emotionality of the lesioned animals and, with the exception of meal frequency—a fact to which I will return—can account for virtually all of our facts about the daily eating habits of these animals. I will, therefore, begin consideration of the hypothesis by examining its implications for those facts that have been most troubling for alternative formulations and by examining those facts that seem to most clearly contradict my own hypothesis.

Let us turn first to the perverse and fascinating fact that though lesioned animals will outeat normals when food is easily available, they simply will not work for food. In my terms, this is an incomplete fact which may prove only that a remote food stimulus will not evoke a food-acquiring response. It is the case that in the experiments concerned with this fact, virtually every manipulation of work has covaried the remoteness or prominence of the food cue. Food at the end of a long alleyway is obviously a more remote cue than food in the animal's food dish. Pellets available only after 256 presses of a lever are certainly more remote food stimuli than pellets available after each press of a lever. If the stimulus-binding hypothesis is correct, it should be anticipated that, in contrast to the results when the food cue is remote, the lesioned animal will work harder than the normal animal when the food stimulus is prominent and compelling. Though the appropriate experiment has not been done on rats, to my delight I have learned recently that such an experiment has been done on humans by

William Johnson (1970), who independently has been pursuing a line of thought similar to mine.

Johnson seated his subject at a table, fastened his hand in a harness, and, to get food, required the subject for 12 minutes to pull, with his index finger, on a ring that was attached by wire to a seven-pound weight. He received food on a VR50 schedule—that is, on the average, a subject received a quarter of a sandwich for every 50 pulls of the ring. Obviously, this was moderately hard work.

To vary stimulus prominence, Johnson manipulated food visibility and prior taste of food. In "food visible" conditions, he placed beside the subject one desirable sandwich covered in a transparent wrap. In addition, as the subject satisfied the VR requirements, he placed beside him quarter sandwiches similarly wrapped. In "food invisible" conditions, Johnson followed exactly the same procedures, but wrapped the sandwiches in white, nontransparent shelf paper. Subjects, of course, did not eat until they had completed their 12 minutes of labor.

As a second means of varying cue prominence, half of the subjects ate a quarter of a very good sandwich immediately before they began work. The remaining subjects ate a roughly equivalent portion of plain white bread.

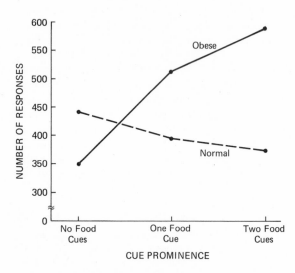

Figure 3. The effect of food cue prominence on effort (from Johnson, 1970).

In Figure 3, you can see the effects of these manipulations on effort. I have arranged the conditions along the dimension of food cue prominence—ranging from no prominent food cues to two prominent food cues—that is, the subjects ate a quarter sandwich and the food was visible. As you can see, the stimulus prominence manipulations have a marked effect on the obese, for they work far harder when the food cues are prominent and compelling than when they are inconspicuous. In contrast, cue prominence has relatively little effect on normal subjects.

Please note also that these results parallel Miller's and Teitelbaum's results with lesioned rats. When the food cues are remote, the obese human works less hard for food than the normally sized human. The fact that this relationship flips when the cues are prominent is, of course, a delight to me, and wouldn't it be absorbing to replicate this experiment on lesioned rats?

Let us turn next to the fact that lesioned rats are hypoactive. If ever a fact were incompatible with a hypothesis, this one is it. Surely an animal that is more responsive to any stimulus should be hyper-, not hypoactive. Yet this is a most peculiar fact—for it remains a fact only because one rather crucial finding in the literature has been generally overlooked and because the definition of activity seems restricted to measures obtained in running wheels or in stabilimeter-type living cages.

Studies of activity have with fair consistency reported dramatically less activity for lesioned than for normal rats. With one exception, these studies report data in terms of total activity per unit time, making no distinction between periods when the animal room was quiet and undisturbed and periods involving the mild ferment of animal-tending activities. Gladfelter and Brobeck (1962), however, report activity data separately for the "43-hour period when the constant-temperature room was dark and quiet and the rats were undisturbed" and for the "five-hour period when the room was lighted and the rats were cared for [p. 811]." During the quiet time, these investigators find precisely what almost everyone else does—lesioned rats are markedly less active. During the animal-tending period, however, lesioned animals are just about as active as normal animals. In short, when the stimulus field is relatively barren and there is little to react to, the ventro-medial animal is inactive; when the field is made up of the routine noises, stirrings, and disturbances involved in tending an animal laboratory, the lesioned animal is just about as active as the normal animal.

Though this is an instructive fact, it hardly proves my hypothesis, which specifies that above a given stimulus intensity the lesioned animal should be *more* reactive than the normal animal. Let us, then, ask—is there any evidence that lesioned animals are more active than normal animals? There is, if you are willing to grant that specific activities such as lever pressing or avoidance behavior are as much "activity" as the gross, overall measures obtained in stabilimeter-mounted living cages.

In his study of activity, Teitelbaum (1957) has distinguished between random and food-directed activity. As do most other investigators, he finds that in their cages, lesioned rats are much less active than are normals. During a 12-hour stint in a Skinner box, however, when on an FR1 schedule, the lesioned animals are more active; that is, they press more than do normals. Thus, when the food cue is salient and prominent, as it is on an FR1 schedule, the lesioned animal is very active indeed. And, as you know, when the food cue is remote, as it is on an FR64 or FR256 schedule, the lesioned animal is inactive.

Since lever pressing is activity in pursuit of food, I suppose one should be cautious in accepting these data as support of my argument. Let us turn, then, to avoidance learning where most of the experiments are unrelated to food.

In overall batting average terms,[5] no area could be messier than this one, for in three of six studies, lesioned animals are better and in three worse at avoidance than normals. However, if one distinguishes between passive and active avoidance, things become considerably more coherent.

In active avoidance studies, a conditioned stimulus, such as a light or buzzer, precedes a noxious event such as electrifying the floor grid. To avoid the shock, the animal must perform some action such as jumping into the nonelectrified compartment of a shuttle box. In three of four such studies, the lesioned animals learn considerably more rapidly than do normal animals. By this criterion, at least, lesioned animals are more

---

[5] Of all the behavioral areas so far considered, avoidance learning is probably the one for which it makes least sense either to adopt a batting average approach or to attempt to treat the research as a conceptually equivalent set of studies. Except in this area, the great majority of experiments have used, as subjects, rats with electrolytically produced lesions. In the avoidance learning area, the subjects have been mice, rats, and cats: the lesions are variously electrolytically produced, produced by gold thioglucose injections, or are "functional" lesions produced by topical application of atropine or some other agent.

reactive than normal animals.[6] Parenthetically, it is amusing to note that the response latencies of the lesioned animal are smaller (Grossman, 1966) than those of the normal animal, just as, in our studies of complex reaction time, obese humans are faster than normal humans.

In contrast to these results, lesioned animals do considerably worse than normal animals in passive avoidance studies. In these studies, the animal's water dish or the lever of a Skinner box are electrified so that if, during the experimental period, the animal touches these objects he receives a shock. In both of the studies we have so far found on passive learnings, the lesioned animals do considerably worse than normal animals. They either press the lever or touch the water dish more than do normals and accordingly are shocked far more often. Thus, when the situation requires a response if the animal is to avoid shock, the lesioned animal does better than the normal animal. Conversely, if the situation requires response quiescence if the animal is to avoid shock, the lesioned animal does far worse than the normal animal. This pair of facts, I suggest, provides strong support for the hypothesis that beyond a given stimulus intensity, the lesioned animal is more reactive than the normal animal. I would also suggest that without some variant of this hypothesis, the overall pattern of results on avoidance learning is incoherent.

All in all, then one can make a case of sorts for the suggestion that there are specifiable circumstances in which lesioned animals will be more active. It is hardly an ideal case, and only an experiment that measures the effects of systematically varied stimulus field richness on gross activity can test the point.

These ruminations on activity do suggest a refinement of the general hypothesis and also, I

[6] Reactive, yes, but what about activity in the more primitive sense of simply moving or scrambling about the experimental box? Even in this respect, the lesioned animals appear to outmove the normals, for Turner, Sechzer, and Liebelt (1967) report that,

The experimental groups, both mice and rats, emitted strong escape tendencies prior to the onset of shock and in response to shock. Repeated attempts were made to climb out of the test apparatus. This group showed much more vocalization than the control group. . . . In contrast to the behavior of the experimental animals, the control animals appeared to become immobilized or to "freeze" both before and during the shock period. Thus, there was little attempt to escape and little vocalization [p. 242].

trust, make clear why I have insisted on inserting that awkward phrase "above a given intensity level" in all statements of the hypothesis. For activity, it appears to be the case that the lesioned animal is less active when the stimulus is remote and more active when the stimulus is prominent. This interaction between reactivity and stimulus prominence is presented graphically in Figure 4. This is a formulation which I believe fits almost all of the available data, on both animals and men, remarkably well. It is also a formulation which for good ad-hoc reasons bears a striking resemblance to almost every relevant set of data I have discussed.

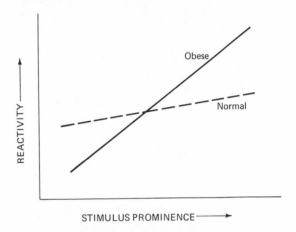

Figure 4. Theoretical curves of relationship of reactivity to stimulus prominence.

For human eating behavior, virtually every fact we have supports the assertion that the obese eat more than normals when the food cue is prominent and less when the cue is remote. In Johnson's study of work and cue prominence, the obese do not work as hard as normals when there are no prominent food cues, but work much harder when the food cues are highy salient. In Nisbett's one- and three-sandwich experiment, the obese subjects eat just as long as food cues are prominent—that is, the sandwiches are directly in front of the subject—but when these immediate cues have been consumed, they stop eating. Thus, they eat more than normals in the three-sandwich condition and less in the one-sandwich condition. We also know that the obese have an easy time fasting in the absence of food cues and a hard time in the presence of such cues, and so on.

About eating habits we know that the obese eat larger meals (what could be a more prominent cue than food on the plate?), but eat fewer meals (as they should if it requires a particularly potent food cue to trigger an eating response). Even the fact that the obese eat more rapidly can be easily derived from this formulation.

For rats, this formulation in general fits what we know about eating habits, but can be considered a good explanation of the various experimental facts only if you are willing to accept my reinterpretation, in terms of cue prominence, of such experiments as Miller et al.'s (1950) study of the effects of work on eating. If, as would I, you would rather suspend judgment until the appropriate experiments have been done on lesioned rats, mark it down as an engaging possibility.

Given the rough state of what we know about emotionality, this formulation seems to fit the data for humans and rats about equally well. The lesioned rats are vicious when handled and lethargic when left alone. In the Rodin (1970) experiment which required subjects to listen to either neutral or emotionally disturbing tapes, obese subjects described themselves (and behaved accordingly) as less emotional than normals when the tapes were neutral and much more emotional than normals when the tapes were disturbing.

All in all, given the variety of species and behaviors involved, it is not a bad ad-hoc hypothesis. So far there has been only one study deliberately designed to test some of the ideas implicit in this formulation. This is Lee Ross's (1969) study of the effects of cue salience on eating. Ross formulated this experiment in the days when we were struggling with some of the data inconsistent with our external–internal theory of eating behavior (see Schachter, 1967). Since the world is full of food cues, it was particularly embarrassing to discover that obese subjects ate less frequently than normals. Short of invoking denial mechanisms, such a fact could be reconciled with the theory only if we assumed that a food cue must be potent in order to trigger an eating response in an obese subject—the difference between a hot dog stand two blocks away and a hot dog under your nose, savory with mustard and steaming with sauerkraut.

To test the effects of cue prominence, Ross simply had his subjects sit at a table covered with a variety of objects among which was a large tin of shelled cashew nuts. Presumably, the subjects were there to take part in a study of thinking. There were two sets of experimental conditions. In high-cue-saliency conditions, the table and the nuts were illuminated by an unshaded table lamp containing a 40-watt bulb. In low-saliency conditions, the lamp was shaded and contained a 7½-watt red bulb. The measure of eating was simply the difference in the weight of the tin of nuts before and after the subject thought his experimentally required thoughts. The results are presented in Figure 5, which, needless to say, though

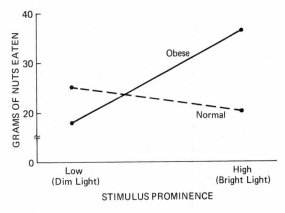

Figure 5. The effects of stimulus intensity on amount eaten (from Ross, 1969).

I will say it, bears a marked resemblance to our theoretical curves.

So much for small triumphs. Let us turn now to some of the problems of this formulation. Though I do not intend to detail a catalog of failings, I would like to make explicit some of my discomforts.

1. Though there has been no direct experimental study of the problem, it seems to be generally thought that the lesioned rat is hyposexual, which, if true, is one hell of a note for a theory which postulates superreactivity. It is the case, however, that gonadal atrophy is frequently a consequence of this operation (Brooks & Lambert, 1946; Hetherington & Ransom, 1940). Possibly, then, we should consider sexual activity as artifactually quite distinct from either gross activity or stimulus-bound activity such as avoidance behavior.

2. I am made uncomfortable by the fact that the obese, both human and rat, eat less bad food than do normals. I simply find it difficult to conceive of nonresponsiveness as a response. I suppose I could conceptually pussyfoot around this difficulty, but I cannot imagine the definition of response that would allow me to cope with

both this fact and with the facts about passive avoidance. I take some comfort from the observation that of all of the facts about animals and humans, the fact about bad taste has the weakest batting average. It may yet turn out not to be a fact.

3. Though the fact that obese humans eat less often is no problem, the fact that obese rats also eat less often is awkward, for it is a bit difficult to see how food stimulus intensity can vary for a caged rat on an ad-lib schedule. This may seem farfetched, but there is some experimental evidence that this may be due to the staleness of the food. Brooks, Lockwood, and Wiggins (1946), using mash for food, demonstrated that lesioned rats do not outeat normals when the food is even slightly stale. Only when the food was absolutely fresh and newly placed in the cage did lesioned rats eat conspicuously more than normal rats. It seems doubtful, however, that this could be the explanation for results obtained with pellets.

4. As with food, one should expect from this formulation that the animal's water intake would increase following the lesion. There does not appear to have been much systematic study of the problem, but what data exist are inconsistent from one study to the next. Several studies indicate decreased water intake; at least one study (Krasne, 1964) indicates no change following the operation; and there are even rare occasional case reports of polydipsia. Possibly my interactional hypothesis can cope with this chaos, and systematically varying the salience of the water cue will systematically affect the water intake of the ventromedial animal. It is also possible that under any circumstance, water, smell-less and tasteless, is a remote cue.

There are, then, difficulties with this formulation. These may be the kinds of difficulties that will ultimately damn the theory, or at least establish its limits. Alternatively, these may mostly be apparent difficulties, and this view of matters may help us clarify inconsistent sets of data, for I suspect that by systematically varying cue prominence we can systematically vary the lesioned animal's reactivity on many dimensions. We shall see. Granting the difficulties, for the moment this view of matters does manage to subsume a surprisingly diverse set of facts about animals and men under one quite simple theoretical scheme.

Since I have presented this article as a more or less personal history of the development of a set of ideas, I would like to conclude by taking a more formal look at this body of data, theory, and speculation, by examining what I believe we now know, what seems to be good guesswork, and what is still out-and-out speculation.

1. With some confidence, we can say that obese humans are externally controlled or stimulus-bound. There is little question that this is true of their eating behavior, and evidence is rapidly accumulating that eating is a special case of the more general state.

I have suggested that stimulus prominence and reactivity are key variables in understanding the realms of behavior with which I have been concerned, and Figure 4 represents a first guess as to the nature of the differential functions involved for obese and normal humans. The specific shapes of the curves are, of course, pure guesswork, and the only absolute requirement that I believe the data impose on the theory is that there be an interaction such that at low levels of stimulus prominence, the obese are less reactive, and at high levels of prominence more reactive, than normals.

2. With considerably less confidence, I believe we can say that this same set of hypotheses may explain many of the differences between the ventromedial-lesioned rat and his intact counterpart. This conclusion is based on the fact that so much of the existing data either fit or can be plausibly reinterpreted to fit these ideas. Obviously, the crucial experiments have yet to be done.

3. Finally, and most tentatively, one may guess that the obesity of rats and men has a common physiological locus in the ventromedial hypothalamus. I must emphasize that this guess is based *entirely* on the persistent and tantalizing analogies between lesioned rats and obese humans. There is absolutely no relevant independent evidence. However, should future work support this speculation, I suspect, in light of the evidence already supporting the stimulus-binding hypotheses, that we are in for a radical revision of our notions about the hypothalamus.

REFERENCES

Brooks, C. McC., & Lambert, E. F. A study of the effect of limitation of food intake and the method of feeding on the rate of weight gain during hypothalamic obesity in the albino rat. *American Journal of Physiology*, 1946, *147*, 695–707.

activity of obese and nonobese adolescent girls appraised by motion picture sampling. *American Journal of Clinical Nutrition*, 1964, *14*, 211–223.

Cannon, W. B. *Bodily changes in pain, hunger, fear and rage.* (2nd ed.) New York: Appleton, 1915.

Carlson, A. J. *The control of hunger in health and disease.* Chicago: University of Chicago Press, 1916.

Decke, E. Effects of taste on the eating behavior of obese and normal persons. Cited in S. Schachter, *Emotion, obesity, and crime.* New York: Academic Press, 1971.

Gladfelter, W. E., & Brobeck, J. R. Decreased spontaneous locomotor activity in the rat induced by hypothalamic lesions. *American Journal of Physiology*, 1962, *203*, 811–817.

Goldman, R., Jaffa, M., & Schachter, S. Yom Kippur, Air France, dormitory food, and the eating behavior of obese and normal persons. *Journal of Personality and Social Psychology*, 1968, *10*, 117–132.

Grossman, S. P. The VMH: A center for affective reactions, satiety, or both? *International Journal of Physiology and Behavior*, 1966, *1*, 1–10.

Grossman, S. P. *A textbook of physiological psychology.* New York: Wiley, 1967.

Hetherington, A. W., & Ranson, S. W. Hypothalamic lesions and adiposity in the rat. *Anatomical Record*, 1940, *78*, 149–172.

Johnson, W. G. The effect of prior-taste and food visibility on the food-directed instrumental performance of obese individuals. Unpublished doctoral dissertation, Catholic University of America, 1970.

Krasne, F. B. Unpublished study cited in N. E. Miller, Some psycho-physiological studies of motivation and of the behavioural effects of illness. *Bulletin of the British Psychological Society*, 1964, *17*, 1–20.

Maren, T. H. Cited in J. L. Fuller & G. A. Jacoby, Central and sensory control of food intake in genetically obese mice. *American Journal of Physiology*, 1955, *183*, 279–283.

Miller, N. E. Some psycho-physiological studies of motivation and of the behavioural effects of illness. *Bulletin of the British Psychological Society*, 1964, *17*, 1–20.

Miller, N. E., Bailey, C. J., & Stevenson, J. A. F. Decreased "hunger" but increased food intake resulting from hypothalamic lesions. *Science*, 1950, *112*, 256–259.

Mrosovsky, N. *Hibernation and the hypothalamus.* New York: Appleton-Century-Crofts, 1971.

Nisbett, R. E. Determinants of food intake in human obesity. *Science*, 1968, *159*, 1254–1255. (a)

Nisbett, R. E. Taste, deprivation, and weight determinants of eating behavior. *Journal of Personality and Social Psychology*, 1968, *10*, 107–116. (b)

Nisbett, R. E. Eating and obesity in men and animals. In press, 1971.

Pliner, P. Effects of liquid and solid preloads on the
Brooks, C. McC., Lockwood, R. A., & Wiggins, M. L. A study of the effect of hypothalamic lesions on the eating habits of the albino rat. *American Journal of Physiology*, 1946, *147*, 735–741.

Bullen, B. A., Reed, R. B., & Mayer, J. Physical eating behavior of obese and normal persons. Unpublished doctoral dissertation, Columbia University, 1970.

Rabin, B. M., & Smith, C. J. Behavioral comparison of the effectiveness of irritative and non-irritative lesions in producing hypothalamic hyperphagia. *Physiology and Behavior*, 1968, *3*, 417–420.

Reeves, A. G., & Plum, F. Hyperphagia, rage, and dementia accompanying a ventromedial hypothalamic neoplasm. *Archives of Neurology*, 1969, *20*, 616–624.

Reynolds, R. W. Ventromedial hypothalamic lesions with hyperphagia. *American Journal of Physiology*, 1963, *204*, 60–62.

Rodin, J. Effects of distraction on performance of obese and normal subjects. Unpublished doctoral dissertation, Columbia University, 1970.

Ross, L. D. Cue- and cognition-controlled eating among obese and normal subjects. Unpublished doctoral dissertation, Columbia University, 1969.

Schachter, S. The interaction of cognitive and physiological determinants of emotional state. In L. Berkowitz (Ed.), *Advances in experimental social psychology.* Vol. 1. New York: Academic Press, 1964.

Schachter, S. Cognitive effects on bodily functioning: Studies of obesity and eating. In D. C. Glass (Ed.), *Neurophysiology and emotion.* New York: Rockefeller University Press and Russell Sage Foundation, 1967.

Schachter, S. Obesity and eating. *Science*, 1968, *161*, 751–756.

Schachter, S. *Emotion, obesity, and crime.* New York: Academic Press, 1971.

Schachter, S., Goldman, R., & Gordon, A. Effects of fear, food deprivation, and obesity on eating. *Journal of Personality and Social Psychology*, 1968, *10*, 91–97.

Singh, D. Comparison of hyperemotionality caused by lesions in the septal and ventromedial hypothalamic areas in the rat. *Psychonomic Science*, 1969, *16*, 3–4.

Stellar, E. The physiology of motivation. *Psychological Review*, 1954, *61*, 5–22.

Stunkard, A., & Koch, C. The interpretation of gastric motility: I. Apparent bias in the reports of hunger by obese persons. *Archives of General Psychiatry*, 1964, *11*, 74–82.

Teitelbaum, P. Sensory control of hypothalamic hyperphagia. *Journal of Comparative and Physiological Psychology*, 1955, *48*, 156–163.

Teitelbaum, P. Random and food-directed activity in hyperphagic and normal rats. *Journal of Comparative and Physiological Psychology*, 1957, *50*, 486–490.

Teitelbaum, P., & Campbell, B. A. Ingestion patterns in hyperphagic and normal rats. *Journal of Comparative and Physiological Psychology*, 1958, *51*, 135–141.

Turner, S. G., Sechzer, J. A., & Liebelt, R. A. Sensitivity to electric shock after ventromedial hypothalamic lesions. *Experimental Neurology*, 1967, *19*, 236–244.

PART V
social problems

Society does not respond in equally benign ways to different kinds of deviance. The odd behavior of a highly creative person may be tolerated, but the hallucinating and delusional psychotic arouses the community's concern, sometimes to the point where he is institutionalized involuntarily. Even though this kind of societal decision seems to be punitive, the personal and interpersonal problems with which Part IV dealt frequently evoke sympathy from most people. Involuntary commitment is almost always rationalized as being in the patient's best interests. Another type of deviance, criminal behavior, is treated more harshly than "mental illness." The convicted criminal is imprisoned for a designated time, the length of which depends mainly upon the act he committed.

Recent years have seen a movement to treat criminals more therapeutically and less punitively. There is far from complete agreement about what constitutes (or should constitute) a crime against society and about what punishment should be meted out to the criminal. Differences of opinion are especially noticeable in cases of "crimes" that may not directly harm others and that are carried out by consenting adults—e.g., gambling, use of marijuana and other illegal substances, homosexuality.

Traditionally, these deviations from community norms have tended to fall within the domain of the sociologist; now, psychologists are directing their attention increasingly to the personal and societal problems that arise when a person's behavior conflicts either with laws or with social mores. In addition to dealing with these deviations, many behavioral scientists are paying more attention to the analysis of society as a product of mutually influencing systems. Thus, the psychologist interested in intelligence cannot ignore the relationship between socioeconomic deprivation and poor intellectual performance. Similarly, the relationships between poverty, overcrowding, aggression depicted in the mass media, and violence are of interest to the student of criminal behavior.

Psychological study of deviations from societal laws and mores takes many directions, and the methods employed can be experimental, developmental, or clinical. The research reported by Mary Cover Jones grew out of an ambitious, long-term developmental project, the Oakland Growth Study. Jones classified the female members of this longitudinal study on the basis of their drinking behavior. Their youthful and adult personality characteristics were assessed psychologically and inquiry was made into the similarities and differences between women who were problem drinkers and those for whom drinking posed no problems. Among the findings were certain similarities between the two extremes in the samples—the problem drinkers and total abstainers. Many significant differences were observed between heavy drinkers and those whose intake of alcohol was more moderate.

The subjects in the Oakland Growth Study were first contacted as children;

at that time, of course, investigators could not envision that the study would yield data and conclusions about the psychological development of drinking problems. Only later did this focus develop. One great advantage of longitudinal studies is that they permit researchers to investigate correlations between behavior in childhood and in adulthood. In this way, they provide an empirical basis for studies of the antecedents of both adaptive and maladaptive behavior.

It is one thing for a person to have a drinking problem and quite another for him to be an alcoholic, a heavy drinker who is unable to maintain himself socially and vocationally. Mills, Sobell, and Schaefer studied a group of thirteen hospitalized male alcoholics, men whose extensive drinking habits had caused them to be institutionalized. Whereas the Jones study exemplifies the developmental approach to behavior, the Mills, Sobell, and Schaefer research was experimental in character. Each subject in the experiment participated voluntarily in experiments designed to modify his drinking behavior—but not by the traditional method of total abstinence. Many nondrinking alcoholics (for example, members of Alcoholics Anonymous) eschew alcohol in any form or amount. Mills, Sobell, and Schaefer sought to replace the alcoholics' habit of drinking straight liquor in large gulps and large amounts with the habits of more acceptable social drinkers —drinking mixed drinks in small amounts. The method selected to achieve this end involved application of basic principles of conditioning and learning. The results suggest that a significant percentage of alcoholics can learn to moderate their drinking practices. As the researchers make clear, their pilot investigation requires additional experimental verification; moreover, social drinking habits acquired in the laboratory must be shown to generalize beyond the laboratory.

Homosexuality, like alcoholism, is a social deviation, but it evokes distinctive reactions from society and from clinical workers. In recent years society has shown an increased willingness to tolerate homosexual behavior between consenting adults when conducted discreetly and privately. Nevertheless, intriguing psychological questions remain: Do homosexuals differ from heterosexuals in their life histories and personal characteristics? Is homosexuality the surface manifestation of a basic weakness in personality? What are the causes of homosexuality? As the article by Ray Evans and the commentaries by Ralph Gundlach and Evelyn Hooker reveal, no small amount of controversy concerns how these questions might best be approached and answered. In his research Evans obtained restrospective self-reports regarding childhood fears and activities, parent-child relationships, and relationships between parents. He found many significant differences between homosexual and heterosexual men.

Research methods are also of interest in these studies. Evans, Gundlach, and Hooker each deal with the close relationship between the results of research and the methodology upon which the results are based. Hooker's comments make especially clear that while it is "results" that count, the "results" may be confusing or meaningless if inappropriate research procedures are employed.

The Vaillant and Nowlis articles treat yet another social deviation, the use of illegal drugs. George Vaillant, integrating the empirical evidence extant, reconstructs the natural history of the narcotic addict with special reference to his rehabilitation. In the process, he uncovers a number of differences between addicts who achieved lasting abstinence and those who did not. Vaillant argues persuasively that, despite speculation about basic defects in the addict's personality, the addict's most outstanding characteristics are his inability to obtain stable jobs, loneliness, and poor interpersonal relationships. Noting the relative lack of success of traditional psychiatric approaches to drug addiction, Vaillant stresses the need to help the addict achieve vocational independence and alternatives to his solitary social existence.

When Helen Nowlis' article was written, a great many people were intensely concerned about the "drug problem" on high school and college campuses throughout the United States. Nowlis presents a reasoned response to this concern. She makes clear the need, first, to define terms such as "drugs" and "drug abuse"; then she points out that the actual "drug problem" may not be so great as the public fears. Beyond these considerations, she stresses the need for well-controlled experiments to determine the effects of different drugs on behavior. The same quantity of a substance—marijuana, for instance—may lead to quite different behaviors in people who have different expectations about the drug's effects. From a psychological standpoint, drug usage poses several important problems. These include not only the effects on behavior of specific drugs administered in specified amounts but also social attitudes toward drugs and public understanding of them.

Human aggression, like drug-taking, may give rise to a variety of opinions among a pluralistic population. Aggression plays a role in family relationships, children's play activities, disputes among groups within a community, and conflicts among nations. Seymour Feshbach's paper on aggression aims at an understanding of violent acts committed by individuals, but it has implications for conflicts and conflict resolutions on a broader social scene. Feshbach emphasizes the need for theoretical and methodological advances in the effort to determine the causes of aggression and the evaluations of aggressive behavior made by different groups within society.

The contribution the psychologist might make to resolving social conflict is implicit in Stanley Lehmann's view of community psychology. Clinicians who work with disturbed people commonly recognize that their behavior may have been caused, to a significant degree, by social forces at work in the community. Artificial distinctions, Lehmann notes, have sometimes been drawn between the individual and his social environment. He suggests that the student of maladaptive behavior go beyond simply recognizing the potency of community variables; he provides a number of examples to support the psychologist's efforts to influence both the community in which he lives and the pluralistic society of which the community is part. Because clinicians are becoming more interested and involved in community problems, the future is likely to see increasing inquiry into problems at the borderline between abnormal psychology and social psychology.

The final article in this anthology gives a provocative picture of the psychologist who contributes to his community's effectiveness and well-being. Beier, Robinson, and Micheletti describe how psychologists helped a community, Susanville, to help itself in creating needed mental health services. Community members, both adults and high school students, were trained to work with families who were experiencing significant stresses and whose children had problems in school. Professional psychologists trained nonprofessional citizens in a variety of clinical skills—how to listen attentively to a person's account of his life stresses, how to show empathy toward him, and how to respond therapeutically to his problems. Beier, Robinson, and Micheletti's community case study is encouraging because it suggests one way of overcoming the current shortage of professionally trained mental health workers. Beyond that, it shows the community-oriented psychologist in action.

personality antecedents and correlates of drinking patterns in women

Mary Cover Jones

A survey of current drinking practices (Jones, 1968) of members of the Oakland Growth Study (Jones, 1938; Jones, Macfarlane, & Eichorn, 1960), now in their late forties, has been the basis of an analysis of concomitant adult psychological variables and of antecedent childhood social and personality factors associated with various adult alcohol-related classifications. On a number of variables, including socioeconomic status, intelligence, and adjustment, no significant differences have been found between the original and the follow-up sample (Haan, 1962).

Information was obtained in a home interview (or in the case of distant members, by mail questionnaire) as to age and circumstances of first use of alcohol, present consumption in terms of amount and frequency, the perceived effects of drinking, the purposes and functions of alcohol use for the individual, the drinking behavior of parents, spouse, friends, and children, and attitudes toward drinking including concern about drinking and driving, and compulsive and excessive drinking.

DRINKING CLASSIFICATIONS

The recent interview data are the principal basis used for drinking classification. However, alcohol-related information obtained on two previous occasions was considered: (*a*) the physician's record in answer to the question, "How much do you drink?" asked when the study members were 33 years old; and (*b*) a question imbedded among others pertaining to present and past health, vocation, and family on an intensive interview schedule at age 38: "How do you feel about drinking?" (The interviewer probed for amount and frequency.) Records for more than 100 individuals were included in the study. Six judges helped with the classification of the data, four of these were involved in drinking practices research, two were familiar with the Ss as well as with the drinking information.[1] For this report, individuals were classified into one of five amount–frequency categories: problem drinkers, heavy drinkers, moderate drinkers, light drinkers, nondrinkers or abstainers.

Problem drinkers were defined as those who had created problems for themselves, their families, or their employers by drinking excessively. Abstainers were those who never drink. For comparative purposes, heavy, moderate, and light drinkers were classified on the amount they drank and the frequency of drinking occasions. Thus heavy drinkers tended to describe themselves as drinking every day or nearly every day. They usually had two or more drinks on these occasions. Light drinkers described themselves as drinking seldom and in small amounts. Moderate drinkers, the largest subsample, fell between the heavy and light drinkers. The patterns of drinking are representative of the age, sex, cultural, and economic

Most of the work on the research reported here was done while the author was a staff member of the Cooperative Commission on the Study of Alcoholism, Nevitt Sanford, Scientific Director. The research was supported by the National Institute of Mental Health Small Grant MH-08684-01. The author wishes to express appreciation to staff and study members of the University of California Institute of Human Development, Oakland Growth Study, for the use of data collected over the past 37 years.

[1] The writer is indebted to Genevieve Knupfer and members of the California Drinking Practices Study, the late E. M. Jellinek, Louis Stewart, and Fred Strassberger, for their assistance in classifying the Ss.

status described in larger survey samples (Cahalan, Cisen, & Crossley, 1967; Knupfer & Room, 1964).

The following excerpts from the women's interview statements illustrate the kind of individual who was judged to belong to each of the drinking categories:

Problem drinker: These last years I have just gone on in alcoholism. I can drink a fifth, without even stopping when I hit the bottle.

Heavy drinker: I like to drink, several drinks before dinner, five to six drinks on a social evening. I've been drunk but never so drunk I didn't know what was going on. I've never passed out but I've been sick.

Moderate drinker: I drink moderately. I stop when I feel woozy, at most three before dinner. I like to have control.

Light drinker: I don't give a hoot for a drink. I don't enjoy it. Occasionally, I have a highball to keep a friend or husband company.

Abstainer: I don't think smoking is absolutely immoral but I think drinking is. You can understand with all the difficulty I had with drinking in the family how I feel about it.

Drinking behavior can be classified in a number of ways. An attempt was made to characterize drinking practices in terms that are theoretically significant and of practical importance.

However, psychologically meaningful categories, for example, the reasons given for drinking, have been less productive of relationships with the available social and personality variables than the more objective quantity–frequency measures based on actual drinking behavior. This may illustrate the fact that, as in many other areas, behavior reflects attitudes and may be more correctly reported. "Actions speak louder than words," and it may be this indirect expression of subjective attitudes which our quantity–frequency categories are measuring. Reasons for drinking vary considerably from one situation to another, and people find it difficult to evaluate their motives. Moreover, the heaviest drinkers give the greatest number of seemingly unrelated reasons for drinking. This presents difficulties when analysis of drinking behavior is attempted, in terms of purpose and function for the individual.

BACKGROUND DATA

Retrospective reports indicate that more women than men had their first taste of alcohol under approved circumstances, usually in the family setting. On the average, they also had this taste at an earlier age than boys. As in other studies of alcohol-related behavior, fewer women report problems with drinking. More women are light drinkers or abstainers. This presumably can be related to the way in which drinking behavior was learned as well as to cultural expectations. In this group, many girls reacted to a parent who overindulged in alcohol by abstaining with disapproval in their youth. They become light drinkers in their forties if their social group (and especially the spouse) set the drinking pattern. There is some evidence in our case histories that the effect of parental drinking is greater on children of the opposite sex. Since more fathers than mothers are reported to have drinking problems, the father–daughter link is more frequent in our material. Mothers' rated characteristics are more closely associated with the later drinking habits of boys. For both sexes, the mothers of problem drinkers are rated as less satisfied with life, less mentally alert, less agreeable. But the mothers of boys in this category are, in addition, rated as less interested in their sons, more fatigued, listless, and dull (Jones, 1965).

Although sex differences in drinking behavior have been found for this sample, they are not as great as reported in most studies. This may be because of the fact that these study members are preponderantly urban, middle class, and middle aged. In addition, the home interview in which information was obtained by an interviewer who had known the Ss for more than 30 years encouraged frank discussion. Studies of alcoholism show that the sex ratio is influenced by the framework of inquiry. For example, in data from a private physician's office, the ratio of women to men problem drinkers is 1 to 3; in hospitals, only 1 to 6; in police custody, only 1 to 11 (Keller & Efron, 1955).

SOURCES OF DATA

We turn now to the sources of the adolescent personality and behavior data. One instrument, Block's (1961) California Q set, provided ratings for three periods; junior high school years, senior

TABLE 1.   Ratings of Mothers—Problem Drinkers versus Others

Characteristic	Men			Women		
	Problem Drinkers	Others	p <	Problem Drinkers	Others	p <
Intelligence	38	32	.10	34	34	ns
Alertness	43	34	.05	36	37	ns
Speed of mental processes	41	33	.05	31	36	ns
Accuracy of thinking	38	35	ns	39	32	.10
Use of language	38	32	.05	38	38	ns
Comprehension of the study	44	30	.01	36	33	ns
Curiosity about the study	45	35	.05	40	35	ns
Satisfaction with lot in life	42	34	.10	45	22	.10
Interest in child	38	30	.05	33	30	ns
Energy output	45	34	.01	29	35	ns
Freshness-fatigue	41	32	.05	40	40	ns
Cheerful	40	34	.10	36	35	ns
Personal appearance	40	28	.05	44	32	.01
Pleasant expression	43	32	.05	43	31	.05

Note: Standard scores based on the total sample. A low score shows a high degree of the trait.

high school years, and adulthood. Separate interpersonal Q sorts were also used on the junior and senior high school levels to cover relationships to adults and peers.[2] The ratings for the junior high school and for the senior high school periods are the combined judgments of three psychologists who independently assessed the extensive data collected during the early or the middle adolescent years. These included periodic measurements of interests, attitudes, and physical and mental abilities, as well as projective tests and personality inventories. Family background information, classmates' impressions, original compositions, and counselor's interviews were also available. Some sources of data such as observational ratings in natural social settings were withheld for purposes of validation. Adult ratings, based on a series of intensive interviews, were made by the interviewer and at least one other psychologist who read the series of interview protocols.

Q-SET FINDINGS

The global approach represented by the Q-set ratings is an attempt to reduce to manageable dimensions the diverse and repeatedly measured variables of longitudinal studies. They have served the drinking practices research well. Agreement and continuity was high for separate measures and over time. The cohorts in various adult drinking categories are differentiated by a core of traits

which are discernible to raters in the early adolescent period.

Tables 2 through 6[3] present samples of data analysis based on the Q-set ratings.

Problem Drinkers and Abstainers

One unexpected finding is that women problem drinkers and women abstainers are more similar than other groups on a number (38) of the 100 standard Q-sort items. Some qualities which women problem drinkers and nondrinkers are judged to have in common suggest inadequate coping devices. The group of items in Table 2 are samples from 25 such ratings which describe problem drinkers and abstainers at the adult level. Many of these have been similarly assessed at earlier age periods. They are self-defeating, vulnerable, pessimistic, withdrawn; they feel guilty, somatize, and project feelings. They are less productive, incisive, independent, and self-satisfied with fewer interests and with lower aspiration levels than normal drinkers. Emotional inadequacies are suggested in their fluctuating moods, anxiety, irritability, and inability to relax.

Although other-directed (Table 3), their behavior would seem to present obstacles to interpersonal associations since they are judged to be sensitive to criticism, judgmental, distrustful, hostile, inexpressive, lacking in generosity, charm, social presence, and perceptiveness. Such qualities as these which are noted in the junior and senior

[2] The author wishes to thank Jack Block and Norma Haan for their generosity in providing the Q-set data.

[3] The author appreciates the contribution of Norman Livson who suggested the format for the tables.

TABLE 2. Comparisons Among Drinking Categories: Coping Items

	Drinking Classification				
Classification	Problem	Heavy	Moderate	Light	Nondrinker
Problem	(3)				
Heavy	Self-defeating (J, A*) Vulnerable (J, S, A*) Pessimistic (J*, A**) Withdrawn (J)	(12)		Self-defeating (J**) Vulnerable (J*) Pessimistic (J**, A**)	Self-defeating (J*, A*) Vulnerable (J, S*) Pessimistic (J, A*) Withdrawn (S, A**)
Moderate	Self-defeating (A**) Vulnerable (A) Pessimistic (A**) Withdrawn (A**)	Self-defeating (S*, A)	(18)	Self-defeating (J) Vulnerable (J*) Pessimistic (J*, A*)	Self-defeating (A*) Vulnerable (J*, S) Pessimistic (S*, A**) Withdrawn (S*)
Light	Self-defeating (A) Vulnerable (A**) Withdrawn (A*)			(8)	Vulnerable (A)
Nondrinker	Withdrawn (A)				(4)

Note: Items below the diagonal are more characteristic of those who drink more; above, of those who drink less in the groups being compared. Items are from either the California Q set at three age levels—Junior High (J), Senior High (S), and Adult (A)—or from the Interpersonal Q set (Junior and Senior High only).

The *N* for each group is in the diagonal cell.

*p < .05.

**p < .01.

school years are more numerous and differentiating at the adult level.

In the case of future problem drinkers, we assume that excessive drinking is one way of mitigating feelings of despondency and inadequacy. Some of the future women abstainers, who in some respects present a similar personality picture, may be reflecting the effect of parental drinking problems in their adolescent years. We know that those who had parents with drinking problems often grew up in economically deprived families. They spent less time in social groups of peers. As adults they tell us they felt ashamed of the excessively drinking parent.

However, there are some qualities which women nondrinkers have and excessive drinkers do not. In these we may find the reason of their radically different approach to alcohol. The former are judged to be responsible, conventional, consistent, ethical, and emotionally controlled. They are also able to accept a dependency relationship at an age when this may be a determining ingredient

TABLE 3. Comparisons Among Drinking Categories: Interpersonal Items

	Drinking Classification				
Classification	Problem	Heavy	Moderate	Light	Nondrinker
Problem	(3)				
Heavy	Other-directed (J*,S) Sensitive (J*, A**) Judgmental (J**, S)	(12)	Judgmental (S*)	Sensitive (J*) Judgmental (S**)	Sensitive (A*)
Moderate	Other-directed (J*) Sensitive (J) Judgmental (J)	Other-directed (J*)	(18)		Sensitive (A)
Light	Other-directed (J) Sensitive (J*, A) Judgmental (J*)	Other-directed (J**)		(8)	Sensitive (A*)
Nondrinker	Sensitive (J) Judgmental (J*)				(4)

Note: Items below the diagonal are more characteristic of those who drink more; above, of those who drink less in the groups being compared. Items are from either the California Q set at three age levels—Junior High (J), Senior High (S), and Adult (A)—or from the Interpersonal Q set (Junior and Senior High only).

The *N* for each group is in the diagonal cell.

*p < .05.

**p < .01.

TABLE 4.   Comparisons Among Drinking Categories: Authority Relationships

	Drinking Classification				
Classification	Problem	Heavy	Moderate	Light	Nondrinker
Problem	(3)				Submissive (S**) Accepts dependency (S)
Heavy	Rebellious (A*) Pseudo-compliant (S) Submissive (S**)	(12)	Pseudo-compliant (S*) Submissive (J*, S*) Accepts dependency (S)	Pseudo-compliant (J) Submissive (J, S) Accepts dependency (S)	Submissive (S*) Accepts dependency (S*)
Moderate	Rebellious (A**) Submissive (J, S)	Rebellious (S*) (18)		Pseudo-compliant (J*)	Pseudo-compliant (J) Submissive (S*)
Light	Rebellious (A*)	Rebellious (S*)		(8)	
Nondrinker	Rebellious (J*, A*)				(4)

Note: Items below the diagonal are more characteristic of those who drink more; above, of those who drink less in the groups being compared. Items are from either the California Q set at three age levels—Junior High (J), Senior High (S), and Adult (A)—or from the Interpersonal Q set (Junior and Senior High only).

The N for each group is in the diagonal cell.

* $p < .05$.

** $p < .01$.

for mental health. Problem drinkers are judged to be submissive as youngsters, rebellious as adults.

Heavy Drinkers

Many studies of alcohol-related behavior concentrate on problem drinkers and on heavy drinkers in whose ranks the problems are assumed to generate. It is interesting, therefore, to analyze by means of Q-set ratings the characteristics of those who drink less than problem drinkers but more than moderate drinkers. They are labeled here as heavy drinkers.

The California Drinking Practices Study (Knup-

fer, Fink, Clark, & Goffman, 1963), an investigation which has used a representative Bay Area sample, designates as heavy drinkers on the amount–frequency continuum "those who drink nearly every day and once in a while three or more drinks at one time." For our Ss, the Q-sort descriptions are very different from those of problem drinkers or of moderate drinkers. They depict the woman who is sure of herself in an upper-middle-class social setting. She tends to be one who is upwardly mobile and says that she drinks more now than formerly because she can afford it. What was she like as an adolescent? This group had the highest ratings on such items as social skills, charm, poise, expressiveness, and

TABLE 5.   Comparisons Among Drinking Categories: Social Items

	Drinking Classification				
Classification	Problem	Heavy	Moderate	Light	Nondrinker
Problem	(3)	Condescending (J*, S*) Social skills (J**, S**, A*)	Social skills (J, A**)	Social skills (S, A**)	
Heavy		(12)			
Moderate		Condescending (J*, S*) Status-oriented (J*, S, A*)	(18)		
Light		Condescending (J**, S**) Social skills (J*, A*) Status-oriented (J*)	Social skills (J, A*)	(8)	
Nondrinker		Condescending (S**) Social skills (J*, S, A**) Status-oriented (S**)	Social skills (A*) Status-oriented (S)	Social skills (J*)	(4)

Note: Items below the diagonal are more characteristic of those who drink more; above, of those who drink less in the groups being compared. Items are from either the California Q set at three age levels—Junior High (J), Senior High (S), and Adult (A)—or from the Interpersonal Q set (Junior and Senior High only).

The N for each group is in the diagonal cell.

*$p < .05$.

**$p < .01$.

interest in the opposite sex. They were judged to be affected, self-indulgent, condescending, opportunistic, power oriented, self-satisfied, decisive, and histrionic. The group of items in Table 5 are illustrative.

Heavy drinkers tend to have low ratings on those items which characterize problem drinkers. They seem to use alcohol more for social than for compensatory purposes. As adolescents, they were significantly different from other categories of drinkers on the greatest number of ratings.

Moderate Drinkers

The items on which moderate drinkers, the classification next lower on the quantity scale, differ from other types, usually favor the former. They appear to be less glamorous and socially oriented

than heavy drinkers, but more likable with usefully adaptive behavior and a satisfactory self-image. They are judged to be sympathetic, straightforward, stable, natural, appealing, insightful, relaxed, productive, and modestly self-satisfied. There are 20 items which describe these women with significant differences for some categories including those positive attributes given above and the lack of handicapping attitudes and behaviors such as deceitfulness, hopelessness, negativism, concern with adequacy, or tendency to withdraw in adversity. Table 6 gives examples.

Light Drinkers

Light drinkers among women are described as most responsible, predictable, fastidious, and overcontrolled. They are least expressive, irritable,

TABLE 6. Comparisons Among Drinking Categories: Adaptive Behavior

Classifi-cation		Drinking Classification				
	Problem	Heavy	Moderate	Light	Nondrinker
Prob-lem	(3)	Wide interests (S*, A**)	Wide interests (S*, A**) Sympathetic (J*)	Wide interests (S, A) Sympathetic (A*)	Sympathetic (S**)
		Responsible (A**)	Responsible (A**)	Responsible (A**)	Responsible (A)
Heavy	Sympathetic (J, S) Arouses nurturance (S*)	(12)	Sympathetic (J*, S*) Arouses nurturance (J*)	Sympathetic (S*) Arouses nurturance (S*)	Sympathetic (S) Arouses nurturance (S*)
			Responsible (S*, A*)	Responsible (S*, A**)	Responsible (J, S*)
Moder-ate			(18)		
Light				(8)	
Non-drinker	Arouses nurturance (S*)	Wide interests (S, A*)	Wide interests (S*, A*)		(4)

Note: Items below the diagonal are more characteristic of those who drink more; above, of those who drink less in the groups being compared. Items are from either the California Q set at three age levels—Junior High (J), Senior High (S), and Adult (A)—or from the Interpersonal Q set (Junior and Senior High only).
The N for each group is in the diagonal cell.
*p < .05.
**p < .01.

and self-indulgent. They have some characteristics which suggest greater adaptability than have the abstainers. For example, they are rated as more self-defeating than moderate drinkers but as less vulnerable (Table 2) and less sensitive to criticism (Table 3) than abstainers. They are rated as less socially skillful, expressive, cheerful, and poised than heavy drinkers or moderates but more so than abstainers (Table 5). They were judged to have less prestige than the average girl among peers in junior high school. Some of the light drinkers are recruited from those who did not drink at all in the 1950s.

OTHER PREDICTIVE FINDINGS

The Q sorts have enabled us to simplify analysis of data and have facilitated comparisons at three age levels. Characterizations in the earliest of these, the junior high school period, have usually proved to be more differentiating of adult drinking patterns than have the intervening high school ratings.

The global approach which composites material from the three years of junior high school lacks certain subtleties. It tends to obscure the transition from childhood, which preponderantly described our seventh graders, to adolescence, which conspicuously transformed our Ss, especially the girls in the eighth grade.

Analysis of separate social and personality measures administered yearly show that eighth-grade measures relate more clearly to adult drinking behavior than do those of earlier or later years. For some purposes, this ability to pinpoint more precisely the predictive power of longitudinal data in terms of age and critical periods is important. The items in Table 7 present a capsule of findings.

CASE SUMMARIES

Perhaps more convincing than ratings are descriptive comments and clinical appraisals of individuals who, in meeting the changing demands of

adolescence, reveal tendencies which will later influence drinking habits. Case summaries based on longitudinal data such as were available for the Q sorts—observations of behavior, self-reports, parental and classmates' opinions—will serve to recapitulate the findings of this study. Individual study members were selected for these sketches because they portray the characteristics delineated for those in the drinking category to which they belong.

A problem drinker as typically described by the Q sort is the girl judged by a clinical psychologist to be

difficult to rate because of marked changes in the junior high school years. At 12 she is convinced that she is smart, attractive, well thought of. At 15 life is full of adolescent self-doubt and confusion. She fears and rejects life, is distrustful of people, follows a religion which accentu-

TABLE 7.   Observational Ratings of Junior High School (J) and Senior High School (S)

| | Drinking classification | | | | |
Classification	Problem	Heavy	Moderate	Light	Nondrinker
Problem	(3)	Expressive (J*) Attractive (J*, S**) Prestige (J*, S) Poise (J**) Buoyancy (J*	Buoyancy (J*)	Buoyancy (J*)	
Heavy		(12)			
Moderate		Attractive (S*)	(18)		
Light		Expressive (J**) Attractive (J**, S**) Poise (S) Buoyancy (S*)	Buoyancy (S*)	(8)	
Nondrinker		Expressive (J*) Attractive (J**, S**) Prestige (J**, S**) Poise (J*) Buoyancy (S*)	Prestige (J**)		(4)

Note: Items below the diagonal are more characteristic of those who drink more; above, of those who drink less in the groups being compared. Most significant differences in eighth grade.

The *N* for each group is in the diagonal cell.

*$p < .05$.

**$p < .01$.

ates judgment and punishment. She escapes into ultra femininity. This protective coloration will keep her going through the mating season but very likely she will recognize the emptiness and impotence in later years.

A heavy social drinker was seen in adolescence as unusually competent and popular in the social area but disturbed (as revealed by the Ror-

schach) under the excellently functioning surface. She is lacking in regard for others and bossy in an energetic and overpowering way; she competitively collects boys as reassurance to her self-esteem.

The summary for a moderate drinker begins:

the amazing thing about this girl is her competence in all spheres; socially, scholastically, artistically. She has had steady, consistent in-fluence and direction from her parents. [Moderate drinkers are judged to conceive of their parents as egalitarian and not conflicted.] She is socially comfortable, kindly to semi-outcasts, nurturant to younger children, gracious with adults, willing to let another take the lead. She takes it for granted that she is liked by boys and girls, not in a hurry to grow up, not boy crazy.

The author of this glowing account, from which this bit is an excerpt, is somewhat uneasy about so much adjustment. Maybe later she will rebel, it is suggested. Such has not been the case!

A light drinker is a girl who is described as well organized, practical, responsible, preoccupied by details; who tries hard but does not quite make the grade socially or intellectually. Her gauche behavior is acceptable to peers because it is coupled with an easy submissiveness and good nature. This girl whose father had a drinking problem is credited with a "fuzzy identity."

In keeping with ratings of abstainers as similar in some respects to problem drinkers, the core of this abstainer's personality is said to be

unquestioning and uncomplaining acceptance of her unimportance and inferiority. She is an old-fashioned neurotic, shy, submissive, with-drawn but cheerful, and friendly.

In view of her good intelligence, her rejection of ambitions is thought of as a waste. Unlike the problem drinker, this girl's qualities are of long standing and not related to an adolescent up-heaval. Her mature judgment is emphasized.

DISCUSSION

This analysis of antecedent and concomitant characteristics of women in relation to their alcohol consumption presents a somewhat different picture than do the findings for men.

In the first place, ratings for men who were problem drinkers differed at significant levels from other drinkers on 41 of 100 traits. For women there were 62 such differences in ratings, suggesting that women who drink excessively are more unlike the normal drinkers of their sex than are male problem drinkers unlike other men who drink. There are 10 characteristics which the problem drinkers of both sexes have in common. These are in the area of unstable, unpredictable

impulsivity. In the Oakland Growth Study sample, of the 20 characteristics attributed to women who drink excessively but not to men who do, the preponderance indicate depressive, self-negating, distrustful tendencies. These qualities are frequently reported in the research literature (e.g., Wines & Edwards, 1964).

Another sex difference in the Oakland Growth Study data is in the relationship between the cohorts in the various drinking classifications. For men there was a decided ordinal trend in scores from problem drinkers through heavy, moderate, and light drinkers to abstainers. The ordinal relationship obtained in 49% of the 100 Q-sort items (Jones, 1968). In general, this means that men in each category rather than displaying unique attributes were frequently judged merely to have more or less of a given characteristic than did those in adjoining categories. On the other hand, for women some distinctive personality syndromes were observed for each category of drinker in early adolescence and continuing into adulthood. This is true especially of the status-oriented heavy drinkers and the "wholesome" moderate drinkers. The similarity between problem drinkers and abstainers among women further disrupts the ordinal trend predominantly found in the data for men.

The circumstances under which drinking is initiated, permitted, and encouraged have some bearing on the drinking patterns which are established in later life. The tendency noted in the literature on this subject—for boys to have their initial drinking experience in less acceptable social situations than girls—is substantiated in the Oakland Growth Study data. Because of early protective experiences and sex differences in cultural sanctions, fewer women than men in this representative sample became problem drinkers. But those who did were judged to suffer profound emotional disturbance and social isolation. The similarity in ratings between problem drinkers and abstainers may be due, as indicated earlier, to the fact that women abstainers more than men seem to have been seriously marked by early unfavorable family situations in which a parent, particularly the father, drank excessively. The characteristics ascribed to women abstainers suggest that abstinence is rather specific to drinking behavior rather than an integrated pattern of negation and over-control. (Their average rating on control was lower than that of moderate drinkers and not significantly different from the score for problem drinkers.)

The personality characteristics associated with

drinking patterns in the Oakland Growth Study sample of women may not be representative of a universal population of drinkers. However, the behaviors associated with the various drinking categories show some common sense and psychological validity.

Alcohol-related behavior is associated in complex ways with other aspects of an individual's living pattern, personality, and life history. Longitudinal studies are essential if we wish to trace the connection between adult drinking behaviors and early tendencies which were formed before the drinking mode has been established. This paper suggests that alcohol-related behavior may be partly predicted from early personality characteristics. It offers the hope that positive mental health approaches instituted in the youthful, formative years may reduce the need for irresponsible drinking and facilitate the development of controlled drinking habits.

REFERENCES

Block, J. *The Q-sort method of personality assessment and psychiatric research.* Springfield, Ill: Charles C. Thomas, 1961.

Cahalan, D., Cisen, I., & Crossley, H. M. *American drinking practices. A national survey of behavior and attitudes related to alcoholic beverages.* (Report No. 3, Social Research Group) Washington, D. C.: George Washington University, 1967.

Haan, N. Some comparisons of various Oakland Growth Study subsamples on selected variables. Unpublished manuscript, University of California, Institute of Human Development. Berkeley, 1962.

Jones, H. E. The California adolescent growth study. *Journal of Educational Research,* 1938, *31,* 561–567.

Jones, H. E., Macfarlane, J. W., & Eichorn, D. H. A progress report on growth studies at the University of California. *Vita Humana,* 1960, *3,* 17–31.

Jones, M. C. Correlates and antecedents of adult drinking patterns. Paper presented at the meeting of the Western Psychological Association, Honolulu, June 1965.

Jones, M. C. Personality correlates and antecedents of drinking patterns in adult males. *Journal of Consulting and Clinical Psychology,* 1968, *32,* 2–12.

Keller, M., & Efron, V. The prevalence of alcoholism. *Quarterly Journal of Studies on Alcohol,* 1935, *16,* 317–319.

Knupfer, G., Fink, R., Clark, W. B., & Goffman, A. S. *Factors related to amount of drinking in an urban community. The California drinking practices study.* (Report No. 6, Division of Alcoholic Rehabilitation) Berkeley: California State Department of Public Health, 1963.

Knupfer, G., & Room, R. Age, sex and social class as factors in amount of drinking in a metropolitan community. *Social Problems,* 1964, *21,* 224–240.

Wines, D. B., & Edwards, A. E. Intemperance: Psychological and sociological concomitants. *Quarterly Journal of Studies on Alcohol,* 1964, *25,* 79–84.

training social drinking as an alternative to abstinence for alcholics

Kenneth C. Mills, Mark B. Sobell, & Halmuth H. Schaefer

Thirteen hospitalized male alcoholics volunteered as subjects for a study to explore whether bar drinking habits typical of alcoholics (drinking straight liquor in large gulps and large amounts) could be changed to bar drinking habits typical of social drinkers (drinking mixed drinks in small sips and small amounts). During experimental drinking sessions in an especially equipped bar the subjects could avoid shock by drinking like a typical social drinker but received painful electric fingershock, 30% above or at individual pain threshold, whenever they behaved like alcoholics. The conditioning contingencies were explained to the subjects before the beginning of the experiment.

Four of the subjects emitted the required behavioral repertoire in an exaggerated fashion from the first day of drinking: they never ordered more than three mixed drinks, and consumed these in exceedingly small sips (30 or more). The remaining nine subjects learned these behaviors over a period of 12–14 sessions. No attempt was made to establish the generalization of this newly acquired behavior after discharge from the hospital. The implications of the findings are discussed.

As with many areas of behavior not previously studied in measurable detail, alcoholism research is hindered by certain implicit assumptions which, despite being unproven, place severe limits on the kinds of operations one can credibly use in experimental studies. This study was an attempt to examine the validity of two of these previously untested assumptions.

The first assumption about alcoholism, long perpetuated by Alcoholics Anonymous, is that, if the habitual drinker wishes to change his drinking pattern, *total* abstinence is the only possible alternative to total inebriation (Alcoholics Anony-

This investigation was supported in part by Public Health Service Grant 1RO1MH16547. The opinions or conclusions stated in this paper are those of the authors and are not to be construed as official or as necessarily reflecting the policy of the [California] Department of Mental Hygiene.

mous, 1955). Social or limited patterns of drinking have been mentioned as rehabilitative efforts in several case studies (Davies, 1962; Kendell, 1965; Bailey & Stewart, 1967; Glatt, 1964; Pattison, Headley, Gleser, & Gottschalk, 1968), but experimental data on social drinking as a possible alternative to abstinence are lacking.

The belief that an alcoholic cannot learn to become a social drinker is widely held by health professionals (Hayman, 1967), public organizations concerned with alcoholism, and by a great many alcoholics themselves. There are essentially three bases from which this belief stems: (1) alcoholism is regarded as a disease which, not unlike diabetes, leaves a human being unable to consume certain foods; (2) the drinking of alcohol, like all human actions, is subject to the will, and alcoholics simply do not have the will power to stop once they have started drinking; and (3) some

Reprinted by permission from C. Franks (Ed.) *Behavior Therapy*, Vol. 2. Academic Press, 1971, pp. 18–27.

alcoholics have actually tried to drink within socially accepted limits and failed.

Upon inspection, however, these bases are not sufficiently supported to prevent the questioning of this widely held belief. There is no evidence that alcoholism really is a disease in the sense in which diabetes is a disease; Skinner (1963) has argued most convincingly that the question of will is merely an unnecessary "waystation" in explaining behavior, and none of the alcoholics who tried social drinking without success reports the use of procedurally established methods of learning in his efforts.

In our culture, strong social pressure endorses drinking socially. This makes matters difficult for the abstaining alcoholic. However, an alcoholic who could successfully be a social drinker would not have to worry constantly that he may be forced into a position of either yielding to temptation or confessing his weaknesses to well-meaning friends. Such a confession may impose strained social relationships between the alcoholic and his friends. Also, the social pressures urging drinking which exist in western society are such that abstinence often requires an unnecessarily restricted selection of friends.

The second new mode of attack derives from a related assumption implicit to the methodology of experimental studies dealing with aversive events and their effects on drinking behavior (e.g., Blake, 1967; Vogler, Post, Johnson, Lunde, & Martin, 1969; Bandura, 1969). Many of these studies use the application of an aversive stimulus (drugs, shock, etc.) designed to suppress on-going drinking activity, with abstinence being the only available escape response. To the authors' knowledge, no study provides the subject with an avoidance situation in which he can perform some socially acceptable alternative drinking response to heavy drinking.

The present study attempted to widen the range of goals and treatment for the chronic alcoholic by providing social (limited) drinking as an acceptable avoidance response to aversive stimuli in a setting previously associated with excessive drinking. It was designed to change three important drinking characteristics of alcoholics so as to be more like the drinking behavior of social drinkers. A previous study (Schaefer, Sobell, & Mills, 1970) indicated that alcoholics differ from social drinkers in at least three quantifiable ways which allow experimental differential reinforcement: (1) The alcoholic typically has a significant preference for straight drinks rather than mixed drinks. (2)

The alcoholic consumes his drinks by gulping rather than sipping; i.e., taking large quantities (1 oz) in any one swallow rather than "nursing a drink." (3) The alcoholic continues to drink well beyond the stage at which the social drinker would have stopped.

The subjects were given alcohol in an experimental bar environment. Undesirable behaviors such as gulping, drinking straight drinks, or excessive drinking were punished on an avoidance schedule of shock reinforcement. The desirable behaviors of sipping, drinking mixed drinks, and limited ordering were successful means for avoiding certain contingencies of shock.

METHOD

Subjects

Thirteen male patients who had been voluntarily admitted to Patton State Hospital for treatment of alcoholism served as subjects for this study. Each patient was a chronic alcoholic and had experienced some sort of withdrawal symptom while in the process of "drying out." Withdrawal symptoms ranged from shakes to convulsions and delirium tremens. The mean age of the subjects was 47.5 years. Each patient had a record of prior hospitalization with a mean number of 6.4 past admissions to either public or private institutions for treatment of alcoholism. The patients had educations ranging from 9 years of grade school to 2 years of college, with a mean of 11.07 years. The average length of stay in the hospital was 63 days. All met the following criteria: (1) No evidence of physical illness at the time of the study. (2) No evidence of poor liver function or erratic EKG. (3) No use of medication concurrent with the study. (4) Not on any other alcoholism program at the time of the study. (5) No evidence of drug addiction. (6) No consumption of alcoholic beverages for a minimum time of 2 weeks before the start of the study. (7) All patients given clearance to participate by the unit psychiatrist.

Apparatus

All subjects lived on an open ward which had facilities for 34 patients. The remaining beds were filled by other patients not on the research program. In the center of the ward was a day hall that had been converted into a cocktail lounge and bar. The room included a padded and varnished serving bar, bar stools, a bottle display behind the bar complete with a full length mirror, diffuse lighting, and a refrigerator to store ice, beer, wine, and soft drinks. Music was available upon request. Subjects reported that the bar simulated so-called neighborhood bars relatively well. An available stock of alcoholic beverages of all kinds was supplied by the Alcoholic Beverage Commission of the State of California.

Located on the underside of the bar were two electrical outlets separated from each other by approximately 26 in., into which a cord terminating in a set of finger electrodes could be plugged. Next to each receptacle and about 18 in. away was a toggle switch which controlled high, low, or no shock output through the receptacle. Additional toggle switches on the bartender's side of the bar were wired in parallel with the switches on the customer's side of the bar allowing the bartender also to deliver shocks to the subjects. Two shock generators (Foringer, voltage attenuated maximum output 800 V ac, 10 mA), as well as equipment for timing and programming shock, were located in an adjacent room. In addition, the experimenter could monitor from the control room all activity and conversation in the bar by means of remote controlled microphones and closed circuit television.

Procedure

All subjects were given a complete explanation of the contingencies in effect before the first session. They were seen in pairs and sat next to one another at the bar, each directly in front of an electrode receptacle. Using electrode jelly to increase conductance, finger electrodes were attached to the thumb and ring finger of the patient's nondominant hand. All subjects were instructed to keep both their hands within view of the bartender–experimenter during the experiment. Female assistants sat on bar stools next to each subject during most sessions of the experiment and administered required shock. If, for some reason, one or both of the assistants could not be present, shock was administered by the bartender. Either the bartender or various assistants in the bar recorded the type and number of drinks ordered for each subject, the number of sips per drink, the number of gulps per drink, and the number of high and low intensity shocks received.

A rough index of shock tolerance was obtained for each patient at the start of the first session. Subjects typically reported their pain threshold to be somewhere between 30–60% of maximum output of the shock generator.

Two levels of electric shock (1.5 sec duration) were used. Low shock was just above the pain threshold. High shock was 30% above pain threshold and, naturally, could not exceed 100%

output of the 800-V generator. Both shock levels were obtained from the same shock generator by wiring a 100-K variable resistor in series with the generator. Pushing a toggle switch upward activated a high shock level output, pushing the same switch downward activated the low level shock by routing the generator output through the variable resistor. Shock was delivered according to the avoidance schedule shown in Table 1. Socially acceptable drinking

TABLE 1. Shock Contingencies During Sessions

Shock Intensity	Drinks No. 1-3	Drinks No. 4-5
Strong	Orders straight drink and gulps	Orders or consumes any alcoholic beverage
Mild	Either orders straight drink and sips or orders mixed drink and gulps	
None	Orders mixed drink and sips	Orders nonalcoholic beverage

was defined as ordering mixed drinks, sipping the drinks, and consuming a maximum equivalent of 3 fluid oz of 86 proof liquor. During the first three drinks of a session, the intensity of a given shock was a function of two variables under the patient's control: the kind of drink ordered (mixed or straight) and the way in which it was drunk (gulped or sipped). Beer and wine were considered to be mixed drinks. A sip was considered to be approximately 1/7 of the total volume of the drink and consumption of any volume greater than this was considered to be a gulp. When the subject exhibited two inappropriate drinking behaviors: namely, ordering a straight drink and gulping that drink, he then received a high intensity shock immediately following the gulp. If he emitted only one inappropriate drinking behavior, i.e., sipping a straight drink or gulping a mixed drink, he received low intensity shocks. When he sipped a mixed drink, he avoided all shock. After three drinks, a new contingency was in effect and the patient now had the option of ordering an additional fourth and fifth drink under the following conditions: in early sessions, the bartender asked the subject if he would like another drink. If the subject replied "yes," he then received a full intensity shock, however, he was served the drink which he had ordered. From then until the end of the session, the subject received 100% intensity shock from the time his hand touched the glass until the time he released the glass. If he consumed a fourth drink, he was then offered a fifth drink by the bartender, and the shock contingencies applied to the fourth drink were repeated.

There was a graded increase in the amount of social pressure put on the patient to order a fourth and fifth drink by the bartender and other persons in the cocktail lounge: (1) in early sessions he was merely asked if he wanted another drink and verbal refusal was sufficient to terminate the session, (2) in later sessions, after he had verbally refused an additional drink, the bartender and other persons in the bar prompted him to accept another drink with statements such as, "oh come on, one more won't hurt you," and finally, (3) if he refused to order additional drinks, a drink was poured for him and the session was only terminated after the subject left the bar without consuming the drink.

The criterion for increasing social pressure on the patient to take an additional drink was his successful refusal of additional drinks for 2 consecutive days. Whenever he successfully refused either to order or consume a drink he was verbally praised by the bartender and others in the bar.

If, at any time, the electric shocks at the intensity level being used did not seem to elicit characteristic aversive responses from the patient, the shock level was raised by 10% increments until such responses were obvious. This was a necessary manipulation as some subjects had significant day-to-day variations in skin resistance. There were a total of 14 experimental sessions, each having a maximum duration of 2 hr.

Follow-up data were gathered on the experimental subjects and a control group of equal size $(N = 13)$ receiving no treatment. Follow-up interviews were conducted at 6 weeks after

discharge for both groups and 6 months after discharge for the experimental group. Whenever possible patients were interviewed in person, a collateral (relative or friend) was also interviewed to verify information given by the subject.

Five categories were used to classify results. They were: (1) Abstinent—No alcohol consumption. (2) Abstinent—Incapacitated—no alcohol consumption due to the lack of opportunity to drink (hospital, jail, etc.). (3) Drunk—Daily consumption of large amounts of alcohol with toxic reactions. (4) Improved—Sporadic excessive consumption of alcohol without prolonged binges or hospitalizations. (5) Social Drinking—Occasional consumption of alcohol without evidence of drunkenness.

Emphasis was placed on longitudinal aspects of the subject's drinking behavior rather than reporting his behavior at the time of the interview.

RESULTS

Figure 1 demonstrates in terms of straight drink responses one of the differences between the subjects who did not complete the experiment and those subjects who completed at least 14 sessions. The noncompleting subjects, who went AWOL from the hospital sometime before the sixth session, showed a very low initial straight drink rate and consequently had no opportunity for shaping in subsequent sessions. These subjects also never ordered more than three drinks and showed exaggerated sipping (up to 30 sips/drink) with mixed drinks. In light of this fact, the results are presented emphasizing the behavior of subjects who completed the experiment.

Figure 2 shows the mean number of mixed drinks, straight drinks, and total drinks ordered by subjects during each session of the experiment. The subjects who completed the experiment began by ordering approximately as many straight drinks as mixed drinks. Around the fourth or fifth session, the subjects were shaped off straight drinks and, from that time on, ordered predominantly mixed drinks. The result of importance is the gradual separation which occurred after the fourth session between the curves for mixed drinks and straight drinks ordered by subjects completing the experiment. Figure 3 shows the mean number of shocks taken in these sessions.

Figure 4 illustrates the ratio of gulps to sips for both mixed and straight drinks during the 14 sessions. Shaping is indicated by the decrease in

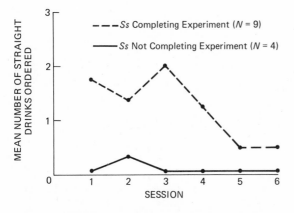

Figure 1. Difference between two groups of alcoholics who at the beginning of experimentation possessed $(N = 4)$ or did not possess $(N = 9)$ the required avoidance criterion in terms of straight drinks consumed.

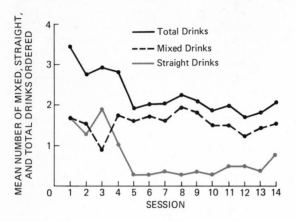

Figure 2. Mean number of straight, mixed, and combined drinks ordered by nine alcoholic patients during 14 avoidance sessions.

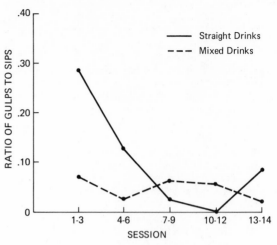

Figure 4. Ratio of gulps to sips for nine alcoholics as a function of progress through 14 avoidance sessions.

the proportion of gulps to sips for straight drinks (high shock) as contrasted to the slightly decreasing and initially low proportion for mixed drinks

The 6-week follow-up data indicate that two of the experimental subjects and none of the control subjects could be classified as social drinkers. When the categories of "abstinent" and "social drinking" were combined, the experimental group had over twice as many subjects ($N = 5$) reporting a favorable change in drinking behavior as

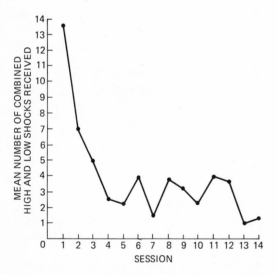

Figure 3. Mean number of shocks received (high and low shocks combined, see text) for nine alcoholic patients during 14 avoidance sessions.

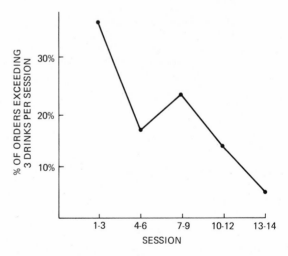

Figure 5. Percentage of all orders exceeding three drinks per session placed by nine alcoholic patients over 14 avoidance sessions.

(mild or no shock contingency). The change from gulping to not gulping straight drinks was evident as the number of sessions increased.

Figure 5 shows a progressive decrease in the percentage of total drinks ordered as a function of sessions for the subjects who completed the experiment.

the control group ($N = 2$). In addition, no subject was reported drunk in the experimental group, while the drunk category had the highest frequency ($N = 4$) for the control group. The 6-

month follow-up also indicated a decrease in subjects reporting less alcoholic behavior and an increase in the drunk category while "improved" frequency remained the same.

DISCUSSION

The most relevant result obtained was the shaping which took place as a result of the avoidance contingencies imposed. The results considered apply only to the group of subjects completing the study. As can be seen in Figure 2, these subjects began the experiment ordering a mean number of nearly four total drinks. Of these drinks, approximately half (usually the first half) were straight drinks, the other half mixed. By the fifth session, a great many of the subjects were already ordering three or less drinks per session, and predominantly mixed drinks were ordered. Sip shaping is evident in Figure 4 in that subjects learned not to gulp as number of sessions increased. That the ratio of gulps to sips increases slightly on occasion is, at first glance, surprising; however, the result can be attributed to the subjects learning to discriminate that an appropriate sip size was defined to be 1/7 of the total drink volume. Although the subjects were informed prior to the first session of the shock contingencies, they were not told in any detail the amount of liquid which would be considered to qualify as a sip rather than a gulp. Figure 5 shows the effect of shaping in that the total number of drinks ordered in a session by the completion group declines steadily for the 14 sessions.

The difference between the subjects who finished and those who did not, clearly evident while sessions in the bar were in progress, was supported by the data analysis. Even during the first session the individuals in the group not completing the experiment never ordered more than three total drinks, almost exclusively ordered

mixed drinks or beer, and typically took from 20–30 sips to consume a drink which they could have consumed in seven sips while still avoiding electric shock. These subjects thus demonstrate that they had extremely exaggerated avoidance responses to electric shock. Of these four subjects, it is also known that three had resumed heavy drinking (to the point of getting sick) within 2 days after leaving the hospital.

The question of how well the methods used in this experiment will generalize to the outside environment is of great importance. The results of this study demonstrate that alcoholics can be taught to drink in the same manner as social drinkers in a hospital environment. Furthermore, the follow-up data indicated partial success in training two subjects to sustain a pattern of social drinking after discharge, again challenging the disease conception of alcoholism dictating that the first drink constitutes failure. The use of a simulated bar and cocktail lounge probably facilitated generalization, but it is likely that more effective generalization would require the addition of at least some of the following characteristics:

1. Additional training sessions to be conducted in which the bulk of the participants are actually social drinkers and the alcoholic is socially reinforced for moderate drinking patterns.

2. Booster treatments, either of the outpatient variety or in the field, will most probably be necessary to maintain any effect achieved in the experimental setting. Helpful in this respect would be a small battery power induction-type shocking device which could probably be constructed for less than $10 and which patients could use to have a friend give booster treatments on the outside. This type of self-administered treatment could avoid one of the major problems which occurs when attempting to give alcoholics booster treatments: if they are functioning well, they don't want to take the time to come to the hospital for treatment.

REFERENCES

Alcoholics Anonymous. New York: Cornwall Press, 1955.

Bailey, M. B., & Stewart, J. Normal drinking reported by persons reporting previous problem drinking. *Quarterly Journal of Studies on Alcohol,* 1967, *28,* 305–315.

Bandura, A. *Principles of behavior modification.* New York: Holt, Rinehart & Winston, 1969.

Blake, B. G. A follow-up of alcoholics treated by behavior therapy. *Behavior Research and Therapy,* 1967, *5,* 89–94.

Davies, D. L. Normal drinking in recovered alcohol

addicts. *Quarterly Journal of Studies on Alcohol*, 1962, 23, 94–104.

Glatt, M. M. Treatment results in an English mental hospital alcoholic unit. *Acta Psychiatrica Scandinavica*, 1964, 37, 143–168.

Hayman, M. The myth of social drinking. *American Journal of Psychiatry*, 1967, 124, 585–594.

Kendell, R. E. Normal drinking by former alcoholic addicts. *Quarterly Journal of Studies on Alcohol*, 1935, 26, 247–257.

Pattison, E. M., Headley, E. B., Gleser, G. C., & Gottschalk, L. A. Abstinence and normal drinking: An assessment of changes in drinking patterns in alco-

holics after treatment. *Quarterly Journal of Studies on Alcohol*, 1968, 29, 610–633.

Schaefer, H. H., Sobell, M. B., & Mills, K. C. Baseline drinking behaviors in alcoholics and social drinkers: kinds of drinks and sip magnitude. *Behaviour Research and Therapy*, 1970, in press.

Skinner, B. F. Behaviorism at fifty. *Science*, 1963, 31, 955–956.

Vogler, R. E., Post, K. L., Johnson, G. R., Lunde, S. E., & Martin, P. L. Electrical aversion conditioning with chronic alcoholics. Paper presented at the Meeting of the Western Psychological Association, Vancouver, B. C., June, 1969.

childhood parental relationships of homosexual men

Ray B. Evans

A major conclusion of a study comparing homosexual and heterosexual men who were all in psychoanalytic therapy was that parental roles are paramount in the etiology of homosexuality (Bieber, Dain, Dince, Drellich, Grand, Gundlach, Kremer, Rifkin, Wilbur, & Bieber, 1962). Those authors described the "classical" pattern as one where the mother is close-binding and intimate with her son and is dominant and minimizing toward her husband, who is a detached (particularly a hostile–detached) father to the son. They concluded that any son exposed to that parental combination will likely develop severe homosexual problems. The Bieber study was based on extensive questionnaires completed by the analysts for each patient; the patients themselves were not aware of the study. Two series of questions proved especially useful in differentiating the homosexual and heterosexual groups, a Developmental Six Score (concerning childhood fears and activities) and a Twenty Questions Score (relating to interparental and parent–child relationships).

There is an obvious risk in generalizing findings from patients in psychotherapy to a nonpatient population. The purpose of the present study was to determine whether questionnaire items adapted from Bieber et al. would differentiate samples of heterosexual and homosexual men who had never sought psychotherapy.

This study was supported in part by the California Foundation for Medical Research. Appreciation is extended to Jessie Marmorston for supplying the heterosexual Ss, and to One, Inc., for their cooperation in recruiting the homosexual Ss. Computational aid was furnished by the Loma Linda University Scientific Computation Facility, supported in part by National Institutes of Health Grant No. FR 00276.

METHOD

Subjects

The sample consisted of 185 American-born, Caucasian men between the ages of 22 and 47, who had at least a high school education, had never sought psychotherapy and were living in the Los Angeles metropolitan area. All Ss were volunteers in a study of cardiovascular disease, but only the 43 homosexuals knew that aspects of homosexuality were also being studied. The latter volunteered, as homosexuals, through the cooperation of a Los Angeles based organization; they did not constitute a representative group of homosexuals. The 142 "heterosexual" Ss volunteered for the cardiac study through a number of sources, and there was no opportunity to develop the kind of rapport needed to elicit information about their sexual preferences and behavior. For purposes of this study, it was assumed they were all heterosexual, though there may have been homosexuals among them, which would tend to attenuate group differences.

The homosexual men ranged in age from 22 to 46, with a mean of 33.8 years ($SD = 7.1$); the heterosexuals ranged from 25 to 47, with an average of 39.3 ($SD = 4.4$), and the difference was significant ($t = 4.84, p < .001$). They were reasonably similar to patients in the Bieber study, where the homosexuals averaged approximately 35 and the heterosexuals approximately 38 years of age.

In education, the homosexuals ranged from 12 to 19 years, with a mean of 14.4 ($SD = 2.2$); and the heterosexuals ranged from 12 to 20 years, with a mean of 15.1 ($SD = 2.1$), with the difference approaching statistical significance ($t = 1.87, p < .10$). Again, they were relatively similar to the Bieber patients, who averaged approximately 15 years of education.

There was an obvious and expected difference between the two groups in marital status. Among the heterosexuals, 5% were single, 87% married, and 8% separated or divorced; 86% of the homosexuals were single, 5% married, and 9% divorced. In the Bieber et al. study, 8% of the homosexuals and 51% of the heterosexuals were married.

As to sibling constellations, there were 12%, 35%, 14%, and 40%, respectively, only, oldest, middle, and youngest children among the homosexuals; comparable figures for the heterosexuals were 8%, 28%, 27%, and 37%. Those distributions were not significantly different. Bieber et al. reported 10% of their homosexuals and 22% of their heterosexuals were only children, which difference was significant at the .05 level.

Proportionately more of the homosexuals

TABLE 1. Questionnaire Content and Item Responses

Questionnaire Item	Bieber Study				Present Study			
	Response	Homo-sexual	Hetero-sexual	p	Response	Homo-sexual	Hetero-sexual	p
Physical make-up as a child	Frail	50	17		Frail	37	11	
	Clumsy	24	08		Clumsy	14	06	
	Athletic	13	33		Athletic	05	45	
	Well coordinated	13	42	.001	Coordinated	44	38	.001
Fearful of physical injury as a child	Yes	75	46		Seldom	23	49	
	No	25	54	.001	Sometimes	51	46	
					Often	19	04	
					Always	07	01	.001
Avoided physical fights	Yes	90	56		Always	56	12	
	No	10	44	.001	Often	30	35	
					Sometimes	14	46	
					Never	00	07	.001
Played with girls before adolescence	Yes	34	10		Never	09	03	
	No	66	90	.001	Sometimes	49	83	
					Often	40	14	
					Always	02	00	.001
"Lone wolf" in childhood	Yes	61	27		Never	12	38	
	No	39	73	.001	Sometimes	35	51	
					Often	42	11	
					Always	12	01	.001
Played competitive group games	Yes	17	64		Never	09	01	
	No	83	36	.001	Sometimes	65	15	
					Often	23	52	
					Very often	02	32	.001
Played baseball	Yes	16	64		Never	19	05	
	No	84	36	.001	Sometimes	70	29	
					Often	09	35	
					Very often	02	32	.001
Father and mother spent time together	Great deal	01	13		Great deal	16	28	
	Average	42	50		Considerable	53	39	
	Little	36	24		Little	26	23	
	Very little	21	13	.002	Very little	05	09	.23
Parents shared similar interests	Yes	20	38		Great many	21	30	
	No	80	62	.01	Several	37	32	
					Few	35	33	
					None	07	05	.70
Mother insisted on being center of son's attention	Yes	64	36		Never	30	18	
	No	36	64	.001	Seldom	37	63	
					Often	16	17	
					Always	16	01	.001
Mother "seductive" toward son as a child	Yes	57	34		Highly	07	00	
	No	43	66	.002	Moderately	07	03	
					Slightly	09	13	
					No	77	85	.02
Mother discouraged masculine attitudes/ activities	Yes	39	17		Often	05	02	
	No	61	83	.002	Sometimes	21	07	
					Seldom	30	14	
					Never	44	77	.001
Mother encouraged feminine attitudes/ activities	Yes	36	12		Never	53	87	
	No	64	88	.001	Seldom	21	11	
					Sometimes	21	02	
					Often	05	01	.001

TABLE 1 *(Continued)*

Questionnaire Item	Response	Bieber Study			Response	Present Study		
		Homo-sexual	Hetero-sexual	p		Homo-sexual	Hetero-sexual	p
Mother considered	Yes	67	51		Strongly	28	11	
puritanical	No	33	49	.05	Moderately	33	35	
					Mildly	23	23	
					No	16	30	.04
Mother's relationships	Frigid	72	56		Frigid	12	00	
with father/other	Not frigid	28	44	.04	Cold	26	23	
men					Warm	63	77	.10
Mother allied with son	Yes	63	40		Often	33	06	
against father	No	37	60	.002	Sometimes	21	18	
					Seldom	16	35	
					Never	30	42	.001
Mother openly pre-	Yes	59	38		Always	12	01	
ferred son to father	No	41	62	.005	Often	14	06	
					Seldom	21	31	
					Never	53	62	.004
Mother interfered	Yes	37	25		Often	12	00	
with heterosexual	No	63	75	.08	Sometimes	16	08	
activities					Seldom	19	20	
					Never	53	71	.004
Son was mother's	Yes	52	36		Never	30	27	
confidant	No	48	64	.03	Seldom	19	32	
					Sometimes	23	36	
					Often	28	05	.001
Son was father's	Yes	08	29		Strongly	09	09	
favorite	No	92	71	.001	Moderately	16	40	
					Mildly	40	37	
					No	35	14	.005
Felt accepted by father	Yes	23	48		Strongly	23	42	
	No	77	52	.001	Moderately	35	42	
					Mildly	23	11	
					No	19	06	.006
Son spent time with	Great deal	03	03		Great deal	02	08	
father	Average	12	39		Considerable	09	39	
	Little	37	31		Little	53	32	
	Very little	48	27	.001	Very little	35	21	.001
Father encouraged	Yes	48	61		Often	26	41	
masculine attitudes/	No	52	39	.07	Sometimes	26	32	
activities					Seldom	23	21	
					Never	26	06	.002
Aware of hating father	Yes	61	37		Never	28	59	
as a child	No	39	63	.002	Seldom	19	20	
					Sometimes	37	18	
					Often	16	03	.001
Afraid father might	Yes	57	43		Often	14	04	
physically harm him	No	43	57	.06	Sometimes	19	23	
					Seldom	30	13	
					Never	37	60	.003
Accepted father	Yes	21	51		Strongly	26	51	
	No	79	49	.001	Moderately	28	37	
					Mildly	33	09	
					No	14	03	.001
Respected father	Yes	30	49		Strongly	37	56	
	No	70	51	.01	Moderately	21	32	
					Mildly	21	08	
					No	21	03	.001

Note: Significance levels based on chi-square, with twofold classifications corrected for continuity. Decimals omitted.

were employed in clerical work and in the arts, and fewer of them in other professions, management, and sales work. The difference in heterosexual–homosexual occupational distributions was significant ($\chi^2 = 42.88$, $df = 5$, $p < .001$). The occupational classifications of the present Ss and the Bieber patients were fairly comparable.

The homosexual volunteers rated their sexual experience on a 7-point scale adapted from Kinsey, Pomeroy, and Gebhard (1948), which ranged from entirely heterosexual to entirely homosexual. Of the 43 Ss, 58% described their experience as having been exclusively homosexual, 35% as predominantly homosexual with incidental heterosexual, and 7% as predominantly homosexual but more than incidental heterosexual experience. For their homosexual patients, Bieber et al. reported 68% as exclusively homosexual, 28% as having some heterosexual experience, and 4% as inactive, so that the proportion of exclusive homosexuals in the two studies was similar ($\chi^2 = .89$, $p = .50$).

The homosexual Ss also completed an 11-item questionnaire designed to determine their sexual identification. In their overall feelings, 40 Ss (93%) considered themselves moderately or strongly masculine, and responses to the other 10 items also indicated essentially masculine identification. Bieber et al. reported that approximately 2% of their homosexual patients were "markedly effeminate," so that seemingly Ss from the two studies were similar in this regard.

Procedure

Each S completed a 27-item questionnaire adapted from Bieber et al. so as to be as nearly comparable as possible. The essential content of the questionnaire appears in Table 1. Included were the Developmental Six (Items 2–7) and Twenty Questions (Items 8–27) scores, and one additional question regarding physical make-up in childhood (Item 1), which had also differentiated the Bieber groups. Four possible choices were provided for each item, whereas the Bieber study used a yes–no dichotomy for all except three items. Following is an example from Bieber et al. completed by the analysts: "Was patient excessively fearful of physical injury in childhood? (yes/no)." The corresponding item modified for the present study, for completion by S himself, was: "During childhood, were you fearful of physical injury? (seldom/sometimes/often/always)."

Questionnaires were used in the analysis only where all 27 items had been answered, which eliminated 11 potential Ss, one homosexual and 10 heterosexual. Differences between groups were calculated by means of chi-square, with twofold classifications corrected for continuity.

RESULTS

The content of each questionnaire item is given in Table 1, together with the proportion of Ss responding in each category, and the significance of differences between the homosexual and heterosexual groups. Comparable figures from the Bieber study are also included, with the significance values calculated from figures in Appendix A (Bieber et al., 1962) using only Ss for whom definite response was available. Differences between the Bieber groups reached at least the .05 level of significance for 24 of the 27 items, and the other three approached significance. (Bieber et al. reported all items significant, and the discrepancy may be due to the method used here of ignoring "No Answer" and "Not Applicable" categories in the calculation of chi-square.)

In the present study, homosexual–heterosexual differences were significant at the .05 level or less for 24 items, one other approached significance, and for two items no difference was found. Thus, despite the very different method of collecting data, the nonpatient status of the Ss, and (perhaps minor) differences due to geographical location, the results were remarkably similar to those reported by Bieber et al.

Specifically, in retrospect, the homosexuals more often described themselves as frail or clumsy as children and less often as athletic. More of them were fearful of physical injury, avoided physical fights, played with girls, and were loners who seldom played baseball and other competitive games. Their mothers more often were considered puritanical, cold toward men, insisted on being the center of the son's attention, made him her confidant, were "seductive" toward him, allied with him against the father, openly preferred him to the father, interfered with his heterosexual activities during adolescence, discouraged masculine attitudes, and encouraged feminine ones. The fathers of the homosexuals were retrospectively considered as less likely to encourage masculine attitudes and activities, and Ss spent little time with their fathers, were more often aware of hating him and afraid he might physically harm them, less often were the father's favorite, felt less accepted by him, and in turn less frequently accepted or respected the father. Unlike Bieber's patients, these homosexuals were no different from the heterosexuals in amount of time they estimated their parents spent together or in the interests shared by their parents.

In addition, a total score on the 27-item questionnaire was obtained for each S by weighting each item from 0 to 3 points, with the higher weighting at the "masculine" end, so there was a maximum possible score of 81. The scores of the homosexuals ranged from 9 to 64, with a mean of 42.9 ($SD = 11.6$); those of the heterosexuals from 36 to 77, with a mean of 57.3 ($SD = 9.2$). Though there was considerable overlap in scores for the two groups, the difference was highly significant ($t = 7.50$, $p < .001$).

DISCUSSION

The results could not be accounted for on the basis of sample characteristics other than sexual orientation; no relationship was found between age and questionnaire scores, and the same was true of marital status, occupational classification, and sibling constellation. The fact that the homosexuals knew homosexuality was being studied might have affected the results, but if there was any tendency to distort in the direction of "normal," it was not sufficient to obscure group differences.

As to preponderance of homosexual experience, no relationship was observed between Kinsey-type ratings (completed only by homosexual Ss) and questionnaire scores ($\chi^2 = 0.0$), perhaps because of the limited variation in proportion of homosexual experience. However, a product–moment correlation of .47 ($t = 3.41$, $p < .01$) was found between the 27-item questionnaire and the 11-item sexual identity questionnaire; the homosexuals with more "desirable" family backgrounds tended to consider themselves as more masculine.

It may be noteworthy that the present results were so similar to those obtained by the Bieber group despite a major difference in the level of observation. In the present study, the data were based on retrospective self-reports of how they now view their childhood, by Ss who had never been in psychotherapy. The Bieber data, on the other hand, were based on psychoanalysts' reconstructions of patients' early life circumstances, derived from impressions during psychotherapy. Arguments could be advanced for the superiority of one method over the other, and certainly both have limitations. The agreement in results could

be interpreted as evidence of validity in both methods, or perhaps as an indication that the two methods are not essentially different.

The results strongly suggested poor parental relationships during childhood for the homosexual men, at least as seen in retrospect; however, the etiological significance of such relationships, or even the etiology of the relationships themselves, is another matter. Bieber et al. considered the chances high that any son exposed to the parental combination of maternal close-binding intimacy and paternal detachment–hostility will develop severe homosexual problems. Nevertheless, only 28% of their homosexual patients had such a parental combination, and the 11% of their control patients who had such parents did not become homosexual. Furthermore, Bieber et al. very much underemphasized one-third of the "triad," the son himself. They reported that "each parent had a specific type of relationship with the homosexual son which generally did not occur with other siblings," and that son was the "focal point for the most profound parental psychopathology." As to why a particular son is singled out, Bieber et al. proposed that son is unconsciously identified by the mother with her own father or brothers, and the son thereby becomes the recipient of sexual feelings carried over from the mother's own early life. Similarly, the father transfers to that son his unresolved hostility and rivalry with his own father/brothers. The above is an oversimplified summary of the Bieber formulation, but it does not exaggerate the neglect of the son's contribution to the triadic relationship, beyond eliciting parental transference feelings.

The personalities and behavior of parents undoubtedly affect a child's personality, but some consideration must be given to the notion that the child's innate characteristics at least partially determine parental reactions and attitudes toward him. For instance, that the father of a homosexual son becomes detached and/or hostile because he does not understand or is disappointed in the son is just as tenable as that the son becomes homosexual because of the father's rejection. Similarly, that a mother may be more intimate with and bind her homosexual son more closely because of the kind of person he is, is just as reasonable as the idea that he becomes homosexual because she is too binding and intimate. Bieber et al. did question whether paternal rejection and hostility were stimulated out of feelings of disappointment and failure because of the son's homosexuality, but concluded that was not likely since only 17% of the fathers were reported to have been aware of the son's homosexuality. Surely most parental reactions crucially affecting the child's personality occur when the child is far too young to be labeled homosexual or heterosexual. The Bieber group also concluded that the father's attitudes were not traceable to the fact that the sons were inadequate and unattractive children, since the mothers did not find them so. That the mothers did not find these sons unattractive is no indication the fathers did not; the evidence suggests the fathers did find them unappealing.

Judging from experience with adult homosexual males, O'Connor (1964) also refuted the idea that lack of a good father relationship was a consequence rather than a cause of homosexuality, on the grounds that would make it difficult to account for the many homosexuals whose fathers were physically absent. Bene (1965) rejected the notion that the lack of a positive father relationship might be due to the son repulsing the father rather than the father repulsing the son, and she cited O'Connor's reasoning. That homosexuality occurs in sons whose fathers are physically absent is irrelevant to the fact that when the father is physically present the relationship with the homosexual son is often a poor one. Furthermore, that homosexuality occurs in the absence of a father not only detracts from the etiological significance of a poor paternal relationship but in fact supports the importance of other causal factors (possibly such as innate physical/personality characteristics of the son).

Information was obtained relevant to another conclusion of Bieber and colleagues, who stated: "We have come to the conclusion that a constructive, supportive, warmly related father *precludes* the possibility of a homosexual son; he acts as a neutralizing, protective agent should the mother make seductive or close-binding attempts [p. 311]." The questionnaire responses gave no full and complete answer as to whether these fathers were constructive, supportive, and warmly related, but there was evidence that the father relationship of some homosexuals was as good as that of many heterosexuals. A score was calculated for each S based on Items 20–27 in Table 1, all of which concern the father–son relationship. With 0–3 points possible for each item, the total scores for the homosexuals ranged from 0 to 22, with a mean of 11.7; and scores for heterosexuals ranged from 3 to 23, with a mean of 16.5. While the difference was significant ($t = 5.95$, $p < .001$), 16% of the homosexuals scored above the heterosexual mean, and 16% of the heterosexuals scored below the homosexual mean. Therefore, it would seem that a moderately good relationship, at least as reflected in the above questionnaire items, does not preclude the appearance of homosexuality, even though it is well established that a poor father relationship is common among homosexual sons. The responses for the Bieber homosexuals on the corresponding questionnaire items suggested their father relationships were poorer than those of the present homosexual Ss, which could merely reflect methodological differences, but more likely is related to the fact that the Bieber Ss had all sought psychotherapy, whereas none of the present Ss had done so.

In a similar fashion, two other questionnaire scores were calculated, one regarding mother–son relationships (Items 10–19) and the other pertaining to development (Items 1–7). With a maximum score of 30 on the 10 mother items, the homosexuals ranged from 4 to 29, with a mean of 18.8; the heterosexuals ranged from 13 to 29, mean 22.9. Although the difference was significant ($t = 5.39$, $p < .001$), 30% of the homosexuals scored above the heterosexual mean, and 12% of the heterosexuals scored below the homosexual mean. As to the seven developmental items, with a possible score of 21, the homosexuals ranged from 1 to 15, with a mean of 8.9; and the heterosexuals ranged from 6 to 19, mean of 14.3. That difference was most significant ($t = 10.39$, $p < .001$), and only 2% of the homosexuals exceeded the heterosexual mean, with 4% of the heterosexuals scoring below the homosexual mean. Of the three content areas, then, the developmental items clearly differentiated Ss best, with the father and mother items similar in their differentiation. The childhood behavior reflected in some of the developmental items, of course, is not unaffected by parents, but the findings suggest the possibility of something more fundamental in homosexuality than a poor father relationship.

The results of the present study agreed closely with those obtained by Bieber et al. but they neither supported nor refuted the Bieber conclusions as to causal relationships. The complicated problem of the etiology of homosexuality probably could be more productively investigated with a prospective study.

REFERENCES

Bene, E. On the genesis of male homosexuality: An attempt at clarifying the role of the parents. *British Journal of Psychiatry*, 1965, *111*, 803–813.

Bieber, I., Dain, H. J., Dince, P. R., Drellich, M. G., Grand, H. G., Gundlach, R. H., Kremer, M. W., Rifkin, A. H., Wilbur, C. B., & Bieber, T. B. *Homosexuality: A psychoanalytic study*. New York: Basic Books, 1962

Kinsey, A., Pomeroy, W. B., & Gebhard, P. H. *Sexual behavior in the human male*. Philadelphia: Saunders, 1948.

O'Connor, J. Aetiological factors in homosexuality as seen in Royal Air Force psychiatric practice. *British Journal of Psychiatry*, 1964, *110*, 381–399.

childhood parental relationships and the establishment of gender roles of homosexuals

Ralph H. Gundlach

It is with considerable satisfaction I learn that Evans' (1969) 27-item questionnaire—taken from the 450 items used by the Bieber team (Bieber, Dain, Dince, Drellich, Grand, Gundlach, Kremer, Wilbur, & Bieber, 1962)—answered by a sample of West Coast male homosexuals and heterosexuals never in psychoanalysis, confirm so solidly our findings on these items. We are grateful to Evans for testing our explicit generalization from a patient population to nonpatients.

In considering Evans' research I am reminded that there are many different and appropriate goals for research and that misunderstandings may occur between researchers because they do not grasp the others' context. I may very well fail to grasp Evans' through inability to get away from my own set. It seems to me that Evans presents his data with admirable objectivity, but I suspect he really did not expect these findings, for he veers off into a discussion which offers no accounting for his data, nor comes to grips with the Bieber et al. data. His arguments are not based on his research.

I see his argument as threefold: (a) he points out that the Bieber et al. findings cannot be taken to prove that parental relationships of the quality indicated have any etiological significance for homosexuality. One could just as reasonably assert, he says, that "the father of a son becomes detached and/or hostile because he does not understand or is disappointed in the son." Likewise, "the mother may be more intimate with and bind her homosexual son more closely because of the kind of a person he is." Although these statements might seem to hold logically for the bare sets of answers to the 27 questions, Evans does not take account of the many cross-tabulations between related questions, and especially such interrelationships that touch differences

in time as presented in Chapter VII, "Developmental aspects of the prehomosexual child" (Bieber et al., 1962). But Evans himself adds—undermining his argument it seems to me— "Surely most parental reactions critically affecting the child's personality occur when the child is far too young to be labeled homosexual or heterosexual."

(b) Evans argues that even though fathers of homosexuals (H) and controls (C), for instance, may be distinguished at the .001 level or higher on a collection of items, the two groups still overlap in part. He thus seems to require that the answers to questionnaire items about relations between parents and child as remembered and categorized in simplified general phrases, whether answered by a psychiatrist or the adult son, should be as firm as a causal connection; as solid as the copper wire between light switch and light bulb.

This position seems to indicate a misconception about the nature of the subject matter of the research and a confusion about the function and meaning of questionnaire data in studies such as these on homosexuality. Evans follows here, perhaps, the old medical model regarding the etiology of a disease, like mumps or yellow fever, and demands no less than the identification of one precise "cause." But the facts show that homosexuality is not a disease, or a syndrome, or a unitary trait; and certainly the questionnaire items are not the causal factors. Evans erects and attacks a straw man so far as he purports that Bieber et al. assert that "a poor father relationship" or a close-binding–intimate mother "causes" homosexuality in a son. The whole tenor of that study was to delineate the multivariate factors that may be involved. Particularly impressive were our findings of a strong

Reprinted from *Journal of Consulting and Clinical Psychology*, 1969, *33*, pp. 136–139. Copyright 1969 by the American Psychological Association and reproduced by permission.

heterosexual interest in many of the H which were sharply inhibited by fears related to female genitalia; and evidence that many H seek pickups not for sheer sexual pleasure and gratification or love, but are driven by anxieties and are acting compulsively. Such neurotic fears are hardly instinctual, but do they also characterize H who never had psychotherapy? Unfortunately Evans did not replicate these most essential items.

(c) Evans' third argument is that the Bieber et al. study overlooked the son himself: one-third of the triad. He asserts "the child's innate characteristics at least partially determine parental reactions and attitudes toward him."

It is hard to understand Evans' objection that the individual personality was left out in the Bieber et al. study, since the patient was the focus of the entire study, triangulated from many vantage points. The study was an attempt to enrich, extend, and systematize clinical material about male homosexuals found in psychoanalytic treatment; the focus was always on the ground level of the particular person. The superposition of an extensive questionnaire was understood as a gross way of collecting disparate persons of family groups. The questionnaire answers and the many tables served to block out the main geography of patterns of male homosexuals and their family of origin patterns, just as a map serves to fix the relative sizes and some of the characteristics of ground-level reality. The statistical material was treated not as primary data but as material to be assessed in the light of clinical experience and to extend clinical insights. Thus, some eight classifications of mother-types and 10 groupings of father-types provided 51 different parental patterns; and these were further collected into four major groupings. Throughout, with every section, the full meaning was illuminated, the clinching material was displayed through some 35–40 cases. We found a remarkable number of conditions and circumstances that may result in homosexuality.

When Evans suggests that there is something within the nature of the homosexual which may be the determining factor ("possibly such as innate physical/personality characteristics of the son"), one could think he was unhappy with his own findings. But the evidence continually mounts against such an "innate" hypothesis. The study of genes, chromosomes, and endocrine secretions have all been largely discredited as determining homosexuality. Perloff (1965) summarizes that "homosexuality is purely a psychological phe-

nomenon, neither dependent on a hormonal pattern for its production nor amenable to change by endocrine substances [p. 68]."

What happens after the child is born is complicated by many factors; there are not only inner biological and emotional factors, parental and familial surroundings, social and cultural circumstances; but the various pressures and expectations shift as the child grows and hardens as he establishes his ways into his eventual adult character structure.

At birth the baby is identified as a boy or girl and the child is reared by the parents with that idea in mind, with whatever doubts, reservations, pleasures, or disappointments, and intentions they carry for the child. So by the age of 2 or 3 it knows that it is a male or a female; its core gender role is established. But at this time, according to Rabban (1950), the child has little of the sex-role characteristics, which are largely established after age 3. Still later come the pressures and anxieties about being acceptable as a masculine or feminine person.

One's sex and gender role are not always consonant, and some most interesting studies have been made of persons caught in this predicament. Money (1965), for instances, describes two cases that were hermaphrodites and biologically the same. But one was raised as a girl and the other as a boy and each developed appropriately and without difficulty into these opposite gender roles. Other more confusing cases arise where the external genitalia give the appearance of one sex—this is announced by the obstetrician at the child's birth—but these conceal internal genitalia carrying the primary characteristics of the opposite sex. The child is reared by parents who have a mistaken idea as to its sex; but when biological difficulties arise, usually at the approach of sexual maturity, the error in sex assignment is discovered. The earlier approach was to proclaim the biological truth, and expect the child to shift its gender role; but this turned out to be usually disastrous, courting psychotic breakdowns. Money (1965) and Stoller (1968) found it proved much better to let the established gender identification prevail, and refit the person's physical and secondary sex characteristics to the person's self-concept. To reverse the psychological structures of the self, incorporated around sexual identity and all the habits, attitudes, values, and ways of living this entails, is extremely hazardous.

Stoller made extensive and precise studies of

some patients with biological abnormalities, and some without biological abnormalities but with gender-role anomalies. In many of these cases not only the child but one or both parents were interviewed, several were in analysis, and the interactions especially of mother and child were discovered in detail. He concluded that differences in gender from biological sex are almost always produced by differences in infant rearing. Most interesting were those male cases he called transsexual. These were male babies that developed within the first year and a half a sense of female identity; and he found and studied adult transsexuals whom he assumed to have been reared as were these males. The adult transsexuals only wanted their male bodies to be changed so as to conform to their feminine outlook. These patients, he pointed out, had no touch of psychosis; they were quite sane. Further, this feminine identity was established not as an adaptation to severe pressures (see Rado, 1965), but under conditions of conflict-free pleasure, provided by an overindulgent, close-binding mother. Stoller points out how these transsexuals are sharply different from transvestites, fetishists who know they are male but periodically take a woman's role for special reasons; different from effeminate homosexuals who like to dress in women's clothing, usually to satirize and make fun of women. In all the child transsexuals he saw, there were some striking similarities. There was a close mother–son symbiosis, with the mothers tending to hold their babies against their own bodies for much too long a time; the mothers all had a special identifiable bisexuality and emptiness; they encouraged cross-dressing of their sons; and their husbands tended to be physically absent from the household, and were unconcerned with the cross-dressing and other behaviors of the son imitative of the mother. These transsexuals, he emphasized, never thought of themselves as homosexuals, since they had the complete sense of being women.

Probably none of the patients in the Bieber et al. study, and none of the women in the Gundlach and Riess (1968) study, had been faced with the biological and social problems just described. The males all accepted the fact they were males, although the H and many C had problems about potency and how masculine they were or were perceived to be; and how, by sexual agression or other behavior, they could promote their social reputation or enhance or protect their self-esteem. Likewise the women studied all knew

themselves as females but their means of establishing or expressing their gender role is quite different in this society than for men. Girls learn femininity by absorption, without effort by imitation of mother (see Lynn, 1962). They do not have to assert themselves to be women.

I would like to end by calling attention to two bits of evidence about female homosexuality, each of which raises interesting questions.

We find that the incidence of homosexuality in relation to birth order depends upon a number of factors (Gundlach & Riess, 1967). For instance, even with our limited sample of about 225 H and 230 C there were significantly (.05) more lesbians who were firstborn among families with only one or two children. However, of families with five or more children, 12 were firstborn but only three of these were H. Of these large families, 22 were fifth or later in rank, 17 H and five C; of the 48 who were in the first four ranks, 16 were H and 32 C ($p < .001$).

What makes this important is that quite different family dynamics must operate with the firstborn girls from small families than for later-born girls from large families. It might be that firstborns are pushed to produce, and feel they must prove themselves with accomplishments as boys must do, while the later-born girls in large families are perhaps largely neglected. (Often the last-born male is the one focused upon by mother, and becomes homosexual.) But furthermore, the question arises as to why it is that the firstborn girls in large families are not as equally prone to being lesbian as within smaller families? I cannot say, but it seems that something about the decision cannot occur until after it is established that there will be five or more siblings; and by that time the firstborn girl must be 10–15 years old!

The other exciting item comes from the study of the patterns of female homosexuality in a prison for women convicted of a felony. Ward and Kassebaum (1965) describe how the majority turned to homosexuality as a way of life: to seek closeness, warmth, and affection from another inmate as the way to survive the loneliness, degradation, and other psychological deprivations and injuries of incarceration. It seemed bound up with emotional needs. Yet 68% of the women were mothers; and only 5–15% were estimated to have been homosexuals "outside."

In men's prisons, on the contrary, males still feel they must demonstrate their masculinity by force: by fighting, sodomizing weaker ones, buying favors, and discharging debts with a sexual "favor." However, the persons who are forced to comply, or traffic in sex, are viewed with contempt by those rated as highly masculine. Yet these forceful leaders, who use the others sexually, do not consider themselves homosexuals.

This brings up the point that some men can have sexual relations only with men, or only with women, or with neither, or both, or with a fetish; and some are willing and able to engage in sexual activity with a great variety of objects and/or persons.

Most women, however, express the feelings that they cannot have sex, or do not wish to, without "love." But many find that they can love a man or a woman. Few are like the majority of male H in treatment, who seem to fear or even have a phobic reaction to heterosexual intercourse. So—what is the (varying) importance of the sex of the sexual partner, to the S's gender role and self-concept?

In the light of evidence of cultural determination of gender role and sexual practices, the possibility of an innate physical/personality characteristic determining homosexuality seems quite remote.

REFERENCES

Bieber, I., Dain, H. J., Dince, P. R., Drellich, M. G., Grand, H. G., Gundlach, R. H., Kremer, M. W., Rifkin, A. H., Wilbur, C. B., & Bieber, T. B. *Homosexuality: A psychoanalytic study.* New York: Basic Books, 1962.

Evans, R. B. Childhood parental relationships of homosexual men. *Journal of Consulting and Clinical Psychology*, 1969, *33*, 129–135.

Gundlach, R. H., & Riess, B. F. Birth order and sex of siblings in a sample of lesbians and nonlesbians. *Psychological Reports*, 1967, *20*, 61–62.

Gundlach, R. H., & Riess, B. F. Self and sexual identity in the female: A study of female homosexuals. In B. F. Riess (Ed.), *New directions in mental health.* New York: Grune & Stratton, 1968.

Lynn, D. B. Sex-role and parental identification. *Child Development*, 1962, *33*, 555–564.

Money, J. *Sex research.* New York: Holt, Rinehart & Winston, 1965.

Perloff, W. H. Hormones and homosexuality. In J. Marmor (Ed.), *Sexual inversion.* New York: Basic Books, 1965.

Rabban, M. Sex role identification in young children in two diverse social groups. *Genetic Psychology Monographs*, 1950, *34*, 81–158.

Rado, S. A critical examination of the concept of bisexuality. In J. Marmor (Ed.), *Sexual inversion.* New York: Basic Books, 1965.

Stoller, R. J. *Sex and gender.* New York: Science House, 1968.

Ward, D. A., & Kassebaum, G. G. *Women's prison: Sex and social structure.* Chicago: Aldine, 1965.

parental relations and male homosexuality in patient and nonpatient samples

Evelyn Hooker

It can no longer be questioned that faulty, disturbed, or pathological parental relationships in early childhood are more commonly reported by male homosexual patients than by a comparable group of male heterosexuals. The studies of West (1959), Braaten and Darling (1965), Freund and Pinkava (1961), O'Connor (1964), and Bieber, Dain, Dince, Drellich, Grand, Gundlach, Kremer, Rifkin, Wilbur, and Bieber (1962) are in agreement on this finding although they differ with respect to the specific critical dimensions of the parental relationships. In some studies, the content of the disturbed relationship is very general and lacks specific behavioral criteria. Thus, for example, West finds that homosexuals more frequently have "overintense" relations with their mothers and "unsatisfactory" relations with their fathers. In O'Connor's study, homosexuals are more attached to their mothers and do not "relate normally" to their fathers. On the other hand, Bieber et al. very carefully delineate a substantial number of behavioral criteria for the close-binding–intimate (CBI) mother and the hostile, detached father as illustrated by the items selected for cross-validation in the Evans (1969) study.

Evans' careful replication of the Bieber study with nonpatients who answer questions directly concerning parental relationships is a very important contribution to the further clarification of the role of parental relationships in homosexuality. The etiological role of parental relationships in producing homosexuality is an *inference* which cannot be justified from psychiatric samples alone, in part because of the contamination

of homosexuality with psychopathology. Similar results with nonpatient samples tend to confirm that inference even though they are not conclusive because of the necessarily large number of other uncontrolled variables in a retrospective study.

Prior to Evans', five studies of nonpatient samples have appeared. As with the patient samples, no precise cumulative picture emerges because the investigators used different dimensions of parental relations. Thus, Westwood (1960) found indifferent or poor relations with the father and an overprotective or possessive mother in approximately 50% of his sample. Unfortunately, the lack of a control group makes it impossible to assess the significance of this finding. In the Schofield (1965) study, homosexual men in a nonpatient sample reported a higher incidence of poor relations with the father and of overprotective or overpossessive mothers than did a similar sample of heterosexual men. Bene (1965) found no evidence that homosexuals were more often attached to their mothers or overprotected and overindulged by them. They more often reported more hostility and less affection from and toward both mothers and fathers than did heterosexual men. In Apperson and McAdoo's study (1968) mothers of homosexuals were found to be less restrictive than were the mothers of heterosexuals, and the fathers were described as more cold and impatient. Thus, the picture of the mother which emerges from these studies is contradictory but that of the father is fairly consistent from one study to another. However, in Greenblatt's (1966) study *no* differences were found between homosexual and heterosexual men in ratings on a semantic differential of attributes of their mothers and fathers. Indeed, fathers of both groups were

This investigation was supported by a Research Career award from the National Institute of Mental Health, United States Public Health Service.

rated by them as good, generous, pleasant, dominant, and underprotective and mothers as good, pleasant, neither subordinate nor dominant, and neither overprotective nor underprotective. None of these studies permits an exact comparison with the investigations of patient samples because of differences in methodology or in the definition of the relevant dimensions.

Evans' study is therefore of special importance as a partial confirmation of the Bieber assumption about causal relation between parental relations in early childhood and adult homosexuality. In my view, Evans is overly cautious in his assertion that his findings neither confirm nor refute the etiological role of parent–child relations as one set of many variables influencing or causing homosexuality in adult life. Indeed, his study necessitates this generalization since it is a replication whereas it is unwarranted from the Bieber study alone. His caution and the lack of appropriate caution in the Bieber study are both unwarranted extremes.

The issue of contaminating psychopathology with homosexuality, unfortunately, is not settled by the Evans study since he did not control for this variable. In fact, the amount of psychopathology other than homosexuality per se in the nonpatient samples thus far investigated is unknown except for Greenblatt's study. Theoretically, nonpatients should show less psychopathology only if it is assumed that greater psychopathology is the impetus to treatment. However, as was demonstrated in the Manhattan and Stirling County investigations, psychopathology may be widespread in an untreated population. Psychopathology is only one set of the complex pattern of variables partially influencing whether treatment is sought.

Greenblatt took this into account in the selection of his nonpatient groups by administering the MMPI as a measure of psychopathology. Both of the homosexual and the heterosexual samples were found to consist of two subgroups: one as "normal" as any group in the MMPI literature and the other showing some psychopathology. However, there was more psychopathology in the homosexual "nonnormal" subgroup than in the heterosexual one. Nevertheless, the total group showed much less psychopathology than is true of neurotic Ss generally. The highest score on any clinical scale for the homosexual group was on the Depression Scale and this mean was only 60.4. Thus, the fact that Greenblatt's data do not confirm the Bieber findings may be due to the comparative lack of psychopathology in the total homosexual nonpatient group. On the other hand, it may be due to differences in methodology.

Some supportive evidence for interpreting the results as due to the relation between parental relations and adult psychopathology rather than to homosexuality per se is given by Schofield's finding that the incidence of disturbed parental relations was greater in the patient than in the nonpatient homosexual samples. Evans' finding that relations with the father were somewhat better, and in fact were "moderately good" in some instances, as compared with Bieber's sample, lends some additional support to the argument. Apperson and McAdoo's findings that mothers of homosexuals were less restrictive than those of the control Ss could also be interpreted in this way. The evidence, however tentative, of the relation between disturbed parental relations and adult psychopathology makes it imperative that further studies include an assessment of psychopathology in the samples studied.

The negative evidence of the Greenblatt study (no difference between parental relations in the homosexual and the heterosexual groups) and the findings in all studies that disturbed parental relations characterize only a portion of the homosexual sample as well as a smaller proportion of the heterosexual sample raise serious questions about the etiological role of parental relations in the genesis of homosexuality. Furthermore, studies of schizophrenic patients have demonstrated that a very similar picture of parental relations characterize the early childhood (Lidz, Cornelison, Fleck, & Terry, 1957).

Thus it appears that disturbed parental relations are neither necessary nor sufficient conditions for homosexuality to emerge. If it should be the case that they are more commonly found in the background of severely disturbed patients than of those individuals who function relatively well, the necessity of looking at other etiological factors should be underlined.

Evans arrives at his position that innate factors may be important by evaluating the significance of the father's role. He argues that because homosexuality develops in sons whose fathers are absent as well as in those with moderately good relations with fathers, the etiological role of the father must be questioned and the contribution of the son's characteristics (perhaps innate) must be assessed. While I am in complete agreement with Evans about potential genetic or other etiological contributions to a homosexual object choice (even though there is no possibility of specifying what they are with the evidence currently available), the force of his argument about the father's role is weak if one considers the function of the father in producing or preventing homosexuality. That is, Bieber et al. assume that the presence of a warm, strong, and supporting father who intervenes on behalf of the son counteracts the effects of a CBI mother. The absence of the father, as well as a poor father, may leave the son in the double bind of maternal sexual seductiveness–maternal sexual restriction.

Finally, there are four major theoretical issues concerning the etiology and determinants of persistent or predominant adult homosexuality. (*a*) Is the human organism psychosexually neutral at birth, so that learning processes determine homosexual object choice in adults, or are there inherent sexual predispositions, which selectively influence the effects of learning? (*b*) What is the nature and content of the learning processes by which homosexual object choice develops? Is the appropriate developmental model a deviant role or a personality system with intrapersonal traits, motives, and gender identifications incompatible with the social-sexual capabilities and self–other expectancies of adult relations with the opposite sex? Does positive conditioning of sexual responses to persons of the same sex, or negative conditioning to persons of the opposite sex, or a combination of both account for homosexuality? (*c*) Are particular periods in the developmental process, such as early childhood or adolescence, critical for homosexual object choice? (*d*) Are parent–child relationships in the nuclear family crucial in determining whether an individual becomes homosexual, or are peer relationships in childhood and adolescence, and deviant subcultures in adolescence and early adult life, of equal or possibly greater importance? These four issues are highly controversial and cannot be resolved by the research evidence currently available.

REFERENCES

Apperson, L. B., & McAdoo, W. G., Jr. Parental factors in the childhood of homosexuals. *Journal of Abnormal Psychology*, 1968, *73*, 201–206.

Bene, E. On the genesis of male homosexuality: An attempt at clarifying the role of the parents. *British Journal of Psychiatry*, 1965, *111*, 803–813.

Bieber, I., Dain, H. J., Dince, P. R., Drellich, M. G., Grand, H. G., Gundlach, R. H., Kremer, M. W., Rifkin, A. H., Wilbur, C. B., & Bieber, T. B. *Homosexuality: A psychoanalytic study*. New York: Basic Books, 1962.

Braaten, L. J., & Darling, C. D. Overt and covert homosexual problems among male college students. *Genetic Psychology Monographs*, 1965, *71*, 269–310.

Evans, R. B. Childhood parental relationships of homosexual men. *Journal of Consulting and Clinical Psychology*, 1969, *33*, 129–135.

Freund, K., & Pinkava, V. Homosexuality in man and its association with parental relationships. *Review of Czechoslovakian Medicine*, 1961, *7*, 32–40.

Greenblatt, D. Semantic differential analysis of the "Triangular System" hypothesis in "adjusted" male homosexuals. Unpublished doctoral dissertation, University of California, Los Angeles, 1966.

Lidz, T., Cornelison, A. R., Fleck, S., & Terry, D. The intrafamilial environment of the schizophrenic patient. II. Marital schism and marital skew. *American Journal of Psychiatry*, 1957, *114*, 241–248.

O'Connor, P. J. Aetiological factors in homosexuality as seen in Royal Air Force psychiatric practice. *British Journal of Psychiatry*, 1964, *110*, 381–391.

Schofield, M. Sociological aspects of homosexuality. Boston: Little, Brown, 1965.

West, D. J. Parental figures in the genesis of male homosexuality. *International Journal of Social Psychiatry*, 1959, *5*, 85–97.

Westwood, G. A. *A minority report on the life of the male homosexual in Great Britain*. London: Longmans, Green, 1960.

the natural history of narcotic drug addiction

George E. Vaillant

The subject of narcotic addiction is now receiving the attention that it deserves. . . . The increase in the number of people addicted to habit forming drugs has been extraordinary within the last five years. . . . The number of victims who directly trace their addiction to physicians' prescriptions is very small. . . . The number of young people addicted is enormous. . . . The charges against dope fiends are usually petty crimes. *P. M. Lichtenstein* (1914).

On the one hand, despite the pessimistic adage "Once an addict, always an addict," a significant number of narcotic addicts recover. On the other hand, despite the optimistic notion that addicts at 40 "mature out of addiction," addiction to narcotics is neither brief nor does it always have a happy ending. Four investigations have followed narcotic addicts long enough to examine the relative validity of these two opposite positions. Two of these studies have been European (17, 20) and two others (15, 23) report long-term follow-ups of patients admitted to the United States Public Health Hospital at Lexington, Kentucky. This review will focus on findings from the latter two studies which fortuitously complement one another and provide an over-view of the eventual fate of American adults addicted to narcotics.

There seem to be many different kinds of narcotics addicts and in each decade patterns of addiction change. At first glance this makes delineation of the natural history of addiction impossible. There are adolescent and middle-aged addicts; there are "criminal" and "medical" addicts; there are heroin and Demerol addicts; there are white Anglo-Saxon Protestant addicts from small towns and black immigrant addicts from urban ghettos; there are male addicts and female addicts; there are high school dropout addicts

Supported by the National Institute of Mental Health through a Research Career Development Award, 5K01 MH38798.

with inadequate personalities and an allergy to employment and physician addicts who self-prescribe and remain employed throughout their addiction. However, one of the conclusions of this review will be that both the addiction pattern and underlying personalities of these disparate groups are more similar than dissimilar. Although these conclusions will rest heavily on the clinical population of one hospital, a wide variety of clinical sub-groups was included in that population.

THE TWO SAMPLES

O'Donnell followed up a stratified sample of all addicts from Kentucky admitted during the period 1936–1959 to the Federal narcotics hospital in the same state (15). His follow-up documented that the hospital served as the principal treatment resource for the state. In the counties he studied, the few addicts who did not obtain admission were not qualitatively different from those who did. His sample included 212 males and 54 females. They were of old American stock, and most had either been originally addicted by a physician's prescription or became addicted in an effort to alleviate alcoholism. At follow-up, half his sample had died. The average addict in his study was 41 at time of admission, had been addicted for 10 years prior to admission and was followed for an average of 11 years after first hospital discharge. In the annals of follow-up studies, his study is per-

From *Seminars in Psychiatry* (Milton Greenblatt and Ernest Artmann, Eds.), 1970, *2*, pp. 486–498. Reprinted by permission of Grune & Stratton, Inc.

haps unique in that only one of the 266 individuals selected for study was unlocated either in person or via tangible evidence of death. In terms of education and father's occupation his sample enjoyed equal or superior socioeconomic status to that of the state as a whole. It included 14 physicians.

In contrast, Vaillant followed up 100 addicts from New York City who in 1952 were first admitted to the Lexington hospital (22–25). In 1952 the hospital at Lexington was a principal, but not the only, voluntary treatment resource for adult New York narcotics addicts. Nine per cent had college education, but most were high school dropouts. Seventy-five per cent sought admission to Lexington voluntarily. However, subsequent to Lexington, 92 percent of the sample were arrested and virtually all who lived became known to the Federal Bureau of Narcotics. Thus, the sample illustrates the difficulty in dichotomizing addicts into criminal and noncriminal categories. Ethnically the sample was probably a fair representation of postwar addiction in New York. Fifty percent of the sample was black and 50 percent white; 30 percent were of Puerto Rican ancestry; all Chinese addicts and those over 50 were excluded. (In order to study at least 50 addicts who had passed their 40th birthday by 1964, Vaillant also studied 32 additional addicts selected so as to have been 28–35 on admission to Lexington in 1952. At points in the text his larger sample of all 132 subjects will be discussed.)

The average age of first illegal drug use was 19; first addiction, 23; and first admission to Lexington, 25. Although 22 percent of the sample was first addicted in adolescence, no addict in the sample was under 20. Thus, both the adolescent addicts who died from their addiction and the relatively large proportion of adolescents (3) who flirt briefly with heroin without becoming seriously addicted are not represented in either study. However, a follow-up of hospital treatment of several hundred adolescent addicts revealed a relapse rate of roughly 95 percent (1). Thus, a majority of severe adolescent addicts in New York were presumably still addicted as young adults, and hence were not necessarily excluded.

In Vaillant's sample 98 percent were followed for 10 years after their first hospital admission. Ninety-six of the 100 addicts were followed until 15 years after the start of their addiction. Of the other four, two were followed for 6 years and one for 11 years at which time each appeared to have achieved stable abstinence. The last addict was still addicted after a 12-year follow-up.

In O'Donnell's sample the decade-long lag between start of addiction and admission to hospital must have served to exclude addicts who rapidly remitted. Similarly, the long distance of the hospital from New York meant that the Lexington hospital probably received only New York addicts who were relatively seriously addicted.

FACTORS PREDISPOSING TO ADDICTION

At least in part narcotic addiction stems from a lack of adequate identification with the adult role. This defective identification seems in part dependent upon childhood events prior to a time when the addiction can be attributed to peer group influence or neighborhood variables (24). Comparison of adolescent addicts with socioeconomically matched controls (3) and the study of physician addicts (14) support this generalization. In both O'Donnell's and Vaillant's study parental loss before six was more frequent than in a nonaddicted but socioeconomically similar segment of the population. In the New York sample addicts tended to be youngest children and to grow up in environments culturally disparate from that of their parents (26); neither observation was true for the Kentucky addicts.

In both samples addicts seemed intellectually superior to appropriate control populations. In Vaillant's sample the addicts as a group were also physically healthy, and three out of four of the allegedly medical addicts were delinquent prior to drug use. In O'Donnell's older middle-class sample 42 percent of the men and 83 percent of the women blamed their original addiction on the treatment of medical complaints. However, their subsequent life history suggested that evidence of persistent medical complaints was evanescent while evidence for personality disorder and persistent addiction was not. At time of follow-up only 2 percent of O'Donnell's medical addicts had medical justification for their addiction. In evaluating the high incidence of medical addicts among women, it is well to remember that symptoms and physical complaints that in men would lead to the diagnoses sociopath and compensation case, in women lead to the diagnoses hysteria and hypochondriasis. A gentleman does not call a lady a character disorder. There is little question, however, that O'Donnell's population did contain more medical addicts than did Vaillant's; and, more important, it contained many more individuals who perceived themselves as *sick* people *needing* drugs rather than *bad* people *indulging* in drugs. Thirty-six percent of O'Donnell's sample maintained their habits entirely via doctors' prescriptions. This was true of only 2 men in Vaillant's sample.

Second, narcotic addicts—even before the passage of the Harrison Act—have much in common with delinquents (12). Long-term study of addicts suggests that the clear distinction between the criminal addict and the a-nice-kid-like-you addict "driven into crime by unwitting addiction" is specious. Certainly, delinquency rates are higher among the poor than the middle-class; adequate identification with adults is more difficult; and the sentences meted out are more severe. Nevertheless, most individuals who use narcotics have a greater tendency than their socioeconomic peers to be delinquent. Studies of physician addicts suggest that they are relatively irresponsible before drug addiction; (14) their MMPIs—especially on the psychopathic deviancy scale—suggest that they have more in common with so-called "criminal" addicts than they do with other physicians. (9, 10) Forty percent of O'Donnell's predominantly white middle-class, middle-aged male addicts had been discharged as unfit from the military (most prior to drug use), and only 36 percent of them were not arrested after the onset of addiction. Twenty-four percent had supported themselves by illegal professions (e.g., gambling and bootlegging) prior to addiction. Fifty percent of Alksne's adolescent addicts (1) and 56 percent of Vaillant's sample (24) *admitted* to being delinquent prior to drug use. The Gluecks' studies of adolescent crime also confirm that drug use of all kinds is a symptom, not a cause, of delinquency. (8) O'Donnell's follow-up data demonstrate that the middle-aged addicts have much less tendency to be overtly delinquent both before or after drugs than do younger addicts, but this may be due to the fact that criminality drops off dramatically after age 30.

Nevertheless, narcotic addiction does vastly magnify preexisting delinquency and maintains it long after an age when criminality of the average delinquent declines. The Gluecks have demonstrated that perhaps a third of delinquents give up criminality as they mature in their thirties but become seriously alcoholic. (7) In O'Donnell's and Vaillant's data the younger addicts tended to be delinquent prior and during drug use but not alcoholic afterwards. The man whose addiction began after 30 tended to be alcoholic prior and subsequent to drug use but not delinquent.

A third premorbid finding is that even prior to addiction, addicts encountered great difficulty in sustaining employment. (15, 17, 23) Not only did dropouts from slum high schools have difficulty with employment but so did the middle-class addicts in O'Donnell's sample. Less than half of O'Donnell's sample were regularly employed prior to addiction, and 15 percent were chronically unemployed. Nearly 50 percent of Vaillant's sample was regularly unemployed prior to addiction.

Addiction itself, however, did not preclude employment. Fifteen percent of O'Donnell's sample worked regularly while addicted and another 40 percent worked part-time. In a group of 50 urban addicts followed for 25 years, Vaillant found that out of 453 man-years during which the subjects were classified as addicted, 11 percent were spent fully employed and another 24 percent spent partially employed. (23) Conversely, during the 275 years during which there was good evidence of abstinence in the community, only 61 percent of the man-years were spent fully employed. Put differently, only an average of 4 out of 25 years were spent regularly employed but an average of 16 of those 25 years were spent *not* addicted.

Disordered lives predispose to narcotic addiction as much as drug addiction leads to disordered lives.

COURSE OF ADDICTION

Most of the existing literature on addiction and virtually all of the treatment programs regard abstinence and addiction as black and white alternatives. Addicts are either sick or well. This is true only if addicts are studied for short periods. Over the long term, most narcotic addicts are gray. Although heroin addiction usually persists for more than a decade, virtually every addict spends some of that time abstinent. Thus, the effectiveness of any treatment must be conceptualized in terms of the proportion of time spent abstinent, rather than in terms of addiction status at a single point in time.

One problem is that there are many ways of looking at the natural history of mental illness. Seeing only the addicts who come to his attention, the police officer feels that addicts never get well. The researcher, if he follows addicts only through their criminal records, believes that most addicts "mature out of addiction." (27) Both are wrong. At an average of 11 years after treatment in Lexington, O'Donnell found 65 percent of living subjects not using drugs; *but* half the subjects in the sample had already died and many were still misusing alcohol. If at point of follow-up only 18 percent of addicts were still addicted to narcotics, an equal number were addicted to barbiturates or confined to jail or hospital. At 12 years after treatment in Lexington, 57 percent of the living subjects in Vaillant's study were in the community and not using drugs. But many others had died from addiction, and of the abstinent some were misusing alcohol and others were to subsequently relapse to narcotics. In the 12 years after Lexington, only 21 percent of Vaillant's sample worked for 3 years or more.

The problem, then, needs to be looked at from other perspectives. The proportion of man-years at risk spent in a given addiction status provides a useful view. Thus, the 1400 man-years after hospital discharge of Vaillant's 100 lower-class, urban, minority group addicts may be contrasted to the 2450 man-years after hospital discharge of O'Donnell's 212 middle-class, rural, Anglo-Saxon male addicts. Interesting similarities emerge. Both groups spent 20 percent of the time in jail or in hospital. O'Donnell's men spent less time fully *abstinent*—18 percent—than did Vaillant's—24 percent—and less time *addicted* to narcotics—32 percent—than Vaillant's group—46 percent. But these differences were due to the fact that O'Donnell's group was older and spent more time addicted to barbiturates and alcohol—30 percent—in contrast to the New York sample who spent only 10 percent of the time misusing alcohol and barbiturates or using narcotics intermittently.

The overall pattern of addiction in women, however, was quite different. (15) Women spent only 7 percent of the time in jail or hospital; they spent 43 percent of the time completely abstinent from any kind of drug misuse. They spent only 14 percent of the time misusing barbiturates and alcohol. However, they spent the same proportion of time as the men in both samples—36 percent—addicted to narcotics.

What of the hypothesis that addicts get better with time? What is the trend of addiction after discharge from hospital? Immediately after leaving Lexington 90 percent of both samples relapsed to the use of narcotics, and a significant proportion of the abstinent 10 percent either died shortly after discharge or had never been physiologically addicted. Over time, however, Vaillant found 22 percent of addicts abstinent and in the community

at 5 years, and 37 percent abstinent and in the community at 10 years. O'Donnell's figures were 15 per cent of addicts fully abstinent at 5 years and 25 percent fully abstinent at 10 years. If ex-addicts using alcohol but not narcotics are included, then O'Donnell's abstinence figures are 44 percent and 52 percent for 5 and 10 years respectively. Studying the course of 343 New York addicts admitted to the Lexington hospital, Duval et al. reported 17 percent abstinent at two years and 25 percent abstinent 5 years after Lexington. (6) Retterstöl and Sund, reporting on 30 Scandinavian morphine addicts, reported 23 percent abstinent at 5 years. (17) In 1932 Schwarz reported on the course of 97 male and 22 female middle-European morphine addicts followed for 5–13 years (average 10); at follow-up he found that 40 percent were abstinent. (20)

These data may be summarized as follows: after first hospital discharge, 10 percent of narcotic addicts will never relapse; on the fifth anniversary of hospitalization another 15 percent will be found to be abstinent; and at the tenth anniversary yet another 15 percent will be abstinent. Roughly 50 percent of addicts who achieve abstinence for a year will subsequently relapse; (11, 22) thus the figures above do not reflect permanent "cures." As the years pass, however, the likelihood of abstinence for a given sample at one point in time goes up.

Active addiction among men showed a steady decline over time. One year after Lexington discharge, 45 percent of O'Donnell's and 62 percent of Vaillant's male subjects were addicted to narcotics. By the fifth anniversary of discharge only 30 percent of O'Donnell's and 50 percent of Vaillant's were addicted. At the tenth anniversary 25 percent of O'Donnell's subjects and 45 percent of Vaillant's subjects were addicted. By the 15th year after Lexington, only 40 percent of Vaillant's subjects were still addicted (but this figure is based on flimsier evidence). The decline of active addiction in Vaillant's sample was artificially gradual due to the relatively large number of potential addicts who were institutionalized at 5 years but who were again at risk on the 10th and 15th anniversary of hospitalization. In O'Donnell's sample 45 percent of the women were addicted at the fifth anniversary after discharge and only 30 percent at the 10th anniversary. The abstinence rates of studies like Winick's that depend upon institutional records are artificially high. (27) Both attrition by death and the fact that some addicts can remain actively addicted and escape notice by the Narcotics Bureau for 5 years makes Winick's conclusions untenable.

But the natural history of addiction is not yet in true perspective. Many addicts alternate between abstinence and addiction. How many addicts become permanent cures? What proportion remain chronically addicted? O'Donnell noted that 30 percent of the men in his sample were addicted virtually the whole period of time after discharged from Lexington, and that 25 percent virtually the whole time abstinent. Another 20 percent spent virtually the whole time addicted either to alcohol and barbiturates or to narcotics. Thus, only 25 percent of O'Donnell's sample showed long periods of both abstinence *and* addiction. Unfortunately, O'Donnell did not specifically report the effect of time on addiction within this group, but his overall figures suggest that this group must have accounted for the decline in addiction within the overall sample.

Vaillant's data were specifically analyzed for the trend toward permanent abstinence over time. But, of course, this sample represents a single, small, selected group of addicts, and the conclusions reported below are only tentative. *During the 18 years after Lexington there appeared to be a trend for 2 percent of addicts at risk to become permanently abstinent each year.* This figure is derived by excluding 8 percent of the sample who were never physiologically addicted, who died shortly after Lexington or who after Lexington returned to a previously established pattern of alcoholism. In Vaillant's sample, the death rate was 1 percent a year, but data from larger samples (2, 6, 15) suggest that at least for the first 5 years of addiction, a more appropriate estimated death rate is 2 percent per year.

By age 28, 17 percent of Vaillant's sample had become abstinent with no known relapse over the next 12 years; 5 years after the start of their addiction 22 percent had become permanently abstinent; 10 years after addiction, at the average age of 35, 31 percent were permanently abstinent. By age 40, 41 percent appeared to have achieved stable abstinence. The figures up to age 35 rest on fairly solid evidence. (25) The figures at age 40 are based on the less firm evidence that: (a) these men have not come to the attention of public health authorities or law enforcement agencies between 1964 and 1970,[1] (b) They have

not been reported to New York city health agencies as narcotics-related deaths. (c) No addict in the sample who achieved 4 years of abstinence was known to subsequently relapse. (d) Emigration out of New York for significant periods of time by active addicts in this sample was rare and is allowed for in the estimate. (e) A more selected sample of 50 older addicts who were definitively followed past their 40th birthday also showed continuation of the same 2 percent per year trend toward permanent abstinence. (23) Certainly there is nothing magical about the age of 40; between ages 20 and 45 there appears no point at which an addict is particularly likely to begin permanent abstinence. A hopeful observation is that the likelihood that an addict chronically addicted for 10 years would become permanently abstinent within the next 5 years, was as likely as the chance that an addict addicted for only 2 years would become abstinent within the next 5. Once a chronic addict, *not* always an addict.

In contradiction to the public's view of narcotics addiction as existing discretely apart from other addictions, the heroin addict is a multiple drug user. Prior to addiction, he has tended to experiment earlier than his peers not only with marijuana but also with tobacco and alcohol. As he passes 30 he has a high likelihood of turning to barbiturates or alcohol. At some point in their lives, 82 percent of the men in O'Donnell's study and 33 percent of the women could be classed alcoholic. Of those who were alcoholic prior to narcotic addiction, only 7 percent were addicted to narcotics at last follow-up; 30 percent, were alcoholic. By contrast, 41 percent of addicts *not* alcoholic prior to addiction remained addicted to narcotics at last follow-up, and only 7 percent were alcoholic. In general, addicts not premorbidly alcoholic constituted a younger group and were more likely to have started drug use for "pleasure."

Similar figures were found in the younger New York sample. Few were premorbidly alcoholic, and 12 years after Lexington 45 percent were addicted to narcotics and 7 percent addicted to alcohol. However, 72 percent of 50 addicts followed past age 40 had also misused alcohol and/or barbiturates at some point in their lives. (23) Young heroin addicts show contempt for the alcoholic; the young car thief scorns the old wino. Both may well be sneering at their own destiny at another point in their life cycle.

[1] Data provided by the Narcotics Register, New York City Department of Health.

Opiate addiction and death are closely linked—both in the minds of the public and in the life of the addict. One explanation for the rarity of narcotic addiction in men over 40 has been ascribed to the high death date. In the world literature, O'Donnell's study provides the most careful and reliable information on the relationship between mortality and opiate addiction. Starting with a population that accurately reflected the population of addicts in an entire state, he identified beyond doubt whether each was alive or dead and obtained the death certificates of each deceased individual. He then matched the age of death with life expectancy tables for the State of Kentucky. The ratio of observed to expected death was 2.54. This figure gives credence to the figure that numerous investigators (6, 17, 19, 21, 23) have derived from smaller, less well-studied samples—namely, that the addict's adult life is shortened by two-thirds. Whether the addicts obtain drugs illegally in the slums, (6) cadge them from physicians (19) or acquire them by prescription from the British National Health Service (2) the death rate is the same. O'Donnell noted conservatively that 6 percent, and perhaps twice that number, of the 130 male deaths in his sample were due to suicide; a third of the deaths were from other than natural causes. From a European sample Rudin noted that 14 percent of 188 deaths of morphine addicts were due to suicide and another 15 percent were also from unnatural causes. (19) Among younger addicts the death rate of the active addicts seems 2 percent a year and very few die from natural causes. For 5 years Duvall followed 453 urban addicts whose source of drugs was illegal and found 11 percent died; 40 percent of the deaths were the direct consequence of addiction. (6) Bewley found an equally high death rate among young English addicts who obtained medically pure heroin by prescription. (2) Twenty-three percent of 69 deaths in Bewley's sample were from suicide; only 17 percent were from natural causes. In short, self-abusive people choose heroin, and even when the means of destruction are provided by a physician rather than a pusher, this does not mitigate the addict's potential for self-destruction.

Yet narcotic addicts are a hardier group than some imagine. Forty addicts in Vaillant's study survived at least 15 years of active addiction (excluding years spent abstinent or protected in institutions) while during the same interval only eight died directly from the hazards of overdose, tetanus, etc., and another seven from causes indirectly associated with that kind of life (e.g., murder, cirrhosis, tuberculosis, alcoholism). Expressed differently, for every two urban addicts who died as a result of addiction, five managed to remain more or less constantly illegally addicted (interrupted, of course, by multiple short hospitalizations and jail sentences) for 15 years!

REASONS FOR ABSTINENCE

A dramatic finding that emerges from the studies of both O'Donnell and Vaillant is that addicts rarely become voluntarily abstinent. The concept of simple maturation out of addiction does not seem tenable and existing evidence suggests that both motivation for abstinence and conventional medical treatment methods for addicts are without much effect. Rather, the principal reason for abstinence among O'Donnell's subjects was the fact that in rural Kentucky narcotics gradually became unavailable. Illegal sources and medical sources alike dried up. For the New York sample, where availability remained unthreatened, the most effective motivation for abstinence was that narcotics were illegal; the most potent treatment was compulsory supervision. Thus, if the addict is followed over time, external coercion of some kind appears a critical variable in facilitating abstinence. This is in contrast to the views both of sociologists like Lindesmith and Chein and the medical profession at large, who, encountering the problem of addiction at one point in time, conclude—quite correctly—that punishment per se is no deterrent.

More specifically several investigators, (1, 6, 15) each studying samples of several hundred voluntary first admissions, observed a relapse rate to narcotics of between 90 and 95 percent. Put differently, in following 132 addicts for 12 years, Vaillant observed that only 3 percent of their 420 voluntarily sought hospitalizations led to abstinence of a year or longer. The same study, however, revealed that short imprisonment was equally ineffective; only 3 percent of 358 short imprisonments meted out to the 132 addicts led to abstinence of a year or longer. (23) Virtually none of the abstinent addicts in either O'Donnell's or Vaillant's studies attributed their abstinence to help from hospitals, physicians or parental intervention. In short, the conventional medical model for the treatment of narcotic addiction is simply not effective.

What then were the factors leading to abstinence? First, there were certain premorbid differences between addicts who achieved lasting abstinence and those who did not. The eventually abstinent addict tends to be more reactive in onset, to exhibit more depression and anxiety and to have been first addicted by a doctor. (15, 17, 25) Never having been physiologically addicted was, of course, a favorable factor; but the length of addiction prior to hospitalization and the daily dose of narcotic was only weakly correlated with outcome. (25) It was not the *amount* of heroin used that determined chronicity.

Ethnic background, voluntary admission, broken homes, family history of addiction, alcoholism or crime were unimportant in affecting prognosis. (6, 25) The absence of criminality prior to addiction predicted abstinence for Kentucky but not New York addicts. As already suggested, a stable pattern of employment prior to addiction was the most important single factor predicting eventual abstinence. (17, 25) Prior employment also happened to be the best predictor of remission from delinquency. (7) A stable childhood before 6 seemed important (25) but difficult to document in retrospect.

Second, certain kinds of "therapeutic" variables seemed to facilitate permanent abstinence; but unfortunately data on permanent abstinence from narcotics are sparse. Although Vaillant has reported on 30 such subjects, generalizations from a single small sample are hazardous. (25) These 30 men were called *permanently* abstinent on the following basis: (a) a minimum of 3 years, and an average of 8 years of documented abstinence in the community by 1964 and (b) a minimum of 9 years without either criminal record or coming to the attention of voluntary treatment agencies reporting to the New York Narcotics Register by 1969. Prior to abstinence, however, each of these 30 men had spent an average of 6 years either addicted or in jail.

Merely taking narcotics away from the addict was not an effective way of inducing permanent abstinence. Length of hospitalization or imprisonment could influence subsequent abstinence over the short but not over the long term. (15, 22) While far more effective than hospitalization, compulsory community supervision was also more effective in permitting short rather than long-term abstinences.

Moving out of areas where addiction was endemic did not powerfully affect long term abstinence. Rather, it seems more important to provide a substitute for addiction than it does to take away what little gratification the addict already has. This fact becomes evident when in Vaillant's sample 27 yearlong abstinences with eventual relapse are compared with the 30 so-called permanent abstinences. (25) A substitute for narcotics (most often alcohol, but also evangelical religious sects, Alcoholics Anonymous and a 50 lb. weight gain) was associated with 60 percent of the permanent but with only 19 percent of the temporary abstinences. It is true that in the Kentucky sample the substitution of alcohol for narcotics was a cure that was often as detrimental as the disease. But among the New York addicts the substitution of alcohol for heroin was often only temporary—perhaps because many such addicts were also on parole. Formation of a close relationship, usually with a new wife, employer or dependent younger relative occurred at the start of 63 percent of the sustained abstinences but was known to be associated with only 26 percent of the temporary abstinences. These findings are in harmony with the therapeutic elements of both methadone-maintenance and Synanon-like programs.

Compulsory community supervision also seemed an important "therapeutic" variable. This was dramatically documented by the fact that 11 of the 30 men who achieved *permanent* abstinences began that abstinence while under at least a year of parole; three others were on some other form of compulsory community supervision. In contrast, only two of the 30 men in Vaillant's sample who remained most persistently addicted received a year of parole. Yet this latter group received 150 voluntary hospitalizations and three times as many jail sentences as the 30 with good outcomes. Thus, poor outcomes were treated more, punished more, but supervised less. Expressed more generally, in 43 instances the 132 addicts in Vaillant's sample received a prison sentence of at least 9 months followed by a year or more of parole. Sixty-five percent of such correctional experiences led to an abstinence of at least a year. The same sample of addicts received 72 imprisonments of 9 months or more *without* a year on parole, and only 14 percent of such sentences led to abstinence for a year. None of the addicts who relapsed on parole ever became abstinent after any other "therapeutic" intervention except a second period of parole. The premorbid background of men who received parole was *not* superior to those who did not receive it. Besides offering addicts compulsory support and an "external super-ego," parole itself was probably a substitute for addiction in that it required ex-addicts to remain regularly employed.

Two short-term studies (4, 11) have reported that only a third of addicts under parole supervision will remain abstinent for a year; the variance of these observations with those of Vaillant can in part be accounted for by the fact that the latter's subjects tended to be older. In evaluating the program of civil commitment in California, Kramer was disappointed that only 20 percent of committed addicts remained abstinent under compulsory community supervision for at least 3 years; 33 percent were abstinent for 1 year. (11) However, even these figures are three to 10 times more successful than those after voluntary hospitalization. Kramer was also concerned that a 7-year civil commitment led to the average addict spending 2–3 years institutionalized. However, this period is not very much greater than the average addict will spend institutionalized; the death rate in his study was only one-third of that expected, and 50 percent of the addicts he traced (in contrast to the expected 25 percent) were abstinent and in the community at the end of 5 years.

Finally, what were the effects of abstinence on the addict's psychological adaptation? There was no evidence that addicts were ever worse off while abstinent. Psychosis, exacerbation of psychosomatic illness and severe depression did not occur. Rather, abstinent addicts resembled personality disorders who have improved. Latent depression might still remain, but even in abstinence the denial of emotional pain, so inherent in addiction, was maintained. Religiosity, altruistic endeavors, a search for silver linings, alcoholism, mild hypomania, and reaction formation were all employed in the service of adaptation to abstinence. The fact that adult addicts do not become psychotic is noteworthy because studies of adolescent addicts suggest that as many as 20 percent are schizophrenic. (1, 3, 24) However, long-term follow-up reveals that such diagnoses are often in error. A study of several thousand felons suggested that addicts were actually far less likely to be psychotic than other delinquents. (13) With the passage of time, then, the psychopathology of the young addicts appears to have been more due to the turmoil of adolescence in an immature, emotionally labile character disorder.

Another facet of the social adjustment of the addicts over time, which militates against a schizophrenic diathesis is the fact that they tended to get married, and if divorced, to get remarried. Unlike the skid row alcoholic or delinquent, only 11 percent lived alone for even half their adult lives. Only 13 percent of the men and 2 percent of the women in O'Donnell's sample never married. In Vaillant's sample 30 percent did not marry, but in this group common-law relationships were more acceptable. In O'Donnell's sample 56 percent of marriages ended in divorce; in those addicts that Vaillant followed to age 40, 67 percent of marriages ended in divorce. Ten percent of the men and 34 percent of the women in O'Donnell's sample married three times or more. In spite of contracting frequent marriages, however, the addicts as a group did not reproduce themselves; the average addict fathered less than two children. (15, 16, 24)

CONCLUSIONS

Perhaps no mental illness is more a product of its social setting than addiction to narcotics. Drugs depend both for their desirability and for their effect on the milieu in which they are taken. Both the modes of and the rationalizations for drug taking depend upon and usually create a subculture. Thus, in part the natural history of drug addiction is like that of a society; it must be rewritten every few years.

It is also well to remember, however, that those who do not read history are condemned to repeat it. Thus, the subculture that spawns the suburban high school addict of the 1970s is different from that spawning the ghetto addict of the 50s or the medical addict of the 30s or the drugstore addict of 1910. Yet the gravity and the common determinants of the malady must be kept in mind. The choice of drug—be it heroin, morphine or alcohol—is a function of the culture, but abuse of that drug is a function of the man. Long-term follow-ups suggest that what is wrong with the addict is *not* that he is addicted to a drug—heroin. Rather, he is an intelligent person unable to sustain employment; he is a suicidal person unable to admit depression; he is a lonely person who inadvertently substitutes drugs for people; he is a person with a paucity of gratifying alternatives rather than a man whose instinctual needs are readily answered by heroin.

The natural history of addiction—like that of adolescence—is that the likelihood of recovery improves with time. In that sense, narcotic addiction differs from most mental illness; but, unlike the adolescent, the addict does not mature spontaneously. The addict needs help both in achieving independence via employment and in discovering means of instinctual satisfaction that are alternative to solitary gratification. Long-term follow-up provides us with certain guidelines for treatment.

The medical model, the casework model of mobilizing family resources and the legal model of punishment are unambiguous failures in the treatment of addiction. Nor can one hope to help the addict by taking away what little he already has—at least not without providing something in return. There appear to be three treatment methods that effectively raise the annual 2 per cent recovery rate and lower the 2 per cent annual death rate that seem to be the fate of the heroin addict. These three treatments are parole, (11) methadone-maintenance (5) and Synanon-like therapeutic communities; (18) all but parole

have too short a history to be encompassed by this review. Over the short term all dramatically appear to facilitate short term abstinence; the success of all three is predictable from the natural history of addiction. All depend upon a backdrop of social prohibition and of legal sanction against narcotic drug abuse. All depend upon close and prolonged supervision, but supervision in the community. Only methadone-maintenance programs fail to require the addict to work as well as prohibiting his use of drugs. All provide some substitute for narcotics. The relative efficacy of these three treatments await scientific comparison. Hopefully, the major centers now working with addicts will conduct such studies and recognize that 1 or 2 years of follow-up will be inadequate to evaluate which one is superior.

REFERENCES

1. Alksne, H., Trussell, R. E. Elinson, J., and Patrick, J.: A follow-up study of treated adolescent narcotic users. Unpublished report of Columbia University School of Public Health and Administrative Medicine, 1959.

2. Bewley, T. H., Ben-Arie, O., and James, I. P.: Morbidity and mortality from heroin dependence. I. Survey of heroin addicts known to Home Office. *Brit. Med. J.* 1:725–726, 1968.

3. Chein, I., Gerard, D. L., Lee, R. S., and Rosenfeld, E.: *The Road to H.* New York, Basic Books, 1964.

4. Diskind, M. H., and Klonsky, G.: *Recent Developments in the Treatment of Paroled Offenders Addicted to Narcotic Drugs.* Albany, New York State Division of Parole, 1964.

5. Dole, V. P., Nyswander, M. E., and Warner, A.: Successful treatment of 750 criminal addicts. *JAMA,* 206:2708–2711, 1968.

6. Duvall, H. J., Locke, B. Z., and Brill, L.: Follow-up study of narcotic drug addicts five years after hospitalization. *Public Health Reports* 78:185–193, 1963.

7. Glueck, S., and Glueck, E.: *Criminal Careers in Retrospect.* New York: Commonwealth Fund, 1943.

8. ——— and ———: *Unraveling Juvenile Delinquency.* New York, Commonwealth Fund, 1950.

9. Hill, H. E., Haertzen, C. A., and Glaser, R.: Personality characteristics of narcotic addicts as indicated by the MMPI. *J. Gen. Psychol.* 62:127–139, 1960.

10. Hill, H. E., Haertzen, C. A., and Yamahiro, R. S.: XXV. The addict physician: A Minnesota Multiphasic Personality Inventory study of the inter-

action of personality characteristics and availability of narcotics. *Res. Publ. Ass. Res. Nerv. Ment. Dis. 46:* 321–332, 1968.

11. Kramer, J. C., and Bass, R. A.: Institutionalization patterns among civilly committed addicts. *JAMA,* 208:2297–2301, 1969.

12. Lichtenstein, P. M.: Narcotic addiction. *N.Y. Med. J.* 100:962–966, 1914.

13. Messinger, E., and Zitrin, A.: A statistical study of criminal drug addicts. *Crime and Delinquency 11:* 283–292, 1965.

14. Modlin, H. C., and Montes, A.: Narcotics addiction in physicians. *Amer. J. Psychiat.* 121:358–363, 1964.

15. O'Donnell, J. A.: *Narcotics Addicts in Kentucky.* Public Health Service Publication 1881, Washington, D.C., U.S. Government Printing Office, 1969.

16. Pescor, J. J.: A statistical analysis of the clinical records of hospitalized drug addicts. *Public Health Reports 143:*1–30, 1943.

17. Retterstöl, N., and Sund, A.: *Drug Addiction and Habituation.* Oslo, Universitetsforlaget, 1964.

18. Rosenthal, M. S.: The Phoenix House Therapeutic Community: An overview. *In* Steinberg, H. (Ed.): *Scientific Basis of Drug Dependence.* London, J. A. Churchill, 1969.

19. Rüdin, E.: Zur sterblichkeit der morphinisten. *Arch. F. Psychiat.* 193:98–116, 1955.

20. Schwarz, H.: Weitere untersuchungen zur prognose de morphinismus. *Mh. Psychiat. Neurol.* 257–280, 1932.

21. Tu, T.: Statistical studies on the mortality rates and the causes of death among opiate addicts in Formosa. *Bulletin on Narcotics 3:*9–11, 1951.

22. Vaillant, G. E.: A 12-year follow-up of New York narcotic addicts: I. The relation of treatment to outcome. *Amer. J. Psychiat. 122:*727–737, 1966.

23. ———: A 12-year follow-up of New York narcotics addicts: II. The natural history of a chronic disease. *New Eng. Med. J. 275:*1282–1288, 1966.

24. ———: A 12-year follow-up of New York narcotic addicts: III. Some social and psychiatric characteristics. *Arch. Gen. Psychiat. 15:*599–609, 1966.

25. ———: A 12-year follow-up of New York narcotic addicts: IV. Some determinants and characteristics of abstinence. *Amer. J. Psychiat. 123:*573–584, 1966.

26. ———: Parent–child cultural disparity and drug addiction. *J. Nerv. Ment. Dis. 142:*534–539, 1966.

27. Winick, C.: The life cycle of the narcotic addict and of addiction. *U.N. Bulletin on Narcotics 16:*1–11, 1964.

student drug use

Helen H. Nowlis

Student drug use is a highly emotional topic for virtually everyone. For an increasing number of people "student" arouses bewilderment, frustration, even anger, and "drug" adds a measure of panic, fear, revulsion, and indignation. Together they provide a climate that is not conducive to clear thinking and constructive action.

I would like to share with you some of the experiences I have had during the past three years as a psychologist, an educator, and an erstwhile psycho-pharmacologist who has been concerned with all aspects of this complex problem. I have managed to become involved with students who use a wide variety of drugs in a variety of ways and for a variety of reasons, with students who do not use drugs, with scientists from biochemists to sociologists, with professionals from medicine and education and the mass media, with judges, with lawyers, with legislators, and with enforcement personnel, as well as with diverse segments of the general public.

I hope that many of you will not be disappointed that I will be discussing only incidentally the prevalence of student drug use, the kinds of drugs they use, and the outcomes of drug use. There are others who can do this better than I. In this connection I would strongly recommend that anyone who is concerned with any aspect of student drug use become familiar with both the methodology and the conclusions of Blum and his associates (1969a, 1969b) in their two important recently published volumes *Society and Drugs* and *Students and Drugs*. My own role has been that of a psychologist analyzing the problem, interpreting the research of others, assessing the current state of our knowledge, and relating

Invited Address presented to the Division of Development Psychology at the Annual Meeting of the American Psychological Association, Washington, D.C., September 2, 1969.

it to what is considered by many to be one of society's major problems. At least a dozen bills related to drug use and abuse have been introduced in the current session of Congress.

Although I shall be discussing one particular problem, I would like to suggest that it is a prototype for many other problems that involve individuals and groups of individuals, society's response to some of the things they do, and psychology's role in contributing to the understanding of these problems and, hopefully, to their solution. I would also suggest that, without being aware of it or without intending to do so, many of us actually contribute to these problems simply by the way we report our research. Once was the time when we could talk only to each other and we developed a special elliptical discourse that, in most instances, communicated effectively and efficiently. We no longer talk only to each other and our discourse (jargon for others) with all of its implicit assumptions is getting us into trouble. Our so-called conclusions are spread abroad by and to people who do not understand sampling and correlation, experimental controls, significance of difference, and the prevalence of error, who do not read or understand our operational definitions, our null hypotheses, or the limited validity and reliability of our measures. They surround every word we use with their own apperceptive mass.

The current "drug problem" is an excellent example of what can happen. One scientist reports chromosome breakage in a "significant" number of white blood cells as a result of adding LSD to blood samples in a test tube and the word spreads across the nation and reverberates in the halls of Congress that LSD is threatening future generations. I am not at all sure how we can cope with this problem, but it might be helpful if each of us reread his "Summary and Conclusions" as if he were John Doe and perhaps added a "may" or an "in some cases," hopefully specified. We may even have to include a new final paragraph, "Cautions." It may not enhance one's ego pleasure over significance at the $p = .01$ level of confidence, but it certainly would help in educating non-scientists in the proper use of scientific information. The real challenge is to do this for individuals who are seeking simple yes-or-no answers to complex questions, and to do it without stretching their tolerance for complexity and uncertainty to the point where they ignore us completely.

"Student drug use" has been widely interpreted as the "spread of narcotic addiction from the ghetto to our middle class and suburban youth," a "threat to the future of our society." In the wake of this increasingly widely held feeling it is almost impossible to discuss student drug use objectively. In the face of society's decision to consider much of this drug use criminal it is difficult even to study it. In estimating incidence of use, of adverse effects, of any drug-related phenomenon we have many numerators but virtually no reliable denominators. The challenges involved in persuading students that their admission to having committed a felony will be confidential and, indeed, in being able to guarantee that confidentiality are sometimes great.

DEFINITION OF TERMS

Within the limits of the space available I would like to discuss the nature and extent of student drug use, its meaning and significance, society's response to it, and some of the problems resulting from efforts to control it. But before we do this we must define some terms lest we add to, rather than reduce, the confusion and controversy that exist.

The first term we must define is "drug." In our society there are two widely accepted definitions of "drug" and both of these contain many implicit assumptions. One defines "drug" as a chemical useful in the art and practice of medicine; the other defines "drug" as a "narcotic," with "narcotic" defined not pharmacologically or medically, but as a socially disapproved substance or an otherwise approved substance used for socially disapproved reasons. Many problems result from definitions based on the purpose for which a drug is used. For example, there is the fact that one and the same substance may be a medicine

under one circumstance and a "narcotic" under another or not even a drug under still another. Second, there is a great temptation to study one type of drug or drug use out of the context of all drugs. Third, there is a tendency to assume that the use of all drugs that fall under one definition has the same significance and the same effects. The use of heroin as a model for all drugs labeled "narcotic" is a case in point. This has led to complete confusion in the design and interpretation of surveys of student drug use. One investigator will define "drug use" as use of any drug without the advice or supervision of a physician; another will define it as use of specific socially disapproved drugs, with the list varying from survey to survey; and at least one has defined it as use of a wide span of drugs, including social drugs such as alcohol and tobacco, home remedies, painkillers, prescription drugs, over-the-counter drugs, as well as exotic and illicit drugs. Only the latter is in any real sense a survey of student drug use. You will note that I have carefully avoided the word "abuse." We will come to that later.

What is needed is a definition of "drug" that is objective and descriptive and does not have within it a variety of implicit value judgments, which are the source of much of the confusion and controversy that abounds in discussions of drugs and drug use. The basic pharmacological definition of "drug" as any substance that by its chemical nature affects the structure or function of the living organism is about as descriptive and objective as one can be. This definition includes a wide range of substances. It includes both medicines and socially disapproved substances. It also includes a wide range of substances that we do not ordinarily call drugs, such as beverage alcohol and caffeine, nicotine, agricultural, industrial, and household chemicals, pollutants, even food. For many purposes this is too broad a definition, but it forms a base from which we can select groups of drugs and it forces us to make explicit the basis on which we make a given classification. Hopefully, it reminds us that a drug is a drug and the principles by which it interacts with the living organism are the same whether we call it a medicine, a "narcotic," or by some other name.

The other term that we must define is "use." Again, there are certain advantages in starting from a descriptive and objective base. "Use" is often defined in terms of frequency—as ever having tried, occasional, regular, or excessive. But even these terms leave plenty of room for value judgments. It is necessary to specify each in terms of actual frequency of use over a specified time. Whatever one's definition of excessive, it is then at least explicit.

This is perhaps the point at which we should consider "abuse" and to recognize that, as currently used, both socially and legally, it has little correspondence to "use" as I have defined it. In other contexts and even for our national drug, alcohol, "abuse" is defined as a pattern of use that interferes with the psychological, social, academic, or vocational functioning of a given individual. As far as many other drugs are involved, if we call them drugs, "abuse" is legally defined as *any* use of a non–medically approved drug or of a medically approved drug for a non–medically approved purpose. Our effort to justify and support this as abuse in terms of "effects" of drugs so used is one of the main factors in the current controversy over drugs. When research indicating that monosodium glutamate injected peritoneally into pregnant mice produces offspring with neural damage, ataxia, obesity, and sterility (Olney, 1969) is presented as evidence that it is dangerous and should not be added to baby food, eminent experts testify that this is irrelevant because it "has no relationship to the amount of MSG consumed conventionally nor does it have any relationship to the usual rate of entry into the body."[1] When the same type of evidence is presented for LSD, it is used as at least partial grounds for labeling LSD society's most dangerous drug, placing it in a category with heroin and singling it out for the severest criminal penalties. I am not making a case for LSD. I am merely pointing out that we are changing the rules to suit our purposes and are inviting controversy and charges of hypocrisy.

SURVEYS OF STUDENT DRUG USE

With all of these qualifications and with the recognition that we have no research from which we can confidently generalize to all students, what can we say about student drug use? Most students use drugs. In Blum's 1967 survey (Blum et al, 1969a, 1969b) of a random sample of approximately 200 students from each of five different west coast colleges and universities, 68–81% had used tobacco one or more times, 89–97% had

used alcohol, 11–32% had used amphetamines, 18–31% had used sedatives, 11–28% had used tranquilizers, 10–33% had used marihuana, 2–9% had used any of a variety of hallucinogens, and 1–2% had used a variety of narcotics and painkillers. Lest you forget, let me remind you that these percentages represent reports of having used once or more. They include both legal and illegal use for most drugs. A follow-up survey in 1968 on marihuana use in the school that had shown 21% marihuana use in the initial survey showed 57% marihuana use. Reports of regular use had increased from 4 to 14%. The rate of hallucinogen experience had increased from 6% to perhaps as high as 17%. Opium use (not heroin) was estimated to have increased from 1 to 10%. Again, a word of caution: We know on the basis of a variety of surveys of institutions around the country that use of illicit drugs varies from institution to institution and from area to area. We also know that the west coast tends to be a relatively high-use area. Even there, it is a small minority of students who are involved in regular use of marihuana or hallucinogens, with regular use defined as more than once a week but less than daily.

There are two surveys in the planning stage that should provide us with more adequate data on which to base generalizations. One will involve a sample of 200 colleges of varying sizes and locations, hopefully with a follow-up after two years. The other will involve a sample of high schools together with their feeder junior high schools in a four-year longitudinal study.

Estimates currently made by Stanley Yolles, Director of the National Institute of Mental Health,[2] on the basis of results of a majority of studies that have been done throughout the country, are that 20–40% of high school and college students have tried marihuana at least once. Of these about 65% are experimenting (from 1 to 10 times and then discontinuing use), 25% are social users, smoking on occasion when it is available, and 10% of those who have tried it at least once use it regularly, with regular defined as devoting a significant portion of their time to obtaining and using the drug. This would mean that somewhere between 2–4% of the students are regular users. This would seem to bear little relationship to statements by prominent people headlined in the

---

[1] P. L. White. Testimony before the Select Committee on Nutrition and Human Needs, United States Senate, 1969. (Quoted in Associated Press Washington dispatch, July 18, 1969.)

[2] S. F. Yolles. Statement before the Subcommittee on Alcoholism and Narcotics, Committee on Labor and Public Welfare, United States Senate, August 6, 1969.

news media that 1 out of 10 students is "hooked" on marihuana.

The National Institute of Mental Health (see Footnote 2) also estimates that the use of LSD, even in relatively high-use areas, is low, with probably not more than 5% ever having tried, and an even smaller percentage country-wide.

There can be little doubt that use of illicit drugs is increasing and that use is spreading both up and down the age scale. In recent years it has begun to appear at the junior high and elementary school levels. A large number of middle class adults are believed to be using marihuana. We do not have and probably will not have good data on this group (or any group) as long as possession of marihuana is a felony. In all cases it is the spread of marihuana use that is predominant. The fact that there is increasing use of a mood-changing drug should not surprise us. Mood-changing drugs are the largest single type of drug used, even in prescriptions. The thing that is significant is that marihuana is a drug that carries the heaviest criminal penalties and a degree of social disapproval equivalent to that of heroin to most people.

The reasons for nonmedical drug use are predominantly the same reasons for which man has used drugs throughout the ages: to relieve pain, to allay anxiety, to produce euphoria, and to modify experience, perception, and thought. It is tempting to speculate that modern man's increased use of mood- and mind-altering substances is at least in part an indication that modern man has more pain, more anxiety, less euphoria, and less satisfying experiences, but this is the kind of speculation that has gotten us into trouble. Many of the reasons that young people use drugs are in large measure the reasons that adults use drugs: for fun, to facilitate social interaction, to feel better, to relieve boredom, to escape from problems, even to protest a little. The main difference is that most adults get their stimulants, sedatives, and tranquilizers legally from physicians and their social drug, alcohol, is legal. Their tension, anxiety, fatigue, and depression are judged to be legitimate consequences of their full participation in pursuit of socially approved social and economic goals or values. That the outcomes of their drug use are not always good is attested to by the fact that increasing numbers of hospital admissions are directly attributable to drug-related illness and that we have 6–9 million alcoholics, depending on how one defines "alcoholic."

CONCEPT OF "DRUG EFFECT"

Please note the use of "outcomes of drug use" rather than "drug effects." The concept of drug effect is an example of a term which may be used to communicate effectively among scientists who understand how drugs act that the "effect" of any drug is a function of dose level, route of administration, and many nondrug factors, and that drugs do not have within them the power to produce a specifiable and reliable effect. The average layman with his "magic-potion-notion" of drugs does not understand that we are really involved in a numbers game. For example, the effective dose (ED50) of any drug is that dosage level or amount of the drug *by* which, not at which, 50% of a given population show whatever effect is desired, among many others. The official toxic dose (TD50) depends on how one defines toxic. Even the lethal dose (LD50) is that dosage level *by* which 50% of a group of animals die under specified conditions. The lethal dose may vary with the temperature under which the animals are kept and with whether they are housed singly or in large groups. The reason for this numbers game is that the "effect" of many drugs is largely a function of many nondrug factors.

"The effect" of any drug is a myth. All drugs have multiple effects. No effects are completely reliable or predictable. All drugs are chemicals that are absorbed into the bloodstream and interact with the complex, delicately balanced biochemical system that is the living organism. It is a system that varies from individual to individual and from time to time in the same individual. It varies with age. It varies with sex. It varies in sickness and in health. One needs only to read the counterindications and the list of idiosyncratic reactions and side effects, the "diseases of medical progress," in the advertisement of drugs in medical and scientific journals to be aware of the complexity of factors influencing the effects of a drug. Effects also vary with psychological characteristics of the individual, with his expectations, and with the setting in which the drug is taken or administered. "Outcomes of" or "reactions to" *use* of a drug at least put the organism, physiologically and psychologically defined, into the picture and leave room for discrimination among patterns and circumstances of use.

Whether outcomes or reactions are good or bad is a value judgment. In some cases there is general agreement, in others, violent disagreement. The widely hailed outcome of treating mentally disturbed patients with the major tranquilizers, that is, "emptying our mental hospitals," is considered by at least one prominent psychiatrist to be the equivalent of putting the patient in a chemical straightjacket and depriving him of his right to attempt to solve his problems. The methadone treatment for heroin addiction is regarded by many, including some addicts, as a bright hope and by other as no treatment at all and as outright immoral, because it substitutes dependency on one drug for dependency on another. It is just a matter of values, to be dependent or to be free of supporting one's habit on the black market. There is bitter disagreement within the medical profession as to the propriety and effectiveness of the use of LSD in therapy.

Somewhat guardedly, Blum (Blum et al., 1969b) concludes from his data,

It is clear . . . that a variety of unpleasant outcomes can occur but one gets the impression that very few suffer anything damaging over the long run. Thus, one can conclude, as we do, that anything but acute toxic ill effects are unlikely and that illicit–exotic drugs when used as students are now doing, for the most part do not seem to pose serious hazards to school performance or to health [p. 378].

He hastens to point out, and properly, that his sample did not include any information on students who had dropped out of school and that those who remained and were studied were a select group. He also points out that his data give no indication of the possible outcomes of long-term low-dosage use.

Yolles (see Footnote 2) reports from NIMH that the incidence of serious adverse reactions to marihuana use appears to be low, but also points out that as the total number of users increases the number experiencing adverse reactions will increase, that the effects of the drug on judgment and perception *might* very well be a factor in automobile accidents, and that users with significant psychiatric problems *might* avoid seeking psychiatric treatment as a result of this form of "self-medication." There are no adequate research data to support the latter statements.

Both of these statements function as projective tests. Those who, because of their personal beliefs, attitudes, and values, believe that illicit drugs are by definition "bad" and that illicit drug use can bring nothing but harm to the individual and to society will dismiss the data and seize on the questions raised by limitations of research design or the absence of research results. Those who hold the other view will seize on the data and dismiss the questions. Those who attempt to be objective will advise caution until we have more data based on research. The irony is that more research will probably leave us with essentially the same dilemma. Such is the nature of drugs, of drug action, and of complex human behavior.

I cannot conceive of a research design that could provide the definitive answers the public wants. The number of and interactions among the independent variables involved in, for instance, the driving performance of individuals who have used marihuana are staggering. Administering marihuana of known composition in known amounts in a double-blind situation in the laboratory to naive subjects of equivalent driving skill as measured on a simulator will tell us very little about the driving performance of individuals who, for a variety of reasons, have chosen to use an unknown amount of an illegal drug of unknown strength and purity obtainable only on the black market, who have expectations and varying amounts of experience as to the "effects" of that drug, who choose to drive cars of varying type and condition under various road conditions at some time after having used some amount of the drug, and who have had varying degrees of experience in coping with whatever reactions they as individuals experience when they "use marihuana."

We do need laboratory research on all drugs. We need to know the ways in which they modify the biochemical and neurochemical organism. But beyond this we need to know how these changes are related to changes in behavior. This is the greater challenge. In the meantime, differences "significantly greater than chance" in situations in which so many important independent variables have been controlled will not provide us with the answers to social problems, especially when they are used inappropriately by people grasping at anything that seems to support what they believe about drugs that have historically been labeled "bad," "dangerous," or "evil."

The use of virtually all drugs involves adverse reactions or bad outcomes, including death or, in some cases, life imprisonment, *at some dosage level in some people under some circumstances.* This includes aspirin, smallpox vaccine, penicillin, alcohol, nicotine, barbiturates, amphetamines, as

well as heroin, LSD, and marihuana. In this regard, it is of interest that, to my knowledge, there
are no verified deaths directly attributable to
either LSD or marihuana as *pharmacological
agents* except for one elephant. Official records
show approximately 185 deaths per year from
aspirin.

SOCIETAL REACTIONS TO STUDENT
DRUG USE

As we turn to the meaning and significance of
student drug use, society's response to it, and
efforts to control it, I want to make it very clear
that I am speaking as one psychologist who is
acutely aware of the fact that background, training and experience, beliefs, attitudes, and values,
even basic beliefs about the nature of man, are
important factors in any analysis and assessment
of these phenomena. One always hopes that
awareness inspires caution. My only special qualifications to comment on this social problem are
that, because of commitments entered into almost
adventitiously, I have been forced to look at student drug use from almost every possible point
of view and have had the privilege of interaction
with many representatives of disciplines and
professions who espouse these many points of
view, including students of all shades of opinion
and involvement.

If one wants to understand drug effect and drug
use, one must look not solely at the pharmacological agent, but at the person who chooses to
use drugs, how much he uses, when and where
and how, and what he expects, wants, or believes
will result from that use. We are learning to our
dismay that to try to control drug use by limiting
the supply of the particular drug used does not
decrease drug use in general. Many users merely
turn to another substance that may involve even
more risk, and in our society drugs are every-
where, legal drugs, illegal drugs, and substances
which we do not call drugs.

In addition, we have mounted a gigantic campaign to persuade the public that there is a drug
for every ill or misery—anxiety, depression, tension, and the physical symptoms associated with
these, irritability, fatigue, lack of success in business, in social life, in the family. If there is not
a chemical cure, there soon will be. This has
rocketed the pharmaceutical industry to the num-
ber-one profit-making industry in the country,
passing the automobile industry in 1967. All of

this, of course, has to do with the promotion of
legal drugs, both prescriptions and over-the-
counter drugs, obtained through legal means. But
I seem to remember learning in introductory psychology about a principle known as generalization. It should not surprise us that young people
do not understand why we are so excited about
their use of drugs for their miseries and ills. It is
also relevant to note that there has been an almost
equally vigorous campaign on behalf of their
drugs via the news reporting of the drug scene.
It has been suggested that the chemical most
responsible for the current drug scene is printer's
ink. Just because most of us who are over 30
do not ordinarily seek adventure, new experience,
insight into one's self, independence, and have
either found or given up looking for new insights,
meaningful social relationships, creative expression, even a dash of rebellion against the restrictions that we accept as inevitable in a modern
technological society, and a pinch of fun, we
should not underestimate the appeal to the young
of anything that promises any or all of these,
regardless of whether those promises can be
fulfilled. This particular characteristic of many
drugs does not seem to deter many of us from
seeking what is promised. In addition, we have
learned that many drugs are much more effective
if we believe that they will be, and that "sugar
pills" have cured great ills and produced profound negative effects. One physician has been
reported to have said somewhat facetiously,
"Whenever a new drug comes on the market, rush
to your physician while both he and you still believe in its powers."

It is almost trite to point out to an audience of
psychologists that drug use serves different functions for different individuals. Despite this, "escape to nowhere" has become the banner for
numerous efforts to dissuade everyone from any
use of certain drugs. It is astounding to note how
often mere use of illicit drugs is taken as an indication that the user needs psychiatric treatment.
This would seem to be, in part, the result of our
concept of drug abuse as a disease and our
definition of any use of illegal drugs as abuse.
We seem to assume both that drugs are to cure
illness and that if one takes drugs, he is, almost
by definition, ill. There is no doubt that some
young people use drugs to escape from pressure,
from anxiety, from impulses which threaten them,
from the stresses and strains of growing up.
There is also no doubt that some people who are
ill use drugs. But unless one defines doing any-

thing that is not socially approved as illness, the great majority of young people who use drugs illegally are not ill and are not in need of psychiatric treatment. Many use them because they think it is fun. Many try them out of curiosity. Many use marihuana much as we use alcohol to facilitate social interaction. Some use them as occasional respite from the pressures of increasing academic demands.

Fun, curiosity, social interaction, and change of pace are all rather normal motivations. There are many ways to satisfy them. The important question is why increasing numbers of students are choosing to risk severe legal penalties by choosing to use illegal drugs. It could have something to do with society's response to their use of drugs or, perhaps more important, society's response to young people.

The very small minority of students who use illegal drugs regularly and who devote a considerable portion of their time to obtaining drugs, to using them, and to talking about their drug experiences are also a varied group. Many of them are bright enough and well enough put together to manage their drug use and still fulfill their academic obligations. Others are not. Some are convinced that drugs will solve any of a variety of problems, some developmental and some pathological. Some are sick. Again we should ask the question, "Why illegal drugs?"

Society's undiscriminating response to all student drug use has been emotional and extremely punitive. It is outraged at many of the things some young people are doing and saying these days. There are those who would pass laws against them and even some who would shoot a few students in the belief that that would serve as a deterrent. If one watches the faces of those who suggest the latter, one gets the impression that shooting students might also serve to reduce their anger and frustration. But there are calmer voices to be heard and as yet the more violent reactions have been held in check in most cases. But the drug issue is different. For a great variety of historical and cultural reasons we have carefully nurtured attitudes, beliefs, and stereotypes about all drugs which are outside of medicine or used for nonmedical reasons. Begining with the Harrison Narcotic Act we have forged a system of criminal penalties, including mandatory jail sentences, denial of probation and parole, for possession and "sale" ("to sell" is legally defined as to sell, to give, or otherwise to dispose) of "narcotics" that would suggest that these were greater

than any crimes other than treason or first-degree murder. I would suggest the hypothesis that the drug issue may represent a rallying point for frustration, resentment, and anger generated by many things that young people are saying and doing and that the existing drug laws and the attitudes that support them are rough-and-ready weapons for retaliation. Many are quick to blame drugs for everything from dropping out, criticizing, and protesting to violence and crime on the streets. If drugs are to blame, we can concentrate on controlling them and look no further. Historically, nonmedical drug use has been associated primarily with minority groups and, with the persistent "magic-potion-notion" of drugs, drug use has been a convenient scapegoat and a ready target for aggression against these groups. Students are our fastest growing and increasingly vocal minority.

Estimates of the number of persons in the United States who have used marihuana vary from 8 to 20 million. The NIMH (see Footnote 2) considers that 8 million is a conservative estimate and that there may be 12 million. All of these people are criminals because they have committed a felony: They possessed marihuana. Psychology has something to say about the effects of labeling. Psychology and common sense certainly have something to say about punishment as a deterrent when the chances of being punished are somewhere between 1 in 500 and 1 in 1,000. But it either is not being said or is not being heard.

Because of these laws, because of the nature of the law enforcement approach to the control of drug use, and because of the persistent attitudes and beliefs which support that approach, the drug issue has also become a target and a rallying point for many young people's frustration, resentment, and charges of hypocrisy against a society that promotes the use of alcohol, is unwilling even to require the registration of guns, and seems unwilling to regulate much behavior that results in thousands of deaths and injuries.

EDUCATIONAL APPROACH TO DRUG CONTROL

The other major approach to control of illegal drug use is that of education. I use the word reluctantly because most so-called drug education has until very recently consisted of preaching and of attempts to scare with statements that are inaccurate and often patently false. Much of it still does. It seems to be designed to preserve and justify our attitudes and beliefs and our laws. It obviously has not reduced illegal drug use. Some of it may even have instigated use.

Drug education is desperately needed: Students need it; parents need it; legislators need it; physicians need it; the general public needs it. We are living in an increasingly chemically dominated environment. Drugs are an important part of that chemical environment. One of our most urgent social problems is to learn to live wisely in that environment, but we cannot learn as long as we do not understand what drugs are and how they act, what risks are involved in all drug use, and how these risks can be minimized. We also need to expand our concept of drug to include the many substances that by their chemical nature affect the structure and function of the living organism.

To do honest, sound, and effective drug education we will need all of our skills in communication and persuasion. We will have to change long-held beliefs and attitudes about drugs. We will have to separate the problem of drugs as pharmacological agents from the problem of people who make value judgments about drugs, about "drug effects," about the reasons for using drugs, and about people who use drugs. The *people* problem will be the more difficult to solve, but a solution to the *drug* problem should make it easier.

CONCLUSION

I would like to close by addressing myself particularly to Division 7, the division of APA primarily concerned with growth and development from infancy to adulthood. The problem of student drug use is extremely complex. It has very little to do with drugs as pharmacological agents. At the core of it is a phenomenon that has relatively recently been created by our society primarily in the interest of technological and economic development. It has recently been intensified by the arrival of the baby boom at college age. This phenomenon is that of increasingly prolonged adolescence. Having created it we generally choose to pretend that it does not exist.

"Nonadulthood" has been stretched 5–10 years beyond physiological maturity. It has been stretched farthest for the brightest and most talented. Our young people between the ages of 16 and 25 are our fastest growing minority, a

minority that has very little power and influence even on their own destinies. In other times they would have been married and dutifully, even happily, contributing to the gross national product or being "liberally educated" while waiting to assume the positions which had been prepared for them.

Our failure to integrate today's young people into society, to give them any significant role except to fight our wars, to provide them with a realistic arena in which to accomplish the tasks of adolescence, however you wish to define them, to examine these tasks in the light of the world in which we now live has left them largely to their own devices. We tend to react violently against many of these.

All is not well with many of our young people. We are not facing the very difficult problems involved in understanding and dealing with the process of becoming an adult in a rapidly changing and highly technological society. No society will flourish whose institutions—family, religion, education, business, government—do not effectively challenge substantial numbers of its most gifted young people to grow, to use their talents in constructive and satisfying ways, to develop a sense of worth and accomplishment, to develop meaningful and humane social relationships, to feel that they have an increasing role in the control of their destinies and some influence on the society in which they must live, work, play, establish a home and raise a family, and eventually to assume responsibility for that society and its problems.

Instead of facing basic problems we are lashing out at symptoms, at drug use, at protest, at dropping out, at manner and dress and language, and are feeling satisfaction and relief at doing "something." Much of what we are doing is at best keeping us from dealing with the basic problems and at worst intensifying those problems. As pointed out by Barber (1967) and many others, social policy is itself one of the major determinants of the nature and severity of a social problem, particularly the "drug problem."

Perhaps we should be among the first to accept George Miller's (1969) advice in his Presidential Address and spread the word that young people are not basically bad and need not be coerced into work and responsibility. Given half a chance they will grow and develop and make wise decisions, but only if we expect that they will and provide the freedom and opportunity for them to learn to do so.

REFERENCES

Barber, B. *Drugs and society.* New York: Russell Sage Foundation, 1967.

Blum, R. H., & Associates (Eds.) *Society and drugs.* Vol. 1. *Drugs.* San Francisco: Jossey-Bass, 1969. (a)

Blum, R. H., & Associates (Eds.) *Students and drugs.* Vol. 2. *Drugs.* San Francisco: Jossey-Bass, 1969. (b)

Miller, G. A. Psychology as a means of promoting human welfare. *American Psychologist,* 1969, *24,* 1063–1075.

Nowlis, H. H. *Drugs on the college campus.* New York: Doubleday, 1969.

Olney, J. W. Brain lesions, obesity, and other disturbances in mice treated with monosodium glutamate. *Science,* 1969, *163,* 719–721.

dynamics and morality of violence and aggression: some psychological considerations

Seymour Feshbach

The intent of this article is to examine, from a psychological perspective, moral as well as more traditional psychological issues pertaining to major manifestations of human aggression. It should be stated at the outset that there are many fundamental questions concerning the antecedents and properties of violence and aggression that remain unresolved. Psychology cannot yet offer definitive statements concerning the nature of human aggression nor can psychological considerations provide the sole or primary basis for the moral evaluations of violent actions. Despite these caveats, psychological research and theory can make a meaningful contribution to the analysis and understanding of violent phenomena. Violence is impressively diverse in the forms that it may take. It includes the physical abuse of a child by a parent, the injury to property and person inherent in so many criminal acts, the eruption of rage and destructiveness in a previously conforming adolescent. To these we may also add the violence exerted by the state, at home, in its efforts to maintain conformity to the rule of law, and abroad, in its efforts to pursue its national interest. Further instances of violence are the destruction of property and manifestations of abusiveness by some college student radicals, the more subtle forms of aggression through which men of one color manage to humiliate and degrade men of another color, and, at another level, the

Based on an address given at the meeting of the Western Psychological Association, Los Angeles, California, April 1970.

The author wishes to express his gratitude to Norma Feshbach and Howard Adelman for their painstaking reading of the manuscript and their helpful comments.

violent fantasies sometimes expressed in dreams and in drama.

It is evident that the range of behaviors subsumed under the category of aggression and violence encompasses actions that differ in their dynamics and morality. There are, however, for several of the behaviors cited, important dimensions of similarity. Although we do not propose to examine each of these examples in detail, a goal of this article is to clarify the basis by which we judge these various forms of violent expression to be similar or different. Pertinent studies, including laboratory experiments, are cited, but the main thrust of this article is analytical. The studies that are referred to largely serve to illuminate ways of conceptualizing complex social phenomena rather than actually accounting for these phenomena.

RELEVANCE OF PSYCHOLOGY FOR MORAL EVALUATIONS OF VIOLENCE

The mere interjection of moral considerations in a scientific discourse is unusual, and it is a reflection of both the maturity of the profession and our rapidly changing social mores that this Convention (see footnote 3) has taken, as its central focus, the moral dimension of behavior. There are still many who would question the relevance of scientific inquiry to moral issues. The scientist is presumably concerned with questions of the "how" and "what" of behavior, while questions of "should" and "ought" have been assumed to be in the domain of theology, philosophy, or cultural tradition. This position is inadequate for the physical sciences, but is particularly superficial for the behavioral sciences. There are, in fact, several points of relevance of psychology and related sciences for the formulation of moral judgments.

At the most obvious level, moral values are the legitimate object of psychological study. With regard to matters of violence, psychologists have begun to investigate individual and cultural differences in the evaluations made of specific violent acts and more general forms of aggressive behavior (Opton & Duckless, 1970). Psychological methods are uniquely suited to describe variations in the moral evaluation of violent acts, to isolate dimensions of the context and of the action which contribute to differences in evaluation, and to determine the degree to which personality and sociocultural factors influence moral attitudes. For example, in the Feshbach and Feshbach (1965) study of reactions to President Kennedy's death, it was found that the respondent who was assessed as high in overt aggressive tendencies was more likely to be pleased by Oswald's death, and to believe that Ruby was a patriot who should be let free or a conspirator who ought to be shot. Evidence was also found of correlations between an aggressive personality disposition, the evaluation of Ruby's act, and a willingness to invade Cuba. Personality factors, however, accounted for only a small part of the variance, with specific attitudinal factors being more closely associated with responses to the assassination. In a subsequent study,[1] these same aggressive personality dispositions were shown to be significantly but not highly correlated with attitudes toward the Vietnam war.

The fact that aggressive people tend to be attracted to the violence of war neither explains nor provides a satisfactory account of attitudes toward war. Psychologists oriented toward personality variables are prone to use a personality correlate of an aggressive value or act as an explanation of that value or act. A well-known example of this tendency was the effort to explain social prejudice through the concept of the authoritarian personality (Adorno, Frenkel-Brunswik, Levinson, & Sanford, 1950). A more recent instance is the effort to explain and evaluate student radicalism solely on the basis of personality characteristics of some militant students.

In investigating the basis for the evaluation of violent acts, one must, of course, be cognizant that such acts take place in a social context and that

the act and its evaluation are multidetermined. A recent example of the multidetermination and complexity of moral judgments is the reactions to the Mylai incident. One might assume that a violent event such as the slaughter at Mylai, so clearly deviant from cultural norms regarding fair play, the appropriate use of force, and the noncombatant status of women and children, would elicit uniform reactions of indignity and condemnation. However, the interviews reported by Opton and Duckless (1970) indicate that a great many people, including some opposed to the Vietnam war, were more disturbed about the disclosure of the events at Mylai than about the events themselves. It is evident that one cannot assume consensus in the evaluations of violent behaviors and that a fruitful problem area for the psychologist is the study of the parameters of moral judgments.

Psychology also relates to moral judgments on a more subtle and more profound level. There is a long philosophical tradition that distinguishes between problems of knowledge or epistemology and problems of value—or ethics. Although the rules and procedures for determining "what is truth" differ from those determining "what should be" or "what is best" (Scheibe, 1970), there are important areas of discourse in which facts and values are intimately related (Churchman, 1964). To cite some illustrative examples, there are certain values, such as those placed on the sanctity of life, on the desirability of a healthy body and a healthy mind, on religious activities, on national prestige, which are independent of the methods of science. However, many values, including some moral statements, are less ultimate and imperative in their structure and are basically subordinate judgments, instrumentally related to the achievement of more fundamental values of the culture. For example, whether physically beating a child is evaluated as "right" or "wrong" or "good" or "bad" is very much dependent on beliefs concerning the effects of the beating on the child's subsequent mental health and social adjustment. If it is believed that repeated physical punishment of a child will result in a youngster who is socially competent and psychologically adjusted, then beating a child would have a positive moral value. This kind of belief is subject, of course, to empirical validation. Thus, while the data are not definitive, there is considerable evidence that repeated physical punishment of a child has a number of undesirable personal and social consequences, including delinquency and serious neu-

[1] M. I. C. Woodson and S. Feshbach. Some Dimensions and Correlates of Attitudes toward War. Unpublished paper, available from author, 1969.

rotic disturbances. In fact, the strongest and most consistent correlate of aggressive problem behavior in children is a history of physical punishment at home, including punishment for aggression (Feshbach, 1970). In socializing a child, as in the political arena, there are instances when violent punishment has the unfortunate consequence of fostering the very behavior it is designed to inhibit.

A similar analysis can be made of many other moral evaluations that have their basis in beliefs that can be subjected to empirical study. For example, the moral judgment of erotic stimuli is likely to be influenced by the results of current investigations of the effect of exposure to pornographic materials on sexual behavior. Thus, there will often be a close relationship between what is "true," what is "desirable," and what "should be." The terms we use in making moral evaluations convey these connections. "Right" and "wrong" are used to describe the truth value of a statement; they are also used to describe the morality of behavior. The ascription "good" and "bad" can carry the instrumental connotation of "good" or "bad" for someone, in terms of the achievement of a superordinate personal or social value. Similar considerations hold for the evaluation of various forms of aggressive expression; and psychology, by delineating the personal and social consequences of violence and other aggressive forms, can thereby help contribute to a rational basis for the evaluation of aggressive behavior.

Freud's (1957, orig. publ. 1930) instinct theory of aggression is a pertinent example of psychological assumptions regarding aggression which have implicit and explicit social consequences. For Freud, aggression was an instinctive biological drive that could be repressed only at the cost of personal integration and pleasure. He felt, however, that the personal price, tempered by the provision of sublimated outlets, must and should be paid in order for social order and culture to be maintained. In *Civilization and Its Discontents*, Freud (1957, orig. publ. 1930) states,

> Civilized society is perpetually menaced with disintegration through this primary hostility of men toward one another. . . . Culture has to call up every possible reinforcement in order to erect barriers against the aggressive instincts of men and hold their manifestations in check by reaction-formation in men's minds. Hence, its system of methods by which mankind is to be driven to identification and aim inhibited love-relationships; hence the restriction on sex-

ual life, and love too, its ideal command to love one's neighbor as oneself [p. 86].

The position enunciated by Freud in this statement, like the philosophy of Hobbes, provides a justification for the exercise by society of strong controls over impulse expression. It also leads to a pessimism about the possibility of reducing violence in human affairs, and, indeed, Freud himself was not very sanguine about the success of these techniques for controlling natural aggressive impulses. However, sharply contrasting views can be derived from a learning model of the origins of violence and aggression, and it should be noted that Freud's pessimism is not shared by a number of other psychoanalytic theorists such as Erich Fromm.

There are at least three related issues implicit in Freud's position which can be distinguished for purposes of theoretical and empirical study: "Is aggression instinctive?"; "Do restraints on aggression lead to internal conflict and maladaptive behavior?"; and "What are the best mechanisms, from the standpoint of personal adjustment and social adaptation, for reducing violent behavior?" The responses to each of these questions have an important bearing on the moral evaluation of aggressive behavior, and, therefore, these issues will be considered in some depth.

DYNAMICS OF AGGRESSION

In order to address ourselves to these and related matters, an elaboration of terminology and theory will be useful. Terminology and theory are interwoven, and, inevitably, definitional distinctions have theoretical implications. The distinctions to be made bear very specifically on the issue of the instinctive nature of aggression and violence. The terms aggression and violence are used similarly in this article, violence being reserved for the more severe forms of physical aggression. At a descriptive level, the label aggression might be applied to any behavioral sequence that results in injury to or destruction of an animal, human, or inanimate object. At the level of construct, or mediating process, this definition is much too broad. One obvious distinction that needs to be made is between acts that are "intentional" or "motivated" and acts that accidentally lead to injury. By unintentional aggression, we refer to acts that, although resulting in injury, were not contingent upon their injurious consequence. The behavior of a clumsy adult may result in physical pain to others and in the destruction of valued property, but we would not consider this behavior aggressive since these injurious effects are incidental and unpredictable consequences of the response. Intentional or motivated aggression does not imply that the individual is aware of or is consciously directing his aggressive behavior; only that the aggressive component of this behavior is an essential part of its function.

Motivated aggressive acts can be further subdivided into instrumental aggression that is directed toward the achievement of nonaggressive goals and aggressive drive for which the goal response is injury to some animate or inanimate object. This distinction between instrumental aggression and aggressive drive is simple but crucial for an understanding of aggressive phenomena. Shooting another man in defense of one's life or bombing a factory in pursuit of military victory are examples of instrumental aggression. The thief who kills his victim to avoid being caught in the act of theft or who, through the use of physical force, steals the victim's wallet is committing an instrumental aggressive act. The rejected suitor who torments his former mistress and the parent who beats an irritating and disliked child are engaging in aggressive drive-mediated behavior. There are many situations, of course, in which both instrumental and drive aggression are present, and it becomes difficult to disentangle their functions. Thus, the thief may get some satisfaction from coercing his victims, while the parent may gain a more docile child. It is possible, through the appropriate analysis of antecedent events and reinforcing stimuli, to distinguish between aggressive acts that are predominantly instrumental in character and aggressive acts that are mediated by aggressive drive (Feshbach, 1970; Feshbach, Stiles, & Bitter, 1967). There is a considerable literature, both animal and human, demonstrating that one can increase or decrease aggressive behaviors through providing or withholding extrinsic reinforcers such as money, food, and social approval (Buss, 1961; Scott, 1958; Taylor, Bowen, & Borden, in press).

There is also a substantial body of research documenting variations in aggressive behavior as a function of insult and physical pain, where the goal response is inflicting injury upon the provocateur, that is, aggressive behavior that is mediated by aggressive drive. Freud, unfortunately, conceptualized all aggression as manifestations of aggressive drive and, as a consequence, gave psychological credence to views of war and riot and prejudice as manifestations of aggressive instinct. As late as 1957, a psychoanalyst could write,

> It should be borne in mind that much of modern man's hatred of war is due to a reactive formation against, or overcompensations for, his own destructive instincts rather than a genuine absence of them ... then too, it must be remembered that the destructive instincts, when all is said and done, are the greatest single cause of war [Strachey, 1957, pp. 265–266].

This proposition, whatever its ultimate validity, is presently an expression of faith (or lack thereof), not observation. It might be useful to see how the average soldier, caught between the Scylla of reaction formation and the Charybdis of impulse expression, would respond if there were no draft and if he could leave the military at any time.

The previous example, assumes that aggression is a drive and that aggression is also instinctive. However, the concept of aggressive drive does not presuppose an instinct theory, or even a modified instinct theory such as the frustration–aggression hypothesis. Animal studies of intraspecies aggression are instructive here. For a given animal species, it is usually possible to identify a signal or behavior by one member of the species which will elicit or release an aggressive response in another member of that species, and the two animals may then subsequently engage in fighting behavior. Of particular interest is the fact that the aggressive sequence is characteristically not terminated by the infliction of injury, but either by the withdrawal of the provocative stimulus or by the presentation of an inhibitory signal. As Tinbergen (1953) and Lorenz (1966) have so amply documented, intraspecies aggression in most animals is regulated by inhibiting stimuli which can divert or modify an opponent's aggressive behavior before serious injury occurs. A deer in the midst of an antler fight will stop the forward movement of his antlers when aimed at the unprotected flank of his rival; a dog who is the loser of a fight may present his unprotected neck to the mouth of the victor (Lorenz, 1966). Intraspecies killing in animals is much rarer than in humans, and the pursuit of a rival over space and time in order to inflict injury upon him is a peculiarly human phenomenon.

The ethological studies suggest that what may be innate or instinctive in human aggression is the evocation of aggressive responses by as yet to be specified stimuli. Thus, an aggressive response, to use an old Hullian concept, may be high in the innate habit family hierarchy of behaviors elicited by particular frustrating stimuli. However, the concept of an instinctive aggressive reaction is quite far from the notion of aggressive drive-mediated behavior, the goal of which is the infliction of injury.

To complete our theoretical model, a further distinction is required between aggressive drive and the affective response of anger. The set of autonomic and motoric responses which we describe as anger is usually a component of the innate aggressive reaction to an eliciting stimulus. However, since there appear to be innate aggressive reactions in which "anger" is minimal (Moyer, 1967), it is useful to separately categorize the anger response. Anger and aggressive drive are often used synonymously and clinical observation would indicate they are intimately related. We suggest that this relationship is a highly probable one in the usual course of development, but it is not inevitable, and there are circumstances in which the anger response can be detached from the motivation to inflict injury.

The anger response is characterized by autonomic changes and by heightened motoric activity. Biologically, its primary adaptive function is expressive, serving as a warning signal to other organisms. It also energizes the musculature, and, in addition, as both Darwin and Freud have suggested, the excited physical activity serves as a means of tension regulation and discharge. As part of the process of socialization, one learns to inhibit the expression of affect, and, in this regard, we can speak of a need for expressive activity when the affect is aroused. When anger is elicited in the young child, he has a drive to hit rather than hurt. Although by maturity anger has become closely associated with the motive to inflict injury, these response modes can still occur independently. One can obtain satisfaction from the infliction of injury without being angry, and one can be angry without wishing to injure the provoking agent. The parent who is angered when his child misbehaves does not necessarily wish to injure the child. The scientist, frustrated and angered by repeated experimental difficulties, may respond with increased vigor and determination in an effort to resolve these difficulties. In short, anger can serve constructive ends. This objective is what William James (1917) had reference to when he advocated a "moral equivalent of war."

To recapitulate our analysis of aggressive in-

stinct, functional distinctions have been made between instrumental aggression, innate aggressive reactions, expressive aggression, and aggressive drive. We have suggested that the concept of instinctive aggression may be applied to innate aggressive reactions and to expressive aggression, but does not account for aggressive drive. The question then arises, "If aggressive drive is not innate, how is it acquired?" For example, how does hurting one's oppressor, enemy, or rival become a source of satisfaction? There is very little research that directly bears on this issue, but merely to raise the question is a critical step toward finding an answer. Sears (1958) suggested that the pairing of the perception of the injury produced by an aggressive response with the successful elimination of the provocation results in the perception of injury acquiring reinforcing properties. It has been argued elsewhere (Feshbach, 1964) that the secondary reinforcement hypothesis does not provide a satisfactory explanation of the origins of aggressive drive. The motivation to inflict injury is rare in animal species other than man, and, in addition, aggressive behaviors in young children are frequently followed by punishment to the aggressor rather than reward. As an alternative or supplementary hypothesis, I would suggest that aggressive drive arises from the pairing of the infliction of injury with counteraggression. This pairing is reinforced by cultural norms which state that retaliation is the appropriate response for an injured party. The child learns that an aggressor must be punished, not merely for the purpose of inhibiting subsequent aggression, but to redress the injury. The *lex talionis* becomes the basis, as it were, for the internalization of aggressive drive.

Other cultural standards and psychological processes add to the satisfactions that humans derive from the infliction of injury. For example, we have said little about the conditions under which aggression becomes a stimulus for sexual gratification. Of greater importance is the relationship between self-esteem and aggression. Violations to self-esteem through insult, humiliation, or coercion are powerful elicitors of hostility, probably the most important source of anger and aggressive drive in humans. Laboratory studies of aggression (Berkowitz, 1962; Buss, 1961) and clinical studies of violent men (Toch, 1969) consistently point to this relationship. Implicit in threats to self-esteem are the impotence and diminished status of the injured party. One way of achieving a restoration of status and demonstrating one's power is to injure the provoking agent. Thus, an instrumental element is introduced into the satisfactions associated with the infliction of injury.

The connection between status and aggression is especially exaggerated for males. The warrior definition of the male image, so characteristic of preliterate societies, is not entirely absent from our own. Not very long ago, a prominent layman was quoted as having stated that what we need are strong men "who love a fight, who, when they get up in the morning, spit on their hands and ask 'whom will I kill today?' [Hoffer, May 9, 1969, p. 2980]." There is some irony in the fact that this individual was a member of the President's National Commission on the Causes and Prevention of Violence when he made the quoted comment. Fortunately, a reading of the Commission's final report suggests that his views were in the minority.

The relationship between manliness and aggressiveness may not be solely a matter of arbitrary cultural definition. It has been argued, on the basis of biological considerations, that a male, to be a fully functioning, effective, adjusted individual, must also be physically aggressive. There is evidence from the study of several primate species that males have a stronger predisposition to motoric aggressive responses than females (DeVore, 1965; Harlow, 1962). At the biochemical level, the administration of the male hormone, testosterone, has been shown to enhance aggressive behavior in very young female rats and female macaques (Harris & Levine, 1962; Young, Goy, & Phoenix, 1964). However, even if further research should confirm the connection between the male hormone and innate aggressive reaction, it would hardly indicate that killing is a male biological requirement. However, it does introduce a basic question: "What are the effects of inhibition of aggression on personal adjustment?" If sex and aggression are closely related, there is the possibility that inhibition of aggression may result in a diminution of male sexual potency. Freud maintained that inhibition of aggressive impulses would result in a reduction of sexual pleasure, and clinical observations can be cited to support this proposition.

A study conducted in our own laboratory [2] indicated that the experimentally induced inhibition of anger and aggression in male college students resulted in a significant decrement on a subsequent measure of sexual arousal in response to erotic stimuli. Research we are currently conducting to explore this effect further is based on the hypothesis that the critical mediating mechanism is the inhibition of aggressive affect or anger rather than instrumental aggression or aggressive drive. Physiological studies of emotion and Schachter and Singer's (1962) work on emotional contagion and labeling indicate that there is substantial commonality in internal psychological cues among the various affective states. Because of this similarity and consequent difficulty of discriminating internal affective cues, the effort to inhibit anger stimuli may also result in the inhibition of sexual feeling. For those subjects who are better able to discriminate affective cues, the inhibition of anger need not generalize to sexual feelings. More generally, it is maintained that before assertions can be made about the effects of inhibition of aggression upon sexual responsiveness or other functions and behaviors, the type of aggression—whether expressive, reactive, instrumental, or aggressive drive—must first be specified.

As an incidental note, the methods we now use to elicit anger in our experiments may be of some interest.[3] Psychologists have become increasingly conscious of the moral implications of their laboratory procedures, and this is especially the case in the experimental investigation of aggression. Like other investigators, we have depended in the past on insult or arbitrary frustrations and similar noxious stimuli to elicit anger so that we might study its parameters and functional properties. These procedures have never been satisfactory. They usually require the use of some deception which may vary in its effectiveness. They sometimes have an artificial quality, and, perhaps most important, the experimental procedures are distressing to the subject, even if only mildly and temporarily. We have currently found that anger can be reliably and effectively aroused by having subjects privately rehearse and briefly describe events in the past which made them angry and which still make them angry when they think of these situations. In this manner, we are able to avoid deception, make use of more naturalistic stimuli, and still arouse anger without being the source of the subject's frustration or pain.

To return to our examination of the effects of

[2] S. Feshbach and Y. Jaffe. The Effects of Inhibition of Aggression upon Sexual Arousal. Preliminary report, 1970.

[3] S. Feshbach, L. King, and C. Hanson. The Arousal of Aggression through a Recall Method. Preliminary report, 1970.

inhibition of aggression on internal conflict and maladaptive behavior, our theoretical model implies that the inhibition of aggressive drive and instrumental aggression may have some negative consequences for male sexual behavior. Instrumental aggression, however, is linked to another behavior category that, at least until recently, has been a male sex-typed attribute—namely, assertiveness. The term aggressive carries both connotations—the infliction of injury and the assertion of one's own self-interests. There unfortunately is very little empirical data bearing on the functional relationship between aggression and assertiveness. The psychoanalytic ego psychologists (Hartmann, Kris, & Lowenstein, 1949) have hypothesized that both of these behavior tendencies emerge from the same developmental structure, while, at an empirical level, they are often treated synonymously during the preschool years (Otis & McCandless, 1955; Patterson, Littman, & Bricker, 1967). By adolescence, however, assertiveness and aggression are usually considered as theoretically and empirically distinct (Kagan & Moss, 1962). In terms of child-rearing practices, it would be important to establish how closely related these two behaviors are. We have no information as to the effects of inhibition of instrumental aggression upon the young child's assertive coping responses. Presumably, it should be possible to modify instrumental aggression through extinction procedures without fostering passivity. However, this possibility needs to be established empirically.

The issue of aggression inhibition and control bears not only on the areas of sexuality and assertiveness, but also on the irrational displacement of aggression and, more broadly, on personal adjustment and effectiveness. There is, certainly, available empirical evidence of displacement of aggression onto innocent targets, but displacement, in most experimental studies, has been a consequence of the stimulation of aggression, not its inhibition. Inhibition of aggression generally tends to reduce aggressive behavior—whether indirect or direct (Berkowitz, 1962; Buss, 1961; Feshbach, 1961). There are findings which suggest that the type of inhibition is important. Thus, in one experiment, while inhibition of instrumental aggression did not result in displaced aggression, guilt over aggressive affect did produce a displacement effect (Kaufmann & Feshbach, 1963). The concern that inhibition of direct instrumental aggression will result in aggression erupting in unpredictable and potentially highly destructive

contexts as in war has little basis in empirical observation. If the issue is the danger of directing one's aggression toward innocent parties, we would do better to be concerned about the effects of reinforcing rather than inhibiting aggressive behavior norms.

The evidence bearing on the relationship between inhibition of aggression and psychopathology is more ambiguous. While there are indications that conflict over expression of aggressive affect may lead to disturbances in perception (Kaufmann & Feshbach, 1963), hypertension (Schachter, 1957; Wolf & Wolff, 1946), and other behavioral and somatic symptoms (Alexander, 1950; Grace & Graham, 1952; Saul, 1956), there is little evidence, clinical or experimental, that the exercise of restraint over instrumental aggression and aggressive drive results in disturbed functioning. Psychologists have differing opinions as to the kind and degree of expression of aggressive affect they feel to be psychologically desirable. Some clinical psychologists would include the direct verbal communication of angry feelings toward the individuals who evoke the anger as part of the expressive aggressive response, and maintain that the inhibition of these direct verbal responses would be therapeutically undesirable. Our own observations indicate that acknowledging and labeling the affect provides a sufficient degree of expression in most instances of anger arousal.

These differences regarding how much expression of aggressive affect is desirable from a criterion of mental health are concerned with niceties when compared to views expressed by some political theorists, psychiatrists, and philosophers who are oriented toward radical social change. Their concern is with the desirability of using violence as a mechanism to foster personal adjustment and social adaptation. The position that violence is necessary in order for the working class and for colonial peoples to bring about genuine political change is a matter for political scientists to resolve rather than psychologists. However, the view that violence directed toward oppressors is essential to personal redemption and the attainment of self-esteem in oppressed individuals is very much within the purview of psychology. This conception of personal transformation concomitant with a violent, apocalyptic transformation of society has its modern origins in the writing of the French social commentator, Georges Sorel (1961, orig. publ. 1908). For Sorel, it is not the act of violence as such that is personally ennobling, but dedication and complete faith in a small cohesive group that is ready to engage freely in acts of violence, regardless of personal risk. In this context, violence becomes forthright, courageous, and a quality of virtuous men. A more contemporary and highly influential treatment of the personal and political significance of violence has been provided by another French writer, the black psychiatrist, Frantz Fanon (1968, orig. publ. 1961). Sartre, in commenting on Fanon in his Preface (see Fanon), states,

> he shows clearly that this irrepressible violence is neither sound and fury, nor the resurrection of savage instincts nor even the effect of resentment; it is man recreating himself; no gentleness can efface the marks of violence; only violence itself can destroy them [p. 21].

The conception of violence as a necessary purge for oppressed peoples is nowhere more clearly expressed. It can be found in different forms in the ideology of various Third World leaders.

As a minor note concerning literary accuracy, I do not read Fanon in precisely the way that Sartre does. Fanon does describe the embitterment and violent feelings of the oppressed natives. A similar description of the feelings of black Americans has been provided by Grier and Cobbs (1968). Fanon also maintains that the oppressed native can achieve power only through destruction of the oppressor. He writes,

> The native who decides to put the program into practice, and to become its moving force, is ready for violence at all times. From birth, it is clear to him that this narrow world, strewn with prohibitions, can only be called in question by violence [p. 37].

This statement is more political than psychological in its implications but is, I believe, representative of Fanon's views. While I am not an expert on Frantz Fanon, I would hazard that it was Sartre rather than Fanon who saw the perpetration of violence as a requisite for personal redemption and growth.

Regardless of the source of this idealization of violence, it requires comment. I would reject it on theoretical grounds, not denying that violent retaliation may be satisfying and a source of pleasure, but questioning its effectiveness as a purge and also offering other alternatives. In terms of the general model of aggression that has been adopted in this article, it is the power to retaliate

rather than the retaliatory act itself and the expression of one's rage rather than the destruction of the humiliating agent that are the critical factors. Clinical comparisons of representative members of emerging black nations that have achieved freedom through negotiation and minimal aggressive tactics with members of nations who have achieved independence through a violent revolution would be useful. These studies could provide data that might, hopefully, render untenable the premise that violence is a prerequisite for the emotional cure of men who have been subjected to repeated violence. Research and theory suggest that there are more effective ways of reducing anger and hostility than through the expression or acting out of aggressive impulses.

When the colonized native becomes a free man in his former colony and attains political power, he is exposed to a very different set of cues than was the case before the liberation. His experiences and perceptions differ, and these should foster new response patterns. The violence may vanish, or be sharply reduced, without it ever being elicited. Aggression—whether drive, expressive, instrumental, or reactive—is evoked by cues. When these cues are not present or are sharply modified, aggression is not elicited and, in a very meaningful sense, has been reduced. Most psychotherapists agree that the reduction in anger that occurs in patients for whom anger has been a major problem is primarily a result of insight and more refined discrimination rather than the cathartic expression of the affect. Cognitive reorganization may be a far more effective means of reducing violence than promoting its sublimated or free expression. Asch (1952) has speculated that if, one morning, a bigot in a Southern town woke to find a complete change in the community in the actions of white men to blacks, his bigotry would soon disappear. Perhaps a comparable change might occur in the anger of the oppressed native when he and his fellows find themselves in totally new role relationships.

EVALUATION OF VIOLENCE IN POLITICAL AND NONPOLITICAL CONTEXTS

The previous discussion has had as its objective the elucidation of the possible psychological consequences of the inhibition versus expression of various forms of aggressive behavior. In our efforts to provide a psychological basis for the evaluation of aggressive behavior, we have considered such issues as the instinctive versus learned nature of aggression, the origins of aggressive drive, the relationship between aggression and masculinity, the effects of inhibition of aggression upon personal adjustment, and the reduction of aggression by nonaggressive means. As was indicated earlier in the article, a second means by which psychology can contribute to the question of the morality of violent behavior is through the analysis of the factors that influence people's evaluation of aggression. These two questions—the implications of psychological findings for the evaluation of aggressive behavior, and second, the bases on which evaluations of aggression are made by the community at large—are concerned with quite different issues, although our discussion of the first question will, at some points, enter in the consideration of the second.

We turn now to an examination of similarities and differences among expressions of violence in various political and interpersonal contexts in an effort to clarify some of the bases by which these aggressive actions are differentially evaluated by members of the community. A cursory examination of reactions to war, murder, revolt, police action, campus disruption, and riots provides an obvious but instructive generalization. Violent acts with the same formal characteristics—for example, one man killing another—are evaluated by most people very differently depending on the context in which the act occurs. The widespread concerns and outcry regarding Violence, writ large, are really concerns about particular forms and uses of violence. In general, violence that is unlawful is disapproved, especially when the goal of the violence is inconsistent with one's own interests and values. Violence carried out as part of society's efforts to insure social order and maintain conformity to its standards will generally be approved, again particularly where one's own interests coincide with law enforcement. However, as the report on *The History of Violence in America* (Graham & Gurr, 1969) documents, when the requirements of law conflict with personal and subgroup interests, the evaluation of the violent act will almost as often be governed by these interests as by the rule of law.

A related dimension is the extent to which violence serves personal interests versus social interests; people tend to evaluate the latter more positively. To rob a bank to obtain money for a political cause is less negatively viewed than robbing for personal gain. Although there is no direct evidence on this issue, attribution theory would suggest that one is more likely to infer social motives when violence is used to enforce the law, and personal motives when violence is used in defiance of the law. Thus, the violence of the black radical and the student radical may not only be negatively valued because it is disruptive of law, but because it is perceived as being personally motivated—to satisfy aggressive drive or as instrumental to the attainment of a self-centered goal. Violence committed in the service of the law is not only more likely to be perceived as impersonal or socially oriented, but carrying out an aggressive act as part of a group mission or in conformity to authority tends to minimize individual responsibility for the commission of the act. The experiments of Milgram (1963, 1965) strikingly demonstrate the extent to which individuals will carry out pain-inflicting behaviors in conformity with norms promulgated by an authority figure.

The degree of personal choice or responsibility entailed in the commission of an aggressive act is then another significant variable influencing the evaluation of the act. The degree of personal choice involved in the activities preceding the act of violence also affects the evaluation of the act. Students participating in a demonstration which erupts in violence over which they had little control may be criticized and punished because of the personal choice exercised in joining the demonstration. However, the action of the accused soldiers at Mylai may be less negatively evaluated, although other soldiers chose not to participate in the killings, because the accused did not choose their mission of perhaps even choose to be in the service.

The dimension of responsibility is complex, embracing a number of relatively independent components, each of which can influence the degree to which aggression is approved or condemned. Thus, the attribution of responsibility is closely related to the question of who initiated the aggressive act. Acts of aggression that are committed in self-defense are considered acceptable since the defender had little personal option. Responsibility, to paraphrase the McNaughten and Durham rules (Roche, 1967, p. 91, pp. 249–274), also encompasses the degree to which the individual was aware of the nature and quality of his acts, his ability to distinguish between right and wrong, and the extent of ego control over his behavior. The concept of responsibility also applies to the intentional versus accidental determination of an act, aggressive acts that are intentional being much more negatively evaluated (Pastore, 1952). One might even consider the minimal force criterion as an instance of the broader dimension of responsibility inasmuch as the agent of the law becomes responsible for the use of aggression in excess of the force necessary to implement compliance.

To summarize, the moral evaluation of a violent act is a function of the lawful status of the act, the extent of personal versus social motivation and the degree of personal responsibility as reflected in the role of authority, the options available to the individual, the defensive or initiated basis of the violence, the degree of emotional disturbance, the amount of force employed, and the intentionality of the act. To these criteria must be added normative considerations of fair play, the degree and manner of the violence, the age and sex of the victim, and, more generally, the appropriateness of the target. Last to be mentioned, but probably most important, is one's attitude toward the objectives of the violence. Thus, the evaluation of an act of violence by a strike breaker versus violence by a striker is very much dependent upon one's attitudes toward the goal of the strike. Often the evaluation is on pragmatic grounds; if violence accomplishes its objectives, it is perceived as good. Broad social consequences of violence are sometimes used as the criterion, and if these are seen as positive, then the revolution, or the sit-in, or the riot that helped produce these consequences acquires a positive value. Judging the ethics of a violent act on the basis of its objectives and its consequences is unlikely to be a reliable procedure. It depends so much on who is the judge. For example, in the initial report made to the National Commission which dealt with *The History of Violence in America* (Graham & Gurr, 1969), a distinction is made between positive and negative violence. The following varieties of violence are included in the positive category: police violence, revolutionary violence, civil war violence, indian wars, vigilante violence, agrarian uprising, and labor violence. In retrospect, the ends always appear to justify the means.

The evaluation of violence that is predominantly instrumental and that is designed to bring about an economic change or a change in the structure of power is a troublesome and, on the whole, inappropriate task to be undertaken by psychologists. Thus, there is little psychological basis for asserting that the actions of the more militant black radicals or student activists are morally inferior or superior to the continuation of the Vietnam war, although on quite personal grounds, I would have no difficulty in assigning the Vietnam war close to the top of my scale of immorality and inhumanity. Psychological considerations are not irrelevant as a criterion for evaluation of these activities, they are simply minor. Because my objectives and my appraisal of options differ from those of the militant radicals, I would place a negative value on their acts of violence regardless of their motives, personality, or intelligence. The evaluation issue in these instances is essentially a political and social question, not a psychological one. It is for the political scientist to determine whether these procedures are effective in bringing about stable political change and for subgroups in the community to determine whether the change is in their interests. This is not to deny in any way the usefulness of psychologists investigating the correlates of these violent events and discovering methods of modifying violence.

Psychologists have developed a number of techniques, varying from intensive psychotherapy to behavior modification, for coping with individual expressions of aggression and also have developed procedures for reducing some types of group conflict (Berkowitz, 1962; Feshbach, 1970). However, we have not been very successful in discovering methods that would reduce warfare and other manifestations of violent instrumental aggression with political objectives. One current approach that appears promising is the development of effective bargaining procedures that are designed to minimize dissatisfaction and maximize compromise. I would like to suggest, in addition, the possible merits of a rather different approach which focuses on the human interaction in interpersonal violence.

In the model of aggression that was presented, a sharp distinction was made between aggressive drive and instrumental aggression, the latter being mediated by nonaggressive goals. However, a closer examination of actual examples of the instrumental use of violence suggests that, except for the hardened criminal, most people find it difficult to deliberately injure another human solely for nonaggressive reasons. To reduce their inhibition, they find it necessary to dehumanize their target and invent beliefs that will enable them to hate the person they must injure. Thus, the policeman becomes a "pig," and the student, a "hippie." The Asiatic becomes a "Gook." Given these rationalizations, it should come as no great surprise that Americans in Vietnam may tend to view and treat friend and foe alike. Mylai is not an aberration. It is an inevitable consequence of the kind of war being fought in Vietnam.

One of the encouraging features of contemporary life is that it is becoming increasingly difficult to view members of other nations and races as nonhumans. I believe this is why there is so much opposition among young people to the Vietnam war. Television has brought foreign cultures directly into their homes; the observations of cultural anthropologists have permeated their textbooks and magazines; and contemporary child-rearing practices tend to foster concern about the feelings and perceptions of others. These developments should be reinforced and supplemented with additional procedures designed to accentuate the attributes that all humans share. Konrad Lorenz (1966) has pointed out that one of the differences between animal and human aggression is the lack, in humans, of the inhibitory mechanisms that control intraspecies aggression in other organisms. Empathy, which has been shown to be negatively correlated with aggression (Feshbach & Feshbach, 1969), may be one such mechanism. The more we perceive another human as like us, the greater is our empathy with him and the more difficult it is to injure him.

The facilitation of empathy may inhibit aggression in the foot soldier, but would be less effective for the bombardier and even weaker for the decision maker, who is too far from the target for empathy to be operative. I have conjectured a procedure, slightly fantastic, which might help war planners, if they would use it, to make rational decisions. Imagine a computer that provides access to pictures of people of all ages, sexes, and races, pictures of violent tactics used in war, and pictures of these same people after they have been crippled in a bombing, accidentally killed in an assault on their village, and subjected to other sufferings. I would have our decision makers watch a before–after sequence daily, with the computer providing unique combinations of victims, violence, and injury so as to minimize adaptation. This procedure is designed to make concrete the casualty estimates of the enemy, noncombatants, and of our own troops which our decision makers decide are tolerable.

Hans Toch (1969), in his study of criminals with a history of repeated violence, has eloquently stated the case for control of the violence of the war planner as well as that of the criminal:

Men who press explosive buttons or who sign bloodthirsty orders are entrepreneurs of violence, and they set the stage for lone operators. The same holds for individuals who coldly plan for inconceivable contingencies, or who produce and disseminate means of destruction. When the roles exercised by such persons have been eliminated from the games societies play, we can attend to our Violent Men with a clearer conscience and a more unambiguous mandate [p. 248].

REFERENCES

Adorno, T., Frenkel-Brunswik, E., Levinson, D., & Sanford, R. *The authoritarian personality.* New York: Harper, 1950.

Alexander, F. *Psychosomatic medicine.* New York: Norton, 1950.

Asch, S. *Social psychology.* New York: Prentice-Hall, 1952.

Berkowitz, L. *Aggression: A social psychological analysis.* New York: McGraw-Hill, 1962.

Buss, A. H. *The psychology of aggression.* New York: Wiley, 1961.

Churchman, C. W. *Prediction and optimal decision; philosophical issues of a science of values.* Englewood Cliffs, N. J.: Prentice-Hall, 1964.

DeVore, I. (Ed.) *Primate behavior.* New York: Holt, Rinehart & Winston, 1965.

Fanon, F. *The wretched of the earth.* New York: Grove Press, 1968. (Originally published 1961.) (Also Preface by J. Sartre.)

Feshbach, N., & Feshbach, S. Personality and political values: A study of reactions to two accused assassins. In B. S. Greenberg & E. B. Parker (Eds.), *The Kennedy assassination and the American public.* Stanford: Stanford University Press, 1965.

Feshbach, N., & Feshbach, S. The relationship between empathy and aggression in two age groups. *Developmental Psychology,* 1969, *1,* 102–107.

Feshbach, S. The influence of drive arousal and conflict upon fantasy behavior. In J. Kagan & G. Lesser (Eds.), *Contemporary issues in thematic apperceptive methods.* Springfield, Ill.: Charles C. Thomas, 1961.

Feshbach, S. The function of aggression and the regulation of aggressive drive. *Psychological Review,* 1964, *71,* 257–272.

Feshbach, S. Aggression. In P. H. Mussen (Ed.), *Carmichael manual of child psychology.* (Rev. ed.) New York: Wiley, 1970.

Feshbach, S., Stiles, W. B., & Bitter, E. The reinforcing effect of witnessing aggression. *Journal of Experimental Research on Personality*, 1967, *2*, 133–139.

Freud, S. *Civilization and its discontents*. (2nd ed.) London: Hogarth Press, 1957. (Originally published 1930.)

Grace, W. J., & Graham, D. T. Relationship of specific attitudes and emotions to certain bodily diseases. *Psychosomatic Medicine*, 1952, *14*, 242–251.

Graham, H. D., & Gurr, T. R. *The history of violence in America*. New York: Bantam Books, 1969.

Grier, W. H., & Cobbs, P. M. *Black rage*. New York: Basic Books, 1968.

Harlow, H. The heterosexual affectional system in monkeys. *American Psychologist*, 1962, *17*, 1–9.

Harris, G., & Levine, S. Sexual differential of the brain and its experimental control. *Journal of Physiology*, 1962, *163*, 42P–43P.

Hartmann, H., Kris, E., & Lowenstein, P. Notes on the theory of aggression. In A. Freud (Ed.), *The psychoanalytic study of the child*. Vol. 3. New York: International Universities Press, 1949.

Hoffer, E. Testimony May 9, 1969 recorded in *Riots, Civil and Criminal Disorders: Hearings before the Permament Subcommittee on Investigations of the Committee on Government Operations, U.S. Senate, ninety-first Congress, first session* (Part 16: May 9, 13, and 14, 1969). Washington, D. C.: United States Government Printing Office, 1969.

James, W. The moral equivalent of war. In, *Memoirs and studies*. London: Longmans, 1917.

Kagan, J., & Moss, H. A. *Birth to maturity*. New York: Wiley, 1962.

Kaufmann, H., & Feshbach, S. The influence of anti-aggressive communications upon the response to provocation. *Journal of Personality*. 1963, *31*, 428–444.

Lorenz, K. *On aggression*. New York: Harcourt, Brace and World, 1966.

Milgram, S. Behavioral study of obedience. *Journal of Abnormal and Social Psychology*, 1963, *67*, 371–378.

Milgram, S. Some conditions of obedience and disobedience to authority. *Human Relations*, 1965, *18*, 57–76.

Moyer, K. E. Kinds of aggression and their physiological basis. (Report No. 67–12) Department of Psychology, Carnegie-Mellon University, 1967.

Opton, E. M., & Duckless, R. Mental gymnastics on Mylai. *New Republic*, Feb. 21, 1970, *162*, 14–16.

Otis, N., & McCandless, B. Responses to repeated frustrations of young children differentiated according to need area. *Journal of Abnormal and Social Psychology*, 1955, *50*, 349–353.

Pastore, N. The role of arbitrariness in the frustration–aggression hypothesis. *Journal of Abnormal and Social Psychology*, 1952, *47*, 728–731.

Patterson, G. R., Littman, R. A., & Bricker, W. Assertive behavior in children: A step toward a theory of aggression. *Child Development*, 1967, *32*(5 and 6).

Roche, P. Q. *The criminal mind*. New York, Wiley, 1967.

Saul, L. J. *The hostile mind*. New York: Random House, 1956.

Schachter, J. Pain, fear, and anger in hypertensives and normotensives: A psycho-physiological study. *Psychosomatic Medicine*, 1957, *29*, 17–29.

Schachter, S. S., & Singer, J. E. Cognitive, social and physiological determinants of emotional state. *Psychological Review*, 1962, *69*, 379–399.

Scheibe, K. E. *Beliefs and values*. New York: Holt, Rinehart & Winston, 1970.

Scott, J. P. *Aggression*. Chicago: University of Chicago Press, 1958.

Sears, R. R. Personality development in the family. In J. M. Seidman (Ed.), *The child*. New York: Rinehart, 1958.

Sorel, G. *Reflections on violence*. London: Collier-Macmillan, 1961. (Originally published in 1908.)

Strachey, A. *The unconscious motives of war*. London: George Allen & Unwin, 1957.

Taylor, S. P., Bowen, R., & Borden, R. Aggressive behavior as a function of physical attack, extrinsic reward, and frustration. In press.

Tinbergen, N. *Social behavior in animals*. New York: Wiley, 1953.

Toch, H. H. *Violent men*. Chicago: Aldine, 1969.

Wolf, G. A., Jr., & Wolff, H. G. Studies on the nature of certain symptoms associated with cardiovascular disorders. *Psychosomatic Medicine*, 1946, *8*, 293–319.

Young, W. C., Goy, R., & Phoenix, C. Hormones and sexual behavior. *Science*, 1964, *143*, 212–218.

community and psychology and community psychology

Stanley Lehmann

Concern over contemporary social problems, and an uncomfortable feeling that the social sciences are remiss in their ability to deal with them, has generated an interest in the community as a subject for psychological study. A number of universities, usually with the encouragement of their students, have installed courses and even programs in community psychology. Twinges of conscience and rumblings of morality feelings—likewise encouraged by the student body—frequently accompany these programs and contribute a heightened air of anticipation.

Psychologists from the relatively new division of community psychology retain their traditional interest in mental health and rehabilitation but recognize the relatedness of broad areas of social problems (see Bennett, 1966). They are confronted with the necessity of studying the community as an organic unit in order to understand as well as to treat disabled members of the community. Community studies abound in the fields of anthropology and sociology but are almost nonexistent in psychology. There have been admonitions about training and about embedding oneself in the community (Kelly, 1970) but few guidelines as to how a psychologist might go about an effective study of community. Behavioral scientists are understandably apt to feel that their good intentions have seriously outdistanced their expertise.

The association of community psychology with the mental health movement is a natural one for several reasons. Studies like those of Hollings-

head and Redlich (1958) and Faris and Dunham (1963) have suggested that both the quantity and quality of behavioral pathology are related to the community from whence it comes. The community can no longer be viewed as an uncompromising set of conditions to which everyone must adjust. Instead, it is an active participant in molding behavior and establishing demands and limitations on it. Modern mental health programs are as interested in the conditions in the community as in the condition of the patients.

A healthy state of affairs seldom calls attention to itself. The widespread public interest in ecology was inspired by the recognition that pollution is threatening to destroy the normal, healthy ecosystem. Civil strife, the dissatisfaction of large segments of the population, and an upsurge of a variety of behavioral deviations are pathologies of the social system, and, similarly, they direct attention to the social system itself. Biologists, however, are already familiar with the normal operation of the ecological community and can contend, at least technically, with its dysfunctions. Social scientists find themselves ill-prepared to deal with anomalies in a system that they barely understand. In spite of the fact that psychologists readily acknowledge the importance of environmental influence on behavior, they have paid little systematic attention to the environmental context of behavior. They have taken little interest in man's habitat: the community in which he lives.

The implication is that there is a need in psychology to study a human ecology that is analogous to bioecology. The ecological approach has become popular and is in danger of meaning everything and nothing. Here, ecology is intended to carry the full import of the study of a life-environment system. Just as bioecology centers its study on the biological community, its psychological counterpart will focus on the human

This paper was supported by the New York State Department of Mental Hygiene which sponsors the Community Research Program at New York University. The author wishes to acknowledge his debt to the staff of the Community Research Program for their inspiration, suggestions, and constructive criticisms.

Reprinted from *American Psychologist*, 1971, *26*, pp. 554–560. Copyright 1971 by the American Psychological Association and reproduced by permission.

352

community. This is the domain of a community psychology that studies man in his environment as a natural system. It is a suitable locus of study for those who would understand pathology by first discovering how the normal, unpolluted system works. Since psychology is a natural science, it seems strange that it is still necessary to suggest that naturalistic study is required, especially when the history of the science is well stocked with similar admonitions. There are serious and effective pressures away from such study. Not only have community studies, or field studies of any kind, been unpopular in this experimentally inclined discipline, but there is a strong suggestion that such studies are not feasible within the rigorous protocol of psychology. It is worth while to examine the influences that have led to the neglect of the inherent subject matter of community psychology for they also make it difficult to conceive of this speciality as a proper area of concern. A look at the traditional attitude of psychology toward field or community studies reveals much that is spurious and outlines the dimensions of a community psychology that remains to be implemented.

COMMUNITY AND PSYCHOLOGY

The traditional psychologist has shown little interest in the community because he has been more concerned with individual dynamics and because he found it easier, and eventually more respectable, to pursue his work in the laboratory rather than in the field. The community might have seemed more relevant to individual dynamics except that it was usually excluded by the laboratory walls. Social psychology expanded concern conceptually beyond the individual, but confinement to the laboratory keeps the numbers that can be practically handled rather small. The community, when it enters the equation at all, is treated as an abstraction under the name of social influence, socialization, or group pressure in the microcosm of the laboratory. Clinical psychologists also have a penchant for remaining within four walls although they presume to expand their vision beyond them. Yet it is not unusual for a clinician to assume that he is recreating a miniature social situation within the treatment room. Such procedures are valid, but there must be some way of verifying that what is simulated in the laboratory or treatment room bears some relation to what exists commonly

in the natural state. Good communication between the laboratory and the field provides a useful sense of proportion to guide theoretical studies.

Not all work in psychology has been so constricted, and there have been some worthy proponents for studying human behavior in a broader context such as Murray (1938) and Lewin (1951). More recently, other voices have been raised to the same end (Barker, 1968; McGuire, 1967; Ring, 1967; Willems & Raush, 1969). These are not campaigns against laboratory research that has proved its own worth by the gains it has produced. Rather, they are appeals for going beyond laboratory research to increase relevance and perspective. Laboratory experiments in opinion change commonly use a captive audience that seldom exists in the natural state. Experimental paradigms of cognitive dissonance usually restrict the available choices so severely that the situation is unlike any that might normally be encountered. Barker (1965) recounts a well-known experiment in which he demonstrated that children frustrated in the laboratory regressed in their behavior (Barker, Dembo, & Lewin, 1941). This finding became incorporated in many theories of child development. Barker adds that a student of his (Fawl, 1963) later examined extensive transcripts of the daily lives of children and found that frustration and hence regression were exceedingly rare events. These are cases in which laboratory findings are veridical except that they do not apply to the normal course of events. Such circumstances make it unlikely that psychology will develop a comprehensive body of knowledge or a generally applicable theory.

Sherif (1970) has objected to the scattered and uneven development of the discipline, which he attributes to the rugged individualism of practitioners who choose to pursue their own exotic interests. Such confusion is probably inevitable if there are no guiding principles. A knowledge of the natural distribution of conditions, behaviors, and psychological states can go a long way toward making psychological studies both relevant and coherent. The lack of any marked concentration of interest has resulted in poorly explored and poorly documented areas of major concern. Beals (1969) has suggested that it is not only ethically proper for social scientists to become involved in public decisions and applications of their work, but that it is also professionally in their best interests. The political arena is not a congenial place for many scientists, but it does offer the possibility of broad empirical tests of theoretical issues which can provide both material and incentive for further development, even if the long-awaited social panacea is not achieved.

Few scientists seem as agoraphobic as the traditional psychologist who clings to the narrow confines of his laboratory or clinic and thinks of field work as highly suspect because it is merely exploratory, descriptive, or even downright unscientific. While field work is not necessarily exploratory or descriptive, much of it is, and it does not need to be defended for so being. Scientific investigation begins with the careful and systematic observation of nature which leads to knowledge of the distribution of phenomena and some plausible formulations about the relationships between them. This, in turn, provides the foundation for theory building that is not trivial. Careful methodological observation is part of the scientific process that has been largely overlooked by psychologists with their aversion to field studies.

Theories, generated in the field, still need to be tested. Field observation can suggest relationships, but it cannot verify them at the same time because it is necessarily dealing with the selected instances that generated the theory. Theory testing requires an experimental paradigm, but this can take place in the community as well as in the laboratory. Each setting has its advantages and disadvantages, and they are not freely interchangeable. The laboratory has the well-known advantage of rigorous control which reduces the ambiguities of the situation to a minimum. The field, on the other hand, affords a test under a broad array of natural conditions that can confirm the generality of the relationship or demonstrate that alternative hypotheses are available. In this sense, the field is more rigorous than the laboratory. Relationships between variables are often affected by ambient conditions that can be ignored or eliminated in the laboratory but that will exercise their full influence in the field. A science like psychology, which is not given to extensive field testing, often fails to specify or even attend to conditions that are important mediators of the relationships under investigation. Better theory will result from more adventurous testing of hypotheses.

The abiding reason for the popularity of laboratory studies is the knowledge that field experiments cannot be controlled properly. It is true that there are frequently many facets in a naturalistic situation that are beyond the direct control of the experimenter, although they can be observed and recorded. There is an ancient and powerful assumption that complex appearances have simple and elementaristic explanations. This Aristotelian logic results in a reductionism that is translated into the experimental technique of varying only one thing at a time. The technique is a valid one only if the assumption that specific effects have independent elementary causes is also valid. The success of the periodic table of elements that predicts all possible chemical combinations on the basis of three elementary particles has contributed to the longevity of an idea that has failed to work in many other instances. Physics has produced a seemingly endless proliferation of elementary particles and has long since forsaken reductionistic explanations. What is often seen as rigorous control in the laboratory, the elimination or suppression of unwanted variables, is neither practical nor desirable in the field if variables are considered to work in conjunction with one another rather than in isolation.

Reductionism is rampant in psychology in spite of many prior admonitions that it is an untenable position. A good reason for this is that the position often works in psychology as it does in molar chemistry. It would be well to understand why it works when it does and, conversely, when it does not. Reductionistic explanations work for states that are either static or can be assumed to be in dynamic equilibrium, as, for example, a chemical combination. Many psychological theories assume an equilibrium or static state. The prediction of behavior from an intelligence test, the prediction of responses from the number of reinforced trials, or the prediction of a response tendency such as conformity from a behavior sample all picture the individual as a reservoir that maintains a prescribed level of the attribute in question. It is a convenient fiction that works much of the time because, for reasons that will be noted later, human behavior tends to maintain itself in a state of dynamic equilibrium. However, disequilibria and change are not uncommon states of the human condition and are becoming increasingly important to contemporary psychologists. Social change, generalized disaffection, mental illness, behavioral deviations, and even socialization represent states of disequilibria and are not amenable to reductionistic explanations.

PSYCHOLOGICAL ECOLOGY

Change is brought about by a new configuration or combination of variables rather than the presence or absence of independent conditions. Alternatives to Aristotelian logic, such as Lewin's field theory, have stressed this difference. They stress the systemic character of the process in which the interrelationships, rather than the components, are prime movers (see Simon, 1969). The system properties of the field theory model are represented by the "life space" which is a subjective representation of the momentary influences (environmental as well as internal) acting on an individual. Being subjective, it is difficult to measure, and Barker (1968), a student of Lewin, has tried to circumvent this difficulty by observing behaviors common to an environmental setting so that the environmental effects can be appreciated directly. He has carried on a programmatic study of environmental settings that he has come to call "ecological psychology." He has cataloged all of the relevant settings of a small midwestern town and has found that some of them almost totally determine the behavior that takes place within the setting. His theory respects the systemic nature of the process, for he sees the individual as mediating the environment, as well as the environment influencing the behavior of the individual. In practice, however, his emphasis is on the result rather than the process. His main interest is in what goes on where. The same directional emphasis is common in social area studies (Shevky & Bell, 1955; Tryon, 1955) and in the epidemiological analysis of behavior (Faris & Dunham, 1963), yet all of these approaches are inherently interactional. Each of these procedures is dedicated to assessing the effect of the integral environment that necessarily includes the effects of individuals on it.

The ecological model is based on the observation that organisms living together in an environment will become adapted to their habitat and to each other in such a way that their essential needs are met. An interlocking system of mutual interdependence such that the organisms contribute to the maintenance of the environment and to each other tends to insure the continuity of the species. The sedentary pond is the classic example of a balanced or "climax" ecosystem where the flora and fauna that inhabit it live together in a relatively enduring system of mutual support (see Amos, 1970). It is the nature of the ecosystem to tend toward a state of equilibrium by way of a series of stages or "successions" as long as conditions external to the system are reasonably constant and appropriate. The popular concern over pollution reflects the fact that changing conditions

may alter the natural ecosystem so that it no longer provides the resources that were previously available.

Human beings, like all other organisms and along with them, live in an ecosystem. Ultimately they are dependent on natural resources in one form or another, but they are distinctive from most other organisms in the extent to which they have transformed and modified their environment. To a very large extent, the modern urban human environment is man made. Men live in concrete cities with central heating, air conditioning, and rapid transit, and their food arrives in plastic packages at the end of a vast technological food chain. They do not have to live entirely at the whim of nature but are, instead, very much at the whim of each other. By far the most important features of the man-made environment are the institutionalized behaviors called social and cultural. They represent collective behavioral adaptations that have become part of the ecosystem. The anthropologist Kroeber (1939) noted the parallel between cultural forms of North American tribes and the ecological areas in which they lived. Some anthropologists have taken the position that many if not most, social customs can be ultimately related to environmental adaptation (Vayda, 1969). As early as the 1920s, the Chicago School of Sociology under Park and Burgess charted the association between behavior and the urban environment. With the development of the study of human ecology, the distinction between the natural and the social environment became blurred, since it was evident that they mutually affected each other (Alihan, 1938). Social patterns derived from environmental adaptations influence other behavioral interactions that lead to a changed environment, and so the process continues. For the behavioral scientist today, human ecology is largely social ecology.

Bioecologists call the minimal network of organisms and their natural resources that are mutually interdependent, a community. In human ecology, this minimal functional unit may coincide with the popular notion of a geographic community in which people live, reproduce, work, and shop together, or it may be poorly localized in space. The sedentary pond is a highly localized community, but that of a migrating species may be very diffuse. Functional rather than geographic integrity is the defining characteristic of the community. For the psychologists, the community is the arena in which the individual acquires his behavioral patterns and carries out the major

functions of his life. During his lifetime, an individual may live in a number of different communities, and some of them, especially if they
are urban, may have little local identity. Nonetheless, at any given time, he is in interaction
with a number of significant others who influence
his behavior, who help to satisfy his needs, who
are influenced by him in turn, and who, along with
his physical environment, make up his community.
The community must work out mutually adaptive
behaviors and roles to support the majority of its
members if it is to endure. Once it has achieved a
functional integrity with sufficient diversity to
sustain its membership, it will tend to maintain
the functional organization that it has achieved.
As a mutually reactive system, the community
will absorb or minimize change insofar as possible.
This tendency often results in the phenomenon
known as "cultural lag," but it also provides enduring behavior patterns and a more stable environment with which to cope. The well-balanced
ecological community is a natural accommodation
that affords its members the maximum opportunity
for survival.

COMMUNITY PSYCHOLOGY

The ecological concept of community provides
a logical base for the naturalistic observation that
is currently missing from psychology. It is no
accident that the ecological community suggests
itself as the "community" in community psychology. This area of specialization developed within
psychology in response to the need to deal with
the intact behavior system as a consequence of
initial concern over dysfunctions within the system. The conscious effort to reintroduce the environmental context into the study of behavior
leads to the inevitable realization that the living
environment is inseparable from those who live
in it. Behavior in context constitutes a system of
highly interrelated components. Nature, unlike
the laboratory, does not admit an easy separation
of the factors that influence ongoing behavior.
Thus, community psychology must be more than
just the study of behavior in the field, or the study
of social problems, or the study of adjustment to a
particular life style. It must have a conceptual
framework that appreciates the complexity of the
interrelationships between a person and his environment, and it must develop the capacity to
deal with such complexity.

The ecological model in psychology will not be
the same as the ecological model of the biosystem,
nor will the methods of study be the same. Psychology has its own subject matter and must
develop its own appropriate methods, but an
ecological framework does provide some guidelines. The model is essentially a functional one.
An ecosystem is an interlocking network of needs,
resources, and facilities. Behavior is to be understood in terms of its function within the person-
environment system. The theory does not insist
that all behavior is functional, but that only functional behavior is meaningful and intelligible.
Most behavior represents a transaction between a
person and his environment in which a person is
influenced by the environment, and the environment, in turn, is influenced by his response to it.
Dewey and Bentley (1949) devised a metaphysics
in which the known is defined exclusively by the
transactional process of knowing: the system of
transactions between the observer and the observed. In a parallel way, the meaning of behavior
is defined exclusively by the transactions that go
on between the person and his environment.

The transactional nature of any behavior must
be assessed in order to understand the function
and hence the meaning of the behavior. Thus,
when a mental patient, a civil rioter, a disaffected
youth, or a stock broker acts in particular ways,
it is assumed that he is responding to internal and
external demands within the possibilities offered
by the available environment in such a way as to
effect a favorable response from the environment,
if possible. It is true that not everyone evaluates
demands, environmental possibilities, and favorable responses in the same way, but these evaluations are largely a function of the individual's role
or niche within the system. When the interrelationships within the system are understood, the
functional regularities will be apparent. The
meaning of behavior and its functional significance
is determined by the system of which it is a part.

The approach considered here does not call for
a new and radical methodology, although methodological innovations, especially in terms of
systems analysis, are always welcome. It is
uniquely necessary to put the problem, or the
questions, in terms of systems relationships and
to investigate the variation among these relationships in response to different configurations of
the system. Some examples may make this abstraction more tangible.

Cross-cultural comparisons often involve very
different physical environments, so it would be
expected that the individual's means of relating
to his environment would also be very different.

The "culture-free" tests frequently used in cross-cultural research are calculated to obliterate the cultural and hence the system differences so they are not suitable for ecological research. Berry (1966, 1967) compared the contrasting cultures of the Temne of Sierra Leone and the Eskimo of Baffin Island on culture-prone perceptual scales and the Asch conformity situation. The Temne live amid bright and variegated tropical vegetation, while the Eskimo live on a monochromatic, barren terrain. Because of the topographic differences, the subsistence economy is also different. The Temne are farmers who cultivate productive fields near their village. The Eskimo are hunters who must travel widely in their sparse environment. Berry found cultural differences that were consonant with the environmental differences. The Eskimo have a more differentiated language in regard to space, and they are more adept at map making, a handy skill in a relatively undifferentiated environment. The Eskimo, with low levels of food accumulation, have socialization practices that encourage self-reliance, while the Temne, with an abundance of food, socialize conformity and obedience. Three psychological tests bore out these differences. The Eskimo exhibit less closure and less field dependence on perceptual tests and less conformity in the Asch situation. This is a revealing demonstration that individual psychological dispositions can be related to systematic differences in the environment.

The examples do not have to be so exotic to relate individual differences to environmental effects. Festinger, Schachter, and Back (1950) investigated the friendship patterns of college students living in two housing projects on an Eastern campus. They found that friendship coincided, not only with the proximity of the neighbors, but also with the architectural design of the project. Architectural features that increased the probability of contact, increased the probability of friendship. Shared attitudes toward common goals developed in the same manner where people had lived in proximity for sufficient time. These relationships will not necessarily hold for different populations with other living arrangements, but they represent an important part of the social dynamics of the students living in this community.

Contextual analysis has been used with social data to extract some of the functional relationships. Such an analysis treats physical, social, or psychological attributes of an area or group as a context or environment for individuals in the area or group. Thus, Cox (1969) examines urban areas with different degrees of political affiliation and, within these areas, classifies respondents according to their formal and informal associations, length of residence, and the amount of discussion and involvement in politics. Cox is interested in the channels of political influence and sees each combination of attributes as different environmental sets or configurations that will affect the flow of political information. Hypotheses about the nature of information flow can be tested by comparing subsets of individuals within the community on their acceptance of the local political norms.

A sophisticated systems model of urban dynamics has been developed by Forrester (1969). Equations have been worked out relating such variables as business, housing, and population to a series of flow variables such as time, aging, construction, demolition, migration, mobility, etc. Since many of these relationships are not known precisely, logical approximations are used so that all of the relationships within the system can be stated. The urban system is then simulated on a computer from time zero through several hundred years, so that the growth and decline of the city can be plotted and compared with that of real cities. Urban planning devices can be tried out on the computer model. In Forrester's model, such typical remedial procedures as supplying more jobs, job training, the construction of low-income housing, and a number of other common panaceas have detrimental long-term effects. These results coincide with the experience of many attempts at urban planning. A device that works on this model is the gradual removal, without replacement, of slum housing. Awaiting the accumulation of concrete knowledge of urban relationships, much of the model is still hypothetical, and the validity of the results depends on how well it reproduces an actual urban system. However, comparisons between the model and a city will test many of the formulations, and simulation makes it possible to investigate a complex and realistic system.

A final example comes from research still in progress. It can be assumed that the orientation of mental patients toward the hospital will affect their behavior in the hospital, and this, in turn, will affect their length of stay. A hospital, however, allows only a limited number of possible behaviors, so that a patient's expectation may or may not be adequately matched by the possibilities. The same is also true in the patient's home community. It follows then that a patient's need system may fit better with the resources available in the hospital or in the community. When the fit is better in the community relative to the fit in the hospital, it would be expected that a patient would remain longer in the community once discharged and also be more symptom free than a patient whose need system found a better fit in the hospital. From the preliminary results that have been gathered thus far, this assumption has been supported. If these findings are strong enough, they contain some obvious implications for a therapeutic milieu.

A diverse set of examples was chosen, but each deals with behavior in the context of a community, and each is devoted to understanding the reciprocal relationship between the behavior and the context. It is this strategy that must underlie any attempt to explore the person–environment system. Sophisticated statistical techniques are available and are often useful, but no quantitative procedure can substitute for an adequate conceptualization of the problem. Community psychology can be a valuable and even necessary adjunct to psychology. Its defining characteristics will be in its transactional and ecological approach to its subject matter.

REFERENCES

Alihan, M. A. *Social ecology.* New York: Columbia University Press, 1938.

Amos, W. H. Teeming life of a pond. *National Geographic,* 1970, *138,* 274–298.

Barker, R. G. Explorations in ecological psychology. *American Psychologist,* 1965, *20,* 1–14.

Barker, R. G. *Ecological psychology.* Stanford: Stanford University Press, 1968.

Barker, R. G., Dembo, T., & Lewin, K. Frustration and regression: An experiment with young children. *University of Iowa Studies in Child Welfare,* 1941, *18,* 1.

Beals, R. L. *Politics of social research.* Chicago: Aldine, 1969.

Bennett, C. C. *Community psychology: A report of the Boston Conference on the Education of Psychologists for the Community Health Program.* Boston: Boston University Press, 1966.

Berry, J. W. Temne and Eskimo perceptual skills. *International Journal of Psychology,* 1966, *1,* 207–229.

Berry, J. W. Independence and conformity in subsistence-level societies. *Journal of Personality and Social Psychology,* 1967, *7,* 415–418.

Cox, K. R. The spatial structuring of information flow and partisan attitudes. In M. Dogan & S. Rokkan (Eds.), *Quantitative ecological analysis in the social sciences,* Cambridge: M.I.T. Press, 1969.

Dewey, J., & Bentley, A. F. *Knowing and the known.* Boston: Beacon Press, 1949.

Faris, R. E. L., & Dunham, W. H. *Mental disorders in urban areas.* New York: Wiley, 1963.

Fawl, C. L. Disturbances experienced by children in their natural habitats. In R. G. Barker (Ed.), *The stream of behavior.* New York: Appleton-Century-Crofts, 1963.

Festinger, L., Schachter, S., & Back, K. *Social pressures in informal groups.* New York: Harper, 1950.

Forrester, J. W. *Urban dynamics.* Cambridge: M.I.T. Press, 1969.

Hollingshead, A. B., & Redlich, F. *Social class and mental illness.* New York: Wiley, 1958.

Kelly, J. G. Antidotes for arrogance: Training for community psychology. *American Psychologist,* 1970, *25,* 524–531.

Kroeber, A. *Cultural and natural areas of native North America.* Berkeley: University of California Press, 1939.

Lewin, K. *Field theory in social science.* New York: Harper & Row, 1951.

McGuire, W. J. Some impending re-orientations in social psychology: Some thoughts provoked by Kenneth Ring. *Journal of Experimental Social Psychology,* 1967, *3,* 124–139.

Murray, H. A. *Explorations in personality.* New York: Oxford University Press, 1938.

Ring, K. Experimental social psychology: Some sober questions about some frivolous values. *Journal of Experimental Social Psychology,* 1967, *3,* 113–123.

Sherif, M. On the relevance of social psychology. *American Psychologist,* 1970, *25,* 144–156.

Shevky, E., & Bell, W. *Social area analysis.* Stanford: Stanford University Press, 1955.

Simon, H. A. *The sciences of the artificial.* Cambridge: M.I.T. Press, 1969.

Tryon, R. C. *Identification of social areas by cluster analysis.* Berkeley and Los Angeles: University of California Press, 1955.

Vayda, A. P. An ecological approach in cultural anthropology. *Bucknell Review,* 1969, *17,* 112–119.

Willems, E. P., & Raush, H. L. (Eds.) *Naturalistic viewpoints in psychological research.* New York: Holt, Rinehart & Winston, 1969.

Susanville: a community helps itself in mobilization of community resources for self-help in mental health

Ernst G. Beier, Peter Robinson, & Gino Micheletti

Susanville is a beautifully located town in Northern California, with approximately 8,000 inhabitants. The major economical support for the town comes from a state prison and the Federal Bureau of Land Management which account for the major portion of employment. Two lumber mills are the single largest private employment source, and there are attempts in the town to utilize its natural beauty as a resort town as well.

With regard to mental health efforts, the town is quite isolated. There are a number of agencies such as the schools, the welfare agencies, the courts, and the law enforcement agencies which have been dealing with mental health problems, but the community is professionally isolated. It has contracted in the past for some monthly consultant visits by a psychiatrist, a psychologist, and a social worker who gave aid with special programs and saw some individuals for diagnosis and treatment. The reaction of the community to this traditional approach was that it was not an efficient way to deal with these problems. Approximately 12 people each year were committed to mental hospitals in Northern California and there were also voluntary commitments.

Since new laws with reference to mental health have been enacted in the State of California, small communities have been encouraged to develop their own programs to deal with mental health problems as they arise in the community. Many of these communities went the traditional way and secured consultants who would diagnose and treat individuals in trouble. In Susanville, the assistant county superintendent of schools, Mr. Micheletti, thought that the community as a whole would benefit by utilizing local resources, rather than their exclusively relying on expensive consultants from the outside. A number of interested citizens, state officials, and an Interagency Council decided they wanted to proceed with a novel plan to bring mental health services to the community. The plan which evolved in discussions between these parties and invited consultants consisted essentially of bringing teacher–therapists to Susanville who would train lay personnel in the use of community resources, to be active in preventive mental health work, as well as to be capable in assisting in working with people in trouble. The proposal was submitted to the California Taxpayers' Association, a nonpartisan group of influential and interested citizens, who sponsored the project with a grant of $11,000.

The final proposal, worked out among the assistant superintendent and the directors of the project (from the Psychology Department of the University of Utah), was accepted with slight modification by the expanded Interagency Council and put into effect almost immediately. The program began on April 2, 1969, and was terminated on June 19, 1969. Theoretical points underlying the program, as well as practical applications, are presented in a detailed form for this report in order to make replication possible.

Theoretical Considerations

The work in Susanville rests on three assumptions which are based on recent theoretical developments and research. These assumptions are quite different from the traditional roles of the helping professions: (a) A person has *learned* his deviant behaviors (which does not rule out the question of a physiological or genetic potential) and he can *unlearn* them; he can learn adequate problem-solving behavior. He can do that best when his natural group (such as his family) is involved in helping in the learning process. (*b*) The layman with some intensive training can become a very effective person in helping another person. (*c*) This training can be done within a reasonably short time such as 50 to 80 hours, provided that there is an opportunity for further supervision in subsequent activity. Beyond these assumptions we had to make a decision about the nature of the "self-help" which would be the most effective and desirable in dealing with the problems of the community. It was felt that the most useful direction would be training toward problem prevention. This would require that the various agencies of the community would have maximum communication with each other (this by itself would be a way of easing problems). Individuals and families who live under an undue amount of stress or find themselves in a crisis would have access to someone who listens to them then and there. There are good reasons to believe that the success of such a program would not only make the community a more desirable place to live in (and perhaps would even counteract the departure of so many of the young people) but that the results eventually should be measurable in dollars and cents both in the productivity of the community and in the lessening of crime, hospitalization rates, and family and school problems.

In accordance with the broad theoretical position, it was the intent of the pilot project to go beyond the individual, to focus on the family unit, and in addition, to involve all possible significant figures in the community in dealing with given problems. Three major desirable effects of this type of program are envisioned: first, help will be given faster and more effectively than when individual patients are treated as if their lives were conducted in a vacuum. Second, those persons involved in the program (patients, peers, youth authorities, teachers, clergy, etc.) will be trained to recognize and deal with behavior patterns which eventuate in behavioral problems, thus reducing the need for "outside" consultants and increasing the efficiency of community members who would ordinarily be involved. The program will benefit a broader catchment area and result in the training of community-based change agents. The third characteristic of the program is evaluative. From a careful evaluation of the techniques applied and an observation of the change which occurs in people and the community, we will be able to contribute to the general knowledge of how self-help applies to mental health and specifically identify training methods which are most useful.

Recent developments in the literature support this position. Dissatisfaction with the effects or "cures" resulting from individual psychotherapy, as well as the tremendous time and expense involved, has caused persons interested in promoting mental health to seek more efficient preventive measures (Ackerman, 1958; Beier, 1966; Boszormenije-Nagy & Framo, 1965; Carter, 1968; Jackson & Sater, 1961; Ullmann & Krasner, 1965). Many workers in the mental health field recognize the shortage of highly trained professional personnel and have encouraged the investigation of the possibility of using indigenous lay people in the community to deal with problems (Albee, 1959; Cowen, Zax, & Laird, 1966; Guerney, 1969; Hobbs, 1964; Langsley, Pittman, Machotka, & Flomenhaft, 1968). That lay people can be effective with rather disturbed patients has also been demonstrated (Carkhuff & Truax, 1965; Poser, 1966; Rioch, Elkes, Flint, Usdansky, Newman, & Silber, 1963).

There have been several attempts in the field to work therapeutically in a whole community. The intervention was most often done by using group therapeutic principles and professional personnel. To our knowledge, the training of an entire community toward self-help has as yet not been reported.

METHOD

Procedure

In order to make this fully a community project, a group consisting of individuals who were working in many of the community's agencies was brought into the project right at the planning stage.

For this pilot project, two groups of change-agent trainees were contacted: (*a*) a group of 18 adult trainees including some who represented the service-oriented agencies in the community; some of the trainees had experience in dealing with problem individuals and families through their agency affiliation, such as the welfare and probation departments and counseling centers of local schools; and (*b*) a group of 14 high school students who had no prior experience with psychotherapy.

Selection of Adult Change-Agent Trainees

It is important to note here that 13 of the adult trainees (9 males, 4 females) were also members of the Interagency Council which was the mental health "power structure" in the community. These trainees participated in the initial planning sessions and helped to establish criteria for recruiting the other five adult trainees from the community.

About one-half of the trainees represented the service-oriented agencies, such as the police department, welfare agency, probation department, schools, etc. The others were lay people as far as mental health work was concerned. The rationale for including so many service personnel in the first training group was that these people are in positions of power in the community, especially where problem families are concerned, and had experience working together as members of the Interagency Council. They were dealing with problem individuals in the community as part of their regular roles. Moreover, if such a pilot project were to develop into a full-time program, more lay people would have to be recruited and they would of necessity work with these agencies. Therefore, it seemed desirable that the leaders of the community and representatives from the agencies become the first to be acquainted with the theoretical orientation of the program. The members of the Council were automatically accepted as trainees for the stated reasons that they were members of the power structure. Selection criteria for the remaining five adult trainees were discussed during the initial planning meeting. Present at this meeting were the Council members, directors of the project, as well as a member of the County Board of Supervisors, and several interested citizens. The following criteria were used as guidelines: trainees should be good listeners, should not be too opinionated, should show concern for people, should be able to accept another person's point of view, and show no undue anxiety. Following the discussion the Council members invited five other people to participate as trainees, three males and two females: the wife of a Board of Supervisors member, the wife of the director of the Welfare Department who is herself a competent social worker, two members of the clergy, and the husband of one of the welfare workers who is the director of the Bureau of Land Management in the area.

It is recognized that the selection of the five adult trainees who were not members of the Interagency Council probably represented the preferences of the Council members rather than an objective choice, but the directors of the project felt a novel project of this sort must be very sensitive to existing power structures and community alignments to be successful. The next group of adult trainees should be selected with more attention to the criteria guidelines rather than to their community status. Adult trainees ranged from 26 to 65 years of age, with an approximate mean of 38 years. They represented the following professions or agencies: Bureau of Land Management; clergy; Counseling Service; high school; County Board of Supervisors; housewife; Police Department; Probation Department (Court); Public Health Department; school districts; Sheriff's Department; Welfare Department.

Adult trainees were given $100 for full participation in the program.

Selection of Families Seen by Adult Trainees

The participating families were selected by their coming to the attention of the school authorities for problems their children had been having in school. These families were contacted by school officials and asked to participate. The directors and school officials agreed that the suggested families might benefit from such a program, on grounds of the following three characteristics: (a) There should be evidence of stress or crisis within the family; (b) there should be evidence that the behavior disturbance be not due to medical conditions or illness; and (c) the family should include school-aged children who manifest reactions to family stress in the school setting.

Upon selection, a discussion regarding the nature of the program was held among the seven families, which strongly emphasized the families' role as helping the community rather than serving as "patients" or guinea pigs. The families were told that the aim of the program was to increase the families' ability to deal effectively with one another and the community. Discussion centered on some principles: to become aware of the consequences of one's actions, and particularly the way one causes others to react. Another tenet was not to wait for other members of the family to make the desired change, but that one can effect that change by providing a different response system.

It was pointed out to the families that they were presently "programming" each other's behavior to maintain their problem situation, and that they could learn to program in a different way to obtain their desired goals more efficiently. They were also told that they were not labeled "patients," but that the goal of the program was to encourage relearning.

The families were a heterogeneous group and ranged in age from 20 to 40 for parents and 1 to 15 for children. Their problems were equally heterogeneous and included temper tantrums, school phobia, retarded speech development, very slow school progress, disciplinary problems in home and community, severe headaches with no medical history, and severe stress states involving husband and wife. At least three members of the participating families were considering hospitalization for their problems at the inception of the program.

Each family was given $50 for full participation in the program. It was hoped the money would serve as an incentive for attendance as well as to help cover any expenses incurred as a result of their regular participation.

Training and Practicum Sessions for Adult Trainees

It was decided not to give the trainees a course in a variety of theories and practices in psychotherapy. Rather, it was our intent to expose them to some fairly specific principles of human interaction presented in terms of a communication model (Beier, 1966). This would allow a maximum amount of time to be used for actual practice of counseling with each other (role playing) as well as working with the families. It should be noted that from the second day of the project, trainees were immediately working (under supervision) with the problem families.

In the first session, the group of trainees became acquainted with the goals of the project and with the theoretical orientation of the directors. They were given then, and repeatedly over the length of the pilot project, the following procedural pointers and principles:

1. Notice the concept of blame whether it is directed at self or others. Point out to the family member when it occurs and discuss the consequences of this behavior as it affects the other members.

2. Do not accept "I am as I am" statements (e.g., I've always been happy go lucky: it's the way I am). These are ways of stopping discussions. Consider people capable of changing, and these comments as excuses.

3. Try to listen to other people, to understand what they are saying rather than what you would like to hear. Observe nonverbal means which people use to manipulate each other. Bring them to the families' awareness descriptively, not critically.

4. Do not give advice—do not present solutions to others. One goal of therapeutic intervention is to allow people to become responsible for themselves, and aware of the consequences of their actions.

5. Do not create dependency on yourself by taking over this responsibility. You clarify, they solve.

6. Do not take sides with any family member. Each person contributes equally to the maladjustment, that is, each person can break up a fight he is involved in.

7. Give equal attention to each family member, whether adult or child. Do not talk exclusively to any one person.

8. Do not become absorbed with historical excuses or reasons for present problems—that is a dead end. Focus on what is happening now to maintain their situation and permit the people to explore what could be done to change it.

9. Ask the family member to consider how he himself should act differently to help the other person, rather than waiting for the other person to change.

10. Consider the specific behaviors each member of the family engages in to cause others to react the way they do. What are the consequences of these behaviors?

11. What could each member do to cause others to behave or respond differently?

During the training sessions, all these points were discussed with some sophistication. After the initial orientation and discussion of the goals of the project, a demonstration was conducted with one of the participating families by the director to which the community at large was invited.

Thereafter for seven weeks the adult trainees met with the directors and families every week for a total of about eight hours. The first meeting of the week of about three hours' duration included a theoretical lecture discussion and role playing. It was held in the early afternoon. During these meetings, trainees would simulate crisis situations in families, such as the teen-age son having stolen the family car and being observed coming home with it at dawn. One trainee would assume the role of the son and two others the roles of his parents. The trainees would then act out the confrontation of parents and child with frequent interjections from the directors and feedback from the other trainees. During and following these interchanges the theoretical points outlined above were clarified. During the following evening, the directors held a similar type of session of 45 minutes, during which time the problem families were also present. The whole group discussed the intervention process, practical problems some members volunteered, as well as the progress families and trainees were making. Two or three trainees then met with each of the seven families in separate rooms for about an hour. During this time the families were encouraged to discuss their problems, and the trainees practiced the application of the principles they had learned. The directors spent 10–15 minutes with each group, supervising trainees while working with the problem families. Following the practicum period, there was a discussion for about 45 minutes among the trainees and directors of the program of what had transpired. The third evening meeting was somewhat different from the other evening meetings. Then another family therapy demonstration was conducted by the directors to give the trainees another example of the therapy model used in this program. During this session, the family of the first demonstration was seen, and the group discussed changes which had occurred in the family. This family professed great if somewhat unrealistic progress, claiming they had the first tranquil week in their married life which became the topic of a very intense discussion.

A third meeting each week was held in the mornings and was reserved for individual trainees, families, or small group appointments with the directors. The time reserved for this was two and one-half hours.

During these meetings, trainees and families as well as individuals from the community at large had the opportunity to discuss problems in human behavior. Often such discussion included problems with supervisors and workers in a particular agency or problems of a more personal nature. Each director scheduled appointments 30 minutes apart for these purposes. Altogether, adult trainees received about eight hours a week of training. However, it should be noted that many of the meetings lasted much longer than the appointed time.

Thus, there were three major meeting times scheduled each week. The meetings included lectures, discussions, seminars, demonstrations, and individual appointments. From time to time interested community members, County Board or Supervisor members, and representatives from the California Taxpayers' Association and the California Department of Mental Hygiene participated as interested observers. All group meetings were open to the public at large and most were held in the library of the Lassen County School Department in Susanville. Meetings were scheduled to accommodate the busy schedules of the trainees, most of whom had demanding full-time jobs in the community.

Youth Trainees

Fourteen high school students were advised of the opportunity to volunteer for training by the counselor in the high school who himself had signed up as an adult trainee. Seven students were juniors and seven seniors. They were selected on the basis of maintaining their residence in Susanville so that they would be available to continue in the fall of 1969, as well as for the other criteria used for the adult trainees. Juniors would continue in the high school as seniors and the seniors selected would attend the nearby junior college. Furthermore, students were selected with a view to their academic performance. Due to the heavy amount of time involved and because of proximity to examination period, only students who could be expected to maintain their studies under these conditions were asked to participate. The group included both boys and girls; the sexes were about equally represented.

Counselees Seen by Youth Trainees

In discussion with the directors, four male counselees were selected by the school counselor. They were to be the training counselees of the youth trainees in the practicum sessions. The boys had been on the "waiting list" and had previously come to the attention of the school counselor because of some academic or behavioral problem in school.

Training and Practicum Sessions for Youth Trainees

Youth trainees met with the directors approximately four hours each week for seven weeks. The meetings were held in the school library during school hours, usually in the morning.

Initially, and throughout the pilot project, the youth trainees were exposed to the same principles of communication analysis as listed above for the adults. The youth trainees had practicum sessions with individual counselees, and the theoretical emphasis was on a better understanding of one's own communication. These were looked at to discover just what sort of responses they elicited in others. A group of youth trainees shared one counselee by acting as a multiple therapist group. One of the directors acted as supervisor.

The meetings with the youth trainees consisted of simple theoretical discussions, role playing (as described for adult trainees), several demonstrations by the supervisor, and practicum sessions with the counselees. Individual appointments were also offered to the youth trainees as well as to the counselees, and about half of the trainees and half of the counselees took advantage of it. Youth trainees were invited to attend the evening demonstration and also the practicum sessions with the adult trainees, and some usually attended and participated in the discussions.

EVALUATION METHODS

In order to obtain information on the effectiveness of training methods for self-help of this pilot project and to determine which characteristics in this training are most worthwhile, four types of data were collected: (a) Interviews were conducted with all participating trainees; (b) interviews were conducted with high school counselees and families: (c) family interactions were video-taped and analyzed; and (d) information was collected from various agencies in the community regarding the type and frequency of community problems. In the seven-week pilot study, it was expected, at best, to obtain leads and indications. Accordingly, we expect from our evaluation suggestive information rather than repeatable statistics, though in some of our evaluation methods surprisingly interesting tentative results were found.

Exit Interviews—Trainees [1]

Sixteen of the total of 27 youth and adult trainees were individually asked a set of standard questions.[2] The questions were sent to the 11 trainees who were unavailable for personal interviews.

The responses of the trainees indicate that the experience had been very important to them. Without exception they felt they were better prepared to understand the way people stimulate and react to each other and were better able to deal with these relationships both in their personal lives and in working with clients. Most trainees felt that they needed more experience and that a longer training period with more opportunity for personal supervision is needed. The most instructive part of the program was thought to be work with actual families in the community.

[1] The authors wish to express appreciation to Jayana Emery who collaborated on the construction of the exit interviews.

[2] Copies of the questionnaire may be obtained from the first author.

Adult trainees generally indicated that it had been difficult to avoid giving advice to families, but that they had learned people are capable of learning to help themselves and that they should be listeners and facilitators and not problem solvers.

Questionnaires of this sort are at best a measure of involvement and perhaps report most accurately just how well the trainees like the project. By and large it was quite clear that they did enjoy the training and that they felt it made them more perceptive human beings. Some of the lay people were particularly proud and surprised at how much confidence they had developed in working with counselees in this short time. The interviews also showed us that the groups gained understanding in the use of psychological tools presented them. Their critical comments on the questionnaires were also quite helpful: that a greater effort should be made to involve the whole community; that continuous supervision was desirable; that the group should be more homogeneous (the professional members felt some of the training was too repetitious, some others felt it was not enough). It should also be stated that some of the trainees' earlier comments were heeded, and the director, with an introduction by a school official, gave several addresses to community-wide audiences.

Of the 18 adult trainees originally contacted, 15 participated fully in the program's heavy schedule and 11 expressed an active interest in continuing working with families in the community. They have organized an independent group to continue working with families and consulting with each other and occasionally with a professional consultant until such time as a regular training and supervision program again becomes available. Of the nine youth trainees, seven participated fully in the program to its termination, and five of them plan to continue seeing high school students in the fall under the direction of the school counselors, regardless of the progress of a full-time community mental health program.

It was the experience of the directors, current members, and all regular participants in the program that enthusiasm continued to increase as the program progressed, despite frequent conflicts with the regular jobs and sacrifices of personal time. One of the signs of the successful climate of the training situation was represented by the many applications for future training received by the school officials. These applications came from both men and women of the community representing a wide spectrum of socioeconomic status.

Summary of Exit Interviews— Families and Counselees

All seven families contacted to participate in the project attended with a high degree of regularity. There were, however, two occasions on which other commitments prevented one of the families from participating.

Only four of the families were available for the personal exit interview, partially due to the limited availability of the interviewers after the termination of the pilot study. Only one of the four high school counselees was available for the personal exit interview, also for the above reason. We wanted to discover from these interviews whether (a) they yielded worthwhile information and (b) how the families felt about their participation.

The responses of the family members and counselees interviewed indicate that while they still have problems, they have learned how they contribute to their own problem situation. They also learned to handle problems more efficiently and with greater skill. There was usually an immediate change for the better, followed by a period of some indecision due to their trying to relate to others in new and sometimes novel and perhaps clumsy ways.

With the exception of one woman interviewed, the reactions of the family members ranged from mildly favorable to very positive to the approach and results of the program. We do not know how much this information represents their true feelings, since they were paid and interviewed by the codirector. Yet, supporting information also came independently to us from friends and occasionally from the service agencies. In general then, the reactions to the questions seem to indicate an increased awareness of how each member contributes to the problems of other members of the family. Each member seemed to be more attuned to his actions, and the families could be characterized as having a greater readiness for change. The responses of the families show that most families were trying out new and less stressful ways of living together, but at this time it would be unwarranted to speak of having achieved permanent changes.

How one mother felt is exemplified by the following:

Mother: I was waiting for the doctor to commit myself to go to the mental hospital, now I am thinking how crazy I was. I am just not the same person now.

The most positive reaction came from a high school counselee who had been seen only once for a three-hour period with two youth trainees and the directors. Some examples from the exit interview three weeks later were:

Q. How is your family getting along now?

A. Much better—have planned to go along to this neighbor town with father and never would have done this before. I could see what I was doing to cause trouble with father—then after trainees took me apart so I could see myself—so naturally once I saw what I was doing, I corrected myself.

Q. What do you do now?

A. If I don't get what Dad is saying and just drop the subject, this gives me the peaceful relation I want—it works well. I was fighting every day with Dad and I haven't had a single fight with him since the program.

We feel the exit interviews were a worthwhile means of discovering how well the families were "tuned in" to the new learning made available to them. While a follow-up study may establish whether there were lasting effects, the interviews do indicate that the families felt better and at least were speaking in terms of personal responsibility. They had gained some meaningful knowledge which had not been available to them before they had come to the meetings.

Video-Tape Recordings of Families

Video-tape recordings were taken of seven families to investigate the usefulness of the technique in representing accurately the families' patterns of communication as well as possibly being a sensitive measure of change in these patterns. The reason for including this measure was that the directors of the program have had experience in systematic measurement of family problems by a content analysis of video samples. The families quickly get over the discomfort of being on TV, and important information of how the members of the family affect each other can be gleaned from their talking with each other.

It was the intent of this approach to video-tape several families who were to be involved in the program and some families not so involved to serve as controls. The families were to be videotaped before and after the program. Further, two kinds of settings were planned: (a) a 10-minute segment of the family talking to each other about things of importance to them, with no direction or guidance from the interviewer, and (b) a 10-minute segment of the family in a stressful problem solving situation (putting together an intricate wooden puzzle).

Only two of the five families taped on TV were selected for participation in the meetings. The video tapes were analyzed by five judges.[3] Observations by these judges strongly suggest video tapes can be used as a sensitive basis for diagnosis and evaluation of family functioning. The inferences drawn from the taped family communication patterns closely coincided with the stated problems for which the families participated in the program. Moreover, observable changes did occur in the two treated families which were not replicated in the control families. It is suggested that this technique should again be used in a future program of this type, particularly if employed in a more systematic and controlled fashion.

Toward Objective Measures of Community Changes

A number of measures which have been considered for the evaluations of changes in the "mental health" of a community follow.[4]

We did not expect to see changes in these statistics during this seven weeks of the pilot study. Most agencies, such as the Police Department, compile their own data only twice a year on such topics as number and type of arrests and their disposition. Also, the limited number of people participating in such a pilot project may not even enter into the statistics of a particular agency. Yet in order to prepare for the possible community-wide application of such a program, we felt an early consideration of such measures to be important in order to forestall the lack of base-rate information. It should be noted that in many cases we found the agency's information not to be current, a problem which threatens the utility of such measures.

Basically, one would expect that an ideally effective self-help program would reduce commu-

nity disturbances, be it truant or delinquency behavior, divorce rate, or need for hospitalization in a mental hospital. Accordingly, comprehensive statistics relating to various problem behaviors in the community (number and nature of crimes, unemployment, welfare recipients, etc.) were collected from the Susanville Police Department, Lassen County Sheriff's Office, Department of Probation, the County Welfare Agency, and various school offices.

Actually, while we did not expect to find changes in these data, we did find some surprises which were of some importance to the community. One such observation from the statistics of Lassen County is reported. In this county, most individuals who are brought before the superior court are in fact convicted. For example, in 1966, 32 out of 34 individuals brought before the court on felony charges, and in 1967, 48 out of 55 persons, were convicted. So we are not dealing here with lax law enforcement. However, it also appears that Lassen County sentences the defendant to prison, probation, bail, or fine almost to the total exclusion of such rehabilitative devices used in other counties such as Youth Authority, California Rehabilitation Center, or referral to Counseling or Mental Hygiene Clinics. To utilize all possible resources available to a court to rehabilitate a convicted person may be an important element in the mental health picture of this community.

Suggestions for Future Evaluation

Some of the measures suggested for inclusion of future research regarding community change may be as follows:

1. Crime report: community members spending time in jail or prison; recidivism; juvenile violations; complaints to the police; types of arrest.

2. School performance: school dropout rate; truancy activity; disciplinary problems; number of college applications; academic achievement tests; grades; teacher ratings.

3. Hospitalization: number of hospitalizations; time spent in hospital; outpatient treatment; reason for hospitalization.

4. Family data: welfare payments; aid to dependent children; food stamps; job attendance; divorce rate; family quarrels which come to attention of police; employment; medical assistance; abandonments.

5. Community morale and involvement: young

[3] The authors want especially to thank James F. Alexander for his help in this analysis.

[4] The authors want to thank Helene Bakewell for her work on this part of the project.

people leaving town; industrial growth; public services; residency turnover; new developments; recreation facilities; agency collaboration; quality of schools; services.

With all the encouragement we obtained, we concluded that a pilot project such as this one should be followed as soon as possible with a broader mental health program in order to maintain the momentum and enthusiasm of the participants and the community in general.

REFERENCES

Ackerman, N. W. Toward an integrative therapy of the family. *American Journal of Psychiatry*, 1958, *114*, 727–733.

Albee, G. W. *Mental health manpower needs.* New York: Basic Books, 1959.

Beier, E. G. *The silent language of psychotherapy.* Chicago: Aldine, 1966.

Boszormenije-Nagy, I., & Framo, J. L. (Eds.) *Intensive family therapy.* New York: Harper & Row, 1965.

Carkhuff, R. R., & Truax, C. B. Lay mental health counseling: The effects of lay group counseling. *Journal of Consulting Psychology*, 1965, *29*, 426–431.

Carter, J. W. (Ed) *Research contributions from psychology to community mental health.* New York: Behavioral Publications, 1968.

Cowen, E. L., Zax, M., & Laird, J. D. A college student volunteer program in the elementary school setting. *Community Mental Health Journal*, 1966, *2*, 319–328.

Guerney, B. G. (Ed.) *Psychotherapeutic agents: New roles for nonprofessionals, parents, and teachers.* New York: Holt, Rinehart & Winston, 1969.

Hobbs, N. Mental health's third revolution. *American Journal of Orthopsychiatry*, 1964, *34*, 822–833.

Jackson, D. D., & Satir, V. A review of psychiatric developments in family diagnosis and therapy. In W. W. Ackerman, F. L. Benman, & S. N. Sherman (Eds.), *Exploring the base for family therapy.* New York: Family Service Association of America, 1961.

Langsley, D. G., Pittman, F. S., Machotka, P., & Flomenhaft, K. Family crisis therapy: Results and implications. *Family Process*, 1968, *7*, 145–158.

Poser, E. G. The effect of therapists' training on group therapeutic outcome. *Journal of Consulting Psychology*, 1966, *30*, 283–289.

Rioch, M. J., Elkes, C., Flint, A. A., Usdansky, B. S., Newman, R. G., & Silber, E. National Institute of Mental Health Pilot Study in Training Mental Health Counselors. *American Journal of Orthopsychiatry*, 1963, *32*, 678–689.

Ullmann, L. P., & Krasner, L. (Eds.) *Case studies in behavior modification.* New York: Holt, Rinehart & Winston, 1965.